AN UNPRECEDENTED ANTHOLOGY OF THE FINEST CONTEMPORARY TRANSLATIONS OF EUROPEAN AND LATIN AMERICAN POETRY

When *Modern European Poetry* was first published in 1966, the work of poets from six European languages appeared, much of it for the first time, in English translation. Since then the stature of many translators and poets has been more firmly established and Pulitzer Prizes, National Book Awards and Nobel Prizes have been conferred upon them. For this edition the poems of Jorge Luis Borges have been added to the Latin American Section.

MODERN EUROPEAN POETRY

"A superb collection of modern European poetry in which virtually every major modern voice is represented. Offered in translation by many of our finest English-language poets, the broad range of the best poetry of this century is spread before us. *Modern European Poetry* is a model of what an anthology should be."

—Breon Mitchell, Chairman of Comparative Literature, Indiana University

"The best anthology of its kind available anywhere. The translations are superior, and the representation of poets generous."

—*International Poetry Forum*

THE EDITORS

WILLIS BARNSTONE, Department of Comparative Literature and Latin American Studies, Indiana University

PATRICIA TERRY, Department of French, Barnard College

ARTHUR S. WENSINGER, Department of German and School of Letters, Wesleyan University

KIMON FRIAR, critic and translator

SONIA RAIZISS and ALFREDO DE PALCHI, Poetry Editors, *Chelsea*

GEORGE REAVEY, translator, author, critic

ANGEL FLORES, Department of Spanish and Comparative Literature, Queens College

MODERN EUROPEAN POETRY

FRENCH / GERMAN / GREEK
ITALIAN / RUSSIAN / SPANISH

Edited by

WILLIS BARNSTONE

PATRICIA TERRY

ARTHUR S. WENSINGER

KIMON FRIAR

SONIA RAIZISS and ALFREDO DE PALCHI

GEORGE REAVEY

ANGEL FLORES

BANTAM BOOKS

TORONTO / NEW YORK / LONDON

MODERN EUROPEAN POETRY

A Bantam Book | January 1966
2nd printing .... March 1967   4th printing . November 1970
3rd printing ... January 1970   5th printing . November 1972
6th printing .... December 1978

Library of Congress Catalog Card Number : 66–12156

ISBN 0-553-12722-5

ACKNOWLEDGMENTS

*1978 Revised Edition published with the cooperation of the
International Poetry Forum.*

*For permission to reprint all works in this volume by each of
the following poets and translators, grateful acknowledgment is
made to the holders of copyright, publishers or representatives
named below and on the following four pages (pages v, vi,
vii, viii), which constitute an extension of this copyright page.*

FRENCH
NEW DIRECTIONS: "I Am Writing to You from a Far-off
Country" by Henri Michaux from *Selected Writings of Henri
Michaux.* "Orpheus," "The Mouse," "The Elephant," "Win-
dows," "Ocean of Earth," "Vitam Impendere Amori," "Twi-
light" and "The Gypsy" by Guillaume Apollinaire from *Selected
Writings of Guillaume Apollinaire.* All rights reserved by New
Directions. Reprinted by permission of the publisher.
CITY LIGHTS BOOKS: "Quartier Libre," "Alicante," "Quick-
sands," "To Paint the Portrait of a Bird" and "The Dunce" by
Jacques Prévert from *Pocketbook Series,* reprinted by permis-
sion of City Lights Books. © 1947 Editions Gallimard.
YALE FRENCH STUDIES: "The Discourse on Peace" and "Picasso
Goes for a Stroll" by Jacques Prévert from *Paroles,* 1949.
RANDOM HOUSE, INC.: "Evadne," "The Rampart of Twigs,"
"Lightning Victory" and "The Woods along the Epte" by René
Char from *Hypnos Waking* © 1956 Random House, Inc. Re-
printed by permission of Random House, Inc.
THE HUDSON REVIEW: "Theatre" by Yves Bonnefoy: © 1961
by The Hudson Review, Inc.
POETRY: "Another Voice" and "Thus We Will Walk" by Yves
Bonnefoy reprinted by permission of Poetry © 1962 by Modern
Poetry Association.
MERCURE DE FRANCE: "Dead Weight," "Beyond Measure" and
"The Winding Road" by Pierre Reverdy from *Main D'Oeuvre,*
1950; "Another Voice" and "Thus We Will Walk" by Yves
Bonnefoy from *Du Mouvement et de l'immobilité;* "The Wind
Is Quiet," "The Iron Bridge" and "Here, Still Here" by Yves
Bonnefoy from *Hier Regnant Desert,* 1959.
ÉDITIONS ALBIN MICHEL: "The Boatmen," "Mountebanks,"
"Festival of the Moon," "Living Light" and "Vegetal Body" by
Robert Sabatier from *Les Fêtes Solaires,* 1955 and "Mortal

ACKNOWLEDGMENTS v

Landscape" and "The Voyages" by Robert Sabatier from *Dedicare d'un Navire*, 1958.

ÉDITIONS SEGHERS: "Elsa at the Mirror" by Louis Aragon from *La Diane française*, 1944; "Bather" by Jean Follain from *Poèmes de L'Année*, 1959; "The Enemy of Spring" by Claude Vigée from *La Corne du Grande Pardon*, 1954.

ÉDITIONS G.L.M.: "Song of the Stairs" and "Common Presence" by René Char.

ÉDITIONS GALLIMARD: Jules Supervielle's "Prophecy" and "Flame Tip" from *Gravitations*, 1925; "The Wake," "Regretting the Earth," "The Poet" and "The House Surrounded" from *Les Amis Inconnus*, 1934; "The Raindrop" from *La Fable du Monde*, 1938; "The Grief of the Death" and "You Disappear" from *1939–1945*, 1945; "Metamorphosis in Blood" and "The Survey" from *L'Escalier*, 1956; Pierre Reverdy's "Sun," "Nomad," "Sound of Bell," "Departure," "Nocturnal Round," "Noon" and "They Alone" from *Les Epaves du Ciel*, 1924; Paul Eluard's "Lady Love," "Second Nature," "They Are Alike," "Evil," "We Have Made the Darkness Ours," "Of No Age" and *Paroles*, 1949; Robert Desnos' "Cuckoo-Clock," "The Great Days of the Poet," "If You Only Knew" and "Nightfall" from *Domaine Public*, 1953, translated by Glauco Cambon © Glauco Cambon; "The Ant," "Sun," "At World's End" and "Last Poem" from *Domaine Public*; Jean Follain's "Fox," "Child's Blackness" and "Voluntary Maiming" from *Usage du Temps*, 1943; "Owl," "The Man Who Stuffed Birds," "These and Those" from *Exister*, 1947; "Death," "Dog with Schoolboys," "October Thoughts" and "Life" from *Territoire*, 1958; "Bather" from *Poemes de L'Année*, 1959; "The Terror," "The Plant" and "The Instant" from *Des Heures*, 1960; René Char's "Play and Sleep . . ." and "Antonin Artaud" from *Les Martinaux*, 1950; "Door of Wholesome Death" and "Alberto Giacometti" from *Recherche de la base et du sommet*, 1955; "The Rampart of Twigs," "Lightning Victory" and "The Woods along the Epte" from *La Parole en Archipel*, 1962. Char translations by Charles Guenther © 1963; Claude Vigée's "The Cosmic Comedian," "The Phoenix of Mozart," "Blues," "Song," "Chorale in December," "April" and "Epiphany" from *L'Eté Indien*.

GERMAN

INSEL VERLAG: Rainer Maria Rilke from *Sämtliche Werke*, Insel Verlag, Frankfurt am Main, © 1961.

OTTO MÜLLER VERLAG: Georg Trakl from *Die Dichtungen*, Otto Müller Verlag, Salzburg, © 1938.

LIMES VERLAG: Gottfried Benn's "Thalassal Regression," "Late" and "Only When," Limes Verlag, Wiesbaden, © 1959.

VERLAG "DIE ARCHE": Gottfried Benn's "Poems That Stand Still," "The Death of Orpheus" and "Ah, the Distant Land" from *Statische Gedichte*, Verlag "Die Arche," Zurich, © 1948.

SUHRKAMP VERLAG: Bertolt Brecht, *Gedichte*, Volumes 1 & 2, © 1960; Volumes 3 & 4, © 1961; Volumes 5, 6 & 7, © 1964, all by Suhrkamp Verlag, Frankfurt am Main; Karl Krolow, *Fremde Körper*, © 1959, *Unsichtbare Hände*, © 1962, both by Suhrkamp Verlag, Frankfurt am Main.

DEUTSCHE VERLAGS-ANSTALT: Paul Celan, *Mohn und Gedachtnis*, © 1961; *Von Schwelle zu Schwelle*, © 1961, both by Deutsche Verlags-Anstalt, Stuttgart.

BECHTLE VERLAG: Heinz Piontek, *Die Rauchfahne*, © 1953, *Wassermarken*, © 1957, both by Bechtle Verlag, Esslingen.

R. PIPER & CO. VERLAG: Ingeborg Bachmann, *Die gestundete Zeit*, © 1953, *Anrufung des grossen Bären*, © 1956, both by R. Piper & Co., Munich.

HERMANN LUCHTERHAND VERLAG: Günter Grass, *Die Vorzüge der Windhühner*, © 1956, *Gleisdreieck*, © 1960, both by Hermann Luchterhand Verlag, Berlin and Neuwied.

THE HOGARTH PRESS: Rainer Maria Rilke, *Sämtliche Werke* in English translation for Great Britain.

FARRAR, STRAUS & GIROUX: "Self-Portrait" and "The Cadet Picture of My Father" by Rainer Maria Rilke, translated by Robert Lowell. Reprinted from *Imitations* by Robert Lowell by permission of Farrar, Straus & Giroux, © 1958, 1959, 1960, 1961.

NEW DIRECTIONS: Gottfried Benn's "Cycle" and "Fragments" from *Primal Vision* by Gottfried Benn, edited by B. B. Ashton. All rights reserved. Reprinted by permission of New Directions. "September," "Tiny Aster" and "Beautiful Youth" reprinted by permission of New Directions.

THE ATLANTIC MONTHLY: Christian Morgenstern's "Palmstrom to a Nightingale Which Would Not Let Him Sleep" translated by William Snodgrass.

THE HUDSON REVIEW: Christian Morgenstern's "The Sandwich Paper" translated by William Snodgrass. Reprinted by permission of The Hudson Review, Vol. XIV, No. 2, Summer 1961, © 1961 by The Hudson Review, Inc.

MADEMOISELLE: Christian Morgenstern's "The Daynightlamp" and "Anxiety for the Future" translated by William Snodgrass, originally appeared in *Mademoiselle*, © 1961 by Street & Smith Publications, Inc.

THE MINNESOTA REVIEW: Rainer Maria Rilke's "Great Night" translated by E. M. Valk.

WAKE: Christian Morgenstern's "The Two Donkeys," "The Moonsheep" and "Ding, Dang, Dong" translated by E. M. Valk.

GREEK

THE CHARIOTEER Summer 1960: "Sparta" by Angelos Sike-lianós; Autumn 1960: "Adolescence of Day," "Drinking the Corinthian Sun," "We Walked in the Fields All Day," "Glittering Day, Conch of That Voice" and "I Know the Night No Longer" by Odysseus Elytis.

POETRY June 1951: "Sparta" by Angelos Sikelianós; "Poem" and "To the Cold Imagination" by Demétrius Antoníou; "The Apprentice of Sorrow" by Níkos Engonópoulos; "I Know the Night No Longer" by Odysseus Elytis.

WAKE NO. 12: "Mathiós Paséalis among the Roses" by George Seféris; "Adolescence of Day" and "We Walked in the Fields All Day" by Odysseus Elytis.

QUARTERLY REVIEW OF LITERATURE Fall 1950: "Gymnopaedia" by George Seféris.

NEW WORLD WRITING NO. 2: "Interval of Joy" by George Seféris; "Drinking the Corinthian Sun" by Odysseus Elytis.

NEW YORK TIMES REVIEW December 7, 1952: "Interval of Joy" by George Seféris.

GREEK HERITAGE Winter 1963: "Of Sleep" and "Landscape" by Alexander Mátsas.

ATHENE Summer 1947: "Picasso" by Níkos Engonópoulos; "Observatory" and "The Saviour" by Míltos Sahtoúris.

ATHENS NEWS: "Poem" by Demétrius Antoníou; "The Apprentice of Sorrow" by Níkos Engonópoulos; "I Know the Night No Longer" by Odysseus Elytis.

THE ATLANTIC MONTHLY: "I Know the Night No Longer" by Odysseus Elytis.

ACCENT Summer 1954: "Heroic and Elegiac Song for the Lost Second Lieutenant of the Albanian Campaign" by Odysseus Elytis.

SHENANDOAH Winter 1954, Washington and Lee University Review: "Beauty" by Míltos Sahtoúris.

SIMON AND SCHUSTER: from *The Odyssey: A Modern Sequel* by Níkos Kazantzákis. Copyright © 1958 Simon and Schuster, Inc. Reprinted by permission of the publishers. Also reprinted by permission of Martin Secker and Warburg Ltd.

ITALIAN

POETRY August 1959: "Land and Sea" and "The Inattentive" by Luciano Erba.

POETRY September 1961: "Sirocco," "Mutable World," "The Sundial" and "Veneris Venefica Agrestis" by Lucio Piccolo.

THE SPARROW MAGAZINE April 1961: "To My Wife" by Umberto Saba.

THE TRANSATLANTIC REVIEW Fall 1961: "Night Encounter" by

Vincenzo Cardarelli; "Lazarus' Dog" by Leonardo Sinisgalli and "For Varvara Alexandrovna" by Salvatore Quasimodo.

LITERARY REVIEW Winter 1960: "The First Man Fallen" by Vittorio Sereni; "Berry" by Mario Luzi.

CHELSEA: "An Italian in Greece" and "On the Road to Zenna" by Vittorio Sereni; "Notes on a Handkerchief's Edge" by Leonardo Sinisgalli; "The Agave" and "Sailing from Greenwich" by Bartolo Cattafi; "Mallow-Warm" and "The Adige Roars" by Rocco Scotellaro; "Love and Death" and "Windy Day" by David Maria Turoldo; "As You Wish" by Mario Luzi; "Lament of the Power Shovel" by Pier Paolo Pasolini; "Lombard-Venetian" and "Super Flumina" by Luciano Erba; "In the Family Circle" and "For a Friend About to Be Married" by Giorgio Orelli; "The Champion Swimmer" by Umberto Saba.

QUARTERLY REVIEW OF LITERATURE: "The Lemon Trees," "Arsenio," "Dora Markus," "The Magnolia's Shadow," "Storm," "The Dead" and "The Eel" by Eugenio Montale.

IL MENABÒ: "The Beautiful Flags" by Pier Paolo Pasolini.

THE NATION: "Hallucination" by Vittorio Sereni; "Death Will Come and Will Have Your Eyes" by Cesare Pavese.

BELOIT POETRY JOURNAL: "To a Childhood Chum" by Vittorio Sereni.

MONDADORI PUBLISHING COMPANY: Vicenzo Cardarelli's "Adolescente," "Incontro notturno," "Stanchezza" and "Alle mura del mio paese" from Poesie, 1943; Giuseppe Ungaretti's "Veglia" and "Giugno" from L'Allegria, 1942; "La Morte meditata" from Sentimento del Tempo, 1943; "Tu ti spezzasti" and "Terra" from Il dolore, 1947; "Cori descrittivi di stati d'animo di Didone" from La terra promessa, 1950; Eugenio Montale's "I limoni," "Arsenio" and "I morti" from Ossi di seppia, 1948; "Dora Markus" from Le occasioni, 1949; "La bufera," "Due mel crepuscolo," "Iride," "L'ombra della magnolia," "L'anguilla" and "Piccolo testamento" from La bufera e altro, 1947; Leonardo Sinisgalli's "L'aurora appena," "Poesia per una cicale" and "Il cane di Lazzaro" from Vidi le Muse, 1943; "Diario sull'orlo di un fazzoletto" from I nuovi campi Elisi, 1947; "Pianto antico" and "Sabato Santo a Manfredonia" from L'eta della luna, 1962; David Maria Turoldo's "Amore e morte" from Gii occhi miei lo vedranno, 1955; Bartolo Cattafi's "L'agave," "Dieppe" and "Partenza da Greenwich" from Le mosche del meriggio, 1959; Rocco Scotellaro's "E' un ritratto tutto piedi," "Alla figlia del trainante," "Per pasqua alla promessa sposa," "E' calda cosi la malva," "Pozzanghera nera il 18 aprile" and "Sempre nuòva e l'alba" from E' fatto giorno, 1954; Luciano Erba's "Lombardo Veneto," "Terra e mare," "Il distratto" and "Super Flumina" from Il male minore, 1960; Giorgio Orelli's "La scolopendra," "Natale 1944," "Estate," "Nel cerchio familiare" and "A un amico che si sposa" from L'ora del tempo, 1962; Lucio Piccolo's "La meridiana," "Sirocco," "Mobile universo di folate" and "Veneris Venefica Agrestis" from Gioco a nascondere a canti barocchi, 1960.

VALLECCHI EDITORE: "Giardino autumnale," "L'invetrata," "La sera di fiera" and "Coi tuo piccoli occhi bestiali" by Dino Campana from Canti orfici e altri scritti; "Italiano in Grecia," "Non sa piu nulla . . ." and "Solo vera e l'estate" by Vittorio Sereni from Diario d'Algeria.

VALENTINO BOMPIANI EDITORE: "Caino" and "Giorno di vento" by David Maria Turoldo from Io non ho mani.

ALDO GARZANTI EDITORE: "Il pianto della scavatrice parte II" by Pier Paolo Pasolini from Le ceneri di Gramsci; "Le Belle Bandiere" by Pier Paolo Pasolini from Poesie in Forma di Rosa, © 1964 by Aldo Garzanti Editore; "Bacca," "Est," "Come tu vuoi," "Las Animas" and "Nell'imminenza dei quaranta anni" by Mario Luzi from Il giusto della vita.

VANNI SCHEIWILLER EDITORE: "Qualcosa di preciso," "Apertura d'ali" and "Sublimazione" by Bartolo Cattafi from Qualcosa di preciso.

NEW DIRECTIONS: Poetry by Giuseppe Ungaretti from Life of a Man and Choruses Descriptive of Dido's States of Mind. "The Lemon Trees," "Arsenio," "Dora Markus," "The Magnolia's

Shadow," "Little Testament," "Storm," "The Dead," "Two Figures in Twilight," "Iris," and "The Eel" by Eugenio Montale.

FARRAR, STRAUS & GIROUX: "Man of My Time," "Auschwitz," "In This City" and "To My Father" by Salvatore Quasimodo from *The Selected Writings of Salvatore Quasimodo;* "Arsenio," "Dora Markus," "The Magnolia's Shadow" and "Little Testament" by Eugenio Montale, adapted by Robert Lowell, from *Imitations.*

GIULIO EINAUDI EDITORE: "A mia moglie," "Una notte," "Mezzogiorno d'inverno," and "La campionessa di nuoto" by Umberto Saba from *Il Canzoniere;* "Il dio caprone," "Paesaggio II" and "Istinto" by Cesare Pavese from *Lavorare stanca* and "Verrà la morte e avra i tuoi occhi" by Cesare Pavese from *Verrà la morte.*

RUSSIAN

G. P. PUTNAM'S SONS. Four poems by Boris Pasternak, translated by George Reavey.

WORLD PUBLISHING COMPANY. Four poems by Vladimir Mayakovsky from *The Bedbug and Selected Poetry,* edited by Patricia Blake, Meridian Books. Copyright © 1960 by The World Publishing Company.

SPANISH

THE NATION: "The Train of the Wounded" by Miguel Hernandez, translated by Hardie St. Martin.

WHIT BURNETT: "Summits of Macchu Picchu" by Pablo Neruda, originally published in English translation in *The World's Best.*

SIXTIES PRESS: © The Sixties Press. "Our Daily Bread," "The Eternal Dice," "To My Brother Miguel in Memoriam" and "I Am Freed from the Burdens of the Sea" by César Vallejo from *Twenty Poems.*

NEW DIRECTIONS: From "Sun Stone" by Octavio Paz, translated by Muriel Rukeyser. All rights reserved. Reprinted by permission of New Directions Publishing Co., Inc. From *Selected Poetry of Federico Garcia Lorca.* Copyright 1955 by New Directions. Reprinted by permission of New Directions Publishing Co., Inc.

LOS AMERICAS PUBLISHING CO.: *Eighty Poems* by Antonio Machado and poems by Rafael Alberti, translated by Mark Strand.

AGENCIA LITERARIA: Poems by Pedro Salinas.

HARCOURT, BRACE & WORLD: "The Horses" by Jorge Guillén, © 1959 by Richard Wilbur. Reprinted from his volume, *Advice to a Prophet and Other Poems,* by permission of Harcourt, Brace & World, Inc.

E. P. DUTTON: "The Watcher," "1891," and "You" ("In all the world . . .") from *The Gold of the Tigers* by Jorge Luis Borges; copyright © 1972, 1975 by Emece Editores, S.A., Buenos Aires. Translated by Alastair Reid; English translation © 1976, 1977 by Alastair Reid.

Published simultaneously in the United States and Canada

Bantam Books are published by Bantam Books, Inc. Its trademark, consisting of the words "Bantam Books" and the portrayal of a bantam, is Registered in U.S. Patent and Trademark Office and in other countries. Marca Registrada. Bantam Books, Inc., 666 Fifth Avenue, New York, New York 10019.

PRINTED IN THE UNITED STATES OF AMERICA

Contents

CONTENTS

SPANISH POETRY 466

CONTENTS

A Note on Prehistory

A book, like all things in art, has two histories: its public history after it is formed and presented to the world; and the prehistory of its formation. The public history has to do with readers and critics, praise and abuse, air-cooled bookstores and stuffy attics. But the prehistory of art is the artist's private world, and only he (or possibly a scholar) knows the many shapes the art object takes before it is fixed and presented to a world of changing tastes.

Occasionally, however, the prehistory of a work becomes public: some old drafts, scores, or preliminary drawings come to light, often to everybody's regret. Here, then, with apologies and diffidence, are a few public words about this volume's prehistory. I feel that they should be said both because of our high adventure and in deference to the many patient participants.

The volume began, in theory, as a periodical. It became, successively, a single tome, six small bilingual editions, and then almost unmanageable. Like the traditional picaresque *mozo,* it changed masters and found a new home. But the odyssey involved much more than the episodic wanderings of an amorphous manuscript from master to master. For as the manuscript grew thick, so the people involved grew many. Each linguistic section was handled by a different editor, and within each section were perhaps twenty or more translators; each separate poem usually involved the original poet, the translator, and the foreign publisher who controlled the rights. Thus the prehistory of this volume has reached a virtual army of poets, translators, editors and publishers, scattered across three continents. Possibly no single book in recent times has been the cause of so much national and international postage, so many letters to and from so many people.

I wish to thank these many friends of poetry, especially the translators and six editors, for their work and their patience. All has been toward one end: a book of good modern poems in English.

I wish to express my gratitude to Nancy Smiler for her patience, good humor and skill in handling the complex mass of editorial work which the international nature of this anthology required.

WILLIS BARNSTONE

Introduction:
An Anthology of Modern Poetry

This is an anthology of modern poetry translated from six languages of Europe and Spanish America. It includes those poets who in time and spirit are part of the twentieth century. Poetry from these particular languages was chosen simply because from our spot on the globe this poetry is better known and has made a stronger impact upon us. But a companion volume might contain poetry of great interest from any number of languages—Dutch, Swedish, Bengali, Japanese.

The linguistic obstacles that separate peoples are so forbidding that most of us accept a nationalistic approach to literature and restrict our interests vertically to one people and one linguistic tradition. The sciences, however, and the non-verbal arts—music, dance, the plastic arts—are not fragmented into small islands. A student of biology or violin or sculpture would never think of limiting himself to works in his own language; yet in belles-lettres, where the literatures of different nations are just as incestuously interrelated, every traditional barrier is present to prevent us from leaving our verbal ghettos.

To rectify this problem, the orderly French invented a discipline to justify a more universal approach to literature: *littérature comparée*. But even here we are burdened with new restrictions, for the comparatists feel compelled to compare. So, while the biologist, musician or sculptor need not hold himself to comparative biology, comparative music, or comparative sculpture, the man of letters again finds himself forced to approach literature with a new set of rules. To speak of world literature will not solve his problem either: no sane musician would wish to carry the burden of world music.

The way out of this verbal labyrinth is to follow the example of those in other arts and sciences, and speak simply of modern poetry, as one speaks of modern music or modern painting, and assume in this title the work of any poet, without regard to language, who comes within the range of our interest. To do this, we must act, as do our friends in other fields, as if the matter of language were no great problem. We may either read poems in their original idiom or circumvent the language barrier by turning to good translations. The aim of this present anthology of modern poetry is to provide just such excellent translations into English verse for readers interested—not necessarily in national, comparative, or world poetry—but simply in modern poetry.

With this in mind, let us turn to the difficult subject of translation (which for the sake of bringing us this far we have had to think of as no great problem). As soon as we begin to look carefully at matters of verse translation, we find many approaches, a whirlpool of doctrines, and a sea of complaints. Yet for all this, there has been, especially in recent years, much good verse translation and some agreement as to intention.

The first principle of common agreement is that good translation does not depend simply on how well the translator knows the original language. One must assume that the work to be translated is thoroughly understood; thus a full understanding of the original is a constant, not a variable, from which the translated is thoroughly understood; thus a full understanding then depend on the translator's own skill in English. He must recreate poetry when he translates; he must be a poet at the moment of translation, which does not mean that he need be a poet outside his duties as translator. Often he is a poet, however, and in this anthology we have been fortunate in having poems rendered into English by many of the very best poets now writing in the English language.

To say further that the poem should not "read as a translation" seems in a way to be denying the dark deed. But by this we mean that the poem in translation should read as a good poem in English. As soon as awkward compromises of misguided literalness are made, the translator is unfaithful to the quality of the original. The original poem, we may assume, is a good one if we wish to translate it, and this standard of excellence is the only acceptable standard for the poem when recreated in English. There may, of course, be many good poems in the original tongue which do not lend themselves to translation. These poems should be left in their native phonemes. The poems must work in English if they are to be presented to a reader.

In this anthology we have tried to be both representative of individual poets and of important literary movements, but we have rejected all poems, whatever their intrinsic or historical importance, if when translated they do not read as excellent poems in English. So it is hoped that this very large anthology from six languages, with all its inevitable omissions and failures,* will be simply a diverse collection of good modern poetry.

W. B.

---

* The most serious and painful omission is that of the Greek poet from Alexandria, Constantine Cavafy, who, for reasons of copyright, could not be included.

Modern European Poetry

French Poetry

EDITED BY *Patricia Terry*

✻ ✻ ✻ ✻ ✻

Introduction

In the beginning was Baudelaire, whose heir was Rimbaud. These were the most powerful determinants of that transfer from the stained-glass attitudes of latter-day Symbolism to the self-consciousness, personal commitment and stylistic freedom which distinguish the poetry called modern. It is essentially a return to the Romantic emphasis on the poet rather than the poem. Baudelaire sought the new beyond the unknown in himself; Rimbaud went further and more deliberately into the irrational and wrapped the explorer in the cloak of a magician. The *"Le Bateau Ivre"* proclaimed, "Sometimes I saw what man believed he saw!" And however forcefully Rimbaud denigrated such visions as not worth their price, the renunciations of *"Une Saison en Enfer"* were never as convincing as the earlier glory.

Between Rimbaud and the surrealists, who acknowledged him as a master, Guillaume Apollinaire (1880–1918) accomplished the esthetic revolution begun by Laforgue, attacking the notion implicit in all symbolist verse that there exists a category of images in themselves "poetic." To these Apollinaire resolutely preferred democracy, ordinary language appropriate to poems in which automobiles and airplanes could circulate as freely as they were beginning to do in the rest of the world. Apollinaire looked at the contemporary scene with approving enthusiasm; he was by nature, and in accordance with Rimbaud's dictum, absolutely modern. It may be that the best of his poems are metrically conservative and traditional in subject (*"Le Pont Mirabeau"* and *"La Chanson du mal-aimé"* are at least the most familiar), but his experiments in literary cubism were of capital importance for the poets of his own and the next generation. LeRoy Breunig has observed that of the poets in orbit around Picasso—Max Jacob, Cocteau, Tzara, Eluard, Reverdy, to name a few of the most devoted—Apollinaire is distinguished by his refusal to claim for himself only the role of a disciple. In any case, the alliance of poetry and painting not only resulted in a liberation of form and imagery but, by causing the aims of poetry to appear less exclusive, made possible the "poetry by everyone" of surrealism.

World War I killed Apollinaire, whose successors found nihilism a more appropriate response than optimism. The dadaist movement, brought to Paris by Tristan Tzara in 1919, would have been productive only of diffuse violence had it not almost immediately begun to transform itself into surrealism whose first manifesto was published by André Breton in 1924. Gerard de Nerval ("Dream is another life"), Rimbaud, Apollinaire whom Breton called "the enchanter" and who gave the movement its name, Alfred Jarry for whose *Ubu-Roi* Breton would have sacrificed Shakespeare and Rabelais, Lautréamont whose *Chants de Maldoror* (1868) is probably the greatest of surrealist texts—these were the literary idols of surrealism, which prided itself, however, on being interested in literature only as a means. Art and beauty were regarded as secondary to knowledge, and knowledge was to be acquired by overthrowing the barriers of reason, the gateway to the subconscious. Man, no longer a prisoner of himself nor restricted by the vast institutions of reason, would be free to recognize and to accomplish his desires.

Accordingly, poetry became, at least in theory, automatic writing, dictated by the subconscious and distorted by no esthetic or moral considerations. Talent as it had previously been understood no longer existed; there was only more or less skill in evading the clinging remnants of logic. Poems could be written by anyone, or by groups—hence the famous surrealist parlor games. However, Aragon's *Traité du Style* (1928) noted in accord with orthodox theory that the use of surrealist techniques was no excuse for writing "sad stupidities"! The enduring value of surrealist poetry is precisely where Apollinaire had said it would be, in its quality of surprise due to the vast reservoir of imagery it made available. According to Gaëtan Picon, the surrealist ideal is in fact that of all contemporary literature which rejects art for art's sake to demand that language function as an act of commitment involving the whole of human experience.

Having formulated a revolutionary doctrine of social reform, the surrealists were bound to seek practical applications. Aragon was very early in desiring the merging of surrealism with communism, while Breton opposed any weakening of the group's autonomy. The violence of this dispute and its repercussions caused the complete dispersal of the surrealists as an organized movement; Breton remains its first and last official representative. The fervent idealism which believed that the world could be remodeled in freedom and by words gave way to the postwar despair and its existentialist interpretations. These, however, apparently had no attraction for poets who have had to recreate for themselves a place in a depleted world.

During the Resistance, arbitrary dictations from the subconscious became an irrelevant luxury, but the efficacy of language intensified by a more accessible poetry was convincing as never before. The words of Aragon, Eluard, Desnos, and many others were directly translated into action, courage, and hope. One lasting result has been an appreciation of eloquence, triumphant in the work of Pierre-Jean Jouve, Saint-Jean Perse, Pierre Emmanuel. Allied to this, confidence in love, derided by Mallarmé and his successor Valéry, and restored to French poetry by the surrealists, has survived the war, particularly through the influence of Eluard.

There is, however, an opposing tendency toward a poetry stripped of embellishment. Sometimes it has the expansive simplicity of common speech, as in the best poems of Prévert, or it may be reduced to aphorisms, fragmentary statements, which in the later work of René Char and in the sparse poems of André de Bouchet has only a minimal concern with communication and seems to begrudge the use of words at all. A greater awareness of the physical world, threatened and therefore the more to be cherished, evokes such a response as the prose poetry of Francis Ponge whose painstaking devotion summons through words the real and not anthropomorphized presence of natural objects. Jean Follain represents the new objectivity also, by carefully erasing the poet from the poem. For other poets, and among the most gifted, reality is the object of a metaphysical quest. The poem becomes an instrument of analysis and synthesis, fusing emotion and intellect, striving to close the gap between words and experience. If the heroic perspective of a Mallarmé is diminished by the skepticism fundamental to our age, it is limited also by an overriding concern for values uncompromisingly human.

This anthology cannot attempt to give full representation to three decades as important for poetry as any in French history. The selection is the result of an esthetic rather than a historical evaluation and so must be attributed more to personal preference than to objective principles. Of the poets who were prominent before 1945, it seemed reasonable to make the necessary omissions from among those more readily available in English. The younger poets, who are in any case much less cohesive than their predecessors, were not chosen to illustrate tendencies or influences but are simply those whose work, in whatever direction, seems the most impressive.

Translations unaccompanied by original texts assume an obligation to the impossible. The precise equation differs with every translator, if not with every line, but the present contributors have unanimously agreed that fidelity at the cost of poetry is no fidelity at all, while the poet's right to his own images deserves a fanatical respect. Which is to say that the translator's uneasy conscience is the best available guarantee of authenticity.

Patricia Terry

BIBLIOGRAPHY

Balakian, Anna. *Surrealism*. New York: Noonday Press, 1959.

Boisdeffre, Pierre De. *Une Histoire Vivante de la Littérature D'Aujourd'hui,* Le Livre Contemporain. Paris: Librairie Academique Perrin, 1961.

Borchardt, Georges (ed.). *New French Writing*. New York: Grove, 1961.

Fowlie, Wallace. *Mid-Century French Poets*. New York: Grove, 1955.

Picon, Gaetan. *Panorama De La Nouvelle Littérature Francaise*. Paris: Gallimard, 1960.

Raymond, M. *From Baudelaire to Surrealism*. New York: Wittenborn, 1950.

Rousselot, Jean. *Panorama Critique Des Nouveaux Poètes Francais*. Paris: Seghers, 1952.

Yale French Studies XXI, Poetry Since The Liberation.

GUILLAUME APOLLINAIRE (1880–1918) Illegitimate Roman birth, Polish blood, schooling on the French Riviera, and extensive travel made Wilhelm Apollinaris de Kostrowitzky a true European. His career and his notoriety belong to Paris. In order to earn a living he engaged in every form of literary activity and made his name in part as the early champion of painters like Picasso, Braque and Delaunay. Active collaboration with futurists and cubists stimulated an experimental bent that led him to eliminate punctuation in his poems and coin the word "surrealist."

Apollinaire wrote the most graceful and delicate lyrics in French since Verlaine; at the same time he developed a muscular free-verse style that suited his strong attraction to prophecy as the poet's major role. Many of his best poems mix the two styles in an alternation of personal and universal themes. The First World War caught him at the height of his powers and sent him to his death at thirty-eight. The acknowledged leader of the younger generation of poets, he portrayed his work as "This long quarrel between tradition and innovation, between Order and Adventure." He earned his motto: "I astonish."

BIBLIOGRAPHY

In French
    L'Heresiarque et Cie. Paris, 1910.
    Alcools. Paris, 1913.
    Les Peintres Cubistes. Paris, 1913.
    Calligrammes. Paris, 1918.
In English
    Selected Writings of Guillaume Apollinaire. Tr. Roger Shattuck. New York: New Directions, 1950.
    Alcools. Tr. William Meredith. New York: Doubleday, 1964.

❊　❊　❊

From THE BESTIARY
ORPHEUS

Admire his display of might
His true nobility of line;
This is the very voice of light
Says Triple Hermes' secret book.

THE MOUSE

Lovely days, the mice of time,
You slowly gnaw my life away.
O God! I shall be twenty-eight,
Years poorly spent, I am afraid.

THE ELEPHANT

As an elephant carries ivory
I bear in my mouth a precious gift.
O purple death! . . . I buy my fame
At the expense of pretty words.

THE PEACOCK

By spreading his tail this bird so fair,
Whose plumage drags the forest floor,
Appears more lovely than before,
But thus unveils his *derrière*.

TRANSLATED BY *Roger Shattuck*

From ALCOOLS
TWILIGHT
To Mademoiselle Marie Laurencin

Grazed by the shadows of the dead
Where day expires on the grass
The columbine takes off her clothes
Looks at her body in the pool

A charlatan out of the dusk
Praises the tricks to be performed
The sky is colorless and set
With Constellations pale as milk

From platform height the harlequin
Wanly salutes the audience
Magicians from Bohemia
Some fairies and some sorcerers

He brandishes with outstretched arms
The star he unhooked from the night
And all the while a hanged man rings
A cymbal with his hanging feet

The blind man rocks a lovely child
The roe walks by with all her fauns
The dwarf regards with sad demean
The magic growth of harlequin

THE GYPSY

The gypsy knew ahead of time
Our secret night-imprisoned lives
We said good-bye to her and hope
Sprang without reason from that well

Love like a lugubrious bear
Danced upright at our slightest will
The blue-bird lost his lovely plumes
And all the mendicants their beads

We knew that we had damned ourselves
But hope which beckoned there
Made us think hand in hand of what
The gypsy had foretold for us

THE FAREWELL

I picked this fragile sprig of heather
Autumn has died long since remember
Never again shall we see one another
Odor of time sprig of heather
And remember I await our life together

THE BETROTHAL

To Picasso

6.

I no longer have pity for myself
Nor can I express my torment of silence
All the words I have to say have become stars
An Icarus tries to rise as high as each of my eyes
And like a sun god I flame between these two nebulae
What have I done to the theological beasts of the mind
At one time the dead came back to revere me
And I hoped for the end of the world
But mine arrived whistling like a hurricane

7.

I have had the courage to look behind me
At the corpses of my days
Which strew my path and I mourn them
Some rot inside Italian churches
Or else in little lemon groves
Which blossom and bear fruit
At the same time and in all seasons
Other days cried before they died in taverns
Where vivid bouquets were wheeling about
Before the eyes of a mulatto woman who improvised poetry
And the roses of electricity still open
In the garden of my memory

13.

Templars I blaze among you on your pyre
Let us prophesy together O it is
For you Grand Master that I am on fire
And spin the night itself in this wild gyre

Flame frees my bonds Only my breath
Can snuff the tongues that lick at forty dead
I sight both shame and glory in my death
And tilt at the quintain that the future holds

Doubt swooped like a feigned and painted bird
Love frolicked with the sun in the village street
Their gay outlandish children built and lit
This pyre of passion where my courage nests

TRANSLATED BY *Roger Shattuck*

From CALLIGRAMMES
WINDOWS

The yellow fades from red to green
When aras sing in their native forest
Pihis giblets
There is a poem to be done on the bird with only one wing
We will send it by telephone
Giant traumatism
It makes your eyes run
There is one pretty one among all the young girls from Turin
The unfortunate young man blows his nose in his white necktie
You will lift the curtain

And now look at the window opening
Spiders when hands wove the light
Beauty paleness unfathomable violet tints
We shall try in vain to take our ease
They start at midnight
When you have time you have freedom
Periwinkles Eel-pouts multiple Stars and Sea-Urchins of sun-
    down
An old pair of yellow shoes in front of the window
Towers
Towers are streets
Wells
Wells are market places
Wells
Hollow trees hide women wandered from Capri
The Octoroons sing songs of dying
To their chestnut-colored wives
And the goose honk honk trumpets in the north
When racoon hunters
Scrape their pelts
Gleaming diamond
Vancouver
Where the train white with snow and fires of the night flees
    the winter

O Paris
The yellow fades from red to green
Paris Vancouver Hyères Maintenon New York and the Antilles
The window opens like an orange
Lovely fruit of light

RECONNAISSANCE

A solitary twilit beech
On the blue rise of my Reason's field . . .
I plot the angle in degrees
From heart to soul to horizon's tree

OCEAN OF EARTH

To G. de Chirico

I built a house in the middle of the ocean
Its windows are rivers which flow out of my eyes
Octopus stir all around its walls

Listen to the triple beat of their hearts and their beaks which
  tap on the window panes
                Humid house
                Burning house
                Rapid season
                Season which sings
          Airplanes drop eggs
          Watch out for the anchor
Watch out for the ink which they squirt
It's a good thing you came from the sky
The honeysuckle of the sky climbs up
The earthly octopus throb
And then we are closer and closer to being our own grave-
  diggers
Pale octopus of chalky waves O octopus with pale beaks
Around the house there is this ocean which you know
And which is never still

TRANSLATED BY *Roger Shattuck*

VITAM IMPENDERE AMORI

Love died in your encircling arms
Do you remember how it was
You will bring back her wayward charms
For you recall the world to her

Another spring out of the past
I think of all its tenderness
Adieu fond season as you pass
You will be back as tenderly

As twilight dies and ancient loves
Rub shoulders in its fading hour
Your fonder memory lies in chains
Far from our shadows which draw back

O hands which memory binds
Hands burning as a flaming pyre
Perfection is a phoenix come
To roost at last within their flame

Link by link the chain wears through
Your memory escapes its bonds
And scoffs in fleeing at our plight
Once more you have me at your feet

My secret is beyond your reach
The cortège wanders slowly on
But we still feel the strange regret
Of not conniving in its grief

The rose floats in the water's spell
And masks have passed in lonely bands
Within me chimes a little bell
The heavy secret you demand

The garden darkens in the dusk
Where women tell their stories to
The quiet night which scornfully
Spreads out the darkness of their hair

Children children while still young
Your tender wings took flight from you
In trying to defend itself
The rose loses its peerless scent

For now is come the hour of theft
Of tresses and of plumes and flowers
Pick from the font the water jet
The roses are its mistresses

The water gleamed where you went down
And I was drowning in your look
The soldier passes she leans out
Turns round and calmly breaks a branch

You float upon the wave of night
Flame is my heart turned upside down
The color of light tortoise-shell
Reflected in the cooling sea

O my fond youth abandoned as
A faded wreath is cast away
Here is the season coming back
Of dark suspicion and disdain

Canvasses compose the scene
Traversed by a false stream of blood
Stars blossom underneath the tree
Only a clown would wander here

A cold light scatters powder on
The décor and your rosy cheek
A gun shot afterwards a shout
And in the dark a portrait smiled

The glass broke in the picture frame
An air which one cannot define
Hovers between thought and sound
Part future and part memory

O my fond youth abandoned as
A faded wreath is cast away
Here is the season coming back
Of reason and of sad regret

TRANSLATED BY *Roger Shattuck*

CHAPEAU TOMBEAU

He spread his smut
In America
This little or-
nithological butt

    But
Enough of this
I'll take a piss

TRANSLATED BY *Roger Shattuck*

JULES SUPERVIELLE (1884–1960) Among the "cosmic" poets, Supervielle is the most human and the least pretentious. He writes with a deft simplicity which can illuminate even the greatest of mysteries. In several of his finest tales and poems death means to recognize the absolute value of the simply tangible—when one can no longer hold a flower or a pebble in one's hand. Elsewhere, however, Supervielle celebrates the power of the intangible: a thought "of terrible intensity" causes a child in *"L'Enfant de la Haute Mer"* to live alone and fixed forever at a point in time and space; or a star depends for its existence on the perceiving mind.

Like Lautréamont and Laforgue, whose influence he acknowledged, Supervielle was born in Montevideo, traveling to France for the first time when he was about ten years old. Europe could never make him forget the freedom and non-humanized expanses of the pampas; but he would be drawn time and again from America to the older, more self-conscious society to which he equally belonged. His work in one of its aspects reconciles these extremes. In the poems of *Gravitations, Les Amis inconnus, La Fable du Monde,* the wilderness of dream and of the cosmos, monsters, planets, even God become personal, intimate, one might say civilized. That Supervielle's raw material included violent manifestations of a universe uninhibited by logic is obvious to readers of his early work *L'Homme de la Pampa,* possibly the best and certainly the funniest of surrealist novels. To this violence his poems prefer coherence, a tranquility which tames but does not banish the monsters of the depths.

BIBLIOGRAPHY

Poems: *Gravitations* (1925), *La Fable du Monde* (1938), *Le Forçat innocent, 1939–1945* (1946), *L'Escalier* (1956), Paris: Gallimard.

Novels: *L'Homme de la Pampa, Le Voleur d'Enfants,* Paris: Gallimard.

Tales: *L'Arche de Noé, L'Enfant de la Haute Mer,* Paris: Gallimard.

Received the Grand Prix de Littérature de l'Académie Française.

Critical studies on Supervielle: Roy, Claude, *Jules Supervielle,* Paris: Seghers; Greene, Tatiana, *Jules Supervielle,* Paris: Gallimard.

PROPHECY

Some day the Earth will be only
A blind space which turning
Mingles night and day.
The vast sky of the Andes
Will float above no mountains,
Not even a small ravine.

All the world's houses will vanish
Except for one balcony,
A boundless grief will stand
For human geography,
And for the late Atlantic
A taste of salt in the air,
A fish flying and magic,
Ignorant of the sea.

In a nineteen-five coupé
(Four wheels without a road)
Three young girls of the day
Who stayed behind as mist
Will open the door quite sure
That Paris can't be far,
And all they will find is the odor
Of sky which sticks in your throat.

Out of the absent forest
Will rise the song of a bird
That no one at all can place,
Prefer, or even hear
Except God—He will listen
And say, "That's a goldfinch."

TRANSLATED BY *Patricia Terry*

FLAME TIP

All during his life
He had preferred to read
By candlelight
And often he would place
His hand over the flame
In order to be sure
He was alive,
Alive.

Since the day of his death
He has kept near him always
A lighted candle
But his hands behind his back.

TRANSLATED BY Patricia Terry

THE WAKE

We could see the wake but nothing of the boat
Because it was happiness that had passed by.

Looking at each other they had come at last
Deep within their eyes to the promised clearing

Where great stags were running at liberty,
No hunters visited this country without tears.

It was the next day after a night of cold
That they were recognized as drowned for love.

But what we might have taken for their grief
Assured us it was not to be trusted.

Part of their sail still floated in the air
Alone and free to take the wind as it pleased

Far from the boat and the oars drifting.

TRANSLATED BY Patricia Terry

REGRETTING THE EARTH

Some day we will be saying, "That was the time of the sun,
Do you remember its light fell on the slightest twig,
The elderly woman or young astonished girl,
As soon as it touched it gave their color to things,
Kept pace with the galloping horse and stopped when he did,
That unforgettable time when we were still on Earth
Where if we dropped something it made a noise,
We would look around us with the eyes of connoisseurs,
And our ears distinguished every nuance in the air,
When the footsteps of a friend approached, we knew,
We used to gather flowers or smooth pebbles,
At that time we never could take hold of smoke,
Ah! What else can our hands do for us now."

TRANSLATED BY Patricia Terry

THE HOUSE SURROUNDED

The mountain hesitates outside my window:
"How can I come in, if I am a mountain,
Extending as I do upwards, with rocks and pebbles,
A piece of the Earth, and changing under the Sky?"
The foliage of woods surrounds my house:
"What have the woods to say about all this?
Our world spread out in branches, leafy world,
What can it do in that room with its white bed,
Where a candlestick is burning at its peak,
Close to that flower sipping from a glass?
What can it do for that man who leans on his arm,
For a hand which writes in the shelter of four walls?
Let us take counsel from our fragile roots,
He hasn't seen us, he searches within himself
For trees which understand what he has to say."
And the river: "This is no concern of mine;
For myself alone I flow and know nothing of men.
Wherever they find me I have already gone,
Always ahead of myself, I fear to linger.
Who cares for people who walk away on their legs—
They leave and they will return the way they came."
But the star says, "Trembling I hang by a thread;
I cease to exist if no one thinks of me."

TRANSLATED BY *Patricia Terry*

METAMORPHOSIS IN BLOOD

While you put on new hands so cruelly
My last sad skin needs no analysis;
I grope in vain toward metamorphosis
In silence where assassins multiply.

Hungry for each other and eating our fill
To extinction, what's morose has come to die
At our feet. Sinners! Watch the endless trial
Where a rose takes the stand to testify.

For what? And to deaf ears the sounds don't reach,
So tangled is this flower's crimson speech,
She makes her point until the echoes hold
In monumental air increasingly cold.

TRANSLATED BY *Patricia Terry*

THE POET

I don't always go alone to the bottom of my self,
Quite often living captives bear me company.
Those who have stepped inside my cold caverns,
Are they sure that they can ever leave again?
Like a sinking ship I pile up in my night
Pell-mell all the passengers and sailors,
Then I extinguish every cabin's light;
The great depths will come to be my friends.

TRANSLATED BY *Patricia Terry*

THE RAINDROP

God speaks:
  I am looking for a raindrop
  Just now fallen into the sea.
  Gleaming the length of its plummet
  More than any of the others,
  This raindrop alone among them
  Had the power to understand
  That very sweet in salt water
  It would soon be lost forever.
  And so I look in the sea
  And on the now vigilant waves,
  Trying at least to do something
  For that fragile memory
  Which entrusted itself to my care.
  But it's no use; there are things
  Which cannot be helped even
  By God, despite His good will
  And the wordless interventions
  Of the sky, the waves, and the air.

TRANSLATED BY *Patricia Terry*

THE GRIEF OF THE DEAD

Lost among the footsteps and ruins of stars
And drawn into the gulf which devours the sky,
I can hear the breathing of stars on the march
In the depths of my, alas, eternal heart.
I have come here from Earth with all my human freight

Of panic-stricken hopes and abrupt memories—
What use in the sky is a heart which carries on
As if still under the sun, and can't learn how to die.
Have you seen my eyes wandering in this place
Where the near and far alike refuse all shore;
Blind and without a cane or strength or faith,
I seek a body, the one I had before.
If only I could keep from avid space
The memories prowling still around my home,
The faces dear to me, and, like a terrace,
Reason from which I overlooked myself.
Let me save at least this vacillating treasure
Like a long-haired dog who grips between his jaws
His little one almost dead, and fights the seafoam.
But closer now the foam of the abyss . . .
The universe around me utters a cruel sigh,
And the deep gorge of the sky rises.
Since all rejects me here, and even dream,
What could this realm, empty of land, promise?

Ah! even in death I have trouble sleeping,
I want to make forever a bit of now;
I'm still too green to be part of nothingness,
Off key among the cosmic harmonies.
How can I renounce those memories
When so much invisible luggage on my mind
Keeps me busier now than when I traveled,
And I float on death instead of sinking down.
Four planks of wood held me under the ground,
But the cemetery still let in the sky.
On the world, now an immense raft, my soul
Goes back and forth, but never quite in balance.
All rises once again when does the tombstone,
A hundred doves are freed by our first glance.
I had only my length in wood to call my own;
Beyond is splendor in the trees alone.

TRANSLATED BY *Patricia Terry*

THE SURVEY

O wrinkled aridity, a face
By a hundred clandestine

Battles laid waste,
And the toothmarks of ruins.
Dawn, the surveyor, begins;
We are naked under those great eyes
Which come to preside over us.
Are we thus to be posthumous?
When it waited for our arrival
The future was a giant,
And, as it turned its face
Toward us, our terraces filled with space.
In its haste to become the past,
Half somber and half of ice,
Thinner with every sunrise
The vaulted future turns aside.
And the present, being a skillful
Mimic, looks like its double.
We may try with our eyes closed
To regain it; the present is so
Absent-minded, so little our own,
It mistakes us for someone else.
Or a countenance with lidless
Eyes the better to penetrate
Seizes our very blood
And could turn it into stone.
It plants those secret pennons
Fixed, until they rot, to stay
In the singing flesh of the poet
Haunted by words which proffer deep
Welcome, until they slay.

TRANSLATED BY *Patricia Terry*

YOU DISAPPEAR

Already closed in mist you disappear
Now as through an evening we must row
Toward your exile among devouring years,
Slender in your arms the last of hope.

There are dead leaves all along your way
Stirred by the failing breath of loves gone by,
The moon behind you steals your strength away
Fading your pallor for the day you die.

Yet what is left to keep your heart alive
Still can penetrate your rueful candor,
And sometimes abrupt, radiant surprise
Awakens from your night the owls of splendor.

TRANSLATED BY *Patricia Terry*

PIERRE REVERDY (1889–1960) Pierre Reverdy has been called realist, surrealist, cubist, and mystic, all four titles being in his case perfectly appropriate and indeed identical in meaning. His life was given over to a quest for the absolute as heroic as Mallarmé's but in an opposite direction, not toward *L'Azur,* the purity of non-being, but toward the ultimate reality of being. The real can be apprehended by the mind provided that we refuse the false impressions offered by the senses. The situation corresponds to that of modern physics which has proved that our immediate experience of matter is illusory. But while the work of a scientist is to describe the real in terms of abstract phenomena uncontaminated by traces of his own intervention, the poet is concerned neither with reality per se nor with himself, but with their encounter which generates significant emotion, the "lyricism of reality." The poem, to re-phrase one of Reverdy's definitions, is a filament through which the diffuse currents of reality are made to pass, giving off light.

A Reverdy poem seems a discontinuous series of images or facts presented with the utmost economy: a door which does not open, a hand simply moving, the sound of a glass breaking, animals without their shadows. Instead of explanations, there is a multiple paradox; the poem is as solid as a physical object and yet intangible, it is dynamic and frozen at an indeterminate point in space and time. The disparate images are held in suspension in the mind, where their logic is made apparent, not by analysis, but by an inexplicable certainty, an emotion. Each poem is a fragment of the spiritual drama which was, for Reverdy, life itself and to which he was totally committed, maintaining through the political and esthetic revolutions of his time the absolute integrity of his vision.

BIBLIOGRAPHY

Poems: *La Lucarne ovale* (1916), *Les Ardoise du Toit* (1918), *Les Epaves du Ciel* (1924), Paris: Gallimard. *Sources du Vent* (1929), *Plupart du Temps* (1945), *Main-d'oeuvre* (1913–1949), Paris: Mercure de France.
Essays: *Self-Defense, Le Livre de mon bord.*
Critical Studies on Reverdy: Balakian, Anna, *Surrealism,* New York: Noonday Press; Rousselot, Jean, and Manoll, Michel, *Pierre Reverdy,* Paris: Seghers.

SUN

Someone has just gone by
And in the room
           has left a sigh
Life deserted
        The street
        An open window pane
A ray of sunshine
On the green plain

TRANSLATED BY *Anna Balakian*

NOMAD

The door which does not open
The hand which passes
      Afar the breaking of glasses
  The lamp is smoking
The sparks which are lighting
     The sky is blacker
        Over the roofs

Sundry animals
Shadowless

     A look
     A dark speck

The house no one enters

TRANSLATED BY *Anna Balakian*

SOUND OF BELL

All is snuffed out
The wind passes singing
     And the trees quiver
The animals are dead
There is no one left
     Look
The stars have stopped shining
     The earth stops turning
A head is leaning
     With hair sweeping away the night
The last bell-tower left standing
     Strikes midnight

TRANSLATED BY *Anna Balakian*

DEPARTURE

The horizon bends
   The days are getting longer
    Voyage
  A heart leaps in a cage
  A bird sings
  About to die
Another door will open
  At the end of the hall
  Where there is glowing
  A star
A dark woman
  The lantern of the train departing

TRANSLATED BY *Anna Balakian*

NOCTURNAL ROUND

A drone comes in from far
Worlds draw nearer one to the other
Stars are dangling from the borders of the steeple
Smoking chimneys in a far corner
Or burning candles
Someone has gone up
     The bells are going to ring
A cloud has touched them off while passing
One gets used to that
    No one is surprised at that
The eyes scan the altitude
   Where you are standing
A free heart has flown away
    You may still choose
    A resting place
    After a long excursion
Lower down there is a spot
     In the night
We were listening
    Did he come
On the horizon someone softly rises to heaven
The stairs are creaking
     it is an artificial thing
A parable or a passageway
The hour that was escaping flies on a single wing

TRANSLATED BY *Anna Balakian*

NOON

The character of man is changing. He can smile. He would extend his hand. One must then seek most peopled places—up there no one takes the offered hand. One makes a noisy entrance.

He scribbled rays in space straighter than the moon's. Moonbeam, he rallied, viewed all, looked down and sideways, then fell on his hard bed, or springless cot, and snored, adding to the night words exhaling vapors of alcohol.

Each step we take is more than a journey
We have no need to be in a hurry

❋   ❋   ❋

Those who are a source of disdain
Those who contain the drop of eternity that life demands
Those who have never known their limitation
Passing along the road with only heaven for a roof
bend their heads
The stars have got caught in their hair
Scorching their heads
And all that passes is a cavalcade
where metal clangs and catches fire

TRANSLATED BY *Anna Balakian*

THEY ALONE

The situation of a man before a wall that is infinite
With no signs on it
The line of the feet and the eyes converging
With no limit
But that is where it will all happen
The door left ajar upon the void
Each time a new wonder
And there quiver a curtain and recognition
What lies behind
Fear holds us back
We'll have no more
Without discontinuity the trees pass along with the sound
All the birds dropped dead
before the first shot was heard
The shot from the dark
The boulevard like a milky way

Street lamps half dimmed
  Eyes drawn with fatigue
Everything was blinking
  We knew not how
Alone the voice and the gait and the balance
of the senses stricken in the night he had felt the turning
of the earth and feared not to leave it

TRANSLATED BY *Anna Balakian*

DEAD WEIGHT *

Sister limpid sister calm
At the sashes of the window
Silhouette frozen whirling with the leaves
Rising with the vapors unrestrained
Lustrous laughter at awakening
Stifled whispers in the mossy fleece
Fearful contours more tightly drawn
Fate's imprints left on your resources
Missed chances tossed overboard
On the hard socle where bees dispute
A heart that has surpassed its weight
Unfathomed regrets rising to the first rung of their ladder
I am unfaithful to all I remember
I deliver chance untying all its strings
The desert is my witness
And all I shatter as I pass on
Is stronger than the pit that calls me
Yet all is sifted by my hunger
By the dire whims of habit
Each day the armed perusal of the horizon
The missing window pane that thrills me
One dies of thirst and ambition
One dies of staying too long in one position

TRANSLATED BY *Anna Balakian*

* It must be remembered that this and the following poem
were written during World War II and contain elliptical allusions to war. The translator has abstained from making the
images clear because that would not have been in keeping with
the character of Reverdy's poetry, which is concrete without
being precise.

BEYOND MEASURE

The world is my prison
If I am far from what I love
You are not far bars of the horizon
Love and liberty in a sky too empty
On a land too marked with grief
A face lights and warms the hard things
That were death's property
From here on I speak
With this face
These ways this voice
With my heart resounding, pounding
A fire-screen, a tender shading
Between the night's familiar walls
Beguiling circle of unfruitful solitudes
Pile of bright reflections
Regrets
All these debris of time crackle in the hearth
One more plan tossed in the fire
One more cue missed
Little left to take
From a man about to die

TRANSLATED BY *Anna Balakian*

THE WINDING ROAD

There is a terrible grayness of dust in the air
A south wind with stormy wings
Droning echoes of the water in the evening light that falters
And in the moist night that lurks around the corners
   harsh voices that complain
On the tongue a taste of cinders
Sound of an organ down the lane
The pitching of a heart at sea
And one's job with its disasters

When the desert fires go out one by one
When eyes are as moist as the blades of grass
When dew treads on the leaves barefooted
When morning is just arising
And someone is searching
For an address dropped on the road
Stars polished bright and flowers all tumble down

Through broken branches
And a secret stream wipes its soft lips barely unsealed
When sounds the step of someone walking on the sundial
Who rules over movement and pushes the horizon on
All the shouting passes all time converges
And I can now walk to heaven my eyes in the sun
There is noise without reason and in my mind there are names
And living faces

        all that happened on the earth

That carnival

       Where I lost my time

          TRANSLATED BY *Anna Balakian*

PAUL ELUARD (1895–1952) The various revelations which altered the course of poetry in his time seem to have been inherent in Paul Eluard's own personality—hence his distinctive ease and simplicity. Not being an iconoclast, he does not insist too much; his surrealism never made a virtue of raw incoherence, and even his later poems of communist inspiration derive more from a sympathetic awareness of poverty than from political dogma. To the surrealist restoration of love he contributed poems in which a sensuous contemplation of the beloved gradually illuminates the very universe and theory is transformed into conviction:

> I sing the great joy of singing you . . .
> I sing to sing, I love you in order to sing
> The mystery where love creates me and goes free.
>
> You are pure, you are even more pure than I.

Eluard always defended the claims of life over literature; or perhaps he understood their values to be identical. Thus the poems of *Au Rendez-vous allemand* or *Poésie et Vérité,* which are among the most effective of the Resistance, are not set apart from his earlier work, as are the wartime poems of Aragon. The Occupation simply brought into sharper focus his concern for human values and his belief in the solidarity of free men. His poems and his active participation as a leader in the publication and distribution of clandestine literature were the natural consequence of responsibilities accepted long before: "The time has come when all poets have the right and the duty to proclaim that they are deeply committed to the lives of other men, to life in common."

BIBLIOGRAPHY

Le Devoir et l'Inquiétude (1917), *Mourir ne pas mourir* (1924), *Capitale de la douleur* (1926), *L'Amour la Poésie* (1929), *L'Immaculée Conception,* with André Breton (1930), *La Vie immédiate* (1932), *La Rose publique* (1934), *Facile* (1935), *Les Yeux fertiles* (1936), *Cours naturel* (1938), *Poésie et Vérité* (1942), *Au Rendez-vous allemand* (1944), *Poésie ininterrompue* (1946), *Le Livre ouvert 1938–1944* (1947), *Le Dur Désir de durer* (1949).

LADY LOVE

She is standing on my lids
And her hair is in my hair
She has the colour of my eye
She has the body of my hand
In my shade she is engulfed
As a stone against the sky

She will never close her eyes
And she does not let me sleep
And her dreams in the bright day
Make the suns evaporate
And me laugh cry and laugh
Speak when I have nothing to say.

TRANSLATED BY *Samuel Beckett*

THE INVENTION

The right hand winnows the sand
Every transformation is possible.

After the stones the sun whets his fever to have done
The description of the landscape is not very important
The pleasant space of harvesting and no longer

Clear with my two eyes
As water and fire.

What is the role of the root?
Despair has broken all his bonds
He carries his hands to his head
One seven one four two one one
A hundred women in the street
Whom I shall never see again.

The art of living, liberal art, the art of dying well, the art of thinking, incoherent art, the art of smoking, the art of enjoying, the art of the Middle Ages, decorative art, the art of reasoning, the art of reasoning well, poetic art, mechanic art, erotic art, the art of being a grandfather, the art of the dance, the art of seeing, the art of being accomplished, the art of caressing, Japanese art, the art of playing, the art of eating, the art of torturing.

Yet I have never found what I write in what I love.

TRANSLATED BY *Samuel Beckett*

GEORGES BRAQUE

A bird flies away,
It discards the clouds like a useless veil,
It has never feared the light
Enclosed in its flight,
It has never owned a shadow.

Shells of harvests broken by the sun.
All the leaves in the woods say yes,
They know only how to say yes,
Every question, every reply
And the dew flows in the depths of this yes.

A man with roving eyes describes the sky of love.
He gathers its wonders
Like leaves in a wood,
Like birds in their wings
And men in their sleep.

TRANSLATED BY *David Gascoyne*

SECOND NATURE

In honour of the dumb the blind the deaf
Shoulderings of the great black stone
The things of time passing simply away

But then for the others knowing things by their names
The sear of every metamorphosis
The unbroken chain of dawns in the brain
The implacable cries shattering words

Furrowing the mouth furrowing the eyes
Where furious colours dispel the mists of vigil
Set up love against life that the dead dream of
The low-living share the others are slaves
Of love as some are slaves of freedom.

TRANSLATED BY *Samuel Beckett*

THEY ARE ALIKE

I change my mind
Following the breezes of fine thread
Following your legs your hands your eyes
The subtle dress which invents you
For you to replace it.

I change my mind
You pass in the street
In a hurricane of sun
I meet you I stop
I am young you must remember.

I change my mind
Your mouth is absent
I speak to you no longer you are asleep
There are fires of terror in your night
A field of clear tears in your dreams
We are not sad together
I forget you.

I change my mind
You cannot sleep
On careless ladders
Interminably
Between the flower and the fruit
In space
Between the flower and the fruit
You seek sleep
The first hoar frost
And you forget me.

I change my mind
You laugh you are living you play
And curious one a desert would people itself for you
And I have trust.

Finished
I have never been able to forget you
We shall never leave each other
To security we must give
The peasant snow the millstone of ruins
A respectable death
The day in pure loss drowns the stars

On the point of a single look
Of the same contemplation
We must burn the sphinx that resembles us
And its seasonable eyes
And its mosses of solitude.

TRANSLATED BY *Denis Devlin*

EVIL

The door was there like a saw
The force of walls was there
Ennui without object
The complacent floor
Facing the winning side which the dice rejected
There were broken windows
Where theatrical flesh of the wind cut itself
There were multiform colors
Boundaries of swamp
Tempo of every day
In a room abandoned a room in check
An empty room

TRANSLATED BY *Bernard Waldrop*

WE HAVE MADE THE DARKNESS OURS

We have made the darkness ours I hold your hand and lie
    awake
I sustain you with all my strength
The star of your powers I grave upon a rock
Deep furrow where the goodness of your body will bear fruit
And to myself I murmur your hidden name your public voice
I laugh still at the haughty woman
You treat like a sorry beggar
At the madmen you respect and the simple folk in whom you
    revel
And in my head that softly blends with yours and with the
    night
I marvel at the strange semblance you assume
A strange woman that resembles you that resembles all I love
And is always new.

TRANSLATED BY *George Reavey*

WARNING

The night that preceded his death
Was the shortest of his life
To know that he still existed
Set the blood in his wrists on fire
The weight of his body sickened him
The strength of it caused him to groan
And then from the uttermost depths
Of that horror he was smiling
He didn't have ONE comrade
But millions of them and millions
To avenge him he could be sure
And the day was dawning for him.

TRANSLATED BY *Patricia Terry*

OF NO AGE

We are close now
In the forests
Follow the street of morning
Go up the steps of the mist

We are close now
The Earth's heart is beating faster

Another day to bring into the world.

The sky will be growing larger
We were tired
Of living in sleep's ruins
In the low shadow of rest
Of fatigue of relaxing

The Earth will assume the shape of our living bodies
We will force ourselves on the wind
The sun the night will pass into our eyes
And never change them

Our sure space our pure air will suffice
To close the hiatus habit wedged in time
We shall enter upon a trackless memory
Together we shall speak a sensitive language.

O my opposite brothers who keep within your eyes
Pervasive night and its horror
Where did I leave you behind
With your heavy hands in the slow lazy oil
Of acts gone by
With so little hope that death is justified
O my lost brothers
As for me I'm going toward life I look like a man
To prove that the world is custom-made for me

And I'm not alone
A thousand images multiply my light
A thousand similar glances sooth the flesh
It's the bird the child the rock the plain
Becoming one with us
The gold laughs to find itself out of the depths
Water and fire go nude for just one season
The brow of the universe bears no eclipse.

Hands to our hands familiar
Lips as one with our lips
With the first warmth of flowers
And the quickening blood allied
The prism is breathing with us
Abundant dawn
On the tips of the grasses queen
On the summits of moss on the crest of the snows
Of waves of astonished sands
Of lingering childhoods
Far beyond all the caves
Beyond ourselves.

TRANSLATED BY *Patricia Terry*

LOUIS ARAGON (1897–) During the time of the Resistance Aragon, the extravagant virtuoso of dadaism, surrealism and communism, became the true poet of France, spokesman with Eluard for that impassioned patriotism which welled up from the underground to inspire courage and revolt. Whatever sacrifices of elegance to polemic, of artistic to political commitment he made after the war, it is nonetheless true that Aragon's had been the most effective voice in France when "for the people" meant for all Frenchmen who still desired to protest and to hope.

After 1940 poetry was valued as a superior means of communciation; freedom for France replaced the surrealists' hectic emancipation of themselves and their verse. For the partisans Aragon wrote dramatic bannerlike ballads, which were later collected in *La Diane française*. More carefully wrought and probably more durable are the poems of *Le Crève-Coeur* and *Les Yeux d'Elsa*, in which his immense technical resources were devoted to themes on which the spiritual survival of his country depended, producing masterpieces in the purest tradition of French poetry. If his poems to Elsa were worth the risks of clandestine circulation, it was not only for their lyrical tenderness which rescued love from the surrounding hatred and despair. Love was itself identified with Liberty, and Elsa became France.

BIBLIOGRAPHY

Poems: *Feu de Joie* (1920), *Le Mouvement perpétuel* (1925), *Hourra l'Oural* (1934), *Le Crève-Coeur* (1941), *Les Yeux d'Elsa* (1942), *Les Musée Grévin* (1943), Paris: Gallimard. *La Diane française* (1944), Paris: Seghers. *En étrange pays dans mon pays lui-même* (1945), *Le nouveau Crève-Coeur* (1948), *Les Yeux et la Mémoire, Mes Caravanes* (1948–54), *Le Roman inachevé* (1956), Paris: Gallimard.

Novels: *Anicet ou le Panorama, Le Payson de Paris, Les Beaux Quartiers, Les Voyageurs de l'Impériale, Aurélien, Les Communistes, La Semaine Sainte* (1958).

Critical studies on Aragon: Roy, Claude, *Aragon*, Paris: Seghers, 1945. Anglès, Auguste, "Aragon the Inopportune," *Yale French Studies XXI;* Josephson, Hannah, and Cowley, Malcolm, *Aragon Poet of Resurgent France,* London: The Pilot Press Ltd., 1946.

❊   ❊   ❊

ELSA AT THE MIRROR

It was in the very middle of our tragedy
And during a long day sitting at her mirror
She combed her golden hair I thought I saw
Her patient hands calming a great fire
It was in the very middle of our tragedy

And during a long day sitting at her mirror
She combed her golden hair and I would have said
It was in the very middle of our tragedy
That she was playing a tune for the harp unthinkingly
During all that long day sitting at her mirror

She combed her golden hair and I would have said
That she was wantonly torturing her memory
During all that long day sitting at her mirror
Rekindling the endless flowers of the great fire
Without saying what another in her place would have said

She was wantonly torturing her memory
It was in the very middle of our tragedy
The world was like that wretched mirror
The comb parted the fires of that shimmering silk
And those fires lit up the corners of my memory

It was in the very middle of our tragedy
As Thursday sits in the middle of the week

And during a long day sitting at her memory
From a distance she saw dying in her mirror

One by one the actors in our tragedy
Who are the best in this wretched world

And you know their names without my telling them
And the significance of the long evenings' flames

And of her gilded hair when she comes to sit down
And comb without words a great fire's reflection

TRANSLATED BY *Muriel Kittel*

THE NEW YEAR'S ROSE

Do you know the moon-rose
Do you know the time-rose
One is as like the other
As in the mirror of the lake
One the other shows

Do you know the bitter rose
Made of salt and refusal
Which blossoms on the ocean
Like rainbow after rain
As the tide ebbs and flows

The dream-rose and the soul-rose
At market in bunches sold
The game-rose the gamut-rose
Gamut of love forbidden
And the rose of wasted steps

Do you know the fear-rose
Do you know the night-rose
Both of them seem painted
As sound is painted on lips
As fruit on the tree grows

All the roses that I sing
All the roses of my choice
All the roses I devise
In vain I sing their praise
To the Rose before my eyes

TRANSLATED BY *Muriel Kittel*

I SHALL DEVISE FOR YOU THE ROSE

For you who are the indescribable rose
At least in words belonging to its usual ritual order
The rose evoked only by words foreign to the rose
Even as the cry that is torn and the pain transmitted
From the stars of pleasure over the abyss love

I shall devise for you the rose of worshiping fingers
That were forming a nave and crossed themselves and lose
   their leaves
I shall devise for you the rose beneath the porch
Of lovers who have no other bed but their arms

The rose at the heart of figures of stone dead without confession
The rose of the peasant blown up by a mine in his field
The crimson scent of a discovered letter
Where nothing is meant for me neither the caress nor the insult

The rendez-vous to which no one has come

An army in flight on a day of high wind

A mother's step in front of a prison

A man's song at siesta time under the olive trees

A cock fight in a foggy country
The rose of the soldier cut off from his country

I shall devise for you my rose as many roses
As there are diamonds in the water of the sea
As many roses as there are centuries in the dust of heaven
As many as there are dreams in one childish head

As many as there can be lights in a sob

TRANSLATED BY *Muriel Kittel*

THEY WILL NOT BELIEVE ME . . .

They will not believe me   In vain
I write it with my blood my violins my rhymes
And since we no longer know how to speak in the night the
    ancient language of oars
Suspended above the waters
To speak the dark dialect of man and woman
To speak to each other like two clasped hands
Like the delirium of happiness
Like the mouth that has lost all words dissimilar to kisses
Like the groaning of unbelief
Like the refusal to be swept away
O perfect word beyond all words
Height of song tessitura of cry
A moment comes when the note reaches unheard regions
The ear can no longer hear music that high
They will not believe me they will not   In vain
I say it with the springtime and the organs
I say it with all the syllables of heaven
With the singular orchestra of common things
And the banality of muffled alexandrines

In vain I say it with barbarous instruments
In vain I say it pounding on the partitions
In vain I say it as if setting fire to the national forests
In vain I say it like a declaration of war
Like an inferno issuing from a gluttonous blaze of cotton
They will not believe me   They have made themselves
An image of me perhaps in their own image
They clothe me in their surplus
They take me about with them and go so far as to quote my
    verse
So that it serves their purposes
Or else they turn it into pretty songs
I am a bit of their property
While waiting to become a street
I am in the dictionaries
And in the schoolbooks
Scandal is forbidden me

In vain I shout that I worship you
And am nothing but your lover

TRANSLATED BY *Muriel Kittel*

HENRI MICHAUX (1899–) Michaux was first published in 1920 but was ignored until after the war, when Gide recommended that he be "discovered." The definition of poetry had to be enlarged to admit him, and in spite of claims for his surrealism (though he makes the official surrealists seem frivolous, literary) and certain similarities to Kafka (though in Michaux man suffers not because he is guilty but because he is weak), Michaux remains unclassifiable. By his own definition he can only be a poet indirectly—"the ambition to write a poem is enough to kill it"—because poetry—which makes the intangible explicit—is a possible means for dealing with the hostile realities never quite concealed by the façade we call everyday life. He writes to exorcise; nameless demons in ambush are still more dangerous than those the poet-magician encounters face to face.

The reader feels rather like an uninvited guest in his own home, fascinated, personally concerned, and uneasy. Michaux writes of the inner world as calmly, as logically as if it were the external world with which it merges from time to time. There are real and imaginary countries, the adventures of the wistfully suffering but always resilient character, Plume, the desperate, matter-of-fact or flamboyant attempts of the magician himself to create and to dominate his creation. But whatever violence or confusion there may be, there is never chaos. The constant presence of Michaux provides the essential perspective, an ironic commentary which is part of the substance of the text.

BIBLIOGRAPHY

Qui je fus (1927), *Ecuador* (1929), *Mes Propriétés* (1929), *Un certain Plume* (1930), *Un Barbare en Asie* (1933), *La Nuit remue* (1935), *Voyage en Grande Garabagne* (1936), *Plume* and *Lointain intérieur* (1937), *Au Pays de la magie* (1941), *Exorcismes* (1943), *Labyrinthes* (1944), *L'Espace du dedans* (1944), *Epreuves, Exorcismes 1940–1944* (1945), *Ici, Poddema* (1946), *Passages* (1950), *Face aux verrous* (1954), *Misérable Miracle* (1955), *L'Infini turbulent* (1957), Paris: Seghers.

Critical studies on Henri Michaux: Gide, André, *Découvrons Henri Michaux*, Paris: Gallimard; Bertelé, René, *Henri Michaux*, Paris: Seghers.

❅ ❅ ❅

MY LIFE

My life, you take off without me.
You roll
while I'm still waiting to take a step.
You carry the battle somewhere else.
You leave me alone like this.
I've never followed you.

I don't see too clearly what you offer.
The little I want, you never bring.
Because of this lack, my ideals go way up
To all sorts of things, to infinity almost . . .
because of this little that's lacking, that you never bring.

TRANSLATED BY *Bernard Waldrop*

MY KING

In the middle of the night I besiege my King, rise by degrees and wring his neck.

He recovers. Once more I turn on him, once more I wring his neck.

I tend him, I tend him as if he were an old plumtree. His crown quakes on his head.

Yet he's my King: I know it and he knows it. Oh I'm his servant, that's for sure.

But in the night the passion in my hands strangles him without let-up. I'm no coward about it, though—barehanded I come, and throttle his regal throat.

And he's my King, whom for eversolong I've been strangling vainly in the stealth of my little room. At first his face turns purple, then in a few minutes resumes its natural hue, and his head comes right back up again, night after night.

In the stealth of my little room, I fart in the face of my King. Then I laugh. He strives to keep his brow serene, bathed clean of every hurt. But I fart in his face with never a stop, except to turn round to him and laugh and laugh in his blue-blood face striving to stay a King's.

That's how I deal with him. That's how my obscure life begins, that never makes an end.

And now I hurl him down on the ground and sit on his face—his august face disappears. My rugged pants all splotched with oil, my behind—for after all, that's its name—untroubledly keep their place on top of that face designed to reign.

And I don't hesitate, not me, to shift my weight to the left or right when I want. What's more, when I do it I don't give a damn if his eyes or nose are in the way. Once I'm seated I don't get off.

And when I turn round, his imperturbable face still—as it always does—reigns.

I swat him, swat him, swat him in the face. I make him blow his nose like a child.

Just the same, it's clear he's the one who's King, and I his subject, his only one.

I drive him out of my room with boots in the ass. I plaster him with tablescraps, turds. I jam his ears with pertinent curses, stab him shamefully to the core with Neapolitan calumny particularly scummy and detailed, whose mere recital leaves a stain that won't ever come out, fits like a cheap suit made-to-measure, the very dungjuice of existence.

And then the next day I've got to start all over again.

He's come back. He's there. He's always there. He just can't seem to pull up stakes for his own good. He absolutely has to impose his cursed presence on me, in my room so little as it is.

TRANSLATED BY *X. J. Kennedy*

NAUSEA OR THIS IS DEATH COMING ON?

Give yourself up, heart.
We've struggled long enough.
Let my life draw halt.
Cowards we were not.
Whatever we could we did.

Oh come on, old soul,
Get you gone or stay,
Up to you to choose.
Quit fingering my vitals so,
Now with attention, now off in space,
Get you gone or stay,
Up to you to choose.

I can take no more.

Sovereign lords of Death
I've neither blasphemed nor huzzahed you.
Pity me, a traveler who's made so many of these suitcaseless
    trips,

With no master, no money, fame gone elsewhere,
Surely you're mighty, can take a joke,
Pity this madman who, before he vaults the barrier, even now
  is shouting you his name,
Catch him in midair,
Let him fit if he can to your customs and to your casts of mind,
And if it please you to aid him, aid him then, I pray.

                              TRANSLATED BY *X. J. Kennedy*

INTERVENTION

In the old days I had too much respect for nature. I put
myself in front of things and landscapes and let them alone.

No more of that, now *I will intervene.*

I was then at Honfleur and was getting bored. So I resolutely brought in some camels there. That didn't seem to be
called for. Never mind. It was my idea. Besides, I put it into
execution with the greatest prudence. I introduced them first
on the days of great crowds, on Saturdays at the market place.
The confusion became indescribable and the tourists said, "Oh,
how it stinks! How dirty the people are here!" The smell
reached the port and began to outdo that of the shrimp. You
emerged from the crowd full of dust and the hairs of nobody
knew what.

And at night you couldn't help hearing the pounding of
camels' feet when they were trying to cross the dikes, gong!
gong! on the metal and the joists!

The camel invasion took place with regularity and sureness.

You began to see the Honfleurians squint every minute with
the suspicious look peculiar to camel-drivers when they are in-
specting their caravans to see if anything is missing and if they
can proceed; but I had to leave Honfleur on the fourth day.

I had launched in the same way a train of travelers. It left
Main Square at full speed, and went resolutely forward along
the water without worrying about the heaviness of the material; it sped onwards, saved by faith.

A pity that I had to go away, but I doubt very much that
calm will immediately reappear in that little city of shrimp
and mussel fishers.

                              TRANSLATED BY *Richard Ellmann*

"I AM WRITING TO YOU FROM A FAR-OFF COUNTRY"

I

We have here, she said, only one sun in the month, and for only a little while. We rub our eyes days ahead. But to no purpose. Inexorable weather. Sunlight arrives only at its proper hour.

Then we have a world of things to do, so long as there is light, in fact we hardly have time to look at one another a bit.

The trouble is that nighttime is when we must work, and we really must: dwarfs are born constantly.

II

When you walk in the country, she further confided to him, you may chance to meet with substantial masses on your road. These are mountains and sooner or later you must bend the knee to them. Resisting will do no good, you could go no further, even by hurting yourself.

I do not say this in order to wound. I could say other things if I really wanted to wound.

III

The dawn is gray here, she went on to tell him. It was not always like this. We do not know whom to accuse.

At night the cattle make a great bellowing, long and flutelike at the end. We feel compassionate, but what can we do?

The smell of eucalyptus surrounds us: a blessing—serenity, but it cannot protect us from everything, or else do you think that it really can protect us from everything?

IV

I add one further word to you, a question rather.

Does water flow in your country too? (I don't remember whether you've told me so) and it gives chills too, if it is the real thing.

Do I love it? I don't know. One feels so alone when it is cold. But quite otherwise when it is warm. Well then? How can I decide? How do you others decide, tell me, when you speak of it without disguise, with open heart?

V

I am writing to you from the end of the world. You must realize this. The trees often tremble. We collect the leaves. They have a ridiculous number of veins. But what for? There's nothing between them and the tree any more, and we go off troubled.

Could not life continue on earth without wind? Or must everything tremble, always, always?

There are subterranean disturbances, too, in the house as well, like angers which might come to face you, like stern beings who would like to wrest confessions.

We see nothing, except what is so unimportant to see.

Nothing, and yet we tremble. Why?

VI

We women here all live with tightened throats. Do you know, although I am very young, in other days I was still younger, and my companions were too. What does that mean? There is surely something horrible in it.

And in other days when, as I have already told you, we were younger still, we were afraid. Someone might have taken advantage of our confusion. Someone might have said to us: "You see, we're going to bury you. The moment has arrived." We were thinking: "It's true, we might just as well be buried this evening, if it's definitely stated that this is the moment."

And we did not dare run too much: Out of breath, at the end of a race, arriving in front of a ditch all prepared, and no time to say a word, no breath.

Tell me, just what is the secret in regard to this?

VII

There are constantly, she told him further, lions in the village, who walk about without any hindrance at all. On condition that we pay no attention to them, they pay no attention to us.

But if they see a young woman running in front of them, they have no desire to apologize for her anxiety. No! They devour her at once.

That is why they constantly walk about the village where they have nothing to do, for quite obviously they might yawn just as well elsewhere.

VIII

For a long, long time, she confided to him, we have been in combat with the sea.

On the very rare occasions when she is blue, soft, one might suppose her to be happy. But that would not last. Her smell says so anyway, a smell of rot (if it is not her bitterness).

Here I should explain the matter of the waves. It is terribly complicated, and the sea . . . I implore you, have confidence in me. Would I want to deceive you? She is not only a word.

She is not only a fear. She exists; I swear it to you; one sees her constantly.

Who? Why, we, we see her. She comes from far away to wrangle with us and to terrify us.

When you come you will see for yourself, you will be very startled. "Well, I'll be . . . !" you'll say, for she is stupefying.

We'll look at her together. I am sure I will not be afraid. Tell me, will this never happen?

IX

I cannot leave you with a doubt, she continues, with a lack of confidence. I should like to speak to you again of the sea. But the obstacle remains. The streams go forward; but not she. Listen, don't be angry, I swear it to you, I wouldn't dream of deceiving you. She is like that. No matter how excited she gets, she will halt before a little sand. She's a great falterer. She would certainly like to go forward, but there's the story.

Later on, maybe, some day she will go forward.

X

"We are more than ever surrounded by ants," says her letter. They push the dust uneasily at top speed. They take no interest in us.

Not one raises its head.

Theirs is the most tightly closed society that could exist, although outdoors they spread out constantly in all directions. No matter, their projected schemes, their preoccupations . . . they are among themselves . . . everywhere.

And up to the present time not one has raised its head toward us. It would rather be crushed.

XI

She writes to him again:

"You cannot imagine all that there is in the sky, you would have to see it to believe it. So now, the . . . but I'm not going to tell you their name at once."

In spite of their air of weighing a great deal and of occupying almost all the sky, they do not weigh, huge though they are, as much as a newborn baby.

We call them clouds.

It is true that water comes out of them, but not by compressing them, or by pounding them. It would be useless, they have so little.

But, by reason of their occupying lengths and lengths, widths and widths, deeps also and deeps, and of puffing themselves up, they succeed in the long run of making a few droplets of water fall, yes, of water. And we are really wet. We run off furious at having been trapped; for nobody knows the moment when they are going to release their drops; sometimes they rest for days without releasing them. And one would stay home waiting for them in vain.

XII

The education regarding chills is not well handled in this country. We are ignorant of the true rules and when the event appears, we are taken unawares.

It is Time, of course. (Is it the same with you?) One must arrive a little sooner than it does; you see what I mean, only a tiny bit ahead. You know the story of the flea in the drawer? Yes, of course. And how true it is, don't you think! I don't know what more to say. When are we going to see each other at last?

— TRANSLATED BY Richard Ellmann

JACQUES PRÉVERT (1900–) There were numerous poets who under the double influence of surrealism and Marxism intended to write a truly accessible, popular poetry in which craftsmanship would give a heightened value to everyday language. The one great success in this line has been that of Jacques Prévert, whose *Paroles* put poetry astonishingly among the best-sellers. Like e. e. cummings, but with much less technical ingenuity, Prévert is concerned with defending the fragile, innocent, or simply human against mechanized aggression and pompous authority. His poems tell stories or praise love and the springtime without ever sacrificing clarity for subtlety. Prévert is absolutely uninterested in metaphysical complications; he walks in a visible world talking of what he sees. His poems are linear, and the reader's experience of them is immediate or not at all. This is not to say, however, that Prévert is either naïf or unsophisticated. The very simplicity and directness of his best poems make them impossible to paraphrase, and the "pips of reality" are not less mysterious for being obvious.

BIBLIOGRAPHY

Poems: *Paroles* (1946), *Spectacle* (1951), *La Pluie et le Beau Temps* (1955), Paris: Gallimard.
Film Scenarios: *Les Visiteurs du Soir, Les Enfants du Paradis, Quai des Brumes,* Paris: Gallimard.

❋   ❋   ❋

QUARTIER LIBRE

I put my cap in the cage
and went out with the bird on my head
So
one no longer salutes
asked the commanding officer
No
one no longer salutes
replied the bird

Ah good
excuse me I thought one saluted
said the commanding officer
You are fully excused everybody makes mistakes
said the bird.

TRANSLATED BY *Lawrence Ferlinghetti*

ALICANTE

An orange on the table
On my rug your clothing
In my bed your breathing
Sweet gift of the moment
The dark is a cool thing
  Spark of my being.

TRANSLATED BY *Andrew Sinclair*

QUICKSANDS

  Demons and wonders
    Winds and tides
  The sea already backward rides
    And you
Like sea-weed in the wind's soft loving
In the sand of the sheet are dreaming and moving
  Demons and wonders
    Winds and tides
  The sea already backward rides
  But, in your half-opened eyes,
  Two small waves remain to keep
    Demons and wonders
    Winds and tides
  Two small waves to drown me deep.

TRANSLATED BY *Andrew Sinclair*

TO PAINT THE PORTRAIT OF A BIRD

Paint first a cage
with an open door
paint then
something pretty
something simple
something handsome

something useful
for the bird
then place the canvas against a tree
in a garden
in a wood
or in a forest
hide behind the tree
silently
motionless
Sometimes the bird arrives at once
but it may also take many years
before making up its mind
Do not be discouraged
wait
wait if need be many years
a speedy or a delayed arrival
bears no relation
to the success of the portrait
When the bird arrives
if it arrives
observe the most profound silence
wait until the bird enters the cage
and when it has entered
close the door gently with a stroke of the brush
then
paint out one by one all the bars of the cage
taking care to touch none of the bird's feathers
Paint then the portrait of a tree
choosing the loveliest of its branches
for the bird
paint too the green foliage and the fresh wind
the dust of the sun
and the noise of insects in the grass in the summer heat
and then wait for the bird to sing
If the bird does not sing
it is a bad sign
a sign that the picture is bad
but if it sings it is a good sign
a sign that you can sign
So you pluck gently then
one of the bird's feathers
and you write your name in a corner of the portrait.

TRANSLATED BY *John Dixon Hunt*

THE DUNCE

He says no with his head
but his heart says yes
he says yes to what he likes
he says no to the teacher
he is on his feet
to be questioned
to be asked all the problems
suddenly he shakes with uncontrollable mirth
and he rubs them all out
the figures and the words
the dates and the names
the sentences and the traps
and despite the threats from the master
amid the jeers of the child prodigies
with all the coloured chalks
upon the miserable black board
he draws the face of happiness.

TRANSLATED BY *John Dixon Hunt*

THE DISCOURSE ON PEACE

Near the end of an extremely important discourse
the great man of state stumbling
on a beautiful hollow phrase
falls over it
and undone with gaping mouth
shows his teeth
and the dental decay of his peaceful reasoning
exposes the nerve of war
the delicate question of money

TRANSLATED BY *Lawrence Ferlinghetti*

PICASSO GOES FOR A STROLL

On a thoroughly round plate of real porcelain
sits an apple
facing it squarely
a painter of reality
tries in vain to paint
the apple as it is
but it's not inclined to submit

it's got a mind of its own
and more than one pippin of a trick up its sleeve
that apple has
and there it poses girating
in its real plate
slyly on its own core
blandly sitting tight
and like a Duke de Guise who assumes the disguise of a gas
   light
to evade certain persons trying to do his portrait despite him
the apple takes the guise of a lovely fruit in disguise
and it's only then
that the painter of reality
begins to realize
that in its every appearance the apple is his enemy
and like the wretched starveling
like the poor pauper who suddenly finds himself at the mercy
   of some philanthropic and charitable association formidable
   in its philanthropy charity and formidableness
the wretched painter of reality
suddenly finds himself to be the pitiful prey
of an endless horde of associations of ideas
And the apple in its girations calls to mind the apple tree
paradise on earth and Eve and finally Adam
a sprayer an espalier Parmentier's potatoes or an escalator
Canada the Hesperides Normandy the Reinette or the Lady
the snake with the brandy glass or the rake in the Garden grass
and original sin
and the origins of art
and the Swiss with their William Tell
And Isaac Newton to boot
grand prize-winner of the Galactic Gravity Fair
and the painter with reeling brain feels his model disappearing
   into thin air
and falls asleep
It's at this very moment that Picasso
Passing by there as he does everywhere
day in day out always right at home
catches sight of the apple and the plate and the dozing painter
Imagine anybody painting an apple
says Picasso
and Picasso eats the apple
and the apple says Thanks

and Picasso smashes the dish
and goes away grinning
and the painter yanked from his reverie
like a tooth
finds himself all alone again facing his unfinished canvas
with in the very midst of the broken crockery
the terrifying pips of reality

TRANSLATED BY *Noelle Gillmor*

ROBERT DESNOS (1900–1945) So great was the affection which Robert Desnos inspired in his contemporaries that he continues to make literary critics aware of the dangers of pedantry which can reduce a human being to literature and literature to a triumph of the abstract intellect. Desnos was a poet in the same way and to the same extent that he was alive; if he was ever theoretical it was after the fact. He had been a practicing surrealist before surrealism was enunciated, and therefore, when the first Manifesto was written, he was the most valued member of the group—the justification, according to André Breton, of their farthest-reaching hopes. Desnos did not, however, conclude from this enthusiasm and his own success in producing chains of spontaneous images that genuine poetry is restricted to the subconscious. "The Night of Loveless Nights," written in 1928, is greatly enriched by surrealist imagery, but its verses are classical in form and its subject is a meditation on solitude and despair.

In 1930 Desnos abandoned the surrealists and his own technical experiments but continued to write poems in which immediate experience is re-created in the belief that a man may speak directly to other human beings and be understood. In spite of the quite extraordinary diversity of his work, it has an unmistakable unity of tone which seems, according to René Bertelé, to prove Desnos' assertion that a poet during his lifetime elaborates one great poem, of which only fragments can be brought to consciousness.

Those who knew Desnos stress unfailingly the generosity which is also apparent to his readers. His poems were among the most appreciated of the Resistance, and he continued courageous, optimistic and fraternal even after his imprisonment by the Gestapo in February, 1944. The last poem of all was sent to his wife Youki by a Polish student who found the poet dying of typhus among survivors of Buchenwald.

BIBLIOGRAPHY

Poems: *Deuil pour Deuil* (1924), *Corps et Biens* (1930), *Les Sans Cou* (1934), *Fortunes* (1942), *Domaine Public* (1953), Paris: Gallimard.

Critical studies on Desnos: Berger, Pierre, *Robert Desnos,* Paris: Seghers; Desnos, Youki, *Souvenirs,* Paris: Fayard, 1960.

CUCKOO-CLOCK

Everything was as if in a childlike picture.
The moon wore an opera hat whose eight reflections bounced
    on the surface of the ponds,
A ghost in a well-tailored shroud
Smoked a cigar at the window of its apartment,
On the last floor of a castle keep
Where the omniscient rook told cats their fortune.
There was the child in her nightgown lost in snowy paths
From having searched her shoes for the silk fan and the high-
    heeled pumps.
There was the fire on which, immense,
The firemen's shadows were outlined.
But, above all, there was the running thief, a big sack on his
    back,
On the moon-bleached road,
Escorted by the barking of dogs in the sleeping villages
And by the cackling of suddenly roused chickens.
I am not rich, said the ghost shaking off the ash from his cigar,
    I am not rich
But I'll bet you a hundred bucks
He'll go far if he keeps at it.
Vanity, all is vanity, replied the rook.
And so's your sister! said the cats.
My sister has beautiful jewels and beautiful spiders
In her castle of night.
A numberless crowd of servants
Comes every night to carry her to bed.
For breakfast she gets sweetmeats, dog-grass, and a small bugle
To blow into.
The moon laid its tall hat on the earth.
And that made a thick night
Where the ghost melted like a sugar cube in coffee.
The thief kept looking for his lost way
And finally fell asleep
And nothing remained beyond the earth
But a smoke-blue sky where the moon rubbed its forehead
    with a sponge
And the lost child who marched into the stars.
Here is your pretty fan
And your dancing shoes
Your grandmother's bodice

And lipstick for your lips.
You can dance among the stars
You can dance for the beautiful ladies
And cross ranges of heavenly roses
From which one falls each night
To reward the sleeper who had the best dream.
Put your shoes on and lace up your stays
Put one of these roses on your bodice
And some pink on your lips
And now flutter your fan
So that on earth there may still be
Nights to follow the days
Days to follow the nights.

TRANSLATED BY Glauco Cambon

THE GREAT DAYS OF THE POET

The scholars of light never invented anything but not very
    thick darkness.
The river rolls the little body of a woman and that means the
    end is near.
The widow in her wedding gown gets into the wrong train.
We shall all arrive late at our tomb.
A flesh vessel sinks into the sand of a small beach. The helms-
    man invites the passengers to silence.
The waves wait impatiently. Nearer, my God, to Thee!
The helmsman invites the waves to speak. They speak.
Night seals her bottles with stars and thrives in the export
    business.
Big stores are built to sell nightingales. But there is no way to
    satisfy the Queen of Siberia who wants a white nightingale.
An English commodore swears he'll never be caught again
    picking sage by night between the feet of salt statues.
With regard to this a small Cérébos salt cellar rises with
    difficulty on its slim legs.
It pours into my dish what is left of my life.
Enough to salt the Pacific Ocean.
You will place a lifebuoy on my grave
For one never knows.

(It's the Seven League Boots
This phrase: "I see Myself")
TRANSLATED BY Glauco Cambon

IF YOU ONLY KNEW

Remote from me and starlike, surflike, equipped with all the
tokens of myth,

Remote from me but present unawares,

Remote from me and steeped in deeper silence from my tireless
imagining,

Remote from me, O my precious mirage and dream without
end, you cannot know.

If you only knew.

Remote from me and perhaps more so through unknowing and
still unknowing.

Remote from me because doubtless you do not love me or,
what is the same, because I doubt it.

Remote from me because you carefully ignore my passionate
desires.

Remote from me because you are cruel.

If you only knew.

Remote from me, O joyous like the water-lily that dances on
its stalk in the river, O sad like seven o'clock in twilit
mushroom-beds.

Remote from me still silent as though in my presence and still
joyous like the hour that swoops from above in the shape of
a stork.

Remote from me in the moment when alembics sing, when
the taciturn sea bends back in clamor on the white pillows.

If you only knew.

Remote from me, O my ever present torment, remote from me
at the magnificent noise of oystershells crushed by the
noctambulist in the inchoate dawn when he passes by
restaurant doors.

If you only knew.

Remote from me, a voluntary and material mirage.

Remote from me there is an island which turns away at the
passage of ships.

Remote from me a quiet herd of oxen strays from its path,
stops obstinately on the brink of a deep ravine, remote from
me, O cruel.

Remote from me, a shooting star falls to the poet's nocturnal
bottle. He promptly corks it and after that spies on the
captive star, he spies on the constellations born on the walls,
remote from me, remote you are from me.

If you only knew.

Remote from me a house is brought to completion.

A bricklayer in a white blouse atop the scaffolding sings an utterly sad song and, suddenly, in the mortar-filled bucket appears the future of the house: the kisses of lovers and double suicides and nakedness in the rooms of the unknown belles and their midnight dreams and the voluptuous secrets surprised by the parquet boards.

Remote from me,

If you only knew.

If you only knew how I love you and, though you do not love me, how joyous I am, how strong and proud of going out with your image in my head, stepping out of the world.

How joyous to the point of death.

If you only knew how the world submits to me.

And you, unsubdued beauty, how you are my prisoner.

O you, remote from me, who subdue me.

If you only knew.

TRANSLATED BY *Glauco Cambon*

NIGHTFALL

You will go away when you like

The bed folds up and unlaces itself with delight like a bodice of black velvet

And the shining insect alights on the pillow

Sparkles and rejoins Night

The hammering wave arrives and keeps silent

Lovely Samoa falls asleep in cottonwool

O burrow, what are you doing with the flags? you roll them in the mud

Under the bare sky at the bottom of all mud

The shipwreck is stressed under the eyelid

I tell and describe sleep

I gather the phials of night and arrange them on shelves

The warbling of the wood bird shades into the wreckage of corks shaped like staring eyes

Never to go there never to die there joy is in excess

An additional guest at the round table in the emerald clearing and clangorous helmets by a heap of swords and ornate armor

A nerve like fond extinguished lamp of sundown

I sleep.

TRANSLATED BY *Glauco Cambon*

THE ANT

An ant ten-six or taller
all decked out in a bowler,
that don't exist, that don't exist.
An ant dragging trucks
full of penguins and ducks,
that don't exist, that don't exist.
An ant who can chat in
French, Greek or Pig-Latin,
that don't exist, that don't exist.
Well but!—why not?

TRANSLATED BY *Bernard Waldrop*

LAST POEM

I have so fiercely dreamed of you
And walked so far and spoken of you so,
Loved a shade of you so hard
That now I've no more left of you.
I'm left to be a shade among the shades
A hundred times more shade than shade
To be shade cast time and time again into your sun-trans-
figured life.

TRANSLATED BY *X. J. Kennedy*

AT WORLD'S END

They're jawing away in the black street at whose end the
water of the
River blithers at barges.
This butt flipped from a window makes a star.
They're jawing on and on in the black street.
Aaaaa, shut your jaws!
Cumbersome night, thick night no man can breathe.
A cry draws close to us, all but touches us, yet
Dies at the instant it breaks through to us.

Somewhere in the world, at the foot of some embankment,
A deserter parleys with sentinels who don't
understand his language.

TRANSLATED BY *X. J. Kennedy*

SUN

Sun in the earth, sunflower,
What have you done with the moon?

She's in the sky, I'm on the ground,
    Yet our two fates are one
For round ourselves we go round
    Like madmen in a pound.

TRANSLATED BY *X. J. Kennedy*

JEAN FOLLAIN (1903–)   The force of Jean Follain's poetry is in its discretion. The poems speak in a low voice, unobtrusively putting things together: a fox—human dreams; the bodies of songbirds—the taxidermist's mistress; a dead soldier—a sack of apples. The art by which these conjunctions are made so curiously compelling is all but invisible. The traditional devices of poetry are rejected; no incantations, no magical patina of music or brilliance of imagery serve to break down the barriers of the rational. Everything is accomplished by a precision in the choice and placing of the simplest words. Metrical formality is replaced by subdued rhythms which construct, out of unpretentious phrases, statements which the reader, like the taxidermist, finds both convincing and strange. That strangeness is the real subject of the poem.

Unlike Reverdy, whose metaphysical anxiety is just beyond an apparently impersonal façade, Follain is almost entirely absent from his own work. The mute surfaces of objects and events, detached from the flux and exhibited in his poems, are made to reveal themselves as signs of a larger order. With the utmost delicacy Follain makes this latent drama verbal, adding neither interpretation nor dialogue. The silence of reality, brought into focus by poems which suggest its definition, is intensified but not broken.

BIBLIOGRAPHY

Poems: *Usage du Temps* (1933–43), *Exister* (1947), *Territoires* (1953), *Tout instant* (1958), Paris: Gallimard. *Poèmes de L'Année 1959,* Paris: Seghers.

Prose: *Chef-lieu,* Paris: Gallimard, 1953.

Critical studies of Follain: Dhotel, André, *Jean Follain,* Paris: Seghers.

❋ ❋ ❋

FOX

Through our nights sometimes a fox roams
who across the drowsing earth
seeks out a hazardous living
grazing the sweet leaf

and from a long dream of rapine
and of childhood and of shame
filled though with mysteries of warm bread
and the live fire of cottages
we wake throats dry.

TRANSLATED BY *Bernard Waldrop*

CHILD'S BLACKNESS

Lights out
his parents gone to the play
a child runs against great wardrobes
against the legs of tables
but no vase is broken;
dressed in black the father
dozes in the old theatre
as his wife putting off every image of death
displays an impassive throat
adorned with cold gems.

TRANSLATED BY *Bernard Waldrop*

VOLUNTARY MAIMING

So he wouldn't have to serve
in the imperial army
one fine night with his axe
the master maimed himself,
took two great fingers off;
his bride a little blonde
tenderly bound his wound,
pansies with yellow hearts
shook in the garden plot,
the master's two hounds bayed
as he was borne to bed,
and then the lamps grew charred
and moth-ringed all around;
however the goodwives, ranged
upon the village square
in front of the red of clouds
declared that what they saw
was the red of soldiers' blood.

TRANSLATED BY *X. J. Kennedy*

THE MAN WHO STUFFED BIRDS

The taxidermist sat
before the pink throats
wings green or mauve
of his songbirds
dreaming of his mistress
with a body so different from
but sometimes so close to
that of the birds
that it seemed to him
strange
in its curves and its volumes
its colors and adornments
and its shadows.

TRANSLATED BY *Bernard Waldrop*

OWL

They say the barn owl
drinks the oil of sanctuary lamps
in village churches
it enters by a broken window
at night
while the soft and violent drowse
while pride and love wear out
while the leaves dream.
The beast warms its blood
with the oil lucent and virginal.

TRANSLATED BY *Bernard Waldrop*

DOG WITH SCHOOLBOYS

For fun the schoolboys crack the ice
along a path
next to the railroad
they are heavily clothed
in dark old woolens
belted with beat leather
The dog that follows them
no longer has a bowl to eat from
he is old
for he is their age.

TRANSLATED BY *Bernard Waldrop*

THESE AND THOSE

Far from the worry of woman affairs
the evening's indifference has joined sometimes
the last garden plots on the road curved inward
the profile of a man with open hands
and the animal sincere
all his days long
While others still prey
to the oldest sorrows
clench their fists around candelabra
throw light on the face of an imaginary guest
and search in broad darkness
for the face of love.

TRANSLATED BY *Bernard Waldrop*

DEATH

From beasts' bones
the factory made those buttons
which held the blouse shut
over a worker's
lively bosom
When she fell
one of the buttons dropped off into the night
and the gutter
carried it
to a private garden
where crumbled
a plaster statue of Pomona
laughing, nude.

TRANSLATED BY *Bernard Waldrop*

OCTOBER THOUGHTS

I like
this fine wine
drunk alone
when evening lights the copper-colored hills
No hunter now sets his sights
on game of the plains
Our friends' sisters
appear more beautiful

There is though menace of war
An insect lands
and again takes off.

TRANSLATED BY *Bernard Waldrop*

LIFE

A child is born
into a great landscape
Half a century later
he's nothing but a dead soldier
This was the man
we saw appear
and then set on the ground
a heavy sack of apples
two or three of which rolled out
sound among a world's sounds
where birds sang
on the stone threshold.

TRANSLATED BY *Bernard Waldrop*

BATHER

Skirt and blouse
of a woman bathing
a stone holds them down
close to these plants
brewed for herb-tea
While along comes
this man busy
eating his dry bread
bit of shade in the shade
on this expectant ground
in a landscape of forget-me-nots
whose blue will tremble.

TRANSLATED BY *Bernard Waldrop*

THE TERROR

On the heart-shaped credenza
a bouquet of paper flowers was placed
one morning during the Ancien Régime
during the Terror it is still there.

The hour is gentle
but of such alarming fragility
that the inhabitant jumps
at the slightest noise from the alleys.
In the evening
the animals are brought back home
the oldest one however
slightly bloodstained.

TRANSLATED BY *S. Gavronsky*

THE INSTANT

So many faces are
at the crossings
of a slow existence
close to the same windows
inviting in the sun.
It is when a man walks by,
his sturdy chest, his legs overborne
his smile
that throbs best
the pure instant
of the single ear of corn
which his indifferent hand picks
letting it escape the scythe.

TRANSLATED BY *S. Gavronsky*

THE PLANT

Savage type called harmful
it raises against the sky
its fluted stem and its tall umbullates
the sap rises bitter in its canals.
The emaciated stroller
fit for war
strikes down such a triumphant plant;
then hearing all those cries of children
who play in the fog
he can't bear it
living and misused every time.

TRANSLATED BY *S. Gavronsky*

RENÉ CHAR (1907–) During the war René Char, a decade and more younger than Eluard and Aragon, was inspired
not to eloquence but to direct action. His war journal,
Feuillets d'Hypnos, was written in those brief moments when
Captain Alexandre of the maquis in Provence could afford to
be "absent." These fragments, like compressed springs, hold
the multifaceted emotions of the occupation years, but Char is
more concerned with accuracy than with the requirements of
immediate communication. The style, like that of his later
poems, is quite opposed to the expansive tendencies of surrealism; it is as economical, as heavy with responsibility and as
wide awake as the gestures of the partisans he led. In spite of
their impersonality, which resists every temptation to be over-
emphatic, these statements, maxims, descriptions, and narrations are stamped with the presence of a man who was
courageous enough to refuse to allow the rescue of a comrade
at the price of a village destroyed, and who earned the right
to say that the poet, inclined to exaggerate, thinks straight
under pressure. Char is strong enough to be independent of
illusions; the claims he makes for poetry, and for love, hope,
and beauty ring true.

Since the war, living for the most part in his native
Provence, he has continued to write poems which are austere
sometimes to the point of being obscure, but which have nevertheless the warm radiance of a Provençal hillside, herb-scented
and dry. The powerful imagery of surrealism is still available
to him, subordinated and intensified by his disdain for anything
in excess of the essential. Often a moralist, he is never didactic
and ranks with Camus among the most convincing defenders
of human values in our times.

BIBLIOGRAPHY

Poems: *Le Marteau sans Maître* (1934), *Feuillets d'Hypnos*
(1946), *Fureur et Mystère* (1948), *Les Matinaux* (1950), *A
une Sérénité crispée* (1951), *Lettera Amorosa* (1953), *Recherche de la base et du sommet* (1955), *Pauvreté et Privilège*
(1955), *Poèmes et Prose choisis* (1957), Paris: Gallimard.

Critical studies of René Char: Pierre Berger, *René Char,*
Paris: Seghers, 1951; Georges Mounin, *Avez-vous lu Char?,*
Paris: Gallimard, 1946.

EVADNE

Summer and life were we in one
The fields consumed the color of your fragrant dress
Hunger and restraint were reconciled
The Chateau de Maubec was sinking into the clay
Soon would subside the rolling of its lyre
The violence of plants made us vacillate
A sculling raven who had left the crew
For the muted flint of quartered noon
Kept pace with the tender movements of our accord
Everywhere the scythe was going to rest
Our rarity was setting up a reign
(The sleepless wind wrinkling our eyelids
Turning every night the consented page
Wishes each part I hold of you prolonged
To a land of famished age and giant tear ducts)

It was the beginning of delightful years
The earth loved us a little I remember.

TRANSLATED BY *Jackson Mathews*

THE RAMPART OF TWIGS

The purpose of poetry being to make us supreme by im-
personalizing us, we reach by grace of the poem the plenitude
of what was only hinted at, or travestied, in the rantings of
the individual.

Poems are those bits of incorruptible being we toss into the
repugnant jaws of death, arching them high so that they rico-
chet and fall into the formative world of unity.

We have lost our way, without a dream. But there is always
a candle dancing in our hands. So the darkness we are entering
is our future sleep, getting shorter and shorter.

When we are fit to climb by the natural ladder toward some
initiatory summit, we leave below the lower rungs; but when
we come down, we bring back with us the rungs from the top.
And we bury the pinnacle in our rarest and most hidden
depths, below the bottom rung, but among more riches and
treasure than our adventure has brought back from the extreme tip of the trembling ladder.

Do not seek the limits of the sea. You contain them. They are given to you at the same instant as your vanished life. As you know, feeling is the child of matter, its marvelously subtle eye.

Young men, choose the dew of women, their lunatic cruelty to which your violence and your love can retort, rather than the dead ink of pen-murderers. Be swift muscular fish, keep to the rapids.

We live bound to the chest of a clock that helplessly watches the course of the sun come to its end and begin. But the clock will bend time, and bend the earth to us; that is our victory.

Though a permanent storm scorches my shores, far out my wave is deep, complex and prodigious. I expect nothing *finite*, I am resigned to sculling between two unequal dimensions. But even so. My markers are of lead, not cork, my trail is salt, not smoke.

To escape the shameful constraint of choosing between obedience and madness, to dodge over and over again the stroke of the despot's axe against which we have no protection though we struggle without stay: that is the justification of our role, of our destination and our dawdling. We must jump the barrier of the worst, run the perilous race, hunt on even beyond, cut to pieces the wicked one, and finally disappear without too much paraphernalia. A faint thanks given or received, and nothing more.

TRANSLATED BY *Jackson Mathews*

LIGHTNING VICTORY

The bird tills the soil,
The serpent sows,
Death, enriched,
Praises the harvest.

Pluto in the sky!

In ourselves the explosion.
There in myself only.
Mad and deaf, how could I be more so?

No more second self, nor changing face, no more season of
flame and season of shadow!

The lepers come down with the slow snow.

Suddenly love, the equal of terror,
With a hand I had never seen, puts an end to the fire,
straightens the sun, reshapes the beloved.

Nothing had heralded so strong an existence.

TRANSLATED BY *W. S. Merwin*

THE WOODS ALONG THE EPTE

That day I was but two legs walking.
Null at the center of my face, my eyes blank,
I set out to follow the stream through the little valley.
A slow runner, that dull hermit did not intrude
On the formlessness through which I moved.

Coming from the angle of a ruined wall left by fire,
Plunged suddenly into the gray water
Two wild rose vines filled with a gentle inflexible will.
There was about them a commerce of beings long ago gone,
now about to return.

The hoarse blush of a rose striking the water
Restored the primitive face of heaven with an ecstasy of
questions,
Woke the earth in the midst of loving words,
Urged me into the future like a hungry and feverish implement.
There was a turning in the Epte woods a little farther on.
But I did not have to leave this dear seedbearer of revival!
On the heel of a half-turn, I breathed the musk of a meadow
where some animal was melting.
I heard the gliding of a timid snake;
I knew—do not think harshly of me—that I was fulfilling the
wishes of everyone.

TRANSLATED BY *Jackson Mathews*

ANTONIN ARTAUD

I haven't the voice to sing your praise, great brother.
If I bent over your body which light is going to scatter,
Your laugh would repel me.
The affection between us, during what we improperly call a
fine storm,
Falls several times,

Kills, digs and burns,
Then is reborn afterwards in the softness of the mushroom.
You don't need a wall of words to raise your truth,
Nor sea-scrolls to anoint your profundity,
Nor this feverish hand that surrounds your wrist
And lightly leads you to cut down a forest
Whose axe is our entrails.
It's enough. Re-enter the volcano.
As for us,
Since we may weep, may assume your relief or ask, "Who's
    Artaud?" of this cluster of dynamite from which no particle
    is broken off,
Nothing is changed for us,
Nothing except this chimera quite alive with the hell that
    takes leave of our anguish.

TRANSLATED BY Charles Guenther

PLAY AND SLEEP . . .

Play and sleep, good thirst, our oppressors here aren't severe.
They joke gladly or hold our arm
To pass the perilous season.
Doubtless the poison has grown dull in them,
To the point of relaxing their cruel disposition.
Yet, how they pursued us until now, my thirst,
And forced us to live in the abandonment of our love reduced
    to a mortal providence!
Aromatics, is this for you? Or all plants who struggle under a
    wall of drouth, is this for you? Or clouds in the great
    expanse, taking leave of the column?
How can we foresee in the boundless?

What can we undertake to give those tyrants the slip, O my
    love?
Play and sleep so that I may take good size of our chances.
But if you come to my aid, I should have to drag you along
    with me, and I don't want to endanger you.
Then let's remain yet . . . And who could call us cowards?

TRANSLATED BY Charles Guenther

ALBERTO GIACOMETTI

Laundry spread out, clothing and house-linens held by
clothespins, hung on a washline. Its indifferent owner let it

spend the night outside. A fine colorless dew was displayed on the stones and grass. Despite the promise of heat, the fields still didn't dare to chatter. Among the deserted farms, the beauty of the morning was total, for the farmers hadn't opened their doors, with large locks and big keys, to wake up buckets and implements. The poultry yard complained. A couple of Giacometti, leaving the nearby path, appeared in the area. Naked or not. Slender and transparent, like the windows of burned out churches, graceful, just as ruins having suffered much in losing their former weight and blood. Yet proud with determination in the manner of those who are engaged untremblingly under the irreducible light of the undergrowth and of disasters. Those passionately fond of oleander stopped before the farmer's bush and inhaled its fragrance for a long time. The laundry on the line was frightened. A stupid dog ran off without barking. The man touched the womb of the woman, who tenderly thanked him with a gaze. But only the water of the deep well, under its little granite roof, rejoiced in that gesture, because it perceived its remote meaning. Inside the house, in the simple guest room, the great Giacometti was sleeping.

TRANSLATED BY *Charles Guenther*

DOOR OF WHOLESOME DEATH

(*Total examination.*)

"Death-cup, O mortal delight,
Sin is placid after its confession."

"I'm only an old pious harnessmaker,
I loved horses, I dressed them up."

"You caused injury and you were a traitor."

"I was alone, I tell you, in my workshop;
I was puncturing and softening leather."

"Guilty or suspect, you will be the one
Of whom History says, 'Thus he wishes to be.
Wouldn't I be rather foolish to question it?' "

Death-cup, luminous prisoner,
You will contribute to our effigy;
On you will rest the burden of our inclemency.

Repeat: "I confess, pardon, punish me."
And you will certify it with all your sleep—

A knife lay near, a danger or good fortune.
The man killed himself with freedom in his grasp.

                          TRANSLATED BY *Charles Guenther*

SONG OF THE STAIRS

It's day in the queen's chamber,
It's nighttime in the king's.
The queen already sings.
The king just fell asleep.

He watches one by one
The shadows chain him down.
The queen, indifferent, pays
No heed there with her gaze.

Their guiding destiny,
At which the king shudders,
Does not disturb the queen.
Below there shine the sea
And, rhythm of her veins,
She who made her burn,
Sister of that same wave.
O minutes so serene,
You serve the king no more!

The memory of an oak
Makes a clear impression
On his anxious brow.
It's in a different life;
When the queen awoke
Against the king's heartbeat.

O close your palace down
Or climb its flights of stairs,
Timid sovereign!
You'll know the reason why
The queen reclines her breast
On a high, wild rock.

You'll know the reason why,
And be consoled thereby.

                          TRANSLATED BY *Charles Guenther*

COMMON PRESENCE

You're in a rush to write
As if you were late for life
If that's how it is provide company to your sources
Hurry
Hurry to communicate
Your share of wonders rebellion benevolence
You're really late for life
Unutterable life
The only thing in the end you agree to join
That's denied you every day by beings and things
From whom you wrest a few meager scraps here and there
After merciless struggles
After that there's only submissive agony rough conclusion
If you meet death during your labor
Receive it like a sweating neck welcomes a dry handkerchief
By bowing
If you want to laugh
Offer your submission
Never your arms
You were created for rare occasions
Change disappear without regret
At the will of the suave rigor
District after district the liquidation of the world goes on

Without interruption
Without distraction

Let the dust swarm
None will reveal your union.

TRANSLATED BY *Charles Guenther*

CLAUDE VIGÉE (1921–) World War II drove Claude Vigée from his native Alsace to America, where he completed his studies and remained to become chairman of the Romance Languages Department at Brandeis University. The Indian Summer of New England furnishes him with the title for one of his books, the season when man and the world achieve a reconciliation. In the prose journal which accompanies the poems he writes, "At fifteen I was torn from what meant for me life, the real world, the future I had chosen for myself. During those interminable years I groped my way in an absence of world, separated even from my language, in the depths of solitude as physical as it was spiritual. Without romantic exaggeration, my life, at certain moments, seemed to me like a slow death."

From the turbulent virtuosity of *La Lutte avec l'ange* through *La Corne du grand pardon* to the limpid poems of *L'Eté indien* there is a triumphant progress toward clarity in depth which coincides with the poet's hard-won victory over exile. The facile solutions ("anywhere out of this world") are rejected; when the world is lost with the homeland, the homeland must become the world. Only long wandering in the desert can reveal the Promised Land, "simply *the earth,* the overwhelming reality of the Creation." Then poetry becomes a gesture of gratitude, the one valid contribution to that glory the human eye has witnessed.

BIBLIOGRAPHY

Poems: *La Lutte avec l'ange* (1950), *La Corne du grand pardon* (1955), Paris: Seghers; *L'Eté indien* (1957), Paris: Gallimard; *Le Poème du Retour* (1962), Paris: Mercure de France; *Canaan d'Exil* (1962), Paris: Seghers.
Translations: *Cinquante Poèmes de Rainer-Maria Rilke.*
Essays: *Les Artistes de la faim, La Condition poétique.*

❊ ❊ ❊

THE ENEMY OF SPRING

"I have never cared
for all those green mouths

which are set to laughing
by the slightest wind

Their thin tongues of grass
hostile to the silence

by their motion disturb
the adamantine dream

endlessly prolonged
into the beds of space

To sow through the night
the seed of nebulae

my white shaft is torn
from absence the black flame

From my peak to roots
I curve into the snow

my spine stretched even
to crack beneath the bark

I fear the air of life
and its so cruel spring

Now the sap is burning
in all of my dark wounds

Birch tree racked by stars
I draw in toward myself

my branches vibrant for
the planets' naked wind:

I am like a lyre
tuned to follow sleep."

TRANSLATED BY *Patricia Terry*

THE COSMIC COMEDIAN

Self-exiled I'll be
transformed to each place,
at a glance colonize

every star with my eyes,
at each moment encounter
the world in surprise.

I am nothing but sight:
the world is the poet,
the sun is the lover

who dazzles my mind.
What's there in the blind
mirror of night?

TRANSLATED BY *Patricia Terry*

THE PHOENIX OF MOZART

Arisen from what childhood
the bird of the source? In the darkest of hells
he sings with the exquisite mouth of the angels.

And that voice alone redeems us from the silence,
silence we wanted to follow, with which we shall die,

we who are deaf to all but our cries in the night
when circlets of wind upon our proffered wrists
turn their alien fires.

TRANSLATED BY *Patricia Terry*

BLUES

So Little Time

Spider, queen of my night,
in my burrow below
the earth I weave
a leaded window.

How shall a single landscape comprise
all that I was in the passage of days?
There are too many names, detours and eyes
in my encounter with life and its face.

To ruins the palace
the garden to urn;
the wine will turn
in its nocturnal chalice.

The dead are not far away; in their night
my shade too rejoins Earth's intimate dust.
Into my song a gag is thrust;
in my bed a monster serves my delight.

To the morning frost
inexhaustible mist
filters across
friable brick.

In the dome of tears
that I weave today
so few hours remain
before the great night,
so little time.

In their rose of stone
on the wall of sleep
if my lidless eyes
but an instant dream
the Earth is their prize,

My glass legs have spun:
my web is my sun!

TRANSLATED BY *Patricia Terry*

CHORALE IN DECEMBER

What dreaming bird
in the tear-drenched wood?
O rising sun,
and the Earth in flower.

Ash, if the tree
is pruned by flame,
fecundates
the rooted star.

Breath of creation,
resonant word,
in the world's winter
incarnate sun,

Come, illuminate
fear and the night,
lone bird alive
in a heart of ice.

Breath of creation
born of abyss,
you leap from the wind,
resonant word.

Naked, alone,
without haven on Earth,
by your birth denied
the maternal breast,

Bird by the night
sheltered for death,
you hold in your open
wing all space.

Life-giving sun
soars on the waves;
terror and ecstasy
merge in one.

Where light invades
the night of the heart
you consummate
the poem, the world,

Breath of creation,
resonant word.

TRANSLATED BY *Patricia Terry*

SONG

In a Rhineland forest
not a bird will sing:
    this is the home of absence
    where my heart is king.

In a few apples summer
loses its last teeth;
    now our days of ardor
    yield themselves to sleep.

The skeleton of fire
takes the leaves for prey:
    upon its blue cloud
    my heart sails away.

On the river willows
snow is balancing;
    in the Rhineland forest
    bird of silence, sing . . .

TRANSLATED BY *Patricia Terry*

APRIL

I am born of turbid blood:
My nature is double.

Kittens of the birch trees
rain through my green night.

On trunks sundered
by the frosted moon,

my solar pollen laughs:
stars, wind and sand.

Mother-water fills my valleys:
O uterine blackness.

But the foamy thickets,
green gold on my summits.

Doves and genistas,
ride my whirlwind!

TRANSLATED BY *Willis Barnstone*

EPIPHANY

I

From a single instant learn the meaning of exile:
in your heart laid waste by utmost solitude,
the dawning of love as at the world's morning.
All song is sacrifice. There are those who deny
the fire by impotence: they are left to our scorn.
But those who cast away the gold which they have known
in the murderous winter of genius will be destroyed.

II

Within the attentive heart the world is consumed,
the lofty night in unison everywhere breathes,
upon the white-washed walls of a mountain chalet
the lunar cat is dancing
before the black circle of forest tents;
a heavy insect rounds the summits of hills,
with green crystal flight a thousand others pierce
caves where the great North is combed by mists.

III

Rivers, overflow of solitary stars—
the universe trying to be.

Can it have patience? Here is the instant for birth.
Already the world has struck through all your windows
wanting to ripen like one fruit of light
with a loving eye for cradle.
You lived in exile from those secret rites;
suddenly you can see, already you are,
the world and you, inseparable creation.

IV

As beauty awakens on a face in love,
the mirror's flame alludes to that of space:
so, the summer's transparent mystery.
Within the nest of morning poem and child,
promises made flesh, are born of the same fire,
wearing the actual crimson of the sun.
The bird if he sings cries out: YOUR HEART IS WORLD,
the double kingdom under one simple crown
and in the human heart the world at home.

TRANSLATED BY *Patricia Terry*

ROBERT SABATIER (1923–)   The source of *Les Fêtes solaires* is confident, total joy: the sensuous exaltation of a child, a prince in a world not so much his possession as an extension of himself, and the more conscious triumph of a poet for whom words can be the language of the sun. The book is like a woodland flickering with wings and glowing with a diffused light in which the lines of verse seem to float. Here every dawn is "the accomplished miracle." Whatever anguish there may be, menace of death or silence of God, is dominated by its very participation in the song which is life itself.

In *Dédicace d'un Navire* the twentieth century dispels the timeless domain of the earlier book; in a "lucid summer" the songs of the birds are crushed under nets. The poet's despair has sharp edges; exiled from his kingdom, he becomes more cerebral, defending himself and his art against a world turned toward darkness. But the bitter violence that strikes at the reader of these poems has its roots in the earlier joy which persists like a dream. Between the bird that has flown and the monster to come, the poet holds in his empty hands the lost beauty of the world.

BIBLIOGRAPHY

Poems: *Les Fêtes solaires* (1955), *Dédicace d'un Navire* (1958). *Les Princes du sang* (in preparation), Paris: Editions Albin Michel.
Novels: *Alain et le Nègre, Le Marchand de Sable, Boulevard* (all translated into English).
Awarded the Prix Guillaume Apollinaire, 1955.
Essays: *L'Esprit poétique,* Paris: Editions Albin Michel.

❊   ❊   ❊

THE BOATMEN

They hauled with such persistence on our limbs
That stretched at length, we glided to the wave
They had been at us rummaging our embers
For stolen fire they'd wanted to retrieve
Not one of us could give it back to them

None of them sang, none of them shouted heave
A bone groaned, now and then bones cracked to bits
By what love sacrificed one sized up love
One took his lover's death for proof he lived
And the Danube was blue with delights

The long night slumbered in the ditch of flesh
Deep in the tow-rope's every upturned row
As each linehandler fallen to the rear
Let go his life we took his weight in tow

We had to haul his body up on land
A bit of fire, for lack of which men sleep
What sun could grudge a man that bit of fire
They hauled with such persistence on the dawns
That one by one the evenings fell away
The boatmen dangle at their hawsers' ends
And can't cry heave and don't know how to pray.

TRANSLATED BY *X. J. Kennedy*

FESTIVAL OF THE MOON

To one who dreamed long kisses with no lips
The wind brought only lips without desires
The adolescent left his tree at night
And slipped into the world to find a virgin
A little snow to offer his first sigh.

Tired of being a tree he was a wall
Against his neck there breathed a stronger wind
Whoever lent an ear to its long hollows
Heard in a thousand bursts of gunfire dawn
Dead children stood erect in the bright sun.

His arms full of names that were like lace
The treasure was his to carry all alone
And every time a new and lovelier rose
Was born to the day he fled into her body
To name her and to lie within her sleep.

He went away to find the lands where white
Sobs of demonic rivers overflow
His mouth was open to the cosmic snows
He held the image that he loved so tight
His body by itself cast two shadows.

The night of the sea pressed his open eyes
The dead man glided down the slopes of day
The dead man drank from the ocean's lips
And lived again because he had known love
In a country where the flags are half-mast always.

To live it was enough that he be named
One could sleep better dreaming of his arms
And he sliding into the human night
Brought sleeping men the dawn and showed the way
Into the splendor of the world's light.

TRANSLATED BY *Patricia Terry*

MOUNTEBANKS

The mountebanks had such convincing grins
One forgot they were dying from nothing to eat
Each slept on the ground without a word
That he might listen to his heart beat.

What is this voice that stirs like a heart
That runs in me like an open vein
They were there and I had no more to fear
As soon as they sang the sea turned green
They were there to inhabit my eyes.

What man here would rather not be born
Than a hundred times to die inside
I face day hardly amazed I exist
I loved them—in front of me they died.

Oh a poplar tree was the tallest of them
He longed for a life free in the air
Another rolled like a flesh-and-blood stone
And the third was as beautiful as dream.

About the woman I'd rather not tell
Blue gardens would flower forth left and right
The mountebanks bed down on their swords
And it's their hands their faces their eyes
That we clasp against us in the night.

TRANSLATED BY *Felicia Borden*

VEGETAL BODY

One must be sun to make homes in these trees
You are mere perfumes in the sleeping night
Rouse up and live—an inch above that star
There is a further sky permitted you
The mouth that sang to lure archangels down
Portends its blossoms to your dazzled eyes
On earth you only need pull down a branch
To hear the nests burst all at once to voice.

Had you such hunger you could feast on shade
You'd give light at the outcome of your roads
You are the kings of kingdoms beyond count
This glinting lute is scepter to your hands
Sun lives in you O voyagers of space
Its every ray flares from your fingertips
Look in my mirror not to see my face
But imaged in my voice the face of spring.

What do I do but feed this living force
A scrap of food? The orange I first knew
Sang in my mouth and made my flesh grow ripe
Here shadow and rain possess the curious power
To turn back short of me. Born of a tear
They go, a coach of mares and seraphim
Waltzing and wheeling on the heart's plains
To fetch my thirst grapes of their garnering.

You voyagers in fate, with such grave eyes
Your voices can engage you in our games
Why dread the sky? What if death root you out?
I know a way to bind her as I wish
Voyagers, voyagers, you'll live a few centuries
No sound cast off can wholly wear away
Deep in their eyepits green plants hold it fast
And swords as well know how to hostel it.

If to exist I sang, better I slept
I sing that this dry rock may give off light
Without my voice, without my lyre I'd live
My songs would sicken me, my skin become
Only the jail of sky, each sightless beast
Enter beneath my nails, invade my pores
Gorge on my voice lest it should live alone
From mouth to ear it would become my flesh.

Yet here I stand who am as none can be
By grace of song; song only, absolute
Fear it no more O you who see it born
You've drunk of it and now your eyes are bare
To others now, your palms are offered forth
Now we are reunited as the child
With fruit he eats—oh, we are nothing more
Than limbs of one who names us in his bones.

TRANSLATED BY X. J. Kennedy

MORTAL LANDSCAPE

The bird is flown, the monster not yet born
where shall we go in this demolished world?
We lie here in position on our death,
flesh bent to flesh in this decrepit light
weary of walking forth to meet the dawns.

Between man and his shadow there remains
a hairsbreadth crack through which his days slip by.
Stars of the night, stars that sink teeth in worlds,
I plant the stolen dagger of my cry
into that breast where Godhead walks its rounds.

Each fit of sorrow yields me up to joy.
Murder or peace—which am I waiting for?
Faces lie hidden in the brake of words
faces I fear so hard, one spring will do
to drive them into the pasture of my lines.

The bird is flown, no look lifts from the ground.
I seek in dirt a hole where I can sleep
and yet so many corpses dreamless lie
that what in man is man has had to die
and even words at last make meals on lips.

TRANSLATED BY X. J. Kennedy

THE VOYAGES

When from a cloud a sudden bird bursts free
Pure fools have but to touch it as it flies
And it's time to inhabit space and be
Flown faster than tears fall or than sighs
To where children and Magi have a country.

Brothers, my fingertips salute you, going
Upon that voyage where spring follows you
One breath, it's earth; one word, it's water flowing,
A murmur and the night is born anew
As long as your mouth thirsts for the Unknowing.

Those dwellers in the eye and in the ear
Have built them palaces of crystal walls
Guests of the forests, of the drowsy mere
Through silent paths and through dark intervals
Bring me your sun, your great burning sphere.

O book open to the pure fool's hand
O book of that hour when love's shining through
I am the child of all that fertile land
Who among flocks of days still waits for you
That body may at last join in the round.

TRANSLATED BY *May Sarton*

LIVING LIGHT

A child speaks and now the lark has come
Collecting all the fire he has spoken
Each goes his way and carries in his eyes
The bright of dawn and of seasons renewed
On the ground the child now sleeps and dreams.

As soon as he says sun, a beach
Becomes his path; the sky is pearl
The shell is a reflection of a star
A god comes to the sea to dance
And dress in seaweed and the waves.

A child speaks or perhaps a rock
Is it a perfume that escapes from him
The mouth that calls these dazzled words
To meet their image has transcended night
Love breaks out and releases dawn.

A child speaks, offering his planet
To the world with all its dangers
Take this face, vulnerable to stone
A single kiss could protect it
And it wakes to the caress of lips.

TRANSLATED BY *Victoria Rippere*

YVES BONNEFOY (1923–) Yves Bonnefoy was immediately recognized as a major poet on the publication of *Du
Mouvement et de l'Immobilité de Douve*. In this century only
Valéry's *"La Jeune Parque"* has evoked a comparable response, and for similar reasons: a stylistic mastery derived
from the classical tradition of French verse and a theme of
great complexity whose façade carries its own sensuous conviction. Bonnefoy's work has the additional persuasive force
of moving along the most vital currents of the literature of
its time; it is not inconoclastic but relevant, obscure only in
the subtlety of its argument and in its refusal to accommodate
crystallizing definitions.

Maurio Maurin has pointed out the resemblance between
Douve and Beckett's *Waiting for Godot* "where what is actually being communicated is a certain structure of experience."
Douve is a woman, merging from time to time with aspects
of Nature; it is also and simultaneously language and the
creative process. The poem illuminates the itinerary implied
by its epigraph, a quotation from Hegel: "But the life of
the spirit is not fearful of death and does not shrink away
from it. It is the life which endures death and in death maintains itself." The affirmation can be realized only by negation,
presence by absence. Douve submits to a minutely physical
death and is reborn, a pure presence in the "true place."
Language reduces itself to silence to become the "greatest cry
a man ever attempted."

BIBLIOGRAPHY

Poems: *Du Mouvement et de l'Immobilité de Douve* (1953),
Hier Régnant Désert (1958).

Essays: *Traité du pianiste* (1946); *Peintures murales de la
France gothique* (1954), *L'Improbable* (1959), *La Seconde
Simplicité* (1961), Paris: Mercure de France.

Translations: *Henry IV, Part I, Hamlet, Julius Caesar* by
Shakespeare, Paris: Mercure de France.

❊   ❊   ❊

THEATRE

I

I could see you run on terraces,
I could see you struggle against the wind,
The cold was bleeding on your lips.

And I saw you break and rejoice at being dead,
  O more beautiful
Than the lightning, when it stains the white windows with
  your blood.

II

The dying summer was chilling you with dull pleasures, we
were scornful of the imperfect drunkenness of life.

"Rather the ivy," you were saying, "the clinging of ivy to
the stones of its night: presence without issue, face without
roots.

"Last happy window ripped by the sun's claw, rather in the
mountains this village to die in.

"Rather this wind . . ."

III

In question was a wind stronger than our memories,
Stupor of dresses and cry of rocks—and you were passing in
  front of these flames,
Head graphpapered, hands split open, wholly
Seeking death on the exultant drums of your gestures.

It was day of your breasts
And you were reigning at last absent from my head.

IV

I awaken, it rains. The wind pierces you, Douve, resinous
heath sleeping near me. I am on a terrace, in a pit of death.
Great dogs of leafage tremble.

The arm you lift, suddenly, on a door, lights me across the
ages. Village of embers, each instant I see you being born,
Douve,

Each instant dying.

V

The arm that is lifted and the arm that is turned
Are simultaneous only for our dull heads,
But these sheets of greenness and mud thrown back,
Nothing remains except a fire in death's kingdom.

The dismantled leg pierced by the strong wind
Driving heads of rain before it
Will light you only to the threshold of this kingdom,
Gestures of Douve, gestures already slower, black gestures.

VI

What pallor comes over you, underground river, what artery breaks in you, where your fall is echoing?

This arm you lift suddenly opens, ignites. Your face draws back. What thickening mist wrenches your gaze from me? Slow cliff of shadow, frontier of death.

Mute arms greet you, trees of another shore.

VII

Wounded one blurred among the leaves,
But caught by the blood of fading paths,
Accomplice yet of life.

I have seen you, beached at your struggle's end,
Falter at the edge of the silence and the water,
And mouth sullied by the last stars
Break off with a cry the horrible nightwatch.

O raising in air suddenly hard as rock
A beautiful gesture of coal.

VIII

The absurd music starts in the hands, in the knees, then there is the cracking in the head, the music swells under the lips, its certainty gets to the underslope of the face.

Now the woodwork of the face is taken apart. Now begins the tearing out of the sight.

IX

White under a ceiling of insects, poorly lit, in profile,
Your dress stained by the venom of lamps,
I find you stretched out,
Your mouth higher than a river breaking far away on the earth.

Broken being whom the invincible being puts back together,
Presence possessed again in the torch of cold,
O watcher always I find you dead
Douve saying Phoenix I am watching in this cold.

X

I see Douve stretched out. At the topmost point of bodily space I hear her rustling. The black-princes hurry their mandibles across the space in which Douve's hands unfold, their unfleshed bones becoming a grey web which the massive spider lights.

XI

Covered by the silent humus of the world,
Webbed over by a living spider's rays,
Already undergoing the change into sand
And cut to pieces secret knowledge.

Adorned for a festival in the emptiness
And teeth bared as if for love,

Fountain of my death, with me, unbearable.

XII

I see Douve stretched out. In the scarlet city of air, where branches are battling across her face, where roots find their way into her body—she radiates a joy strident with insects, a frightful music.

To the black tread of the earth, Douve, ravaged and exultant, returns to the gnarled lamp of the plateaus.

XIII

Your face tonight lighted by the earth,
But I see your eyes' corruption
And the word face makes no sense any more.

The interior sea lighted by turning eagles,
This is an image.
I hold you cold at a depth where images do not take any more.

XIV

I see Douve stretched out. In a white room, eyes dark-circled with plaster, mouth dizzy and hands condemned to the luxuriant grass invading her on all sides.

The door opens. An orchestra advances. And faceted eyes, wooly thoraxes, cold heads beaked and pincered, flood over her.

XV

O gifted with a profile in which the earth is raging
I see you disappearing.

On your lips bare grass and flintsparks
Invent your last smile,

Deep knowledge in which the ancient
Bestiary of the mind burns to ashes.

XVI

Home of a dark fire where our slopes converge! Under its vaults I see you glimmering, motionless Douve, caught in the vertical net of death.

Masterful Douve, thrown down: to the march of suns through funeral space, she accedes slowly to the lower levels.

XVII

The ravine enters the mouth now,
The five fingers disperse in casual woods now,
The original head flows among the grasses now,
The throat paints itself with snow and wolves now,
The eyes blow on which of death's passengers and it is we in
  this wind in this water in this cold now.

XVIII

Exact presence, whom no flame again could restrain; bearer of secret coldness; living, by that blood which revives and grows where the poem is destroyed,

It was necessary for you to appear, thus, at the mute limits, and to undergo the ordeal of this land of death where your light increases.

O most beautiful, and death in your laughter! I dare now to meet you, I can face your gestures' flashing.

XIX

On the first day of cold our head escapes,
Like a prisoner fleeing into the higher air,
But, Douve of one instant, this arrow falls
And breaks its crown of palms on the ground.

Thus we had dreamed of reincarnating our gestures
But the head gainsaid we drink a cold water,
And bankrolls of death are buntings on your smile,
Attempted rift in the thickness of the world.

TRANSLATED BY *Galway Kinnell*

ANOTHER VOICE

Shaking your hair or Phoenix's ashes
What gesture do you venture now everything is halting,

And the inner midnight is lighting the tables?

What sign do you keep on your black lips,
What poor speech now all is growing still,

Last brand now the hearth is flickering and closing?

I will learn how to live in you, I will tear
All light out of you,

All incarnation, all reefs, all law.

And in the emptiness where I raise you I will open
The roadway of lightning,

Or greatest cry a man ever attempted.

TRANSLATED BY *Galway Kinnell*

THUS WE WILL WALK

Thus we will walk on the ruins of a vast sky,
The distant landscape will come into fullness
Like a destiny in the vivid light.

The long-sought most beautiful country
Will lie out before us—land of the salamanders.

Look, you will say, at that stone:
Death is in it.
This is the secret lamp burning under our gestures,
Thus we walk lighted.

TRANSLATED BY *Galway Kinnell*

THE WIND IS QUIET

The wind is quiet, lord of the oldest keening,
Shall I be the last to arm myself for the dead?
Already the fire is memory only and ashes
And sound of a wing folded, and sound of a face dead.

Are you willing to love only iron of the grey water
When the angel of your night will come to close the harbor
And shed in the motionless water of the harbor
The last flickers of light caught in the dead wing?

Oh, suffer at least from my hard word,
And for you I shall conquer sleep and death,
For you I shall hail to the breaking tree
The flame that will be the ship and the harbor.

For you I shall raise the fire of no place nor hour,
A wind seeking the fire, the tree tops of the dead wood,
The horizon of a voice where the stars are falling
And the moon meddling in the disorder of the dead.

TRANSLATED BY *Jackson Mathews*

THE IRON BRIDGE

No doubt there is still at the end of a long street
Where I walked as a child a pool of oil,
A rectangle of thick death under the black sky.

Since then, poetry
Has divided its waters from the other waters
No beauty, no color can hold it,
It anguishes for iron and night.

It nourishes
A long yearn of dead river bank, an iron bridge
Leaping for the other bank into still darker night
Is its only memory and its only love.

TRANSLATED BY *Jackson Mathews*

HERE, STILL HERE

Here, the home of light. No longer dawn,
It is day already, with its speakable desires.
Of the mirages of song in your dream, there remains
But this sparkle of stones to come.

Here, until evening. The flower of shadows
Will turn on the walls. The rose of the hours
Will drop its soundless petals. The bright flagstones
Will lead where they will these steps in love with day.

Here, still here. Stone on stone
Has built the country told of by memory.
Hardly does the sound of simple fruits falling
Stir in you again the fever of time that will soon be cured.

TRANSLATED BY *Jackson Mathews*

German Poetry

EDITED BY *Arthur S. Wensinger*

✳ ✳ ✳ ✳ ✳

Introduction

Different from the few other recent anthologies of modern German poetry in translation, this one cannot be said to have any one specific guiding theme. In the selection of our ten poets no particular light is meant to be shed on the expressionists, the impressionists, the neomystics, or any other group. This may be left for such later collections as are bound to come with the resurgence of our interest in German, Austrian, and Swiss poetry. The only limitation imposed here is one of period—the twentieth century—and length—twenty-five hundred lines. Beyond that the selection is a result of preference.

Why Trakl and not George; why Rilke and not Hofmannsthal; why Morgenstern and not Lehmann or Heym or Däubler or Hesse or Jünger or Eich or Loerke or Werfel or Weinheber? In a word, it seemed better to have a handful of poems from ten than merely a smattering from thirty. In the simplest terms, it was decided to take two of the early great poets of the century (Rilke and Trakl), a whimsical leavener (and a good deal more: Morgenstern), the two important middle expressionists (Benn and Brecht), four from among the perhaps ten best contemporaries (Piontek, Krolow, Celan, and Bachmann), and finally one whose great current popularity has yet to demonstrate whether it will surmount ephemeral acclaim (Grass).

Because of the somewhat random nature of the selection and its deliberate untendentiousness, and because the selections from each poet represented are accompanied by separate short introductions, it is felt that only brief and general observations about the German poetry of this century are indicated here. Of more value will be a list of other, larger, anthologies and of recent critical studies likely to be of interest to the American reader (both in German and English).

There are qualities inherent in modern German poetry (one is tempted to emphasize the adjective) which do indeed set it apart from that of the other European countries. The feeling about this uniqueness has for a long time been a strong one. It is not, of course, that these qualities individually are unique to *die deutsche Lyrik* or even markedly different from those of English or French or Polish poetry; it is the sum, the congeries, of these qualities which is distinctly German and which may be said to have been distinctly German since roughly the 1870's, at the time when Germany was born as a modern nation and (ironically) died a noisy death as an international partner. As much as anywhere else it is in the work of the younger poets in Germany today that we may detect the hopeful signs of its resurrection. It may be true that when a German poet can again express in a beautiful poem a love for his own (and his whole) country, a love which does not redound to the detriment of others, expressly or implicitly, nor stem from the quirksome and even pernicious collective self-consciousness which has so often beset the nation and its continent, a kind of literary millennium at least will be at hand. Meanwhile this brand of liberality and generosity cannot yet be said generally to obtain among the qualities alluded to above.

What, then, are these qualities which together seem to mark German poetry as "German"? (In listing what are perhaps the most obvious, it need hardly be mentioned that none of them applies in equal measure to the poets represented here; some of them may have little application at all.) One is the unusual privacy of modern German poetry, its retreat in the face of cumbersome reality. Except perhaps briefly in the case of some of the expressionists, the dadaists, the dreary excesses of the *Blut-und-Boden* poets, the concept of a united aesthetic "togetherness" front cannot even remotely be said to be part of this poetic sphere. *Einsamkeit* (solitude or loneliness) is really a more genuine watchword of twentieth-century poetry than of the great romantic lyricists who wrote so much (and often so refreshingly) of it. The sempiternal wandering and seeking of the German poet, after either the "blue flower" ahead or his own childhood behind him, is nearly always a very private, if not to say introverted, affair. Emotionalism is another hallmark of much of German poetry: sometimes supercharged and unmistakably evident, sometimes subterranean and bottled, sometimes tempered or in a state of suspension between vigorous protest and sardonic or nostalgic resignation. Closely allied is the tendency in much German poetry (as in much else German) to universalize and to speak in abstractions, the opposite in a certain sense of the German *Biedermeier* penchant to observe quietly and to learn from the fine and the particular. Immodesty is frequently correlative here. Brooding and earnestness looked at from another direction can be called a lack of levity, humorlessness. There is much wit in modern German poetry—but not much that is funny; even when it is joyous it is rarely gay. The German brands of urbanity and sophistication are still far from their French and Anglo-Saxon counterparts. Finally, nature and the mystic approach to it remain a vital legacy from the Middle High German poetry of the twelfth and thirteenth centuries, the baroque mystics of the sixteenth and seventeenth, and the supreme romanticists of the early nineteenth century; the inheritance can be traced directly to a contemporary such as Ingeborg Bachmann.

There are many other general, and perhaps less dire-sounding, claims to be made for modern German poetry. If the foregoing characteristics seem negative, so be it. The "positive" characteristics, insofar as they are discrete from the ones above (many are imbedded precisely within these "negative" qualities) are more difficult to enumerate without the list's appearing even more cumbersome and sweeping. A recital of them here would be little better than useless. The poetry itself must simply first be read, even if only in translation. Until then the assertion must be taken on faith that no Western literature can with justification lay claim to any greater body of modern poetry.

There follows a list of anthologies (in the original and/or in English translation) of modern German poetry. The reader interested in a specific poet is urged to check the annual PMLA bibliography (especially inclusive since the mid-1950's) for particular studies. Three of the best recent general considerations are the introduction to the Hamburger-Middleton anthology, the introduction by Victor Lange in the Schwebell anthology (see below), and an article by poet-critic Hans Magnus Enzensberger in the September 1963 issue of *Encounter* (no. 120), "In Search of the Lost Language."

Arthur S. Wensinger

BIBLIOGRAPHY

Anthologies in English Translation

Flores, Angel (ed.). *An Anthology of German Poetry from Hölderlin to Rilke*. New York: Doubleday, Anchor Book, 1960.

Forster, Leonard (ed. and trans.). *The Penguin Book of German Verse*. Suffolk: Penguin Books, 1957. Bilingual.

Hamburger, Michael, and Middleton, Christopher (eds. and trans.). *Modern German Poetry, 1910–1960*. New York: Grove, 1962. Bilingual.

Kaufman, Walter (ed. and trans.). *Twenty German Poets. A Bilingual Collection*. New York: Random House, 1962.

Rothenburg, Jerome (ed. and trans.). *New Young German Poets*. San Francisco: City Lights, 1959.

Salinger, Herman (ed. and trans.). *Twentieth Century German Verse*. Princeton: Princeton University Press, 1952. Bilingual.

Schwebell, Gertrude C. (ed. and trans.). *Contemporary German Poetry*. New York: New Directions, 1964. Introduction by Victor Lange.

Recent German Anthologies of Modern Poetry

Abt, Georg (ed.). *Deutsche Gedichte der Gegenwart*. Gütersloh: Bertelsmann, 1954.

Bender, Hans (ed.). *Widerspiel. Deutsche Lyrik seit 1945*. Munich: Hanser, 1962.

Bender, Hans (ed.). *Junge Lyrik 1956: eine Auslese* (Erste Folge). Munich: Hanser, 1956.

Benn, Gottfried (ed.). *Lyrik des expressionistischen Jahrzehnts von den Wegbereitern bis zum Dada*. Wiesbaden: Limes, 1955. Introduction by Gottfried Benn.

Bingel, Horst (ed.). *Deutsche Lyrik. Gedichte seit 1945*. Stuttgart: Deutsche Verlags-Anstalt, 1961.

Best, Otto (ed.). *Deutsche Lyrik und Prosa nach 1945*. Berlin and Frankfurt: Fischer, 1957; paperback in series "Fischer Schulausgaben moderner Autoren."

Fehse, Willi (ed.). *Deutsche Lyrik der Gegenwart*. Stuttgart: Reklam, 1955; 3rd enl. ed., 1960.

Groll, Gunter (ed.). *De Profundis. Deutsche Lyrik in dieser Zeit: eine Anthologie aus zwölf Jahren*. Munich: Desch, 1946.

Hohoff, Curt (ed.). *Flügel der Zeit. Deutsche Gedichte 1900–1950*. Frankfurt: Fischer, 1956.

Höllerer, Walter (ed.). *Transit. Lyrikbuch der Jahrhundertmitte*. Frankfurt: Suhrkamp, 1956.

Holthusen, Hans Egon, and Kemp, Friedhelm (eds.). *Ergriffenes Dasein. Deutsche Lyrik 1900–1950*. Ebenhausen: Langewiesche-Brandt, 1953; enl. ed., 1957.

Ibel, Rudolf (ed.). *Das Gedicht. Jahrbuch zeitgenössischer Lyrik 1954–55*. Hamburg: Wegner, 1955.

Kraus, Wolfgang (ed.). *Frage und Formel. Lyrik einer jungen österreichischen Generation.* Salzburg: Müller, 1963.

Lehner, Peter (ed.). *Ensemble. Ein Schweizer Beitrag zur zeitgenössischen Lyrik.* Bern: Benteli, 1958.

Leonhard, Kurt, and Schwedhelm, Karl (eds.). *Lyrik aus dieser Zeit 1961. Ein Jahrbuch mit bisher unveröffentlichter Lyrik.* Munich: Bechtle, 1961.

Michael, Friederich (ed.). *Jahrhundertmitte. Deutsche Gedichte der Gegenwart.* Wiesbaden: Insel, 1955; paperback ed., Insel-Bücherei.

Niedermayer, Max (ed.). *Geliebte Verse. Eine Auswahl deutscher Lyrik von 1900–1950.* Wiesbaden: Limes, 1952.

Pinthus, Kurt (ed.). *Menschheitsdämmerung. Ein Dokument des Expressionismus.* Hamburg: Rowohlt, 1959.

Schönwiese, Ernst (ed.). *Oesterreichische Lyrik nach 1945.* Frankfurt: Fischer, 1960.

Schwedhelm, K., and Leonhard, K. (eds.). *Lyrik aus dieser Zeit 1963–64 (Zweite Folge).* Munich: Bechtle, 1963.

Tschesnohell, Michael (ed.). *Neue deutsche Lyrik. Gedichte aus unserer Zeit.* East Berlin: Verlag Kultur und Fortschritt, 1952.

Weyrauch, Wolfgang (ed.). *Expeditionen: deutsche Lyrik seit 1945.* Munich: List, 1959.

Zimmer, Dieter (ed.). *Mein Gedicht: Begegnungen mit deutscher Lyrik (Die Umfrage der "Zeit" nach den schönsten deutschen Gedichten).* Wiesbaden: Limes, 1961.

CHRISTIAN MORGENSTERN (1871–1914) Naturalistic, patriotic, Nietzschean, Rilkean, ironic, sentimental—each in turn—Morgenstern, despite all these variations in style, is primarily known today for his humorous poetry (which all but defies translation). As a man of broad and inventive disposition, he ventured into many areas of expression, always, however, severely separating what he thought of as his serious from his comic work. By the end of his life he had rejected the humor and become a poet of a naïve and pious *Weltanschauung.*

He was born in Munich as son and (on both sides) grandson of eminent landscape painters. His background was Protestant Hamburg. His eventful but irregular upbringing culminated in a split with his jovial father, who was to outlive him by many years. His mother had long before died of tuberculosis, the disease which plagued the poet throughout his short life. By the time Morgenstern began his period of military training (a course decided upon by his father but soon abandoned by the son) his gift for whimsy had already produced some of the fanciful language and people (Palmström, Korf, Palma, Kunkel, the raven Ralf) of his later verse. After studying law at Breslau and while studying art history in Berlin, he was suddenly and powerfully influenced by the writings of Nietzsche, which seem to be present in the "cycles of humoristic fantasy" early praised by Theodor Fontane, Richard Strauss, Rilke, and Nietzsche's mother.

In striving to get "beyond the planets and behind the stars," the poetic freedom Morgenstern eventually attained is not to be found in his theosophic or Zarathustrian work but in the sometimes surreal, sometimes mordant humorous poems and in his earnest grotesques (*Galgenlieder,* 1905; *Palmström,* 1910; and *Palma Kunkel* and *Gingganz,* not published until 1916). The poet himself, who had taken this aspect of his work least seriously, was the most astonished at the remarkable popularity it soon enjoyed. The first of the collections was dedicated to Nietzsche's *"Kind im Mann,"* suggesting perhaps that we should be quite wrong in taking the poems as occasional verse, rather that from the first they were meant to be essentially more earnest parodies on a dangerous pedantry, a faltering society, a dissolving civilization. Their inventiveness, marvelous word plays, and "Berliner lightning-logic" (Curt Hohoff) go far beyond mere nonsense. There are a few in which (possibly unique in German poetry) fancy and lyricism achieve identity. These poems reflect their author's conviction that "time and space are not realities" and, read carefully, help us understand his subsequent refuge in a private mysticism (deriving from Boehme, Eckehart, Buddha, and the Gospel of St. John) and finally in a feeling of new-found spiritual salvation and community in his friendship with Rudolf Steiner, the Anthroposophist. After a number of soulful volumes of confessional love poetry, religious and philosophic values seem to have replaced those of literary creativeness for Morgenstern.

BIBLIOGRAPHY

Alle Galgenlieder. Wiesbaden: Insel Verlag, 1947. This contains the collected humorous poetry.

❄ ❄ ❄

KORF'S JOKE

Korf has invented a new kind of joke:
The point comes only many hours after.
All listen to them with disdain and boredom.

But like the light that shineth in the darkness
They rouse you from your slumbers wildly gurgling,
Holding your sides and laughing like a drain.

TRANSLATED BY *R. F. C. Hull*

THE SANDWICH PAPER

A sandwich paper, in the glen,
besnowed upon, feels cold and then

in its fear, although it never
before, in any sense, had ever

thought about thinking, naturally,
as a thing of rags, et cetera, be

-gan, from fear, as I just men
-tioned, thinking, started and commen

-ced to think—think what that means!—in fear, it
became, as I just mentioned, spirit;

that is, you understand, not mere
-ly down from up in Heaven somewhere;

rather, in consequence of a rather
precisely evolved gray brain matter

which out of wood, protein, flour, grease
(through fear) by skipping the otherwise

normal geologic ages, found
within this paper vessel and ground—

within and on it found, by special
skipping of ages, ground and vessel.

Benefitted by this benefaction,
the paper decided itself toward action—

toward Life, toward—started, anywhy,
to walking—like a butterfly . . .

to creep, first, flying thereupon
till over the underbrush and on

up over the highway and criss
and cross and left, from that to this

the way such creatures turn toward Life
(as winds or other things connive).

And yet, dear Friends! now blanche with me!—
a bird, quite fat and greedily

sees it (this is January . . .)
and sets himself, both hide and hairy,

and sets himself both hair and hidey
(who could end here!) (Dear God Almighty!)

(consider how much was necessary!)
and sets himself, both hide and hairy—

In the woods, a sandwich pape
-r, won, by fear, a natural shape . . . .

Enough! The wild woodpecker gobbles
The product, irrecoverable.

TRANSLATED BY *William Snodgrass*

ANXIETY FOR THE FUTURE

Korf, whom worry easily attacks,
Can already see the skies
Filled by balloons of every size,
So all day he prepares whole stacks
Of draughts for bylaws and statutes
Of a society for resolute
Maintenance of a zone designed
To keep balloon-egress confined.

Yet even now he can smell doom:
His club already falls behind;
The air, it seems to him, goes blind,
All the landscape turns gloom and tomb.
Therefore he puts down his pen,
Turns on the light (they *all* will, THEN!)
And goes at once to Palmstrom's place;
They sit together, face to face.

After four long hours, finally,
This nightmare is overcome.
First to break the spell is Palmstrom:
"Be a man now, Korf;" says he,
"You've got hold of the wrong era;
As yet, this is a vain chimera
That tricks your intellect away,
Bobbing over your head today."

Korf recovers his own clear sight—
No one is flying in the golden light!
He snuffs his candle, silently;
Then, points to the sun suddenly
And speaks: "If not today, sometime!
One day you will no longer shine,
At least for us—it makes one's teeth
Chatter—the masses underneath! . . ."

Thereafter, von Korf once again
Sits in his room and takes his pen
Drawing up a vast design
For the protection of sunshine.

TRANSLATED BY *William Snodgrass*

THE EMPORIUM

Without mail, Palmstrom would pass away;
It is his meat and drink each day.

Three times a day, he goes all tense;
Every day, that same old dance.

How seldom does a letter slide
Into his mailbox, dark and wide.

He scolds, morosely, that poor man
Who does, we know, the best he can.

Finally, he comes back to this:
"The Emporium for Small Gladnesses."

Fresh from the grill, he makes his order:
Mixed Mail—enough to last a Quarter.

Now, dawn to sunset, without fail,
Comes every variety of mail.

People all think of him and write
To keep in touch, noon and night.

He sees himself suddenly enter
The world of things at their dead center;

Already he feels addled, sore—
The "E. for S. G."—nothing more.

TRANSLATED BY *William Snodgrass*

THE KNEE

A knee is roaming through the world;
No more; it's just a knee.
It's not a tent; it's not a tree;
It is a knee; no more.

There was a man once in a war
Got killed and killed and killed.
Alone, unhurt, remained the knee
Like a saint's relics, pure.

Since then, it roams the whole world, lonely;
It is a knee, now, only;
It's not a tent; it's not a tree;
Only a knee, no more.

TRANSLATED BY *William Snodgrass*

PALMSTROM

Palmstrom, standing beside the brook,
Unfolds a handkerchief wide and red
On which a mighty oak is shown
And someone with an open book.

Blow his nose?—he would not dare!
For he belongs to that sort of men
Who are so often, nakedly,
Stricken by beauty, unaware.

What he has only just outspread,
Tenderly, now, he has to close;
No sensitive spirit will condemn
Him, marching on with unblown nose.

TRANSLATED BY *William Snodgrass*

THE TWO DONKEYS

A donkey at his gloomiest
his spouse as follows once addressed:

"I'm so dumb, you're so dumb,
let's go and die now, come!"

Yet as so frequently turns out:
Both gaily stayed alive throughout.

TRANSLATED BY *E. M. Valk*

THE SPHERES

Palmstrom takes some paper from a drawer,
Distributing it artfully around the floor,

And after he has formed it into tight
Spheres, artfully distributed for the night,

He so distributes, for the night, these spheres
That he, when he wakes up suddenly in the night,

That he, waking in the dead of night, then hears
Paper crackling and a secret shuddering fright

Attacks him (so that in the night terrible fears
Attack him) being spooked by packing-paper spheres.

TRANSLATED BY *William Snodgrass*

DING, DANG, DONG

The peal of bells flies through the night
as though with wings endowed,
in Roman vestments soaring to a height
above vale, hill and cloud.

DANG is chasing after DING
who had preceded him,
i.e., a very serious thing:
she was unfaithful to him.

"O come," he calls, "your DANG
is waiting in great pain.
Come back, DING darling, love's pang
rends your DANG's heart in twain."

But DING, I'll have you know,
has given DONG her whole affection,
an equally good Christian, though,
that's just the rub in this selection.

DANG through the night pursues his course
high above glade and wooded intersection—
in vain, alas, because his very force
propels him in the wrong direction.

TRANSLATED BY *E. M. Valk*

THE DAYNIGHTLAMP

Korf has a daynightlamp,
His own invention, which
At one flick of the switch,
Turns day, however bright,
To blackest night.

When, at the convention
He displays it on the ramp,
No man of comprehension
Who understands his field
Can fail to see, revealed—

(Brilliant day turns to night;
Applause storms through the house)
(Someone starts to shout
for the janitor, Mr. Camp:
"Lights! Lights!")—to see, outright,

The facts: aforesaid lamp,
Indeed has powers which
At one flick of the switch
Turns any day, how bright,
To blackest night.

TRANSLATED BY *William Snodgrass*

THE MOUSETRAP

I

Palmstrom hasn't a crumb in the house;
Nevertheless, he has a mouse.

Von Korf, upset by his friend's distress,
Builds a room out of trellises

And places Palmstrom there, within,
Fiddling an exquisite violin.

It gets late; the stars shine bright;
Palmstrom makes music in the night,

Till, midway through the serenade,
In strolls the mouse, to promenade.

Behind it, by some secret trick
A trapdoor closes, quiet, quick.

Before it, Palmstrom, immediately,
Sinks into slumber, silently.

II

Von Korf arrives in the early dawn
And loads this useful invention on

The nearest medium-sized, as it were,
Moving van for furniture,

Which is hauled then, by a powerful horse,
Nimbly, into the distant forest.

There, profoundly isolated,
This strange couple are liberated:

First the mouse comes strolling out,
And then Palmstrom—after the mouse.

The animal, with no trace of fright,
Takes to its new home with delight.

Palmstrom, meanwhile, observing this,
Drives home with Korf, transformed by bliss.

TRANSLATED BY *William Snodgrass*

PALMSTROM TO A NIGHTINGALE
WHICH WOULD NOT LET HIM SLEEP

Why do you not transform
Yourself to a fish; and,
In this matter of song, perform
Accordingly? For otherwise,
Through the long nights, how can
Slumber restore my eyes
And blossom on my pillow,
Which is most needful? Then,
Do; if you are a noble fellow.

And your wife, too, on the nest—
How sweetly you will astound her
When you shine forth like a flounder
Blissfully at rest
On the top branch of your tree—
Or when you flutter around her
Like a flying mackerel,
Heavenly Philomel—
You will do me this courtesy?

TRANSLATED BY *William Snodgrass*

PALMSTROM GIVES PRAISE

Palmstrom greatly praises the bad weather—
Then, things are much more quiet upon earth:
Frenzies willingly pull themselves together;
Man walks with dignity, and knows his worth.

Even the umbrella's little sky
Symbolically acts upon man's core
Because, alas! the real one is still high
And distant from the mobs that thrash and roar.

In meadows, through the streets, across the common,
Palmstrom wanders while the torrents fall,
Delighted by the image of the human
That can behave so cosmo-logical.

TRANSLATED BY *William Snodgrass*

THE PIKE

Reformed by sainted Anthony,
A pike decided, morally,
Together with his wife and son,
To try and feed himself upon
The vegetarian ideal.

Since that day, he would only eat
Seagrass, searose and seaoatmeal.
Horrors! Soon as he had dined,
Seagrass, searose, creamofseawheat
Flowed out again horribly behind.

The pond was soon polluted, wholly;
Five hundred fish expired in pain.
Saint Anthony, however, when
Hurriedly summoned back again,
Said only, "Holy, holy, holy."

TRANSLATED BY *William Snodgrass*

THE MOONSHEEP

The moonsheep stands in the open plain,
waiting, waiting, for the shears' refrain.
    The moonsheep.

The moonsheep pulls a single blade
and then goes home to his alpine glade.
    The moonsheep.

The moonsheep, dreaming, does with himself converse:
"I am the dark space of the universe."
    The moonsheep.

The moonsheep in the morn lies dead.
His body's white, the sun is red.
    The moonsheep.

TRANSLATED BY *E. M. Valk*

RAINER MARIA RILKE (1875–1926) Within the long-recognized trinity of great German poets in the first part of our century—George, Hofmannsthal, Rilke—Rilke inevitably and properly has been granted first place. Indeed, there can be few to dispute the assertion that he is the greatest poet of the German language in the past 125 years. Among the European poets in our time perhaps only the names of Yeats and Valéry can begin to suggest an approximate degree of lyrical intensity and achievement. That to many of the postwar German poets Rilke seems now to be "without the walls" and that he is seldom named by them can only be a temporary reaction and the current guarantee of his unassailable dominance. Like his contemporaries in prose, Mann and Kafka (Rilke, like Kafka, was a native of Prague), Rilke is fashionable as a famous name in pseudo-academic circles; but, unlike them, his work cannot really be said to be known here, despite the valiant efforts of translators and critics. Instead, the overpowering mass of European and American scholarship on Rilke seems to stand in the way of something more than awed admiration of the ten marmoreal *Duino Elegies*, the thrilling (and admittedly arcane) *Sonnets to Orpheus*, the "existential novel" *The Notebooks of Malte Laurids Brigge*. These are the titles generally known and named here. There are many more.

The poet's astounding gift was born well before its control and its apposite themes were found. From the first, Rilke's entire emotional and productive life was determined and dominated by his poetry. The seductive, obsessive, gorgeous, sentimental, and too numerous and facile works of the first twenty-five years lived to plague and in part to be renounced by the poet; for he was soon to be sobered and staggered by the immensities of the real space in which man dwells (Russia, 1900) and shortly afterward to learn under the tutelage of Rodin in Paris to *see* and to *be* and to interpret the things of this world which are far beyond undigested, private religiosity and egocentric sympathizing. From seer to see-er, he wrote now of animals, statues, classical and biblical figures and artifacts, trees and flowers, buildings, the poor and suffering, the Angel, the Life and Passion, childhood, landscapes of history, the present, the soul, deaths and Death (*Buch der Bilder, Neue Gedichte*). Rilke has shown us his

and our *Weltinnenraum*. He does not preach at us to feel—
his poetry makes us feel. It has broadened the limits of
human perception through a language which is in every sense
new: a realization and a creation which by the time of
World War I exceeded the capacity of all others writing in
German.

Finally—after the agonies of the war, his almost insane
movement from place to place, up, down, and across Europe
and over North Africa (there are fifty addresses within one
four-year period), the fitful ten-year struggle with the *Elegies*
(1912–1922), the release and replacement of Christ by the
Orpheus-Poet—the now famous Rilke, correspondent and
protegé of princesses, looking like a thyroidal and Slavic
mandarin, knowing more than ever the centrality of *Geduld*
and *Einsamkeit,* settled in his tower in Switzerland and sub-
mitted for the first time, it seems, to his peers in Goethe and
Hölderlin. During his last few years Rilke produced those
poems (*Nachgelassene Gedichte*) which many have come to
consider his finest achievement: sparser, more economic, more
anchored and secured against the exposures of the *Elegies,*
they are a reduction and a whittling down, as in the final
Rembrandt self-portraits, the final *pietás* of Michelangelo—
somehow more palpable and more mystical at the same time.
The central theme and point remain: the transmutation (by
the poet) of the world into spirit through feeling, possible
only because we (and he) are mortal and remembering.

Only the slightest suggestion of Rilke can be conveyed here.

BIBLIOGRAPHY

Rilke's poetry is collected in the first three volumes of the
Sämtliche Werke (complete works), edited by Ernst Zinn for
the Rilke Archiv (Wiesbaden: Insel Verlag); Volume I,
Gedichte Erster Teil, 1955; Volume II, *Gedichte Zweiter Teil,*
1956; Volume III, *Jugendgedichte,* 1959.

❊   ❊   ❊

GREAT NIGHT

Often I would stand and stare from the window begun yes-
    terday,
stand there and stare at you. As yet the new city
felt as if barred to me, and the unpersuaded country

slid into darkness as though I didn't exist. Nor would
the nearest things reveal their meaning to me. By the lantern
the alley rose up: alien my eyes said it was.
Across, a room accessible to response, luminous in the lamp-
      light—
I was already among them: they sensed it, closed the shutters.
Stood there. And then a child cried. And I knew of the
      mothers
in the houses round about, what they could do, and knew
together with all the weeping the causes beyond comfort.
Or a voice was singing, extending some distance
past expectation, or from below an old man's cough
full of reproach as if his body were in the right
against a world more gentle. Then the hour struck—
but I counted too late, it passed me by.
As a boy, an outsider, when finally allowed to join in,
one doesn't after all catch the ball and knows none of the
      games
which the others are playing among themselves with such ease,
stands there, looking away—where?—so stood I, and suddenly
it was *you*, I realized, accompanying, playing with me, adult
night, and I stared at you. Where the towers were
shaking with anger, where with averted destiny
a city was hemming me in and mountains that couldn't be
      guessed at
were lying athwart my path, and where, closing in,
a starved strangeness encircled the haphazard flickerings
of my feelings: there was, exalted one,
no shame in it for you to know me. Your breath
swept over me; your smile dispersed among
farflung gravities became lodged in me.

                              TRANSLATED BY *E. M. Valk*

EVA

Simply she stands, by the cathedral portal
over its arch and near the window's rose,
with the apple in the apple pose,
forever guiltless-guilty of the mortal

growing thing she thus had brought to birth
when from the eternal circle wide
she went forth loving, now to strive and stride
like a young year walking through the earth.

Ah! in that land she could have wished to stay
yet for a while among the beasts whose breath
breathed peace and understanding of their way.

But when she found the Man determined, they
went, she with him, turning her face toward death;
and she had known God like a passing day.
                    TRANSLATED BY *Herman Salinger*

MUSIC: BREATHING OF STATUES

Music: breathing of statues. Perhaps
stillness of pictures. Language where languages
end. Time,
erect on the pathway of hearts
towards extinction.

Feelings for whom? Transformation
of feelings to what? Into audible landscape.
Strange land: Music. Space grown from our hearts,
Ours most intimate,
stepping beyond us,
striving afar.
            Sacred Farewell,
when the Within is around us as distance most distant,
Air's other side,
pure,
gigantic,
and not for us to inhabit.
                    TRANSLATED BY *Anneliese Braun*

PORTRAIT

For fear that her renouncing face unloose
and drop a single of its *grandes douleurs,*
she slowly carries through her tragic *tours*
her features in a lovely dry bouquet,
wildly tied, already almost parting;
sometimes a forlorn smile weakly starting,
loose, a sort of tuberose, drops away.

And she calmly moves from where it lies,
weary, with her lovely hands supine,
that know they could not find it, being blind,

And she utters pure invention, in whose guise
fate totters, willed or otherwise, her own,
and from the sense and heart that she supplies,
this fate bursts out, a marvellous unknown,
like screaming from a stone—

And she lets all these words and cries,
her chin held up in hauteur, fall again,
without their staying; for not one can feign
a pathos equal to that desolation
which her own properties contain,
that, like a vase without a pedestal,
she must hold high above her reputation
and the pace these evenings constrain.

TRANSLATED BY *S. A. Corngold*

SELF-PORTRAIT

The bone-build of the eyebrows has a mule's
or Pole's noble and narrow steadfastness.
A scared blue child is peering through the eyes,
and there's a kind of weakness, not a fool's,
yet womanish—the gaze of one who serves.
The mouth is just a mouth . . . untidy curves,
quite unpersuasive, yet it says its *yes,*
when forced to act. The forehead cannot frown,
and likes the shade of dumbly looking down.

A still life, *nature morte*—hardly a whole!
It has done nothing worked through or alive,
in spite of pain, in spite of comforting . . .
Out of this distant and disordered thing
something in earnest labors to unroll.

ADAPTED BY *Robert Lowell*

THE CADET PICTURE OF MY FATHER

There's absence in the eyes. The brow's in touch
with something far. Now distant boyishness
and seduction shadow his enormous lips,
the slender aristocratic uniform
with its Franz Josef braid; both the hands bulge
like gloves upon the saber's basket hilt.
The hands are quiet, they reach out toward nothing—

I hardly see them now, as if they were
the first to grasp distance and disappear,
and all the rest lies curtained in itself,
and so withdrawn, I cannot understand
my father as he bleaches on this page—

Oh quickly disappearing photograph
in my more slowly disappearing hand !

ADAPTED BY *Robert Lowell*

BEHIND THE INCULPABLE TREES

Behind the inculpable trees
Slowly the old Fatality
Works out her silent face.
Wrinkles are drawing that way . . .
What down here a bird screeches
Bends off as a woe-line
At the hard soothsaying mouth.

O and the soon-to-be lovers
Smile on each other, ignorant of farewells.
Over them sets and rises
Starlike their destiny,
Night-inspired.
Still unoffered to them as experience
It dwells
Poised in the course of spheres,
An airy configuration.

TRANSLATED BY *Francis Golffing*

WALK

My eyes already touch that hill, sun-gold,
ending the path I've scarcely started. We're
thus gripped by what we could not grasp and hold,
full of its immanence when far from here—

and changed by it, though never reaching there,
into those selves, scarce guessing, we conceal:
a sign waves, answering the sign we bear . . .
And yet the counterwind is all we feel.

TRANSLATED BY *Herman Salinger*

EXPOSED ON THE ALPS OF THE HEART

Exposed on the alps of the heart. See how small there,
see: the last hamlet of words, and higher,
but how small too, a last
farmstead of feeling. Can you discern it?
Exposed on the alps of the heart. Stoneground
under your grip. True, something still
flowers here: out of the mute slope,
chanting, an ignorant herb comes forth.
But the sage? Ah, he who has begun to *know*
grows silent now, exposed on the alps of the heart.
There pass indeed without peril,
led by uninjured awareness, the mountain deer,
pass and abide. And the huge secure bird
circles around the peaks' pure denial.—But
insecure, here on the alps of the heart . . .

TRANSLATED BY *Francis Golffing*

BUDDHA

As though he might be listening. Quietude:
remote . . . We pause and soon our hearing's spent.
And he is star. And other amplitude
of stars beyond our sight is his extent.

He is the sum. And do we really stay
that he might see us? Is he then in need?
And like an inert beast he would not heed,
profound, if prostrate we before him lay.

For that which now impels us to his feet,
has whirled around in him a million years.
It's he forgets what brings us tears,
and we're rebuked where he's replete.

TRANSLATED BY *D. C. Travis*

LONELINESS

Loneliness is like a rain.
Towards dusk it leaves the sea where it has lain;
It mounts to skies unslaked by all they gain,
From far-off plains, unvisited retreats.
Soon from the sky it drops on city streets.

It rains down here in those ambiguous hours
When all the lanes wind onward into morning,
And saddened bodies, emptied of their powers,
Unlink in disenchantment, lords of nothing;
And couples who are couples in their loathing
Must search in one bed for their warring dreams:

Then loneliness flows with the streams . . .

TRANSLATED BY *Edwin Morgan*

SENSE OF SOMETHING COMING

I am like a flag in the center of open space.
I sense ahead the wind which is coming, and must live it
    through,
While the creatures of the world beneath still do not move in
    their sleep:
The doors still close softly, and the chimneys are full of silence,
The windows do not rattle yet, and the dust still lies down.

I already know the storm, and I am as troubled as the sea,
And spread myself out, and fall into myself,
And throw myself out and am absolutely alone
In the great storm.

TRANSLATED BY *Robert Bly*

APPARITION

What, today, compels your return
to the restlessly rustling garden
through which, a moment ago,
there sped a shower of sunlight?
See all the green growing grave in its wake.
Come! that I might, like you,
disregard the weight of the trees.
(If one of them were to fall
across the path, one would have to
call for men to lift it again.
What, in the world, is as heavy?)
The many stone steps
you descended more loudly: I heard you.
Now you again make no sound.
I am alone in hearing,
with myself, with the wind . . . On a sudden

a nightingale sings
in the sheltered thicket.
Hear, in the air, how the towering song
stands crumbling or not completed.
Are you listening with me—
or does even now the other side of the voice,
which turns away from us, keep you preoccupied?

TRANSLATED BY *Ruth Speirs*

WHEN CATCHING . . .

When catching what you throw yourself, it all
is mere dexterity, dispensable attainment;
only when all at once you catch the ball
which she, eternal fellow-player,
has flung to you, your centre, with a throw
exactly mastered, in an arc like those
of God's great bridges: only then
ability to catch becomes achievement—
not yours, a world's. And if you even
had strength and courage to return the ball,
no, still more wonderful: forgot both strength and courage
and *had* already thrown it . . . as the year
throws birds, the swarms of migratory birds
an older warmth hurls far across the seas
to young, new warmth—then only, in such daring,
you play at last a valid part.
You make the throw no longer easier for yourself;
no longer harder for yourself. Out of your hands,
a meteor hurtles on its course through space . . .

TRANSLATED BY *Ruth Speirs*

IMAGINARY LIFE

First, childhood, boundless, with no aim,
no renunciation. O unconscious bliss!
Abruptly, terror, limits, school and bondage,
and headlong falling to temptation and to loss.

Defiance. He who had been bent bends others—
inflicts, on others, vengeance for his own defeat.
Loved, feared, he rescues, wrestles, wins
and overcomes, with rapid blow on blow.

Alone, a weightless cold expanse about him.
But deep within his upright body he draws breath
now that the first, the old deed has been done . . .

Then God rushed forward from His ambush.

TRANSLATED BY Ruth Speirs

EXPERIENCE OF DEATH

Nothing is known to us about this passing;
it does not share with us. We have no cause
for showing admiration, love, or hate
to Death disfigured strangely by a tragic

mask's lamenting mouth. As yet,
the world is full of parts for us to act.
As long as we concern ourselves with pleasing,
Death also acts although he does not please.

But, as you went, a segment of reality
flashed in upon our stage by that same crevice
through which you passed: the green of real verdure,
the real sunshine, and the real wood.

We go on acting, and reciting lines
learnt with anxiety and painful effort,
and now and then we raise our hands in gesture;
but your existence, far from us, removed

out of our play, can sometimes come upon us,
descending like experience of reality,
and for a brief while we act life itself,
carried away, not thinking of applause.

TRANSLATED BY Ruth Speirs

PARTING

How I have felt what parting means! How well
I know it still: dark, cruel, never overcome,
it shows once more a perfect union, holding
it out to us, and tearing it apart.

And how defenceless I was, watching
what, calling to me, let me go
and stayed behind as if it were all women,
yet small and white and nothing more than this:

a waving which applied to me no longer,
a slight continued waving—and already
barely explainable: perhaps a plum-tree
from which a cuckoo rose in hasty flight.

TRANSLATED BY *Ruth Speirs*

SPANISH DANCER

As in one's hand a sulphur-match,
white, before blazing, darts in all directions
convulsive tongues: her round dance starts,
precipitate, bright, hot, to spread convulsively
within the narrow circle of spectators.

All of a sudden it is all ablaze.

And with a glance she sets her hair alight
and suddenly, with daring art, she whirls
her whole attire into this conflagration
from which there reach like frightened snakes
her bare arms, rattling, wide awake.

And then: as if that fire did not suffice her
she gathers it together, flings it off
very imperiously and with a haughty gesture,
she gazes: raging, there it lies,
refusing to surrender, still a blaze—
but, sure, triumphant, with a sweet
saluting smile, she lifts her face,
and stamps it out with small firm feet.

TRANSLATED BY *Ruth Speirs*

LATE AUTUMN IN VENICE

No longer does the city drift like bait
that catches all emerging days.
The glassy palaces ring out more brittle
against your gaze. The summer hangs

from gardens, like a heap of puppets,
head foremost, wilted, done to death.
But from the forest-skeletons, deep down,
determination rises: overnight

the General of the Seas would have to double
the galleys in the wakeful Arsenal,
to tar the morning air with all his fleet

which throngs with threshing oars, and on a sudden,
all flags unfurled to greet the day, sweeps on
before a great wind, radiant, charged with fate.

TRANSLATED BY *Ruth Speirs*

BLUE HYDRANGEA

Like green left over in a pot of paint,
the leaves look dry and dull and rough
behind the clustered blooms that have no blue
but merely mirror it from far away.

Their mirroring seems blurred with tears, and vague
as though they were to lose it all again,
and as in old blue, faded writing-paper
there is some yellow in them, mauve and grey;

a washed-out colour as in children's pinafores,
no longer worn, when nothing can befall it any more:
how it conveys to us a small life's brevity!

But suddenly the blueness seems renewed
in one of all the clusters, and we see
a touching blue rejoice before the green.

TRANSLATED BY *Ruth Speirs*

SONNETS TO ORPHEUS, II/5

Flower-muscle, gradually admitting
the anemone's whole meadow morning
till the loud skies' polyphonic
light pours forth into its lap—

muscle of an infinite reception,
tautened in the quiet starry blossom,
sometimes overpowered by such fullness
that the sunset's call to rest

scarcely can turn back to you
rims of petals sprung wide open:
you, resolve and strength of *many* worlds!

We, the violent, continue longer.
But in which of all lives, *when* at last
are we open and receptive?

TRANSLATED BY *Ruth Speirs*

SONNETS TO ORPHEUS, II/6

Rose, enthroned, to those in Antiquity
you were a calyx with one single rim.
To *us* you are the full numberless flower,
the ever inexhaustible thing.

Opulent rose, like robes upon robes
about a body of nothing but lustre,
your single petal yet an evasion
and a disowning of any attire.

For centuries has your fragrance been calling
its sweetest names across to us here,
suddenly floating like fame in the air.

Yet, name it we cannot, we try to guess . . .
And recollection goes out to meet it,
granted by hours we can still recall.

TRANSLATED BY *Ruth Speirs*

ARCHAIC TORSO OF APOLLO

We did not know his unfamiliar head
Where hung the ripening apples of his eyes,
But still his torso candelabra-wise
Glows, where his gazing, screwed back from the dead,

Holds itself back and gleams. The bow of the breast
Could not else blind you, nor in subtle turning
Of loins could a smile break that goes there yearning
To that mid-place which held the seeds at rest.

Else would this stone, short and disfigured, cower
Under the shoulders' dropped, transparent power
Nor shine like sparkling skins of beasts of prey

And would not from all contours of the knife
Break starlike out: for there is no place, nay,
Which does not see you. You must change your life.

TRANSLATED BY *Vernon Watkins*

THE BLIND MAN. PARIS.

Look, where he goes he interrupts the town
—which *is* not where his darkness is—
like a dark crack going through a clear
light-coloured cup. And the reflection

of things is painted on him as on paper;
he does not take it in.
Only his feeling stirs as if it caught
the world in little waves:

a silence, a resistance; waiting,
he seems to choose somebody, lifts his hand
devotedly and almost festive
as though to give himself in marriage.

TRANSLATED BY *Ruth Speirs*

LOVE SONG

How should I hold my spirit back, how weight
it lest it graze your own? How should I raise
it high above your head to other things?
Oh gladly I would simply relegate
my soul to something lost that darkly clings
to a strange silent place, a place that stays
quite still when your own inmost depths vibrate.
But all that grazes us, yourself and me,
is like a bow to us and joins two strings
together, so that one voice only sings.
To what stringed instrument have we been bound?
And in what player's hands do we resound?
Sweet melody.

TRANSLATED BY *Michael Hamburger*

ROSA HORTENSIE

Who, then, received the rose? Who knew that there,
Into this umbel thrust, it pressed its mould?
Like things laid under gold that lose their gold,
Softly lose lustre, as things do by wear.

Because they ask no boon for such a rose,
Does it remain for them and smile from air?
Are angels there to take it when it blows,
Great-hearted as a breath, into their care?

Or do they rather yield it up unseen
That it may never learn of its own fall?
But underneath this rose meanwhile a green
Has listened, that now withers and knows all.

                    TRANSLATED BY *Vernon Watkins*

THE APPLE ORCHARD. BORGEBY-GÅRD

Come, come quickly now the sun has set:
See the green of evening on the lawn.
Is it not as if we'd gathered it
Long ago and saved it for our own,

Out of feeling now and recollection,
Out of new hope, half-forgotten joys,
Mingled still with dark from introspection,
Here to lay it, strewn before our eyes

Under trees, as if by Dürer, which,
Burdened by a hundred working days,
Take the weight the fruits full-swollen pitch,
Serving, full of patience, finding ways

Still, the utmost measurement surpassed,
Something more to raise and to release,
If man through a long life to the last
Wills the one and grows and holds his peace?

                    TRANSLATED BY *Vernon Watkins*

A YOUNG GIRL'S TOMB

Still we think of it. It is as if
All this once again would have to be.
Like a tree upon the lemon-cliff
You dared your light and little breasts to lift
Into the tumult of his blood's wild sea:

—that god burning.
                    And it was the slender
Fugitive, the thief of girls' despair,
Sweet and glowing, as your thought was, tender,
Shadowing your early flank's surrender,
Arched above you as your eyebrows were.

                    TRANSLATED BY *Vernon Watkins*

EVER AGAIN . . .

Ever again, although knowing the landscape of love
and the small churchyard with its complaining names
and the abyss where the others end, where dread silence
reigns—ever again we set forth, two together,
under the ancient trees, ever again we rest
among flowers, facing the sky.

TRANSLATED BY *Anneliese Braun*

DEATH OF THE POET

He lay. Propped high upon the pillowed bier,
pale was his countenance and it denied,
since now the world and knowledge there implied,
was flayed from senses, nullified,
reverting to the uncommitted year.

Who saw him living were in ignorance
how much he was at one with all these things,
for such as these: these meadows and these springs,
these waters always were his countenance.

His face was this whole amplitude which waits
on him and woos him still; his mask that dies
afraid is like the flesh of fruit that lies
out open to the air that penetrates
its soft inside, and then it putrifies.

TRANSLATED BY *D. C. Travis*

GEORG TRAKL (1887–1914) The theme and style of no other poet since Rilke have exerted a more profound influence on German letters than those of the enigmatic, despairing Trakl. Unlike the poetic triumvirate, however, and unlike others, such as Benn and Brecht, he never lived to reap the public (and more than a very few of the private) rewards of his now famous poetry. These came only with the publication in 1919 of his collected poems and with a sudden realization that here had been a lyricist of the stamp and nearly the scope of Friedrich Hölderlin. By then it had been five years since Trakl's death from an overdose of narcotics, the poet's final gesture in the face of baffling existence and the horrors of war on the Galician front, where, as a pharmacist and orderly, he had been posted to watch helplessly over the dying of dozens of wounded soldiers.

Like others of his fellow Austrians—the great novelist Robert Musil, for example—Trakl is a writer of decay. Although true in a sense also of Heym, Stadler, Werfel (others in the vanguard of expressionism), his particular evocation of *Verfall* (decay)—especially in the later poems, when the melancholy folksong is now less insistent and the syntax becomes a spread of colors, tones, and private metaphors and images drawn from an ominous mental landscape—has informed some of the most limpid yet hermetic, serene yet agonizing poetry of our time. It is poetry which, willed or not, resolutely sets him apart from any program or movement. His German forebears are Novalis, Lenau, Hölderlin; his French sources are Baudelaire, Verlaine, Rimbaud; and the contemporaries whose work is demonstrably influential on his own are Heym, Maeterlinck, and the poetess Elsa Lasker-Schüler. But nothing ties him to any of them.

He produces a rotting and clanging autumnal world—a Christian world, moribund, fragmentary, and ineffably melancholy, dissolving into dream and insanity. As the critic Curt Hohoff has put it, he seems to have known only one theme, that of the negative idyll in a sick age altogether bereft of magic and protective mystery. Yet he urgently believed in the Orphic power of the poet, and his tortured life was given over to piecing together those fragments he was able to preserve for his shattered world.

BIBLIOGRAPHY

Die Dichtungen. 8th ed., Salzburg: Otto Müller, 1955.

❊   ❊   ❊

DE PROFUNDIS

There is a stubble field on which a black rain falls.
There is a tree which, brown, stands lonely here.
There is a hissing wind which haunts deserted huts—
How sad this evening.

Past the village pond
The gentle orphan still gathers scanty ears of corn.
Golden and round her eyes are grazing in the dusk
And her lap awaits the heavenly bridegroom.

Returning home
Shepherds found the sweet body
Decayed in the bramble bush.

A shade I am remote from sombre hamlets.
The silence of God
I drank from the woodland well.

On my forehead cold metal forms.
Spiders look for my heart.
There is a light that fails in my mouth.

At night I found myself upon a heath,
Thick with garbage and the dust of stars.
In the hazel copse
Crystal angels have sounded once more.

TRANSLATED BY Michael Hamburger

NOCTURNE

Beneath the stars a man alone
his pathway through the midnight takes.
Out of wild dreams a boy awakes;
under the moon his face is stone.

With streaming hair a lunatic
weeps at her staring window-bars.
On pale pond-water sewn with stars
lovers are floating past, love-sick.

The murderer drinks his wine wide-eyed.
Invalids shake with fear of death.
A nun prays nude with baited breath
before the savior crucified.

A sleeping mother sways and sings.
Her child looks toward the moon's soft light
with eyes still truth-filled in the night.
Out of the whorehouse laughter rings.

By candle in the cellar deep
from fingers of the freshly dead
on walls a grinning hush is spread.
The sleeper whispers in his sleep.

TRANSLATED BY *Herman Salinger*

TOWARD NIGHTFALL MY HEART

At nightfall one hears the crying of bats,
Two black horses frisk in the meadow,
The red maple rustles.
To the wanderer the little wayside inn appears.
Glorious new wine and walnuts taste to him,
Glorious: to stagger drunk through the dusking wood.
In its black branches the grievous bells are pealing.
Dew-drops fall on his face.

TRANSLATED BY *Michael Hamburger*

TO THE SILENCED

Oh, the great city's madness when at nightfall
The crippled trees gape by the blackened wall,
The spirit of evil peers from a silver mask;
Lights with magnetic scourge drive off the stony night.
Oh, the sunken pealing of evening bells.

Whore who in her icy shivers sheds a still-born child.
With raving whips God's fury punishes brows possessed.
Purple pestilence, hunger that breaks green eyes.
Oh, the horrible laughter of gold.

But silent in dark caves a stiller humanity bleeds,
Out of hard metals moulds the redeeming head.

TRANSLATED BY *Michael Hamburger*

ELIS

I

Absolute is the stillness of this golden day.
Under old oak trees,
Elis, you appear, one resting with round eyes.

Their blueness reflects the sleeping of lovers.
Against your mouth
Their rosy sighs died down.

At nightfall the fisherman hauled in his heavy nets.
A good shepherd
Leads his flock along the forest edge.
Oh how righteous, Elis, are all your days.

Softly sinks
The olive tree's blue stillness on bare walls,
An old man's dark song subsides.

A golden boat
Sways, Elis, your heart against a lonely sky.

II

A gentle chiming of bells resounds in Elis' breast
At nightfall,
When to the black pillow his head sinks down.

A blue deer
Bleeds in the thorny thicket quietly.

Aloof and separate a brown tree stands.
Its blue fruits have fallen away.

Symbols and stars
Softly go down in the evening pond.

Behind the hill winter has come.

At night
Blue doves drink the icy sweat
That trickles from Elis' crystal brow.

Always
God's lonely wind sounds on black walls.

TRANSLATED BY *Michael Hamburger*

TO THE BOY ELIS

Elis, when the ouzel calls in the black wood,
This is your own decline.
Your lips drink in the coolness of the blue
Spring in the rocks.

No more, when softly your forehead bleeds,
Primaeval legends
And dark interpretation of the flight of birds.

But you walk with soft footsteps into the night
Which is laden with purple grapes,
And move your arms more beautifully in the blue.

A thorn-bush sounds
Where your lunar eyes are.
O Elis, how long you have been dead.

Your body is a hyacinth
Into which a monk dips his waxen fingers.
Our silence is a black cavern

From which at times a gentle animal
Steps out and slowly lowers heavy lids.
Upon your temples black dew drips,

The last gold of perished stars.

TRANSLATED BY *Michael Hamburger*

SUMMER

At evening the complaint of the cuckoo
Grows still in the wood.
The grain bends its head deeper,
The red poppy.

Darkening thunder drives
Over the hill.
The old song of the cricket
Dies in the field.

The leaves of the chestnut tree
Stir no more.
Your clothes rustle
On the winding stair.

The candle gleams silently
In the dark room;
A silver hand
Puts the light out;

Windless, starless night.
                    TRANSLATED BY *James Wright and Robert Bly*

THE SUN

Each day the gold sun comes over the hill.
The woods are beautiful, also the dark animals,
Also man; hunter or farmer.

The fish rises with a red body in the green pond.
Under the arch of heaven
The fisherman travels smoothly in his blue skiff.

The grain, the cluster of grapes, ripens slowly.
When the still day comes to an end,
Both evil and good have been prepared.

When the night has come,
Easily the pilgrim lifts his heavy eyelids;
The sun breaks from gloomy ravines.
                    TRANSLATED BY *James Wright and Robert Bly*

NEARNESS OF DEATH

O the evening deep in the darkling hamlets of childhood.
The pond beneath the willows
Fills with the tainted sighs of sadness.

O the wood which softly lowers its brown eyes,
When from the solitary's bony hands
The purple of his enraptured days ebbs down.

O the nearness of death. Let us pray.
This night the delicate limbs of lovers
Yellowed with incense on warm cushions untwine.
                    TRANSLATED BY *Michael Hamburger*

IN HELLBRUNN

Following once again the evening's blue lament
Along the hillside, along the vernal pond—

As if the shades of those long dead, the shades
Of prelates and of noble women hovered over them—
Already their flowers are in bloom, the earnest violets
In the evening's depth, the blue source's
Crystal wave purls on. So religiously
Do the oaks grow green over forgotten paths of the dead,
The golden cloud over the pond.

TRANSLATED BY *Michael Hamburger*

AT THE EASTERN FRONT

Like the wild organs of winter storms
Is a people's dark wrath,
The crimson wave of the battle,
Of leafless stars.

With broken brows, with silver arms,
To dying soldiers waves the night.
In the shades of the autumnal ash tree
Sigh the spirits of the slain.

Thorny wilderness strangles the town.
From bloodstained steps the moon
Harries the frightened women.
Wild wolves have broken through the gate.

TRANSLATED BY *Ingo Seidler*

GRODEK *

At nightfall the autumn woods cry out
With deadly weapons and the golden plains,
The deep blue lakes, above which more darkly
Rolls the sun; the night embraces
Dying warriors, the wild lament
Of their broken mouths.
But quietly at the meadow's end

---

* A town in Galicia, Poland, where Trakl served as a
pharmacist with the Austrian army. A battle was fought there,
after which he was placed in charge of a large number of
serious casualties, whose sufferings he could not relieve; he tried
to shoot himself but was prevented. This was his last poem;
soon after writing it, he was sent to Cracow to be placed under
observation as a mental case; he died there of an overdose of
drugs.

Red clouds in which an angry God resides,
The shed blood gathers, lunar coolness.
Every road leads to blackest carrion.
Under golden twigs of the night and stars
The sister's shade now sways through the silent copse
To greet the ghosts of the heroes, the bleeding heads;
And softly the dark flutes of autumn sound in the reeds.
O prouder grief! You brazen altars,
Today a great pain feeds the hot flame of the spirit,
The grandsons yet unborn.

TRANSLATED BY *Michael Hamburger*

GOTTFRIED BENN (1886–1956) Gottfried Benn was the
T. S. Eliot of modern German poetry—an assertion which
must of course be immediately barricaded with reservations.
Cerebral and resigned, he was a profoundly serious player,
whose work was expressionist from beginning to end as it
moved toward ever more rarified zones of polished statement.
Born in Brandenburg of North German and French-Swiss parents, he first studied philosophy in Marburg, then medicine in
Berlin. He entered the army medical corps in World War I
(as he did again in World War II) and, unlike other physician-
poets of the era, continued his practice (in dermatology and
venereal diseases) from 1918 to the end of his life. By 1956 he
had gained an international reputation as poet and essayist.

The greatest puzzle to Benn and his central preoccupation
was the ascertaining of the nature of reality and of man's perplexing and pathetic brain. His outlook, a thoroughly intellectual one, was early stamped and regulated by the cynicism
of medical jargon. Looking at the world through his micro-
scope he saw man as creature, "a poor braindog, draped and
encumbered by God," and found that man's genius had brought
him (differently from Trakl's *Verfall*) to *Zerfall,* total dissolution. For the poet the only answer to this was the work of the
formative, expressive artist. Clearly the so-called world of
reality was not the true one. Benn's concern from the first was
not the empirical but the metaphysical "I"—*"das lyrische
Ich,"* as he called it; and his work was aimed at the annihila-
tion of the rational, causal, logical world. He performed au-
topsies on history and man's intellectual heritage as he did on
the bodies which we see in his earliest poems. Artistically his
goals became "the transmutation of words" and "the creation
of a new lyrical syntax"—not unheard-of goals in our century,
but ones which he attained through greater gifts and with more
success than any other expressionist lyricist.

His mark is absolutely unique. From 1912 to his silence in
the mid-thirties, we move from raw and shocking tours through
morgues and wards through flights of pestilential and withering
satire to strangely elliptical excursions into voluptuous and
exotic botanical landscapes. There are blinding snapshots of
the metropolis in the jazz age, of Europe's *Kulturgeschichte,*
of classical mythology, of Benn's own childhood. In his terse,

songlike, strongly rhythmic, almost (but not quite) "beautiful," sometimes severely parodistic poems, studded with neologisms, he has raised a latter-day Darwinian literature, so to speak, to its loftiest artistic level. With bitter mockery and an absolute ethics he attacked everything idiotic, "Bolshevist," everything smacking of artificially and sanctimoniously postulated "human freedoms" and thus went in quite another direction from yet another "expressionist" in Berlin, Bertolt Brecht. After a brief, altogether disillusioning, and much misinterpreted involvement with the Nazi regime in 1933, from which Benn emerged sobered (in 1936 his work was condemned and then banned), there began a period of withdrawal as poet— not as physician. During this silence Benn became only more thoroughly convinced of his recognition that the one constant factor in all the illusory and transient workings of "reality" is art, for him the expressive poem, the only telling act against the void. In the face of the phenomenal world the poems, which first appeared again in 1948, now seem denser, more obscure, associative, abstract, narcotic, elegiac. The works of this period then give way to a final turn to poetry of more simplicity, grace, and gravity. They are Benn's reduction to an all-inclusive lyrical remnant, the only thing that still seemed to matter: the palpable creation.

BIBLIOGRAPHY

Gesammelte Gedichte, Wiesbaden: Limes Verlag, 1956, contains the poet's own selection. *Primäre Tage* (*Nachlass*), Wiesbaden: Limes Verlag, 1958, is a posthumous volume. The poems likewise appear in the four-volume *Gesammelte Werke*, Wiesbaden: Limes Verlag, 1959.

❈   ❈   ❈

THALASSAL REGRESSION

No, not in you, not in the forms
of love, in the child's blood,
nor in a word, nor in an order
is something in which your dark may rest.

Gods and beasts—so much nonsense.
Creator and pimp, you and I—
wreck, catafalque, with barnacles are
the eyes amended.

But there are times it dawns: in odors
from the beach, coral-coloring,
in fissions, in disintegrations
you lift the heavy lid of night:

on the horizon the hazy passage,
Stygian blossoms, sleep and poppy,
the tear is buried in the oceans—
for you: thalassal regression.

TRANSLATED BY *Edgar Lohner and Cid Corman*

POEMS THAT STAND STILL

A coolness to the coming of generations
is the depth of the Wise Man,
children and the children of children
do not bring him unrest,
do not pierce him.

To represent some party,
Busy-ness,
Travelling to, and from,
is the distinguishing stamp of a world
which does not see well.
Before my window,
the Wise Man said,
a valley lies,
the shadows gather together there,
two poplars show a road,
you know—where.

Perspective
is another word for his way of standing still:
to mark down lines,
the lines grow farther on
according to the laws of plants which put out shoots—
Jungle plants throw out shoots—
multitudes of birds also, crows
thrown out in winter dawn from early heaven—

then to allow them all to sink—

you know—for whom.

TRANSLATED BY *Robert Bly*

CYCLE

The solitary molar of a whore
who had died incognito
wore a gold filling.
(The rest had decamped
as if by silent agreement.)
That filling was swiped by the mortician's mate
and pawned, so he could go to a dive
and dance, for, as he put it:
"Earth alone should return to earth."

TRANSLATED BY *Francis Golffing*

SEPTEMBER

I

You, bent over the fence with phlox,
(cleft by heavy rains,
curious smell of game),
who likes to walk on stubble
and go to the old men,
gathering balsamine,
who breathes on the fields
smoke with lust and sorrow—

whose rising masonry
still wants its roof by snow and winter,
wants to call out an: "alas, in vain"
to the men laying the mortar,
but procrastinates—

stout rather than vertical,
with a filthy pumpkin nude at the foot,
fat and faceless, this vegetable toad—

risen from the level fields,
moon-end of all flames,
the increase of fruit and fever
fizzling out, an already darkened face—

fool or baptizer,
the summer's fool, late blabberer, last notice
or the pre-song of the glacier,
at least the nutcracker,
reed-reaper,
employer of rushed conclusions—

before You the snow,
high silence, unproductive
the unfertilizable distance:
there your arm extends,
still bent over the fence
the press of weeds and beetles,
the yearning for life,
spiders and fieldmice—

II

You, veiled by the mountain ash
of early fall,
stubble-webbed,
cabbage-fly in your breath,
let all the hands run,
cuckoo-clocks strike,
startle with vesper-clang,
ring
the hour, so golden in its fastness,
so surely yellowed away,
into a trembling heart!

You—: Different!
So only the gods lie
or the garments
of unshakable Titans
fashioned to endure,
butterflies and blossoms
embroidered so deeply
into the paths!

Or a sleep of an earlier kind,
when there was no wakening,
only golden warmth and purple berries,
nibbled by swallows, eternal,
that never hence migrate—

Strike this, ring,
this hour,
for
when you are still,
the poplar-planted borders will
advance and will be cooler.

TRANSLATED BY *Edgar Lohner and Cid Corman*

Three Poems from MORGUE
TINY ASTER

A freshly-drowned beer-driver was hoisted onto the table.
Somehow someone had left him a dark lilac-brightened aster
caught between his teeth.
When from out of the chest
under the skin
with a nice long blade
I cut his tongue and palate out,
I must have shaken it loose, for then it slid
into the neighboring brain.
I packed it into his chest-cavity
among the wood-shavings,
when they sewed him up.
Drink your fill in your own vase!
Rest in peace,
tiny aster!

TRANSLATED BY *Edgar Lohner and Cid Corman*

BEAUTIFUL YOUTH

The mouth of a girl, who for long had lain in the sedge,
looked so badly nibbled at.
When they broke open her chest, her esophagus was so full of
    holes.
Finally in one bower under her diaphragm
they found a nest of young rats.
One dear little sister lay dead.
The others lived on liver and kidneys,
drank the cold blood and had
here a beautiful worn-out youth.
And pretty quick their death came too:
they were thrown all at once in water.
Ah, how the small snouts squeaked!

TRANSLATED BY *Edgar Lohner and Cid Corman*

LATE
I

The heavy old trees
in the wide parks
and the flowergardens,
the moist confusion—

Autumnal essence.
Matting of heather
along the highway's length,
all of it's Lüneburger
Heath, lilac and unfruitful,
illuminations, that lead to Nothing,
introverted vegetation,
that soon deeply brown
—a question of a month—
as if never bloomed.

This is Nature.
And through the City
in friendly light
the beertrucks convey
final faint notes, and unconcernment
with excitation, thirst and unappeasement—
what's not appeased? Just minor circles!
The large ones wallow
in excesses.

II

So ends the looking, the looking backwards:
fields and lakes grown to be a part of your days
and the first songs
from an old piano.

Experiences of the soul! Youth!
then self perfected
bad faith, failures, corruption—
the backgrounds of fortunes.

And Love!
"I believe that you would've preferred to remain with me,
but it wasn't possible,
I absolve you of any guilt"—
yes, Love
harsh and multiform,
for years hidden
we keep calling to one another: "don't forget,"
till one of us is dead—
so roses end,
petal by petal.

III

Once again to be as before:
irresponsible and unaware of the end,

to feel the flesh: thirst, affection, triumph, defeat,
to reach way over into that Other—into what?

Sitting some evening, looking into the night's jaws,
they begin to contract, but on the ground are flowers,
they waft a fragrance, fleet and wavering,
behind which of course the putrefaction,
then there is full darkness and you know once more your lot,
fling your gold down and go—

so many lies beloved,
so many words believed,
that only came from the round of the lips,
and your own heart
so changeable, bottomless and momentary—

so many lies beloved,
so many lips besought
("wipe the lipstick from your mouth,
give me it pale")
and always more questions—

IV

Little old Lady
in a big red room
little old Lady—
Marion Davies hums,
while Hearst, her friend for 30 years,

in a massive copper-casket under the protection of a strong
  escort
and followed by 22 black limousines
arrives at the marmormausoleum,
distant cameras softly buzz.

Little old Lady, big red room,
henna-red, gladiola-red, royal-red (snail-purple),
bedchamber in Santa Monica Castle
à la Pompadour—

Louella, she cries, radio!
the blues, jitterbug—zigzag—!
the bourgeois in the Atlantic region:
marriageable daughters and obliterated sex,
Palazzos by the bays, eiderdown quilts on the couches,
the world is divided into Monde and Demimonde—
I was always amongst the latter—

Louella, my mixture—very potent!
What's it all about—
humiliated, reached the top, suffered like a dog—
the features, hideous features, to which the copper-casket now
　　puts a stop,
were overrun by light, when he saw me,
the rich love too, tremble, knowing perdition—

Very potent—the glass by the silver-apparatus,
he will be still from now on at that hour,
which only we two knew—
witticisms issued from the shell,
"life is determined at the breakfast-table,
"at the beach in a bathingsuit it hails granite,
"the unexpected usually occurs,
"the hoped-for never happens—"
these were his Stories.

Stop parading around! Only a few more flagstones,
on the foremost the glass
very potent, tinkles, last rhapsody—
Little old Lady
in a big room—

V

Feel, but understand, ages have felt—
sea and animals and the headless stars
wrestle it down today as once—

Think, but understand, the most illustrious
drive on upon their own keels,
are only the yellow of the buttercup,
and other colors have played their part—

understand all this and learn from the hour,
none is like this one, each is alike,
men and angels and cherubim,
the darkwinged ones, the heavenly-eyed,
none was yours—
not yours ever.

VI

Don't you see, how some of them stop,
many turn their backs to it,
curious tall slender shapes,
all are wandering toward the bridges.

Drop their sticks, stop their watches
short, the ciphers require no light,
dwindling crowds, dark figures,
all are weeping—don't you see it?
                    TRANSLATED BY *Edgar Lohner and Cid Corman*

THE DEATH OF ORPHEUS

How you desert me, dearest—
cast out of Erebos,
from the inhospitable Rhodope
through forests travelling,
two-coloured berries,
fruit glowing red—
providing foliage,
plucking the lyre
my thumb upon the string!

Three years already in the northerly gale!
To think of the dead is sweet,
thus removed
more purely one hears the voice,
feels the kisses,
the casual ones and the deep—
but you astray among shades!

How you desert me—
up rush the river nymphs,
the rock beauties beckon,
cooing "In the dreary wood
only fauns and sprites, but you,
singer, up-vaulter
of the bronze light, of the swallow skies—
put away your music—
oblivion—!"

—threaten—!

One of them stares so strangely.
And one who is tall and mottled,
the bright-skinned ("yellow poppy")
lures with meek gestures, with hints of chastity
combined with unbridled lust—(purple
in the chalice of love!)—in vain!

—threaten—!

No, you shall not melt away,
not be merged in
Iole, Dryope, Prokne,
nor mingle your features with Atalanta's,
so that indeed Euridice
I might gasp out beside Lais—

but: threaten—!

and now the stones
no longer obeying the voice,
the singer,
draping themselves in moss,
the branches appeased with leaves,
the pick-axes soothed with corn—:
naked blows—!

now defenseless against the thrust of the bitches,
the wild—
and now the eyelash moist,
the palate bleeding—
and now the lyre
drifting downstream—

the banks resound—

TRANSLATED BY *Michael Hamburger*

ONLY WHEN

Neither the olive-landscape
nor the Tyrrhenian sea
are the great experience:
the white towns are empty,
everything lies in dumb
cellar-vaults of substance,
and no shadows dim
the ungoverned brilliance.

The wine-cistern's empty;
with its flow disconcerted,
it offers no distance
and nothing overwhelming
and nothing to help expose
whatever sleeps in the brain:
it offers the South's ways,
but not the South's motif.

A yard of polar debris,
ice-ages, walls of ice
around the Villa d'Este too
and the torches of its broom:
only when creation's wound
has quietly opened itself
does the streaming hour rise
from the edge of the white town.

TRANSLATED BY *Edgar Lohner and Cid Corman*

AH, THE DISTANT LAND

Ah, the distant land,
where the breaking heart
at rounded pebble
or reed-flats flown by dragonflies
makes murmur,
and the moon
with its cunning light
—half hoar, half white-tufted—
sets up so comfortingly
the doubleground of night—

ah, the distant land,
where from the shimmer of lakes
the hills are warmed,
just think of Asolo, where Duse lies,
from Pittsburgh the "Duilio" took her home,
all the warships, even the English, had their flags at halfmast,
when it passed Gibraltar—

there soliloquies
without relationship to what's near,
self-consciousness,
early mechanisms,
totem fragments
in the gentle air—
some raisinbread in the coat—
so the days drift down,
till at the sky the bough stands,
on which the birds perch
after long flight.

TRANSLATED BY *Edgar Lohner and Cid Corman*

FRAGMENTS

Fragments,
Refuse of the soul,
Coagulations of blood of the twentieth century:

Scars—interrupted cycle of early creation,
The historic religions of five centuries pulverized,
Science: cracks in the Parthenon,
Planck with his quantum theory merging
In the new confusion with Kepler and Kierkegaard—

Yet there were evenings that went in the colours
Of the Father of all, dissolute, far-gathering,
Inviolate in their silence
Of coursing blue,
Colour of the introvert;
Then one relaxed
With the hands caught up round the knee
Peasant-wise, simple,
And resigned to the quiet drink
And the sound of the servants' concertina—

And others
Provoked by inner scrolls of paper,
Vaulted pressures,
Constrictions in the building of style
Or pursuits of love.
Crises of expression and bouts of eroticism,
That is the man of today,
His inwardness a vacuum;
The survival of personality
Is preserved by the clothing
Which, where material is good, may last ten years.

The rest fragments,
Half tones,
Snatches of melody from neighbours' houses,
Negro spirituals
Or Ave Marias.

TRANSLATED BY *Vernon Watkins*

BERTOLT BRECHT (1898–1956) Of all the sensational expressionist dramatists of the second and third decades of this century in Germany (Sternheim, Toller, Sorge, Johst, Unruh, Hasenclever, and the rest—even Kaiser and Barlach), Brecht's is the only name really vigorous and alive today. His fame only began under the aegis of that movement; he has far outlasted the era, founded his own style and school, and—as the outstanding dramatist-theater man of his age—has laid claim to the world's stages as no other.

The communist Brecht was born into a thoroughly bourgeois family (which he was soon to reject) in the Bavarian city of Augsburg. Medical studies in Munich led to a fearsome and enlightening experience toward the end of World War I, in which he was an army orderly. By 1920 he was working with the theater in Munich. He won the coveted Kleist Prize for his first dramas in 1922, and from about this time he began a career as an independent writer. His earlier extreme nihilism was altered through an intensive and thenceforth all-embracing involvement with Marxism, first in Berlin where he lived, famous and infamous, from 1924 to 1933. He fled to Switzerland, France, and then Denmark after the burning of the Reichstag (and his books) by the Nazis. When Denmark, his home for seven years, was occupied by Germany, he fled to Finland and then "out Europe's back door," across Siberia to the ocean and eventually to California. Here he spent the next seven unsettled years in fitful contact with such people as Lion Feuchtwanger, Thomas Mann, Charlie Chaplin, Charles Laughton, Hanns Eisler. After his curious hearing before the House Un-American Activities Committee in 1947, he returned to Switzerland and in 1948 to East Berlin, where he established with his wife, Helene Weigel, the great "Berliner Ensemble" at the Theater am Kurfürstendamm. Theater work occupied him almost exclusively for the rest of his life. He died in Berlin in the summer of 1956 and is buried near the grave of Hegel. During this final period he wrote little to compare with his dramatic work from 1925 to 1945. However, much from the last decade has yet to be appreciated and properly evaluated in the West. The image of Brecht as a shattered and disillusioned tool of the Soviets is altogether absurd. In Brecht's poetry (from 1918 on), as in his dramas, the central, indeed almost the only, concern is for humanity's welfare. His precise formulations of questions about the value of life and men are too demanding to be ignored. Until lately his great plays (themselves full of verse) tended to cast the poetry into the shadow. Now, with the piecemeal appearance of the seven volumes of collected verse, critics are having to confront the necessity of reappraisal. For as a poet Brecht was infinitely more than a malcontent and adroit rhymester. In the newest studies of German literature we are beginning to read with insistent frequency that Brecht must be recognized as "the great and major lyricist" (Soergel-Hohoff) that he was. Yet, despite their seeming simplicity, it is all but impossible to transfer his lyrics and "Songs" from their native language.

Brecht's considerable poetic range encompasses the lugubrious *"Moritat,"* the didactic ballads, parodies on sanctimonious theologizing, veiled autobiography, the sparse and cynical but loving confrontation of urban man and nature, the haiku glimpse. It is frequently maintained and in part true that his poems are "antipoems," a sort of inverse snobbery, consciously unliterary and folksy. But it is likewise true for a very large number of poems unknown here that such a claim is altogether misplaced. In style and theme the ones best known go back frankly to Kipling and Villon; less known is the influence of Rimbaud. And it is surprising to those who do not know German to learn that Luther's Bible is probably the strongest single literary influence. Paradoxically, too, the anarchy of early Brecht is very close to the *"Sturm und Drang"* Goethe and the medievalizing romantics he tended to satirize. His special manipulation of the South German tone is impossible to catch in translation.

Ethically opposed to the vices of excessive self-analysis and wasteful introspection, Brecht was among the very few of the New Objectivists in the late 1920's to decry by new examples the ever more private ecstasies of the inbred expressionists. Freed from a movement as such and in a sense freed from himself, he eventually turned his work into a weapon of real concern, less clamorous than earlier, often shrouded — but decisive, friendly, relaxed, and ever ready.

BIBLIOGRAPHY

Gedichte (*Gesammelte Ausgabe*). Frankfurt am Main: Suhrkamp Verlag, 1960 ff. To comprise seven volumes when complete.

CONVERSATIONS ROWING

It is evening. Two folding-boats
Glide past, with two young men in them,
Naked. Rowing side by side
They talk. Talking
They row side by side.

TRANSLATED BY *Edwin Morgan*

THOSE WHO DEPRIVE THE TABLE OF MEAT

Teach men to be content with their lot.
Those who are certain to gain by the offering
Demand a spirit of sacrifice.
Those who have risen from a banquet are loquacious
Before the hungry about the good times to come.
Those who lead the State over a precipice
Call governing too onerous
For the plain man.

TRANSLATED BY *Edwin Morgan*

GERMANY

Let others speak of her shame,
I speak of my own.

O Germany, pale mother!
How soiled you are
As you sit among the peoples.
You flaunt yourself
Among the besmirched.

The poorest of your sons
Lies struck down.
When his hunger was great
Your other sons
Raised their hands against him.
This is notorious.

With their hands thus raised,
Raised against their brother,
They march insolently around you
And laugh in your face.
This is well known.

In your house
Lies are roared aloud.
But the truth
Must be silent.
Is it so?

Why do the oppressors praise you everywhere,
The oppressed accuse you?
The plundered
Point to you with their fingers, but
The plunderer praises the system
That was invented in your house!

Whereupon everyone sees you
Hiding the hem of your mantle which is bloody
With the blood
Of your best sons.

Hearing the harangues which echo from your house, men
    laugh.
But whoever sees you reaches for a knife
As at the approach of a robber.

O Germany, pale mother!
How have your sons arrayed you
That you sit among the peoples
A thing of scorn and fear!

TRANSLATED BY *H. R. Hays*

A WORKER READS, AND ASKS THESE QUESTIONS

Who built Thebes with its seven gates?
In all the books it says kings.
Did kings drag up those rocks from the quarry?
And Babylon, overthrown time after time,
Who built it up again as often? What walls
In dazzling gilded Lima housed the builders?
When evening fell on the completed Wall of China,
Where did the stonemasons go? Great Rome
Is thick with triumphal arches. Who erected them? Who was
    it
The Caesars triumphed over? Had famous Byzantium
Nothing but palaces, where did people live? Atlantis itself,
That legendary night the sea devoured it, heard
The drowning roaring for their slaves.

The young Alexander took India.
By himself?
Caesar hammered Gaul.
Had he not even a cook beside him?
Philip of Spain cried as his fleet
Foundered. Did no one else cry?
Frederick the Second won the Seven Years War. Who
Won it with him?

Someone wins on every page.
Who cooked the winners' banquet?
One great man every ten years.
Who paid the expenses?

So many statements.
So many questions.

TRANSLATED BY *Edwin Morgan*

THE LANDSCAPE OF EXILE

And yet I too, on that last boat,
Watched the same cheerful dawn glow through the rigging
And the greyish skins of the dolphins riding
Through the Sea of Japan.

The little gilded horse-drawn carts
And the rosy veils on the matrons' arms
In the alleys of Manila, that marked place:
These the fugitive rejoiced to see.

By the high oil derricks and thirsty gardens of Los Angeles
And the twilight gorges of California and its fruit-markets
The bearer of bad luck
Was not left cold.

TRANSLATED BY *Edwin Morgan*

SONG ON BLACK SATURDAY AT THE ELEVENTH HOUR OF THE NIGHT BEFORE EASTER

In the springtime, under a green sky, already
Somewhat brutal, wild loved winds I buried
Within me as I entered the blackness of the cities,
Upholstery of cold proverbs in me I carried.

I filled myself with beasts from the black pavements,
I filled myself with water and with loud outcry,
But it left me very cold and light, my boy,
Utterly unfulfilled and light was I.

Indeed they knocked holes through all my walls
And, cursing, crept outside of me again:
There was nothing in me but much space and silence,
I was nought but paper: they shrieked, and cursed me then.

Grinning, I rolled down between the houses
Into the open, soft and festively
The wind blew—more swiftly through my walls,
And still it snowed. It rained in me.

The mean snouts of cynical fellows have discovered
That in me nothing at all exists.
Wild swine have paired in me. Often in me
Out of milky heavens ravens have pissed.

Frailer than clouds! Lighter than the winds!
Invisible! Light, brutal and gay the while,
Like one of my poems, I flew through the heavens
With a stork that flapped in somewhat quicker style!

TRANSLATED BY *H. R. Hays*

OF SWIMMING IN LAKES AND RIVERS

In the pale summertime, when far above you
In only the largest trees the winds are sighing,
You must float inert in a pool or in a river
Like the waterweeds in which pike are lying.
Your flesh grows light in water. Thrust your arm
Softly from water into air and now
The little wind cradles it forgetfully,
Seeming to take it for a brown bough.

At midday the sky proffers a great stillness.
You close your eyes when the swallows pass you.
The mud is warm. When the cool bubbles rise up
You know that a fish has just swum across you.
Your body, your thigh and motionless arm
Lie in quiet unity, only when the cool
Fish are swimming lazily across you
Can you feel the sun shine down upon the pool.

In the evening when, from long lying,
You grow so lazy that all your limbs prickle
Without a backward glance you must fling yourself,
Splashing, into a blue river where the rapids ripple.
It is best to hold out until evening comes
For then, like a shark over stream and shrubbery,
The pale sky looms, angry and gluttonous,
And all things are just as they should be.

You must, of course, lie on your back quietly
As is usual and let yourself go on drifting.
You must not swim, no, but only act as if
You were a mass of flotsam slowly shifting.
You must look up at the sky and act as if
A woman carried you, and it is so.
Quiet, without disturbance, as the good God himself does
When at evening he swims in his rivers here below.

TRANSLATED BY *H. R. Hays*

THE MASK OF EVIL

On my wall hangs a Japanese carving,
The mask of an evil demon, decorated with gold lacquer.
Sympathetically I observe
The swollen veins of the forehead, indicating
What a strain it is to be evil.

TRANSLATED BY *H. R. Hays*

1940

My young son asks me: Must I learn mathematics?
What is the use, I feel like saying. That two pieces
Of bread are more than one's about all you'll end up with.
My young son asks me: Must I learn French?
What is the use, I feel like saying. This State's collapsing.
And if you just rub your belly with your hand and
Groan, you'll be understood with little trouble.
My young son asks me: Must I learn history?
What is the use, I feel like saying. Learn to stick
Your head in the earth, and maybe you'll still survive.

Yes, learn mathematics, I tell him.
Learn your French, learn your history!

TRANSLATED BY *Edwin Morgan*

ON WATERING THE GARDEN

O watering of the garden, to put the green in good heart!
Spraying of thirsty trees! Give more than enough and
Never forget the shrubbery, not even
The shrub without berries, the exhausted
Niggardly bearers. And don't overlook
The weed between the flowers, it too
Knows thirst. Nor should you pour
Only on the fresh turf or only on the parched turf:
You must refresh the naked earth itself.

TRANSLATED BY *Edwin Morgan*

THE PLUM-TREE

The back-yard has a tiny plum-tree,
It shows how small a tree can be.
Yet there it is, railed round
So no one tramps it to the ground.

It's reached its full shape, low and meagre.
O yes, it wants to grow more, it's eager
For what can't be done—
It gets too little sun.

A plum-tree no hand's ever been at
To pick a plum: it strains belief.
It is a plum-tree for all that—
We know it by the leaf.

TRANSLATED BY *Edwin Morgan*

KARL KROLOW (1915–) Krolow is the elder among the "young" German lyricists who, to oversimplify, have turned away from Rilke and followed the lead of Wilhelm Lehmann (1882–), Elisabeth Langgässer (1899–1950), and Georg Britting (1891–) in the field of modern nature poetry. His earlier and again his more recent poems have a strict purity of line and image, contain a highly stylized yet talkative quality, play rhythmically with and against normal stress patterns, and seem now to project, now to conceal the poet's persona. The poems of his "middle" period are larger, looser, and chunkier and seem to lie in a magnetic field equidistant from the poles of nature-as-magic and a German surrealism clearly influenced by the French moderns—Apollinaire, Michaux, Jouve, René Char, Eluard, Max Jacob—all of whom (together with a good deal from modern Spanish poetry) Krolow has translated. His recent critical essays (*Aspekte deutscher Lyrik,* 1961) reveal also his indebtedness to and continued interest in modern American and British poetry. They show, too, his deep concern for poetical subject matter, the problem of "permissible" sounds and vocabulary, the limits of experimental play—in short, substantive gain and loss in regard to the "new poetry."

The poet was born in Hannover, Germany, and studied German and Romance literatures, philosophy, and art at Göttingen and Breslau. He fought in World War II and since 1956 has been living as an independent writer in Darmstadt.

BIBLIOGRAPHY

Gedichte. Konstanz: Südverlag, 1948.
Heimsuchung. Berlin: Verlag Volk und Welt, 1948.
Auf Erden. Hamburg: Ellermann, 1949.
Die Zeichen der Welt. Stuttgart: Deutsche Verlags-Anstalt, 1952.
Wind und Zeit. Stuttgart: Deutsche Verlags-Anstalt, 1954.
Tage und Nächte. Düsseldorf: Eugen Diederichs Verlag, 1956.
Fremde Körper. Frankfurt am Main: Suhrkamp Verlag, 1959.
Unsichtbare Hände. Frankfurt am Main: Suhrkamp Verlag, 1962.

❀ ❀ ❀

DEAD SEASON

It happened
That the ancestral portraits
Fell from the wall
Because it was so quiet.
The bottle of Beaujolais
Joined itself
With a few burst pears
Into a still-life.

It was the hour of the carp
And of the dying flies.

Afternoon blinked
Under heavy eyelids.
Yet the sounds of the heart were
Audible for a while
By the sail-boat pond of the boys
Who here, yesterday, had given out
Their nautical commands.

Day-before-yesterday anyhow
Everything had been different.
The dead season
Still lived in the legend-light
Smell of the grass.

Now they wait on the floor:
The broken pictures, waiting
For someone to step
Out of the wall
And pick them up, laughing!

TRANSLATED BY *Herman Salinger*

LOVE POEM

Flesh painted with the chalk of sleeplessness,
Painted white with the death of time, which
Is dying at this hour.
Painted with mortar that crumbles on your face,
Painted with night-watches,
The sound of caresses full in the ear,
Of whistles on street corners,
Of minutes that move with the tread of cats in the jungle,
Between three and four in the morning.

I don't see you any longer.
You don't exist any longer.
You have fallen among the savage cats
Who claw at your temples, your breasts, your hands—
The murderous minutes of this night.

Company comes through the window:
Summer with young crickets and black cries
From the steaming water.
I turn around to the wall
With its shadowplay of obscene pictures, pythagorean symbols,
tokens of your absence.

And the death of time comes up to my bed,
And I hear how he buries the final minute
In the gulf of an eternity
To which you don't belong.

TRANSLATED BY *Jerome Rothenberg*

WORDS

Candor of words invented,
Said behind doors out of sight,
From windows and against blank walls,
White-washed with patient light.

Reality of words spoken,
Of two syllables or of three:
Carved from the riddles of heaven,
From a vein in the stone set free.

Deciphering of strangers' faces,
With lightning under the skin,
With beards in which the wind stands,
By a sound, whispered within.

But the names, still remaining,
A hum in the ear, so slight,
As of bees and of cicadas,
Returning into the night.

Vowels—humble insects,
Invisible in the air.
Floating down as ashes,
As quince scent lingering there.

TRANSLATED BY *Ingo Seidler*

WALK

Someone, in the twilight, is taking a walk
And singing.

The wolf from the fable
Is in flight.

The wild plum thickets
Hover before him.
The man in the moon
Starts up out of the yellow straw
Whenever anyone goes past.

The wind's hand rubs
The hazel nuts
Whenever the darkness
Likes anybody.

Somebody takes the night
Upon his shoulders,
Gives love her names,
And the hands of the dead
Begin again in the dust
To stir.

TRANSLATED BY *Herman Salinger*

POEMS AGAINST DEATH

I

The elongated fruits of the jasmine bush, pressed against the
   breast,
Hung with alchemistic mussel-shells like ghostly playthings,
And the sugar of the year's seasons on the lip—

Anima candida:
You stand straight before the sky and the wind,
Catching innocent fishes by the wall,
The shadow of your own security in your arm.

On benches you sit in comfort.
The straw of the stubble does not press your skin.
You are alive and show your teeth to the grapes
That hang down before your eyes.

But a dead-man is not made of milk and blood;
And you will be like him

In the midst of wrist-watches, which indicate the hour,
Hour without an Above or Below,
Without heaven and wind,
With soot in the fire, with a groaning into the blue night,
No longer calmed by barbiturates.

A dead-man is no rhyme for tenderness.
A bundle of weeds on the flat palm of the hand
Is clearer.
He still exists only
In lights they light for him.
In the unmade bed which he has left,
In the smell, which lasted for the woman when he was tired
of her.
You will be like him.

II

A deck of cards the lyric landscape—easy to shuffle,
Easy to hold in the hand in the dream
Of green leaf-fingers.
And the one, the most worn card in the deck,
With the princes of this world in the picture,
Over which no angels unfold themselves like sailboats—

Death, unshuffled, marked with fear-sweat
And old laughter,
Death with a leather-coat smell on the mahogany-painted
wall:
Smoke before my eyes and already vanished again,
Blown away into a confused landscape,
Held by green leaf-fingers . . .

III

Scratched into the angles of the horizon,
Above the glowing of rose and poppy,
Above the heat in the flesh of invented fruits, the flesh of life;
Into the passing sweetness of an immature face, engraved in it,
With traces of night and still a man and on some morning,
Lizard-cool and green-faced.
Scratched into the epidermis of the sky,
White as snow that tastes of the knife's edge:—

Your hostile image,
Your invisible gestures and jokes,
With hands at the throat,
In ambush behind the bend of the tree-lined walk!

Your pain in the left heart-chamber
In the midst of perfect joy,
At the laugh of a seventeen-year old mouth,
Under eyes of fever and ice.

Closer than bodily closeness: you,
Noise in the blood, no chatter of eternity
But the cruel singing of deathless gnats.

Above the glowing places of rose and poppy,
In a colored shirt that gleams through the bushes,
Stripped off by a love that does not want to die:—

Your old countenance without color
Terrible and lonely!

IV

Like bird-swarm in the blue sea-oats, a light cloud:
Ill humor—a cloudbank—weakly at my two temples—

Thus you are there, quite unexpectedly,
In a noon that is like a rising dolphin,
Or evenings, smelling of tobacco-smoke,
Innocently between two pulse-beats,
A slight murmur in my blood,
Just while, forgetting, I let myself go in the game:—

Forgotten those leaves of the plane-tree, bright-bellied as a
    virgin,
Forgotten the leaf-breath by night on the skin
In the wind that blew for strange soldiers,
Forgotten the face of a woman, out of a Breton legend, face
    bared by the lamplight,
As all is quickly forgotten and turns to light cloudwork.

Death, linnet-light in the blue sea-oats.

V

The sweet seeds of the early dawn
Scatter through the thicket of the night-sky.
I can gather them up
And feel joy within me, like the wind,
The wind that has no fear of death.

The darkness has laid her head into her hands.
She gives way to the song-bird swarm of ecstasy,
Which in me beats its wings.

Every morning speaks its verdict over death;
And the flight-smell of the night wafts away.
I seize time with my finger.
Time rests—a mobile dust-grain—in the cup of my hand:
Perfect like the red sweet-pea
That is hung with blossoms and with pods,
With the dry, split lip of the earth
That has been crossed by heat.

Existence is stronger now in the growing horn of the nails,
In the blond-and-black beard-stubbles
And in women whose nipples stiffen under their blouses.

Every morning speaks its verdict over death.
The seeds of the dawn I have gathered up
And against the morning wind I sing:
Dead is Death!

VI

In a face the flickering of joy,
Silent ship that sails out never to return home:—

So evening comes.

Its life does not weigh heavy against the shoulder.
Gold cloud-mass in arm, evening is there;
And once more death has patience:
A seer of ghosts whose own hide hates him
As long as the water-aloes with white wombs blossom
And the twilight-dusk is light as a sand-wasp.

Darkness trembles its lips:
Beautiful, like the woman who doesn't exist.
Death it makes insecure, turns him a while away with its
    whispering.

So evening comes.
Its life weighs lightly against the shoulder.

And night has the color of Jenny's eyebrows.
She is not like that friend who changes her perfumes.
She is not like that friend in whose eyes the sea-fires flit.
She has little teeth, little teeth that gleam.
She has a mouth of exultation and stillness.

And once more death has patience . . .

TRANSLATED BY *Herman Salinger*

PAUL CELAN (1920–) German poetic surrealism has reached a high point in the work of Paul Celan. More than any other contemporary poet writing in the language, he has been influenced by the French surrealists. Primary among his "native" forebears are Trakl and the important Franco-German Jewish poet and dramatist Yvan Goll (1891–1950), with whom Celan was for a time in direct contact in Paris. It is probably correct to say that the fate of Europe's Jews has been the most powerful formative influence upon his art. His famous *"Todesfuge"* is the most realized expression of this concern in modern German poetry. Firmly controlled imagery, metrics, and metaphorical structure are the earmarks of his visionary and frequently antirational poetry.

Celan was born in Czernowitz (Bukovina), lived in Paris after 1938 (where he studied medicine briefly), and in Vienna after the war, where he published his first poems. In 1948 he returned to Paris and studied German literature and linguistics. He continues to live in that city, where he lectures in language at the École Normale, writes his own poetry, and translates extensively from others: Rimbaud (1958), Alexander Blok (1958), René Char (1959), Mandelshtam (1959), Paul Valéry (1960), Serge Esenin (1960), and a number of others.

BIBLIOGRAPHY

Der Sand aus den Urnen. Stuttgart: Deutsche Verlags-Anstalt, 1948.

Mohn und Gedächtnis. Stuttgart: Deutsche Verlags-Anstalt, 1952.

Von Schwelle zu Schwelle. Stuttgart: Deutsche Verlags-Anstalt, 1955.

Sprachgitter. Frankfurt am Main: S. Fischer Verlag, 1959.

Niemandsrose. Frankfurt: S. Fischer Verlag, 1963.

❀ ❀ ❀

IN THE SHAPE OF A BOAR

In the shape of a boar
Your dream stamps through the woods on the rim of the evening.

And his tusks,
Like the ice through which he has crashed,
Flash lightning.

He roots
For a bitter nut under the leaves
That his shadow tore down from a tree,
A nut
As black as the heart your foot kicked along
When you walked here yourself.

He gobbles it up
And fulfills those woods with his fateful grunting,
As it drives him
Below to the beach,
Far out where the sea
Is holding its gloomiest feast
On the reefs:

Perhaps
A fruit not unlike his own
Once enchanted that celebrant's eye
Into weeping such stones as these.

                    TRANSLATED BY *Jerome Rothenberg*

EYE OF TIME

This is the eye of time:
it squints cross-eyed
under a seven-colored brow.
Its lid is fire-washed,
its tear is steam.

The blind star flies at it
and melts away against the hotter lashes:
world waxes warm
and the dead
bud out and blossom.

                    TRANSLATED BY *Herman Salinger*

CORONA

Out of my hand autumn is eating his leaf: we are friends.
We crack time out of the nuts and teach it to run:
and time returns to its shell.

In the mirror it's Sunday,
in dreams there is sleeping,
the mouth speaks the truth.

My eye descends to the sex of my love:
We look at each other,
We speak what is darkness,
we love one another like poppies and memory,
we sleep like wine in the sea-shells,
like the sea in the blood-red ray of the moon.

We stand at the window, embracing, they look at us from the
 street:
It is time that they knew!
It is time that the stone decided to blossom,
that a heart beat for unrest.
It is time to be time.

It is time.

TRANSLATED BY *Ingo Seidler*

FUGUE OF DEATH

Coal-black milk of morning we drink it at sundown
we drink it at noon and at dawning we drink it at night
we drink it and drink it
we'll shovel a grave in the heavens there's no crowding there
A man's in the house he plays with his serpents he writes
he writes back home when the dark comes your golden hair
 Margareta
he writes it and then leaves the house and the stars are
 atwinkle he whistles his dogs to come near
he whistles his Jews to come here and shovel a grave in the
 earth
he commands us play sweet now for dancing

Coal-black milk of morning we drink thee at night
we drink thee at dawning at noontime we drink thee at sundown
we drink thee and drink thee
A man's in the house he plays with his serpents he writes
he writes back home when the dark comes your golden hair
 Margareta
your ashen hair Shulamite we'll shovel a grave in the heavens there's no crowding there

He shouts you there get the earth open deeper you here sing
  and play for the dance
he grabs at the gun in his belt he lifts it his eyes are bright blue
you there get the earth open faster you others play on now
  for dancing

Coal-black milk of morning we drink thee at night
we drink thee at noon and at dawning we drink thee at sundown
we drink thee and drink thee
a man's in the house your golden hair Margareta
your ashen hair Shulamite he plays with his serpents

He shouts play death very sweet now Death is a proud German
  master
he shouts make the fiddles sing darker you'll rise as grey smoke
  in the air
your grave will be high in the clouds there's no crowding there

Coal-black milk of morning we drink thee at night
we drink thee at noontime and Death is a proud German master
we drink thee at dawning and sundown we drink thee and
  drink thee
and Death is a proud German master his eyes are bright blue
he'll get you with missile of lead he will pierce you right
  through
a man's in the house your golden hair Margareta
he'll sic his big dogs on us all he'll give us a grave in the sky
he plays with his snakes he dreams nightly and Death is a
  proud German master

your golden hair Margareta
your ashen hair Shulamite

TRANSLATED BY *Donald White*

LIFE CYCLE

The suns of half-sleep are blue as your hair an hour from
  morning.
For they grow as fast as the grass on the grave of a bird.
For they're lured by the game that we played in dreams on the
  ships of desire.
For the daggers are waiting for them on the chalk-cliffs of
  time.

The suns of deep-sleep are bluer: your hair was like them just
    once.

Like the night-wind, I paused in the saleable lap of your sis-
    ter;

Your hair hung down from the tree just above us, though you
    weren't there.

We were the world, as you were a shrub at the gates.

The suns of death are white as the hair of our child:

He rose from the waves while you set up your tent on the
    dunes.

He brandished the knife-blade of joy and held us with fireless
    eyes.

TRANSLATED BY *Jerome Rothenberg*

THE TANKARDS

At the long tables of time
The Tankards of God carouse.
They empty the eyes of the seeing and the eyes of the blind,
The hearts of the ruling shadows,
The hollow cheek of evening.
They are the most mighty tipplers:
They drink up the full and they drink up the empty
And never foam over as you do and I.

TRANSLATED BY *Ingo Seidler*

WITH CHANGING KEY

With changing key
you open the house in which
the snow of the unsaid is drifting.
And with the blood that may run
from your eye, or your mouth, or your ear,
your key will be changing.

Changing the key is changing the word
that may drift with the snow-flakes.
And in the wind that rejects you,
round the word gathers the snow.

TRANSLATED BY *Ingo Seidler*

HEINZ PIONTEK (1925–)   The vital and refreshing lyrics of Heinz Piontek derive, as with a number of his contemporaries, in large part from the *Naturmagie* of Lehmann, Langgässer, Britting, Oskar Loerke. Yet Piontek's is on the whole a more positive, perhaps a more "manly" approach than that of most of the others now working in this vein. He writes briskly of memories of his homeland and is not convinced by the mocking rejection (since Benn?) of the poetic preservation of the past and the celebration of a vibrant present. In his neat, generally strophic and rhymed poems he manipulates people and things in such a way as to render plastic his grasp on the images of reality and to make us understand his perception of nature. The author more often than not is concealed behind his metaphorical language. At the same time he will assert his "infinite importance as a human being," whose roots ultimately go deeper than literature itself. He does not shy away from what others might think of as truisms or as images too transparent for our convoluted and refined perceptions and sensibilities. Nor do his meditations exclude speculations on immortality. At the same time he is painfully aware of the rootlessness and horror of much of our age. The sudden breakdown of stanza and rhyme in a number of late poems reflects his constant awareness of the transitory quality of human life. Still, his answers lie closer to Keats', whom he has translated and with whom he has found an answer to the inexorable flow in his discovery of the vitality of the South, Rome, our heritage of classical artifacts, the music of the Mediterranean.

After the war Piontek, a native of Kreuzberg in Upper Silesia, held a variety of jobs; he was a construction worker and a sign painter and worked with native arts and crafts. He then decided to complete his secondary-school education and subsequently studied literature, philosophy, and history of art at the University of Munich. He works as a literary critic for press and radio, has written short stories and radio plays in addition to his poetry and essays, and lives at present in Dillingen on the Danube.

BIBLIOGRAPHY

Die Furt. Munich: Bechtle Verlag, 1952.
Die Rauchfahne. Munich: Bechtle Verlag, 1953.
Wassermarken. Munich: Bechtle Verlag, 1957.
Mit einer Kranichfeder. Stuttgart: Deutsche Verlags-Anstalt, 1962.

❄   ❄   ❄

WIND'S BRIDE

Shy in limb,
the neck and back
a willow-wand.

You are
the stupefying one.

A squall
of grace.
A smoke signal
of beauty.

Entangled
in your own hair.

Shrouded
in a swirl
of blackbirds.

TRANSLATED BY *Emery George*

MERLIN'S TRAVELS

"Everywhere connections, combinations,
fluid transitions . . ." Heraclitus.

Chestnut trees whisper the wind
over beaches of sea-weed
and trickling sand.
The imprint of toes leads
to useless discoveries.
In the sweltering bath-house
the steam conceals the rustling of fabrics,
the hurried embraces,
the wild odor of sperm.

Under the planks of the bridge,
the river splashes
the figures of nymphs.
Sorcery flitting about coils
through the unexpressed words of the shepherd,
while the sheepdogs move in a circle.
The pressurized Summer,
condensed into sweat,
gleams on his temples.

Over softening asphalt—
marshlands,
a vitrified garden:
jungle aroma starts taking form,
the young men hold whispered meetings
and sink in a web of liana.
Green pollen pumps the sky
full of twilight
—soon.

Declining landscape,
where a newly started town
tenaciously grows in the marshgrass,
the fragile voice of the vegetation
is drowned out by electrical music—
feebleness wears down the riverbanks,
debased time
flows around the shallow, satisfied lives,
the black crayon sketches equations
on the wall of the contractor's hut—
pragmatic illusion.

TRANSLATED BY *Jerome Rothenberg*

KORSCHINSKY POTTED

His belongings: quart bottle with a wire stopper,
the coarse glass green as pine brush.
His wish: eighteen score charitable bartenders per year,
or bad booze from the clouds.

He knows the parts: takes his bearings wisely
by the smoke of the hangouts, and by the hounds
(those pink-tongued ones) they set loose on him.

Veteran that lets himself be led into bottle-battles,
and snoozes on the wood benches the livelong day.
—Children in swarms at his coattails.

Lives by his adorable white hair
that hangs in fringes under the brim.
—On the rack with the devil in the bottle.

Flunkey to fat landlords with the skittle-shooting
when he is not all befuddled.
Snivels at his mother's grave,
and throws her a fistful of stars in her apron.

One of these days he'll steal a tame rooster,
and it will turn out to be an eagle.

One of these days he'll fling his crooked knife into the air,
but will not hit the lightning.

Later they'll find him: one morning,
and dead between the fences.

TRANSLATED BY *Emery George*

THE ROUTES OF FATE

The routes of fate, with my life I take their measure
And reflect on them with one half of my mind.
Days when the green wheat rolls and billows,
When the cuckoo's call counts out what cannot be lost
And the farmers follow the wind with their ploughs—
With gentle understanding these I have linked together.

Gladly I bend under my burden of nettles and dead wood,
The sky is a crystal tambourine which softly your fingers
    shake,
Lombardy poplars escort me on my way.

Your goodness is like old sunshine on twigs that will soon be
    sprouting.
I am quiet with you.
White doves fly up to your heart.

TRANSLATED BY *Michael Hamburger*

JOURNEY WITHOUT END

Where to? Swaying under the wind, the inclines turn;
Against the blue parchment the coasts are light and hot.
When enroute? In the cart a docile servant train
To the dust: flour and salt. (Sharp, the way this skin burns!)

There go parched steers, a peaceful mule stud with each yoke.
The rivers transport gold. Just one woman on board.
Fires cast torrents of shadows against the sky
From the campers: their trail creaks on through campers'
    dreams.

And still enroute! In smoke from the files of motors
We follow, feverish, through the trampled meadows.
Extolled country! a sign, a breeze, sweet to acknowledge—
Here Miriam sinks down, with her eyes wild and moist.

TRANSLATED BY *Emery George*

SHADOWS AND TRACKS

Over streets and squares,
today in autumn when the smoke bursts open;
the squall gathers strength;
bleached jackets, hoisted as signals, flutter in the stands—
Today a girl, tall, with her hair undone,
on a bewitched and foolish path that
we walk, to gloomy babble: embrace and
farewell—stricken with love,
with lips greedy for echo.

Past faces of pregnant women
and their sneers, their wild compassions; past hollow shanties:
Children skip lightly through the gates of heaven
they scrawled with blue chalk.
The silhouettes of cranes wander in the harbor—
and yet, thoughts are birds of soot pinned to the wind,
higher than all impatience: making silence itself grow dumb,
and changing faint hearts.
Then finally behind the mildew of the docks
the deep park, and a man in a loose shawl:
a man with green eyes and green hands,
standing still, waiting—

A few steps more
between empty cisterns and crumbling gods—
and then, the leaves on your temples
and on your coat.
Nothing can begin and nothing has ended
as long as time will hammer out a single shadow
and swirl over the battlements!
Still: when don't we founder?
—And not earth, but air guards over the tracks
of hands and knees . . .

TRANSLATED BY *Emery George*

INGEBORG BACHMANN (1926–)   The two slim volumes of highly polished, sinewy poems by Ingeborg Bachmann assure her pre-eminent position among today's numerous woman poets writing in German (Elisabeth Borchers, Christine Busta, Hilde Domin, Marie Luise Kaschnitz, Christine Lavant, Dagmar Nick, Christa Reinig, Martha Saalfeld, Silja Walter, and others). Her work is charged with powerful imagery, surreal metaphors, and a depth and earnestness of *Zeitkritik* rarely attained by her contemporaries.

Ingeborg Bachmann is a native of Austria. She was born in Klagenfurt and grew up in a valley town in Carinthia. She completed her study in philosophy in Vienna in 1950 with a dissertation on the critical reception of Martin Heidegger's existential ontology. Her poetry was first published one year later in Viennese newspapers while she was working for the Rot-Weiss-Rot broadcasting station in the capital. As a result of her extensive travels, she has herself become a symbol of the *"unbehauste Mensch"* (Goethe's "homeless man") of our era, one of her major themes. She has spent time in England and America and has lived in Paris, Munich, and Frankfurt (where she was guest lecturer for poetry at the university). At present she lives mostly in Rome and Zurich.

Bachmann is a difficult but rewarding poet. Far from being modishly obfuscatory, her unique and curiously dreamlike imagery is the sincerest attempt to distill a new precision from words which, even as her raw material, she distrusts and at the same time to which she is confined and by which she is essentially fascinated—a fact which reflects an affinity closer now to Wittgenstein than to Heidegger. In her resonant, melancholy lyrics she speaks of man's loss of connection with other men and with his land, the unreality of love, the demon history, dreams, the sea, and of a nocturnal phantasmagoria peopled with her own prophet-birds and visionary animals which seem immune to the overwhelming feeling of the evanescence which is modern man's lot. Despite all this, her distillation cannot be called despair. She works with the polar tensions reminiscent of Keats, Baudelaire, Rilke, Benn, Eliot (past and present, immortality and transcience, protection and exposure, salvation and rejection); the result is the very fact of the poem. For Bachmann, as for Benn, it is enough.

BIBLIOGRAPHY

Die gestundete Zeit. Munich: Verlag Piper, 1953.
Anrufung des Grossen Bären. Munich: Verlag Piper, 1956.

❊ ❊ ❊

THE RESPITE

A harder time is coming.
The end of the respite allowed us
appears on the skyline.
Soon you must tie your shoe-lace
and drive back the dogs to the marshland farms.
For the fishes' entrails
have grown cold in the wind.
Poorly the light of the lupins burns.
Your gaze gropes in the fog:
the end of the respite allowed us
appears on the skyline.

Over there your loved one sinks in the sand,
it rises towards her blown hair,
it cuts short her speaking,
it commands her to be silent,
it finds that she is mortal
and willing to part
after every embrace.

Do not look round.
Tie your shoe-lace.
Drive back the dogs.
Throw the fishes into the sea.
Put out the lupins!

A harder time is coming.

TRANSLATED BY *Michael Hamburger*

MESSAGE

From the thresholds of the sky, warmed still by corpses, rises
    the sun.
Not the immortals dwell there, we are told,
but the war dead.

And rays are not reflected from such dissolution.
Our Godhead. History, has tilled a tomb for us
from which there is no resurrection.

TRANSLATED BY *Marcel L. Mendelson*

FOG LAND

In winter my beloved
is one of the beasts of the wood.
That I must return before morning
she knows, the vixen, and laughs.
How the clouds shiver! There falls
on my winter coat
a layer of brittle ice.

In winter my beloved
is a tree in the forest and calls
the crows, forsaken by fortune,
to her beautiful boughs. She knows
that the wind, when evening falls,
raises her stiff and frost-trimmed
gown and harries me home.

In winter is my beloved
a fish among fishes and dumb.
Slave to the waters that stir
at the stroke of her fins,
I stand on the bank and watch
her sinuous dives and turns,
till the ice floes drive me away.

Or else by the hunting bird's cry
struck down, as over my head
she arches her wings, I fall
on the open field: she plucks
the hens' feathers and throws me a white
wishing-bone. I hang it around my neck
and go off through the bitter down.

Faithless is my beloved,
I know she sometimes glides
on high-heeled shoes to the town,
in bars she kisses the glasses
deep on the mouth with straws,
and is free with her words to all.
But that language I do not know.

Fog land I have seen,
Fog heart I have eaten.

TRANSLATED BY *Janice Orion*

TO THE SUN

More beautiful than the remarkable moon and her noble light,
More beautiful than the stars, the famous medals of night,
Much more beautiful than the fiery entrance a comet makes,
And called to a part far more splendid than any other planet's
Because daily your life and my life depend on it, is the sun.

Beautiful sun that rises, his work not forgotten,
And completes it, most beautifully in summer, when a day
Evaporates on the coast, and effortlessly mirrored the sails
Pass through your sight, till you tire and cut short the last.

Without the sun even art takes the veil again,
You cease to appear to me, and the sea and the sand,
Lashed by shadows, take refuge under my eyelids.

Beautiful light, that keeps us warm, preserves us, marvellously
    makes sure
That I see again and that I see you again!

Nothing more beautiful under the sun than to be under the
    sun . . .

Nothing more beautiful than to see the stick in water and the
    bird above,
Pondering his flight, and, below, the fishes in shoals,

Coloured, moulded, brought into the world with a mission of
    light,
And to see the radius, the square of a field, my landscape's
    thousand angles

And the dress you have put on. And *your* dress, bell-shaped
    and blue!
Beautiful blue, in which peacocks walk and bow,

Blue of far places, the zones of joy with weathers that suit my
    mood,
Blue chance on the horizon! And my enchanted eyes
Dilate again and blink and burn themselves sore.

Beautiful sun, to whom dust owes great admiration yet,
Not for the moon, therefore, and not for the stars, and not

Because night shows off with comets, trying to fool me,
But for your sake, and endlessly soon, and for you above all

I shall lament the inevitable loss of my sight.
                          TRANSLATED BY *Michael Hamburger*

CURRICULUM VITAE

Long is the night,
long as the shame of the man
who can't manage to die, long
under the lamp post his naked
eye swung, and his eye, blind with the breath of gin
and the smell of a blonde girl's wet flesh
under his nails, oh God, long is the night.

My hair won't turn white,
for I dropped from a womb of machines,
Rose Red smeared tar on my forehead
and curls, they had
strangled her snow-white sister. But I,
the oldest, marched through a town
of ten hundred thousand souls, and my foot
stepped on a soul-louse under the leather sky from which
ten hundred thousand peace-pipes
were hanging, mutely. And often
I wish for angels' repose
and hunting grounds, sick
of the powerless cries
of my friends.

With wide-straddling legs and wings,
youth like some marsh grass shot up
over me, over ordure, over jasmine it went
on those towering nights with their square-
root dilemmas, breathing
the wisdom of death on my window each hour,
giving me wolf's milk, and pouring
old age's ridicule into my throat,
when I fell
over folios in sleep,
in a disconcerting dream
where I wasn't found worthy of thought,
playing with tassels
whose fringes were snakes.

And our mothers would also
dream of the future of their men,
they would see someone powerful,
revolutionary, withdrawn,
and mostly after prayers in the garden,
while bending over the burning weeds,
hand in hand with the howling child
of their love. Oh my gloomy father,
why were you always so silent then,
nor ever thought past tomorrow?

Forsaken in the fire fountains,
a night of crouching near a gun
that misses fire, so goddamn long
a night, under the refuse
of a jaundiced moon, whose light
stunk gall, there rumbled in the shadow
of a dream of power (why hide it now?)
the bobsled of our ornamented
past, and cut me down.
Not that I slept: awake
under the icy bones I trailed it
homeward, wrapped my arms and legs
in ivy and daubed the ruins
white with droppings from the sun.
I kept the holy festivals,
and only after prayers
did bread appear.

In a self-righteous decade
a man moves faster from one light
to another, from one country
to another, under the rainbow,
the compass points stuck in his heart,
towards the radius labeled the night.
Wide open. From the mountains
one sees oceans, in the oceans
mountains, and where the clouds line up
in pews, the swinging of the bells
of the one and only world. Which world
I was commanded not to know.

It happened on a Friday—
my life ran down with fasting,

the air oozed with vapors of lemon
and the fishbone stuck in my craw—
when out of the gutted fish, I lifted
a ring which, thrown away at the time
of my birth, fell in the river
of night, where it sank.
I threw it back to the night.

O if I had no fear of death!
If I had the word
(nor knew its loss)
if I had no thorns within my heart
(but battered out the sun)
if I had no greed within my mouth
(nor drank from the wild water)
if I waited without blinking
(nor saw the threads before me).
Must they drag the sky away?
Let the Earth not play me false,
but lay me long in stillness,
long in stillness, for Night
with its black snout to nose me,
and dream the next caress
of its devouring arms.

TRANSLATED BY *Jerome Rothenberg*

GUNTER GRASS (1927–) Grass, one of the outstanding members of Gruppe 47 (the most important new literary guild in Germany), would surely be West Germany's nomination for its most irascible, vigorous, and "angry" writer. So far his role seems in great measure to be to break society's religious and sexual taboos. He has been very successful. His novels *The Tin Drum* (1959) and *Dog Years* (1963) have gained a very wide audience in Europe and now in the United States. In his fiction he pays more attention to content than to style, more to sensation than to "composition." In his mighty and much-translated novels and his novella *Katz und Maus* (1961) he sees recent history as a universal manifestation of perversion; his work amounts to grotesque travesty in the picaresque mode on abnormal politics and its equivalent in sexual behavior. He is unquestionably a fascinating writer and one who transmits a feeling of infinite vitality. But there seems as yet no time for digestion and reflection. The energy is all directed at being free, liberal, mad. Although the ornamentation of his writing is predominantly surreal, its matrix is kept generally naturalistic. In his poetry, on the other hand, all seems surreal until we work our way further into it. The form is stricter and the impact, if often a puzzling one, is direct and immediate. The spirit of Grass the novelist and the poet is one.

Born in Danzig in 1927, he became an apprentice stone-mason and then sculptor before enrolling at the art academies in Düsseldorf and Berlin. After the war he held a variety of jobs as farm worker, miner, and jazz musician. Beside his novels and poetry he has written short stories, a play, and the book for a ballet. Since 1960 he has been living in Berlin with his wife and children.

BIBLIOGRAPHY

Die Vorzuge der Windhuhner. Neuwied: Luchterhand, 1956.
Gleisdreieck. Neuwied: Luchterhand, 1960.

❋   ❋   ❋

FOLDING CHAIRS

How sad these changes are.
People unscrew the name plates from the doors,
take the saucepan of cabbage
and heat it up again, in a different place.

What sort of furniture is this
that advertises departure?
People take up their folding chairs
and emigrate.

Ships laden with homesickness and the urge to vomit
carry patented seating contraptions
and unpatented owners
to and fro.

Now on both sides of the great ocean
there are folding chairs;
how sad these changes are.

TRANSLATED BY *Michael Hamburger*

OPEN AIR CONCERT

When the interval seemed to have been overcome
Aurelia arrived with the bone.
Look at my flute and my white shift,
Look at the giraffe peering over the fence,
Those are my blood, which is listening.
Now I'll defeat all the thrushes.

When the yellow dog ran across the meadow
The concert expired.
Later the bone could not be found.
The score lay under the chairs,
The conductor seized his air-gun
And shot all the blackbirds.

TRANSLATED BY *Michael Hamburger*

IN THE EGG

We live in the egg.
We have covered the inside wall
of the shell with dirty drawings
and the Christian names of our enemies.
We are being hatched.

Whoever is hatching us
is hatching our pencils as well.
Set free from the egg one day,
at once we shall draw a picture
of whoever is hatching us.

We assume that we're being hatched.
We imagine some good-natured fowl
and write school essays
about the colour and breed
of the hen that is hatching us.

When shall we break the shell?
Our prophets inside the egg
for a middling salary argue
about the period of incubation.
They posit a day called X.

Out of boredom and genuine need
we have invented incubators.
We are much concerned about our offspring inside the egg.
We should be glad to recommend our patent
to her who looks after us.

But we have a roof over our heads.
Senile chicks,
polyglot embryos
chatter all day
and even discuss their dreams.

And what if we're not being hatched?
If this shell will never break?
If our horizon is only that
of our scribbles, and always will be?
We hope that we're being hatched.

Even if we only talk of hatching
there remains the fear that someone
outside our shell will feel hungry
and crack us into the frying pan with a pinch of salt.—
What shall we do then, my brethren inside the egg?

TRANSLATED BY *Michael Hamburger*

THE OPEN WARDROBE

The shoes are on the bottom.
They stand in terror of a beetle
On the way out,
Of a penny on the way back in,
Of a beetle and a penny on which they can step
Till it makes an impression.
On top is the kingdom of headwear.
Head where it's safe. Head nowhere.
Impossible feathers,
Tell me the bird's name,
Where did his eyes roll
When he found himself trapped in so much color?
The tiny white balls, asleep in your pockets,
Are dreaming of moths.
Here a button was lost,
The snake in the girdle grew tired.
Sorrowful silk,
Asters and other highly combustible flowers,
Autumn transformed to a dress,
Every Sunday stuffed full of meat and the
Salt of ruffled panties.
Before the wardrobe grows still, turns wooden,
A distant kin of the pine tree—
Who's going to wear your topcoat
Someday when you're dead?
Moving an arm through your sleeve,
And every movement so friendly?
Who will turn up your collar on top,
Will continue to stand in front of the pictures,
And be alone under the windy bell?

TRANSLATED BY Jerome Rothenberg

FOOD FOR PROPHETS

When the locusts occupied our town,
no milk came to the door, the dailies suffocated,
our jails were opened to release
all prophets.
They streamed through the streets,
3800 prophets,
talking and teaching without restriction,
and eating their fill of that grey

& jumpy mess
we called the plague.
So everything was fine and up to expectations.

Soon our milk came again; our papers reappeared;
and prophets filled our jails.

TRANSLATED BY *Anselm Hollo*

TO ALL GARDENERS

Why would you force me to stop eating meat?
You come here with your flowers,
stuff me with asters etc.
as if autumn didn't leave a bad enough taste.
Keep the carnations in your garden.
Your almonds are bitter as hell,
and the gas drums
you'd pass off as pies—
why, you keep me shut in
till I'll even settle for milk.
You cry: vegetables!
then you sell me a rose by the pound.
You say health and mean tulips.
What should I do with the poison
you wind into nosegays,
should I eat it with salt?
Should I die from chrysanthemums?
And the lilies you'd strew on my grave—
who's going to save me from all these vegetarians?

Let me keep eating meat.
Let me head off alone with a rib,
let me work off its shame till it stands there naked.
And then, when I've pushed back my plate
and made a long speech to the cow,
that's when you open your gardens
and put those flowers on sale—
because they're only good when they're rotten.

TRANSLATED BY *Jerome Rothenberg*

CRACK-UP

Stags were roaring where the road curved.
Sunday morning threw a damper

On the woolens, on the watches.
Coins fell down as spoons were deafened,
Coins that sounded where the road curved,
When they screamed and chrome and nickel
And a handkerchief were crumpled.
But the chauffeur ate the dashboard,
Died and froze and wrapped himself
In the quartz-shawl of his bride.
Black shellac, the waiter's rose,
Was blooming, and the cobblestones
Had grated love down to a fine powder.
The whore, propped inside her oil can
That a man would pay three shots
To pump with gas, chattered about lilacs.
Oh ten cents, you ancient wonder,
In the poems in coin dispensers,
Silverfoil and cotton rhymed,
And the white-carnationed doctor
Came too late, the ambulances
Had dissolved like salt or sugar.

TRANSLATED BY *Jerome Rothenberg*

FROST AND BITE

With cheeks gone blue, in a shrinking shift,
with breath as a shawl (knitted for whom?)—
with feet like bare bones on the paving stones,
on which the tubercular cripple hops,
because of which the organ moans,
subzero chiming, no amen.

The Credo gasps through a siege of chills,
the Miserere rattles its R,
a pig, newly resurrected in aspic,
chatters, clatters,
as long as two teeth can find each other
in the gelatine depths.

Machineguns lie awake in their beds,
no rest for the weary,
groping with bony salvos
towards night and a railway yard in dreams.
Shoving against the wall
the leaden, death-sentenced morning.

A metal screen gets shaken loose.
Frost and bite, pot-lid and pot.
The clock throws up in the bucket,
the bucket wants more to eat—
RATTLING OF TEETH is the name
of the first and final poem.

TRANSLATED BY *Jerome Rothenberg*

Greek Poetry

EDITED AND TRANSLATED BY *Kimon Friar*

❊ ❊ ❊ ❊ ❊

Introduction

The architectural lines of ancient Greece are not to be found in the imitative grandeurs of Washington, D. C., but in the severe and functional lines of such buildings as flank Rockefeller Plaza or in the chrome, glass, and utilitarian grace of the Lever and Seagram buildings in New York City. And though the ancient ruins of Greece are dazzling in their splendor, the living classical architecture is best found in lines and proportions of peasant island homes; the pyrrhic dances are still to be seen in living transformation any evening at a Greek *tavérna* when a worker rises to tread the intricate steps of the *zeïbékiko;* the Lydian and Doric modes are still to be heard in the modern strains to which he dances; pagan ritual and symbol are still worshiped in the liturgies of the Greek Orthodox Church; and the best echoes of the ancient Greek language itself are to be heard, not in any of the purist revivals like the *katharévousa,* but in the demotic tongue of the goatherd and commoner whose mountain or city ballads continue Homeric traditions and motifs. In the same manner, ancient Greek poetry shows an unbroken line of tradition from Homeric days through classical, Christian, Byzantine, and Medieval times, finding an outlet in folk ballads during the four hundred years of the Ottoman Occupation, and bursting into full renaissance after the Greek War of Independence of 1821, in Andréas Kálvos (1792–1867), Dhionýsios Solomós (1798–1857), Kostís Palamás (1859–1943), Constantine Caváfis (1863–1933), Ángelos Sikelianós (1880–1951), and Níkos Kazantzákis (1883–1957).

In this small anthology of poets, all of whom are living (except for Sikelianós and Kazantzákis, with whom I collaborated before their deaths), the reader will find a diversity of talent, yet it is impressive to see how the racial Greek mind has remained almost integral throughout four thousand years of development and still shows the same qualities of clarity, precision, logic, and realism, though tempered with idealism and counterbalanced with romantic and symbolist grace. The greatest modern influence has been the French surrealist and symbolist schools, combined with an English and American metaphysical density. Any overly romantic manifestation may be taken to be not the indigenous expression of the race but the inevitable reaction to central Doric starkness, whether once found in *The Bacchae* of Euripides, the Eleusinian mysteries, or in contemporary surrealism. The Western World has made Greek myths part of its culture, but only the Greek himself, of whatever time, may use them with genuine validity, not as adornments of an outmoded religion, but as symbols still alive in the land and consciousness of the people. The best example of this is in Kazantzákis' *The Odyssey: A Modern Sequel,* or in the poems of Seféris.

Just as one should perhaps not speak of the ancient Greek or modern Greek languages but of the present state of Greek, so one should not speak of ancient Greek myth but only of the present state of Greek myth. The myths of the Greeks, and the literature inseparably connected with them, are used by modern Greek poets for the expression of a thoroughly modern sensibility, influenced, as Greeks have been since Homeric times and the long and various occupations, by the cultures of both Occidental and Oriental countries. This may be noted in almost all the poems of this collection, but particularly in the poetry of Seféris and the *Odyssey* of Kazantzákis. Ancient and modern streams meet in the Greek poet as in a swirling whirlpool, casting up marble fragments of the past but crushed into new molds by the pressures of modern life. He struggles with a language unique in world development, so very old yet so alive and changing that it slides like mercury in his hand, slipping and transforming itself like Proteus, taking on many shapes but keeping the same identity. The symbols of Proteus, of metamorphosis, of Odysseus, of the eternally restless wanderer on the frontiers of mind and spirit are still passionately alive in Greece today. Transformation, metamorphosis, and finally transfiguration, wherein the old and the new are blended into a compound light and insight distilled from thousands of years of unbroken tradition in language and myth, both pagan and Christian, are keywords to the complex, constantly striving, ever-wandering Greek mind which, like the self of an individual, changes momentarily but is always the same.

I am indebted to all of the poets represented here, without exception, not only for their assistance with the first draft of their poems, but also with the many revisions and the final version. I have nowhere fettered myself with any theory of translation, trusting to my feeling for the original and to my knowledge of English versification and rhythms, adapting my style to the temperaments and techniques of differing poets.

Note on the Language

No introduction to contemporary Greek literature is possible without some word about the language problem. In no other country of the West has this problem been of such long duration or aroused quite so much passion, beginning in Hellenistic times with the split between the Attic dialect and the Koine; that is to say, between the classical Greek of the educated and the common parlance of the people in which the New Testament was written. This chasm has been widening for over two thousand years, for the "common" tongue constantly evolved in syntax, grammar, and vocabulary, while the "pure" tongue remained faithful, by and large, to ancient Greek modes. After the Greek War of Independence of 1821, an artificial language constructed in the late eighteenth century and named the *purist,* was to all intents the official tongue of the newly formed nation and was taught in all the schools. The purist is the official language used on all formal occasions by those in government, business, radio, newspapers, and universities, although the same persons who use it speak at home or among themselves in the demotic.

By the time of the eleventh century, the demotic had closely approximated its present form, which in grammar today varies slightly from that spoken during the downfall of the Byzantine Empire in the fifteenth century. The purist is condensed and synthetic; the demotic is periphrastic and analytic, rich in many concrete words and phrases but poor in those abstract words of the arts and sciences which were not the concern of the common people who kept it living. Today this lack of abstract words is the despair of the modern poet who wishes to express a thought of any metaphysical nicety; he is driven to paraphrase or symbol. Since the eighteenth century, when the demotic had crystallized into folk poetry, the battle between the use of purist and demotic has raged, but the battle has finally been won by the demotic. Today the contemporary poet may mold his expression on a living language, and borrow his vocabulary as he can from a rich tradition of some three thousand years. But since he cannot proceed much beyond the capacity of the people to assimilate, the new living language in its vocabulary must be formed gradually by a constant interreaction between poet and public. If in all this confusion, poverty, and richness the modern Greek poet sometimes despairs, he may remind himself that in periods of language formation great poets have arisen—a Chaucer, a Dante, even a Shakespeare.

Kimon Friar

BIBLIOGRAPHY

Books in English

Kazantzákis, Níkos. *The Odyssey: A Modern Sequel.* New York: Simon and Schuster, 1958. Translated, introduction, synopsis and notes by Kimon Friar.

Prevelákis, Pandelís, *Níkos Kazantzákis and His Odyssey: A Study of the Poet and the Poem.* Translated by Philip Sherrard. Preface by Kimon Friar. New York: Simon and Schuster, 1961.

Seféris, George. *The King of Asine and Other Poems.* London: Lehmann, 1948. Translated by Bernard Spencer, Nanos Valaoritis, and Lawrence Durrell, with an introduction by Rex Warner.

Seféris, George. *Poems.* Boston: Little, Brown and Co., 1960. Translated by Rex Warner.

Sherrard, Philip. *The Marble Threshing Floor, Studies in Modern Greek Poetry.* London: Vallentine, Michell, 1956.

Sherrard, Philip, and Keeley, Edmund (ed. and trans.). *Six Poets of Modern Greece.* New York: Alfred A. Knopf, 1961.

Books in Greek

Dhiktéos, Áres. *Search for Poetic Personality.* Athens: Féxis, 1963.

Dhiktéos, Áres. *Theory of Poetry.* Athens: Féxis, 1962.

Karandónis, Andréas. *Around Modern Greek Poetry.* Athens: Féxis, 1961.

Karandónis, Andréas. *Introduction to Modern Poetry.* Athens: Dhíphros, 1958.

Meraklís, M. Y. *Our Poetry, Disagreement, Midpoint.* Kalamáta: Nestor, 1959.

Paráskhos, K. V. *Greek Lyric Poets.* Athens: Sotíris Spirópoulos, 1953.

Spandhonídhis, S. *The Newest Poetry in Greece*. Athens: Ikaros, 1955.

Thémelis, George. *Our Newest Poetry, 1930–1960*. Athens: Féxis, 1963.

Anthologies in Greek

Apostolídhis, I. N. (ed.). *Anthology, 1708–1952*. Athens: Estías, 1933, 1956.

Apostolídhis, I. N. (ed.). *Supplement to the Anthology*. Athens: Estías, 1959.

Dhiktéos, Áres, and Phaédros, Barlás (eds.). *Anthology of Contemporary Greek Poetry*. Athens: Féxis, 1961.

Panayotoúnis, Pános N., and Nathanaíl Paúlos N. (eds.). *Contemporary Poetry*. Athens: Dhíphros, 1961.

Pános, Panayótis, K. (ed.). *Anthology of Poetry*. Athens: Panayótis Pános, 1963.

Porfíris, K. (ed.). *Anthology of Poetry, 1650–1964*. Athens: Tákis Dhrakópoulos, 1964. Prologue by Nikiphóros Vrettákos.

Yorghoudhís, Dínos, and Yennatás, K. (eds.). *Anthology of Post-War Poetry*, Athens: P. Fragoúlis, 1957. Introduction by Aléxandros Aryiríou.

ÁNGELOS SIKELIANÓS (1880–1951)   Ángelos Sikelianós was born in 1880 in Lefkas, one of the Ionian islands, and died in Athens in 1951. For many years he roamed throughout the length and breadth of Greece, confirming his knowledge and mastery of Greek tradition and the demotic tongue. The central action of his life was the formation of the Delphic Festivals in 1927 and 1930. At Delphi, where the Amphictyonic Council (the first League of Nations) used to meet, Sikelianós hoped to found a cosmic center where, through a dedication to a religious view of life without dogma, the nations of the world might meet to insure peace and justice. Aeschylus's *Prometheus Bound* and the *Suppliants* were lavishly mounted, Olympic contests were held on the heights of Mt. Parnassos, Byzantine music was played, Greek demotic songs were delivered and danced, and an international university was planned. The author of nine books of poetry and of seven poetic dramas, Sikelianós was a poet in the grand tradition, a Yeats-like figure, a prophet and seer, a man of high visions and noble actions, one who had assimilated the cultural traditions of his own nation and those of the modern world, a revolutionary democrat and mystic who acted beyond the particular political creeds and religious faiths of the world. His vision was pantheistic and panhellenic, and his poetry, with its wide rhetorical sweep and unequaled command of language, encompassed both the lyric (of which he was a modern master), the philosophic poem, and in his later years, the poetic drama.

BIBLIOGRAPHY

Consecrated Bread. Selected Poems. Athens: The Greek Publishing House, 1943; Athens, Galaxy Publications, 1961.
The Lyric Life. 3 Vols. Athens: The Friends of Books, 1947.

❊   ❊   ❊

ATTIC

On our two horses, brother,
the black-maned Orion,
and the blond Demogorgon, on the drop
of deathless noon,

we trotted on the road to Eleusis,
slowly conversing,
like two ancient priests of Athens, astride . . .

"Is this perhaps chimerical?
I see not from the measured light
but from a lightning prodigal
which has from all sides wrapped me round . . .

And where is Time? From out my brain
the slightest breeze has taken it . . .
These pines are from eternity, this breeze
eternal that from the fresh thyme blows . . .

And this same rhythm with which we trot
is as it were the same whose master mold
some ancient horses left faint traces of,
treading upon this holy ground . . ."

"Only that body which from death
can rise may gaze upon and face
such earth as this, in silence such as this,
victorious body that shall loose

even those final chains that wind it round
as by its thread the caterpillar that
shall burst with wings, or by his mind
the thought of man that blooms with inner vision.

No, it is not chimerical that we
on this divine day are astride a dream
where all, invisible, visible, our horses, the gods and we
breathe in the same cool crystal sphere!"

"Would I might never waken from this dream . . .
Soon, as we reach the sea at that hour when
out of the heat we goad our horses on,
thrusting their flanks into the waves

like prows, we shall awaken, it may be,
once more amid the impediments of time
to scatter once again the miracle amid
rejoicings mystical and the enormous strife . . ."

"Do you live still in the divisible tumult,
brother? and have you still from out
the thin soil of this earth not yet
redeemed the body mystically achieved,

like the cicada which, emerging from its tomb,
enthroning itself upon the topmost bough,
stands sentry over earth and sun and gods
with its brief frugal hymn of resurrection?

But we who have so often conquered death,
brother, and have the darknesses dissolved
of times like these, now for the indivisible push on,
and grow, the more we speed, younger than youth!

And it may be that our horses now have here
divined all this which we as yet do not
perceive, for now behold them in the road's midst
how they begin to chew their bridles and to dance

lightly, as if and suddenly they sought
to change their pace and, on this ancient lane
—hold fast to your bridle, brother, and push on—
to change their steady gallop and to take wing.

No, it is not chimerical that we
on this divine day are astride a dream where all,
invisible, visible, our heroes, the gods and we
rush in the same eternal sphere. . . ."

SPARTA *

"As if from ambush now for a long time
I've held you in my eye, and from all others
have chosen you as if you were a star;
your countenance has gratified my heart.
Hearken: now let me tightly grasp your hand,
for youth is like a stallion thus subdued:
for one night only shall you lie upon
my bed, and be my own wife's counterpart.

Go; she is small in waist and as compact
in beauty as majestic Helen was,
and fill her generously with your seed.
For one night take her in your strong embrace,
and then uplift my desolate old age
before all Sparta with a worthy son."

* See Plutarch's *Life of Lycurgos:* "The old husband of a
young woman was permitted to introduce her to a handsome
and virtuous young man whom he esteemed, and to recognize
the offspring of their generous blood as his own."

PANTARKES

"Ο ΠΑΙΣ ΚΑΛΟΣ" *

Deep was the mystic valley, and the wet woods
   of Kronion had donned
shadows both dim and clear from the mild wind
   that blew after the rain.

Along the gutters of the temples where
   rills sang like nightingales
the swallows gathered in a slow, sad dance
   then sat in a long row.

Fragrance of honey struck the nostrils from
   old hollows of tree-trunks,
and breathed forth from the dry pine-needles that
   from each forked bough hung low.

One quick wing-footed burst of wind roused up,
   another strewed perfumes,
and from the incomparable bliss of flowers
   unseen, the earth became

one fragrant mouth, for as the wind's heel swirled
   with unapparent grace
luxuriously, it spread out everywhere
   an endless mystic feast.

The breast and throat of a young man whose teeth
   gleamed, as he deeply breathed,
like bitter orange bloom, glowed from the cold
   after the sudden rain;

who felt his teeth like unripe almonds set
   within his tightened gums
till his chaste mind rejoiced to its far depths
   to feel the freshened world.

Later, when cooling darknesses spread far
   and wide, a sudden flash
of silent lightning lit up everything
   like dry twigs blazoning,

* "The virtuous young man." Καλός in ancient Greek is
almost untranslatable, meaning "good," "virtuous," and "beautiful."

and from the resin of the dampened trees
   a perfume breathed as if
with loving inclination toward the earth
   the locks of Zeus hung down.

And the dew-laden eyelids opened wide
   in meditation, sleep
would not draw near, so full refreshing were
   the feasts of fragrances;

and in the workshop on a tripod stood
   a lamp with triple flame
that lit up all the thought of that one man
   who leant on his open palm,

and before whose calm Olympian eye a bright
   young athlete slowly paced
naked among the various tools before
   the flickering triple flame.

But still the artisan remained serene,
   sublimely cool, awake,
long since accustomed how to eat at mystic
   banquets with all the gods.

And in the splendor of his mind, which flowed
   like Alpheus noiselessly,
the chryselphantine treasure stirred and glowed
   slowly before him. Then,

like the flax flower or pale sapphire stone
   of indigo, there shone
bright gems within him with a hard cold light,
   mystic and myriad,

that for the indescribable nude stare
   of those Olympian eyes
confronting all of Nature, he might choose
   of diamonds the most blue.

And as the darknesses upon his closed
   eyelids now wove the myriad
and multicolored flowers, he fancied how
   the valanced ebony

upon the throne would glitter and how all
   the constellation's wealth,
which breathed a deep serenity, would close
   about it like the tail

turning about a peacock's legs. So did
  the God appear to him,
the Eternal Benefactor of all youth,
  and in whose smile his mind

was laved as the Archer of Aegina who,
  kneeling, exults and grasps
the bow within his hands as if it were
  the bowstring of a lyre,

and life and death a double star. He raised
  his eyes and saw the youth,
and his soul filled with peace Olympian and
  the fading fragrant night.

Then, as an eagle swoops to lust, his eyes
  fell on the young man's breast,
shoulders, arms, thighs, and murmuring he said:
  "Zeus, if I should erect

you in that high Olympian style, then let
  that joy be mine, to write
but on a corner of your foot: *Pantarkes*
  is the most beautiful boy.

"HAUTE ACTUALITÉ"

"When the new King of Egypt, Farouk, ascended the
throne, he thought of transferring the mummies of the
Pharaohs from the museums to their original tombs with
great official pomp and splendor."
        —Newspaper account of 1936

Here where the final Lotus sprang for me,
in this desolate cape where I have turned
my face, that it may be hammered out,
at dawn, in the illimitable ocean and the sun,
and in the breaths of stellar wastes at night;

here where the wind blows without end
in the dry grasses round about me,
and a voice whispers, as if it were the very
language of my soul,

how was I suddenly turned,
so deeply immersed in listening,
to this distant message from the world?

"The new
King of Egypt has decreed that the holy
corpses of the forty
dynasties of the Land of the Nile
shall from their crystal tombs be raised
where they have lain so many years enclosed,
gaped at by the irreverent multitude,
and with magnificent pomp
shall in their primal tombs once more be buried.

There shall precede, chosen amid all
the territories of Ape, the greatest female mourner,
who will from time to time burst out in great lament,
—as if Osiris for the second time endured
his death at Typhon's hands—

and there shall follow, behind the royal orchestras,
a Chorus of Youths and Maidens,
slowly,
upon their golden-woven pillows holding
the emblems of the Pharaohs;

and like a silver-swirling river,
a little behind,
the Egyptian priests, each with his white tiara
and on his breast the multi-colored jewels
inlaid with gold,
shall chant
funeral dirges from the Book of the Dead;

until the Desert is reached,
and there,
like the ostrich who thrusts her eggs in the sand
and waits for the Sun to hatch them,
they shall rethrust their holy dead
into the revolving centuries to await
from Osiris their glowing resurrection.

And then, with head unbared,
unarmed,
the King shall kneel upon the sand,
raising his hands amid the dead and living,
and call
upon the Spirit of his Ancestors
to descend like a blessing on the Land of the Nile,

on his own bared head,
and on all his people.
And with blood
and spirit so renewed
from the great Ceremony,
all shall return to their homes and their work,
to continue with faith,
again, the toil of the forty
dynasties of the Land of the Nile."

This is what I heard
in that one moment that took me
out of my listening, away from the wind's whispering
in the dry grasses,
from the illimitable ocean and the sun,
from drifts of wind in my face in the starry Desert,
and I said:
"In truth, it profits me to follow this funeral
of Pharaohs into the Desert,
and with denuded mind
to lean the Polar Star
of my Thought
on their magnificent and resurrectional expectation."

But for a moment only!

For behold, the wind's breath once more about me
scatters from the dry thistles
their star-shaped fluff into the distance,
and once more,
with my whole mind, now freed
from this greatly imagined Phantasm of Time,
that for a while had bewitched me,

like a snake
lately emerged out of its molting
with skin renewed,
I plunge,
—a dragon now—
into the eternal coolnesses about me
of earth and of sea,
and with my entire being,
like a naked body

that for the first time leans
upon another beloved body,
whose touch redeems the infinite within me
and annihilates
all the horizon of the world around me,

I raise myself aloft, holding within me deeply enclosed
my own Eternity,
while here where the final Lotus sprang for me,
and the dry grasses about me whisper in a tongue
which is the very language of my soul,
I feel on my mouth suddenly and again
flaming and ready to be born
with invincible pulse my new Word,
lip on my lip glued,
flaming, burning,
the virginal kiss of the Abyss!

NÍKOS KAZANTZÁKIS (1883–1957) Níkos Kazantzákis was born in Heracleion, Crete, in 1883 and died in Freiburg, Germany, in 1957. He studied law at the University of Athens, philosophy under Henri Bergson at the College de France, and literature and art in Germany and Italy. In 1919 he served briefly in the Ministry of Public Welfare and in 1919 as Minister of National Education, without portfolio. In 1947 he was appointed Director of Translations from the Classics for UNESCO. The greatest man of letters of modern Greece, Kazantzákis wrote some nine novels (of which *Zorba the Greek, The Greek Passion, Freedom or Death, The Last Temptation of Christ, St. Francis,* and *The Rock Garden* are available in English), five books of travel, sixteen poetic dramas, three philosophical treatises (including *The Saviors of God: Spiritual Exercises,* available in English translation by Kimon Friar), and his great epical poem of 33,333 lines, *The Odyssey: A Modern Sequel,* hailed unanimously as a world masterpiece immediately on its American publication in a translation by Kimon Friar. In addition, he has translated into modern Greek Homer's *Iliad* and *Odyssey,* Dante's *Divine Comedy,* Goethe's *Faust,* Darwin's *Origin of the Species,* and innumerable other books.

BIBLIOGRAPHY

Odyssey. Athens: Pirsós, 1938; Athens: Y. S. Hrístou & Sons, 1957; Athens: Dhorikós, 1960.

The Odyssey: A Modern Sequel. Translated by Kimon Friar. New York: Simon and Schuster, 1958.

The Saviors of God: Spiritual Exercises. Translated by Kimon Friar. New York: Simon and Schuster, 1960.

Terza Rimas. Athens: F. Konstandinídhis & K. Mihalás, 1960.

❊ ❊ ❊

From THE ODYSSEY: A MODERN SEQUEL

THE ASCENT

What joy to climb the mountain's holy solitude
alone, in its clear air, a bay leaf in your teeth,

to hear the blood pound in your veins up from your heels
and speed on past your knees and loins to reach your throat
and there spread like a river to wash your mind's roots!
Never to say, "I'll go to the right," "I'll go to the left,"
but let the four winds range the crossroads of your mind,
and as you mount to hear God breathing everywhere,
laughing beside you, walking, kicking at sticks and stones;
to turn, and like a hunter out for grouse at dawn,
see not a single soul, not even a wing in air,
though all the mountain slopes about you cackle and caw.
What joy, when earth shakes like a flag in the dawn's mist,
and your soul sits astride a steed, sword-sharp and strong,
your head a castle of great power, while from your chest
the sun and moon hang down like gold and silver charms!
To hunt for that uncatchable high bird, to leave behind
your mind and jangling life, and joy, that faithless whore;
to say farewell to virtue, to all-numbing love,
to leave behind the moldy and worm-eaten earth
the way new cobras shed their flimsy skins on thorns.
The lackwits laugh in taverns and the girls grow pale,
the landlords shake their velvet caps with threatening looks
and envy your red apples, soul, but dread the cliff,
but you strike up a gallant tune and like a bridegroom
walk straight toward solitude with bridal gifts in hand.
Lone man, you know that God avoids the herd and takes
the desert paths alone nor casts a shadow there;
you've learned all crafts, most wily man, and neither God's
own traces nor man's tracks can make you change your road;
you know the forest clearings where dark demons eat,
the wells which water the dread phantoms of the breast;
you hold all weapons in your mind, seize what you want:
ambush, bewitching spells, harehounds or feathery shafts.
That day as you climbed up at dawn and walked with light,
both of your rude palms itched, your cunning eyes cast flames
and beat among the bushes everywhere to flush
that savage bird, your wild waste's god, with its rich plumes.
Light-footed on the mountains, the cool hours passed
and leapt like kids among the crags with their bronze bells;
the sun paused in mid-heaven, the day cast off its yoke,
and twilight slowly settled on cool, azure mists
till with his friend, the light, the archer also stopped
on a sharp barren mountain peak with clawing crags,
precipitous and parched, no water and no grass,

wild nest well suited to his eagle-grappling mind.
At length the first star fluttered in the darkling air,
a golden housefly caught in the night's spidery web
which slowly, slowly caught still more till the black dome
in marble traceries spread like webs after a rain.

                                        Book XIV, 1–50

From THE ODYSSEY: A MODERN SEQUEL

ODYSSEUS AND HELEN MEET AGAIN IN SPARTA

Cunning Odysseus, meanwhile, stole through palace rooms
where torches had not yet been lit in scented halls,
and like a stealthy thief groped columns and dim walls.
In misty darkness, gold-wrought inlays gleamed like snakes,
mother-of-pearl glowed softly like fine, human flesh,
and as his fingers suddenly touched an amber's gloss,
he started back, as though he'd touched fair Helen's arms.
Trailing their languorous blazing tails, the peacocks screamed
like strutting ladies of the court, as in dark night
Odysseus passed and trembled like a still green youth
who fumbles through his sweetheart's house for the first time.
And as the burning doves above him sighed with love,
and fountaining waters fell within the fragrant night,
and one bird warbled in the garden close, he felt
suddenly sheathed and lost in Helen's enclosing flesh.
In truth, a slender lady loomed there by the threshold;
her motionless white hands, her face and throat were bathed
in misty moonlike glow by the door's golden mouth.
The savage solitary's temples throbbed like wings
for Helen stood awaiting him on the deathless threshold.
For a long time they held each other's hand, nor spoke,
but tasted the fine flavor of unhoped reunion,
till like a tree's soft rustling Helen spoke at last:
"Good is the earth, life in this world is sweet, most sweet.
Dear God, I hold Odysseus' hands in both my hands!"
"I love earth, too, for now I hold your hands in mine,"
and as he spoke his keen eyes strove in the dark to see
if her black hair had grayed, her flashing eyes grown dull.
"Do you recall that night you saved me, dear, when all,
mortals and gods, had cast me off before death's door?
Blond Menelaus had drawn his sword to pierce my throat."
On her full lips, round as a ring, the stars rained down,

but the heart's tempter had already spread his nets:
"The past has fled, all totally vanished, sunk in earth,
and in this holy hour, complete and stripped of evil,
I'm blessed to stand with my gray hairs in this famed court
and hold within my mortal palms the immortal moon.
I swear—I see and touch you for the first time, Helen!"
Then both fell silent; time stood still above their heads
like a gray eagle hovering on the air's high peak.
Perhaps a lightning moment passed, perhaps ten years,
those ten years that had flashed to take those toppling towers;
all things now turned to stone and in the heart lay still,
and dull life burst with stars and turned to fabled myth.
This was not gore and conflagration, no grand castle,
no brash young blade had seized the swan-born maiden yet;
a rich field of red lilies, reed-pipe of a small
and love-sick shepherd had softly swept their brains like clouds
then set them gently on far-distant mountain tops.

                                        Book III, 1033–1081

From THE ODYSSEY: A MODERN SEQUEL

ODYSSEUS BECOMES ONE WITH NATURE

Untamed Odysseus raised his head on high and hung
above the chasm and sank into the terror of thought.
The contours of his brain glittered like mountain peaks
till the earth shook, and darkness like a spool unwound;
his eyes sank inward, his white head swayed sluggishly,
his soul cut cleanly from the worm, became all silk
and slowly wove its fine cocoon in the empty air.
As the fierce outer sun grew dim, his memory grew sweet,
leopards passed by like sighs, and the world's holy myth
like an enchanted prince was drowned in the swift stream.
His inner rose burst into bloom and sucked his heart,
his mind grew light, and his starved flesh turned into spirit;
light formed a scorching ring about him, the woods shook
as in the center, motionless, hopeless, the archer crouched;
the woods wrapped round him like green flesh, his mind flung
    leaves;
when dewdrops gleamed on boughs, Odysseus also gleamed,
for his whole body in the dewdrops swam and glowed.
Ants scurried in thick swarms with insects, eggs, and seed,
and he, too, strove and fetched and hid his treasures deep;

he watched snakes coil and sun themselves on stones and
    knew
the sleep of poisonous snakes was holy as a child's;
he fondled grass as though it were a loved one's hair,
his snake-mind gently slid and coiled on warming stones,
and in that nestling sweetness he heard words of love:
"A white black-headed worm deep in the forest bores
through a sweet apple, and I crouch on stones and wail
because a white black-headed worm gnaws at my brain.
In damp tree-hollows coupling scorpions, newly wed,
keep motionless, nor eat nor drink, dizzy with lust;
the males watch death approaching in the females' eyes,
and ah, deep down, both in their male and female orbs
I watch my own face fill with death and deathlessness."
He pressed his ears to earth and heard the small seeds toil
flat on their backs, fighting the soil courageously,
thrusting through stifling stones, groaning for life and freedom.
"I, too, am a small seed! I strive to lift the earth!
I hear the roots of trees grope mutely in the dark
like long blind worms that softly suck, I hear my veins
spill on the ground and suckle softly too, I hear
the birds of air, I hear the insects of the earth
opening their wings in close embrace, and my head gapes
that all might enter, warm their eggs, and hatch them soon.
Now the great forest sups and clacks its tongue with greed,
varied sweet fruit perch on its palate, slowly melt,
and on its bitter lips bees drip their pure wild honey."
Far off a pomegranate softly burst and flung its fruit
and the archer's breast was filled with pomegranate seed.
His nostrils quivered as he smelled deeply in woods
fragrance of rotted leaves, waters, and steaming soil,
white hidden jasmine sprays that blossomed in dark wells,
until the great ascetic's eyes brimmed full of tears
and his brains smelled of laurel, thyme, and golden furze,
his fingers dripped with the thick musk of too much love.
Though motionless, he grabbed with greed at the whole grove,
his body cooled, his palms were filled with herbs and plants,
and round his neck a twisting ivy slowly curled.
His cool feet ran like flowing streams, his chest flung grass,
and like hushed pools of jet-black water his eyes gleamed
behind the morning-glory blooms that twined his beard.
He turned his head right, and the forest, too, turned right,
he turned his head left, and the forest, too, turned left,

he yelled "I!" in his heart, and the whole forest quivered.
For the first time he felt that he lived and had a soul.
Odysseus brimmed with waters, trees, fruit, beasts, and snakes,
and all trees, waters, beasts and fruit brimmed with Odysseus.

Book XVI, 412–477

From The Odyssey: A Modern Sequel

DYING ODYSSEUS SAYS FAREWELL TO HIS FIVE ELEMENTS

He gathered all his memories, held Time in his hands
like a thick ball of musk and smelled it in the wastes
with flaring nostrils till his mind was drenched with scent.
Time melted in the lone man's fingers till his nails
dripped with aromas like the birds of inner Asia
flown from rich woods of nutmeg blooms and pepper root.
He was drained pure till life turned to immaculate myth
and into tranquil princesses his fearful thoughts,
for in his mind dread God distilled like oil of roses.
And as Odysseus smelled the ripe and flaming fruit,
a sweet swoon seized him, all his entrails came unstitched,
his full veins opened with unutterable relief,
and all his body's armored nets which once he cast
to snare the world—nerves, bones, and flesh--became disjoined.
The five tumultuous elements, that strove for years
to forge the famous form of the world-wandering man,
shifted and parted now and slowly said farewell—
earth, water, fire, air, and mind, the Keeper of Keys.
Like five old friends who have caroused the whole night through
then stand at dawn by crossroads, for the talk is good,
and make half-hearted stray attempts to part at daybreak
but find still more to say and stand with door ajar
and still hold hands and twine their fingers, lingering still—
thus like these five old friends who had caroused all night,
the archer's five strong elements, his five proud friends,
stood at the crossroads of his brain and could not part.
The mighty athlete then caressed his white-haired head:
"O nacreous, pearl-lined jewel-box, O brimming head,
in you the seeds of the whole world became one kin,
for trees, birds, beasts, and man's own gaudy generations

all rushed to sprout within you, not to plunge to Hades,
but now that they've all sweetly met and merged like brothers,
it's time, dear head, that you were smashed! Fall down and
 break! . . ."

Odysseus spread his hands and blessed his famous body,
his five night-long carousing friends, and said farewell:
"O Loam, thick prudent dowry of mud-mother earth,
O strong hutch of the homeless mind that like a tramp
roams far and rots in sun and rain, by ghosts devoured,
dear Loam, who open your arms wide to take him in,
I feel you like mute heavy ballast in my bowels,
gripping with strong foundations so the mind won't wreck
 me. . . .
You hear the mad heart flap its wings and long to fly,
but you plod on, speak with coarse words and mock the bird:
'What shame, you dolt, to long for skies when earth's at hand!
What a great crime if now my heels should sprout with wings,
for the green earth is sweet, and I have heard it said
that even in the Elysian Fields souls weep for earth.
My belly, my coarse hands, my feet adore the earth,
nor do wild wings torment me nor far gods enchant me,
for if our eyes are made of clay, they shine like stars! . . .'"

Then the mind-archer ceased and his sad heart felt light
as though his ballast of mud, stones, and heavy earth
had suddenly sunk and his freed body had sprung in stature.
He stretched his hands and blessed his second element:
"O Water, wandering female source of life, I cup
your flux to give you a firm face and say farewell.
You warble swiftly, vanish, fluctuate and slide,
you turn all the mind's mills and all its fantasies,
nor condescend to faith, nor know what pity is.
You pierce through the black earth with rage, play with the
 sun,
you make the rainbows and the water-kingdoms bloom
then blot them out once more and play with other toys.
You are no peasant to strike earth's roots in my heart
but a swift-vesseled sailor who's squandered all his wealth,
glad to set sail at daybreak in a walnut shell
and leave behind all certain good, his home, his son,
virtues and feasts and comforts, all his useful gods,
and roam nude through stark foreign strands, a weathercock.
'I'm neither flesh nor mind,' you roar, 'I pass and flow

like laughter after rain, the seven-stringed sky's bow! . . .
Some call me sea, and when a ship plows through my waves,
I close its blue wake, and my honor once more blooms;
some with due reverence call me soul, an inner sea,
and deck me like a bride with breastless and dry virtues.
They call me deathless, pure, without one lump of earth,
they say I long to flee from the frail body's shame,
and though I listen to their words, I clasp flesh tight
the way a fierce girl clasps her sweetheart in the dark. . . .
Archer, I've loved you much, and now that you must go
don't leave me your strong hands or even your virile thighs;
don't sigh, my tight-twined love, our time has been well
    spent.' "
Thus did the deep voice murmur in the archer's heart,
and when it ceased and the wave closed his bleeding wound,
the deeply bitter voice of the flesh-wrecker rang:
"O my heart's female element, O washing wave
that waters me, you draw me with you night and day,
but now we've reached that parting where embracements
    end."
He spoke, bent down and scooped some water in both palms
then joyed to watch it falling from his fingertips
drop by slow drop, sad, multicolored, in the sun-washed sea.

When his palms emptied, he turned then to his third friend,
to this third inner element, and said farewell: . . .
"O Fire, O noble dancer, dance-adoring flame, . . .
you know the inmost secret that has burned my heart:
I don't love man, I only love the flame that eats him! . . .
You flapped above my bold heart like a tattered flag,
you shouted and I shouted too as your tongues leapt
till earth's and the heart's foundations tumbled down and left
but warm ash slowly smouldering in my hollow hands.
Wipe out whore-mongering earth, O Fire: my sons have
    shamed me,
my daughters have shamed me too, and I shall blot them out!
I watch the crimson thread that slowly mounts the earth,
the bloody turbid phosphor of glowworms that crawl
and squirm with lust and couple in the mud, then fade
within the rain-drenched ruts of man's imagination;
I watch, but scorn to play here on this whorish earth!
Soul, country, men and earth, gods, sorrows, joys and thoughts
are phantoms made of water, loam, and the mind's froth,

good only for those cowardly hearts that hope and fear
and those air-pregnant brains that belch their sons to birth.
Our trembling bowels groan: 'From whence, and why, and
   where?'
our heads groan too, resounding in the boundless night,
and now a voice within me leaps in bold reply:
'Fire will surely come one day to cleanse the earth,
fire will surely come one day to make mind ash,
fate is a fiery tongue that eats up earth and sky!'
The womb of life is fire, and fire the last tomb,
and there between two lofty flames we dance and weep.
In this blue lightning flash of ours where our life burns,
all time and all space disappear, and the mind sinks,
and all—hearts, birds, beasts, brain and loam—break into
   dance,
although it's no dance now, for all blaze, spin, and fade,
are suddenly freed to exist no more, nor have they ever
   lived! . . ."

The archer hailed this conflagration like a dew
then turned with calm to say farewell to his fourth friend:
"O Air, who gently rest on conflagration's dome,
who hold light like a mystic task, flame's final fruit,
invisible secret stature high above our heads,
descend, amass yourself in the head's crown, then vanish!
You hold the cool pure light, you conjure smoke away,
for as the lily stares on its mud-roots in earth,
you look down on the smoking flame and rise up purely.
You take the still warm ash that drifts in my coarse palms
and scatter it like a good plowman who sows his seed
till ash turns wheat once more and the world once more
   sprouts. . . .
You sprang from my deep entrails like a bridegroom bee,
like a proud drone in springtime when the heather blooms
till the chaste honeyed Queen-Bee with her fragrant body
secretly sighs, within her regal cells constrained,
and spreads and tries her wings, then licks her body well,
for honey-cells have brimmed and all await their spawn.
Then the drone dons his armor, arrays himself in sun
and wraps himself in love's most sacred panoply.
His eyes dilate like a gold cap, spread round his head,
then swiftly sweep, though motionless, through the sky's dome
and spy on the whole azure globe to catch the bride.

His small ears open wide, and if a feather fall,
he hears the whole wood ring as if a tree had crashed;
he hears how the Queen dresses and adorns herself,
he hears how her whole working army buzz about her,
rasp secret counsels in her ear, then see her off.
His taste augments and plunders fields like honeycombs,
his tongue flicks even about the sun like harvest knives,
his nostrils swell till in the springtime air he feels
his bridal body soaring in the wedding pomp
as honeyed premonitions burgeon through his body.
Earth is a buzzing beehive grove, the dripping sun
a golden honeycomb he gleans until he feels
about his sticky feet and fuzzy happy belly
her regal body merge with his and fill with seed.
Aye, honey-drone, good was the wedding, good the game,
old Honey-Mother Earth brimmed with transplendent seed,
nor now has need of you but rushes to give birth,
and all your empty guts hang from her sated thighs.
O honey-drone Odysseus, air, light, unseen form,
I raise my eyes on high and see with trembling joy
Death riding the most violent nuptial lightning bolt!"

For hours the dying man watched the sun's lonely wheel
graze the sky's level rim, nor rise nor sink in waves
as a continuous dawn poured in the pearly sea.
Without once touching the smooth waters, the sun turned,
pale, hopeless, weaponless, about his snow-white head.
In his skull's secret lair, the suffering man approached
with calm the fearful scorpion with its sting raised high: . . .
"O Mind, your four steeds, water, fire, earth, and light
strain at the bit and leap, but you hold the reins firmly
and temper savage strength with the brain's prudent thoughts.
Though your steeds snort and fly with wingèd hooves to reach
those fat stalls which they think await them at road's end,
and though you know the secret well, for your eyes brim
with chasms and despair and death and gallant deeds,
your hand is firm, you spur the swiftly dying steeds
and feed them well, caress them, deck them handsomely,
then all together, road, steeds, chariot, charioteer,
plunge swiftly headlong, tumbling down the bottomless
     gulf! . . .
In the fine scales of your mid-brow you weigh all things,
and in your every sorrow, every joy, you temper all

with your wise thinking—water, fire, earth, or air—
for you know well that life is but a game of scales.
If a grain more of earth should fall, man's mind grows heavy,
the poor soul's caught in the lime twigs of mud, and drowns;
if a drop more of water falls, man's firm face breaks,
its dough sags, it can't grip, it spills, and flows, and rolls,
it tastes with no sure memory, clasps with no real arms;
if a flick more of flame falls in fate's kneading trough,
alas then to the immoderate heart, for the whole world
burns down, and life turns ash within our palms once more;
if in our ripe heads boundless light should overblaze,
then pallid and pellucid life, that star-stitched veil,
flutters and plays above us like a drifting cloud;
but our strong fists will never deign to be deceived
or rise to grasp air-phantoms like the firmest flesh,
and life will fade in air like a soft shadowy dream.
O Mind, great charioteer, you hold the myriad reins
of sacred virtue and of shame, of fear, of hope
in your strong hands and drive on toward the plunging cliff;
I thank you, for you've ended your hard duty well;
now that the cliff looms close, O Guide, let loose your steeds
to plunge with chariot and charioteer in the dark gulf,
for we've arrived with luck at length at our long journey's
    end!"

    Book XXIII, condensed version of lines 234–1068.

GEORGE SEFÉRIS (1900–)   George Seféris, pseudonym
of George Seferiádhis, was born in Smyrna in 1900 and in
1926 entered the Ministry of Foreign Affairs where he has
served ever since. At present he is the Royal Greek Ambassador to England. In 1961 he was awarded the William Foyle
Poetry Prize in England, and in 1963 the Nobel Prize in Literature. The author of eight books of poetry and two of critical
essays, he is a poet of evocative symbols and metaphysical dis-
tinctions who has superbly translated Eliot's *The Waste Land*
and other poems. All of his mature poetry is written in a free
verse of great sinuousness, rhythmical yet modulated, which
never rises in tone or diction beyond the "conversation between
intellectual men," as Ezra Pound has it. His is a poetry of
understatement and hesitation, dealing with recurring themes
of expatriation, the disintegration of the modern world. His
poetry is brooding and contemplative, precise yet subtle in
thought and image. He has often attempted to define what
Greece *is* as a "state of being." Yet in the center of each poem
is the poet himself, looking back into the mythological past
of his country and her symbols, retracing her history, and telling a story which has the independent validity of imaginative
fiction.

BIBLIOGRAPHY

Poems, 1924–46. 5th ed. Athens: Íkaros, 1964.
Cyprus . . . Where He Prophesied That I. . . . Athens:
Íkaros, 1955.
The King of Asine and Other Poems. London: John Lehman,
1948. Translated by Bernard Spencer, Nanos Valaorítis, Lawrence Durrell, with an introduction by Rex Warner.
Poems. Boston: Little, Brown and Company, 1960. Translated and introduced by Rex Warner.
Six Poets of Modern Greece. New York: Alfred A. Knopf,
1961. Edited, translated, and introduced by Edmund Keeley
and Philip Sherrard.

❊　❊　❊

GYMNOPAEDIA

Thyra [the ancient name for Santorin] is geologically composed of pumice-stone and porcelaneous clay. In her bay

. . . islands have appeared and disappeared. It was the center of an ancient religion where lyric dances of a strict and heavy rhythm were performed, called "Gymnopaedia."

—*A Guide to Greece*

I. Santorin

Stoop if you can to the dark sea forgetting
the sound of a flute to naked feet
that trod in your sleep in the other the sunken life.

Write if you can on your last shell
the day the name the place
and cast it to sink in the sea.

We found ourselves naked on pumice stone
watching the islands emerging
watching the red islands sinking
in their sleep, in our sleep.
We found ourselves naked here holding
the scales tilted on the side
of injustice.

Heel of power unshadowed will meditated love
plans that ripen in the noonday sun,
road of destiny with the stroke of a young hand
on the shoulder;
in the land which has crumbled away which does not endure
in the land which had once been ours
the islands are sinking ashes and rust.

Altars overthrown
and friends forgotten
leaves of the palm tree in mud.

Here in the turn of time, if you can,
let your hands voyage with the ship
that touched the horizon.
When the dice struck the slab
when the lance struck the breastplate
when the eye recognized the stranger
and love dried up
in pierced souls;
when you look about you and find yourself
circled with sickled feet
circled with dead hands
circled with darkened eyes;
when it is no longer even possible to choose

the death you have sought as your own,
hearing a cry
even the cry of a wolf,
your due;
let your hands voyage if you can
tear yourself away from the unfaithful time
and sink,

he sinks who carries the huge stones.

II. Mycenae

Give me your hands, give me your hands, give me your hands.

I saw in the night
the pointed peak of the mountain
I saw the field in the distance flooded
with the light of the unapparent moon
I saw, turning my head
the black stones clustered
and my life stretched like a catgut
beginning and end
the last moment;
my hands.

He sinks who carries the huge stones;
these stones I carried as long as I could
these stones I loved as long as I could
these stones, my destiny.
Wounded by my own earth
tormented by my own shirt
condemned by my own gods,
these stones.

I know they do not know, but I
who have followed so many times
the road from the murderer to the murdered
from the murdered to the punishment
and from the punishment to the other murder,
groping
the inexhaustible purple
that night of homecoming
when the Furies began to whistle
in the sparse grass—
I saw snakes crossed with vipers
entwined on the vile generation

our destiny.
Voice out of stone out of sleep
deeper here where the world darkens,
memory of toil rooted in a rhythm
that beat on the earth with feet
forgotten.
Bodies sunken in the foundations
of the other time, naked. Eyes
riveted, riveted on a spot
which you cannot discern however you try;
the soul
that struggles to become your soul.

Even the silence is no longer yours
here where the millstones stopped.

MATHIÓS PASĆALIS AMONG THE ROSES

I have been smoking since morning without break
if I stop the roses will embrace me
with thorns and with fallen petals they will choke me
they all grow crookedly with the same rose color
they are staring; they are waiting to see someone; no one
    passes;
behind the smoke of my pipe I watch them
on a weary stalk without fragrance,
in the other life a woman would say to me you may touch this
    hand
and this rose is yours it is yours you may take it
now or later, whenever you wish.

I descend ever smoking, the stairs
the roses descend with me in excitement
and there is something in their manner of the voice
at the root of shrieking at the point where man
begins to cry out "mother" or "help me"
or the small white cries of love.

It is a small garden full of rose bushes
a few square yards that sink with me
as I descend the stairs, skyless;
and her aunt would say to her, "Antigone, you forgot to do
    your exercises today

at your age I never wore a corset, not in my time."
Her aunt was a pitiful creature with protruding veins
she had many wrinkles about her ears and a moribund nose
but her words were full of prudence always.
One day I caught her touching Antigone's breasts
like a small child stealing an apple.

Will I meet the old woman perhaps as I am descending?
She said to me when I left, "Who knows when we shall meet
    again?"
later I read of her death in some old newspapers
of Antigone's wedding and the wedding of Antigone's daughter
with no end to the stairs nor to my tobacco
that imparts to me the taste of a haunted ship
with a mermaid crucified, while she was still beautiful, on the
    wheel.

INTERVAL OF JOY

We were happy all that morning
O God how happy.
First the stones the leaves and the flowers shone
and then the sun
a huge sun all thorns but so very high in the heavens.
A nymph was gathering our cares and hanging them on the
    trees
a forest of Judas trees.
Cupids and satyrs were singing and playing
and rosy limbs could be glimpsed amid black laurel
the flesh of young children.
We were happy all that morning;
the abyss was a closed well
on which the tender foot of a young faun stamped
do you remember its laughter: how happy we were!
And then clouds rain and the damp earth;
you stopped laughing when you reclined in the hut,
and opened your large eyes and gazed
on the archangel wielding a fiery sword

"I cannot explain it," you said, "I cannot explain it,"
I find people impossible to understand
however much they may play with colors
they are all black.

AN OLD MAN BY THE RIVER BANK

And yet we must consider how we are advancing.
To feel is not enough, neither to think nor to move
nor to endanger your body in the old embrasure,
when molten lead and scalding oil gutter the walls.

And yet we must consider toward what we are advancing,
not as our pain would have it and our hungry children
and the chasm of our comrades' calling from the opposite
  shore;
nor as it is whispered by the bluish light of the provisional
  hospital,
the clinical glitter on the pillow of the brave youth who was
  operated on at noon;
but in some other way, perhaps what I want to say is—like
the long river that rises out of the great lakes locked in the
  depths of Africa
which was once a god and afterwards became a thoroughfare
  and a giver of gifts and a judge and a delta;
which is never the same, as ancient scholars taught,
and yet remains always the same body, the same stratum, the
  same Sign,
the same orientation.

I want nothing more than to speak simply, to be granted this
  grace.
For we have burdened even our song with so much music that
  it is slowly sinking
and we have embellished our art so much that the goldwork
  has eaten away its face
and it is time to say our few words because tomorrow our
  soul sets sail.

If pain is the human lot we are not made men merely to suffer
and that is why I think on the great river so often these days
on this meaning advancing amid herbs and grasses
and animals that browse and quench their thirst and men who
  sow and who reap
and even among the grand sepulchres and humble habitations
  of the dead.
This stream which goes on its way and is not much different
  from the blood of men
and from the eyes of men when they look straight ahead
  without fear in their hearts,

without the daily anxiety of trivial things or even of great;
when they look straight ahead like the wayfarer accustomed
   to gauging his road by the stars,
not like us the other day who were gazing at the closed garden
   of a sleeping Arabian house,
the cool small garden changing shape behind the window
   lattice, growing larger and smaller,
and we too changing, as we watched, the shape of our desires
   and the shape of our hearts,
we, at the height of noon, the patient dough of a world which
   casts us out and which molds us,
caught in the embellished nets of a life which had once been
   true and became dust and sank in the sand
leaving behind it only that vague rocking of a tall palm tree
   which made us giddy.

HELEN

"The nightingales won't let you go to sleep in Platres."

Shy nightingale, amid the respiration of leaves,
bestower of music, the dew of the forest
to bodies separated and to souls
of those who know they will not return.
Blind voice, who in the night-glooming memory grope
at footsteps and gestures; I would not dare say kisses;
and the bitter turbulence of the female slave grown savage.

"The nightingales won't let you go to sleep in Platres."

What is Platres? who knows this island?
I have lived my life hearing names for the first time heard:
new places, new insanities of men
or of the gods;
                  my fate which wavers
between the final sword of an Ajax
and another Salamis
has brought me here to this seashore.
                  The moon
rose out of the sea like Aphrodite,
covered the stars of the Archer, now goes to find
the Heart of the Scorpion, and changes everything.
Where is truth?
I also was an archer in the war;
my fate: that of a man who missed the mark.

Nightingale, minstrel,
on such a night as this by the sea's rim of Proteus
the Spartan slave—girls heard you and dragged out their
    lament,
and among them—who would have thought it?—was Helen!
She whom we pursued for years by the Scamander.
She was there, at the desert's edge; I touched her, she spoke to
    me:
"It's not true, it's not true," she cried.
"I never boarded that blue-prowed vessel.
I never set foot on valiant Troy."

With full breast-band, sun on hair, and this stature of hers
shadows and smiles everywhere
on shoulders on thighs on knees;
animated skin, and those eyes
with their large eyelashes,
she was there, on the bank of a Delta.
                                        And at Troy?
Nothing at Troy—a phantom.
That's how the gods willed it.
And Paris lay with a shadow as though it were solid flesh;
and we were slaughtered for Helen ten years.

Great suffering had fallen on Greece.
So many bodies cast
into the jaws of the sea, the jaws of the earth;
so many souls
given over to the millstones, like wheat.
And the rivers swelled with blood amid the mire
for a linen undulation for a cloud
for the fluttering of a butterfly, the down of a swan
for an empty garment, for a Helen.
And my brother?
                        Nightingale nightingale nightingale,
what is god? what is not god? and what is between the two?

"The nightingales won't let you go to sleep in Platres."

Tearful bird,
            by sea-kissed Cyprus
so ordained as to remind me of my country,
I anchored alone with this fable,
if it's true that this is a fable,
if it's true that men will not again be caught

by the ancient deceit of the gods;
                                    if it's true
that some other Teucer, years afterwards,
or some Ajax or Priam or Hecuba
or someone quite unknown, anonymous, yet one
who saw a Scamander overbrimming with corpses
is not fated to hear
messengers who come to say
that so much suffering so much life
plunged into an abyss
for an empty garment for a Helen.

NOTES

According to an ancient legend, Helen was not abducted to Troy at all. Aphrodite had promised Helen to Paris because he had given her the golden apple for beauty in preference to Hera or Artemis. To avenge herself for the slight, Hera formed an image of Helen out of pure air with which she duped Paris and spirited the real Helen away to Egypt, where she remained chaste and untouched until her husband Menelaus found her there after the Trojan war.

After the title of his poem, Seféris has placed the following quotation from Euripides' *Helen:*

TEUCER
. . . . for the sea-girt land
of Cyprus, where Apollo prophesied that I
should found and name New Salamis from my island home.

. . . .

HELEN
It was an image of me. I never went to Troy.

. . . .

MESSENGER
                      you mean
it was for a cloud, for nothing, we did all that work?

(Lines 148–150, 582, 705–706. These and all subsequent lines from *Helen* are translated by Richmond Lattimore.)

Ancient writers are unanimous in asserting that the port of Salamis in Cyprus was founded by Teucer, the son of Telamon, King of the famous island of Salamis in Greece, on his return from the Trojan war.

Nightingales: for the various references to nightingales, and especially for *tearful bird,* see the Chorus in *Helen,* 107 ff.:

To you, who deep forested, choired in the growth
of singing wood hide nested,
to you I utter my outcry,
to you, beyond all other birds sweet in your singing,
O nightingale of the sorrows
come, with brown beak shaken,
to the beat of your melody, come
with song to my sad singing
as I mourn for the hard sorrows
of Helen, for all the suffering,
all the tears of the daughters of Troy
from spears held by Achaeans . . .

Platres: chief summer resort in Cyprus of the wealthy
Cypriots and visitors from abroad.

Blind voice: compare with Milton's "Blind mouths,"
Lycidas, 119.

*That's how the gods willed it; the ancient deceit of the
gods:* see in *Helen,* "Wretched men of Troy / and all you
Achaeans who, day after day, went on / dying for me beside
Scamander, by Hera's craft . . ." (608–610); and "it was by
the arts of gods / that they were ruined," (930–931).

Into the jaws . . . of the earth: from a mural painting in
the church of Asinou, in Cyprus.

Down of a swan: Helen was the daughter of Leda and Zeus,
who made love to her in the form of a swan.

What is god . . . the two: line 1137 in *Helen.*

THREE MULES

And the queen mounted on the wonderful mule called
Margarita, which had belonged to her husband King
Pierre, and she sat upon the wonderful mule as women do;
and she ordered her squire who was called Putsurello to
bring her spurs with him, and she signed to him to turn
her foot over so that she would sit like a man . . .

—*The Chronicle of Makhairas*

In Damascus one sleepless night
there appeared before me the procession of Umm Harám
the deeply esteemed kinswoman of the Prophet.
I heard the patter of hooves like silver dinars
as though she were crossing over hills of salt
towards Lárnaka, astride her mule.
I waited amid cool branches
biting the fruit of the myrtle;
my eyes were stung by a whiteness

perhaps the salt perhaps her ghost. And then
a whispering in the bushes:
　　　　　　　　　　　"This is where
my animal slipped. This is the stone
that broke my illumined neck
and I gave up my soul victorious.
I was filled with God's will;
a mule cannot bear such weight;
don't forget this and don't condemn her unjustly."

She spoke and vanished. Yet even now
her mule is always browsing in my brain
just like that other one whose heart stopped
when they unloaded her of two coffins,
of those two brothers unjustly slain
by the public executioner there on Koutsovéndi.

But of the most magnificent one, how shall I speak of her?
In that country where those who lived below the castellos
were forgotten like last year's upturned earth,
she sails still on the wings of fame,
that renowned animal of Queen Eleanore.
Against her belly those golden spurs,
on her saddle those insatiable loins,
in her gallop those jolting breasts
bursting like pomegranates with murder.
And when Neapolitans, Genoese and Lombards
brought to the royal table
on a silver tray the bloody
shirt of the murdered king
and made away with the wretched John,
I can imagine how she neighed that night,
beyond the impassivity of her tribe
the way a dog howls,
doubly caparisoned, golden rumped, in her stable,
the mule Margarita.

NOTES

Leontios Makhairas, a native of Cyprus, was probably born
in Nicosia not much before 1380. He wrote, in Cypriot Greek,
*Recital Concerning the Sweet Land of Cyprus, Entitled
"Chronicle."* This has been edited with a translation and
notes by R. M. Dawkins, 2 vols., Oxford at the Clarendon

Press, 1932. It chronicles primarily the reign of the Lusignan dynasty, 1359–1432. Quotations are from Dawkins' translations. Queen Eleanore of Aragon was the wife of Peter I, 1359–1369. Her husband had been killed by his own knights, and she was later captured by the Genoese and held at Famagusta. At first she intrigued with the Genoese to avenge herself on the knights, but when she discovered that they intended to dispossess her son of his kingdom, she changed her plans. She offered to lead the Genoese soldiers in an attack on the Castle of Kyrenia, and set out from Nicosia at their head, having provided herself with her late husband's mule, the strongest and swiftest in Cyprus. When the Queen approached the castle, she signaled to Putsurello, who helped her to ride astride the horse so that she dashed ahead and then taunted the Genoese from the castle walls. (Makhairas, p. 445)

Umm Harám; Lárnaka. Larnaka is one of the most ancient cities of Cyprus, the Chittim of the Bible, the birthplace of Zeno, and where Kimon died while besieging the town. About three miles from Larnaka is a famous salt lake and the Tekke, or Tomb, of Umm Haram, daughter of Milhan, grandmother of the Prophet Mohammed, who visited Cyprus in 694 and died of a fall from her mule. See *Journal of the Royal Asiatic Society.* Jan., 1897.

Two brothers: Perot and Wilmot de Montolif, two of the twelve knights who managed the kingdom after the death of Pierre II, and who would not agree with the rest of the council that the seneschal, James de Lusignan, should be chosen to be his successor. They were cast into a dungeon. "After he was crowned, King James sent to the castle and they cut off their heads; they put them into a chest and set them on a mule and brought them to Cava: and the mule died, and there they buried them." This took place in 1385. (Makhairas, p. 603)

Koutsovéndi: Castle of the Lion, or Castle of Buffavento, perched on a crag 3,135 feet high, east of Kyrenia.

The wretched John: Queen Eleanore's brother-in-law, the Prince of Antioch, killed in 1375 during the reign of her son, Pierre II. Queen Eleanore invited John to dine with her son, and then advised Pierre to have him killed because he was to blame for the death of his father, Pierre I. "And they sat down to table. And she arranged that, when they took off the napkin, the shirt of the king, her husband, whom they had killed, should be there in the dish; and she said to the men whom she had put in hiding: 'As soon as I show him the shirt, you must be ready to kill him.' And so it was done." John was killed in the same room where Pierre I was assassinated. (Makhairas, p. 547)

GEORGE THÉMELIS (1900–) George Thémelis was born on the island of Samos in 1900, studied literature at the University of Athens, and has been teaching in the high schools of Salonika since 1930. He is the author of ten books of poetry and of several books of essays and the translator into modern Greek of *Prometheus Bound* and *Oedipus the King*. In 1955 he was awarded the Second, and in 1961 the First National Award in Poetry. Essentially a metaphysical poet, Thémelis explores the esoteric country of the spirit, the individual conscience, and in so doing emphasizes less man's agony and disintegration and more man's progress from struggle to hope, from death into birth, affirmation, and salvation.

BIBLIOGRAPHY

Naked Window. Salonika: M. Stouyannákis, 1945. *Men and Birds,* 1947. *The Return,* 1948. *Odes By Which to Remember Heroes,* 1949. *Escort,* 1950. *Conversations,* 1953. *The Orchard,* 1955. *The Face and the Image,* 1959. *Mona is Playing,* 1961. *Chiaroscuro,* 1961. All but the first were published in Salonika by N. Nikolaïdhis.

❊ ❊ ❊

TOUR

As you proceed in the late twilight . . .

(Hour when the light invests you
With a sad uncertainty, like something troublesome,
As though you had lost something and cannot find it.
You don't know exactly what—neither when nor where—
You have a suspicion it is looking at you from somewhere,
    but you cannot see it.
You feel it is weighing on your flesh somewhere, when you lie down,
As though you had killed someone and do not know it.)

You may stumble, suddenly, on a certain body . . .

(Eyes closed, keeping in all the light
Which you once possessed and with it illumined the midnight . . .)

You stoop to raise it with your fingers and you lose it
(The way you lose a pencil or a button . . .)
You take to the street and search, you stop the pedestrians.

You study their features, you listen to the noises,
You walk and gaze into your most secret suspicion.
You stare at your hands, you touch your skin.

Within you someone is crying inconsolably . . .

The dusk is thick and you cannot be recognized
Amid so many derelict things, unsought for,
A dead man, a thing more of a thing than things themselves,
Waiting for daybreak, that distances may be illuminated.

DESOLATION

Outside of us things die.

No matter where you walk at night you hear
Something like a whisper coming out
Of streets you have never walked upon
Of houses you have never visited
Of windows you have never opened
Of rivers over which you have never stooped to drink water
Of ships on which you have never sailed.

Outside of us die trees we have never known
The wind passes through vanished forests
Animals die from anonymity and birds from silence.

Bodies die slowly, slowly, by being abandoned
Together with our old clothes laid away in coffers.
Hands we have never touched die out of loneliness.
Dreams we have never seen, from lack of light.

Outside of us begins death's desolation.

SEARCH

Our footsteps will not be heard in an encounter . . .

As though we have lost our souls and are seeking to find them
(On streets through which we walked, in dwellings where we
passed the night . . .)
As though we return from going out and turn on the light
And talk, as we used to talk—strolling,
Or pausing to listen to a certain noise.

(We are small noises and make noises,
We are small wings and beat the wind . . .)

We touch one another and then fall silent for a long time
Leaning into our faces that we may recognize each other.

(Our acquaintance is a secret affair which has no ending . . .)

Sleep comes slowly, slowly, and winds us round.

The faces we have known, the things we have touched,
Features, encounters, lost lightning flashes,
The earth which glittered in our hearts,
Enter into our naked souls and share them . . .

I do not know if it is the wind we raised,
Which we filled with our small cries and which mourns us
    now
On streets through which we walked, in dwellings where we
    passed the night.

I do not know if it is snow which is coming to cover us . . .

(Where shall we be found in the morning, when the bells
    begin to ring? . . .)

DEMÉTRIUS ANTONÍOU (1906–) Captain Demétrius Antoníou was born in Mozambique, South Africa, in 1906 but is descended from generations of sea captains from the island of Cassos in the Dodecanese. Most of his poems were written on cigarette boxes and scraps of paper aboard ship during his travels throughout all parts of the globe. His poems are metaphysical, terse and precise in style, crabbed and gnarled in diction—an attempt to arrive at what he defines as the "specific gravity" of expression.

BIBLIOGRAPHY

Poems. Athens: Seryiadhís, 1936.
Poems. Athens: Anglo-Hellenic Review, 1954.

❊ ❊ ❊

THE BAD MERCHANTS

Lord, we were simple men,
we sold merchandise
(and our souls were the material
no one bought).
We did not fix prices according to the selvage
measurements were exact by yard and inch
we never sold remnants at half-price.
This was our sin.

We dealt only in merchandise of quality
a small corner in life was all we wanted
the precious things in life take little room.
Now with the same rule by which we measured,
measure Thou us. We have not enlarged our premises.
Lord, we were bad merchants.

POEM

But my heart, alas, freed finally from all things, finds the ancient torment more cruel than that upon the first day.
—Goethe, *Wilhelm Meister*

To conquer this blank paper! now
securing in words that fill it this bruised

necessity, in half-feelings and in the mirror
of resolution that becomes an immovable mountain in our
way . . .
What do you long for?
The star will no longer rise nor turn to sleep
as your road is ending, there where you
shall say: and a little more and day will break . . .
The simple daisy in the green meadow does not stay you,
nor shall you weep ever again
over the nameless small flowers of the field.
Thus drunk with melancholy
we murmured until yesterday, strolling in the countryside:
we recall all of this today and pass it by
as we might consent to the course of the wind in a blossomed
    almond tree,
your ring turning to rust on the finger of another.
Your pleading voice brings our years to their knees,
those years I spent in an open sea blossomed by sails of return.

TO THE COLD IMAGINATION

The walls of my room fell down and left me in the garden,
disclosing its interior to space like an opening flower;
so many centuries embalmed, the light of the moon
leapt; and with forces restrained for so many years
flooded the interior, dark but a while before,
there where I stood not yet comprehending,
clinging to silence like a bulwark to change.
Amid arcs and broken lines and this rain
of forms in a shifting wind I stood,
half in shadow and more and more mastered with light,
and heard less and divined more my unrhythmical heart
then knew myself for the first time to be without rhythm
lacking that rhythm which had always tyrannically ruled my
    heart,
and for the first time felt the music of Bach to be without
    meaning;
only ruins wept over the redemption within me.

Dazzling is a work of art
rising out of the flames that create it,
unalterably serene in the triumph of our eternity.

YÁNNIS RÍTSOS (1909–) Yánnis Rítsos, born in Monem-
vasía, a town of the Peloponnesos, in 1909, fell ill at the age of
eighteen of tuberculosis and spent many years in various sana-
toriums. His heritage is a tragic one, for both his mother and
elder brother died of tuberculosis and his father and sister
died insane. Because of his left-wing activities, he spent the
years 1948–1952 in various detention camps in Greece. The
author of twenty-three books of poetry, two volumes of *Collected Poems* (1961), of two plays and a poem for dance, he
won the National Award for Poetry for 1956 for *Moonlight
Sonata*.

BIBLIOGRAPHY

Poems, 1930–1960. 2 Vols., 1961. *The Window*, 1960. *The
Bridge*, 1960. *Testimonies*, 1963. *Twelve Poems for Cavafis*,
1963. All were published in Athens: Kédhros.

❊ ❊ ❊

THE AUDIBLE AND THE INAUDIBLE

An abrupt unexpected movement: his hand
clutched his wound to stop the blood,
though we had not heard a single shot
nor the whistling bullet. In a little while
he dropped his hand and smiled;
but again he placed his palm slowly
on that same place. Then he took out his wallet,
paid the waiter politely, and left.

The coffee cup cracked by itself.
This at least we heard quite clearly.

A LONE MAN'S NIGHT

How sad the furniture in a lone man's room.
The table is an animal frozen stiff with cold,
the chair a child lost in a snowfilled forest,
the sofa becomes a naked tree again felled in the courtyard by
   the wind.

And yet in a little while within there
a round, translucent silence will be formed,
as in the glass-bottom bucket of a fishing boat,
and you, bent wholly by your bitterness within that hollow,
gaze through the glass at the diaphanous and luminous sea-
depths
with their crystalline, deep-green crevices,
with their exotic sea vegetation,
gaze so long at the rose-colored, indifferent, enormous fish
with their wide, noble movements
that you do not know whether they are lying in ambush, or
exploring, whether they are sheltering themselves or dreaming,
because their eyes are opened so wide they seem tightly closed.

In the last analysis, this does not matter.
Isn't it perhaps enough that their movement is like beauty and
like immobility?

ESTRANGEMENT

Only a flower immersed in its fragrance,
a face anchored in its smile,
—does it exist? doesn't it exist?—lost.
If you speak to it, it will turn, as though from thousands of
years,
perplexed, awkward, nor know where it is, nor know
what expression to assume, which might be some kind of
answer.
It is a stone shrine on an old, abandoned road.

Sometimes, at dusk, he walks down his marble stairway,
gathers wild flowers amid the stones,
weaves a wreath and hangs it over his own icon. Sometimes
a stray sheep stands there as though it were praying,
and slowly chews, uncomprehendingly, the withered wreath.

DIPTYCH

I. Immobility of a Voyage

Great nocturnal ships halted amid their lights—
the stewards, porters, automobiles, deckwatch,
leathern valises with foreign labels,
local baskets of reed or wicker, with distracted goats,
with farewells late in coming above the masts.

Not a voice or sob could be heard—perhaps you did not notice?
All silent and shadowy; unshaken
in their movements—wraiths of another age and place.
The harbor enmarbled in its ever-moving lights
amid the reflections of the sea-depths. The wharf
a monstrous, pure white cube of silence,
and the voyage neither arrival nor departure—an airy bridge
above familiar and foreign names. On this bridge
the young captain walked slowly in his white uniform (or was
  it the moon?).

II. A Movement

Well then, did no one ever leave? Will no one leave?
This justle among the nightlong coffeehouses of the wharf,
among the push carts, the trucks, the kiosks, the decks,
among the intertwined tracks of the street cars and the blind
  alley eyes,
among the harbor women and the lights,
among the bundles and the ruminating horses unaccustomed to
  the holds,
among the blowing of sirens and the newly cut tickets—the air
  is squeezed tight.

The ships are immobilized by the general strike,
with their enormous anchors; berths, for a time, of seaweed
  and shells,
with their thick chains, a series of linked zeros untroubled in
  the sea-depths.
And if an explosion should occur in the ammunition dumps?

A ship could bear it no longer; it raised anchor
and all alone, brilliantly lit in its silence,
set sail without explanation in the open sea.

Then everyone, the harbor women, musing strollers, ruffians,
sailors, skippers, bus conductors,
pointed out to sea, and murmured: *"The Strike Breaker!"*

A few moments of hesitation, expectation, irritation,
and then all the mouths of the shore batteries swerved toward
  it.
But it had vanished amid its many-voiced silence and its light,
and the gunfire (if it fell) was never heard.

ALEXANDER MÁTSAS (1910–) Alexander Mátsas, born in Athens in 1911, studied political science and Ancient Greeks at Oxford and entered the Greek diplomatic service in 1934. He served in various posts in Egypt, London, Paris, The Hague, and Rome, was Royal Greek Ambassador to Turkey, Iran, and Pakistan, and is at present Royal Greek Ambassador to the United States. He has published three books of poetry (the first written in French) and three poetical dramas on ancient themes, of which two—*Clytemnestra* and *Croesus*—have been produced by the State Royal Theatre of Athens in 1957 and 1963 respectively. The multiplicity of human nature, the successive metamorphosis of the individual in character and personality under the stress of circumstance and time seem to Mátsas the most striking element in life. Sleep and love are an escape into time. Because he believes that communion with life is best attained through the world of the senses, his poetry is often a lament on the passage of time and the dispersal of the body. For Mátsas poetry is a precise art, yet permeated with suggestive disintegrations under which precise meaning crumbles away and vague unanswered questions of death and decay obtrude.

BIBLIOGRAPHY

Poems. Athens: Notebook, 1946.

❈ ❈ ❈

OF SLEEP

I

Sleep came and lay between us like a rival.
He took your radiant eyes
and closed them; he took your lips
and swept away your smile and your kiss.

Your pale hair was combed by the tranquil
waters of Lethe that bore your beloved body
away to the world of stars and shadows.

Filters of silence are forcing your sealed lips,
sleep-living voices your ears; and in your veins
I hear the deep rumor of the voyage.

II

You have emerged from the depths of sleep
with stars and seashells in your hands
and in your eyes the dark coolness
     of the seas.

As you open them, I want to be the first to receive
their glance, so as to capture before it fades
the meaning of the world which has kept you away
     all night.

TRANSLATED BY the author

LANDSCAPE

Here, in this mineral landscape
of rock and sea, sapphire and diamond,
which to the wheel of Time offers nothing
     that's perishable;

here in the great victorious light
whose only stain is your own shadow,
and where only your body carries
     a germ of death;

here perhaps for a moment the idols
will vanish; perhaps once again
in a dazzling flash you may stare
     at your true self;

that self hidden by so many masks,
distorted by necessities and yokes,
which you betray, and everyone robs you
     with violence and seduction.

Thus cleansed like an earthen jar
or bones stripped bare, your clay shall escape
for a brief moment the implacable weights
     of life and of death.

ANTHROPOS

However far you may advance, the mystery
recedes; and you always remain
at the same distance from the mirrors which block
   the mortal vision.

Nailed to the moving escalator of Time
like a hurried buyer in some huge supermarket
you speed motionless and laden
   with useless purchases;

with food and drink which will not deceive
your hunger or your thirst; with clothing
which cannot cover nakedness, and cosmetics
   which will not convince.

And you always fear you have lost some
of your packages, those fraudulent wares
once more expensively purchased with Time,
   that priceless coin.

Thus you proceed toward the fatal solution
in a dimension which chokes and scorns
the one you had once felt unfolding
   within you.

Elusive and most fulgurant
sole diamond that could ever tear
the transparent and deceptive walls
   of your jail.

NÍKOS ENGONÓPOULOS (1910–) Níkos Engonópoulos, born in Constantinople in 1910, ranks as the foremost surrealist painter in Greece and in the Biennial Exhibition of Modern and Fantastic Art in Venice in 1954 was represented by seventy-four canvases. But he is also the author of eight books of poetry. His main effort is toward self-expression, no matter what the means: if he finds himself without colors, he will turn to words; if without words, to action. Paints, words, action are for him the mediums of a single expression. He believes that the more personal a work of art, the more universal its significance; that the fundamental thing is the responsible presence of a man in a work of art, which is the expression of loneliness. Though he has a profound sense of and love for tradition, he understands that what was revolutionary and fertile in one generation may become reactionary and stifling in another, that traditions and institutions inevitably decay. He therefore believes in revolution in the name of tradition.

BIBLIOGRAPHY

Do Not Speak to the Conductor. Athens: Kíklos, 1938.
The Pianos of Silence. Athens: Ippalektrión, 1939.
Seven Poems. Athens: Ghláros, 1944.
Bolívar: A Greek Poem. Athens: Íkaros, 1944; 2nd ed., 1962.
Return of the Birds. Athens: Íkaros, 1946.
Eleusis. Athens: Íkaros, 1948.
The Atlantic. Athens: Anglo-Hellenic Review, 1954.
In a Blossoming Greek Language. Athens: Íkaros, 1957.

✻　✻　✻

THE APPRENTICE OF SORROW

this statue
arose and left in the morning
—at daybreak—
that he might steal
the stars
he arose and left
in the night
and killed
all the dreams

—and his bare feet
as he walked
became entangled
in the brambles
and bled among the thorns—

and his noble god-blessed hands,
the very birds of spring, caressed
the geranium she named during a night of love
and the secret clasps of her virginal dreambook

and of her breasts {
the cries
of crimson
and the hidden
fringes

STREET-CAR AND ACROPOLIS
le soleil me brûle et me rend lumineux *

through the monotony of rain
the mud
the ashy atmosphere
the street cars pass
and through the deserted market-place
which the rain has deadened
they proceed towards
the
terminals

my thought
filled with emotion
follows them lovingly until
they reach
there where the fields begin
where the rain is drowning the fields
at the terminals

what grief it would have been, my God,
what grief
if my heart was not consoled
by the hope of marble
and the prospect of a shining sunray
which shall give new life
to the splendid ruins

* *The motto*—"The sun burns me and renders me luminous"
—is the author's.

exactly like a red flower
amid green leaves.

PICASSO

now at last the toreador lives in Elassóna
in the cobblestone square under the plane trees
and the coffee-vendor comes and goes unceasingly and fills and
   refills
the coffee in the coffee-cup and the tobacco in the narghileh of
   the toreador
until the hours of the day
shall pass away nostalgically
and myriad birds shall gather
in the thick foliage of the plane trees
a sign that the sun is setting

one by one the conspirators then glide into the alleys
silently as the night falls and assists them
that they too might gather unseen like
the birds
there where they wish to be
and heavy tears roll from their wretched eyes

and the mother who wants to outwit the fascists
in the dark room where the conspirators whisper
and peppers hang from the ceiling to dry
takes off the glass of the lamp and lights it
with her calloused hands that rosaries adorn
then slowly slowly wipes on her apron again
her calloused hands which the kerosene had soiled

and as we have said before she wants to outwit the killers
the old woman takes the lamp from the table
and opens the windows quickly
and stretches outside
—into the night—
the enormous hand that holds the lamp

old mother! they call to her
where do you take the lamp?
but in the fields of Avila see suspicious shadows
are moving with machine-guns under the armpits
and as the light thrusts out of the window
and blazes from afar like a star
little by little guitars begin to play

and the gypsies begin to dance
with beautiful buttocks and many-hued wide flouncing dresses
and at the same time from their hot painted lips like cries of
   pain
pour the words of the song:
"I shall tell you of my loneliness with soleares."

and the majos played on the guitars in a frenzy
and the fascist filth were machine-gunning the gathering
and they with their silken slippers
—with their high heels—
down there upon the cobblestones were trampling my heart

then it happened: you would have gone out of your mind
as a red-haired bull flung himself in their midst
the flames spouting from his nostrils
and the banderillas needling his neck and his back with pain
and he began to charge here and there
to gut out entrails
to rip up flesh with his horns
to toss high into the air
all those he hit
and a mountain of corpses piled up about him
of men and horses
in rivers of blood

(his neck and his back the banderillas ADORNED with pain)

and the girls with beautiful breasts lay on their backs on the
   ground
and within their beautiful eyes were setting
and rising
suns

ODYSSEUS ELÝTIS (1912–) Odysseus Elýtis, pseudonym of Odysseus Alepoudhélis, was born in Heracleion, Crete, in 1912, of a well-known industrial family, and studied law and political science at the University of Athens. In the period 1940–1941 he served as a second lieutenant on the Albanian front in the Greek-Italian war. In 1938 he represented Greece at the eleventh International Congress of Writers in Geneva, and in 1950 at the first International Congress of Art Critics in Paris. He has spent many years in France and several months touring the United States in 1961 under the auspices of the State Department. The author of five books of poetry, his work marks the joyous return to nature, to summer and the sea, to the blaze of the noonday sun over the Aegean, to the praise of adolescence and its sentiments. His second book was entitled *Sun the First*, as one might refer to an emperor. Though his poetry is rhythmical in effect, he is more interested in the plastic use of language and imagery, both of which still reflect his earlier preoccupation with surrealism. His experience on the Albanian front during the war brought greater depth and sobriety to his poetry and resulted in one of the best elegies written about the war. He was awarded the National Prize in Poetry in 1960 for *Worthy It Is*.

BIBLIOGRAPHY

Orientations. Athens: Pirsós, 1940; Athens: Galaxy, 1961.
Sun the First. Athens: Ghláros, 1943.
Heroic and Elegiac Song for the Lost Second Lieutenant of the Albanian Campaign. Athens: Tetrádhio, August–September, 1945.
Worthy It Is. Athens: Íkaros, 1959.
Six and One Regrets for the Sky. Athens: Íkaros, 1960.

❋   ❋   ❋

WE WALKED IN THE FIELDS ALL DAY

We walked in the fields all day
With our women our sons our dogs
We played we sang we drank water
Fresh as it sprang from the ages

In the afternoon we sat for a moment
And looked each other deep in the eyes
A butterfly flew from our breasts
It was whiter
Than the small white branch at the tip of our dreams
We knew it was never to vanish
That it did not remember at all what worms it dragged along

At night we lit a fire
And round about it we sang:

Fire lovely fire do not pity the logs
Fire lovely fire do not come to ash
Fire lovely fire burn us
               tell us of life.

It is we who tell of life, we take her by the hands
We look into her eyes which look into our own
And if this which makes us drunk is a magnet, we know it
And if this which gives us pain is misfortune, we have felt it
It is we who tell of life, we go forward
And say farewell to her migrating birds

We come of a good stock.

ADOLESCENCE OF DAY

Adolescence of day first lily of joy
The ancient myrtle flutters its flag
The breast of skylarks shall open to the light
And a song shall hover in mid-air
Sowing the golden barley of fire
To the five winds

Setting free a terrestrial beauty.

DRINKING THE CORINTHIAN SUN

Drinking the Corinthian sun
Reading the marble ruins
Striding over vineyard seas
Aiming with my harpoon
At votive fish that elude me
I found those leaves which the psalm of the sun memorizes
That living land which desire opens
With joy.

I drink water, cut fruit
Plunge my hands through the wind's foliage
Lemon trees quicken the pollen of summer days
Green birds cut through my dreams
And I leave, my eyes filled
With a boundless gaze where the world becomes
Beautiful again from the beginning according to the heart's
    measure.

GLITTERING DAY, CONCH OF THAT VOICE

Glittering day, conch of that voice which created me
Naked, to walk on my daily Sundays
Amid the welcoming cry of seashores
Blow on the first-known wind
Spread out an affectionate green meadow
On which the sun may roll his head
And light up poppies with his lips
Poppies which proud men will pluck
So there may be no other mark on their naked chests
Than the blood of carefree disdain which erases sorrow
Reaching as far as the memory of freedom

I spoke of love, of the rose's health, the sunray
Which alone finds the heart straightway
Of Greece that walks the sea with surety
Of Greece which takes me on voyages always
To naked snow-glorious mountains

I give my hand to justice
Translucent fountain, spring on the mountain summit
My sky is deep and unchanging
Whatever I love is born unceasingly
Whatever I love is always at its beginning.

I KNOW THE NIGHT NO LONGER

I know the night no longer, the terrible anonymity of death
A fleet of stars moors in the haven of my heart
O Hesperos, sentinel, that you may shine by the side
Of a skyblue breeze on an island which dreams
Of me announcing the dawn from its rocky heights
My twin eyes set you sailing embraced
With my true heart's star: I know the night no longer

I know the names no longer of a world which disavows me
I read seashells, leaves, and the stars clearly
My hatred is superfluous on the roads of the sky
Unless it is the dream which watches me again
As I walk by the sea of immortality in tears
O Hesperos, under the arc of your golden fire
I know the night no longer that is a night only.

HELEN

With the first drop of rain summer was killed
Those words were drenched which had given birth to starlight
All those words whose unique destination was You!
Where shall we stretch out our hands now that time is no
    longer concerned with us
Where shall we rest our eyes now that distant lines have
    foundered on the clouds
Now that your eyelids have closed on our landscape
And we are—as though the fog had gone through us—
Alone all alone surrounded by your dead images.

Forehead on the windowpane, we keep sleepless vigil over this
    new grief
It is not death which shall cast us down, for You exist
For a wind elsewhere exists to live in you wholly
To clothe you close by as our hope clothes you from afar
For there exists elsewhere
The greenest of meadows stretching beyond your laughter to
    the sun
Telling it in confidence that we shall meet again
No it is not death we shall have to face
But the smallest drop of autumn rain
A blurred emotion
The smell of damp earth in our souls which draw apart the
    farther they go.

And if your hand is not in ours
And if our blood is not in the veins of your dreams
The light in the immaculate sky
And music within us invincible O! melancholy Lady
O Passer-by—of all things which bind us to this earth still
It is the moist wind the autumnal hour the separation
Which appears when night sets out to part us from light
Behind the square window that gazes toward sorrow

That sees nothing
Because it has already become an invisible music a flame in the
    fireplace
A chiming of the great clock on the wall
Because it has already become
A poem a verse followed by another verse
A sound parallel with rain tears and words
Words unlike all others, but even these have only one destina-
    tion: You!

ANNIVERSARY

I brought my life this far
To this spot which struggles
Always near the sea
Youth upon the rocks, breast
To breast against the wind
Where can a man go
Who is none other than a man
Summing up his green moments
With coolnesses, the visions of his hearing
With waters, his remorses with wings
Ah, Life
Of a child who becomes a man
Always near the sea when the sun
Teaches him to breathe toward that place where
The shadow of a seagull vanishes.

I brought my life this far
White measurements ink-black total
A few trees and a few
Wet pebbles
Light fingers to caress a forehead
What forehead
Anticipations wept all night and are no more
There is no one
That a free footstep may be heard
That a restful voice may dawn
That sterns may splash by the quays, inscribing
A name in deeper azure on their horizon
A few years, a few waves
Sensitive rowing
Amid the inlets surrounding love.

I brought my life this far
Bitter gash in the sand which will vanish
—Whoever saw two eyes touching his silence
And mingled with their sunlight enclosing a thousand worlds
Let him remind the other suns of his blood
Closer to the light
There is a smile which remunerates the flame—
But here in this ignorant landscape which fades away
In an open and pitiless sea
Success moults
Whirlwinds of feathers
And of moments which have become attached to the earth
Hard earth under the soles of impatient feet
Earth made for vertigo
A dead volcano.

I brought my life this far
A stone pledged to the liquid element
Farther than the islands
Lower than the waves
In the neighborhood of anchors
—When keels pass splitting with passion
Some new obstacle and triumph over it
And hope is resplendent with all its dolphins
The sun's gain in a human heart—
The nets of doubt draw up
A figure of salt
Carved with effort
Indifferent, white
That turns toward the sea the void of its eyes
Upholding infinity.

From HEROIC AND ELEGIAC SONG FOR THE LOST SECOND
LIEUTENANT OF THE ALBANIAN CAMPAIGN

IV

He lies down now on the scorched battle-coat
With a halted breeze on his quiet hair
With a twig of forgetfulness on his left ear
He resembles a garden suddenly abandoned by the birds
He resembles a song muzzled in the darkness
He resembles a clock of an angel stopped
Just when the eyelashes said: "So long, boys"
And amazement turned into stone . . .

He lies down on the scorched battle-coat;
The black centuries about him
Bark with the skeletons of dogs at the dreadful silence,
And the houses which have again become stone pigeons
Listen with attention;
But laughter was burned, but the earth was deafened
But no one heard the very last shriek
All the world was emptied with the last shriek.

Under the five cedars
With no other candles
He lies on the scorched battle-coat;
The helmet empty, the blood muddy,
At his side the half-finished arm
And between his eyebrows—
A small bitter well, fingerprint of fate
A small bitter black-red well
Well where memory grows cold.

O do not see O do not see from where his
From where his life has fled. Do not say how
Do not say how the smoke of the dream rose high
In this way then the one moment In this way then the one
In this way then the one moment abandoned the other.
And the eternal sun in this way suddenly left the world.

VI

He was a handsome lad. On the first day of his birth
The mountains of Thrace bent down to show
The cheerful wheat on the shoulders of firm earth;
The mountains of Thrace bent down and spat on him
Once on the head, once on the chest, and once amid his crying;
Greeks came forth with terrible arms
And raised him up in the swaddling clothes of the North
    Wind . . .
Then the days ran, to see who could cast the farthest stone
They jumped about, riding the young mares
Then morning rivers rolled
Until the gypsy windflowers ranged everywhere
And from the ends of the earth
The shepherds of the sea came to take the flocks of jib-sails
To where a sea-cavern breathed deeply
To where a great stone sighed.

He was a sturdy lad;
In the arms of the bitter-orange girls at night
He would soil the large garment of the stars,
Love was so huge within him
That in wine he tasted all the flavors of earth
Joining in dance later with all the white-poplar brides
Until dawn should hear and spill the light into his hair
Dawn who with open arms would find him
Scratching the sun on a saddle of two small branches,
Painting the flowers,
Or with love singing a slow lullaby
To the small owls that lay awake all night . . .
Ah what a strong thyme was his breath
What a map of pride his naked chest
On which seas and freedom burst . . .

He was a valiant lad:
With his dull gold buttons and his pistol
With a manly air in his stride
With his helmet, a glittering target
(They entered so easily into his brain
He who had never known evil)
With his soldiers to left and right
And revenge for injustice done before him
—Flame upon lawless flame!—
With blood above the eyebrows.
The Albanian mountains thundered
Then they melted snow to wash
His body, silent shipwreck of dawn
And his mouth, small songless bird
And his hands, prairies of desolation
The Albanian mountains thundered
They did not weep
Why should they weep
He was a valiant lad.

IX

Bring forth new hands, for who shall go now
On high to lullaby the infants of the stars?
Bring forth new feet, for who shall join now
First in the folk dances of the angels?
New eyes—my God—for where shall the small lilies
Of the beloved go now to bow themselves down?

New blood, for with what joyous greeting shall they all light up,
And mouth, cool mouth of brass and amaranth
For who among the clouds will say now "Your health, boys!"

In the day, who will defy the peach tree leaves
In the night, who will domesticate the green crops
Who will scatter green church lamps in the fields
Or shout courageously, confronting the sun
That he might wear tempests, astride an invulnerable horse
And become the Achilles of the shipyards?
Who will ascend the black and mythical desert island
To kiss the pebbles with reverence
And who will sleep
To pass by the Euboeans of dream
To find new hands, feet, eyes
Blood and speech
To erect himself again on the marble threshing floors
And to fall upon—ah this time—
And to fall with all his holiness on Death!

X

The sun, the sound of brass, and the holy mistral
Vowed on his breast, "Life may I take joy of you!"
There was no room here for a darker power
Only with light spilled from a laurel bough
And silver from coolness, only there the cross
Flashed like lightning, as Greatness was dawning
And Goodness appeared with a sword in hand
To say from within his eyes and their flags, "I live!"

Hello there river who would at daybreak see
A similar child of God with a twig of pomegranate
In his teeth, perfuming himself with your waters;
And a hello to you, wild medlar tree who waxed manly
Whenever Andróutsos wished to enter into his dreams;
And you, small spring of midday that reached up to his feet
And you, O maiden who were his Helen
Who were his bird his Madonna his Pleiades
For if the love of man in life
Should ring but once only, lighting up
From star to star the hidden firmament,
Then everywhere always the godly echo shall reign
To adorn the woods with the small hearts of birds
And the words of poets with lyres of jasmine

And torment secret evil wherever it might be
And blazing up, torment secret evil wherever it may be.

XII

With a morning stride on the growing grasses
He ascends alone and blazing with light . . .

Flowers and tomboys wave to him secretly
And speak to him in a high voice which turns into mist on
    the air
And even the trees bend toward him lovingly
With their nests thrust into their armpits
With their branches dipped in the oil of the sun
Miracle—what a miracle, low on the earth
White races with an azure plowshare cut the fields
The mountain ranges flash like lightning far away
And farther away the inaccessible dreams of the mountains of
    spring!

He ascends alone and blazing with light,
So drunk with light that his heart shows through
And the true Olympos can be seen amid the clouds
And the hosannahs of his comrades in the air around . . .
The dream now beats more quickly than blood
On the sides of the footpaths the animals gather
They rasp like crickets and seem to be speaking
All the world is in truth enormous
A giant who fondles his children

Bells of crystal are ringing far away
Tomorrow, tomorrow they say: the Easter of the Heavens!

NOTES

VI, *spat on him:* In the Greek baptismal ceremony the infant
is spat on to indicate the eviction of the devil through the
mouth, according to medieval belief.

X, *Andróutsos:* Odysseus Andróutsos, one of the greatest and
most violent guerilla heroes of the Greek War of Independence.

NÍKOS GÁTSOS (1915–   )   Níkos Gátsos was born in a
small village in Arcadia and took his degree from the School
of Letters at the University of Athens. From early childhood
he grew up in the heroic traditions of his countryside, made
vivid for him by the ballads and folksongs of the region. He is
the author of only one longish poem, *Amorgós,* but it has had
a disproportionate influence among the writers of his generation. In *Amorgós,* the practice of surrealism, the rhythms of
the Bible, and the traditions of Greek folk ballads were combined for the first time in a strange, arresting, and elegiac
manner. Profoundly influenced by the Ionian philosopher
Heracleitos, Gátsos believes that the essence of life and art is
to be found in nothing static, but in an eternal flux. In the
brooding long lines of his lamentations, however, there is
always to be found the sprig of basil or rosemary, symbols of
hope and resurrection, a joyful melancholy.

BIBLIOGRAPHY

Amorgós. Athens: Aïtós, 1943; Athens: Íkaros, 1963.

❊   ❊   ❊

From AMORGÓS

I

With their country tied to their sails and their oars hung on
the wind
The shipwrecked slept tamely like dead beasts on a bedding
of sponges
But the eyes of seaweed are turned toward the sea
Hoping the South Wind will bring them back with their
lateen-sails new-painted
For one lost elephant is always worth much more than the
quivering breasts of a girl
Only if the roofs of deserted chapels should light up with the
caprice of the Evening Star
Only if birds should ripple amid the masts of the lemon trees
With the firm white flurry of lively footsteps

Will the winds come, the bodies of swans that remained immaculate, unmoving and tender
When steamrollers rolled through shops, when hurricanes
  whirled through vegetation
When the eyes of women became coal and the hearts of the
  chestnut hawkers were broken
When the harvest was done and the hopes of crickets began.

And indeed this is why, my brave young men, with kisses, wine,
  and leaves on your mouth
I would like to stride naked by the rivers
To sing of the Barbary Coast like the woodsman hunting the
  mastic shrub
Like the viper slithering through gardens of barley
With the proud eyes of irritation
Like the lightning-bolt as it threshes youth.

And do not laugh and do not weep and do not rejoice
And do not squeeze your shoes in vain as though you were
  planting plane trees
Do not become DESTINY
For the king-eagle is not a closed drawer
It is not the tear of the plum tree nor a smile of the water-lily
Nor the undershirt of a pigeon or a Sultan's mandolin
Nor a silken shawl for the head of a whale
It is a saw of the sea which rips the seagulls apart
It is a carpenter's pillow, a beggar's watch
It is a flame in the blacksmith's shop teasing the wives of the
  priests and lulling the lilies
It is a wedding procession of Turks, a festival of Australians
It is the hideaway of Hungarian gypsies
Where the hazel trees in autumn secretly congregate
They watch the sensible storks painting their eggs black
And then they also weep
They burn their nightgowns and dress themselves in the duck's
  petticoat
They strew stars on the earth for kings to walk upon
With their silver amulets with their crowns and their purple
  mantles
They strew rosemary in garden plots
That mice may pass on their way to other cellars
And to other cathedrals to eat of the Holy Altars
And the owls, my lads,
The owls growl

And dead nuns rise up to dance
With tambourines and drums and violins, with bagpipes and
  lutes
With bannerets and censors, with wimples and magic veils
With the pantaloons of bears in the frozen valley
They eat the mushrooms of martens
They play heads or tails with the ring of St. John and the
  gold florins of the Blackamoor
They mock all witches
They cut off the beard of a priest with the yataghan of Koloko-
  trónis
They bathe themselves in the vapors of incense
And afterwards, slowly chanting, enter the earth again and fall
  silent
As waves fall silent, as the cuckoo bird at dawn, as the oil
  lamp at evening.

And thus in a deep jar the grape shrivels and in the belfry of
  a fig tree the apple turns yellow
And thus flaunting a gay-colored necktie
Under a grapevine bower the summer suspires
And thus naked among white cherry trees a tender love of
  mine lies sleeping
A girl as unwithering as a branch of almond
Her head resting on her elbow and her palm on her golden
  treasure
On its dawning warmth while slowly and softly like a thief
From the window of spring the Morning Star comes to awake
  her.

NOTE

Amorgós: An island in the Aegean Sea, used only as a symbol of evocative beauty.

MÍLTOS SAHTOÚRIS (1919–)   Míltos Sahtoúris was born on the island of Hydra in 1919, studied law at the University of Athens, and has published eight books of poetry. Though he began as a surrealist, Sahtoúris has more recently tried to create a more personal idiom based on a clearer lyric and dramatic line. When asked to make a statement about his work, he wrote, characteristically, "Poetry, without my being aware of it, was like a mirror of my inner self, and behold, I held in my hand another mirror in which everything I saw was reflected. I shattered both mirrors, and from the splinters built my own Orpheus-Mirror, in which true poetry now stands reflected, my own life. . . . My poetry is fundamentally erotic. It is composed of two bodies which embrace until they suddenly discover that their faces are black and besmirched with blood. My poetry is many things which elude me, and which I do not understand. If I did understand, I would not wish to reveal it."

BIBLIOGRAPHY

The Forgotten Lady. Athens: Íkaros, 1945.
Paraloyés. Athens: Taroussópoulos, 1948.
With the Face to the Wall. Athens: Taroussópoulos, 1952.
When I Speak to You. Athens: Taroussópoulos, 1956.
The Phantoms or *Joy in the Other Street.* Athens: Taroussópoulos, 1958.
The Stroll. Athens: The Brothers Taroussópoulos, 1960.
The Stigmata. Athens: The Brothers Taroussópoulos, 1962.
The Seal or *The Eighth Moon.* Athens: A. and P. Klisioúnis, 1964.

❋ ❋ ❋

THE GIFTS

Today I wore a
warm red blood
today men love me
a woman smiled at me
a girl gave me a seashell
a boy gave me a hammer

Today I kneel on the sidewalk
and nail the naked white feet of the passers-by
to the pavement tiles
they are all in tears
but no one is frightened
all remain in the places to which I had come in time
they are all in tears
but they gaze at the celestial advertisements
and at a beggar who sells hot cross buns
in the sky

Two men whisper
what is he doing is he nailing our hearts?
yes he is nailing our hearts
well then he is a poet

BEAUTY

He sprinkled ugliness with beauty
he took a guitar
he walked along a riverbank
singing

He lost his voice
the delirious lady stole it
who cut off her head amid the crimson waters
and the poor man no longer has a voice with which to sing
and the river rolls
the tranquil head with its closed eyelids

Singing

EXPERIMENTS FOR THE REPETITION OF NIGHT

My friends are leaving
they have come to say goodbye

I shall never see my friends again

one of them is leaving for the adjacent room
his face turned black
he wore a dark green material
night has fallen
he no longer speaks

the other is leaving for the other room
to find the pins
first however he hid himself behind the curtains
he became frightened
afterwards he climbed on the window
to sleep

the other took off his shoes
with trembling hands
he took the warm
statue
he took it into the bedroom
he does not know how to make it stand upright

my friends have gone far away

I shall not see my friends
again

LIFE

Night
in a pharmacy
a kneeling
horse
eats
the floor boards
a girl
with a strange
green
burn
is receiving first aid
while
the ghost
in despair
weeps
in the corner

OBSERVATORY

Burglars of the sun
they had never seen a green twig
they had never touched a burning mouth
they do not know what the color of the sky is

In darkened rooms locked up
they do not know if they will die
they lurk in ambush
with black masks and heavy telescopes
with stars in their pockets dirty with crumbs
with stones of cowards in their hands
they lurk in other planets for the light

Let them die

Let every spring be judged by its gladness
by its color every single flower
by its caress every single hand
by its trembling every single kiss

THE SAVIOUR

I count on the fingers of my severed hands
the hours in which I have strayed in these rooms of the wind
I do not have other hands my beloved and the doors
do not want to close and the dogs are unrelenting

With my bare feet I splash in these dirty waters
with my bare heart I seek (but not for myself)
a skyblue window
how did they ever build so many rooms so many tragic books
without a crack of light
without a breath of oxygen
for the sick reader

Since every room is also an open wound
how shall I descend the stairs again which are crumbling
to bring through the mud again and the wild dogs
bandages of rose and medicines
and if I should find the pharmacy closed
and if I should find the pharmacist dead
and if I should find my heart displayed in the pharmacy window

No no it is ended there is no salvation

The rooms shall remain as they are
with the wind and the reeds of the wind
with splinters of glass faces that groan
with their colorless bleeding

with porcelain hands that are stretched out toward me
with unpardonable oblivion

My own severed and f l e s h l y hands were forgotten
That very moment when I was counting up their agony

ELÉNI VAKALÓ (1921–)   Eléni Vakaló, born in Athens
in 1921, studied archeology at the University of Athens and
esthetics and the history of art in Paris. Since 1949 she has
been art critic of various newspapers and periodicals, and
since 1958 she has taught the history of art and techniques
in the Free School of Painting and Decoration in Athens. She
is married to the painter George Vakaló. The author of eight
books of poetry, she agrees with MacLeish that "A poem
should not mean / But be" and most emphatically with
Marianne Moore's statement about poetry: "I too dislike it!"
Like Moore's, her poetry concentrates on the thing seen, for
she feels that the rhythm of life resides within objects, as in
herself, until her rhythms become refined beyond harmony
and become the tendons of the thing described, lean and
muscular.

BIBLIOGRAPHY

Theme and Variations. Athens: Íkaros, 1945.
Recollections of a Nightmare City. Athens: Íkaros, 1948.
In the Form of Theorems. Athens: Taroussópoulos, 1951.
The Forest. Athens: A. Karavías, 1954.
Frescoes. Athens: The Friends of Literature, 1956.
Journal of the Age. Athens: Dhífros, 1958.
Description of the Body. Athens: Dhífros, 1959.
The Meaning of the Blind. Athens: Dhífros, 1962.

❋   ❋   ❋

MY FATHER'S EYE

My father had a glass eye.

On Sundays when he stayed at home he would take other
eyes out of his pocket, polish them with the edge of his sleeve
and then call my mother to make her choice. My mother
would giggle.

In the mornings my father was well satisfied. He would toss
the eye in his hand before he wore it and would say it was a
good eye. But I did not want to believe him.

I would throw a dark shawl over my shoulders as though I were cold but this was that I might spy on him. At last one day I saw him weeping. There was no difference at all from a real eye.

> *This poem*
> *Is not to be read*
> *By those who do not love me*
> *Not even*
> *By those*
> *Who will not know me*
> *If they do not believe I existed*
> *Like themselves*

After this episode with my father
I became suspicious even of those who had real eyes.

AGE OF THE POLYP

I have been thinking that the species polyp
Has similarities to our own work.

                      In such manner

Must events occur which
In depositing unrelated strata—
Fossilized seashells
Dry pieces of sponges
Perhaps twigs which weary birds
Passing above have dropped—
Penetrate into the joints of cellular tissue;
Dead organisms in the sea
Unite among themselves
Form vertebrae out of empty broken shells
Which pass into other offshoots
Salt accumulates
Twisting seaweed turns to bone before it can crumble
The imprint remains
Whiter threads pierce through these fossils
Protrusions, hollows remain
Sea reptiles once again make their nests there
Barnacles
And those fragments, which but lately glued themselves,
Waver still at edges, back and forth, in the water.

The appropriation of spaces between joints
Is heard in poems quietly like a creaking.

NÁNOS VALAORÍTIS (1921–) Nános Valaorítis, the great-grandson of one of the national poets of Greece, was born in Lausanne, Switzerland, in 1921, studied law at the University of Athens, English literature at London University, and worked in various capacities for the BBC and on film commentary. He is the author of two books of poetry and two poetic dramas, and, in collaboration with his wife, Marie Wilson, wrote a book of texts on her line drawings. Tersely, Valaorítis says that for him "poetry helps the living to die and the dead to live."

BIBLIOGRAPHY

Punishment of the Magi. London: Hermes Press, 1947.
Central Arcade. Athens, 1958.

❋   ❋   ❋

HOMECOMING

One morning we woke by the side of those who neither
Sleep nor wake, like the trees,
Though we speak they do not hear our voices
They understand only the language of the winds
They groan when the strong winds blow
In our small seaside country
Driven by waves into the mercy of the sea.

From here in the flower of their youth they set sail
Into the archipelago with their deep ships;
The starting is easy but the returning is a difficult game
And autumn, which bars and bolts its doors,
Swooped like a hawk to eat of our hearts,
And women yearning for virile bodies
Old men mumbling in empty rooms
And we, competing in running and the shotput
Never noticed the gross faces of the hired mercenaries.

They went away, and the scales tilted behind them
And the seed of vengeance grew into a plane tree
And we saw the chasm they left behind them widening

And those who remained were planning the disappearance of
   those who had gone
Though we never felt that in our sturdy bodies
The poisoned blood had assumed control.

Afterwards one morning we saw those arriving
For whom, like the years of man, there is no returning;
The gods will not permit them to approach closer
And to grasp the land with their hands.
The houses they long for seem close by like fruit
But disappear when they reach greedy hands
In pursuit of a land forever retreating.

And those also for whom their returning is that death
Who comes to receive them sweetly like a woman
And leads them from the threshold deeply within
The dark corridors toward the murderer's bed
As their lips still murmur
The remnants of an old devotion.
Blind as oxen and almost happy, they proceed to their de-
   struction.

And when everything has come to pass as was foretold us
And everything remains to be done all over again,
Each in its turn, for the blood to flow,
To be cleansed and to flow again, to flood over
Without ever once filling the huge jars of pain,
And when after endless toil those wounds quiet down
Which of themselves open after many years
Like doors which lead us to a stained past,
For the earth to be cleansed and that knot untied
Which bound together so many souls, like bats, one with the
   other
While we watch the last, the most dreadful murder
Being justified and which still writhes within us like a
   wounded viper
Since no man could be found to judge him
Since no vengeance exists, since it becomes dream, a statue
   and a city
In our small seaside country
Driven by the winds into the mercy of the sky.

NÍKOS KAROÚZOS (1926–) Níkos Karoúzos, born in
Nauplion in 1926, studied law and political science at the University of Athens and has written six books of poetry. Essentially a religious poet, he feels that his poetry wells up within
him from a nostalgic reach for God. What he most wishes in
his poetry is to immerse his inner world in the glory of God
and to serve those mysterious qualities of words which lead to
song.

BIBLIOGRAPHY

Poems. Athens, 1961.
Stag of the Stars. Athens: Prótipon Publishing Company,
1962.

❊　❊　❊

TOUCHING THIS YOUTHFULNESS

All night long I waited with frankincense
a woman had died
at break of dawn
the unemployed were waiting with their shovels
a bit of darkness still remained
in the morning square of the post office
and that warmth was now setting
which one unhappy heart gives to another—
the small restaurants of dawn
with light misted on their window panes.
Attica was weaving the new day in every eye
footsteps hurt on every empty street
this deep and early morning.
Joy was once a river far deeper
with solitary crystals on its surface
with a god hidden clearly
and trees but barely
reflected.
But now I walk the streets in a deep
river of sound and men have no words
with which to speak—what can they say . . .
Stocky Greek women, listless mothers, charwomen

go to the hushed buildings
with little defence of clothing against the cold, so little,
they have no flowers on their cheap dresses.
And other women wait in vain for
love, death, money;
it is late, the night has kept its cruelty
I give money and vanish
I go far, far away—do not call me
my desolation is a filthy white.
And other women wash
the doors where the devil will enter,
from early morning they stoop to his service.
Hell, then, is our country,
the black smoke of factories
rises, a sin
high in the dawn.
Yet once joy was my river,
not here on the waste earth but in the celestial
worlds above with my solitary soul.

CONTINUING CITY

*For here we have no continuing city, but we seek one to
come.*   —Hebrews, XIII, 14.

The lesser guide has written on a rock
with whitewash, "moon, sea, land."
The water in the silence was seawater—
I happened to be passing by with a rose held in my fingers . . .
I shall always hear this music, I whispered,
always at the end my soul shall triumph.
I have no body, I am naked;
O moon
how many earthen days still,
years with death portioned out bit by bit!
I have a humbled body
O moon
I am burned by colors, by my own voices.
Only the rock's message
the lost guide
these clouds with their primeval rain . . .
the clouds ready to burst.
A November night bristling with thorns surrounds me,
color of ash;

I feel it as I descend
to the nocturnal harbor
where lights melt gold on the waters.
I am alone resembling
your mystical surface O sea.
Whoever wants my help
in this earthen desolation
will find me beside him.
Who are you? I sing the mystery,
I am the one confined in fire, I fulfill
ancient prophecy;
it rains
the bestial sky crumbles.

DÍNOS CHRISTIANÓPOULOS (1931–) Dínos Christianópoulos was born in Salonika in 1931 and studied ancient Greek literature at the university there. At present he is working in the public library of the same city and is the editor of a literary quarterly, *Diagonal*. The author of several books of poetry, he has been deeply influenced by Cavafian attitudes and techniques. Like Cavafis, his earlier poetry deals with historical characters and situations to express some ironic view of life, but in his later poetry he has stripped his versification, diction, and emotions to the bone, writing with the confessional directness of a diary.

BIBLIOGRAPHY

Poems, 1949–1960. Salonika: Dhiaghónios, 1962.
The Body and Remorse. Salonika: Dhiaghónios, 1964.

❊　❊　❊

THEY ARE TRACKING DOWN EVERYTHING PICTURESQUE

they are tracking down everything picturesque

gentlemen came with portfolios and measuring rods
they measured the ground spread out their papers
workers shooed away the pigeons
ripped up the fence tore down the house
mixed lime in the garden
brought cement raised scaffolding
they are going to build an enormous apartment house

they are wrecking the beautiful houses one by one
the houses which nourished us since we were small
with their wide windows their wooden stairs
with their high ceilings lamps on the walls
trophies of folk architecture

they are tracking down everything picturesque
chasing it away persistently to the upper part of town
it expires like a revolution betrayed
in a little while it will not even exist in post cards
nor in the memory or souls of our children

DISMISSED FROM MILITARY SERVICE

now there is no ESA * any more
voices of sergeants to rip away your dreams
wives of majors who want their kitchens scrubbed
no thirsting for a little warmth in the barracks every night
smoking one cigarette after another

now
without military belt or beret
the dirty army boots give me a notion of freedom
an unbuttoned chest means that I am my own master
and here's the small cord with which I cleaned my gun
I shall keep it to remind me of inspections

I'd like to buy something before I leave
a bit of ribbon for my sister a toy or two for the children
but my pockets are as empty as my heart
I'd like to wander through the streets once more
and see Salonika for the last time
but I've no feet any more I've no eyes
I'm not even in the mood for talk
my mind is always sailing off to my village

horses 8, men 40
(let this be our last ordeal
the last reward from our country)
but why does this sudden jolt so squeeze my heart?
all we have gone through is nothing in comparison
to what we may face before us
unemployment, drought, crop failure
the daily agony for a loaf of bread
the children crying and father's pension small
and our uncle in America merely promises

there is no end to this military service

INTERVAL OF JOY

just as I was saying I would stop writing about love and lust
and write something instead about the unhappiness of my
    neighbor
I met you and fell into complete confusion
and all my resolutions went up in air

* ESA are the initial letters in Greek representing the "Greek
Military Police."

now see where I sit and write songs again
burning for your somewhat green eyes
thirsting for your saliva
recollecting our one love-walk in the country
when the mosquitoes bit us in confused bewilderment
at this incomparable devotion of ours
and the thorns pierced into our bodies
astonished at the extent of our indifference

it was an interval of joy
may the unhappy forgive me for it
I have not yet suffered enough
for the pain of my neighbor to touch me

FROM BODY TO BODY

I said I would yield to a smile
to see where two lips would lead me, which open like an
    embrace;
and from concession to concession and from smile to smile
and from body to body
I have arrived here where death becomes one with your blood
it takes your features it wraps you round it breaks you
it makes you more wretched it brings you to the *amen*

until at last neither silence can save you
nor honesty

THE CENTURION CORNELIUS

Lord, do not wonder at my great faith;
it is love that dictates my faith.
I do not beg you for Nikítas or for Harílaos,
nor for Nikólaos who has not had time yet to be bored with
    prayer.
Only make Andónios well, Andónios;
this is all so painful for me—
when he was young and a free man
he also concerned himself with letters and the arts;
he was conversant with ancient Greek and loved to play the
    accordion
on nights when the sky slept and the drowsy moon
leaned her head on the house with the lilac bushes.
But now he is my slave—do not ask me how.

I have authority over him to bind or to free.
I can do with him whatever I please;
I can even set him free, though this would be most painful for
   me;
besides, he works efficiently with his great strength.
For these reasons, Lord, and for many others,
make Andónios well, slave of your slave.
If need be, I can even turn Christian.
Only make him well, all I ask of you, nothing else.
Anything else I might dare ask of you would be immoral.

Italian Poetry

EDITED BY *Sonia Raiziss and Alfredo de Palchi*

❋ ❋ ❋ ❋ ❋

Introduction

A conversant American audience has long accepted Pirandello as a symbol of modern theater. His heirs, like Diego Fabbri and Ugo Betti, attract the attention of Broadway and off-Broadway companies. Italian novelists—Moravia and Lampedusa, to name only two—not infrequently make the best-seller lists and are courted by Hollywood. And of course the Italian film, the brilliant firstborn of postwar realism—*Open City, Paisan, The Bicycle Thief*—with such later troubled children as *Rocco and His Brothers, La dolce vita,* has reached through the sophisticated to the general audience. Paintings and sculptures from Italy visit our contemporary galleries: Giorgio Morandi's modulated bottles, Marino Marini's equestrian tensions, Alberto Burri's nonobjective thoughts. Italy's fashions are the rage with Americans at home, as are her incomparable splendors when they travel abroad.

Where during this exportable renascence have her poets stood, between the scattered d'Annunzian star and the comet Quasimodo? The wild weather after World War II (which Italy otherwise challenged with alacrity and spirit) left their names waiting in shadows on a vague landscape, until their rather recent and still modest acknowledgment here.

The fault belongs both to the circumstance of an unwarranted indifference in others and to the conventional character of Italian poetry, that fateful complicity of inner and outer events. With roots reaching back to Dante's time and straggling through a precarious modern history into the fallow years of the Fascist regime,—which strained to resurrect grandeur, not glory—Italy's literature for generations glossed living facts and mistook destiny, her poets wasting themselves in verbal homesickness. (There were always some powerful single talents like Ungaretti, Montale, Alvaro, Pavese, who raised their early unyielding towers. Those staying out the dictatorship were only sporadically molested, for this temporizing coercion had not sunk deep into the Italian soul.)

That futile era—eventually a civil war that turned the land into a battlefield for two ideas and for aliens—reflected its political shifts and spiritual anomalies in literary equivocation. Once the dire diversion of Fascism was played out, the expectant personalities of the poets loomed in the new uncertain morning. And fiction, first to review the disaster, often cursed both their houses. When the hollow structure had toppled and Italy began repairing, her prose arts came to terms faster, more effectively than her poetry—which had the Italianly reluctance to discard shapes of a bygone beauty. Such fidelity had the advantage of historical continuity but was embarrassed by an outdated look. Certain unimaginative critics, along with the still complacent reading public, wavered before the unfamiliar long enough to compromise or retard the potential urgencies.

Yet a whole world and two wars back, it was Italian futurism, with F. T. Marinetti's brash manifesto in the Paris *Le Figaro* in 1909, that antedated dadaism and surrealism. In a coeval appearance, *La Voce,* founded by Giuseppe Prezzolini and Giovanni Papini, welcomed native debutant writers as well as already shining names, such as Benedetto Croce and G. E. Borgese. Its innovations absorbed futurist techniques, but its aims implied social awareness and an outlook on European vistas beyond the provinces. Poets of various allegiances and related to other movements were attracted to the *vociani.* Thus Corrado Govoni and Aldo Palazzeschi belonged as well to the *crepuscolari* by temperament. Identified chiefly with the precocious Guido Gozzano and Sergio Corazzini, the "twilight" group had their effective season of ironic regrets. They expressed their personal and public languors, however, in a descriptive style that had the ease of prose and a conversational, often colorful idiom. This Janus-faced school made the first notable gestures to loosen the grasp of d'Annunzio, incumbent arbiter, whose tenable but inflated fame died years before his death. His baroque eloquence fell away in company with the sounder romanticism of Giosué Carducci and Giovanni Pascoli —and thus the triumvirate ended. Each had his respective lingering influence, if only in the form of intense reactions.

But the single-minded revolution against all Italianate decorums, including crepuscularism, resided in one man—Ungaretti—among the first and foremost in the European vanguard. He cleansed the poem of its effete lyricism, he condensed the image, symbolist in mood and pointillist-impressionist in form (think of W. C. Williams' lighted reverberant word clusters and spaces). Baffled critics applied the epithet "hermetic" (first used by Francesco Flora in 1936) to what was already the most telling new mode in contemporary Italian poetry. Writers of the opposite persuasion carped at a seemingly perverse obscurantism. But this hovering allusive fragmented style, confirmed by time and prevalence and by the very disputes it provoked, lost its esoteric wonder. It joined the tradition, while changing it. Now it was understood, not as a deliberate retreat, but as an intense excursion into the poet's universe, with its frontiers on the actual world, elemental or sophisticated. The unconscious had made its contacts with the fortuitous outside. But, as in symbolism or surrealism, intermediate steps outward downward inward were omitted.

The major hermetics themselves moderated these initial astringencies but still enjoyed that useful ambivalence which had served to cut the flat overripe diffuseness. For Vincenzo Cardarelli, who launched *La Ronda* (1919–1922), there was another way to approach novelty and freshen jaded habits. He chose to return to a classic Leopardian clarity; by thus appearing to move backward, he could take a firmer step forward to invigorate poetry with the directness of daily idiom and candor. Two other poets disregarded current vogues: Umberto Saba, who kept aloof and spoke with an unassuming confiding simplicity that sounded a special lone note in modern classicism; and Dino Campana, at first associated with the *vociani* but always a true original and still a legend, who did not reflect the sunset so much as the hot colors of his own tragic personality.

Though not a school with formal tenets, *ermetismo* was certainly the major movement in a half-century of Italian poetry and a centrifugal force that governed even the anti-hermetics. It fanned out from the initiators to the posthermetics on the periphery—from Ungaretti's poetic generation; to the next of Montale and Quasimodo; to that of Gatto, Sinisgalli, Luzi, Caproni, Sereni. . . . The first configuration traveled in time and temper with English-American imagism, the advent of Pound and Eliot. The cluster of posthermetics absorbed the refracted techniques and inquiring attitudes, ac-

commodating the innovations to the demands of poetry after
World War II. Latter-day neorealists, such as Pier Paolo Pasolini and Elio Pagliarani, who are detailed, more discursive, and
surely more outspoken, have not missed the master classes.
Their driving immediacy of tone may be deceptively à la mode.
What seems more obviously recent is not the bitterness—deep
and purgative in Montale, patiently and lyrically urgent in
Quasimodo, strenuous in the new social poets—but the sore
jerking irony in a writer such as Nelo Risi, the disenchantments
tensely oblique in Bartolo Cattafi and Luciano Erba.

The pre-World War II poets have shrunk the distance between them and their sons, having shifted position since the
1940's from experimental postures and refinements, or remote
broodings, to a nearness both human and literary. Ungaretti
expanded and complicated his line and stanza syntax as darker
emotions gathered. Quasimodo succeeded himself and developed from the closed hermetic man into the communicative
humanist engaged in world turbulence (a change similarly
experienced and expressed by Archibald MacLeish). Only
Montale, it would seem, had found his universal forms
"squared off" from the start—harsh angular pieces of creation
beside the symbolic sea or restless beings metaphysically revealed in lightning bolts.

So these poets offer a breathing palpable heritage to others
at work today, as Cardarelli and Saba might also provide, with
their unpretentious language. The middle poets, who are seeing further truths (surely Vittorio Sereni and Franco Fortini),
can urge what they need to: their private crises and those of
our most cruel age. If such legatees or the youngest of the
rebels (the *novissimi*) are driven by other considerations, if
they want to go back or ahead to recital argument polemic or
passion—with a difference—they at least have leave to talk
out loud. They live in a less anxious land but a more anxious
world and should have things to say and say them naturally
in other ways. They can mind their elders or stand up to them.
And this too will be a compliment to certain formidable talents—among the strongest and purest in Europe.

This can be only an indicative anthology. The poets whose
arbitrary exclusion is painful, and for which the editors ask
pardon under the pressure of space, should otherwise some day
range from a Sibilla Aleramo to an Andrea Zanzotto, in a
truer perspective of contemporary Italian poetry reaching for

some impossible point of convergence in the back distance and running its lines out wide to the presumptive foreground tomorrow.

Sonia Raiziss and Alfredo de Palchi

BIBLIOGRAPHY

Works in English

Bergin, Thomas G. *Italian Sampler*. Montreal: Mario Casalini Ltd., 1964.

Brandeis, Irma (ed.). *Quarterly Review of Literature*. Montale Issue, Vol. XI, No. 4, 1962.

Buzzi, Giancarlo. "Vittorio Sereni," *Italian Quarterly*. Vol. 6, No. 22, Summer, 1962.

Cambon, Glauco. "Eugenio Montale's Poetry," *The Sewanee Review*. Winter, 1958.

Gilbert, Creighton. (guest ed.). *Perspective*. Italian Issue, Vol. 3, No. 3, Spring–Summer, 1950.

Golino, Carlo L. (ed.). *Contemporary Italian Poetry*. Berkeley and Los Angeles: University of California Press, 1962.

"Italian Number," *The Literary Review*. Vol. 3, No. 1, Autumn, 1959; see also No. 2, Winter, 1959–1960.

Kay, George (ed.). *The Penguin Book of Italian Verse*. London: Penguin Books, 1958.

"Literature and the Arts in Italy: Contemporary and Avantgarde," *Chelsea 18*, 1966.

Lowell, Robert. *Imitations*. New York: Farrar, Straus & Giroux, 1961.

Miller, Peter. "Italian Poetry of the Novecento." Introduction to *Italian Poets: An Anthology, folio*, Vol. XXIII, No. 3, Summer, 1958.

Pacifici, Sergio (ed.). *The Promised Land and Other Poems*. An anthology of four contemporary Italian poets. New York: S. F. Vanni, 1957. Introduction by Sergio Pacifici; preface by Henri Peyre.

Poggioli, Renato. "Contemporary Italian Poetry," *Voices*. No. 128, Winter, 1947.

Poggioli, Renato. "The Italian Success Story," *Wake 12*. 1953.

Sampoli, Maria Simonelli. "An Italian Contemporary Poet: Mario Luzi," *Italian Quarterly*. Vol. 6, No. 23–24, Fall–Winter, 1962.

Williamson, Edward. "Contemporary Italian Poetry," *Poetry*. December 1951–January 1952.

UMBERTO SABA (1883–1957) We now associate Trieste with the humanity of Saba's poetry. In this city of his birth and death, Umberto Saba gave a lifetime's secluded devotion to books as the proprietor of a *"libreria antica e moderna."* He left it only for that period during World War II when he was forced, because of his half-Jewish parentage, to keep hidden in Florence. This experience and the tension implicit in the severe character difference between his parents, roughened the otherwise mild surface of those long domestic years in his adored city.

For all its seeming peaceable tenor, his autobiographical poetry betrays some of this conflict, the griefs and fatigues of existence. Feelings yearn between the natural affection he knew for animals, objects, home, and their refracted melancholy. The ingenuous quality of Saba's work, intimate and familiar, is misleading. His sensibility is more simply seen than explained, his method more canny than one would think. That apparent psychological innocence, that spontaneous approach to things, people, places, the effortless conversational manner, all gather symbolic meaning in the end. And his personal way has a lineage from Petrarch (who named his evolving book) to Tasso to Leopardi to the later lyric realists he anticipated. Saba's old-new language is a classic technique that in fact balances substrata in the man and the style.

BIBLIOGRAPHY

Poesie. Florence: Casa Editrice Italiana, 1911.
Mediterranee. Milan: Mondadori, 1946.
Uccelli, quasi un racconto. Milan: Mondadori, 1951.
Il Canzoniere (1900–1947). Trieste: 1921; Turin: Einaudi, 1957.

❈   ❈   ❈

WINTER NOON

That wink of time when I was happy still
(happy!—may God forgive the grand rash word)
what was it dashed to the very brink of tears
my momentary joy? You'll say, "Oh some

etty young thing just happened to be passing,
ith a bright smile for you." No, a toy balloon
ther, a turquoise wandering balloon
) high in the azure air, and the skies of home
ver so wholly brilliant as that day—
ry cold they were, very clear, that winter noon.
heaven with just a trace of fine white cloud,
id the city windows bright as fire in the sun,
id a wisp of smoke from a chimney or maybe two—
id up there high over all those things—divine
ings!—that globe that had slipped from the heedless hand
 a little boy (he was all in tears, I'm sure,
 the thick of the crowd somewhere, for his grief, his grief,
r his mighty grief)—slipped into the sky between
ie Commercial Bank and the Coffee House I sat in,
aring there, lost in reverie, through the pane,
yes bright, as it dipped and soared away—his treasure.

TRANSLATED BY *John Frederick Nims*

THE CHAMPION SWIMMER

Vhoever saw you in the sea called you
iren.

efore the curtain of my humiliated life
ou appeared, disappeared, triumphant winner
f the race.

 cord, tenuous and unbreakable,
inds me to you as you pass by smiling
 front of me, unseeing, surrounded by numerous
iends, young like you, making a lot of noise
mong yourselves in the bar. One day
 sad shadow descended—for an instant!—
rom your lashes, a maternal shadow
ent at the angles of your lovely, proud mouth;
nd your dawn was married to my evening.

TRANSLATED BY *Lynne Lawner*

ONE NIGHT

f only sleep would come, as it has come
n other nights: already slipping through
ıy thoughts.

Instead now,

like an old washerwoman wringing clothes,
anguish wrings another pain from my heart.
I would cry out, but cannot. As for torment—
suffered once—I suffer on in silence.

And that which I have lost, only I know.

TRANSLATED BY *Felix Stefanile*

TO MY WIFE

You are like a creamy pullet,
my white hen,
whose plumes the wind disturbs
when she stoops to drink
or peck at the ground,
yet proceeding over the grass with measured step
just like a queen:
full-bosomed and superb
and better than roosters;
she is like all the females
of the peaceful animals,
close to God.
And so if eye and judgment
do not fool me,
among these your equal will be found,
and in no other woman.
And when the evening makes them comfortable,
the peaceful cluck of their troubles
reminds me of you
complaining,
and unaware
that like the hens
your voice makes sad and gentle music.

You are like a pregnant heifer,
happy still and without dullness,
even frisky,
who if you pet her
turns her neck where the coat glows,
a tint of rose.
Or, coming on her and listening to her moans,
so sad is her lament,
you are driven to gathering grass
to make her a gift.
And so it is I offer you my gift when you are sad.

ou are like the sleek bitch
sweet of stare
t tough at heart.
hen she lies down
e seems a saint
rning with unconquerable religion,
oking at you as though
u were her Lord and Master.
t when she follows you
rough the house, in the street,
ould anyone dare to approach,
res her lily teeth.
ve. Love and jealousy.

ou are like the scared rabbit
ho in her narrow cage
ises herself erect at sight of you
d stretches her ears,
eping them stiff,
though begging you to bring her the leavings,
dishes,
d when denied
rls up in the corner by herself,
uggling the dark.
ho would hold food from her?
ho would rob her
the fur she nips from her back
line her nest with
here she shall give birth?
who would ever make you suffer?

ou are like a swallow
turning in Spring,
eparting in Autumn—
ut you've not learnt this trick!)
nd, like the swallow, you have your light ways,
when, the time I was feeling my age
d becoming ancient,
u predicted another Spring.

ou are the thrifty ant
f whom, when they go to the country,
randmother speaks to the baby
s they take their walk.
nd so too I find you in the bees,

as in all the females
of the peaceful animals,
close to God;
and in no other woman.

TRANSLATED BY *Felix Stefanile*

VINCENZO CARDARELLI (1887–1959) At nineteen Vincenzo Cardarelli came from Etruscan Tarquinia to Rome where he led a somewhat disorganized life of intermittent work. Eventually he found his way into journalism and literary circles. Here he was the most important among those who launched the avant-garde *La Ronda,* its "nearly personal expression" (Giansiro Ferrata). The program of this magazine consisted of a return to order, modernized and renewed, and the shedding of a tired grandiloquence, Cardarelli's procedure in his own lyric prose and unaffected poetry. He took a determined view of what to do with tradition and crusty convention, learning from Leopardi to come closer to the prose virtues of poetry.

But he was also temperamentally prepared to speak straight out on the page, as he used to at a party. Yet his verse is more varied than one might suppose from its commonplace look and level tone, as it moves along in a forthright, no-nonsense approach to life and literature. What is honest in his work comes to us with seeming artlessness; yet it carries a sense of the eternal, understated. The simplicity is neoclassic only in its composure, contemporary in its unadorned language. He said of his own poetry: "Light without color, existence without attributes, hymns without interjections, impassivity and distance, order and not images. . . ." Cardarelli should be recognized as the antecedent of certain present-day realists in Italy.

BIBLIOGRAPHY

Prologhi. Milan: S.E.L., 1916.
Poesie. Rome, 1926; Milan: Mondadori, 1943.
Prologhi, viaggi e favole. Lanciano: Carabba, 1929; Milan: Mondadori, 1946.

❊   ❊   ❊

ADOLESCENT

Over you, young virgin, broods
a holy shadow.

Nothing is more mysterious
and adorable and becoming
than your naked flesh.
But you keep shut in your careful dress
and live aloof and far off
with your favors
not knowing who will reach you there.
Surely not me, who turn giddy
if I see you pass by
at such a proud distance,
with your hair loose
and your whole person guarded:
sleek tight-skinned creature
whose very breath comes heavy
with an obscure rapture of flesh
that can hardly bear its fullness.
In your blood suffusing
your face like a burn
the laughter of the cosmos darts
as in the swallow's black eyes.
Your pupils are branded
with the sun that hives there.
Your lips are locked.
Your white hands are innocent
of the shameful sweats of contact.
And I think how your body
unbending and wanted
makes love despair
in a man's heart!

Still, someone will deflower you,
mouth of a wellspring.
Some undiscerning
sponge fisher
will find this rare pearl—
to him the grace and good luck
not to have searched for you
and not to know what you are
nor how to enjoy you
with the subtle knowledge
that offends a grudging God.
Yes, the brute will be
simple enough not to

die sooner than touch you.
And it's always like this.
Even you don't know who you are.
You will let yourself be taken
only to see how the game goes,
and laugh together a while.
Like a flame fading in daylight,
in the starkness of truth
your promised mysteries
dissolve into nothing.
So much unconsumed
pleasure will slip by!
You'll give yourself, you'll be lost
to the first one who charms you,
for a whim that will never guess why.
Time loves the joke
in its favor, not the cautious
will that lags and considers.
So it's youth
must keep the world rolling.
And the wisest man is just a boy
who grieves that he's grown up.

TRANSLATED BY *Sonia Raiziss and Alfredo de Palchi*

NIGHT ENCOUNTER

Ah hobo, mortals like you!
with your white sneakers
and enormous corduroys,
and that dead cigar
dangling between your lips
like a forgotten notion;
bug-eyed zany of every town,
its aimless dog drifting
curiously through the crowd
distracted by the newest smell—
you might have called at
all the ports of the world.
You've made a dozen
dozen voyages of Columbus
around the globe.
Did you learn the oceans

before you sailed them,
and experience the lives of so many
so many cities?
On what map
strolling the earth with your finger
did you plot the routes of your travels?
Whole Continents confront you,
talk big like a daft
stubborn explorer!
Hardly ashore you would follow
necessity's blind rut
that seems like home
whatever the place
not even asking—where are we?
Cast off here, you settled right down.
And I won't question your trades.
You've endured them all
let's say, and never had any.
Like those brothers of yours
wherever the latitude
who acknowledged you without wonder
welcomed you without a greeting
and watched you go with no regrets
(look, you've done it too)
o lonesome one!
Life's like that
among your kind, all linked
to the same chain.
In steamy taverns
you spooned it from the common dish;
then evenings in a party
took pleasure in the streets.
Huddled for a couple of days
on transient cots
naked, together, you lay down
under the same sheets
and traded belongings
next to the skin,
and forced shoulder to shoulder
you loosened your tongues,
but the heart said nothing.
For weariness racked you,
each loathed his anguish in the other

and munched his own silence,
and mankind was a long way off.
You kept in touch
like cargo waiting at the piers
wondering on what shore it would unload.
These neutral sojourns
of your life, reluctant
salamander flights through flame,
little by little forlornly
fill all time.
And now you shuffle like a scared
boy not knowing if he's done wrong.
And awkwardly you chew your butt . . .
For solace, you go glancing
sideways at the tart
across the street,
who bears her parallel loneness
with less grudge.

TRANSLATED BY *Sonia Raiziss and Alfredo de Palchi*

TIRED

On the page I've written
—I scrawled it in a fever—
how much I must do over
to cool the bite of remorse.
To advance myself a little
with one short jump
what a long hard run it takes!
Back and forth
through phases and decisions,
through seasons, eternity,
I'm forever beginning:
a Lazarus risen
a convalescent relapsing,
with my precocious mornings
vital, exultant,
and perpetually spoiled:
I make an orgy of time.
The challenges spurned
in my life, the launchings
and shipwrecks!

My days are
pieces of odd worlds
that won't fit together,
deadly toil.

TRANSLATED BY *Sonia Raiziss and Alfredo de Palchi*

DINO CAMPANA (1885–1932)   The aberrant life of Dino Campana began in Tuscany and ended there, where he died in a hospital for the insane. To his doctor he gave these hints and unhappy highpoints of his existence: "At fifteen I went to a college near Turin. Later to the University of Bologna. I didn't do well in chemistry. If I'd gone in for letters, I could have made a living. . . . Then I started to write a little, roam a little. . . . I was driven by a kind of vagabond mania. . . . An instability impelled me to constant change. . . . I was imprisoned in Switzerland for brawling. . . . Then a month in a Parma jail, around 1902. Four months in a hospital in Imola for dementia praecox. . . . I took odd jobs—doorman, stoker, fireman, triangle player in Argentina; a vendor at fairs in Odessa and companion of gypsies. I peddled my *Canti Orfici* in cafés, out of hard need. . . . I was a writer once, but had to give up, being of unsound mind. I don't connect ideas, I don't follow. . . ."

His one significant book, published and posthumously augmented in the long span between 1914 and 1952, sets him apart in Italian poetry. Here is an erratic and often lush lyricism—impulsive, sometimes automatic notations delivered in an impassioned Rimbaud-like excess. Though his musical echoes recall other decades, there is a modern originality in the verbal pyrotechnic tumble. Out of some feverish limbo, his figure returns from homesick shadows to touch contemporaries with elliptic suggestions of style that diverse poets like Ungaretti and Montale have perfected. He leaves a nightshade in the memory.

BIBLIOGRAPHY

Canti Orfici. Marradi: Ravagli, 1914; Florence: Vallecchi, 1928, 1941.
Inediti. Florence: Vallecchi, 1941.
Canti Orfici e altri scritti. Florence: Vallecchi, 1952.

❅   ❅   ❅

THE WINDOW

The smoky summer evening
Riddles the gloom with a dazzle of glass from the window
  above,

Sears a token of fire in my heart.
But who has (on the terrace on the river there's lamplight)
  who has
To the Little Madonna of the Bridge who is it who is it who's
  lighted the lamp?—there's
An odor of rot in the room: there's
A lagging red wound in the room.
The stars are buttons of mother-of-pearl and the evening is
  dressing in velvet:
And it shimmers, an evening all folly and will-o'-the-wisp: it
  shimmers, but there's
In the heart of the evening there's
Forever a lagging red wound.

TRANSLATED BY John Frederick Nims

AUTUMN GARDEN

To the ghostly garden to the laurel mute
green garlands shorn
to the autumnal country
now a last salute!
Up the parched falling lawns
harsh scarlet in the sun's last rays
struggles a torn
deep-throated roar—life crying far away:
it cries to the dying sun that sheds
dark blood on the flower-beds.
A brass band saws
the air: the river's gone
between its golden sands: in a great calm
the dazzling statues that the bridgehead bore
are turned away: there's nothing any more.
Out of profound silence, something like
a chorus soft and grand,
longing, soars to the terrace where I stand:
and in redolence of laurel,
of laurel languorous, laurel piercing, where
those statues in the sunset loom immortal,
she appears, present there.

TRANSLATED BY John Frederick Nims

THE NIGHT OF THE FAIR

Tonight my heart told me, don't you know?
The bewildering rose brunette
gilded with yellow hair and spangles
in her brown eyes: that regal grace of hers
ravished the coral
freshness of the mornings:
and you would follow on the air
the cool incarnation of a morning dream:
and she would roam when dreams
and perfumes veiled the stars
(the night's feeble stars
you loved to stare at behind the gates):
she used to flow by quiet
and candid as a flash of doves—
she must be dead now, don't you know?
It was the night of the fair
perfidious Babel climbing
a piled sky in bundles a paradise of flame
in lewd and grotesque hoots
and tinklings of angelic bells
and shrieks and whorish voices
and Ophelian pantomimes
distilled from simple tears of electric lamps

A common little song was dead
and left my heart bereaved
and I've gone roving loveless
to leave my heart from door to door:
she who was not born and yet is dead
has left my haggard heart here
and yet in sorrow bears it:
leaving my heart from door to door.

TRANSLATED BY *Sonia Raiziss and Alfredo de Palchi*

YOUR ANIMAL EYES

You watch me with your narrow
animal eyes, silent and waiting,
then draw near, and stare and keep silent.
The weight of your flesh drowses, clumsy, dazed
in primordial dreams. Who called you to life,
harlot . . . where do you come from?

—sour Tyrrhenian ports,
the singing fairs of Tuscany,
or did your mother wallow in the hot
sands under the sirocco?
Immensity engraves wonder on your
savage face of a sphinx—
the teeming breath of life
tragically shakes like a lioness
your somber mane
and you look at the blond profane angel
you don't love, who doesn't love you
and suffers from you and wearily kisses.

TRANSLATED BY *Sonia Raiziss and Alfredo de Palchi*

GIUSEPPE UNGARETTI (1888–) Giuseppe Ungaretti was born of Tuscan parents in Alexandria, Egypt. Much of his formative youth was spent in pre-World War I Paris, where he studied at the Collège de France under Bédier and Bergson and at the Sorbonne under Lanson and Jeanroy. There he was in intimate touch with European culture, especially French poetry, through such friends as Apollinaire. While he was a soldier in Italy, then in France, his long luminous career began out of the heart of the war with a book of verse in 1916. A progressively widening literary activity involved him in polemics in both countries. He has been an editor and a professor of Italian literature at the universities of São Paolo and Rome, where he now lives.

Ungaretti has a formidable show of volumes: translations that range in time and genre from the French classics to the moderns to Brazilian folksongs; and a body of his own poetry under the title of *Vita d'un uomo* which already looms as a contemporary masterwork. He still holds his early position as one of Europe's surest exponents of the organic image, of the pristine use of the word itself in its historic authority. The phrase—sometimes one word, one syllable—has a special personality in an Ungaretti poem. This spare chosen impression runs as a clear river of print (and pause) between the white banks of the page. These brevities that might seem so fugitive are among the best-defined of our imagist integers: real and verbal life in compounded essence. Here was a successful experiment in the distillation of experience, drastic and too soon for the traditional Italian at first. When he had done his essential work of purification, a shift occurred in his diction, hinted at in *Il dolore* (1947), obvious in *La terra promessa* (1950). The lean syntax grew complex, the tenuous surface opaque, and the heart of the matter crowded, contorted with sorrows and perplexities. Once a controversial hermetic stylist in his own country, he emerged as a major craftsman of both the word-image technique and the more richly weighted, figured manner.

BIBLIOGRAPHY

Il porto sepolto. Udine: Stabilimento Tipografico Fruliano, 1916.

Allegria di naufragi. Florence: Vallecchi, 1919; Milan: Mondadori, 1942.

Sentimento del tempo. Florence: Vallecchi, 1933; Milan: Mondadori, 1943.

Il dolore. Milan: Mondadori, 1947.

La terra promessa. Milan: Mondadori, 1950.

Un grido e paesaggi. Milan: Mondadori, 1954.

Il taccuino del vecchio. Milan: Mondadori, 1960.

Life of a Man. Translated by Allen Mandelbaum. New York: New Directions, 1958.

❅ ❅ ❅

DEATHWATCH

All night long
thrown against
a buddy
slain
with his gnashing
teeth
bared to the full moon
with his bloated
hands
penetrating
my silence
I was writing
letters full of love

Never have I hugged
life
so hard

Cima Quattro, December 1915.
TRANSLATED BY *Sonia Raiziss and Alfredo de Palchi*

YOU WERE BROKEN

I

The many, monstrous, tumbled, dun-grey boulders
Stunned even yet from the catapults that flung them
From the ancient fires of earth, long dungeoned, or
From terror of raw cataracts, virgin surge
Hauling off all in the hug that nothing softens:
—Over the dazzle of sand, on a blind horizon
Looming stiff in their trance—you don't remember them?

And that jutting hunchback, swollen over the only
Clotting of gloom in the hollow, the araucaria
—Wild pine—racked by its anguish to great size,
But, tougher than other victims of that inferno,
Its exiled fibers turning to fierce flint;
The dark maw, rotted out where the roots were wounded
Now all a freshness of butterflies and grasses:
—Its silent contortion of madness, not remember?
Perched on a ball of a boulder three palms wide
Balanced uncannily,
Trick of a witch?

Gay little light little bird, from branch to branch,
With eyes that were giddy with wonder, never weary,
You mounted in triumph to its tettered top,
Rash little song-loving boy,
Only to see again in the glossy gulf
Of a sunk and silent crater in the ocean,
The fabulous murk of turtles
Stirring to life in the seaweed.

Tension of nature wrought to extremes
And that solemn ado in the deep,
Funereal premonitions.

II

You lifted your arms like wings
And called every breeze into being
As you sprinted in lulls of the air.

Nobody ever saw lagging
Your light little foot in its dance.

III

Happy grace,
No way but for you to be broken
In a blindness denser than stone,
You, simple breath, and a crystal,

Too human a glow for the rancorous,
Shaggy, berserk, and reverberant
Roar of the stark-naked sun.

TRANSLATED BY *John Frederick Nims*

JUNE

When
this night
dies for me
and I can observe her
with the eyes of another
and doze off
to the rustling
of the waves
that end their coiling
at the sash of acacias
round my house

When I wake again
in your body
that modulates
like the voice of the thrush

and is drawn fine
like the glittering
color
of ripe grain

In the water's
transparence
the thin gold
of your skin
will frost over darkly

Balanced
on resounding
slabs
of air you'll wait
like a
panther

At the restless
mowing
of shadow
you will unleaf

Mutely
raging in
that dust
you'll smother me

Then
halfway shut your eyelids

We'll see our love reclining
like the evening

Assuaged then
I'll see
on the mineral horizon
of your irises
my pupils dying

Now
the sky is closed
as are
the jasmines
at this hour
in my African land

My sleep is gone

I waver
at the street corner
like a firefly

Will this night ever
die for me?

TRANSLATED BY *Sonia Raiziss and Alfredo de Palchi*

From the Sequence THE MEDITATED DEATH
FIRST SONG

O sister of the shadow,
Nocturnal most as light is brightest,
Death, you do pursue me.

In a pure garden
The ingenuous longing brought you to light
And peace was lost,
Pensive death,
Upon your mouth.

From that moment
In the flow of mind I hear you,
Deepening the distances,
Suffering rival of the eternal.

Venomous mother of the ages,
In the terror of the throbbing
And the solitude,

Beauty punished, smiling,
In the drowsing of the flesh,
Dreamer fugitive,

Sleepless athlete
Of our greatness,

When you have tamed me, tell me:
In the melancholy of the living
Will my shadow's flight be lengthy?

TRANSLATED BY *Allen Mandelbaum*

EARTH

A glistening might flash upon
The scythe, and by degrees the sound
From grottoes might return and err
Astray, the wind
With other brine might redden the eyes . . .

You might hear the keel submerged
Moving out at sea,
Or an angry seagull pecking,
Fled his prey, the mirror . . .

Of the grain of nights and days
Full-laden you displayed your hands,
Painted dolphins did you see
On Tyrrhenian ancestors'
Secret walls immaterial,
Then behind the ships beheld them
Living flying,
And, earth, you are still of ashes
Of inventors without repose.

Cautious in the olive-trees the rustling
Might, at any instant, wake hypnotic
Butterflies,
You will remain inspired wakes of those extinct,
Of absent ones the sleepless interventions,
The force of ashes—shadows
In the swift sway of the silvers.

Though the wind still roar,
From palms to firs the clamour
Forever desolate, the silent
Outcry of the dead is louder.

TRANSLATED BY *Allen Mandelbaum*

CHORUSES DESCRIPTIVE OF DIDO'S STATES OF MIND

I

The shadow disappearing,

In a distance of years,

When grief did not wound,

You hear the then childish
Breast swell, longed for,
And your alarmed eye
Unveil uncautious fire of April
From a perfumed cheek.

Scorn, diligent specter
That makes time inert
And its fury known at length,

—Leave the bitten heart!
But could, silent struggles
Abated, Night fade from age?

II

The evening is prolonged
By a suspended fire
And a shudder in the grass little by little
Seems to reunite the infinite with fate.

Then unperceived, a moonlike echo
Was born and was fused with the shiver of the water.

I don't know what was more alive,
The grumbling up to the drunken stream
Or the expectant echo that was tenderly silent.

III

Now the wind has become silent.
Silent also is the sea;
All is quiet; but I cry out
The cry, alone, of my heart,

Cry of love, cry of shame
Of my heart that burns
Since I watched you and you looked at me
And I am nothing any more but a weak thing.

I cry and my heart is afire without peace
Since the time when I have become only
A thing in ruins and abandoned.

IV

Only I have in my spirit hidden wounds,
Wooded equators, on swamps
Brumal clots of vapors where
There rages the desire,
In sleep, never to have been born.

V

As yet unweaned, but infants
Whose impatience increase too hastily,
We were transported by anxiety, along sleep
Toward what other, elsewhere?
It took on color and the aroma began to sprinkle
Those first-fruits
So that, through tender tricks
Disclosing itself surprised in the light,
It offered its true richness only
Later, when we were already maddened in our vigils.

VI

All its tricks mystery has lost,
Accustomed crown to long life,
And, changed in himself,
Concedes the bile of remorses drop by drop.

VII

In the darkness, silent
You walk in fields empty of any wheat;
No more do you wait for anyone, proud, at your side.

VIII

From my face to yours your secret comes;
Your dear features are repeated in mine,
Our eyes contain nothing else
And, in despair, our love ephemeral
Eternal shudders in the sails of a delay.

IX

No more am I attracted by the wandering landscapes
Of the sea, nor by the searing

Pallor of dawn upon these leaves or those.
Nor do I fight any longer with the heavy stone,
Past night that on my eyes I bear.

Images, what use are they
To me, who am forgotten?

X

Do you not hear the plane-tree's
Leaf, do you not hear it suddenly creaking
As it falls along the river over the flints?

I will embellish my decline, tonight;
They will see, joined to the dry leaves,
A roseate glow.

XI

And restless
Since their space offered
To our intimate fires a cloud's refuge,
Cherishing each other,
Our ingenuous twin
Spirits were awakened, already in flight.

XII

In a squall there opened, in the dark, a harbor
Supposed to be safe.

It was a starry gulf
And its heaven seemed unchangeable:
But now, how changed it is!

TRANSLATED BY *William Weaver*

EUGENIO MONTALE (1896–) To contemporary Italian poetry Eugenio Montale has given a strong personal accent, the most distinctive (said Robert Lowell) since Leopardi. The decisive somber strokes in *Cuttlefish Bones* proved his first and lasting signature; and all his subsequent books, few but of urgent impact, have been unmistakably Montalian. They show the northerly nature of his Ligurian coast and acknowledge his own complex nature in a rugged original idiom, almost un-Italian.

The facts of his life—his birth in Genoa; his experience as an infantry officer in World War I; his connections with various periodicals as poet, critic, translator; the eleven-year curatorship at the Vieusseux Library in Florence; and since 1948 the regular stint of literary and musical criticism for *Il Corriere della sera*—these scarcely skim the compelling inward events. What he sees and what happens in the outside world assume an intense symbolic existence.

Explicit details, in plain or technical terms, or the large-muscled metaphors of beach, boulder, storm—insistent meanings made tangible—correspond to Eliot's objective correlatives. And though reached independently and manipulated in his own way, they confirmed the critical cliché of Montale's kinship with Eliot, whom he introduced to Italian readers. This is valid as to their common penchant for the symbol and their questing metaphysical temper. But Montale's art is more personal and passionate; and his world view, now seen arching from negativism to a kind of exalted resignation, holds without Eliot's visible stanchions of faith. A hoarseness of despair is heard through Montale's work, and a brooding atmosphere still darkens it. Yet a consoling vision lights up the abstract face of a woman or a stoic godhead. From book to book the drama of a man's history has grown more allusive and oblique. The earlier elemental detachment and then the deeper subjective involvements have joined in an apocalyptic whole.

After a stage of comparative stylistic formalism—paired rhymes, correct stanzas, though always phrased with resilient vigor—Montale's prosody broke free. It was a deliberate release from traditional Italian melodies and manners. The "asperities of rhythm . . . phonetic harshness" (Sergio Solmi),

sometimes poem-long bold stanza blocks, all the irregular rich
sculpture of mood and method, are peculiarly his own.

BIBLIOGRAPHY

Ossi di seppia. Turin: Gobetti, 1925.
La casa dei doganieri e altre poesie. Florence: Antico Fattore,
1932.
Le occasioni. Turin: Einaudi, 1939.
Finisterre. "Quaderni di Lugano," Lugano: 1943.
La bufera e altro. Venice: Neri Pozza, 1956.
(These five books have all been reissued under the imprint
of Mondadori.)
La farfalla di Dinard. Milan: Mondadori, 1960.
Satura. Verona, 1963.
Accordi e pastelli. Milan: Scheiwiller, 1963.

❊   ❊   ❊

ARSENIO

Roof-high, winds worrying winds
rake up the dust, clog the chimney ventilators,
drum through the bald, distracted little squares,
where a few senile, straw-hatted horses wheeze
by the El Dorado of the rooming houses' windows in the sun.
You are like an acid clash of castanets
disturbing by fits and starts our workaday hours,
today, as you go down
our main street, fronting the bay—
now you are sloshed with the dreary drizzle, now you dazzle us.

It's a sign of quite another orbit: you follow it.
A gusher of lead hangs over
the ungraspable gorges, and you go down,
more rootless than the winds.
A shower of salt spray, a whirlpool,
lifts, heavy with its element rebellious to the other.
Your step through the pebbles is a creaking,
the mop-headed, beach-tossed seaweed snags you.
Iron link in a chain! Perhaps, powerless to walk,
this moment,
you finally evade finishing your journey's
all too well publicized delirium of inaction.

Here and there among the papery palm trees
you hear the wavering outcry
of the violins, dying as the thunder slams in
with the shudder of the shops closing metal shutters.
How imposing the storm now, when Sirius sparkles
garishly against the indigo heavens, far out
where the evening is already importunate.
Like some delicate tree entering the reddening light,
lightning etches a crash of pruned branches.
The strings of the two-bit orchestra grumble for silence.

You go down to a gloom that precipitates
and changes the siesta hour into night;
globelike lanterns rock on the gunnels of fishboats
in the offing, where a single darkening presence
clasps sea and heaven. Acetylene pulses
from a few perforated, rusty funnels.

The sky trembles with raindrops.
The dry soil, turning to water, steams.
Everything near you is smoke,
a rustling hoes the earth,
capsizes the sopping pavilions,
douses the Chinese lanterns hissing on the esplanade.

You are flung aside
among wicker porch furniture and dank mats—
like a water-lily dragging its roots,
sticky, never sure-footed.
Hysterical with life, you stretch
towards an emptiness of suffocated sobbing.
You are knotted in the rings of the fish-net,
gulped by the gasping spent water . . .
Everything you grab hold of—
street, portico, walls and mirrors—
glues you to a paralyzed crowd of dead things.

If a word fells you,
if a gesture ruins you now, Arsenio,
it's a sign that this is the hour for letting go
of the life you were always disposed to throttle.
A wind carries its ashes to the stars.

ADAPTED BY *Robert Lowell*

THE LEMON TREES

Listen, the poets laureate
walk only among plants
of unfamiliar name: boxwood, acanthus;
I, for my part, prefer the streets that fade
to grassy ditches where a boy
hunting the half-dried puddles
sometimes scoops up a meagre eel;
the little paths that wind along the slopes,
plunge down among the cane-tufts,
and break into the orchards, among trunks of the lemon trees.
Better if the jubilee of birds
is quenched, swallowed entirely in the blue:
more clear to the listener murmur of friendly boughs
in air that scarcely moves,
that fills the senses with this odor
inseparable from earth,
and rains an unquiet sweetness in the breast.
Here by a miracle is hushed
the war of the diverted passions,
here even to us poor falls our share of riches,
and it is the scent of the lemon trees.

See, in these silences
in which things yield and seem
about to betray their ultimate secret,
sometimes one half expects
to discover a mistake of Nature,
the dead point of the world, the link which will not hold,
the thread to disentangle which might set us at last
in the midst of a truth.
The eyes cast round,
the mind seeks harmonizes disunites
in the perfume that expands
when day most languishes.
Silences in which one sees
in each departing human shadow
some dislodged Divinity.
But the illusion wanes and time returns us
to our clamorous cities where the blue appears
only in patches, high up, among the gables.
The rain falls wearying the earth,
the winter tedium weighs on the roofs,

the light grows miserly, bitter the soul.
When one day through a half-shut gate,
among the leafage of a court
the yellows of the lemon blaze
and the heart's ice melts
and songs
pour into the breast
from golden trumpets of solarity.

TRANSLATED BY *Irma Brandeis*

DORA MARKUS

I

It was where a plank pier
pushed from Porto Corsini into the open sea;
a handful of men, dull as blocks, drop,
draw in their nets. With a toss
of your thumb, you point out the other shore,
invisible, your true country.
Then we trailed a canal to the outlying shipyards,
silvered with sun and soot—
a patch of town-sick country, where depressed spring,
full of amnesia, was burning out.

Here where the old world's way of surviving
is subtilized by a nervous
Levantine anxiety,
your words flash a rainbow,
like the scales of a choking mullet.

Your restlessness makes me think
of migratory birds diving at a lighthouse
on an ugly night—
even your ennui is a whirlwind,
circling invisibly—
the let-ups non-existent.
I don't know how, so pressed, you've stood up
to that puddle of diffidence, your heart.
What saves you, perhaps,
is a charm, which you keep
near your lipstick, puff and nail-file—
a white mouse made of ivory . . .
Thus you exist.

II

In your own Carinthia now
your corsage is the crescent
hedges of flowering myrtle . . .
You sashay on the curb of a stagnant pond,
and watch the timid carp swallowing, swallowing,
or saunter under the lime trees,
and follow the kindling night
along the frowzy shorefront.
The purple and orange awnings of landings
and *pensioni* throw
a bonfire on the water.

Night blanketing
the fogging lake coves
brings only the catcalls of geese,
the put-put-put of the outboards.
The snow-white majolicas of your interior
have seen you alter,
and tell your fly-blown mirror
a story of cool miscalculations,
now engraved where no sponge can expunge.

That's your legend, Dora!
But it is written already
on the moist lips of sugar daddies
with weak, masculine side-burns,
in the ten inch gold frames
of the grand hotels—
it lives in the asthma
of the sprung harmonica
at the hour when daylight muddies, each day later.

It is written there!
The evergreen laurel lives on
for the kitchen, the voice doesn't change;
Ravenna is far away. A ferocious faith
distills its venom.
What does it want from you?
Not that you surrender
voice, legend or destiny . . .

ADAPTED BY *Robert Lowell*

THE MAGNOLIA'S SHADOW

The shadow of the dwarf magnolia
is a scarecrow now that the turkey-wattle
blossoms are blown. Like something wired,
the cicada vibrates at timed intervals.
It is no longer the Easter of voices in unison,
Clizia, the season of the infinite deity,
who devours his faithful, then revives them in blood.
It was more facile to expend one's self,
and die at the first wing-flutter, at the first
hectic rumbling from the adversary—a nursery game.
The hard way begins now; but not for you,
eaten by sunlight, rooted—yet a fragile thrush,
flying high over those frogskin mudbanks,
not for you to whom zenith, nadir, capricorn
and cancer rush together, so that the war may be
inside you, and in your adorer, who sees on you
the stigmata of the Bridegroom—the shiver
of snowfall doesn't jar you. Others
shy backwards and hold back. The artisan's
subtle file shall be silent; the hollow husk
of the singer shall be powdered glass
under your feet; the shadow is neutral.
It's autumn, it's winter, it's the other
side of the sky that leads you—there
I break water, a fish left high and dry
under the new moon.
                                        Goodbye.

ADAPTED BY *Robert Lowell*

LITTLE TESTAMENT

This thing the night flashes
like marshlight through the skull of my mind,
this pearl necklace snail's trail,
this ground glass, diamond-dust sparkle—
it is not the lamp in any church or office,
tended by some adolescent altar boy,
Communist or papist,
in black or red.
I have only this rainbow
to leave you, this testimonial

of a faith, often invaded,
of a hope that burned more slowly
than a green log on the fire.
Keep its spectrum in your pocket-mirror,
when every lamp goes out,
when hell's orchestra trembles,
and the torch-bearing Lucifer
lands on some bowsprit
in the Thames, Hudson or Seine—
rotating his hard coal wings,
half lopped by fatigue, to tell you, "Now."
It's hardly an heirloom or charm
that can tranquillize monsoons
with the transparent spider web of contemplation—
but an autobiography can only survive in ashes,
persistence is extinction.
It is certainly a sign: whoever has seen it,
will always return to you.
Each knows his own: his pride
was not an escape, his humility
was not a meanness, his obscure
earth-bound flash
was not the fizzle of a wet match.

ADAPTED BY *Robert Lowell*

THE DEAD

The sea crashing on the opposite shore
heaves up a cloud that foams
until the flats absorb it. There
one time on the iron coast we hurled
wilder than the ocean, our hardbreathing
hope!—and the barren vortex turns
green as in days that saw us still living.

Now that the north wind levels the sullen
tangle of salt tides and whips them back
where they reared, someone nearby throws
nets over the brushwood, uncoiling
along the roadway that sinks
out of sight;
bleached nets dried by the slow
chill touch of the light; and above them

the thick lens of the sky blinks
and drops to a curve of the flogged
horizon.

      Deeper than seaweed that drags
in the eddy disclosed to us, our life is
troubled by this lull: whatever once stopped
in us, resigned to its cage
still swirls; between strands that link
one branch to the next, the heart fights
like a marsh hen
trapped in the meshes;
and a freezing deadlock holds us
rigid and wandering.

           So too
perhaps the dead in the sod are cheated
of rest: from there a force more ruthless
than life pulls them, and all round
the ghosts tortured by human reminders
are driven as far as these beaches, breaths
without substance or sound
betrayed by the darkness; and their cropped
flights hardly cut off from us now
skim by and in the sieve
of the sea go under . . .

    TRANSLATED BY *Sonia Raiziss and Alfredo de Palchi*

STORM

"Les princes n'ont point d'yeux
*   pour voir ces grands merveilles,*
leur mains ne servent plus qu'à nous persécuter . . ."
               Agrippa D'Aubigné: "A Dieu"

The storm that pelts the tough leaves
of the magnolia with long
March thunders, with hailstones,

(crystal sounds in your nighttime
nest startle you; what's left of the gold
doused on the mahogany, on the tooling
of bound books, still burns
a grain of sugar in the shell
of your eyelids)

the lightning blaze that candies
trees and walls surprising them in this
forever of an instant—marble, manna
and destruction—which you bear carved
inside you, your condemnation, and lashes
you to me, strange sister, more than love—
and then the rough crash, rattles, thrill of
timbrels over the hidden pit,
the stamp of the fandango, and beyond it
some groping gesture . . .

                 The way it was when
you turned, your forehead cleared
of a cloud of hair,

and waved to me—and stepped into darkness.

TRANSLATED BY *Sonia Raiziss and Alfredo de Palchi*

TWO FIGURES IN TWILIGHT

Flowing between us on the terrace
an underwater light distorts the hills'
profile, and your face.
On a shifty backdrop every move of yours
hovers, cut off from you; without a trace enters,
fades, in the element that floods
each track and closes on your step:
you here with me, in this atmosphere
which stoops to seal
the torpor of boulders.

                 And I drawn back
into the power that bears down, succumb
to the spell of recognizing nothing
of myself outside me: if only I lift
my arm, the act changes
splintered on a crystal, its memory anonymous
and gone pale, and now the gesture
is not mine any more;
if I speak, startled I hear that voice
run down the full scale
or snuffed out in the air that won't hold it.

At such moments resisting the day's
dissolution
bewilderment lingers: then a gust
rouses the valleys in a frantic
impulse and draws from the leaves a
jangling that scatters
through driven smoke and the first
lights define the docks.

          . . . words
fall weightless between us. I watch you
in the supple reflection. I don't know
if I know you: I know I was never
detached from you as now in this late
return. A few seconds have burned
us whole: except two faces, two
strained masks that are etched
in a smile.

TRANSLATED BY *Sonia Raiziss and Alfredo de Palchi*

IRIS

When suddenly St. Martin's * summer topples
its embers and shakes them down low in
Ontario's dark hearth—
snapping of green pine cones in the cinders
or the fumes of steeped poppies
and the bloody Face on the shroud
that separates me from you:
                    this and little else (if very
little is in fact your sign, a nod, in the struggle
goading me into the charnel house, my back
to the wall, where the sapphires of heaven
and palm leaves and one-legged storks don't shut out
the brutal sight from the wretched
strayed Nestorian);
                    this is how much of you gets here
from the wreck of my people, and yours,
now that the fires of frost remind me of your
land which you've not seen; and I have
no other rosary to finger, no other flame
has assailed you, if it's not this,
of berries and resin.

   * Indian summer.

The hearts of others are nothing like yours,
the lynx not like the striped tabby, beautiful,
stalking the hummingbird above the laurel;
but do you believe them the same breed, when you
venture outside the sycamore's shade
or maybe that mask on the white cloth
has guided you, that image in crimson?

So that your work (a form born of
His) might bloom under new suns
Iris of Canaan, you were gone
in that nimbus of mistletoe and thornbush
ushering your heart through the world's
nighttime, past the mirage
of desert flowers, your first kin.

If you turn up, here's where you'd bring me, the arbor
of stripped vines, next to our river's
pier—and the ferry does not come back again,
St. Martin's sun is blacked out.
But it won't be you should you return, your earthly
story has changed, you don't wait for
the prow at the crossing,

> you have eyes for nothing, and have no
> yesterdays no tomorrows;

because His work (which translates
into yours) *must be kept going.*
        TRANSLATED BY *Sonia Raiziss and Alfredo de Palchi*

THE EEL

The eel, the
siren of sleety seas, abandoning
the Baltic for our waters,
our estuaries, our
freshets—to thresh upcurrent under the brunt
of the flood, sunk deep, from brook to brook, and then
trickle to trickle dwindling,
more inner always, always more in the heart
of the living rock,
needling in ruts of the mud, until, one day,
explosion of splendor from the chestnut groves
kindles a flicker in deadwater sumps,
in ditches pitched

from ramparts of the Apennine to Romagna;
eel: torch and whip;
arrow of love on earth,
which nothing but our gorges or bone-dry
gutters of the Pyrenees usher back
to edens of fertility;
green soul that probes
for life where only
fevering heat or devastation preys,
spark that says
the whole commences when the whole would seem
charred black, an old stick buried;
brief rainbow, twin
to that within your lashes' dazzle, that
you keep alive, inviolate, among
the sons of men, steeped in your mire—in this
not recognize a sister?

TRANSLATED BY *John Frederick Nims*

SALVATORE QUASIMODO (1901–)   Now professor of Italian literature at the Milan Conservatory of Music, Salvatore Quasimodo, Sicilian-born, shifted the interrupted course of his education from technical training to the study of Greek and Latin begun at the age of twenty. Though the first discipline may have accommodated his onetime position as a surveyor of public works, his schooling in the classics served him as a poet and brilliant translator. His local and international awards, culminating in the 1959 Nobel Prize, have drawn world attention to his country's literary resurgence.

After his first book in 1930, its successors followed steadily, with the 1940 *Lirici greci* fixing his reputation at once as a rare craftsman in the jewels of antiquity and, later, those of our day, which he reset in a clear contemporary idiomatic Italian. Quasimodo's early lyrics are paradigms of the then endemic hermeticism: rarefied, deflected, private, maybe arbitrarily abstruse. But the sometimes elliptic metaphors, the exquisite melodies of the south, are held within the fine outlines of his classic practice. A frugal décor, foreshortened or elongated images, suggest a quasi-surrealist vista where the atmosphere is both sharp and shadowed. After the war and since *Giorno dopo giorno,* he has filled in and peopled his landscape —a denser background, a nearer human presence, a middle distance. But his sense of destiny is always transmitted with "intellectual rigor, almost acid" (Sergio Solmi). Now wide with sympathy, his work in its more relaxed but still careful style has turned fully toward the social and tragic problems of life.

BIBLIOGRAPHY

Acque e terre. Florence: Solaria, 1930.
Oboe sommerso. Genoa: Circoli, 1932.
Erato e Apòllion. Milan: Scheiwiller, 1936.
Poesie. Milan: Primi Piani, 1938.
Ed è subito sera. Milan: Mondadori, 1942.
Giorno dopo giorno. Milan: Mondadori, 1947.
La vita non è sogno. Milan: Mondadori, 1949.
Il falso e vero verde. Milan: Mondadori, 1956.
La terra impareggiabile. Milan: Mondadori, 1958.
Tutte le poesie. Milan: Mondadori, 1960.
The Selected Writings of Salvatore Quasimodo. New York: Farrar, Straus and Cudahy, 1960. Translated by Allen Mandelbaum.

METAMORPHOSES IN THE URN OF THE SAINT

The dead mature;
with them, my heart.
Self-pity
is earth's final humor.

Stirring in the glass of the urn,
a light of lacustrine trees:
Dark mutation devastates me,
unknown saint: in the scattered seed moan
green maggots:
my visage is their springtime.

A memory of darkness
is born at the bottom of walled-in wells,
an echo of buried drums.

I am your suffered
relic.

TRANSLATED BY *Allen Mandelbaum*

MAN OF MY TIME

You are still the one with the stone and the sling,
man of my time. You were in the cockpit,
with the malign wings, the sundials of death,
—I have seen you—in the chariot of fire, at the gallows,
at the wheels of torture. I have seen you: it was you
with your exact science persuaded to extermination,
without love, without Christ. Again, as always, you
have killed, as did your fathers kill, as did
the animals that saw you for the first time, kill.
And this blood smells as on the day
one brother told the other brother: "Let us
go into the fields." And that echo, chill, tenacious,
has reached down to you, within your day.
Forget, o sons, the clouds of blood
risen from the earth, forget the fathers:
their tombs sink down in ashes,
black birds, the wind, cover their heart.

TRANSLATED BY *Allen Mandelbaum*

AUSCHWITZ

There, at Auschwitz, distant from the Vistula,
love, along the northern plain,
in a camp of death: funereal, chill,
the rain upon the rusty poles
and the tangled iron of the fences:
and neither tree nor birds in the grey air
or above our revery, but inertia
and pain, that memory bequeaths unto
its silence without irony or ire.

You seek no idylls, elegies: only
motives for our destiny, you tender
here before the contrasts of the mind,
uncertain at a clear
presence that is life's. But life is here,
in every no that seems a certainty:
here we shall hear the angel weep, the monster,
hear our future hours
beating on the beyond, that now is here
in movement and eternity, not in
an image of dreams, of possible piety.
And here the metamorphoses, the myths.
They bear no name of symbols or a god,
are chronicle, are places of the earth,
they are Auschwitz, love. How suddenly
to smoke of shadow altered
dear flesh of Alpheus and Arethusa!

From that inferno opened by a white
inscription: "Labour will make you free"
issued continually
the smoke of thousands of women, from the kennels
forward thrust at dawn against the target
wall or suffocated howling mercy
unto water with the skeletal mouth
under the showers of gas.
You will find them, soldier, there within
your history, within the forms of streams,
of animals, or are you, too, but ash
of Auschwitz, medal of silence?
Long braids remain enclosed in urns of glass,
still crowded by amulets and infinite

shades of little shoes and shawls of Jews:
they are relics of a time of wisdom,
of man who makes of arms the measure, they
are the myths, our metamorphoses.

Upon the plains, where love and lamentation
rotted and piety, beneath the rain,
there, a no within us beat, a no
to death, at Auschwitz dead, that from that pit
of ash, death not repeat.

TRANSLATED BY *Allen Mandelbaum*

IN THIS CITY

This city has even got the machine
that grinds out dreams: with a quick
token, a little disk of pain,
in no time you're off, upon this earth,
unknown in a pack of raving shadows
on phosphorus seaweed, mushrooms of smoke:
a merry-go-round of monsters
revolving on conch shells
that fall to putrid pieces when they play.
It's in a bar down there at the turn
of the plane trees, here in my metropolis
or elsewhere. Come, the switch is on!

TRANSLATED BY *Allen Mandelbaum*

TO MY FATHER

Where Messina lay
violet upon the waters, among the mangled wires
and rubble, you walk along the rails
and switches in your islander's
cock-of-the-walk beret. For three days now,
the earthquake boils, it's hurricane December
and a poisoned sea. Our nights fall
into the freight cars; we, young livestock,
count our dusty dreams with the dead
crushed by iron, munching almonds
and apples dried in garlands. The science
of pain put truth and blades into our games
on the lowlands of yellow malaria
and tertian fever swollen with mud.

Your patience, sad and delicate,
robbed us of fear,
a lesson of days linked to the death
we had betrayed, to the scorn of the thieves
seized among the debris, and executed in the dark
by the firing squads of the landing parties, a tally
of low numbers adding up exact
concentric, a scale of future life.

Back and forth your sun cap moved
in the little space they always left you.
For me, too, everything was measured
and I have borne your name
a little beyond the hatred and the envy.
That red on your cap was a mitre;
a crown with eagle's wings.
And now in the eagle of your ninety years
I wanted to speak to you—your parting
signals coloured by the night-time lantern—
to speak to you from this imperfect
wheel of the world,
within a flood of crowded walls,
far from the Arabian jasmine
where you are still, to tell you
what once I could not—difficult
affinity of thoughts—to tell you (not only
the marshland locust, the mastic tree can hear)
as the watchman of the fields tells his master:
"I kiss your hands." This, nothing else.
Life is darkly strong.

                    TRANSLATED BY *Allen Mandelbaum*

FOR VARVARA ALEXANDROVNA

The dry branch of a birch tree
beats on my window in whirling Moscow.
By night Siberia sets free a shining wind
against the cold glass. The wind plays
a tune on my fretted nerves, in my mind.
I am sick. I can die from one minute to the next.
I go with you, Varvara Alexandrovna,
making your rounds in little felt shoes
with your quick eyes, nurse of my chances.
I am not afraid of death,

just as I have never feared life.
I think somebody else is lying here.
Perhaps, if I can forget love and pity,
the grinding earth and the pale sound
of solitude, I can let go of life.
In the dark your hands burn me, Varvara
Alexandrovna. You have the fingers of my mother,
pressing hard to leave the long peace
after pain. You are the human Russia
of the times of Tolstoy and Mayakovsky.
You are Russia. Not this country of snow
caught now in a hospital mirror.
You are a multitude of hands reaching out for others.

TRANSLATED BY *George Garrett*

ON THE ISLAND

A hill, the symbols
of time, the continuous motionless
mirror of the mind,
hear themselves, await
the future answer. The hour we have
springs up without warning, a sharp beam
in the harmonic labyrinth.

It's March with bursts of blue,
the man leaves his bed of brushwood
and goes in search of stone and mortar.
On his hair he has the morning star
which shines in the water, in his pocket a folding
ruler of yellow wood, barefoot—
he can close curves, incline eaves,
he squares, joins corners, trusses.
Workman and architect, he's alone,
the donkey carries stones, a boy
breaks them and lets off sparks. He labors
three four months before the mistletoe
the sultriness and the rains, dawn and dusk.

Of all the hands that built walls
on the island, Swabian and Greek hands
hands of Spain Saracen hands,
walls of the dog days and autumn,
of all the anonymous hands and hands adorned

with signets, now I see
those which laid foundations
on the seashore of Trabia. Vertical lines,
the air's twistings bent
by acacia and almond leaves.

Beyond the houses, there among the mastic
trees of the hares is dead Sòlunto.
I'd climb that hill mornings
with other boys, through
inner silences. I still
had to discover life.

TRANSLATED BY *Charles Guenther*

CESARE PAVESE (1908–1950) Cesare Pavese was born near Turin and died there. After a term of political banishment by the Fascists, he returned to that city at twenty-eight, with a then obscure book of poems to his credit, the beginnings of a diary posthumously published as *The Burning Brand,* and a masterly translation of *Moby Dick.* During his years as translator and teacher, and later as an editor for Einaudi, Turin publisher, he wrote those nine volumes of prose which earned him a reputation as one of the most vivid and artful writers in the Italy of his day. But a few weeks after receiving the desirable Strega prize, he crumpled under the accumulated weight of political disillusionments and his personal love-and-death obsessions, "an immense and complex mistrust of men and life" (Giacinto Spagnoletti), and committed suicide, an act he had long contemplated in the perverse dichotomy of a successful novelist and an unsuccessful human being.

It could be that Pavese's true concern was his poetry rather than his fiction which is, however, far better known; for it is a poet who writes the fiction. Themes in the verse written between 1931 and 1935, and gathered in *Lavorare stanca,* were expanded in his novels, where the settings and characters are fully developed. The "landscapes" are lively examples of the prevailing temper of this book of poetry, and the gusty colloquial sketches anticipated the vogue of postwar neorealism. His later poems show his moodier and more lyrical cast and a muted anguish that finally estranged him from the world.

BIBLIOGRAPHY

Lavorare stanca. Florence: Edizione di Solaria, 1936; Turin: Einaudi, 1943.
Verrà la morte e avrà i tuoi occhi. Turin: Einaudi, 1951.
Poesie. Turin: Einaudi, 1961.

❄   ❄   ❄

INSTINCT

The old man, frustrated in everything, sitting by the doorstep of his house in the warm sun watches a dog and a bitch giving free play to instinct.

Flies scurry around the man's toothless mouth. His
wife has been dead for some time. She, like every other
bitch, never wanted to know anything about it, but the
instinct was there. The old man—not yet toothless then—
had a nose for it; night would come, they'd go to bed.
Instinct: it was beautiful.

What's admirable in a dog's life is the great freedom:
to rove the streets morning to night; eat a little, sleep
a little, climb up on some bitch's tail a little, not even
waiting for night. A dog reasons the way he sniffs, and
the smells that he gets are for him.

The old man thinks back on an occasion he did it in the
daytime dog-style in a wheatfield. He no longer knows with
what bitch but recalls the high sun and the streaming
sweat and the desire never, never to stop. It was just
like in a bed. Turn back the years and he would always
do it in the fields.

A woman coming down the street stops to watch; a priest
passes and turns aside. Anything can happen out in the
open. Even a woman, shy when face to face with a man,
stands there. But a boy, without patience for the game,
starts pelting stones. The old man rages.

TRANSLATED BY *Norman Thomas di Giovanni*

LANDSCAPE II

The hilltop whitens toward the stars in open land;
thieves would be seen up there. Here below between the slopes
the aisles are all in shade. Up above where there's plenty
and the land belongs to men who have no troubles, nobody
    climbs;
here in the dampness on the pretext of going for truffles
they come inside the vineyard and plunder the grapes.

My old man has come upon two grape stalks thrown
among his plants and tonight he grumbles. The crop's already
    short;
day and night in dampness nothing comes but leaves.
Between the plants at the line of the sky bare ground is visible,
daily robbing him of sun. Up there the sunlight burns
all day and the land is chalky; even in the dark you see it.
There no leaves come, the sap goes all to the grape.

My old man, leaning on a walking stick in the wet grass,
holds one hand clenched: if the thieves come tonight
he'll leap to the middle of the rows and break their backs.
People who deserve the treatment of beasts, they are;
besides, can they go telling about it? Now and then he lifts his
    head,
sniffing the air; out of the darkness he seems to feel
a smack of earthy odors will arrive—freshly dug truffles.

Up above on the little hills that spread to the sky
no stain of shade is cast by trees, the grape trails the ground
it weighs so much. There no one can stay hidden;
on the summit the shapes of trees are outlined,
black and sparse. If he had his vineyard up there
my old man could stand guard from the house, in bed,
with his shotgun pointed. Here at the bottom not even a gun
serves him, for in the darkness there is nothing but leaves.

TRANSLATED BY *Norman Thomas di Giovanni*

THE CATS WILL KNOW

Still the rain will fall
on your sweet cobble pavements,
a rain light
as a breath or a step.
Still the breeze and sunrise
will flower lightly
beneath your step
when you come in again.
Among the flowers and sills
the cats will know.

There will be other days,
there will be other voices.
You will smile by yourself.
The cats will know.
Old, old words you will hear,
weary and vain
like the costumes cast aside
from yesterday's revels.
You too will make gestures.
You will answer words—
visage of spring—
you too will make gestures.

The cats will know,
visage of spring;
the light rain
and dawn the color of hyacinth,
that tear the heart
of one who hopes for you no longer,
are the sad smile
you smile by yourself.
There will be other days,
other voices and awakening.
We will suffer in the sunrise,
visage of spring.

TRANSLATED BY *Norman Thomas di Giovanni*

DEATH WILL COME AND WILL HAVE YOUR EYES

Death will come and will have your eyes—
this death which attends us
from morning to night, sleepless,
deaf, like an old remorse
or absurd vice. Your eyes
will be a vain word,
a stilled cry, a silence.
So you see them each morning
when upon yourself alone you bend
into the mirror. O dear hope,
on that day we too will know
you are life and nothingness.

For all death has one glance.
Death will come and will have your eyes.
It will be like quitting a vice,
like seeing in the mirror
a dead visage unfold,
like heeding closed lips.
We will descend into the abyss muted.

TRANSLATED BY *Norman Thomas di Giovanni*

THE GOAT-GOD

The country is a place of green mysteries
to the boy who comes there summers. The she-goat, chewing
certain flowers, gets a swollen belly and must run it off.

When a man has enjoyed himself with some girl—
they have hair down below—a baby swells her belly.
Grazing the goats, they leer and lead each other on,
but at dusk both start watching out behind.
The boys can tell when a snake has passed
by the winding streak it leaves along the ground.
But nobody knows when a snake slips
through grass. There are goats that stop still
over a snake in the grass and like being sucked.
The girls like it too—being touched.

At moonrise the she-goats are no longer quiet
and must be herded and driven home,
otherwise the buck is aroused. Leaping into the pasture
he gores the flock of females, then disappears. Girls in heat
come alone into the woods at night
and the buck, if they bleat lying in the grass, runs to find them.
Should the moon come up, he becomes aroused and gores them.
The bitches bark under the moon,
for they have heard the buck, as he leaps
on the crests of the hills, and have smelled the odor of blood.
The cattle stir in their sheds.
Only the bravest of the old mongrels bite at their ropes
and some free themselves and run pursuing the buck
who spatters them, driving them wild, with blood redder than
    fire.
Then all dance together, standing tall and baying at the moon.

When in the morning one of the mongrels comes back, snarling,
    his hair torn out in patches,
the villagers taunt him with kicks from behind.
As for the daughter who runs around at night, and sons who
    stay out late—
should a female goat be lost—they get their necks broken.
Village men knock up their women, toiling without consid-
    eration.
They keep moving day and night and are not afraid
of hoeing even under the moon or of lighting a fire
in the dark with weeds. This is why the land
is so beautiful when green and, tilled, takes on the color
in the dawn of sunburnt faces. Go to the grape harvest
and there's dancing and drinking. And the girls are laughing,
for someone remembers the buck. Up on the summit, in the
    woods,

among the rocky slopes, the villagers have seen him
looking for a she-goat and butting his head against the trees.
Because when a beast has no knowledge of work
and is kept only as a stud, he takes pleasure in destruction.

TRANSLATED BY *Norman Thomas di Giovanni*

LEONARDO SINISGALLI (1908–)   There is no ostensible
correlation between the two major interests in the working life
of Leonardo Sinisgalli, born in Lucania. His professional training in mathematics and engineering, in which he took a degree,
disposed him in 1952 to found and edit *La civiltà delle mac-
chine,* a sumptuous Roman review of the mechanical arts and
crafts, illustrated by paintings that express our machine culture. Soon after leaving the magazine, he joined the airline
Alitalia as its publicity consultant.

The business of his poetry is a thing apart. Its clean line
shows the bent of his early studies, though he deliberately
avoids their terminology. Sinisgalli's post-Ungarettian style is
neat, bridled, illuminated—sometimes lightly ironic. His balanced images and explicit subject matter admit a prickling
if restrained playfulness, even a dry touch of the marvelous.
This "laic mystery" evokes not only native scenes, acts, and
creatures of childhood and youth, but goes back into god-
remembering. Whatever is emblematic and ranging in his
poetry is also localized in shape and sound and leaps from the
page. The two aspects of this poet concur in a natural elegance
close to the senses.

BIBLIOGRAPHY

18 poesie. Milan: Scheiwiller, 1936.
Campi Elisi. Milan: Scheiwiller, 1939.
Vidi le Muse. Milan: Mondadori, 1943.
I nuovi Campi Elisi. Milan: Mondadori, 1947.
La vigna vecchia. Milan: Mondadori, 1956.
L'età della luna. Milan: Mondadori, 1962.

❊   ❊   ❊

MORNING HAS JUST GROWN

Morning has just
grown from the ovens.
Then there starts out of sleep
with the first hum of wind
a whimpering of wheatspears.
No longer watchful, grace

falls from your hand
a gold sickle. Hugging the ground
your breast warms to it.
Your head looms in the light.
Now at sunup the earth
is heavy, sex strong.

TRANSLATED BY *Sonia Raiziss and Alfredo de Palchi*

LAZARUS' DOG

You rove alone in the night
and leave no savor
no spoor among the black rose-
briers that make me bleed.
You are your shade,
your shoulders
lighter, more futile
than butterfly shadows
over the waters.

I'll scent you I'll find you
beyond the red banks,
and suddenly start at your horn.
I used to bring you
the first goodmorning
a muzzle seasoned with thyme.

And in my mouth I'd bring
fish from the dry shore,
the wounded coots in the fern.
Your blood was quicker
than my legs, your shoulder
firmer than the bar
where the river's voice founders.
Handsome and proud, you were
all over new
and straight as the quills
of the sparrow hawk shot down.

TRANSLATED BY *Sonia Raiziss and Alfredo de Palchi*

OLD TEARS

To the old, weeping comes easy.
In midafternoon,

in some hiding-place in the empty house
they sit, and burst into tears.
An infinite despair
takes them by surprise.
They raise to their lips
a dry slice of pear, the pulp
of a fig dried on the roof-tiles.
Even a sip of water
can resolve their crisis
or the sight of a snail.

TRANSLATED BY *William Weaver*

HOLY SATURDAY AT MANFREDONIA

No one from here is left.
The ducks slip away,
one after the other,
towards the dark shore.
Our friends are founding a celestial city.
They leave us at the windows
against the sea, brown
as a mountain.
Messengers between life and death,
the children plunge
to catch worms under water,
and the old shepherd
waits for them to rise again
with a twig of blood
in their fingers.

TRANSLATED BY *William Weaver*

NOTES ON A HANDKERCHIEF'S EDGE

I

Like your eyelids' commotion
the blood moves at the nape
the nape of your neck, when down
your back there pours the marvel
your combing reveals.

II

In my hand the traits
of your heart, memento
of when you were here
in the hand that I bite.

III

The butterfly encumbering
your sky each evening
with its shadow's
transience, lights on your shoulder
to look like a rose.

IV

Your spotless soul,
your lazy essence of an
angel! Hot as flame
your ear of a tigress
rests against my cheek.

V

The fiery
flower lies tattered in the gardens.
You finger the branches. And dive
in a thicket of shade, in love
with the dark.

TRANSLATED BY *Sonia Raiziss and Alfredo de Palchi*

MARIO LUZI (1914–) A man of cultivated discrimination who searches his own work as well as another's, Mario Luzi has been teaching in his native Florence, which gave him his degree in literature. In the endeavor to go beyond his marked hermetic attitude, he contributed his share to the soul-sounding arguments of revisionist or rebel poets in the 1950's and had this to say: "After the germinal experience—which the war was—both for its recognition of reality, a living continuum, and for its moral dramatization, I felt the need to give my work a more essential look and substance, based on the nature of man's experience and of the language that expresses it: I felt the need to make all this the very aim of poetry . . . in an ideal identity between subject and object."

Appropriate to his purpose, there has been a reaching downward rather than an obvious striking change from his already mature earlier work (but with its still lyrical-literary tone, as in "Berry") to the work that appeared in 1952 and after. A more wryly intellectualized realism and focused use of language placed him critically (together with Sereni) on the bridge between their generation and the younger incoming poets. In over twenty-five years, his range suggests the restrained sweep but vibrant asymmetry of modern music, with its cool metaphysical brilliance.

BIBLIOGRAPHY

La barca. Modena: Guanda, 1935.
Avvento notturno. Florence: Vallecchi, 1940.
Un brindisi. Florence: Sansoni, 1946.
Quaderno gotico. Florence: Vallecchi, 1947.
Primizie del deserto. Milan: Schwarz, 1952.
Onore del vero. Venice: Neri Pozza, 1957.
Il giusto della vita (collected poems). Milan: Garzanti, 1960.

❊　❊　❊

BERRY

Heavy with pears autumn will return
to the edges of the roads
hunting you out even on the nighttime
wall warm with heaped fodder.

From the sky the weeping September
spray will hang in vain along the branches
near the closed doors turning your
temples purple with dying meteors.

Songs ebb from you if the time
of the grape grows black
in the arbors, high in an austral
veil the Arno swells

the random chatter of the rowlocks;
and in the young juniper fire
gleams the yard acrid with hares
fled from the minty woods.

If some day the blond voice falls mute,
voice shaping nonexistent suns and
broken moons, who will revive the brown
torpors of my heart?

But you ask for a life, you also ask,
just like your own lament, a wing from the day
which frees from the mountains
the dawn enhanced in its red horn.

And where melancholy is most vast and strange
you hear Sirius bearing it away through time
and fires of love,
drawing back in his purple wind.

To be more sad I linger
between you and me like the disheartened
blue of your gaze at the garden's edge.

TRANSLATED BY *Eric Sellin*

ALL SOULS' DAY

Fire everywhere, a low brushwood fire, fire
over the walls where a dim shadow flows
too weak to leave its imprint, a farther
fire which in needlefuls ascends and descends
the hill through its brim of ashes,
fire with tufts from the branches, from the arbors.

Here neither sooner nor later at the exact time
now that everything around the gay
and sad valley loses life, loses
fire, I turn, I count my dead
and the procession seems longer, it trembles
from leaf to leaf down to the bole.

Give them peace, eternal peace, carry them
to a safe place, away from this turbulence
of ashes and flame which presses together
strangled in the gorges, is scattered
on the paths, flies fitfully, disappears;
let death be death, nothing else
than death, without struggle or life.
Give them peace, eternal peace, quiet them.

Down where the dry havoc of leaves crowds in
they till the soil, drive casks to the fountains,
muttering in the still changes
from hour to hour. The puppy stretches out
by the corner of the dooryard and dozes.

A fire so moderate is hardly enough,
hardly enough, to illuminate this life of
the undergrowth while it endures. Another,
only another could do the rest
and the most: could consume those remains,
change them into clear, incorruptible light.

Peace from the dead to the living, peace
of the living and dead in a single flame. Fan it:
here's night, night spreads,
it stretches its quivering web between mountains,
soon our eyes serve no more and there remains
knowledge by fervor or darkness.

TRANSLATED BY *Charles Guenther*

ON APPROACHING FORTY

Thought pursues me in this dark
town where a wind runs off the plateau
and the swallow's plunge cuts the fine
thread of the mountains in the distance.

Soon there will be forty years of worry,
boredom, gaiety, sudden and swift
as the gust of March wind
which scatters light and rain, soon the delays,
the wrench, with yearning hands, from those I love,
from my haunts, my habits of years
abruptly broken, which I now must understand.
The tree of regret shakes its branches . . .

The years rise over my shoulders
in swarms. It wasn't in vain; this is the work
each accomplishes alone and all together,
the living and the dead, to enter the obscure world
along plain roads and subterranean ways
dense with fleet encounters and casualties
either from love to love or in a single one
from father to son until it be clear.

And having said this, I can set out
freely in the eternal company
of all things that live and die,
I can leave off in dust or fire
if fire endures beyond its flame.

TRANSLATED BY *Charles Guenther*

AS YOU WISH

The north wind cracks the clay,
it presses, it hardens the farmlands,
it disturbs the water in the basins; it leaves
hoes fixed, plows inert
in the field. If someone goes out for wood,
or changes places with difficulty or stops a while
shrunk up in cowl and cape,
he clenches his teeth. What prevails in the room
is the silence of the mute testimony
of the snow, the rain, the smoke,
the immobility of change.

Here I am putting pine cones
on the fire, I listen
to the shuddering windows, I'm neither calm
nor anxious. You who come
through long promise and occupy the place

left by suffering
not to despair either of me or you,
search in the nearness of the house,
try the gray folds of the door.
Little by little the measure is filled,
little by little, little by little, as
you wish, the solitude overflows,
you come and enter, draw with downward hands.

It's a day of this year's winter,
one day, one day of our life.

TRANSLATED BY *Charles Guenther*

VITTORIO SERENI (1913–) A doctor of letters, formerly a professor of literature and now editorial director at Mondadori, Vittorio Sereni was born in the Lombardy region that colors his work. He was one of the young Italians repeatedly called up for army duty and destined for North Africa. But from 1941 to 1943 he was moved about in a Camus-like ambience from Tuscany to Greece to Sicily; and only as a prisoner of the Americans did he reach the Africa of Oran and Casablanca for a two-year internment.

With his first book of poems, Sereni's style if not his substance was confirmed: a late pure version of hermeticism, subtle and poised, but with little of its obscurity or literary slyness. His themes are not extravagant, and are shaped with tact and taste and truth. The war poetry in *Diario d'Algeria,* among the best of its kind in his generation, naturally exposed new and shaken emotions. This further dimension is felt even more in the social and civic concerns of certain late poems included here. The pace is still fastidious, the sentiments disciplined. Because his words and moods often look so matter-of-fact yet are oddly affective, they must in the making exude an aura. At the same time the important hard reactions to a warring society are curbed into a poignant forbearance.

BIBLIOGRAPHY

Frontiera. Milan: Edizione di Corrente, 1941.
Poesie. Florence: Vallecchi, 1942.
Diario d'Algeria. Florence: Vallecchi, 1947.
Gli immediati dintorni. Milan: Il Saggiatore, 1962.

❊　❊　❊

AN ITALIAN IN GREECE

First evening in Athens, a long goodby
of convoys that trail at your sides
full of heartache in the dragging gloom.
Like a sorrow
I have left summer at the bend
and tomorrow is sea and desert
without future seasons.

Europe Europe watching me go down
helpless and absorbed in my
frail myth among the ranks of brutes,
I am a runaway child of yours who knows
no enemy but his own sadness
or some reviving tenderness
of lakes and leaves left behind
his lost footsteps,
I am clothed in dust and sun
I go forth to years of damnation, of sand . . .

TRANSLATED BY Sonia Raiziss and Glauco Cambon

THE FIRST MAN FALLEN

The first man fallen on the Normandy beach
doesn't know anything now, he's high on wings.
That's how tonight someone
touched my shoulder murmuring
to pray for Europe
while the New Armada
came to the coast of France.

I answered in sleep: it's the wind,
the wind which makes strange music.
But if you were really
the first to fall on the Normandy beach,
pray if you can, I am dead
to war and to peace.
This is the music now;
of tents shaking on their poles.
It's not a music of angels, it's
my only music and is enough.

Campo Ospedale 127, June 1944
TRANSLATED BY Eric Sellin

ON THE ROAD TO ZENNA

Why do those worried trees trouble me?
Perhaps in repeating that the green each
spring comes back, but hardly the blooms of joy?
It's not my lament this time,
not spring, it's summer
the summer of my years.

Under my eyes the shoreline
unfurls in the ride, forever unchanged and
created, and my noise cannot alter it
nor, deeper, the sudden bothering wind
that perhaps shies off at the next turn.
And I could despair for all that changes,
my head burning with a bandage of pain . . .
Yet I can guess back there a dim
succession of things: the groaning wellrope,
the cable car shuttling in the woods,
the least of their acts, poor
human tools hooked to the chain
of necessity, the fishing line
vainly cast out into centuries,
the meager lives that happen over and
over for one who returns and finds
nothing is different, nothing—
those flailing arms that will soon sink back,
those hands that start new to no purpose
that reach out and reproach me
for the privilege of motion . . .
So, pity for the uneasy trees
evoked in a spiral of wind for a while
soon falling away away from me,
goodby.
And here the uproar I came with
already transmuted stumbles an instant and then
breaks loose from a great sleep
and another landscape swirls and passes.

TRANSLATED BY *Sonia Raiziss*

THE BEACH

to a lost friend

They have all gone away—
the voice over the receiver talked big.
And then, in the know—They won't come back any more.

But today
on this stretch of beach never walked before
those sun patches . . . Signals
from the ones who have not left at all?
And so quiet when you turn round, as if it were nothing.

The dead, that's not what is squandered day after
day, but those patches
of non-being, lime or ashes
ready to become motion and light.   **Don't**
you doubt it—the sea invests me with this strength—
they will speak out.

TRANSLATED BY Sonia Raiziss

EXPECTATION

It was no dream, I tell you—
                              unless a dream
is a town where they're having supper on time,
doormats blinds iron shutters,
nobody in the doorways (and what was it, suddenly
on the first sure day of spring,
that sad gale shivering the trees and hedges?)
a town that unwinds infinitely
with strange landmarks and signboards
in the suffering of slow motion
or a dread we don't understand.
But now, first clues, coming toward us
familiar landmarks and signs and
faces at certain parapets halfseen in midair
droll tender mute in the little light still left
until they showed up clear—
Carlo maybe, or Piero or someone like Sergio
and others I won't name for reasons of discretion
and for one that's most crucial . . .
what if I tell you
there was Maurizio among them
a bit of Italy's old quicksilver
a covered fire and still hot.
I say it was no dream.
They were all there, almost, the faces in my life
numbering those that are gone
and others who were already in sight of it,
a few steps from the border
not quite on the outskirts of death.

TRANSLATED BY Sonia Raiziss

HALLUCINATION

I was close to crossing the bridge
over a river which might be the Magra
where I go summers, or even the Tresa
where I come from, between Germignaga and Luino.
My way was blocked by a faceless one, a leaden figure.
"Your papers" he ordered. "What papers" I said.
"Let's have them" he was steely, he clinched it
seeing me flustered. I tried to placate him:
"I've got prospects, a town that expects me,
things to remember, some friends still living,
my dead decently buried."
"Great stories" he said, "without a program
nobody passes," and scornfully weighed in his palm
the few pages that were all my assets.
I tried again. "I'll make good
on my way back if you'll let me go now,
let me keep working." There was no
coming to terms with each other: "Have you"—
he growled—"taken your ideological stand?"
At the bridge rail we locked and grappled
alone, in dead silence.
Shame on me, the fight's not over.
I can't say
who'll end in the river.

TRANSLATED BY *Sonia Raiziss*

ONLY SUMMER IS REAL

Only summer is real and this
light that levels you all.
And may each for himself find
the evergreen tree, for the cone of shadow,
the lustral waters—
and may the cobweb woven of tedium
over the treacherous ponds remain
a rainbow shroud. Down there
is the shifting hedge, a halo
of red dust,
but like a dirge the intoning of German
stragglers for the lost force.

Each leaf is mute
the shell of oblivion tight
the circle perfect.

St. Cloud, August 1944
TRANSLATED BY *Sonia Raiziss*

TO A CHILDHOOD CHUM

I

There's not much more to say—
and time and again the same landscape.
Nothing is left but to roam it, yelling
futile secrets between us in the wind
believing them the whole
truth and pageantry of life.
               "But you have your glory . . ."
                    "Gibberings
in the gloomy wind, the piety
of death: years passing
such as they are, the hill inflamed with fall,
bell towers
sunlit and calm,
the stony bones of the dead, our roots
too close and too far back
for grieving apart when that wind
afflicts them . . ."

Soon a highway will run some other
wind through these ecstatic names—Creva
Germignaga Voldomino
Trebedora—they'll rally
with a changed sound and meaning
in a boast of light . . .
Not that beauty is this,
               but
the clean cut of the whiplash, the imperative
gesture
toward the anger twisting absurdly in us,
knowing that beauty is always
a step beyond in the pungent air:
this,
which the profligate dimly seek
and I've worked hard to learn.

II

Goodby the trees keep harping.
It's my turn now to tell you goodby
with the same fondness
and fervor, the same humility of trees
though they'll go on muttering
time out of mind out of sight.
Seems no one's at the bridge
I'll soon be crossing: not that fellow
with a mask of nonentity, not one rueful traveler.
So the way's clear, and I'm done with visions!
In the Sunday confusion
at the river's mouth they scuffle in me
for my own good . . .

TRANSLATED BY *Sonia Raiziss*

DAVID MARIA TUROLDO (1916–) The poet-priest
David Maria Turoldo was born in a rustic environment at
Coderno del Friuli. He dedicated himself to the religious life
from the age of twenty and entered the Order of the Servi
four years later. A degree in philosophy entitled him to teach
his subject at the Catholic University in Urbino and later in
Florence. During the painful time of the *dopoguerra* he published the book that projected him into the small company
of forceful poets then beginning to flourish.

Both the poet and the person win you at once and wrap you
in spiritual and creature warmth. There is nothing either
severe or smug in this man's love for living things, for the
earth itself. The soil mixes with his compassionate dry tears
for every anguish—of man, animal, or his God. And his almost laic sympathies with his themes and material, expressive
in his sensuous uninhibited imagery, have placed him in an
equivocal position between the secular and the religious, both
at less ease than he is. But whereas, he says, "his religious
experience is lived in the fullness of humanity," by the same
token his natural and historical sensibilities are to be seen
in a "supernatural perspective." The gentleness nerved with
the vigors of his life, as of his poetry, have been gathered
into a film telling the story of the humble Friulani who suffered hard in the world crisis of the 1930's.

BIBLIOGRAPHY

Io non ho mani. Milan: Bompiani, 1948.
Udii una voce. Milan: Mondadori, 1952.
Gli occhi miei lo vedranno. Milan: Mondadori, 1955.
Se tu non riappari. Milan: Mondadori, 1963.

❊ ❊ ❊

THE SECRET OF CAIN

Now I am
a man without mystery.
Already
in the first burnt noon
I saw the face of God.

Now I am
absolute emptiness:
a frightful evening desert
with nothing but the bitter joy
of meeting myself
no more.

Now night hangs heavy over me
but I still walk vigorously
only to leave tracks
on the burning dune;
and have them say, "Even beyond there
he went exploring . . ."

Oh! if I had stayed
with the beasts I love most
to plow the fields, and then tired,
to sleep sound on any heap of stones,
would this
perhaps
have contented me?

Tortures of my heart
set me on my shepherd brother,
to pity him;
the voluptuous pity of testing
what it was to kill; then
to run away
from the tortures of God.

I didn't kill
to be alone (my solitude
is the putrid seething of a rivermouth
clogged by the filth
of rotten seaweed).

Howling
to drown the absurd silence
that dogged me
I fled the woods
to build cities.

I didn't kill
from envy of God:
holding out to Him the first fruits,
stubbornly
I hid my face.

Nor that I might see
beast leap at beast; I remember
all was still calm,
immersed in deep peace
like a sleeping virgin.
The world
still wore
an innocent smile.

Suddenly my veins
turned black, a mysterious being
danced in me.
The unbearable balance at last
was shattered. The silence
of the soul's life shattered
at last
by Cain.

And from that moment
my own hands dug my ditch
but I did not die:
in there the immense roar
of all those memories tracks me.
Now I seek the infinite silence
and I wait to be hurled in
by someone.

TRANSLATED BY *Margo and Anthony Viscusi*

WINDY DAY

I have no pity
for this naked heart of mine;

just as one windy day
a tree was beating the glass
with insane arms
the sea was one huge sob;

and there on the shore
foam-covered stones
were scarcely breathing,
and there was wreckage
of boats and branches
and a shoe tossed among pebbles
and the tatter of a dress;

and I from my cell window
watched laughing.

TRANSLATED BY *Margo and Anthony Viscusi*

LOVE AND DEATH

But when I pass from death into life,
I already know I'll agree with you, Lord.
And this sea of days
will be as a speck in my memory.
Then I shall understand
how beautiful were the psalms at evening;
and the dew that unseen you scattered
on meadows with delicate hands at night.
I shall remember the lichen
that one day you spread
over the crumbling wall of the convent:
then I shall see it as a gigantic tree
covering the ruins. Then I shall hear again
the sweetness of morning bells
that awakened such melancholy in me
at every encounter with the light.
Then I shall know with what patience
you waited for me; and with what love
you prepared me for marriage.
And death refused to take me.
I wept from my loneliness
but you fed on it.
Never did my heart intone a song of joy,
dazed by the fragrance of things created.
Every voice of love was a sob. Instead
it was You I smelled in my flesh,
You hidden in every desire,
O Infinite, who weighed on my embraces.
The same quiver, or storm, on the surface
of the sea as within the waves of the chalice.
You were everywhere. And while the kisses of others
stopped at the mouth,
I ate You at every dawn.
And why then, why then
was I so sad?

TRANSLATED BY *Margo and Anthony Viscusi*

PIER PAOLO PASOLINI (1922–) As the son of a career officer, Pier Paolo Pasolini, born in Bologna, had the vivid experience in early life of knowing many towns and the sounds of their dialects—serviceable to his earthy public sympathies and neorealistic work. There was room and time for him to acquire a degree in letters. Critic, novelist, philologist, at one time a teacher, he has now become a director of offbeat movies picturing the squalor of Roman suburbs.

One of these films, *The Beggar,* suggests the major concern of his writings: the social ills and interests of life. At twenty he began with a little volume of verse in the speech of his mother's town, in Friuli. After several other books in dialect, interspersed with more standard poetry and after the furor stirred up by his novel, *Children of Life,* flavored with Roman localisms, Pasolini produced his distinctive book of poems, *Gramsci's Ashes.* Here he speaks a social and political language discharging the excited lava of living history. There is all the rush of passion in his diction, but held within the line's long rhythmic breath, the stanza's unobtrusive compromise between an established form and the casual flow of prose.

BIBLIOGRAPHY

Poesie a Casarsa. Bologna: 1942.
I diarii. Casarsa, 1945.
I pianti. Casarsa, 1946.
La meglio gioventù. Florence: Sansoni, 1954.
Le ceneri di Gramsci. Milan: Garzanti, 1957.
L'vsignuolo della Chiesa Cattolica. Milan: Longanesi, 1958.
La religione del mio tempo. Milan: Garzanti, 1961.

❊ ❊ ❊

From LAMENT OF THE POWER SHOVEL

II

Poor as a cat in the Colosseum,
I lived in the outskirts all lime
and dust, far from the city

and countryside, squashed every day
in a death-rattling bus;
and each going and returning

was a calvary of sweat and anxiety:
long walks in a hot thick fog,
long twilights in front of the papers

heaped up on the table, through muddy
streets, low walls, little houses wet with lime,
lacking fixtures, with curtains for doors.

The olive-vendor and the ragpicker
would pass by, from some other slum
(their dusty merchandise

looking like stolen goods) and the cruel faces
of boys grown old among the vices
of whoever has a hard hungry mother.

Renewed, as I was, by a new world, freed,
a flame, an indescribable breath
gave a sense of serene pity

to the dirty and humble,
confused and immense reality
teeming on the southern fringe.

A soul within me not entirely mine,
a little soul in that reckless world,
grew up, nourished by the joy

of whoever loved, even if not loved in return.
Everything was lighted by this love
perhaps still heroically young,

yet matured by the experience
born at the feet of history.
I was at the center of that world

of sad bedouin slums
and yellow grasslands rubbed
by an always querulous wind

that would blow from the hot sea at Fiumicino,
or from the plain, where the city
disappears among hovels, a world

that the Penitentiary alone could dominate:
square yellowish specter
in the yellowish haze,

pierced by thousands of similar rows
of barred windows,
among old fields and drowsy farmhouses.

Waste paper and dust
the blind breeze dragged here and there;
impoverished, echoless voices

of womenfolk come from the Sabine
Mountains or the Adriatic
to camp here with swarms

of worn-out, tough, strident kids
in ragged undershirts
and grey threadbare trousers;

African suns and agitated rains
that turned streets to muddy torrents,
buses sunken in corners

at the end-of-the-line, between
the last stripe of white grass
and some acid, ardent trash heap—

this was the center of the world
just as the center of my story
is the love I bore it;

and because of a maturity
still love, since newly born,
everything was about to be clear,

in fact, *was* clear! That slum naked in the wind,
neither Roman nor southern
nor working-class, was life

in its most actual light:
life, light of life, full
of a chaos not yet proletarian

(as it's called in crude newspapers
of the Cell, or the latest
fluttering of pulp sheets)

but essential bone of daily existence,
pure in its being almost too near,
absolute in its being

almost too miserably human.

TRANSLATED BY *Lynne Lawner*

From THE BEAUTIFUL FLAGS

The dreams of morning: when
already the sun reigns
in a ripeness
which only the pushcart vendor knows,
who for hours now has walked the streets,
a sick man's beard
hung on the wrinkles of his washed-out youth:
when the sun reigns
over the green kingdoms already hot, on exhausted
awnings, on crowds
whose clothes already taste faintly of misery
—and already hundreds of trams have gone and come back
on the avenue tracks which encircle the city,
inexpressibly perfumed,

the dreams of 10 o'clock in the morning,
in the sleeper, alone,
like a pilgrim on his pallet,
an unknown corpse
—Greek characters appearing in brilliance,
and, in the simple holiness of two or three syllables,
full, precisely, of the whiteness of the triumphant sun—
they divine a reality,
ripened in the depths and now already fully ripe, like the
    sun,
to be enjoyed, or to give fear.

And, meanwhile, I am alone.
Lost in the past.
(Because man has one period, only, in his life.)

Suddenly, my friends, the poets,
who share with me the ugly whiteness
of these 60s,
men and women, just a little older,
or a little younger—are there, in the sun.

I haven't been able to have the grace
to hold them close to me—in the shadow of a life
which unfolds too attached
to the rooted sloth in my soul.

The whole world is my unburied body.
Atoll crumbled
by the blue-grained blows of the sea.

What to do if not, during the vigil, to have dignity?
The hour of exile has come,
perhaps: the hour in which an ancient would have given reality
to reality,
and the loneliness which had grown around him
would have had the form of loneliness.

And I, instead—as in the dream—
persist in giving myself illusions, painful,
like an earth-worm paralyzed by incomprehensible forces:
"no! no! it's only a dream!

reality
is outside, in the sun, triumphant
in the avenues and empty coffee houses,
in the extreme aphony of 10 o'clock,
a day like all the others, with its cross!"

My friend with the pope's chin, my friend
with the chestnut eyes . . .
my dear friends from the north
rooted in elective affinities, sweet as life,
—they are there, in the sun.

Even Elsa, with her blond sorrow,
she—wounded steed, fallen,
bleeding—is there.

Like a wife stretched out on the funeral pyre with a king,
or buried with him
in a tomb which sails away like a little boat
toward the millenniums—the faith of the 50s
is here with me, already lightly beyond the limits of time, crumbling also
from the raging patience of the blue-grained sea.

And . . .
my loves, purest sensuality,
repeated in the sacred valleys of lust,
sadistic, masochistic, the pants
with their warm sack
wherein a man's destiny is marked
—these are acts which I discharge only
in the middle of a sea stupendously convulsed.

Slowly, the thousands of sacred gestures,
the hand on the warm swelling,
kisses, each time on a different mouth,
always more virginal,
always closer to the enchantment of the species,
to the standard which makes of sons tender fathers,
slowly,
they have become monuments of stone
which by the thousands crowd my loneliness.

Thus I awake,
one more time:
and I dress, and I sit at the desk to work.
The sun's light already is riper,
the pushcart vendor already further away,
sharper, in the markets of the world, the luke-warmth of
    greens,
along avenues of inexpressible perfume,
on the shores of the sea, at the feet of volcanoes.
All the world is at work, in its future.

But that "white" something
which came to me
in Greek letters, irrevocable, the knowing dream,
stays with me—dressed,
at the work table.
Marble, wax or lime
on the eyelids, at the corners of the eyes:
the whiteness, radiantly romanesque,
desperately-lost baroque, of sun while in sleep.

The true sun was of that whiteness,
the factory walls were of that whiteness . . .

On those walls, in those streets,
dense with a strange perfume,
where apples, where cherries flowered red
in the tepid air: and their red color
had a burnishing, as if
it had been immersed in the hot air of a storm,
a red almost brown, cherries like plums,
apples like plums, which swivel-eyed,
among the darks, the intense
conspiracies of the foliage, calm, as though spring
was not in any hurry,

and wished to enjoy that luke-warmth in which the world
    breathed,
burning, in the old hope, for a new hope.

And, over everything, the flapping,
the modest, lazy flapping
of the red flags. God! the beautiful flags
of the 40s!
Fluttering one upon the other, in a crowd of wretched
cloth, reddening, a true red,
which shone with the dazzling misery
of silk bed spreads, of the wash of workmen's families,
—and with the fire of cherries, of apples, violet
in the dampness, sanguine in the little sunlight which struck
    it,
burning red, jumbled and quivering,
in the heroic tenderness of an immortal season!

TRANSLATED BY *Charles Wright*

BARTOLO CATTAFI (1922–) Born in Sicilian Barcellona, Bartolo Cattafi had a classical education and took a law degree but never practiced. In the years that followed he has gone from country to country in Africa and Europe, from one occupation to another, at times trying publicity and freelance journalism. His restiveness and predilection for the roving life at home and in countries of his choice (such as England, Ireland, Spain) have produced poems topically and geographically oriented as well as symptomatic of the tense human predicament today.

This temperament is reflected in the prolific invention of images which sometimes jostle each other in enigmatic charged contacts. A mordant outlook on the adventure of life sees through nostalgias of place and time. What might have been generalized allusions contract into acute nervous metaphors, actual in reference, arresting in their aptness. His analogical method is even more penetrating and centripetal in his latest book. His name counts now among the best of two poetic generations.

BIBLIOGRAPHY

Nel centro della mano. Milan: La Meridiana, 1951.
Partenza da Greenwich. Milan: La Meridiana, 1955.
Le mosche del meriggio. Milan: Mondadori, 1958.
Qualcosa di preciso. Milan: Scheiwiller, 1961.
L'osso l'anima. Milan: Mondadori, 1964.

❊   ❊   ❊

THE AGAVE

Forsake the sands of Sicily, the music and honey
of Arabs and Hellenes,
break the sweet ties, this drowsy
milk of roots,
go down to the sea, somnolent queen
green beast with arms of sorrow
like one ready for the crossing; in the great
cities, in the snows, in the wood, in the desert
there are caravans walking on forever;

travel along with the cold
soul of seagulls
with the sprouting heart with the pregnant fish
that enrich the farthest net
and the most slow hand of God
that came winging from a nest of fog.

TRANSLATED BY *Glauco Cambon*

DIEPPE, JULY

I can imagine what winter cold
behind the rainy panes of the bistro,
the Channel roaring on France,
a fringe of wool round round
your bed . . .
The black ship boils, all set
in the sun and in its smoke, a prelude
to Newhaven, England.
By now a shadow insistent at my temples
with the ultimate tinkling of jewelry
with a sound of memory, and you enter,
you take your place beside
the old thoughts to be borne
in the midst of future years,

you are what
the heart loses at the threshold
of the sea, in farewell,
and again a sign meeting me on the course
a feather afloat on the sea, a leaf
of the felicitous tree
that all the lookouts miss
hoisted as they are, roped
to the somber fleet.

TRANSLATED BY *Glauco Cambon*

SAILING FROM GREENWICH

One always sails from Greenwich
from the zero marked on every map and in this
gray mild color of England.
Bag and baggage, all the bright
hopes of youth at the prow,
disdaining the tabulated numbers

the calculations that click smooth
like doorlocks loosened by
harmonious oil, in a precise
prison.
Too many are prey wandering among
the fires of the Isles, and ships offshore,
full to the brim, portly, made
to be boarded by the crew
that swarmed to the Tropics
under a pledge to capture
the fierce and difficult dreams.
And seaweed, whitecaps,
the blue background where
the gull of memory goes fishing
set beside the gray
dilated color
of the eyes, the heart, the mind,
austral bird-dung for the surviving
seeds of the world.

TRANSLATED BY *Glauco Cambon*

WINGSPAN

What about wingspan?
It varies; it can be
microns, inches, yards wide.
Depends on the model, on materials, on
motor power; the aim, to attain altitude.

Folded, shut away, discarded
under the greenest wreath, a meal
in Eden for the lucky maggots;
or else with wreckage under the ice, royal
bones, mammoths, dead flies
deep in the amber of time.
We walked longer than we could,
often we saw memorized aloft, a sorrowful
white formation of fragments . . . (just
a game, a call for help, an illusion
if fire in a desert scene
catches the victims' skin
if frost clots the dehumanized names).
A pulsing of wings up the vast

walls of memory doesn't save us
from the stalking shadows; the hyena,
the wolf, the abject
angels in devious procession.

TRANSLATED BY *Sonia Raiziss*

SUBLIMATION

Through years and more years,
on the patient ellipse circling the sun
for a handful of reasons
for some love or other which day after day
is drained of red corpuscles,
a slow-burning tree of fire
with white flames, flames under control.
That's how you live,
honoring the seed
which bears fruit, a different kind, in the sky,
the budding of cryptic springtimes.
In the air that consumes and strengthens
you are trained for austere altitudes.
You raise statues to the greatness
of Lavoisier.

TRANSLATED BY *Sonia Raiziss*

A THING OF PRECISION

A powerful contour
spare, handsome, on the trigger,
something precise
made of steel or whatever else
might show icy lights.
And there, on the thread of the machine, the outrage
of the puniest rusty star
that darkens the more it gnaws and corrupts.
A point to clear up—man's
blood, a wretched crumb or an everlasting
clot, a block of courage.

TRANSLATED BY *Sonia Raiziss*

ROCCO SCOTELLARO (1923–1953) Rocco Scotellaro passed too quickly through the very heart of one of Italy's ugliest and most controversial periods. He had scarcely time to live deeply or develop diversity in substance and style. His sympathies from the start embraced the economically and socially dispossessed. In *"Sempre nuova è l'alba"* and *"Pozzanghera"* he wrote poetic manifestoes of the peasant movement, with something of the expected oversimplification but with much downright warmth and poignance. He took an active part in the fortunes of his native southern region, Lucania, and of his hometown, Tricarico, whose youthful mayor he became at twenty-three. His "hard experiences culminated in 1950 in a prison term for political reasons . . . and his liberation as well as exile in Naples" (Carlo Levi).

If Scotellaro's poetry, contained in one volume edited and introduced by Levi, and a winner of the Viareggio prize, is ostensibly proletarian, it is also essentially the poetry of the plain people who belong to the old culture of the south. His poems are not generally hard-fisted, but are modest deeply cut prints of the humble life. In him, rebellion is resolved in a wider acceptance of man's fate.

BIBLIOGRAPHY

É fatto giorno. Milan: Mondadori, 1954.

❋ ❋ ❋

A PORTRAIT ALL FEET

In the cave at the alley's end
they sit around the old woman, dead.
They have tied together the toes
of her shoes with their oil-cloth soles.
You can see the face distant on the pillow
the belly swollen with camomile.
It is a portrait all feet
from this doorway where there is dancing.

TRANSLATED BY *William Weaver*

TO THE CARTER'S DAUGHTER

I can live near you no longer
someone binds the voice in my chest
you are the carter's daughter
who take the breath from my mouth.
Because below us in the stall
the mules move in their sleep
because your father snores near us
and does not go yet, high on his cart
to chase off the stars with his whip.

TRANSLATED BY *William Weaver*

TO HIS FIANCÉE, FOR EASTER

The day will come to ripeness, Isabella.
You will yet hear the tree toads beating out
the time, concealed among the violets.
And if you'll see that I am not alone
when the air takes on the color of the squall
and the kestrels clash and mingle in affray
and only tongues of defiled angels sing
the passion of our Lord, why then with all
the longing I can't tell for all I try,
together we may hope to live and die.

TRANSLATED BY *Thomas G. Bergin*

MALLOW-WARM

There is left the fragrance
of your flesh in my bed.
It has a warmth like the mallow
that we store up to dry
against the ills of winter.

TRANSLATED BY *Thomas G. Bergin*

THE ADIGE ROARS

Have you noticed how over the Trentine Mountains
the wind plays its thieving games
on men as they quietly talk
under the bell towers?
The streets are lacerated wounds.

The Adige comes roaring this side of the barrier.
This is the foreign land
of the friars in white,
the high peaks of snow.
Here melancholy may die of fatigue
since here I have lost myself and my cry
freezes to ice in the cage of the chair-lift.

                    TRANSLATED BY *Thomas G. Bergin*

DIRTY PUDDLE, APRIL 18TH

Dazzling papers and dirty puddles.
They've painted the moon
on our walls that flake plaster!
The bosses dished out food
that day, we were all brothers,
as on holy festivals
we had a fire and a band.
But it's all over, it's over
this other hot festival
we're alone here to cry over our lives
we're alone in the storm.

And if death smothers us
no one will be with us,
and if we're sick and down on our luck
no one will be with us.
They've barred the gates to us,
the ravines are thrown wide open.
Today and two thousand years from now
we'll still wear the same clothes.
We'll still be the mob
the mob of beggars,
who rip the masks off the bosses
with our teeth.

                    TRANSLATED BY *Charles Guenther*

THE DAWN IS ALWAYS NEW

Never again cry inside me,
don't blow your warm breath
in my heart, my people.

Let's drink a full cup of wine together,
so our desperate wind may quiet down
in the evening's good time.

Outlaws' heads still crop up
on poles, and the cave,
that green oasis of hope,
keeps a neat stone pillow.

But we don't turn back in our trails.
Other wings will take flight
from the straws of the nest,
for along the perishing of the ages
the dawn is new, is new.

TRANSLATED BY *Charles Guenther*

LUCIANO ERBA (1922–) Luciano Erba was born in Milan, where he has lived most of his life except for two signal absences: when like many other dissidents during the German occupation he moved to Switzerland (1943–1945), and when he spent two years in Paris (1948–1950) between his baccalaureate and his appointment at the Catholic University of Milan to teach French literature. His special interests are the baroque period, on which he has published research studies, and the lyric poetry of chivalry. He is presently teaching at the University of Washington.

Erba's poetry has an evocative quality not consonant with his detached expository manner. Or perhaps this technique of understatement plays tricks. An emotional theme—an intimately disquieting recollection, for instance—is delivered casually or cryptically. The effect in reverse is of something drawn from far back of the ordinary experience. Sober meanings are respected but exercised through irony; an irony less crepuscular or metaphysical than profoundly artful in the best sense—used by a tender mind to guard its vulnerable side. The feelings that balance on the line of his words leave a subtle, slight malaise concerning the spirit in a worldly situation.

BIBLIOGRAPHY

Il male minore. Milan: Mondadori, 1960.
Lineak. Modena: Guanda, 1951.
Il bel paese. Milan: La Meridiana, 1955.
Il prete di Ratanà. Milan: Scheiwiller, 1959.

THE INATTENTIVE

But when and how will they arrive?
and who will send them among us?
you find them, one day, near at hand
in visored cap, red scarf around the neck,
hands pushed forward in trouser pockets—
new companions for our games,
mute but smiling playmates
smaller than ourselves, and paler,

tired out after a short run, clumsy
at wrestling and jumping, weightless.
I remember one on an October morning
climbed with me up to Horse Mountain,
his cheeks were red with pain around the heart,
he smiled, running to keep up with us.
And another, or perhaps the same, I can't say,
knowing that way they all have of walking and
the blue sweaters they wear:
he followed me through vineyards to the valley
of trout streams—where the river
branches in bright channels.
Till evening we stayed in the water
and he never once asked me to try
fishing; then he disappeared
by a path I could never find now.
And a third—or again the same one,
going by that big knot in the woolen scarf
and the way he stood beside me, silent,
in the yellow meadows outside town—
imaginary Africa—
one motionless long day.

                      And a fourth . . .
All gone. Destroyed by pitiless fevers,
consumed by an unknown ill, and far away.
I don't know. Nor do I know
if they will come again, nor when, nor how—
the friends, the days, the bright season,
if life lost by inattention
will come again.

              TRANSLATED BY *Robert Fitzgerald*

LAND AND SEA

Schooner, most gracious craft, O swift
prodigy! if the heart only
knew how to sail as you do
among the azure island chains!

But I go back to my house above the harbor
around six, when my Lenormant
pushes an armchair forward on the terrace
and settles down to her embroidery—
new napery for the altars.

Blue seafaring, days of summer,
evenings behind a curtain coarsely knit
just like a net! Full-rigged ship models
among seashell reefs, in bottles,
and the reading of Giordano Bruno
in the rush-lined parlor, *nominatim*
Concerning the First Cause and the One!

TRANSLATED BY Robert Fitzgerald

LOMBARD-VENETIAN

The women
who come down to county capitals
to be maids in riverside inns
(the river green, running among stones
under long wooden balconies),
and who were once as clever as priests
in going in search of mushrooms
with secret step over the mountain,
now dust the purple and yellow panes
on a veranda, roebuck-heads,
and card tables in a vestibule.
Hearing dogs bark last night
made them suspect a starry sky;
at dawn they were already running a bath
for some salesman, smoke from chestnut-wood
filling the attic:
how they laughed! what a foresty smell there was!
And once I read in a newspaper
that the women in these parts
are victims of the Industrial Revolution.

TRANSLATED BY Lynne Lawner

SUPER FLUMINA

I will see years, faces, and countries
circling in step to a dance,
if I ever have a velvet jacket,
a pipe of clay,
and red wine from my own land,
if I have a tower, and apples in the drawers.

That day I will be "a friend of the people."
But today is a time of necessary triangulations.

We leave for a Sunday ride on the river
and, once the suburbs are out of sight,
climb the whole of an inclined plain
of roads and clouded-over country,
take a step onto the first high borders
surrounded by an impetuous flood,
which shatters the rock and overwhelms it,
or splinters it to ashes at the river-bends.

The women bathers beached in gravel
wear flowered suits; exiled couples
come and go through deeper ruins
among whitened, fruitless thorns.
Sisters keep on emptying a leaking
boat, but the ferry stays put
over there. Here's a goodhearted guy
scaling to the naked ledge,
slowed up by a lunch basket
and a golden-sandaled partner—
another futile adventure if he climbs up
alone among the brambles, peers down, goes.

I wish he wouldn't try again, that the boat
of counterdanaïdes would go away,
and a broken Ixion lie no more
in the cog-wheeled shadow of a dredge.
I wish there were no Tartarean tortures
on the banks of the Adda on a holiday,
but this is a time of inevitable triangulations.

Now, one who is king of neither quail nor partridge
rises, grey-feathered, from the deep
on tardy wings, his flight
saturated with antique blood: thus he flies
above the hump of each bald hill.
Three Chinese hunters
have already aimed long rifles:
is there no one who understands
that ignorance is a minor evil
for the faithful subjects of the emperor?

TRANSLATED BY *Lynne Lawner*

GIORGIO ORELLI (1921–) Giorgio Orelli belongs of course to Italian poetry, although he was born in the Swiss canton of Ticino and has been teaching since 1945 in the secondary school of Bellinzona, Switzerland. His studies, pursued at the University of Fribourg, were interrupted by military service; and of this time he remembers the warmth of the friendships he made with Italian refugees, like the critics Giansiro Ferrata and Dante Isella. *"Professore di frontiera,"* Orelli guards his Italianism, moreover, by writing critiques for Italian as well as Swiss reviews and newspapers.

With the appearance of his first verses (1944), Orelli's books have attracted prizes: the Lugano for *Né bianco, né viola,* the Città di Firenze for *Nel cerchio familiare,* the Libera Stampa for a book of short stories. His poetry regards life, and death too, almost as vignettes: a ghost of the ancestral, a rural street, animal agony, Christmas in wartime. These closecut and edgy views are worked with the delicate sharpness of certain precious stones. The poems in a given volume seem related through theme or attitude—as if strung on a moodily glittering bracelet.

BIBLIOGRAPHY

Né bianco, né viola. Lugano: La Collana di Lugano, 1944.
Poesie. Milan: Meridiana, 1953.
Nel cerchio familiare. Milan: Scheiwiller, 1960.
L'ora del tempo. Milan: Mondadori, 1962.

❈ ❈ ❈

SUMMER

Once-ignored swallows
confidently play, then swiftly flee.
Over there in the apple tree their cries descend
in a gentle shell down to where grass
surrenders to the neat swing of the sickle,
and slows up, greener.
It might rain and it might not. There's no anxiety
in the farmers' toil, only hope stretched taut
as a saw, when a trunk is felled.

The oldest woman exits
with her cat from the house, runs her hands over her face,
gazes deeply at meadows and hills,
then strays into the orchard to caress radiant
peonies and weigh them in her hand;
while doing the washing in cold clear water,
a little maid lights up
love's kisses in her songs and,
after crying, is happier than before.

Few in number, a shepherd
counts us every evening at the usual turning
of the road,
touching each back with his stick.
Separated birds chirp,
then vault beyond the limits of our day,
leaving an emptiness, where the mind inscribes
the slow eagle who signals the end
of another summer and another year.

                              TRANSLATED BY *Lynne Lawner*

FOR A FRIEND ABOUT TO BE MARRIED

Tonight I want you to remember Isolde
clinging to Tristram on a scooter
between Tuscany and Emilia
                              (we had left
behind a yelping storm at sea,
and, used as we were to fir trees, the light
                    from wind-struck olives ravished us), Isolde
gently poised, suspended, the heels
of her tiny feet submissive
as if she were a rung higher than a merry-go-round;
then hail through hazel trees and beloved locusts,
snow revealing some green along the way.
But the world changed before long,
a new wind blew up and showed us
the sun's passing;
and in the darkening air, in land already Lombard,
on the bridge above us as we arrowed past, we saw
two shadows embraced against the sky.

                              TRANSLATED BY *Lynne Lawner*

CHRISTMAS 1944

quare rubicunda sunt vestimenta Tua (Isaiah)

You were born. Were your clothes red?

But here the snow conserves no trace
of the blood You spilled, nor of any blood
spilled by men.
And the angel-hair glitters
on the evergreen foliage;
aged birds of glass
and bewildered bells tremble;
if a child touches them, they give forth a sound
fainter than infancy.

As I turn back to look, night falls
like so many other nights uselessly
luminous in the vast embrace of the moon.

TRANSLATED BY *Lynne Lawner*

THE CENTIPEDE

Where only once you passed,
and the brunette light of your eyes
struck me in my absentmindedness,
a kind of anticipated joy
explodes, disperses.
Or maybe it's only a case of light
and there's nothing new,
except the grass that fumes and shouts
and the red-bellied centipede
moving its legs wildly in the blue.

TRANSLATED BY *Lynne Lawner*

IN THE FAMILY CIRCLE

An extinguished funereal light
frosts once more the fir trees
whose bark survives past death;
and everything is still in this shell
dug sweetly from time,
in the family circle
from which it is senseless to escape.

Within a silence known so well,
the dead are livelier than the living:
they descend from neat rooms smelling
of camphor, through trapdoors into heated
wood-lined cubicles,
adjust their own portraits,
then return to the stables to view again the heads
of a pure dark breed.

But

without a mole's tools or umbrellas
to ensnare swallows, after what carillon
have you boys run through numbed meadows,
neither cautious nor forgetful in your pursuits?

The whetstone is in its horn.
The henroost leans against its elder tree.
The spiders have been entangled
a long time on the church walls.
The fountain keeps itself company with water.
And I am restored
to a more discreet love of life.

TRANSLATED BY *Lynne Lawner*

LUCIO PICCOLO (1903–)   Lucio Piccolo di Calanovella remained unpublished until late in life, like his cousin the Prince of Lampedusa, author of *The Leopard*. Like him, too, he belongs to a vanishing breed, the nobleman of complete culture. A taciturn "cosmopolitan gran signore and country gentleman," he lives and writes in the solitude of his estate at Capo d'Orlando, Messina, in the Sicily where he was born.

With his first plaquette of *9 Poems,* privately printed on poor paper, Piccolo sent a letter to Montale, saying it was his intention "to evoke and fix a particular Sicilian world—now about to disappear—that world of baroque churches, of old convents, of the souls proper to these places. . . ." This remote Greco-like figure, presented by Montale in 1956, is "an accomplished musician, a student of philosophy . . . a reader of Hopkins and Yeats, whose esoteric inclinations he shares." His afflatus reminded Montale of "the better pages of Dino Campana . . . of those Welsh poets, of Dylan Thomas—who seemed to draw out of the very pit a primordial speech. . . ." But Piccolo is an original, and any inadvertent echoes of voices past or present are transmuted into his own extravagant harmony of "a modern polytonal composer."

BIBLIOGRAPHY

Canti barocchi e altre liriche. Milan: Mondadori, 1956.
Gioco a nascondere e canti barocchi. Milan: Mondadori, 1960.

✲   ✲   ✲

MUTABLE WORLD

Mutable world of gusty
rays, of hours without color, of perennial
flux, the pomp
of clouds: an instant and look—the changed
forms dazzle, millenniums sway.
     And the low door's arch and the worn
sill of too many winters, are a fable in the abrupt
glory of the March sun.

TRANSLATED BY *Sonia Raiziss and Alfredo de Palchi*

SIROCCO

And over the mountains, away on the horizon
a long saffron streak:
the moorish mob of winds breaks in,
rushes the big doors
the watchers on the glazed roofs,
batters the façades from the south,
convulses the kites, scarlet curtains, bloodred
pennons, opens brief interims of blue domes,
imagined forms, startles the arbors, the blazing
tiles where springwater rests in pearly jugs,
burns the buds, turns shoots into sticks,
makes trumpets of tree aisles,
swoops on the timid beginnings
of gardens, claws forsaken leaves
and infant jasmines—then grows milder
taps small drums; tassels, ribbons . . .

But when in the west the wild pontifical
closes its flaming margins and the last
channel of rust flakes off, on all
sides the hot night rises from ambush.

TRANSLATED BY *Sonia Raiziss and Alfredo de Palchi*

From VENERIS VENEFICA AGRESTIS

She springs from the crouching bushes, her face
—exultant, surly—pinched in a black kerchief
looks like a dried chestnut, her straggling
hair is no soft fleece
but a goat's tangle; when she goes by
(who knows if straight or stooped) her dark gnarled foot
is a root that suddenly thrusts from the ground and walks.
  Mind she doesn't hand you a gourd
with water tasting of roots, sticky leaves,
or blackberry, or sorb apple, a woody fruit that tempts
the mouth but binds the tongue.
  She governs it seems
the pull of dilating moons
that swells tree bark and alternates
the invincible yeasts
flood tides, the rising of sap . . .
  Pronubial like the birds

bringing distant seeds
she bears mysterious grafts . . .
        TRANSLATED BY *Sonia Raiziss and Alfredo de Palchi*

THE SUNDIAL

Behold water the inscrutable:
                buttress, tower, throne of
granite, branch plume wing pupil
everything loosened, splintered, multiplied;
                in the eager flexion
what once was stone, a massed bulwark,
is a vain whirlpool passing, a rainbow flicker, a gurgle
dispelled with the leaf's adventure;
it dreams of spaces . . . and where it reaches, soft and brilliant,
is but an infinite fracture of drops, a transit of bubbles.
        Behold water the inscrutable:
                the Universe slips at its touch.
And when the lamp goes out and each
thought drowns weightless in darkness,
you hear it run agile and deep
humming back of your dream.

    In the brimmed hour, in the noonday streets
(where the shadow is, at the blackened masks
at the eaves the sea air ruffles the grasses)
the fountains answer,
from the nearby courtyard (nighttime left
on the sweating walls its stucco of salts,
constellations scattered by sunbeams),
from the roof gardens where greenness anchors
arches of crystal hover and meet
in the charmed breath of the squares
over the horses of frosted foam,
vaults of glittering sound surge up
that an instant shatters and repairs
—the tender octopus, the liquid flower emerges, eludes
the silence and clears a corridor between singing and dozing;
solitudes open, zones of transparence,
and the leaning cane at the bench, reposes
and the reverie ascends . . .

    The shadow of the roadbridge pulses
on the simmering pavement.

Now level now steady, you see yourself blissfully mirrored
in the high gallery wall—neat as a sail—in the loggia,
and the gallery, the dome, the gable that strains
taller, are washed in the sun's wind;
the sky seeps through the worn rafters,
the stairway climbing to the cell: it makes of the eyeholes
of the riddled walls, of the arches—blue glances,
and the saddle horses rest in the mown hay;
exuberance of calla lilies, banana and wayfaring trees,
on embankments where the mulberry plays
arpeggios of shadow and along the banisters
soft avalanches
of honeysuckle fall,
(behind the iron gate among orange trees
a secret water talks in birdnotes)

 And the mountains, mountains melted in a choral of rays
by the resins, sweet herbs, savage smells . .
. . the sun pitches bristling rings
into jars where water spangles,
and as one sinks another rises,
—harmonica of gold—
the Scales barely swing
almost even.

 The old men wait;
under the domeshape at the circular sign
(in Gemini) the hour flashes an echo of cosmos
and along the hedges of the world
there runs a shuddering splendor,
cracks the cruel spread of heaven;
vibrates, fades, expires,
wind not holding—and silence.

 But if transience is dread
eternity is terror.

TRANSLATED BY *Sonia Raiziss and Alfredo de Palchi*

Russian Poetry

EDITED AND TRANSLATED BY *George Reavey*

✻ ✻ ✻ ✻ ✻

Introduction

The Russian Revolution, when it finally came in its double-edged form in 1917, cut across the cultural scene with little regard for the cultural amenities. It soon became clear that the Revolution would involve a severe and radical break with the cultural past of Russia and certainly with the idealistic outlook of the old Russian intelligentsia. And censorship, far from being abolished, became an organic part of the new regime. The Soviet period of Russian literature may be said to begin in the early twenties. Soviet literature can be roughly divided into three phases: an initial and transitional phase up to 1932; the Stalinist phase of literary dictatorship or Socialist Realism up to 1953; and the post-Stalinist phase of somewhat insecure and tentative liberalism up to 1965. On February 21, 1965, a new policy seems to have been proclaimed in *Pravda*—a policy which affirmed that "genuine creativeness is possible only through search, experimentation, free expression and clashes of viewpoints." It is obviously too early to be able to judge the practical effects of this new policy, which would appear at last to give up the principle of literary dictatorship that in some ways had survived the demise of Stalin. Some of the poets of the third phase, such as Martynov, Yevtushenko and Voznesensky, had already gone about their work in the past decade very much in the spirit of February, 1965, though they had often been the targets of the Stalinist type critics. However, most of the poets of the preceding generation had to suffer gravely from the handicaps imposed upon them by arbitrary critics and the frequent purges of the 1930's and 1940's.

The Revolution had come in the middle of what can be described as a poetic revival, which had begun with the symbolist poets at the turn of the century. The symbolist movement was already past its zenith in 1917, and it may be said to die out with Alexander Blok in 1921. In *The Twelve* and *The Scythians,* both written in the cruel and critical year of 1918, Blok succeeded not only in bidding farewell to old Russia, but also in contributing to the beginning of a new epoch. But symbolism was not the only aspect of the poetic revival. There were other poets who had grouped themselves around other poetic theories and movements.

As from 1912 Mayakovsky had become the leader of the Russian Futurists. Poets such as Anna Akhmatova and Osip Mandelshtam rallied to the standpoint of Acmeism, which stressed craft and concrete experience as against the mystical experience and the vague musicality of the symbolist poets. Even Yesenin had promulgated a poetic theory of his own in Imaginism. However, the effect of the Revolution in the 1920's was to bring to an end the interplay of "isms" and to make these poets individually face each in his own way the consequences of the Revolution, which had the effect of gradually stamping out the lyrical impulse. By the middle 1930's very little remained of the lyrical revival. If there was some renewal of the lyrical impulse during the war, it was soon arrested after Zhdanov's savage attack in 1946 against those surviving lyric poets of the older generation such as Anna Akhmatova and Boris Pasternak. But a lyrical revival did come again. It may be said to coincide with Stalin's death. This lyrical revival had several aspects. On one hand, some of the surviving poets of an older generation, such as Boris Pasternak, Anna Akhmatova, Nikolai Zabolotsky, and even Leonid Martynov, found themselves again in a position to speak out and publish the type of poetry they could not before. On the other hand, a new generation of younger poets— Yevgeny Yevtushenko, Andrey Voznesensky, Victor Bokov, Bella Akhmadulina, and others, emerged in rapid succession and made their voices heard. Yevtushenko was undoubtedly the spearhead of this younger avant-garde group, which proclaimed its intention of speaking the truth about the immediate past and of seeking new poetic forms and absorbing those aspects of the modern world from which they had been cut off as a result of the Stalinist restrictions. It was also clear that neither the older nor the younger poets were to have it all their own way. Their claim to speak the truth at last, as Akhmatova does in *Requiem* and as Yevtushenko does in *Babii Yar,* was bitterly resented in certain quarters. Many a battle was waged and many new restrictions were threatened, but it must be admitted that, in spite of such incidents as the Pasternak-Zhivago affair, Khrushchev's denunciation of the "modern" artists at the December 1963 exhibition in Moscow, the recall of Yevtushenko from Paris in March 1963, and the no-exit policy for the avant-garde poets and artists since then, the new poets seem largely to have stuck to their positions and to have won in the end if we are to take the *Pravda* statement of February 21, 1965, at all seriously. For *Pravda* does say: "Communist criticism must rid itself of the tone of literary command. The party must in every way eradicate attempts at homebred and incompetent administrative interference in literary affairs." This sounds too good to be true, but if it is true it is so largely because of the brave and lyrical fight put up by the younger poets with the support of some of their less compromised elders.

George Reavey

BIBLIOGRAPHY

Alexandrovna, Vera. *History of Soviet Literature: 1917–1962.* New York: Doubleday, 1963.

Blake, Patricia, and Hayward, Max (eds.). *Dissonant Voices in Soviet Literature.* New York: Pantheon, 1962.

Blake, Patricia, and Hayward, Max (eds.). *Half-way to the Moon, New Writing from Russia.* New York: Holt, Rinehart & Winston, 1964; London: Weidenfeld & Nicolson, 1964.

Bowra, C. M. *The Creative Experiment.* London: Macmillan, 1949.

Forgues, Pierre. "The Young Poets," Survey No. 46. London: January 1963.

Muchnic, Helen. *From Gorky to Pasternak.* New York: Random House, 1961.

New Voices in Russian Writing. *Encounter* No. 115, 1963.

Poggioli, Renato. *The Poets of Russia (1890–1930).* Cambridge: Harvard University Press, 1960.

Reavey, George. *Soviet Literature Today.* London: Drummond, 1946; New Haven, Yale University Press, 1947.

Reavey, George, and Slonim, Marc (eds.). *Soviet Literature Anthology.* London: Wishart, 1933; New York: Covici Friede, 1934.

Slonim, Marc. *The Epic of Russian Literature: From its Origin Through Tolstoy.* New York: Oxford University Press, 1964.

Yarmolinsky, Avram (ed.). *An Anthology of Russian Verse 1812–1960.* Revised as *A Treasury of Russian Verse.* New York: Doubleday, 1961.

ALEXANDER BLOK (1880–1921) Alexander Blok, the greatest poet of the Silver Age of Russian poetry, just managed to cross the bridge separating the old from the new Russia. In doing so, he wrote and published in 1918 his memorable *The Twelve* and *The Scythians,* poems which implied a historical acceptance of the Revolution. After that, with his health failing in the trying conditions of those days, his poetic inspiration dwindled. His death may be attributed to criminal negligence and stupidity; he was not granted an exit visa to go abroad in time when his health demanded it. Blok remains, however, the greatest Russian lyrical poet of the twentieth century. In restrospect, he was also a poet of wide critical acumen, who was deeply concerned with problems of culture and civilization, of Russia and its destiny. Poetically, his development as a whole may be compared to that of W. B. Yeats. He progressed from a rather misty interpretation of symbolical forms to a more realistic apprehension of the world.

Alexander Blok represents the best type of poet and intellectual to issue from the background of the Russian gentry and the intelligentsia. On his father's side he came from a gentry family of military men and officials who were descended from a Lutheran German doctor who had immigrated to Russia in the seventeenth century. His father, A. L. Blok (d. 1909), was Professor of Law at the University of Warsaw. His mother, the daughter of Professor A. N. Beketov, a botanist and Rector of the University of St. Petersburg, was a noted translator from the French. The Beketov family was steeped in literary traditions. After Blok's parents had separated, he was brought up by his mother and maternal grandfather, "an idealist of the purest water," on their estate at Shakhmatovo, near Klin in the province of Moscow. By 1906 Blok had completed his studies at the philological faculty of the University of St. Petersburg. Blok was distinctly a product of Petersburg rather than Moscow. He had begun to write poetry in 1897–1898, but his literary career dates from 1901–1902, when he began to emerge as a poet already deeply attracted to the symbolist ethos and the poetry and philosophy of Vladimir Solovyev. In 1905 he published his first book, *Poems About A Beautiful Lady.* From then on, Blok began to assume a dominating position, not only as the poet of the

Silver Age, but also as one of the chief spokesmen for the symbolist movement. However, by 1910 symbolism was in full crisis and, in 1911, Blok started his long poem *Retribution* (1911–1921), which in its historical idea, tone, and style marked a departure from the language of the symbolists. Blok was not striving to grasp the world in its historical and realistic aspects as well. The crisis of symbolism, as well as in Russian life in general, deepened. Blok, as the poet of "the spirit of music," could only foresee threatening disruption and chaos, "the end of humanism." In *The Twelve* he caught the elemental music of mass events, which culminated in the revolutionary turmoil of 1917–1921 and which did, in fact, destroy the illusions of the old world.

It should be added that Blok also tried his hand at lyrical drama, wrote a number of penetrating essays of cultural problems, and left a wealth of diaries and correspondence. Thus, his activity was of major importance in the arena of twentieth-century cultural development.

BIBLIOGRAPHY

In Russian
   Stikhi o Prekrásnoy Damé (Poems About a Beautiful Lady). Moscow, 1905.
   Nechayannaya Radost (Unpremeditated Joy). Moscow, 1907.
   Zemlya v Snegu (Snow-Bound Earth). Moscow, 1908.
   Liricheskie Drami (Lyrical Dramas). Petersburg, 1908.
   Nochniye Chasi. Stikhi 1908–10. (Nocturnal Hours. Poems). Moscow, 1911.
   Sobraniye Stikhotvorenii (Collected Poems). 3 Vols. Moscow, 1911–1912; 1916.
   Theatr (Theater). Moscow, 1916.
   Dvenatzat. Skify. (The Twelve. The Scythians). Petersburg, 1918.
   Rossiya i Intelligentsia (Russia and the Intelligentsia. Seven Essays). Moscow, 1918.
   Sedoye Utro (Gray Morning). Petersburg, 1920.
   Sobranie Sochinenii (Collected Works). 15 Vols. Leningrad, 1932. The latest of a number of new Collected Works was published in Moscow in 1960–63.
In English
   Blok, Alexander. *The Spirit of Music.* London: Lindsay Drummond, 1946. Translated by I. Freiman.
   Bowra, C. M "Alexander Blok," *The Heritage of Symbolism.* London: Macmillan and Co., 1943.
   Kisch, Sir Cecil. *Alexander Blok, Prophet of the Revolution.* London: Weidenfeld and Nicolson, 1960.

THE TWELVE

I

Black, black evening,
White, white snow,
Wind, what wind!
A man can hardly keep his feet!
Wind, what wind!
Wind the whole world over!

Restless wind
Sweeping up white flakes.
Under the flakes—hard ice!
Slippery, hard going,
Each pedestrian
Slithers here and there—ah! poor fellow!

From building to building
A cable is stretched.
From the cable a banner hangs:
"All Power to the Constituent Assembly!"
An old crone in a quandary weeps,
She can't make head or tail of it:
What does the banner mean or say?
Such a large piece of material!
It could keep a lot of children warm,
Children without clothes or shoes . . .

Like a fussy hen the crone
Stumbles over the deep snow.
"O Mother of God! Save me, save!
The Bolsheviks will dig my grave!"

Wind-the-slasher!
Frost no better!
The bourgeois at the crossroads
Tucks his nose into his fur.

And who is that?—A fellow with long hair,
Talking in a modulated voice:
"Oh the traitors!
The end of Russia!"
Must be a writer—
A speechifier . . .

And there goes one in a long cassock—
Sneaking in the shadows through a snowdrift . . .
"Why so downcast nowadays,
  Comrade priest?"

"Remember how it was in days gone by
When you stuck your belly forward,
And the cross upon your belly
Shone upon the people brightly?"

There, a lady in Persian lamb
Turns to address another:
  "How we wept and wept . . ."
  Slipped and tripped
And—crash!—she sprawls on the ground!

  Ai, ai!
  Pull her up, haul away!

  Wind, skittish wind,
  Playful and angry,
  Billowing the skirts,
  Crumples, rips, and carries
  The big banner:
"All Power to the Constituent Assembly" . . .
  And wafts to us phrases:

  "And we also held a meeting . . .
  Here in this very building . . .
  We debated . . .
  And agreed:
Ten rubles for a short one, twenty-five the night . . .
  And we won't take less from anyone . . .
  Let's go to bed" . . .

  Late evening.
  Emptying street.
  Only one tramp
  Huddling down there,
While the wind whistles . . .

  "Hey, you poor bum!
    Come here—
  Let me embrace you . . .
    Here's bread!
  What is there ahead?
    Go your way!"

Black, black sky, black sky.

Spite, insidious spite,
Boils in the breast . . .
Black spite, holy spite . . .

Comrade! Keep your eyes
Peeled!

II

The wind's out walking, flakes are whirling.
Twelve men go marching down the street.

Their rifle straps are of black leather.
Around them—lights and lights and lights . . .

A crumpled cap, a butt between his teeth,
A convict's diamond patch might fit his back!

Freedom, freedom,
Ah, you freedom without the Cross!

Tra-ta-ta!

"It's cold, comrades, bloody cold!

But Vanka's in a tavern with his Katya . . .
She's got some bills stuffed in her stocking!"

"Vanka damn him is well off, . . .
He was one of us, but joined the army! . . .

"Vanka, you son of a bitch, you bourgeois,
Just you try to paw or kiss my girl!"

Freedom, freedom,
Ah, ah, without the Cross!
Katya's busy with her Vanka—
Very busy doing what?

Tra-ta-ta!

Around them—lights and lights and lights . . .
Sling your rifles on your shoulders . . .

Keep the revolutionary step!
Tireless enemies are not asleep!

Don't be yellow, comrade, grip your rifle!
Let us fire a bullet at our Holy Russia!

At Russia the stolid,
The wooden-hutted,
Fat-rumped and stolid!

Ah, ah, without the Cross!

III

When our lads went off
To serve in the Red Guard,
To serve in the Red Guard,
To offer up their heady heads!

Ah, you bitter grief,
  Life not very sweet!
Soldier's weathered coat,
Little Austrian rifle!

To give all bourgeois a shock,
We'll stoke up a world-wide fire,
Such a world-wide fire of blood—
            Bless us, Lord!

IV

Snow is swirling, coachman yelling,
Vanka with his Katya go speeding—
An electric light
      Glimmers on the shaft . . .
      Ah, ah, just you look!

He is wearing a soldier's coat;
Looking like a bloody idiot,
Twirls and twirls his black mustache,
      Twists and twists about,
      Wriggles like he made a joke . . .

There's your Vanka—so broad-shouldered!
There's your Vanka—such a talker!
      Foolish Katya he embraces,
      Turns her empty head . . .

And she lets her head fall back,
And her teeth are pearls that glitter . . .
      Ah, you Katya, my own Katya,
      Little dumpling face . . .

V

There's a scar upon your neck,
Katya, a scar made by a knife!
Under your breast, sweet Katya,
That scratch is freshly red!

Ai, dance, stamp your feet!
What fine legs you've got!

You had undies all of lace—
Walk about now, take a walk!
With the officers you whored—
Whore around then, whore around!

Ai, ai, whore around!
Something grips the heart!

Katya, that officer d'you recall?
He did not escape the knife . . .
Or perhaps you don't, you doll?
Or is your memory less fresh?

Ai, ai, come refresh me too,
Let me get in bed with you!

You wore a pair of gaiters gray,
Munched the best of "Mignon" candy.
With subalterns you whored round—
Are we privates now O.K.?

Ai, ai, go and sin!
It will ease your soul!

VI

Again to meet them at a gallop
A screeching sleigh comes dashing by . . .

"Hey there, stop, stop! Andryusha, help!
Petruha! catch them in the rear! . . .

Crack-crack-a-rack! the shots ring now!
Then skyward spiral flakes of snow! . . .

The sleigh—with Vanka—rushes faster . . .
Once more! Your finger pull the trigger!

Crack-crack-a-rack! That will teach you how

. . . .

To take my girl out for a ride!

He's gone, bastard! Missed you now!
I'll settle my accounts tomorrow!

But where is Katya?—Dead, she's dead!
That bullet bore right through her head!

Katya, are you glad?—No peep from her . . .
Lie in the snow, you offal, there! . . .

March in revolutionary step!
The tireless enemy is not asleep!

VII

And once more the twelve advance,
Rifles slung on their right shoulders . . .
But the murderer, poor chap,
Keeps his face averted from us . . .

Quicker ever, ever quicker,
Haste his ever quickening steps.
Round his neck he pulls his muffler—
He just can't believe he did it . . .

"What's the matter, comrade—sad?"
"Why so bloody dumb, old chum?"
"Why, Petruha, that long face?"
"Or does Katya stir your pity?"

"Ah, my comrades, my good friends,
Of that wench I was right fond . . .
Many dark and drunken nights
With that wench I used to spend . . .

"It's because of desperation
In her devilish eyes of fire,
It's because of the bright purple
Birthmark under her right shoulder,
I destroyed her, mindless fool,
I hotheadedly destroyed her" . . .

"Stop shooting the breeze, you carrion.
Petka, say, are you a woman, Petka?"
"Are you spewing up your soul
Or what? It's no bloody good!"
"Try and keep your bearing!"
"Exercise control!"

"It's no time to play the nurse,
Coddling such weak idiots!
Harder times now lie ahead,
Comrade dear, for all of us!"

And Petruha slows his pace,
Checks his rapid hurrying pace . . .

Up he throws his youngish head,
Growing cheerful now instead . . .

　　ah, ah!
It's no sin to have some fun!

　　Bolt all your apartment doors,
　　Soon we'll ransack all the floors!

　　Open up the liquor cellars—
　　We're taking over, ragged fellers!
VIII

　Oh, you grief so bitter!
　　Life so tedious,
　　　So deadly!

Now I'll paint the town,
Paint it red, the town . . .

Scratch my head, I will,
Scratch and scratch until . . .

Sunflower seeds I'll spill,
Crack them at my will.

Slash with a knife I will,
Slash and slash my fill.

Fly away, you sparrow—sparrow-bourgeois!
　I'll drink up your blood
　To eke out this cold,
　Black-browed maiden cold . . .

O Lord, have mercy on her soul . .
　　　What a bore!
IX

The restless city now is quiet,
A hush descends on the Nevsky Tower,
And no policeman is in sight—
Take over, fellows, without liquor.

The bourgeois standing at the crossroads
Tucks his nose inside his fur.
Beside him a mangy mongrel huddles,
With wiry coat and tail between its legs.

The bourgeois stands, a famished cur,
Stands speechless like a question mark.
And the ancient world behind him stands,
A cur with tail between its legs.

X

Now the blizzard is rampaging,
  Oh, you blizzard, swirling blizzard,
At a distance of four paces
  You can't see a man at all.

The snow is twisting, funnel-shaped,
The snow is rising like a pillar . . .

"Oh, Lord save us, what a blizzard!
"Petka! Cut that drivel out!
What did it ever save you from,
That icon framed in gold?
You've no sense at all, that's sure,
Try to think aright and ponder—
Your hands, are they not stained in blood
Because of Katya and your fondness for her?"
  Keep the revolutionary step!
  The tireless enemy is near!

Forward, forward, forward,
  The Working People!

XI

They march on, all twelve, afar,
With no holy name for star.
    Ready for everything,
    Pitying nothing . . .

At the enemy unseen they aim
The steel of their small rifles . . .
Through dark side-streets where
Blizzard only whirls . . .
Through the downy snowdrifts
Where you sink up to your knees . . .

    A red flag flutters
    Before their eyes.
    Their steady tread
    Resounds there.

    Any moment now
    Savage foes will wake . . .

And the blizzard whips their eyes

Days and nights
Without cease . . .
Forward, advance,
The Working People!

XII

On they march with sovereign tread . . .
"Hey, who's skulking there? Come out!"
That's the wind with banner red
Tossing in the stormy rout . . .

Freezing snowdrifts lie ahead.
"Hey, who's skulking there? Come near!"
A wretched, mangy cur unfed
Slinks and shambles in the rear . . .

"Scuttle fast, you mangy cur,
Or with bayonets we'll make you skip!
Ancient world and mangy cur,
Hustle, or you'll feel the whip."

Like a famished wolf it scowls,
Slinks behind with gaping jaws,
Famished vagrant cur, it howls . . .
"Hey, who's there? Reply, who goes?"

"Who advances, flaunting red?"
"Look, how black it is ahead!"
"Who runs on with shifty tread,
Skulking in among the houses?"

"We shall get you, no mistake,
Better come, or curse your lot!"
"Comrade, out, or never wake,
We shall rake you with our shot!"

Crack-crack-crack! The echoes peal,
Startling houses in their rows . . .
Only blizzard laughs and reels,
Laughing vastly through the snows.

     Crrack-crack-crack!
     Crrack-crack-crack!

. . . On they march with sovereign tread:
     And behind the mongrel lean;

In advance—with flag blood-red,
    And because of blizzard all unseen,
    And unharmed by hail of lead,
Over snow with soft step light,
Showered in myriad pearls of snow
    Crowned with wreath of roses white—
    Jesus Christ walks on ahead.

SERGEY YESENIN (1895–1925) Sergey Yesenin was born in the village of Konstantinovo in the province of Ryazan, southeast of Moscow. In 1912 his parents brought him to Moscow as a boy of seventeen, and from 1914 to 1918 he lived mainly in Petersburg. His talent was noticed early and he mixed in literary circles before he was twenty. His first works were published in literary magazines in 1915. However, he remained a rural poet in the sense that his mind was almost entirely filled with the images and the feelings excited by the recollections of his native countryside. He might have remained a provincial poet but for the tensions built in him by his life in the city. These tensions created that dramatic background in which he saw himself as a tragic figure torn between the old world of "wooden Russia" and the new mechanical world of the Soviet Union. This underlying tragic tone of many of his later poems lifted him above being a mere "country poet." His tragic dilemma had an immediate appeal to thousands of Russians who themselves had been tied down on the anvil of history. Yesenin's first book of poems, *Radunitza (Spring Rite)*, was published in Petersburg in 1916. In 1918 Yesenin, with a number of other poets, founded the Imaginist group whose theories of poetry resembled somewhat that of the Imagists. Some of his poems exemplify this theory which attaches an importance to the image as a creative principle of poetry. In 1918, he also greeted the Revolution with his long poem *Inonia,* in which he accepted the event but saw the future in an entirely unbolshevik way—Russia as a sort of peasant paradise rather than a twentieth century industrialized land. The duality inherent in Yesenin's vision of the world culminated in *Tavern Moscow* and in his final pessimistic poem *The Black Man* (1925). In some poems, it is true, as in those included in *Strana Sovietskaya (Soviet Land)*, 1925, he also attempted to come to terms with Soviet reality, but he could not resolve in the end the dilemma in which he found himself. His suicide was a prelude to that of Mayakovsky's, the latter poet who earlier, in 1926, had condemned Yesenin's act. It should be noted that Yesenin was married briefly three times: first, to Zinaida Reich, who later became the wife of the famous theater director Vsevolod Meyerhold and who was found brutally murdered after Meyerhold's arrest; second, to Isadora Duncan, with whom he visited Europe and the United States in 1922–23; and third, to a grand-daughter of Leo Tolstoy.

BIBLIOGRAPHY

Radunitza (Spring Rite). Petersburg: 1916; Moscow: 1921.
Goluben (The Dove). Petersburg, 1918.
Preobrazhenie (Transfiguration). Moscow, 1918.
Selskii Chasoslov (Country Breviary). Moscow, 1918.
Treryadnitza. Moscow, 1920.
Pugachev (A Dramatic Poem). Moscow, 1921; Berlin, 1922.
Sobranie Stikhov i Poem (Collected Verses and Poems). Berlin: Grzhebin, 1922.
Stikhi Skandalista (Poems of a Scandalist). Berlin, 1923.
Stikhi 1920–24 (Poems 1920–24). Moscow: Krug, 1924.
Moskva Kabatzkaya (Tavern Moscow). Leningrad, 1924.
Rus Sovietskaya (Soviet Rus). Baku, 1925.
Strana Sovietskaya (Soviet Land). Tiflis, 1925.
O Rossii i Revolutzii (About Russia and the Revolution). Moscow: Sovietskaya Rossiya, 1925.
Persidskie Motivi (Persian Motifs). Moscow: Sovremennaya Rossiya, 1925.
Chernyi Chelovek (The Black Man). Poem published posthumously in *Novy Mir* No. I, 1926.
Sobranie Stikhotvorenii (Collected Poems). 4 Vols. Giz. Moscow-Leningrad, 1926–27; 3 Vols. Leningrad: 1927.
Izbrannoye (Selected). Moscow: Goslitizdat, 1946.
Yesenin. Stikhotvoreniya (Poems). Leningrad: Sovietsky Pisatel, 1953.
Sochineniya (Works). 2 Vols. Moscow: Gosizdat, 1955, 1956.
Sobranie Sochinenii (Collected Works). 5 Vols. Moscow: 1961.

❊   ❊   ❊

TAVERN MOSCOW

I

Yes, I've decided at last! For ever
I've forsaken my fields and my home.
The poplars will sound no longer
Their fluttering leaves over my head.
My hovel will fall down without me,
And my old dog has croaked long ago.
God has condemned me to die
On the tortuous streets of Moscow.

But I love this old town, be it muddy,
Be it decrepit, tawdry, decayed.
Asia, drowsy and golden,
Sleeps on its gilded domes.
And when the moon shines out,
Shines . . . the devil knows how!
I stumble with my head hanging down
Through a lane to a tavern I know.
Screaming and noise in that den,
And all the night through till dawn,
I recite my verses to whores
And brew spirit with bandits.
My heart pounds faster and faster
Till soon I falter and say:
"Like you, I am one of the lost.
For me there is no turning back."
My hovel will fall down without me,
And my old dog has croaked long ago.
God has condemned me to die
On the tortuous streets of Moscow.

2

Once more they quarrel and weep
To the gloomy accordion's wailing;
And remembering Muscovite Russia,
They endlessly curse their lot.
My head sinks lower and lower,
And I drown my eyes in vodka
To avoid facing squarely my fate,
To think of something else for a while.
Oh Russia is so merry this day!
The home-brew spills like a river!
The accordionist with his rotting nose
Sings of the Volga and the Cheka.
There's spite in these people's crazed eyes,
And their speech rings proud and unbroken.
They pity the foolish young men
Who threw away their life for a passion.
They regret that ruthless October
Has led them astray in merciless blizzards;
And boldly they sharpen anew
The knives they keep tucked in their boots.
Where are you, who have left us behind?
Does our light now shine brightly on you?

The accordionist with his vodka
Treats the pox he caught in the Kirghiz steppes.
No! Such men will never be crushed!
Decay only makes them more wild!
You, Russia . . . My Rus-sia,
Asiatic land.

3

Play, accordion, play! What boredom, boredom . . .
The player's fingers ripple like waves.
Drink with me, you mangy bitch,
Drink with me.
You've been fingered and soiled
More than I can bear!
What are you goggling at
With those blue sparks of your eyes?
Do you want a black eye?
You're just a scarecrow.
And you won't lay off.
Play there, accordion! Play on forever!
And you, bitch, come drink, knock it back!
I'd rather have the one with the bubs—
She's more stupid.
You're not the first woman.
There's a crowd of you.
But it's the first time
I've gone with a bitch like you.
Sting well and sharply, pain!
Here or there, what's the odds.
But I'll not end my days, not yet!
Go to hell!
It's time to cool off
Towards your dog's pack . . .
Dearest . . . I'm crying . . .
Forgive me . . . Forgive . . .

4

Sing! On that damned guitar
Let your fingers dazzle and dance.
If only we could choke in these fumes,
My faithful, my only friend!
Don't look at her quivering bangles,
Or at her shoulders' shimmering silk.
I tried to find joy in that woman,
But I found my ruin instead.

I didn't know love was contagion,
I didn't know love was a plague.
She sidled up with narrowing eyes
And drove the hooligan mad.
Sing, Sandro! Sing once again
About our former riotous youth!
Let her go, that spent, beautiful trash,
Let her make love to another!
But, hold! I don't blame her.
But, hold! I don't curse her.
Oh, let me sing of myself
To the twang of those agonized strings . . .
Of my days the rose cupola shimmers,
And my heart's full of golden dreams.
How many girls I have fondled,
How many women embraced!
Yes, the earth has one bitter truth:
With the eyes of a child I observed
Dogs sniffing a bitch in turn.
So why should I then be jealous?
Why then should I sicken at heart?
Our life's but a sheet and a bed!
Our life's but a kiss and oblivion!
Sing, then, sing! Those hands' fateful swing
Holds all destined misfortune . . .
Only be sure . . . send them all to hell . . .
But never, my friend, shall I die.

FAREWELL, MY FRIEND *

Farewell, my friend, until we meet
Again, I hold you in my heart.
Our long appointed separation
Foretells reunion over there.

No word, no handshake, till we're met;
Don't grieve, my friend, or look so black—
In life it's nothing new to die,
And living is, of course, not newer.

---

* This is Yesenin's farewell poem, written in blood just before he hanged himself in the Hotel d'Angleterre in Leningrad.

VLADIMIR MAYAKOVSKY (1893–1930) Vladimir Mayakovsky was born of a Russian family (his father was a forester) in Bagdadi, near Kutais, Georgia. He first attended secondary school in Kutais and later in Moscow, where the family had moved after his father's death. He never finished his formal education. While at school, he became involved in minor revolutionary activity and was arrested three times. On his final release from the Butyrki prison in 1910, he enrolled in an art school, having had for some time an eye for modern art and a distinctive, though limited, pictorial talent of his own. His artistic training served him later in the days of the civil war when he also worked for *Rosta* (the early Soviet equivalent of *Tass*) and produced several thousand propaganda posters. He also began to seriously study literature. The language and imagery of Symbolism, and of the other contemporary literary movements was not Mayakovsky's forte. The dynamic rhythm of Futurism, as well as its accent on modernity and machinery, were more to his heart. At this time he also met the poet Khlebnikov, a wizard of language and verbal associations, the painter Burlyuk, and the writer Kruchenykh, and began to appear with them in Futurist magazines. In 1910, two of Mayakovsky's poems were printed in *Sadok Sudey*, the first Russian Futurist anthology. By 1912, Mayakovsky was firmly seated in the Futurist automobile: he became one of the four signatories of the Russian Futurist Manifesto, *A Slap to Public Taste*, which proclaimed that "We Alone are the face of our time," and insisted on the right to verbal innovation. By 1914, Mayakovsky was already working on his iconoclastic poem "The Cloud in Trousers," of which the first, a heavily censored version, appeared in 1916. It was followed by "The Backbone Flute," "Man," and "War and the World." In 1915 he also met O. M. Brik, the critic, who published "The Cloud" and "The Backbone Flute," and certain other of his works. After 1917 the Revolution was to provide Mayakovsky with an additional theme, which he began to use in poems such as the hyperbolic and challenging "150,000,000," as well as in the rhymed posters he did for *Rosta*. In 1923 he started the *Lef* magazine, which was intended to be a sort of laboratory for applying the techniques of modern verse to the development of social themes. In other words, Mayakovsky, who believed that a new society should be reflected in *new* forms of art, was trying to build a bridge between Futurism and some of the social requirements of the new Soviet society. He was also trying to close the gap between the backwardness of old Russia, the "wooden" Russia of Yesenin, and the modern world of new techniques and industrialization. Mayakovsky was essentially international in spirit and was always interested in the Western world. He made a number of trips abroad, visiting Paris many times and, in 1925, Mexico and the United States, where he wrote "Brooklyn Bridge" and "My Discovery of America." "Brooklyn Bridge" is a good example of Mayakovsky's later style.

A poet of extraordinary sensibility for the "new," Mayakovsky combined a sense of fantasy and a dynamic approach to language and imagery. Essentially a lyrical poet, Mayakovsky strove at times to write on larger more objective themes in an attempt to achieve a more epic strain. His satirical ability found, perhaps, its best expression in his plays *Klop (The Bedbug)*, 1929, and *Banya (The Bath-House)*, 1930, in which he satirized certain aspects of Soviet society—mainly the persistence of "old traits." But the poet, who had been increasingly subject to tension and anxiety, could not himself bridge the transition to Stalinist Russia and its return to more traditional forms. On April 14, 1930, he shot himself.

BIBLIOGRAPHY

In Russian

  Ya. Stikhi. (I. Poems). Moscow: Lithographicheskoye Izdanie G. Kuzmina 1 S. Dolinskogo, 1913.

  Vladimir Mayakovsky. Tragedia. Moscow: Izdanie Pervogo Zhurnala Russkikh Futuristov, 1914.

  Oblako v Shtanakh. (Poem). Petersburg: O. M. Brik, 1916; 2nd ed., 1918, uncensored.

  Fleita Pozvonochnik. Poema. (The Backbone Flute). Petersburg: Izd. Vzyal, 1916.

  Misteria Bouffe (Mystery Bouffe). "Heroic, epical and satirical portrayal of our age." Petersburg: IMO, 1918, 1919; Moscow, 1922.

  Mayakovsky Izdevaietsia. (Mayakovsky Mocks). Moscow: Moscow Association of Futurists. Vhutemas, 1922.

  13 Let Rabot. (13 Years of Work). Moscow: Vhutemas M.A.F., 1922. Vols. I, II.

  Stikhi o Revolutzii. (Poems about the Revolution). Moscow: Krasnaya Nov, GPP, 1923.

  Lirika. (Lyrics). Moscow: Krug, 1923.

  Satiry. (Satires). Moscow: Krug, 1923.

Izbrannyi Mayakovsky. (*Selected Mayakovsky*). Berlin: Nakunune, 1923.

Gallereya Mayakovskogo. (*Mayakovsky's Gallery*). Moscow: Krasnaya Nov, GPP, 1923.

255 Stranitz Mayakovskogo. (*255 Pages of Mayakovsky*). Moscow: Giz., 1923.

Veshchi Etogo Goda. (*Things of This Year*). Berlin: Nakunune, 1924.

Vladimir Ilyich Lenin. Poema. Leningrad: Giz., 1925.

Razgovors Fininspektorom o Poesii. (*Conversation with a Tax Inspector about Poetry*). Tiflis: Zak. Kniga, 1926.

Moye Otkritie Ameriki. (*My Discovery of America*). Moscow: Giz., 1926.

Izbrannoye iz Izbrannogo. (*Selections from Selected*). Moscow: Ogonyok, 1926.

Amerikantzem dlya Pamyati. (*To Americans in Memory*). New York: Novy Mir, 1926.

No. S. Noviye Stikhi. (*No. S. New Poems*). Moscow: Federatzia, 1928.

Sobranie Sochinenii. (*Collected Works*). Moscow-Leningrad: Gosizdat, 1927–30.

Polnoye Sobranie Sochinenii. (*Complete Works*). 12 Vols. Moscow: Goslitizdat, 1939–40.

Polnoye Sobranie Sochinenii. (*Complete Works*). Moscow: Gosizdat, 1955–58.

In English

Marshall, Herbert (ed.). *Mayakovsky and His Poetry.* London: Pilot Press, 1942, 1945.

Blake, Patricia (ed.). *The Bedbug and Selected Poetry.* New York: Meridian, 1960, bilingual; London: Weidenfel and Nicholson, 1961. Translated by Max Hayward and George Reavey.

❈   ❈   ❈

THEY DON'T UNDERSTAND A THING

Entering a hairdresser's, I calmly said:
"Please, be good enough to comb my ears."
The slick barber bristled at once,
his face growing long as a pear.
"Crazy man!"
"Fool!"
Words leapt about.
Abuse flew from squeak to squeal,
and for a l-o-o-ong time
someone's head giggled,
jerked out of the crowd like an old radish.

COULD YOU?

Immediately I painted this day's map,
splashing on paint from a glass;
on the studio's dish I daubed
the slanting cheekbones of an ocean.
I read the summons of fresh lips
on the scales of a tin fish.
But you—
could you play
a nocturne
on the waterpipes' flute?

BROTHER WRITERS

Seemingly I shall never grow accustomed
to sitting in the "Bristol,"
sipping tea,
fibbing by the line.
I shall knock down the glasses,
clamber on the table:
"Listen,
literary brothers!
Here you sit,
eyes drowning in tea,
velvet elbows worn with scribbling.
Raise your eyes from the unemptied glasses!
Disentangle your ears from those shaggy locks!
Darlings,
what has wedded you to words,
you who sit glued
to walls
and wall-paper?
Do you know
that François Villon,
when he had finished writing,
did a job of plundering?
But you,
who quake at the sight of a penknife,
boast yourselves the guardians of a splendid age.
What have you to write about today?
Any solicitor's clerk finds
life

a hundred times more fascinating.
Gentlemen poets,
have you not wearied
of palaces,
pages,
love
and lilac blooms?
If such as you
are the creators,
then I spit upon all art.
I'd rather open a shop,
or work on the Stock Exchange
and bulge my sides with fat wallets.
In a tavern rear
I'll spew up my soul
in a drunken song.
Will the blow tell,
cleave through your sheaves of hair?
But you have only one notion
under that mop of hair:
to be slick-combed! But why?
For a short while it's not worth the labour,
and to be combed
eternally
is impossible."

MAYAKOVSKY IN HEAVEN

Stop!
I throw down on a cloud
the burden
of things
and of a weary body.
Propitious places I have never visited before.
I look around.
This surface
so smoothly licked down,
is this then the heaven so vaunted?
We'll see, we'll see!

It glistened,
and glittered,
and sparkled,

and a rustling crept—
a cloud
or bodiless people
glided quietly by.

"If a beauty pledges her love . . ."

Here,
in the heavenly firmament,
to hear the music of Verdi?
A chink in a cloud.
Peeping through—
I see angels singing there.
Angels live importantly.
Importantly.
One of them quit the throng
and very amiably
broke the drowsed numbness:
"Well, Vladimir Vladimirovich,
how do you like our abyss?"
And I answered as amiably:
"A charming abyss.
The abyss—what a rapture!"
Irritation at first:
there's no
corner of comfort,
no tea,
and no newspapers.
Gradually I grew accustomed to the heavenly ways.
I emerged with others
to watch for new arrivals.
"Ah, so that's you!"
A joyful embrace.
"Greetings, Vladimir Vladimirovich!"
"Welcome, Abraham Vassilievich!"
"Well, and how did you meet your end?
"Not too badly?
"Are you comfortable?"

Nice little jokes, ah?

I grew to like this.
Stood by the gates.
And if
acquaintances

showed up, after their demise,
accompanied them,
explaining the order of the constellations
and the mighty props of the universe.

The central station of all the phenomena,
a tangle of wires, handles and levers.
A tug here—
and the worlds stop idle;
a tug there—
and they spin faster and steeper.
"Give a turn"—they beg.
"Let the world die away.
What are they about?
Flooding the fields with blood?"
I laugh at their heat.
"Why bother!
Let them spill it,
I don't care!"
The chief depot of all sorts of rays.
A place to junk burnt-out stars.
An ancient sketch—
author unknown—
the first unsuccessful draft of a whale.

So serious, everything.
Busy.
Some mend the clouds,
others stoke the sun's furnace.
Everything is in such terrifying order,
at rest,
in its proper place.
No shoving.
Anyhow, there's nothing to shove with.

At first they scolded me.
"He does nothing but loiter!"
For heart's sake—
but do the bodiless have hearts!?
I suggested:
"If you like,
I'll spread
my body
on a cloud

and contemplate everyone."
"No," they answered, "that does not suit us!"
"Well, if that doesn't suit you, it's your affair! Mine
is merely to suggest."

The bellows blow the forges of time—
and the new
year
is ready.
From here,
thundering, plunges
the terrible landslide of years.
I lose count of the weeks.
We,
preserved in the frame of the ages,
we do not divide our love into days,
nor change the names of our loves.
I sank into stillness.
In moonbeams on shallows
laid me down,
with dreams diverting my emotion.
As on a southern beach,
but far more numbed,
and over me,
caressing deeply down,
the sea's eternities roll on.

From THE CLOUD IN TROUSERS: A TETRAPTYCH
PROLOGUE

Your thought,
musing on a sodden brain
like a bloated lackey on a greasy couch,
I'll taunt with a bloody morsel of heart;
and satiate my insolent, caustic contempt.

No gray hairs streak my soul,
no grandfatherly fondness there!
I shake the world with the might of my voice,
and walk—handsome,
twentytwoyearold.

Tender souls!
You play your love on a fiddle,
and the crude club their love on a drum.

But you cannot turn yourselves inside out,
like me, and be just bare lips!

Come and be lessoned—
prim officiates of the angelic league,
lisping in drawing-room cambric.

You, too, who leaf your lips like a cook
turns the pages of a cookery book.

If you wish,
I shall rage on raw meat;
or, as the sky changes its hue,
if you wish,
I shall grow irreproachably tender:
not a man, but a cloud in trousers!
I deny the existence of blossoming Nice!
Again in song I glorify
men as crumpled as hospital beds,
and women as battered as proverbs.

I

You think malaria makes me delirious?

It happened.
In Odessa, it happened.

"I'll come at four," Maria promised.

Eight.
Nine.
Ten.

Then the evening
turned its back on the windows
and plunged into grim night,
scowling,
Decemberish.

At my decrepit back
the candelabras guffawed and whinnied.

You would not recognize me now:
a bulging bulk of sinews,
groaning
and writhing.
What can such a clod desire?
Though a clod, many things!

The self does not care
whether one is cast of bronze
or the heart has an iron lining.
At night the self only desires
to steep its clangor in softness,
in woman.

And thus,
enormous,
I stood hunched by the window,
and my brow melted the glass.
What will it be: love or no-love?
And what kind of love:
big or minute?
How could a body like this have a big love?
It should be a teeny-weeny,
humble, little love;
a love that shies at the hooting of cars,
that adores the bells of horse-trams.

Again and again
nuzzling against the rain,
my face pressed against its pitted face,
I wait,
splashed by the city's thundering surf.

Then midnight, amok with a knife,
caught up,
cut him down—
out with him!

The stroke of twelve fell
like a head from a block.

On the windowpanes, gray raindrops,
howled together,
piling on a grimace
as though the gargoyles
of Notre Dame were howling.

Damn you!
Isn't that enough?
Screams will soon claw my mouth apart.

Then I heard,
softly,

a nerve leap
like a sick man from his bed.
Then,
barely moving
at first,
it soon scampered about,
agitated,
distinct.
Now, with a couple more,
it darted about in a desperate dance.

The plaster on the ground floor crashed.

Nerves,
big nerves,
tiny nerves,
many nerves!—
galloped madly
till soon
their legs gave way.

But night oozed and oozed through the room—
and the eye, weighed down, could not slither out of the slime.

The doors suddenly banged ta-ra-bang,
as though the hotel's teeth
chattered.

You swept in abruptly
like "take it or leave it!"
Mauling your suede gloves,
you declared:
"D'you know,
I'm getting married."

All right, marry then.
So what.
I can take it.
As you see, I'm calm!
Like the pulse
of a corpse.

Do you remember
how you used to talk?
"Jack London,
money,

love,
passion."
But I saw one thing only:
you, a Gioconda,
had to be stolen!

And you were stolen.

In love, I shall gamble again,
the arch of my brows ablaze.
What of it!
Homeless tramps often find
shelter in a burnt-out house!

You're teasing me now?
"You have fewer emeralds of madness
than a beggar has kopecks!"
But remember!
When they teased Vesuvius,
Pompeii perished!

Hey!
Gentlemen!
Lovers
of sacrilege,
crime,
and carnage,
have you seen
the terror of terrors—
my face
when
I
am absolutely calm?

I feel
my "I"
is much too small for me.
Stubbornly a body pushes out of me.

Hello!
Who's speaking?
Mamma?
Mamma!
Your son is gloriously ill!
Mamma!
His heart is on fire.

Tell his sisters, Lyuda and Olya,
he has no nook to hide in.

Each word,
each joke,
which his scorching mouth spews,
jumps like a naked prostitute
from a burning brothel.

People sniff
the smell of burnt flesh!
A brigade of men drive up.
A glittering brigade.
In bright helmets.
But no jackboots here!
Tell the firemen
to climb lovingly when a heart's on fire.
Leave it to me.
I'll pump barrels of tears from my eyes.
I'll brace myself against my ribs.
I'll leap out! Out! Out!
They've collapsed.
But you can't leap out of the heart!

From the cracks of the lips
upon a smoldering face
a cinder of a kiss rises to leap.

Mamma!
I cannot sing.
In the heart's chapel the choir loft catches fire!

The scorched figurines of words and numbers
scurry from the skull
like children from a flaming building.
Thus fear,
in its effort to grasp at the sky,
lifted high
the flaming arms of the *Lusitania*.

Into the calm of an apartment
where people quake,
a hundred-eyed blaze bursts from the docks.
Moan
into the centuries,
if you can, a last scream: I'm on fire!

ORDER NO. 2 TO THE ARMY OF THE ARTS

This is for you—
the fleshy baritones
who, since the days
of Adam,
have shaken those dens called theaters
with the arias of Romeos and Juliets.

This is for you—
the *peintres,*
grown as robust as horses,
the ravening and neighing beauty of Russia,
skulking in ateliers
and, as of old, imposing Draconian laws on flowers
and bulking bodies.

This is for you—
who put on little fig leaves of mysticism,
whose brows are harrowed with wrinkles—
you, little futurists,
imaginists,
acmeists,
entangled in the cobweb of rhymes.
This is for you—
who have exchanged rumpled hair
for a slick hairdo,
bast shoes for lacquered pumps,
you, men of the Proletcult,
who keep patching
Pushkin's faded tailcoat.

This is for you—
who dance and pipe on pipes,
sell yourselves openly,
sin in secret,
and picture your future as academicians
with outsized rations.
I admonish you,
I—
genius or not—
who have forsaken trifles
and now work in Rosta,
I admonish you—

before they disperse you with rifle-butts:
Give it up!

Give it up!
Forget it.
Spit
on rhymes
and arias
and the rose bush
and other such mawkishness
from the arsenal of the arts.
Who's interested now
in—"Ah, wretched soul!
How he loved,
how he suffered . . . "?
Good workers—
these are the men we need
rather than long-haired preachers.
Listen!
The locomotives groan,
and a draft blows through crannies and floor:
"Give us coal from the Don!
Metal workers
and mechanics for the depot!"

At each river's outlet, steamers
with an aching hole in their side,
howl through the docks:
"Give us oil from Baku!"
While we dawdle and quarrel
in search of fundamental answers,
all things yell:
"give us new forms!"

There are no fools today
to crowd, open-mouthed, round a "maestro"
and await his pronouncement.
Comrades,
give us a new form of art—
an art
that will pull the republic out of the mud.

BROOKLYN BRIDGE *

Give, Coolidge,
a shout of joy!
I too will spare no words
               about good things.
Blush
    at my praise,
           go red as our flag,
however
          united-states
              -of
-america you may be.
As a crazed believer
          enters
             a church,
retreats
    into a monastery cell,
             austere and plain;
so I,
    in graying evening
          haze,
humbly set foot
        on Brooklyn Bridge.
As a conqueror presses
         into a city
           all shattered,
on cannon with muzzles
         craning high as a giraffe—
so, drunk with glory,
         eager to live,
I clamber,
     in pride,
        upon Brooklyn Bridge.
As a foolish painter
        plunges his eye,
sharp and loving,
       into a museum madonna,
so I,
    from the near skies
        bestrewn with stars,

  * Written during Mayakovsky's visit to America.

gaze
    at New York
            through the Brooklyn Bridge.
New York,
       heavy and stifling
               till night,
has forgotten
         its hardships
              and height;
and only
      the household ghosts
ascend
      in the lucid glow of its windows.
Here
    the elevateds
            drone softly.
And only
      their gentle
           droning
tells us:
     here trains
           are crawling and rattling
like dishes
      being cleared into a cupboard.
While
   a shopkeeper fetched sugar
from a mill
       that seemed to project
             out of the water—
the masts
      passing under the bridge
looked
   no larger than pins.
I am proud
      of just this
         mile of steel;
upon it,
     my visions come to life, erect—
here's a fight
      for construction
         instead of style,

an austere disposition
                    of bolts
                                and steel.

If
    the end of the world
                        befall—
and chaos
                smash our planet
                                to bits,
and what remains
                    will be
                            this
bridge, rearing above the dust of destruction;
then,
        as huge ancient lizards
                                are rebuilt
from bones
            finer than needles,
                                to tower in museums,
so,
    from this bridge,
                    a geologist of the centuries
will succeed
            in recreating
                        our contemporary world.
He will say:
            —Yonder paw
                        of steel
once joined
            the seas and the prairies;
from this spot,
                Europe
                        rushed to the West,
scattering
            to the wind
                        Indian feathers.
This rib
        reminds us
                    of a machine—
just imagine,
            would there be hands enough,

after planting
>> a steel foot
>>>> in Manhattan,
to yank
> Brooklyn to oneself
>>>> by the lip?
By the cables
>> of electric strands,
I recognize
>> the era succeeding
>>>> the steam age—
here
> men
>> had ranted
>>> on radio.
Here
> men
>> had ascended
>>> in planes.
For some,
> life
>> here
>>> had no worries;
for others,
> it was a prolonged
>>>> and hungry howl.
From this spot,
>> jobless men
leapt
> headlong
>> into the Hudson.*
Now
> my canvas
>> is unobstructed
as it stretches on cables of string
>>>> to the feet of the stars.
I see:
> here
>> stood Mayakovsky,

---

* The poet meant the East River.

stood,
      composing verse, syllable by syllable.
I stare
      as an Eskimo gapes at a train,
I seize on it
         as a tick fastens to an ear.
Brooklyn Bridge—
yes . . .
      That's quite a thing!

PAST ONE O'CLOCK . . .*

Past one o'clock. You must have gone to bed.
The Milky Way streams silver through the night.
I'm in no hurry; with lightning telegrams
I have no cause to wake or trouble you.
And, as they say, the incident is closed.
Love's boat has smashed against the daily grind.
Now you and I are quits. Why bother then
to balance mutual sorrows, pains, and hurts.
Behold what quiet settles on the world.
Night wraps the sky in tribute from the stars.
In hours like these, one rises to address
The ages, history, and all creation.

---

* Found in Mayakovsky's pocket after he shot himself. It was
part of a larger poem he was working on at the time.

OSIP MANDELSHTAM (1891–1940) Osip Mandelshtam was born into a Jewish middle class family in Warsaw, Poland (then part of the Russian Empire). He spent his childhood and youth in St. Petersburg where, in 1911, he began studying languages and history at the University of St. Petersburg. He was particularly interested in the study of Greek, and many of his later poems have an Hellenic feeling and tone about them. He had already traveled in Europe: in 1907 he visited France, where he read the French symbolists; and in 1910 he spent two semesters at the University of Heidelberg. In the 1920's his knowledge of languages made it possible for him to translate works by Upton Sinclair, Jules Romains, André Barbusse and others. He had also written imaginative prose and literary articles and reviews; but poetry was his main work and achievement. As a poet, he began publishing in 1909, and by 1910 he was included in such distinguished literary magazines as *Apollon,* just as later he was included in the leading Soviet monthlies *Krasnaya Nov* and *Novy Mir.* His first volume of poetry, *Kamen (Stone),* appeared in Petersburg in 1913. The bulk of his work, both poetry and prose, was published in the Soviet Union in the 1920's. His reputation as a poet was firmly established with his volume, *Tristia* (1922). His last three books all appeared in 1928, his culminating year in print. He continued to be published in literary magazines until 1932, when his life became a nightmare. He was arrested and deported to Voronezh, where he lived in difficult circumstances until 1937. Here he managed to write a new cycle of poems (which was published in Russian in New York in 1961). On his return to Moscow, where he had lived after leaving Petrograd in 1918, he was again arrested and, this time, deported to the Far East in the vicinity of Vladivostok. There he met a tragic death, one of the many victims of the Stalin terrorism. In his *Memoirs, People, Years, Life,* Ilya Ehrenburg gives the date of Mandelshtam's death as 1940, but so far no official account of his death has been forthcoming.

Mandelshtam was an early member of the acmeist group. He is above all a lyric poet of richly sounding, many-voweled sonorous lines. His rhythms, in contrast to Pasternak's, are slow and undulating. He is more concerned with musical harmony than Akhmatova, and his images are on the whole more striking. To the last he preserved his poetic independence. He was largely ignored by Soviet critics after his death, and has not been included in either the 1943 or the 1957 anthologies of Soviet poetry.

BIBLIOGRAPHY

In Russian

   Kamen (Stone). Petersburg: Akme, 1913; Second edition. Petersburg: Giperboroy, 1916; Third edition. Moscow-Petrograd: Gosizdat, 1923.

   Tristia. Berlin: Petropolis, 1922.

   Vtoraya Kniga (Second Book). Moscow-Petersburg: Krug, 1923.

   Shum Vremeni (The Noise of Time. Prose pieces). Leningrad: Vremya, 1925.

   Egipetskaya Marka (The Egyptian Stamp. Prose pieces). Leningrad: Priboy, 1928.

   Stikhotvoreniya (Poetical Works). Moscow-Leningrad: Gosizdat, 1928.

   O Poesii (About Poetry. Articles). Moscow: Akademia, 1928.

   Sobranie Sochinenii (Collected Works). New York: Chekhov Publishing House, 1955.

   Vozdushniye Puti (Aerial Ways, II. Almanac). New York, 1961. This issue contains "Fifty Seven Poems by Osip Mandelshtam." These poems, written in the 1930's, were to have been included in a new book which was never published.

In English

   Bowra, C. M. (ed. and trans.). *A Book of Russian Verse.* London: Macmillan & Co., 1943.

❋ ❋ ❋

WE SHALL DIE

We shall die in transparent Petropolis,
Where Proserpine at present is sovereign;
With every sigh we exhale a fatal breath,
And every hour affirms the year of our death.

Mighty goddess of the sea, dread Athene,
Put aside your imperious helmet of stone.
We shall die in transparent Petropolis,
Where not you, but Proserpine is sovereign.

ON THE DREAD HEIGHTS

On the dread heights a fire wanders;
But is it a star that twinkles so?
Translucent star and wandering fire,
Petropolis, your brother, now is dying.

Earthly dreams are burning on dread heights,
A green star twinkles there.
If you are a star—brother of the sky and water,
Petropolis, your brother, now is dying.

On the dread heights a monstrous ship
With wings spread wide is speeding:
Green star, in beauteous indigence
Your brother, Petropolis, is dying.

Translucent spring above the black Neva
Has broken, and immortal wax is melting.
O if you are a star—Petropolis, your town,
Your brother, Petropolis, is dying.

I WAS LIKE A CHILD

I was like a child in that world of sovereign power;
I was afraid of oysters, glanced askance at guardsmen,
And spiritually owe nothing to that world,
Save I may have suffered in the semblance of others.
In a beaver miter, impressive, stupid, and sullen,
I've never stood under the Egyptian porticoes of a Bank,
And never, never, has a gypsy girl danced for me
To the crackling of hundred ruble bills above the lemon Neva.
Foreseeing executions, the turmoil of mutinous events,
I decamped to the nereids on the shores of the Black Sea.
Much confusion, anguish and pain, I have suffered
From the beauties of that day—those fond European ladies!
Why then does this city still impose
On my mind and emotions as of ancient right?
Fires and frosts only add to its arrogance,
City vain and accursed, hollow and callow.
Is it because as a child I once saw a print
Of Lady Godiva with abundant red tresses cascading,
That, like a hurdy-gurdy, I keep repeating:
Lady Godiva, farewell . . . I don't remember, Lady Godiva.

THIS AGE

My age, my beast! Who now can try
To look you in the eye,
And with his blood together glue
The backbones of two centuries?
Blood-the-builder gushes from
The throat of all terrestrial things;
What has no backbone merely trembles
On the threshold of new days.

The creature must, while there's still life,
Give all support to the spine he bears,
And on that invisible backbone
The wave will play for all it can.
As if a child's tender cartilage
Were the earth's own age of infancy,
They've brought the very crown of life,
As lamb, in sacrifice again.

To wrench life from its captive state,
And to begin a world that's new,
We must bind together with a flute
The generations of nodal days.
It is the age that stirs the waves
With all the anguish of human life,
And a viper in the grass will hiss
The golden rule of our present age.

The buds will swell with sap again,
And shoots of green will sprout,
But that spine of yours is cracked,
O age of beauty and of anguish.
A fatuous grin upon your face,
You glare behind you, weak and rapacious,
Like a beast that once was lithe,
At the tracks your paws have made.

LENINGRAD

I returned to my city, familiar as tears,
As my fibres, as the swollen glands of my childhood.
You've returned here—then gulp all the faster
The codliver oil of Leningrad's riverside lamps.

Quickly get to know this December day,
Wherein the yolk is mixed with sinister tar.
Petersburg! I have no wish to die—not yet!
My telephone numbers are in your keeping.

Petersburg! I still possess a list of addresses,
Which will help me to hear the voices of the dead.
I live on a black staircase, and the doorbell
Ripped out with the flesh hits me on the temple.

Fingering the rustling irons of the door chains,
I stay up all night expecting the dear guests.

EDUARD BAGRITZKY (1885–1934) Eduard Bagritzky is the pseudonym for Eduard Dzyubin, who was born in Odessa of a family of artisans. His parents were poor and he had some difficulty in getting a good education, but he had already begun to write verse at the age of fifteen. His first poems were published in the collection *Serebryaniye Trubi* (*Silver Trumpet*) in 1914 and in other Odessa collections of 1915. During World War I he served in the Russian army on the Persian front in 1917. Then he joined the Red army and served in a partisan detachment and with the Red Cavalry. On returning to Odessa after the civil war, he continued to write poetry and took part in the literary life of that city, which was rich in literary talent at the time. In 1925 he headed for Moscow and, settling down in the country at Kuntzevo nearby, began to be published in the literary magazines. For a time he was a member of the constructivist group. His first book of poems, *Yugo-Zapad* (*Southwest*), appeared in 1928. Two further collections of his poetry were published before he died of a lingering illness in 1934. Apart from his own work, Bagritzky also translated various works from the English and, in particular, some of the poems of Walter Scott, Thomas Hood, and his favorite, Robert Burns. Bagritzky's selection of these poets was not accidental: he was at heart a romantic; and he used the romantic ballad style to excellent effect in a long civil war poem, *Duma pro Opanasa* (*The Lay of Opanas*), 1926. Opanas, the hero of this poem, is not a "commissar," but a peasant who has chosen the wrong side in the conflict. Imbued with the romantic spirit of the early days of the Revolution and concerned with the theme of the contemporary generation which had witnessed the Revolution, Bagritzky expressed alarm and anxiety for the passing of a heroic epoch in poems such as "By Our Black Bread" written in the mid-1920's. In other poems he was much concerned with the contrast between the old and the new. Bagritzky had a natural and attractive lyrical gift. His death at forty-nine was a distinct loss to Soviet poetry.

BIBLIOGRAPHY

Yugo-Zapad (*Southwest*). Moscow, 1928.
Pobediteli (*The Conquerors*). Moscow, 1932.

Posledniya Noch (The Last Night). Moscow, 1932.

Duma Pro Opanasa (Lay of Opanas. Libretto for Opera based on poem of the same title). Moscow, 1933.

Sobranie Sochinenii (Collected Works). 2 Vols. Moscow-Leningrad, 1938.

Stikhi i Poemi (Verses and Poems). Moscow: Goslitizdat, 1956.

Stikhotvoreniya (Poetical Works). Leningrad: Sovietsky Pisatel, 1956.

Stikhotvoreniya i Poemi (Poetical Works). Moscow, 1958.

❊ ❊ ❊

SWEETLY I FAINT

Sweetly I faint
       from the still air and dreams,
From long pervasive tedium
         and halting song;
I like the cockerels
       embroidered on white linen,
And the austere icons'
        agelong soot.
With devout humility
       day follows day
Beneath the sultry buzz of flies.
A quail mutters
      under the low ceiling,
And raspberry jam scents the holidays.

At night soft goose-down makes us stuffy,
And the stifling icon-lamp blinks in torment.
And, neck outstretched,
        the cockerel embroidered

On the linen starts his endless crowing.

You vouchsafed me there, O Lord, an humble shelter
Beneath a generous roof,
       exempt from daily worries
Where heavy days,
      like spoons of jam,
Flow thickly drop by drop.

BY OUR BLACK BREAD, OUR FAITHFUL WIFE

By our black bread, our faithful wife,
With a pallid impotence we are infected . . .

The years were tried with hoof and stone,
With deathless wormwood the waters saturated.
And bitter wormwood taints our lips . . .
The knife's not for us to handle,
The pen not ours by inclination,
The spade does not become our honor,
And fame not our repute:
We are the rusty leaves
On rusty oaks . . .
The least breeze,
The least breath of North—
And we fall scattered.

Upon whose path are we now strewn?
Whose feet will trample down our rust?
Will the young trumpeters tread us down?
Will alien constellations rise above us?
We are the discarded comfort of the rusty oaks . . .
With our harsh, homeless chill, we banish comfort . . .
We soar into the night!
We soar into the night!
Blindly we fly like ripened stars . . .
Above us the young trumpeters now thunder,
Above us alien constellations rise,
Above us alien banners flutter . . .
The least breeze,
The least breath of North—
Tear off in their pursuit,
Rush off in their pursuit,
Roll on through the fields,
Chant in the steppes!
Follow the gleam of bayonets glancing in the clouds,
Follow the thud of hoof through forest fastness,
Follow the trumpet's song drowning in the forests . . .

ANNA AKHMATOVA (1889–) Anna Akhmatova, a consistently lyrical poet, has survived many tragedies to emerge in the 1960's as perhaps the outstanding living Russian poet of today. Her achievement was recently recognized in the West when she was awarded the Catagna international prize for poetry in December, 1964.

Anna Akhmatova (née Gorenko) was born near Odessa. Her father was a retired naval engineer who finally settled in Tsarskoye Selo, not far from Petersburg. There Akhmatova spent her childhood and school years. Then she completed her education at the universities of Kiev and Petersburg. In the spring of 1910 and 1911 she lived in Paris; in 1912 she toured northern Italy. She returned to Italy in 1964, to receive the poetry prize at Catagna.

In 1910 she married the well-known acmeist poet, Nikolai Gumilev (d. 1912), who inspired many of her earlier lyrical poems. She has lived mainly in Petersburg (Leningrad, as of 1924), and most of her poems reflect in various ways the peculiar atmosphere and traditions of this northern city. After being besieged there for some months in 1941, she was evacuated to Tashkent, where she was able not only to continue writing but also to publish her *Selected Poems* (1943). In 1944–1945 she went to Moscow before returning to Leningrad.

Anna Akhmatova began writing in 1907. A few years later her poems began to appear in *Apollon,* a magazine which had opened its pages to the acmeist poets Gumilev, Kuzmin, Gorodeszky, and Mandelshtam, who had reacted against the symbolist school of poetry.

Akhmatova's poetry is essentially lyrical and intimate in tone. Much of it is love poetry. But a note of sad meditation and even tragedy creeps into some of her later poems, especially the long elegiac poems which she completed in the 1940's and 1950's—poems such as "Poem Without A Hero" (1913–1942) and "Requiem" (1939–1957). "Requiem" is an elegy for her son and other victims of the 1937–1938 Stalinist purges; it has not yet been fully published in the Soviet Union. It should be remembered that Anna Akhmatova was unable to publish her work between 1922 and 1940 and that she was also one of the main targets of Zhdanov's attack in 1946. But time was on her side, and the impact of her poetry grows stronger with the years.

BIBLIOGRAPHY

In Russian
  Vecher (Evening), 1912.
  Chetki (Rosary), 1914.
  Belaya Staya (The White Flock), 1917.
  Anno Domini, 1922.
  Podorozhnik (The Plantain), 1921.
  Stikhi (Poems), 1940.
  Izbrannye Stikhi (Selected Poems). Tashkent, 1943.
  Stikhi (Poems) 1909–60, 1961.
  Poema bez Geroya, Triptykh. (Poem Without A Hero. A Triptych). Vozdushnye Puti (Airways). New York, 1960.
  Rekviem. Tzikl stikhotvorenii. (Requiem. A Cycle of Poems). Grani, No. 56, October, 1964, Possev. Frankfurt-am-Main.
In English
  Forty-Seven Love Poems. Tr. by N. Duddington. London: Cape, 1927.
  Poems. In C. M. Bowra (ed.). *A Book of Russian Verse.* London, 1943.
  Poems. In G. Shelley (ed.). *Modern Poems from Russia.* London, 1942.

❅ ❅ ❅

OF THE CUCKOO I INQUIRED

Of the cuckoo I inquired
How many years I had left for living . . .
The tops of the pine-trees trembled,
A yellow sunbeam fell on the sward.
But no sound disturbed the clearing . . .
I then walked homeward,
And the cool breeze fondled
My brow which was burning.

FROM YOU I HID MY HEART

From you I hid my heart
As though I'd jumped into the Neva . . .
Now tamed and wingless, I
Am living in your house.
But . . . I hear a creaking in the night.

What's happening in the alien dusk?
—The Sheremetyev linden trees.
Household spirits calling to each other . . .
With furtive steps approaching,
As creeps the lapping water,
The black whisper of misfortune
Bends feverishly to the ear
Muttering as if its business were
To be disturbing here all night:
"You yearn for a little solace!?
But where is he now, your solace?"

THE DEATH OF SOPHOCLES

From the nocturnal sky an eagle swooped
 Upon the house of Sophocles,
And from the garden there in mourning
 A choir of cicadas rang out.

But the man of genius at this hour
 had stepped into immortality,
Escaping the enemy host encamped
 before the walls of his own city.

The besieger king dreamed a strange dream:
 Dionysus bade him raise the siege—
That the funeral rites be not upset,
 And Athenians pay their last respects.

REQUIEM

No, under no alien sky, under the shelter of no alien wings—
I was then together with my people, where my people
found itself to its misfortune.

Dedication

Before this grief the mountains stoop;
no more the majestic river flows.
But prison bars are doubly strong,
and hide behind them "convict burrows"
and the tedium of deadly days.
For some a fresh wind blows,
for some a sunset dallies and delays—
but we don't know, we're everywhere the same,
hearing only the hateful clank of keys

and the soldiers' * heavy tread.
We rose as if for matins,
Trudged through the now savage capital,
Met there, more breathless than the dead,
the sun now lower and the mistier Neva,
while hope still sang ahead . . .
The sentence then . . . and tears will gush at once,
and now she's separated from them all,
and it pains like a wrenched out heart
like a brutal blow that knocked one down,
but she still walks on . . . And staggers . . . All alone . . .
Where are they now, those friends unfree
of my two excruciating years?
What do they see now in the Siberian blizzard?
What strange glimmer in the aura of the moon?
To you I send my farewell greeting.

Prologue

It was a time when only the dead
could smile, glad of their repose.
And like a superfluous appendage,
Leningrad dangled close to its jails.
And when, crazed by torture,
the regiments of the condemned tramped on,
and the hooting locomotives
sang out their brief song of separation.
The stars of death stood over us,
and guiltless Russia shrank and shriveled
under those bloodied boots
and the tyres of the Black Marias.

I

They took you away at dawn.
I followed as though behind a coffin;
in a dark room children sobbed,
the icon-candle guttered.
An icon's chill was on your lips.
I can't forget the deadly sweat on the brow.
Like the wives of the Streltzi,† I shall howl
beneath the Kremlin towers.

---

* Not the ordinary wardens, but NKVD troops.
† The Muscovite musketeers in the days of Peter the Great.
They revolted and Peter had them tortured and executed in
Red Square.

2

Gently flows the quiet Don.
In comes the yellow moon,

comes into the house with cap askew,
the yellow moon, and sees a shadow.

There's a woman, and she is ill;
There's a woman, and she's alone.

Her husband's dead, her son in jail.
Say a prayer, a prayer, for me then.

3

No, it's not I, but another who suffers.
I couldn't bear it. As for what happened,
let a black pall cover it all,
and let the street lamps bear it away . . .

Night.

4

If one could have shown you, so fond of mocking
and so loved by all your friends,
sprightly sinner of Tsarskoye Selo,*
what your life held in store for you—
how, three-hundred number in a queue,
you would wail with your package under walls of Kresty †
and with a searing tear
burn a hole in the New Year's ice.
How like a prison poplar swaying,
and making no sound . . . and how many lives,
innocent lives find their end there . . .

5

For seventeen months I have cried,
calling you home;
I've thrown myself at the executioner's feet.
You are my son and my terror too.
Within me all is confused forever,
And I can't sort out who
is the beast now and who the man,
and how long it will be to the execution?
All that is left are dusty flowers,
the tinkling censer and the footsteps
leading somewhere into nowhere.

---

* Akhmatova spent her youth in Tsarskoye Selo.
† A notorious prison in Leningrad. *Krest* means "cross."

And staring me straight in the eyes
a huge star menaces me
with imminent destruction.

6

Weightless weeks sped by.
I don't understand how it came about
that the white nights gazed down
into your prison, dear son;
that they gaze again
with feverish hawklike eye,
telling of death
and your high cross.

7 The Sentence

And the stone word fell
on my yet throbbing breast.
No matter, I was prepared.
I'll manage somehow.

Today I have much to do:
I must kill off memory;
my soul must turn to stone,
and I must learn to live anew.

Otherwise . . . Sultry summer rustles
like a holiday beneath my window.
I have long foreseen this
bright day and emptied house.

8 To Death

You'll come all the same—why not now?
I'm waiting for you—I find it hard.
I've put out the light and opened the door
to receive you who are so simple and strange.
Come in whatever guise you wish—
burst in like a poison-gas shell,
or creep up like a bandit with brass knuckles
or poison me with typhus fumes.
Or with some denunciation you've contrived,
one so familiar it sickens—
that I might see the top of a blue cap *
and the *upravdom* † pale with fear.

* Refers to NKVD.
† A house superintendent who must also report anything unusual to the police.

It's all one now. The Enisei * goes swirling.
The Polar star shines bright.
An ultimate horror covers over
the blue gleam of beloved eyes.

9

Already madness with its wing
has enveloped half the soul,
and plying me with fiery liquor,
lures into the dark valley.

Listening to my delirium
as if it were another's,
I understood I must
yield victory to him.

And he will not allow me
to carry anything away
(pester him with prayer,
implore him as you may):

Neither my son's dread eyes—
suffering turned to stone—
nor the day the storm broke,
nor the hour of my prison visit,
nor the cool feel of dear hands,
nor the lindens' agitated shadows,
nor any slight sound in the distance—
the last words of consolation.

10 Crucifixion

"Weep not for me, Mother, I shall seek you out in the grave."

I

The choir of angels has glorified the great hour,
and the heavens have gaped in fire.
"Why hast thou forsaken me?" he implored the Father.
And to the Mother he said: "Why weepest thou for me?"

2

Mary Magdalene writhed and sobbed,
the favorite disciple turned to stone,
and no one even dared to glance
at the Mother standing there in silence.

Epilogue

I learned how faces sag,
how fear peeps under the eyelids,

* River in Arctic Siberia.

how suffering marks the cheeks
with hard cut cuneiform characters,
how black and ashen hair
turns silver of a sudden,
a smile withers on submissive lips
and a wry laugh is shot with trembling fear.
And not for myself alone I pray,
but for all who stood with me then,
in savage frost and in July's blaze,
beneath that red blinded wall.

2

Again the hour of remembrance comes.
I see, I hear, I feel you all:
they could barely lead her to the window,
and her who walks her native soil no more,
and her who, tossing her handsome head,
said: "I come here as if it were my home."
And I'd like to name them all
but they took the list, and there's nowhere to ask.
For them all I've woven a broad pall
out of the poor words I overheard them speak.
Always and everywhere I remember them:
I shall not forget them even if misfortune strikes again
and they shut my tortured mouth,
through which a hundred-million people cry.
And let them also remember me
on the eve of my burial day.
And if in this country they will ever
think of erecting a monument to me,
I shall at once accept this honor,
but only on one condition: that the monument be not
placed by the seashore where I was born: *
my last ties with the sea were broken
not in the Tsar's garden by the hallowed tree stump
where an inconsolable shadow seeks me,
but here, where I stood three hundred hours
and where they did not unbolt the doors;
because even in blessed death I am afraid
to forget the rumbling sound of the Black Marias,
to forget how the hateful door clanged shut,

* Akhmatova was born near the port of Odessa on the Black
Sea.

and the old woman howled like a wounded beast.
And from the immobile eyelids of stone
let the thawing snow flow like tears;
and let the prison dove coo in the distance,
and ships gently glide on the Neva.

BORIS PASTERNAK (1890–1960) Boris Pasternak was born in Moscow. His parents, of Jewish descent, came from Odessa. The father, Leonid Pasternak, a noted academical painter of his day, was a friend of Leo Tolstoy, Scriabin, and Rainer Maria Rilke. His mother had been a professional pianist. As a result, Boris Pasternak was brought up in an intense atmosphere of cultural activity. At one time he nearly became a pianist himself. After completing his secondary-school studies, Pasternak entered Moscow University. He studied philosophy there and also at the University of Freiburg under the philosopher C. M. Cohen. But in 1912 he abandoned his philosophical studies in favor of languages and literature. He had already begun to write poetry, and his first published poems date from 1912. By 1914 he had published his first volume of poems, *A Twin in the Clouds*. His next volume was *Over the Barriers* (1916). By 1923 Pasternak had published four books, of which the last two, *Sister My Life* and *Themes and Variations*, were largely responsible for establishing a firm reputation for him as a poet of unusual gifts, lyrical intensity, and modern vision. By this time, however, the Russian Revolution was six years old; it was entering a period of comparative stabilization; a new Soviet literature was beginning to emerge in the works of such prose writers as Leonov, Babel, and Olesha and such poets as Mayakovsky, Tikhomov, Yesenin, and Pasternak. But the new revolutionary environment posed special problems, and in this second period of his creative work Pasternak may be said to have been grappling with the realities of the Soviet world. The results were his long poems such as *1905* and *Lieutenant Schmidt*, in which the poet attempted to combine lyrical poetry with epic subject matter. In his sequence of poems *The Waves* (1932), Pasternak returned to a more purely lyrical note. *The Waves* may be said to mark the end of his second period of poetic activity. From then until 1943, hardly any new poetry by Pasternak was to appear in print, although two editions of his *Collected Works* and other reprints of previous works were published by 1936. Nearly a decade passed during which Pasternak tried to perfect a more realistic style for his work. His previous poetry had been characterized by ebullient and dynamic word play and verbal musical effects which only a virtuoso could produce. His poetry of the 1940's and after takes on a rather different, more sober aspect—that of deeper feeling more simply expressed. In fact, Pasternak went so far as to diminish the value of his earlier work. In the 1940's he had time to publish two slender books of poems, *On Early Trains* and *Spacious Earth,* before he was obliged to keep silent again during the so-called "anti-cosmopolitan" drive which ended only with Stalin's death. It was during this period of silence that the idea of *Doctor Zhivago* began to take final shape and form. The poems that compose the *Zhivago* cycle have a deeply religious and ritualistic note about them, and differ greatly in tone and feeling and style from any of Pasternak's previous poetry. Very few of these poems ever saw the light of day in the Soviet Union. *Doctor Zhivago* was first published in Italy. Pasternak's last cycle of poems—that of *Kogda Razgulyatsia (A Rift in the Clouds)*— continued in the vein of short, deeply felt lyrics expressed in simple and sustained language. It is clear from certain discussions in *Doctor Zhivago* and from certain statements in his autobiographical *I Remember* that Pasternak had now thrown all excess poetic baggage overboard and was serving the ideal of a Pushkinlike lyrical purity and simplicity.

BIBLIOGRAPHY

In Russian
  Bliznetz v Tuchakh (A Twin in the Clouds). Moscow: Lyrika, 1914.
  Poverkh Barierov (Over the Barriers. Poems 1914–16). Moscow: Centrifuga, 1917; Moscow: Giz, 1931.
  Setra Moya Zhizn (Sister My Life). Berlin: Grzhebin, 1923.
  Themi i Variatzii (Themes and Variations. Fourth Book of Verse). Berlin-Moscow: Gelikon, 1923.
  Raskazi (Stories). Moscow: Krug, 1925.
  Izbranyii Stikhi (Selected Poems). Moscow: Uzel, 1926.
  1905 (Verses). Moscow: Giz, 1927.
  Dve Knigi (Two Books). Moscow: Ogonyok, 1929.
  Spektorsky (Poem). Leningrad: Izdanie Sovietskikh Pisateley, 1931.
  Okhrannaya Gramota (Safe Conduct). Leningrad: Izd. Sovietskikh Pisateley, 1931.
  Vtoroye Rozhdenie (Second Birth). Moscow: Federatziya, 1932; Moscow: Sovietskii Pisatel, 1934.
  Poemi (Poems). Moscow: Goslitizdat, 1933.
  Sobranie Sochinenii (Collected Poems). Leningrad: Izd. Sovietskikh Pisateley, 1933.

Vozdushniye Puti. Povesti (Aerial Ways Tales). Moscow: Gosizdat, 1933.

Povest (Tale). Leningrad: Izd. Sovietskikh Pisateley, 1934.

Sobranie Stikhov (Collected Poems). Moscow: Gosizdat, 1936.

Na Rannikh Poezdakh (On Early Trains). Moscow: Sovietskii Pisatel, 1943.

Zemnoy Prostor. Stikhi (Spacious Earth. Poems). Moscow: Sovietskii Pisatel, 1945.

Izbrannyii Stikhi i Poemi (Selected Verse and Poems). Moscow: Goslitizdat, 1945.

Znamya No. 4, 1954 (Ten poems from a novel in prose, *Doctor Zhivago*).

Znamya No. 9, 1956. "New Lines."

Novy Mir No. 10, 1956. "Bread."

Literaturnaya Moskva No. 1. Almanac. Two poems from the *Doctor Zhivago* cycle.

Den Poesii 1957 (Day of Poetry 1957).

Poeziya. Izbrannoye (Poetry. Selected). Frankfurt-am-Main: Posev, 1960. Introduction by N. Anatolievna. This edition includes the 25 poems of the Zhivago cycle.

Stikhotvoreniya i Poemi (Verse and Poems). Moscow: Gosizdat, 1961. Posthumous edition of selected poems 1912–1960. This volume includes most of Pasternak's last cycle of poems *Kogda Razgulyatsya (A Rift in the Clouds)* 1955–60; but excludes all of the poems of the Zhivago cycle.

Pasternak, Boris. *Sochineniya (Works).* 4 Vols. Ann Arbor: University of Michigan Press, 1961. This is a four-volume edition of the almost complete poetry and prose in Russian.

In English

The Collected Prose Works. Arranged with an introduction by Stefan Schimanski. Tr. Beatrice Scott and Robert Payne. London: Lindsay Drummond, 1945.

Doctor Zhivago. Tr. J. M. Cohen. London: Lindsay Drummond, 1946; Benn, 1958.

An Essay in Autobiography. Tr. Manya Harari with an introduction by Edward Crankshaw. London: Collins and Harvill, 1959.

"First Essay Towards Pasternak," George Reavey. Cambridge: Experiment No. 6, 1930.

The Last Summer. Tr. George Reavey. London: Peter Owen, 1959; New York: Avon Books, 1959.

The Poetry of Boris Pasternak. Selected, edited, and translated by George Reavey. New York: Putnam and Capricorn, 1960.

I Remember: Sketch for an Autobiography. Translated with a preface and notes by David Magarshack. New York: Pantheon Books, 1959; Meridian Books, 1960.

Selected Writings. New York: New Directions, 1958.

THE DROWSY GARDEN

The drowsy garden sprinkles beetles
Like a brazier bursting with bronze ash.
And level with me and my taper
Whole worlds in flower hang suspended.

And as by some surprising faith,
I am converted by this night,
Where grayly the weather-beaten poplar
Has curtained off the moonlit zone,

Where the pond's a mystery revealed,
Where apple-trees are whispering surf,
Where hangs the garden propped on piles,
Holding up the sky before it.

From "MARBURG"

Why then am I coward? For, like grammar, I know
Insomnia well. They'll save me if anything happens.
Reason? Why, *he*'s drawn to the moon like a lunatic.
We are friends, but I'm no mere vessel of his.

For the nights settle down to play chess
With me on the moon-flooded parquet floor;
There's scent of acacia, and windows wide open,
And passion, the witness, turns gray in a corner.

And the poplar is king. I play with insomnia.
The queen is nightingale. I move to nightingale.
And the night is victorious, the chessmen fall back.
And I meet face to face the white morning.

SPARROW HILLS

As to kisses, bare your breast to an open tap.
Not for an age, unstopping, will summer gush like a spring,
Not every night we raise low accordion notes
From dust, stamp our feet, and lure others to dance.

I've heard of old age. What alarming prophecies!
No billow can throw up its arms to the stars.
They say you don't believe. The meadows are faceless,
Heartless the ponds, and no God in the woods.

So you'd split the soul! Stump it out this day!
It is the world's noonday. Where are your eyes?
See how thoughts gather high in a white froth
Of woodpeckers, clouds and heat, pine cones and needles.

Here the rails of city trams come to a stop.
Further, pines will serve. Further, they cannot go.
Further on is Sunday. Breaking off branches,
A clearing starts to run, slithering on the grass.

Sifting the noon, Trinity Day goes on parade.
A grove from us craves belief: the world's always thus.
Conceived thus by the grove, suggested to the meadow,
Spilled from the clouds on satin dresses and us.

SISTER MY LIFE *

Sister my life, to this day overflowing,
You burst on all things with springtime rain,
But men with watch fobs are highly fastidious
And, like snakes in the grass, politely sting.

Our elders for this have good reasons,
But yours without doubt the strangest:
That eyes and lawns in lilac are bathed;
And the horizon's fragrant with moist mignonette.

That, when you read the timetable in May
While traveling on the Kamishinsky line,
It makes a grander impression than the Holy Writ,
And you cannot tear your eyes from the text.

That, when the sunset lights up the peasant
Women who come crowding on the track,
I hear them say it's not my stop as yet,
And the sun, as it sets, expresses regret.

That the bell, striking three, swims away
In apology: Not your stop, I regret.
Then the night, burning out, creeps under the shade.
And the steppe crumbles from a step to a star.

* Also the title of Boris Pasternak's third and perhaps best-
known book of poems. This translation follows the revised text
of 1957.

Winking and blinking, sleep can be gentle,
And like Fatamorgana the beloved is asleep
At the hour when the heart, splashing the platforms,
With the carriage doors sprinkles the steppe.

PROLOGUE TO "1905"

Into our prose with its deformations
From October the winter wanders in.
The skies drop lowering to earth
Like a curtain with fringed hems.

First snow is still close and crisp of weave,
Still sensitive, uncanny—like the news.
In these days of unearthly novelty,
Revolution, you are your own immediate self.

A Joan of Arc fresh from the Siberian mines,
Once convict, you're now a leader, one
Who plunged into the well of existence
Before you had time to gage the leap.

A socialist, emerging from the dusk,
You struck fire from a heap of iron.
Your basilisk face shook with sobbing
As you illumined and froze us to the bone.

Distracted by the crackling of shots,
Flickering there to life in the distance,
Aloofly you make the fires waver
As if spinning the streets in your hand.

And in orgies of fluttering snow-flakes
You make the same proud gesture of reserve:
Like an artist dissatisfied with himself,
You turn your back on all solemn occasions.

Like a poet, who's cooled off and reflected,
You seek your distraction in walking.
Avoiding not merely the money-bags,
You also loathe all trivial things.

THE POET

Had I but known what lay in store—
That verse with clotting blood could kill;
Yes, kill, and throttle too, what's more—
And kept untried my debuts still;

I'd said, "O never, never, no!"
To jokes with this dread spore of all;
But I had still long way to go,
And shy the heart took up the call.

Now this grey age is Rome—the same,
That stands no quirks, insists no fleet
Applause for actor win acclaim,
But death ungrudging and complete.

So when blind passions lines dictate,
They thrust a slave upon the stage;
Then blood alone beats out his fate—
For art dies choked with swelling rage.

THE CITY

A wintry kitchen. Petya's piping,
A frozen room and blizzards' waste—
All these may grow past daily bearing,
And leave at last a bitter taste.

The tracks are snowbound past all reason;
And snowdrifts, death and slumber tell
That this is not a proper season,
But of the times the end and knell.

On slippery steps unchipped ice still,
And frosty bands the well chain down.
A magnet draws us in this chill
Toward the warm expectant town.

In winter country life's no life—
I need not stress this or insist:
With unconcern the city's rife
To imperfections that persist.

A thousand fantasies in gyre
He spun, and need not feel the cold;
And, like a ghost, he is inspired
By swarming souls that thronged his fold.

From railway sidings he seems now
To lonely stacks of frozen logs
Just such a vision's distant glow
Amid the night's effulgent fogs.

Although I thought him rather young,
His pertness pleased me anyway.
The tales of history, on his tongue,
Appeared unfinished till his day.

The twinkling stars he loved to ape
With nightly show of promised good,
And even heaven assumed his shape
In boyish dreams that were my mood.

WIND

(*Two Fragments About Blok*)

1

Who will survive and be accepted,
Who censured and accounted dead,
Such is the province of our toadies—
Of them alone, empowered thus.

No one would know, let us assume,
That Pushkin's honored or indited
Without their doctoral dissertations
Which throw on all things so much light.

But Blok, thank God, is different;
His essay is of a different kind:
From Sinai he did not descend
To adopt us as his rightful heirs.

For fame depending on no lecture,
By no school or system deemed eternal,
He has escaped all manufacture,
And no one thrusts him down our throat.

2

He's as windy as the wind. And like the wind
That whistled through the estate in the days
When Filka the outrider still galloped
At the head of a team of six horses.

Then the Jacobin grandfather was still living,
That old radical of crystalline soul,
And his windy grandson did not lag far behind—
Not even by one finger's length.

The wind, which seeped beneath the ribs
And into the soul as years went by,
Finds mention both in good and ill repute
In poems where that wind is celebrated.

That wind is everywhere. It's present in
The house, in trees, in the countryside and rain,
In the poetry of his third volume,
In *The Twelve,* in death, and everywhere . . .

AFTER THE STORM

The air's sonorous with the storm departed.
Here, as in Eden, all's alive and breathing blithe.
With broken mauve of branches thickly clustered
To drink the freshened air the lilac strives.

All is made quick by weather's alteration.
With rain the gutters of tin roofs are brimmed,
But ever brighter show the sky's transitions
And zenith blue above the cloud's black rim.

The artist's hand, more masterful in power,
From all things purges dust and dirt.
From his own vats of dye, transfigured more,
Reality and life rise fable-girt.

The fifty years that have in tempest passed,
Fade in the memory fainter every day.
And as our century matures at last,
We to the future must give right of way.

So neither cataclysms nor upheavals
Can cleanse a path to usher life's new claim,
But what is shown in generous traits and trials
Of some man's soul aspiring to flame.

HAMLET *

Talk is hushed. I tread the boards.
Leaning on the post of the door,
Distantly I catch the stir
Of what will happen in this age.

Darkly night admonishes
With a thousand lenses trained.
Abba Father, if Thou wouldst,
Bear this chalice past my lips.

I adore Thy strict design,
And consent to act this part.
But another drama's playing:
So, for once, may I dismiss.

But the acts have been ordained,
Irreversible the journey's end.
I'm alone. The Pharisees swamp all.
Living is no country stroll.

From 1905
PART I: THE FATHERS

That was in our time.
With us it turned into proverb.
And it will pass.
Yet, however,
In the rapid turnover of years,
The trace was obliterated,
As if that year
Showed a *nought* between the *nine* and the *five* . . .
Obliterated the trace,
No true story is left,
No sign of the true story remains.

Night is still under arms,
And dawn has not yet grasped the rifle.
But let us
Look closer:
There's more light to this story.
This darkness under arms

* From "The Poems of Yury Zhivago," first printed in
"Znamya" in 1954.

Lies plunged
In half-sleep
By the strike.
This night
Is our childhood
And the youth of our teachers.

The evening of derailments,
Of groups and heroes,
Dynamiters,
Daguerrotypes,
Burning souls,
Had preceded.
Troikas gallop over the new highways,
Savvas * rise up,
and in remote parts *Vikulas* † see the light.

Railway-line signals
Muffle the beat of drums.
The rumbling of tumbrils ‡—
The rattling of the first freight cars.
The Russia of serfdom
Steps out
From its strict confinement
Into the wilds,
And is called
"Russia After The Reforms." **

It is the men of "The Popular Will" party:
Perovskaya,
The nihilists in
Ambush,
Students in pince-nez.
The story of our fathers,
Like a tale
Of the age of the Stuarts,
More remote from us than Pushkin,
But still perceptible
As in a dream.

* Savva Morozov, mill owner and capitalist, who secretly subsidized the revolutionary movement.

† Name symbolizing illiterate rural types.

‡ Literally, "shameful carts": the carts in which condemned men were driven to their place of flogging or execution.

** After 1861, the year in which the serfs were emancipated.

Impossible to see closer.
Twenty-five years spent underground.
A buried trove.
On the surface—
A mere soulless kaleidoscope.
To dig up the trove,
We strain
Our eyes till they pain.
Submitting to its will,
We ourselves must descend into the sap.

Here Dostoyevsky had been.
Those female eremites,
Never expecting
That each police raid
Would uncover relics for the museum,
Went to their execution
And accepted the fact
That Nechaeyev, the conspirator, would inter
Their beauty under the ground,
Concealing it
From the times, enemies and friends.

That was yesterday.
Had we been born thirty years earlier,
And approached through the courtyard
In the dim light of the kerosene lamps,
We'd have found,
Amid the glimmer of retorts,
That those women in the laboratory
Were indeed our mothers
Or
Our mothers' best friends.
It's drizzling outside.
The commotion has died down in the palace.
The lampions go out.
The weather is mild.
The town seems dead and deaf.
The night breathes
Fallen leaves and graveyard thistles.
Not a soul.
The square is drowsy,
Dreaming bad dreams.

But they still write reports
In formal language;
And with no foreboding of the future
A private carriage rattles on the other side of the Neva.
But the September night
Is being stifled
By the secret of that trove,
And dynamite prevents
Stepan Halturin * from sleeping.

This night
Will remain in oblivion
Until the time of Port Arthur.
The telegraph poles
Will have the scaffold for guide.
The whisper of victims and of telegrams,
Becoming more frequent,
Will make the secret agents drowsy,
And then that winter
Will come,
Bringing all things to life.

We were born into the world.
One day
The sun in the late afternoon
Will beckon us to the window.
By chance we shall spiritualize
An unusual sunset
And, at the sight of the chimneys,
Tremble
As some man
Might have trembled
If he could have looked back a hundred years.
Laocoon-like,
The smoke,
Stripping
Like a wrestler

---

* Stepan Halturin (1856–1880), a worker and leading revolutionary figure of the 1870's. In 1878 he organized "The
Northern Union of Workers." Later he joined the Popular Will
Party, which induced him to become a terrorist. He tried to
dynamite Alexander II in the winter palace. In the same year
he killed the military prosecutor Strelnikov and was himself
executed.

In the crackling frost,
Will grapple with and throw the clouds.
The slip-away day
Shall glide past
On the iron runners
Of the telegraph wires
As observed by the attics.

But a little while after,
As if lighting the way for a prodigal son
To prevent him breaking his neck
That day on the roadway,
The lanterns on buildings
Will walk out with their lamps into the night
And, through the mist,
Will slap him on the back.

YEVGENY YEVTUSHENKO (1933–)   Yevgeny Yevtushenko is undoubtedly the voice of the younger generation of Soviet poets and the spearhead of the lyrical revival in the last decade. A poet with an authentic lyrical gift, Yevtushenko has also tried to be a "civic" poet in the sense of adopting a very definite ethical and social position *vis-à-vis* the discredited writers of the Stalinist era. Ethically, Yevtushenko attacks hypocrisy, falsehood, boot-licking and brutality. He supports the ideal cause of the Revolution and the notion of a "guiltless" Russian people, which has been much sinned against. His poetry is informed with compassion for ordinary Russians and the victims of terror, be they Russians or Jews. This aspect of his work is, perhaps, seen most clearly in such poems as "Babii Yar" (1961), "The Heirs of Stalin" (1962), and "The Execution of Stenka Razin" (1964). In "program" poems like these, with political overtones, Yevtushenko is yet able to preserve a high lyrical quality. In other poems, he can be more purely lyrical and write of love and nature, which has been much neglected as a subject in Soviet poetry except in the work of Zabolotzky and Pasternak. Yevtushenko has revived the theme, and it appears even more strongly and lyrically in his latest cycle of poetry. Love is another theme, considered "too personal" by many Soviet ideologists, which has seen a revival not only in Yevtushenko's work, but also in that of his fellow poets Voznesensky, Akhmadullina, Vinokurov, and others. A characteristic feature of Yevtushenko's poetic attitude and work is his love of life, exuberance, and expansiveness, his eagerness to embrace and include an ever greater world of experience in his lyricism. His eager interest has expanded beyond Russia, and he has written poems on French, African, Cuban, and American themes. Yevtushenko is still in his early thirties, and his poetic development has shown a steady deepening of his lyrical feeling as well as an extended grasp of the possibilities of language.

Yevgeny Yevtushenko was born in Stanzia Zima (Winter Station), situated on the Transiberian railway in the region of Irkutsk. The family was originally Ukrainian, but his great-grandfather had been exiled to Siberia. On his mother's side he is of Latvian descent. In his long autobiographical poem, *Zima Station* (1956), Yevtushenko tells us a great deal about his birthplace and family background. In it he also raises some of the issues that have separated the younger generation from their Stalinist "fathers." He began writing early, and his first poem was published in 1949. He was only seventeen then, but he was already beginning to attract attention. It was made possible for him to study at the Gorky Literary Institute in Moscow and, while there, he published his first book *Prospectors of the Future* (1952). He had already published five books when his *Poems of Various Years* appeared in 1959. The initial phase of his poetry was over, but he was in the vanguard of Russian poetry. In the next two years he became internationally known through such poems as "Babii Yar." He traveled and even read his poems in France, England, Germany, and the United States. By 1962 he had published three further books of poems and his *Precocious Autobiography* (1963). The autobiography and some of his poems had provoked so much controversy that the Soviet authorities clamped down on him. From March, 1963, to June, 1965, he did not travel abroad. However, he was able to travel within the Soviet Union and has continued to publish his new poems in magazines. The lyrical quality of his poetry has, if anything, improved.

BIBLIOGRAPHY

In Russian

Razvedchiki Gryadushchego (*Prospectors of the Future*). Moscow: Sovietsky Pisatel, 1952.

Tretii Sneg (*Third Snow*). Moscow: Sovietsky Pisatel, 1955.

Shossé Entusiastov (*Highway of the Enthusiasts*). Moscow: Moskovskii Rabochii, 1956.

Obeschanie (*Promise*). Moscow: Sovietsky Pisatel, 1957.

Luk i Lira (*The Bow and the Lyre*). Tiflis: Zarya Vostoka, *Stikhi Raznikh Let* (*Poems of Various Years*). Moscow: Molodaya Gvardia, 1959.

Yabloko (*Apple*). Moscow: Sovietsky Pisatel, 1960.

Vzmakh Ruki (*A Wave of the Hand*). Moscow: Molodaya Gvardia, 1962.

Nezhnost. Novyii Stikhi (*Tenderness. New Poems*). Moscow: Sovietsky Pisatel, 1962.

"Babii Yar." The Russian text was originally printed in *Literaturnaya Gazeta*, September 19, 1961.

In English

Selected Poems. Tr. by Robin Milner-Gulland and Peter Levi, S.J. London: Penguin Books, 1962; New York: Dutton, 1962.

A Precocious Autobiography. Tr. from the Russian by Andrew R. MacAndrew. London: William Collins & Sons, 1963; New York: E. P. Dutton & Co., 1963. This autobiography first appeared in French in Paris. A small Russian edition was published in Toronto. It has not yet appeared in the Soviet Union.

Reavey, George (ed. and trans.). *The Poetry of Yevgeny Yevtushenko. With An Essay on the Life and Poetry of Yevgeny Yevtushenko*. Bilingual edition. New York: October House Inc., 1965.

❊   ❊   ❊

THERE'S SOMETHING I OFTEN NOTICE

To M. Roschin

There's something I often notice,
and someone apparently gloats over this,
that I'm rather scatter-brained,
and untidy in my way of living.
Among the, in appearance, harmless
half-desires
       and half-feelings,
my pinching worry is:
          I do all right?
What if I don't pull through?
I am disturbed by all the waste of meetings
that nourish neither heart nor mind,
by the sloth,
       not the festive spirit,
that has taken lodging in my house;
by my mistrust for many books,
and the warring strains in all my moods,
and the far too suspect
non-enthusiasm for myself . . .

I'll break with all I lived with up to now,
forget my various mishaps,
with arms spread out
          fall down
on the warm
       and steamy earth.
Oh those who are my generation!
We're not the threshold, just a step.
We're but the preface to a preface,
a prologue to a newer prologue!

Oh you in years my equal,
                        my true friend!
My fate's
            contained in yours.
Then let us be extremely frank,
and speak the truth about ourselves.
Let us share our anxieties together,
discuss between us, tell others too,
what sort of men we can't be any longer,
what sort of men we now desire to be.
Fallen out of love with self-conceit,
we shall not regret the loss.

Character
            begins to form
at the first pinch of anxiety about ourselves.

OTHERS MAY JUDGE YOU

Others may judge you with ironic smile:
"Well, who denies he's got
                        a gift?
But he's so young,
                so very young.
                        There are older men about.
What's he after in such a hurry?"
Petulantly
            they shake their heads:
"Yes, youth eternally—
                        it can't be helped!—
tries to look older than its years . . ."
Listen to them,
                but take no heed.
                        Older!
Be equal to your talent, not your age.
At times let the gap between them be embarrassing.
Fear not
        to be young, precocious.
To be young and tardy—
                    that is wrong!
What if ironic smiles do multiply;
more mature,
            fear not to make them laugh;

more mature,
            while you still have time to grow,
make haste,
            while there's somewhere you can hurry.

ENVY

I envy.
      This secret
I have not revealed before.
I know
      there is somewhere a boy
whom I greatly envy.
I envy
      the way he fights;
I myself was never so guileless and bold.
I envy
      the way he laughs—
as a boy I could never laugh like that.
He always walks about with bumps and bruises;
I've always been better combed,
                        intact.
He will not miss
                all those passages in books
I've missed.
            Here he is stronger too.
He will be more blunt and harshly honest,
forgiving no evil for any good it may bring;
and where I'd dropped my pen:
                        "It isn't worth it . . ."
he'd assert:
        "It's worth it!"
                    and pick up the pen.
If he can't unravel a knot,
                    he'll cut it through,
where I can neither unravel a knot,
                        nor cut it through.

Once he falls in love,
                he won't fall out of it,
while I keep falling in
                and out of love.
I'll hide my envy.
            Start to smile.

I'll pretend to be a simple soul:
"Someone has to smile;
someone has to live in a different way . . ."
But much as I tried to persuade myself of this,
repeating:
"To each man his fate . . ."
I can't forget there is somewhere a boy
who will achieve far more than I.

WHEN I THINK OF ALEXANDER BLOK

To I. Glazunov

When I think of Alexander Blok,
and grow nostalgic for him,
I then remember—not some line of verse,
but a bridge, a carriage, and the Neva.
And above the voices in the night
a rider's figure is clearly etched—
the rings under his startling eyes,
and the outline of a black frockcoat.
Lights and shadows fly to meet him,
and stars in splinters fall on the roadways,
and the waxen fingers of his clasped hands
show something higher than dismay.
As in some very enigmatic prologue,
whose deep meaning is not too clear,
a mist envelops the rattling carriage,
the cobblestones, the clouds, and Blok . . .

ROCKETS AND CARTS

We should not sniff at carts.
The cart has done good service.
But how often,
though hardly fitting now,
I still perceive the cart in art.
How depressing to stare at a colleague
and at his cart-
the-novel.
We've already shot a lunic into the sky,
but our operas
still retain a cart-like style.

O cart-grease spirit!
                    Spirit of routine!
Carts do exist—
                  no pictures.
And yet rumbling like a battering ram,
carts push their way on to the screen.
O you who are so pleased with carts,
what a cart-like mind you own.
You want no rockets in your art;
it's carts you want,
                    just carts.
Your art's most diligent,
wrapped in the label of "vocation";
but all the same
                  it's like a cart,
and in an age of rockets
                        doomed.

CONVERSATION WITH AN
AMERICAN WRITER

"You have courage,"
                    they tell me.
It's not true.
          I was never courageous.
I simply felt it unbecoming
to stoop to the cowardice of my colleagues.

I've shaken no foundations.
I simply mocked at pretense
                          and inflation.
Wrote articles.
              Scribbled no denunciations.
And tried to speak all
                      on my mind.
Yes,
    I defended men of talent,
branding the hacks,
                    the would-be writers.
But this, in general, we should always do;
and yet they keep stressing my courage.
Oh, our descendants will burn with bitter shame
to remember, when punishing vile acts,

that most peculiar
> time,
>> when
plain honesty
> was labeled "courage" . . .

BABII YAR

No monument stands over Babii Yar.
A drop sheer as a crude gravestone.
I am afraid.
> Today I am as old in years
as all the Jewish people.
Now I seem to be
> a Jew.
Here I plod through ancient Egypt.
Here I perish crucified, on the cross,
and to this day I bear the scars of nails.
I seem to be
> Dreyfus.
The Philistine
> is both informer and judge.
I am behind bars.
> Beset on every side.
Hounded,
> spat on,
>> slandered.
Squealing, dainty ladies in flounced Brussels lace
stick their parasols into my face.
I seem to be then
> a young boy in Byelostók.
Blood runs, spilling over the floors.
The bar-room rabble-rousers
give off a stench of vodka and onion.
A boot kicks me aside, helpless.
In vain I plead with these pogrom bullies.
While they jeer and shout,
> "Beat the Yids. Save Russia!"
some grain-marketeer beats up my mother.
O my Russian people!
> I know
>> you
are international to the core.

But those with unclean hands
have often made a jingle of your purest name.
I know the goodness of my land.
How vile these antisemites—
                              without a qualm
they pompously called themselves
"The Union of the Russian People"!
I seem to be
              Anne Frank
transparent
              as a branch in April.
And I love.
              And have no need of phrases.
My need
        is that we gaze into each other.
How little we can see
                      or smell!
We are denied the leaves,
                          we are denied the sky.
Yet we can do so much—
                        tenderly
embrace each other in a dark room.
They're coming here?
                      Be not afraid. Those are the booming
sounds of spring:
                  spring is coming here.
Come then to me.
                  Quick, give me your lips.
Are they smashing down the door?
                                  No, it's the ice breaking . . .
The wild grasses rustle over Babii Yar.
The trees look ominous,
                        like judges.
Here all things scream silently,
                                  and, baring my head,
slowly I feel myself
                      turning gray.
And I myself
            am one massive, soundless scream
above the thousand thousand buried here.
I am
      each old man
                  here shot dead.

I am
　　　　every child
　　　　　　　　here shot dead.
Nothing in me
　　　　　　shall ever forget!
The "Internationale," let it
　　　　　　　　　thunder
when the last antisemite on earth
is buried forever.
In my blood there is no Jewish blood.
In their callous rage, all antisemites
must hate me now as a Jew.
For that reason
　　　　　　I am a true Russian!

LOVE'S MATURITY

Love's maturity, you say?
　　　　　　　　　Is that so?
Straining,
　　　　I wait.
　　　　　　　You come.
Glances meet!
　　　　　　No shudder even!
Instead, repose . . .
　　　　　　　　ready to howl, I run.
Fingers touch!
　　　　　　No explosion even!
Instead, repose . . .
　　　　　　　　I run, ready to howl.
Is that all
　　　　between you and me?
Are ashes
　　　　the maturity of fire then?
Is love's maturity
　　　　　　　no more than affinity,
and that only
　　　　　in the best of cases?
Who's playing the monster
　　　　　　　　over us,
wicked and leering?
Who, with cold efficacy,
dared fabricate a false definition?

Love has its birth and death.
Love has no maturity.
Love roars,
        stoking
the menace of extinction for us,
and it breathes
                not with equanimity,
but huskily
gasps—
        begging for mercy
and no mercy—
as the stifling earth gasps,
abandoned by reason,
half smothered by the world's creation . . .

OTHER TIMES HAVE COME

Other times will come.
Other names will rise.

They push and shove and run.
Making hard-baked enemies,
they create difficulties,
and give rise to spite and malice.

That's why they take the lead,
and girls wait for them in the rain,
and, peering through the dusk,
with furtive fingers wet their eyebrows.

Where are your foes, where are they?
You'd have trouble finding them again . . .
Ah, there they go, so blandly
cordial with their nodding heads.

Where are your girls, tell me where?
The rainy weather's dangerous
for their health, that's the matter—
baby-sitting, they'd rather stay at home.

All your enemies have been stolen.
Stolen, too, the tripping steps,
stolen the whispering of a voice . . .
Only the experience remains.

But why take it to heart and grieve?
Tell me—have you never thieved,
and, failing to keep accounts,
stolen these things from someone else?

Youth is a form of thieving.
Therein lies all the magic of life.
Nothing passes entirely away,
but is simply a transition.

Be wiser then. Don't fall for envy.
Feel sorry for the lucky thieves.
However much they play the devil,
They'll end by being robbed themselves.

Other times will come.
Other names will rise.

ANDREY VOZNESENSKY (1933–) Andrey Voznesensky's name is often coupled with that of Yevgeny Yevtushenko. Though born in the same year as the latter, Voznesensky began publishing much later; and it was not until 1960 that he began to attract public attention. His early poetry has much in common, both in theme and attitude, with that of Yevtushenko. He was one of the "new generation," an *avant-garde* poet eager to express the emotions, the aspirations, and the style of post-Stalinist Russia. But he was not as all-embracing or fluent as Yevtushenko. Nor did he plunge into the vortex of social and political issues as readily as his fellow poet. He was more reticent, less provocative, and quieter—more intimate and purely lyrical perhaps, more immediately concerned with the effects of language, with modern imagery and new forms. This aspect of Voznesensky becomes more clearly evident in 1962, after his first trip abroad, when he published his *Triangular Pear*, undoubtedly the most modern and westward-looking book to appear in the Soviet Union since the 1920's. By 1965 Voznesensky's poetic world has become rather different from Yevtushenko's, but there is no point in arguing which is the "better" poet, as some will tend to do. Both are good poets. Each represents a somewhat different aspect of the new Soviet poetry. Voznesensky has perhaps more of Pasternak in him, while Yevtushenko has more of Mayakovsky and Yesenin.

Andrey Voznesensky was born in Moscow. Intending to become an architect, he attended the Moscow Institute of Architecture in 1957–1958. But he had also begun to write poetry. In 1958 his poems began to be printed in the literary magazines. As a result of this, perhaps, he abandoned architecture and concentrated on literature. In 1960 he published his first book, *Mosaika* (*Mosaic*) in Vladimir, a provincial town not far from Moscow. In the same year he also published his second volume. Two further books of his appeared in 1962 and 1964 respectively. In 1961 he had visited the United States together with Yevtushenko. In 1962 he read his poems in Paris. He fell under the same ban as Yevtushenko and was confined to the Soviet Union until 1965. After a period of rustication in Vladimir, he has been publishing again. His fourth volume, *Antimiri* (*Antiworlds*) appeared in the autumn of 1964. Voznesensky is certainly a poet of quality and imagination, and his development is worth watching.

BIBLIOGRAPHY

In Russian

   Mosiaka. Stikhi i Poemi 1959–60 (Mosaic. Verses and Poems 1959–60). Vladimir, 1960.
   Parabola. Stikhi (Parabola. Poems). Moscow: Sovietsky Pisatel, 1960.
   Treogolnaya Grusha (Triangular Pear). Moscow: Sovietsky Pisatel, 1962.
   Antimiri. Izbrannaya Lirika (Antiworlds. Selected Lyrics). Moscow: Molodaya Gvardia, 1964.

In English

   Encounter No. 115, April 1963. Nine poems by Voznesensky.
   Odyssey Review Vol. 2, No. 4, December 1962. Andrey Voznesensky. Six Digressions from the poem, "The Triangular Pear." Translated by Natasha Bienstok.
   Selected Poems of Andrey Voznesensky. Translated by Anselm Hello. New York: Grove Press, 1964.

❋   ❋   ❋

WEDDING

Young girls get married, marry
Not someone but some thing.
Youth will creak and strain
After a fashionable coat.

After the golden mountains,
And curls pinned up in silver.
And Oh! boots will trample on
The finest broken porcelain.

Where people drink they smash things,
Smash cups and mugs on the floor;
Under the young men's heels
Pots will break to smithereens—
Some one person's happiness
Shatters into shards.

And you in the transparent skirt,
So young and milk-white,
You quiver like a glass
On the edge of a table.

A smile like a small crack
Plays up and down your lips.
And little tears have left
Dark smudges on your cheeks . . .

Tranquil on the surface,
You are not yourself at all.
Your bracelets are like handcuffs,
Your beaded necklace like a noose.

"Bitter, bitter, bitter!" *
It's not such an easy game.
And what's it for? A what-not
All inlaid with silver? . . .

Oh how many of you, girls,
Beautiful idiots and fools,
Have perished for epaulets,
An apartment and the furnishings!

And how many girlish tears,
As on this occasion,
Are interrupted by the wailing
Of a brisk dancing tune repeated!
Where people drink, there's spilling,
Tears, tears, tears, are spilling . . .

* "Bitter!" (*Gorko!*)—a traditional Russian wedding toast.

PARABOLIC BALLAD

Fate-the-rocket describes a parabola
In darkness mostly, more rarely on a rainbow.

Fiery-haired Gauguin the painter lived
As a bohemian, though once he'd been a stockbroker.
To get into the royal Louvre
                from Montmartre,
He
    turned a somersault through Java and Sumatra!
He rushed off, forgetting the craze for money,
the clucking wives, the stale air of Academies.
He conquered
             the gravity of earth.
The augurs guffawed over their steins of beer:
"A straight line is shorter, a parabola steeper.
Isn't it better to copy the groves of paradise?"

And he sped away, a roaring rocket,
Though the wind ripped off coat-tails and ears.
And he landed in the Louvre, through no main entrance
But in a parabola
                    fiercely
                              smashing in the ceiling!
Bravely each man in his fashion seeks truth:
A worm crawling through a crack, man in a parabola.

There was a girl who lived in my quarter.
We attended school together, sent in our term papers.

Where had I gone?!
                    And the devil made off with me
In between the ponderous, ambiguous stars of Tbilisi!
Please forgive me this foolish parabola.
Those frail shivering shoulders in best evening black . . .
O how you rang out to me in the black Universe,
Direct and resilient—like the rod of an antenna!
But I was still flying,
                    getting my bearings to land
From your earthly, chilled, persistent summonses.
How hard it is for us to execute this parabola! . . .

Sweeping aside canons, prognoses, paragraphs,
Art, love and history speed along
A parabolic trajectory.

Galoshes sink in the Siberian spring . . .
Perhaps the straight line is shorter after all?

GOYA

I'm—Goya!
Gliding down upon a bare field,
A raven pecked my eyes out of their funnel sockets.
I'm—Grief.
I'm—the groan
Of war, the charred guts of cities in the snow of "forty-one."
I'm—hunger.
I'm the gasp
Of a hanged woman, whose body clanged like a bell above the
     naked square . . .
I'm—Goya!
O grapes

Of wrath! Westward in a salvo I raised the ash of the intruder!
And into the memorial sky I hammered strong stars—
Like nails.
I'm—Goya!

PREGNANT YOU SIT

Pregnant you sit, and pale.
How you have changed, poor girl.

Plucking at your dress, you sit
And want to go on weeping, weeping . . .

What makes you women spoil us
And, falling, give us your lips,

Then run beyond the platforms,
Outstripped by speeding trains? . . .

How hard you tried to keep up
With the blurring carriage windows . . .

Trains rattle by, express and mail,
Trains to Khabarovsk and elsewhere . . .

From Moscow all the way
To Ashkabad, like numb idols,

Women stand as if turned to stone,
Their bellies proffered to the moon.

And swinging into the light,
In the unpeopled life of the night—

How well the moon, with her
Big belly, understands them.

EVENING ON A CONSTRUCTION SITE

They try to frighten me with formalism.

How remote you are from life,
You experts, smelling high
Of incense and formalin.

In you there may be some "virgin land,"
But you have no pearls of grain to hand.

Art is dead without a spark,
Human rather than divine—
The sort bulldozer men can hear
In the impassable taiga.

It had been tough and sweaty for them;
But to stand up as they do now,
They had to go unshaven as the sun
And shed their husk as pine trees do.

The sort of spark a Chuvashi girl,
Brushing away a blue tear,
Brushing it clean or smudged,
Brushing it off like a dragonfly,
Might applaud resoundingly . . .

For the sake of this, I do not mind
The abuse that's slung at me,
Nor all their outrageous labels.

TAIGA

You have such bold teeth,
And a knife of a smile.
And the gold of your eyes
Hums like a flight of hornets.

We stroll away from the huts,
Up to our ears in the tall grass.
My parents and friends, you predict,
Will haul me over the coals.

But you're hardly a nun
Even among hermit retreats.
But here the furry bees wander too,
Bending the flowers beneath them.

I don't know the taiga any more.
I don't know my parents any more.
I only see the pupils of your eyes.
Your teeth are all I know.

The dew glistens on the daisies
As on a Buddhist bowl.
How lovely she looks in
The dewdrops upon the cyclamen.

On every drop of each fibril,
Reflected and naked,
You tremble minutely,
Making the flowers bend.

You are the living water
On the lips, on a leaf.
To the last drop—you have given
To the Taiga all of yourself.

FIRST ICE

A girl freezes in a telephone booth.
In her draughty overcoat she hides
A face all smeared
In tears and lipstick.

She breathes on her thin palms.
Her fingers are icy. She wears earrings.

She'll have to go home alone, alone,
Along the icy street.

First ice. It is the first time.
The first ice of telephone phrases.

Frozen tears glitter on her cheeks—
The first ice of human hurt.

TWENTIETH CENTURY

The twentieth century,
Out of gloom and fire,
Goes speeding through me
In an uranium rocket.

With metal and sledge-hammer
The earth is lashed red-hot.
But the heart is Thermopylae,
Where war shall not pass by.

ARCHITECTS

Beyond the forests and the seas,
Beyond the blue expanses,
Billowing sails under their vaults
Whisk architects away.

They cut and shape in stone
Rows of Venetian arches—
Russians over in Venice,
And Venetians here in Ryazan.

And high above the cities,
Making the stone glow bright,
They fused in their inward hearts
Poppy-colored cupolas of flame!

With furious, devilish zest,
Architects, you cherished the people.
Out of your own hearts you've shaped
Many a miraculous palace.

My heart I have now apprenticed
To the mystery of a generous calling.

NEW YORK BIRD

With moonbeams garlanded
an aluminum bird—
　　　　　　　　with fuselage
　　　　　　　　　　　　body—
alights on my window,

And above her screw-neck,
a woman's face
　　　　　　flares
like a tongue of flame
over a gigantic lighter!

(Tucked in a capitalist sheet,
my friend is sound asleep.)

who are you cybernetic delirium?
half-robot? half-spirit?
an amalgam of a queen of the blues
and a flying saucer?

America's soul, perhaps,
weary of all the fun?
who are you, teenage chimera,
a cigarette stuck in your teeth?

but they stare unblinking—
and the night cream is not wiped off yet—
those eyes like a certain girl's
on Lake Michigan.

Such gassy bags
she has under her eyes.
Bird, what do you prophesy?
Tell no lies now, bird.
Tell us what you know.
A very strange thing from the outside
surges up in me
as in a connecting vessel.

the atomic age moans in the bedroom . . .

I yell. And, swearing,
my room-mate, as if scalded,
sits up on the mattress.

SECOND MONOLOGUE:
THE REVOLT OF THE MACHINES

To E. Neizvestny

Run—into the self, to Haiti, inside R.C. churches, into privies,
    Egyptian deserts.

Run!

In dark ignorance, like Khan Batyi,
the machines enslave us.

In law courts their barefaced agents
gulping crude oil from wine-glasses
calculate: Who was it in England
led the revolt against machines?
Let us run! . . .

And in the night, mastering his modesty,
the cybernetic robot makes demands
on his creator:

"Give me your wife!" he says.
"I have a weakness for brunettes," he says. "I make love
at thirty revolutions. Better be accommodating! . . ."

O the rapacious things of this age!
The soul is vetoed.
We bolt it into the hills, hide behind beards,
              dive naked into the water,
              but the rivers dry up, for
              the fish are dying in the seas . . .
              women give birth to Rolls Royces . . .
              Radiation! . . .

              . . . My soul, my little beastling,
              behind the city scenes
              you scamper about, scowling
              like a puppy dragging a broken lead!

              And handsomely time whistles
              above fiery Tennessee
              as enigmatic as a harpy
              with a duralumin chassis.

INTRODUCTION: OPEN UP, AMERICA!

Open up, America!
Eureka!
Let me do some pioneering,
                        discover,
                                  snorting,
In America—
              America,
Me—
    in myself.
Wrenching off the earth's skin,
              I brush away dust and mold,
plunge in the depths
                        of the subject,
as into a subway.
There I find triangular pears,
                        seek bare angular souls.
I take the trapezoid fruit,
                        not to swallow it,
but to make the glass of the core
shine like an altar!

Search, get things done,
                        don't twiddle your thumbs.

Let them lie, claiming it's an emerald—
It's really bright red, your watermelon.
I bite into it like a setter,

                cleave deep as an axe.
Is the artist behaving like a hooligan?
Play along with me, Columbus!
My sixth sense

              blows me to shore . . .
Bound for India,
you discover

        America!

Spanish Poetry

SELECTED AND EDITED BY *Angel Flores*

✳ ✳ ✳ ✳ ✳

Introduction

After 1898, when Spain was ingloriously defeated in a war with the United States, the last illusions of national grandeur blurred and disappeared. This low in Spanish morale came, however, at a moment of change, an awakening—as if the stimulus of defeat had kindled the latent forces of revival.* The years that followed saw a new spirit in Spanish education, music, and painting, and Spanish writers came into the twentieth century in a highly critical mood, intent both upon ending cultural insularity and discovering the landscape of Castile and Andalusia. In poetry the so-called generation of 98 and the more French-oriented modernists initiated a rebirth in Spanish letters more intense than any known in Spain in three hundred years.

Antonio Machado, Juan Ramón Jiménez, Miguel de Unamuno were the saints—at times outrageous, humorous, or diabolical—of modern Spanish literature. Much has been written to place these figures in schools: generation of 98, modernism, or a little of both. But by now the academic terms have worn thin and have little more accurate meaning than that of indicating the writers of the first two decades of our century. Machado, Jiménez, and Unamuno rise above classroom labels—*les catégories vides*. In reality their most unifying quality is the diversity of the sources to which they went for nourishment; thus, we find Machado going from the medieval poet Berceo to Emily Dickinson, Jiménez from the

---

* It should not be inferred, however, that a miracle occurred after 1898, but rather that these latent forces—Giner de los Ríos in education, Galdós in the novel, Bécquer in poetry—began to have a more general effect upon education and the arts.

baroque poet Góngora to Tagore, whom he translated into Spanish, and Unamuno from Emerson to Kierkegaard, whom he learned to read in Danish.

It was Juan Ramón Jiménez who dominated Spanish poetry before World War I. Ironically, he was writing perhaps his best poems in the years immediately before 1956 when he won the Nobel Prize, but by then his influence was negligible and even the prize was given for work of his early years.

After World War I new movements in the arts, new isms, were rampant in Europe: futurism, dadaism, cubism, surrealism, and Spanish versions of dada and surrealism in Huidobro's creationism and the related ultraism. In addition to surrealism, Spanish poets were under the spell of both Gongorism and popularism (folksong and ballad) and, later, Marxism.

Surrealism offered a vision of reality particularly at home in a Spain which had produced the phantasmagoric world of Quevedo's *Sueños* (*Dreams*) and nightmarish figures of the late Goya. But the Spanish poets who were at one time affected by surrealism—Lorca, Aleixandre, Miguel Hernández, Alberti, Cernuda—tamed the beast of the unconscious, gave it full imaginative range but more order and immediate meaning. Ultimately the Spanish poets used surrealistic imagery with much greater success than their French counterparts.

Lorca found in surrealism the wild images of anger, despair, and grim laughter to express the impact of New York City of the early 1930's on a Spanish poet. Aleixandre used surrealism to convey the wonder and helplessness of man in lone struggle with the cosmos. Hernández, the shepherd boy who became a master craftsman of poetry, drove surrealism into the confines of the Petrarchan sonnet, combining masculine fury, grace, and discipline in a sequence of love poems unmatched in the Spanish language.

Among Spanish-American poets, surrealism also won its devotees. Unlike Europeans, who saw the beginnings of modern poetry in the orderly sorcery of Poe, Spanish Americans were more attracted to the expansive energy and free forms of Whitman and were at once taken by the revolutionary freedom permitted in surrealism. The Chilean poet Pablo Neruda invented a kind of Whitmanesque surrealism to express dark and shining images of a social nightmare. The Peruvian Vallejo, intense as Hernández and dramatic as Lorca, used the

imagery of surrealism to express the agony of his personal
voyage in hostile lands and among alien lovers. For the Mexi-
can Octavio Paz, surrealism was a natural vehicle for the color
and baroque exuberance of his verse.

Folk poetry also affected the modern poets—anonymous
romancero (ballad book) and *cancionero* (songbook), which
had in the past been imitated by Lope and Góngora and
others. Lorca wrote popular songs of the gypsy and the sierra,
Alberti of the sailor and the sea. Andrade described the In-
dians of his native Ecuador in the popular form of the *copla*.
In Lorca's poem *"Remanso, canción final,"*

> *Ya viene la noche.*
>
> Golpean rayos de luna
> sobre el yunque de la tarde.
>
> *Ya viene la noche.*
>
> Un árbol grande se abriga
> con palabras de cantares.
>
> *Ya viene la noche.*
>
> Si tu vinieras a verme
> por los senderos del aire.
>
> *Ya viene la noche.*
>
> Me encontrarías llorando
> bajo los álamos grandes
>   Ay, morena!
> Bajo los álamos grandes.

are all the ingredients of the anonymous popular song—
simple candor, pathos, and the refrain. In the sixteenth century Saint John of the Cross used a similar refrain, *"Aunque
es de noche"* in poetry which, like Lorca's, was at once popular and highly sophisticated. Often, however, the popular or
folkloric element was blended in the same poem with other
very different poetic traditions. In Lorca's *"Romancero
gitano,"* for example, we see very clearly three figures operating in his verse: the surrealist, the gypsy, and Góngora.

Góngora was a third decisive factor in the poetry between
the wars. The year 1927 was the three-hundredth anniversary
of Luis de Góngora's death. At that time Dámaso Alonoso
brought out a pioneer study of the rehabilitated baroque
poet. The poets publishing at this time—Guillén, Salinas,
Diego, Lorca, Alberti—found in Góngora a model for their

work. In his elemental and symbolic snows, diamonds, feathers, metals, Góngora provided a fresh imagery for the young poets. In the use of hyperbole and hyperbaton, Góngora had extended the linguistic and musical limits of the Spanish language. His extremely sensorial poetry was neither romantic nor sentimental but crisply extravagant, somewhat hermetic despite explications, and, by the taste of the time, very modern.

In addition to Luis de Góngora, there were other classical poets who left their mark on contemporary poetry. Indeed, one of the fascinating qualities of recent poetry has been its return, not simply to one period in vogue, but to the great figures from the twelfth to the nineteenth century. Thus we find in Machado clear echoes of Berceo, Manrique, Fray Luis de León and Bécquer—early and late middle ages, renaissance and romanticism; or we see Lope as well as the verse forms of Andalusian Arabic poetry in Lorca whose last book, *Diván de Tamarit,* contains Spanish imitations of the *qasida;* in like manner, Pedro Salinas entitled one of his early books, *Razón de amor,* after a thirteenth-century narrative lyric of the same title. Guillén went to Saint John of the Cross for the title of his main work, *Cántico (Canticle).*

Finally the years preceding World War II saw the impact of political movements on poetry. Like Eluard and Aragon in France, Neruda, Vallejo, and Alberti turned from surrealism to Marxism, and their poems expressed political beliefs and social events. As with the mural painters of Mexico, the artist took upon himself the mission of social reform. Neruda at one point forbade the translation into other languages of his earlier bourgeois poems from *Residencia en la tierra,* which had made him famous. In the spirit of the time, Machado also turned to Marxism—Christ would come to Moscow rather than Rome, he wrote—and in January, 1939, a few days before he died, in exile, in Collioure, France, he wrote to José Bergamín, stating that while he would prefer to stay in France because of the language, he would go to Russia where he was assured of at least economic survival.

In the same year, 1939, the civil war ended in all parts of Spain, and Miguel Hernández was arrested, condemned to death, and then had his sentence commuted to thirty years. Hernández had also had a stage of politically oriented poems, those of *Viento del pueblo,* but now he went beyond partisan political verse and was writing some of the most moving

poems in the Spanish language since Saint John of the Cross
began his poems of light and darkness in a Toledo dungeon.
Hernández' poems were smuggled out of prison. When he
died in 1942, he was only thirty-two years old. He was the
last of the major poets to appear between the wars. After
Hernández, poetry in Spain changed.

The condition of Unamuno's death while under house ar-
rest, of Lorca's senseless execution, of Machado's death in
French exile and of Hernández' tuberculosis and death in a
Spanish prison was symbolic of the internal convulsions which
racked the body of Spain with the coming of civil war. The
flowering of poetry in Spain, which had begun at the turn of
the century, came to an end. Unamuno, Machado, Lorca, and
Hernández were dead, and the others—Jiménez, Salinas,
Guillén, Moreno Villa, Altolaguirre, Cernuda, Alberti,
Prados—were henceforth poets in exile. The main figures of
modernism and the generation of 98, whoever they were and
however clear or unclear their attachment to one group or the
other, ceased to represent these movements in Spain. The four
most highly esteemed poets of the New World—Neruda, Paz,
Andrade, and Vallejo—who had been living in Spain, were
gone. Of the poets of some reputation, Aleixandre, Diego and
Dámaso Alonso alone remained in Spain to write poems that
could be printed in magazines and books. Spanish letters
suffered actually and symbolically the fate of the Spanish
people.

Under Franco, literature in Spain has taken on a new character. With the disappearance of the leading prewar figures,
with the experience of the postwar generation wholly distinct
from prewar or exiled figures, the younger generation has
necessarily rejected the immediate past in order to confront a
stark present. In prose, the result has led to a novel of much
greater vitality and variety than the prewar novel in Spain.
In poetry there has been a division into two camps: social
and personal poetry.

The new political poetry, uniformly anti-franquista, is a
natural reaction to life under a government unjust and repressive, although not so repressive as to intimidate or censure
away all statements of protest. The poetry of protest is represented by Gabriel Celaya, Leopoldo de Alas, Carlos Barral,
and Blas de Otero, who is presently in exile in France—following a very old Spanish custom. With the exception of
Blas de Otero's work, much of the political poetry, however,

is second-rate and provincially anachronistic. The political realities of Spain—a harsh totalitarian government with pious traditionalist illusions of the grandeur of Isabel la Católica—make little sense outside of Spain, and so do even the violent reactions of its poets to the illusions and propaganda.

The personal or existential poetry, as it is called, began weakly. Much of the religious poetry of Valverde and others also appears local and remote from the preoccupations and metaphysical directions of European literature after the war. Formally much of the experimentation and invention of the 1920's and 1930's was put aside, and poetry was largely formless or unimaginatively traditional: loose free verse or the sonnet, and little in between.

In recent years, however, new things are stirring in Spain and Spanish America. In both areas poetry is again less local, more international, as it were; and concrete poetry, American far-out howls, and French anguish are in the air. Neruda is still producing at a legendary speed, a new *monstruo de la naturaleza* singing the praises of South America. In Spain the personal poets have come upon original areas of form and content. No longer obsessed, as were so many writers in the past, with the Quixotic mission of defining the Spanish soul, they have broken out of the shell of Spain and write incisively about individual man. In so doing, such poets as Bousoño, Cabañero, Claudio Rodríguez, Luis Feria, and Francisco Brines share that obvious turn to simple metaphysical statement which characterizes much poetry of this generation, from Lowell and Roethke in America to Bonnefoy, Sabatier, and Vigée in France. Of these poets, José Hierro, with ties in each of the camps, personal and social, and Blas de Otero stand out today as the most promising poets of their generation.

While literary prophecy is both a pompous and a foolish game, and while the most significant artists inevitably rise above and form anew the tradition about them—Shakespeare, Goya, Cavafy—nonetheless, given the present vitality of letters in Spain and Spanish America, it is certain that new figures of the stature of Machado, Lorca, and Vallejo will suddenly surprise us by their presence in the coming years, shame us for not recognizing them sooner, and give Spanish and Spanish-American poetry a new direction and quality.

Willis Barnstone

BIBLIOGRAPHY

Alonso, Dámaso. *Poetas españoles contemporáneos.* Madrid, 1952.

Alonso Schokel, L. *Introducción a la poesía moderna.* Santander, 1948.

Aub, Max. *La poesía española contemporánea.* Mexico, 1954; *Una nueva poesía española.* Mexico, 1957.

Cirre, José F. *Forma y espíritu de una lírica española.* Mexico, 1950.

Durán Gili, M. *El superrealismo en la poesía española contemporánea.* Mexico, 1950.

Fitts, Dudley. *An Anthology of Contemporary Latin American Poetry.* Norfolk, Conn., 1942 and 1947.

Flores, Angel. *An Anthology of Spanish Poetry from Garcilaso to García Lorca.* New York, 1963.

Hays, H. R. *Twelve Spanish American Poets.* New Haven, Conn., 1943.

Monterde, Alberto. *La poesía pura en la lírica española.* Mexico, 1953.

Sainz de Robles, F. C. *Historia y antología de la poesía española.* Madrid, 1950.

Salinas, Pedro. *Reality and the Poet in Spanish Poetry.* Baltimore, Md., 1940; *Literatura española. Siglo XX.* Mexico, 1941.

Turnbull, Eleanor L. *Contemporary Spanish Poetry. Selections from Ten Poets.* Baltimore, Md., 1945.

Valbuena Prat, Ángel. *La poesía española contemporánea.* Madrid, 1930.

Vivanco, L. F. *Introducción a la poesía española contemporánea.* Madrid, 1957.

ANTONIO MACHADO (1875–1939) Antonio Machado was born in 1875 in Seville, capital of Andalusia. Although his father, an anthologist of Andalusian folksong, took the family to Madrid when Antonio was only eight and enrolled him in the progressive *Institución de Libre Enseñanza* of Giner de los Ríos, the childhood memory of Andalusia remained to dominate his first book, *Soledades* (1903). As a young man he made several trips to Paris, where he attended courses with Henri Bergson, worked as a translator with Garnier, and met Rubén Darío and the French poets of the day. Bergson's philosophy marked his poetry; France gave him its language and so his profession of French schoolmaster; and the mood of Paris colored his early poetry in the form of Spanish modernism and French symbolism.

Machado took his first teaching post in the city of Soria in 1907. There he fell in love with Leonor and with the Castilian landscape. Leonor was sixteen when he married her and died but three years later. Although he left Soria the same year, 1912, for Baeza in northern Andalusia, the obsessive memory and conscious daydream of Leonor and Castile stayed with him throughout his life.

The impact of Soria is recorded in *Campos de Castilla* (1912), a volume of solitude, bare Castilian landscapes, painful memories of Leonor, and Spain seen through the reforming eyes of a poet of the generation of 98. The language is sparse, exact, yet sonorous, throbbing with a grave, contained emotion. After 1919, don Antonio was in Segovia, and in 1931, when the Republic was declared, he came to Madrid. During these years he collaborated with his brother Manuel in several plays, and published both poetry (*Nuevas canciones,* 1917–1930) and an extraordinary book of philosophy, wit and poetry called *De un cancionero apócrifo,* followed by *Juan de Mairena.*

Machado has been considered the poet of Castile. But recently he has been increasingly recognized as the poet of both Andalusia and Castile: of both wit and gravity, of Andalusian childhood and dream and Castilian manhood and love. In the later years of his life, a new love, Guiomar (Pilar Valderrama), brought in an element of immediate erotic drama, not found in earlier poems. When civil war came,

Machado remained loyal to the Republic. The war separated him from Guiomar and eventually from Spain itself. He crossed the French border when Catalonia fell and died soon after in Collioure, in early February, 1939. Among his most perfect poems were those written during the war, lines fused with pathos and calm, painful and peaceful recollection, and images of a startling clarity. Today Machado is the most highly esteemed poet in Spain.

EDITOR'S NOTE. Works by the first three poets in this section were selected by Willis Barnstone. The poems by Machado were all translated by Willis Barnstone.

BIBLIOGRAPHY

Soledades. Madrid, 1903.
Soledades, galerías y otros poemas. Madrid, 1907.
Campos de Castilla. Madrid, 1912.
Nuevas canciones. Madrid, 1925.
Poesías completas. 6th Ed. Madrid, 1946.

❊　❊　❊

A YOUNG FACE ONE DAY APPEARS

A young face one day appears
before our house.
We tell her: why do you return
to the old home?
She opens a window and all the fields
in light and fragrance waft inside.
On the white path
the tree trunks grow black;
the top leaves
are green smoke dreaming far away.
A pond seems
like a broad river in the white mist
of morning. Across the livid mountains
another chimera.

NAKED IS THE EARTH

Naked is the earth,
and the soul howls to the pale horizon
like a hungry she-wolf. Poet, what do you seek
in the sunset?

Bitter walking, for the road
weighs upon the heart. The frozen wind
and coming night, and the bitterness
of distance! On the white road

a few stiff trees blacken;
in the distant mountains there is gold
and blood. The sun is dead. Poet, what do you seek
in the sunset?

AND HE WAS THE DEVIL OF MY DREAMS

And he was the devil of my dreams,
the handsomest angel. His eyes
of victory shone like steel,
and bloody flames from his torch
lighted the deep crypt of my soul.

"Will you come with me?" "Never.
Tombs and the dead terrify me."
Yet the ferrous fingers
seized my right arm.

"Will you come with me?"—And in my dream
I went forward, blinded by his red lantern.
And in the crypt I heard the ringing chains
and the stirring of imprisoned beasts.

SUMMER NIGHT

A beautiful summer night.
The tall houses
leave their balcony shutters
open to the wide village plaza.
In the large deserted square,
stone benches, burning bush, and acacias
trace their black shadows
symmetrically on the white sand.
In its zenith, the moon; in the tower,
the clock's illuminated globe.
I walk through this ancient village,
alone, like a ghost.

SILVERED HILLS

Silvered hills,
gray heights, dark violet rocks
where the Duero twists
a bow around Soria, somber oaks,
fierce stony ground, bald peaks,
white roads and river poplars,
Sorian afternoons, mystical and warlike,
today I feel deep sadness for you,
sadness of love. Fields of Soria
where the rocks seem to dream,
come with me. Silvered hills,
gray heights, dark violet rocks!

TO JOSÉ MARIA PALACIO

Palacio, good friend,
is spring
already dressing branches of the black poplars
by the river and the roads? On the steppe
by the deep Duero, spring is late,
yet so lovely and soft when it comes!
Do the old elms have
a few new leaves?
The acacias must still be bare
and the sierra mountains with snow.
O white and pink mass of Moncayo,
there, so handsome in the Aragon sky!
Are brambles in flower
among the gray rocks,
and white daisies
in the slender grass?
In those belfries
the storks must be arriving.
The green wheatfields
and brown mules in the seeded furrows,
and with April rains the farmers
who plant the late lands. Now bees
are sipping rosemary and thyme.
Are the plums in bloom? Violets left?
Furtive hunters, with partridge
decoys under their long capes

cannot be missing. Palacio, good friend,
are nightingales already on the riverbanks?
With the first lilies
and first roses in the orchards,
on a blue afternoon, climb to the cemetery
of Espino, high Espino, where she is in her earth.

IN THE BLUE

In the blue
a bank of black birds
that shriek, flutter, and alight
on a stiff poplar tree.
In the naked grove
the grave quiet jackdaws
write cold black notes
on February staffs.

THE BLUE MOUNTAIN, THE RIVER, THE ERECT

The blue mountain, the river, the erect
coppery staffs of slender aspens,
and the white of almond trees on the hill.
O flowering snow and butterfly on the tree!
With the aroma of bean plants, the wind
runs in the joyful solitude of the fields.

RAINBOW AND BALCONY

Rainbow and balcony.
                    The seven chords
of the sun's lyre tremble in dreams.
A child's kettledrum strikes seven times—
water and windowpane.
                    Linnets in acacia trees.

Storks on towers.
                    In the plaza,
rain has washed the dusty myrtle.
Who put this smiling group of virgins
in the wide rectangle,
and above—hosanna!—the serene blue
and golden palm leaf in the broken cloud?

WHO PUT BETWEEN THE ASHEN ROCKS

Who put between the ashen rocks,
as honey for a dream,
those genistas of gold
and those blue rosemary flowers?
Who painted
the violet range and the saffron of the sky
in the sunset? Beehive, hermitage,
the gorge above the river, the eternal
rolling of water between great boulders,
the blond greenness of new fields,
and all, even the white pink earth
at the foot of the almond trees!

THE DRAB BROWN OAK

The drab brown oak
and the wasteland of stone.
When the sun sinks,
the river wakens.

O distant mountains
of mauve and violet!
In the shadowed air
only the river sounds.

Livid moon
of an ancient afternoon,
in the cold fields
more moon than earth!

BESIDE THE SIERRA IN FLOWER

Beside the sierra in flower
the broad sea bubbles.
In my honeycomb of bees
are small grains of salt.

BESIDE THE BLACK WATER

Beside the black water.
A scent of sea and jasmine.
Malaguenean evening.

YOUR FACE ALONE

Your face alone
like white lightning
in my somber night!

In the glossy sand
near the sea,
your rose and dark flesh
suddenly, Guiomar!

In the gray of the wall,
prison and bedroom,
and in a future landscape
only your voice and the wind;

in the cold mother-of-pearl
of your earring in my mouth,
and in the shivering
of a mad dawn, Guiomar,

you appear on an embankment
dashed by the sea of a dream,
and below the arching frown
of my vigil, treacherously,
always you!

Guiomar, Guiomar,
see me punished in you:
guilty of having created you,
now I cannot forget you.

THE CRIME WAS IN GRANADA

I

He was seen walking between rifles
down a long street,
coming upon the cold field
which still held stars of early dawn.
They killed Federico
when daylight came.
The squad of executioners
dared not look upon his face.
All had shut their eyes.
They prayed: Not even God can save you!
Dead fell Federico—

blood on his forehead and lead in his entrails.
. . . Oh, that the crime was in Granada.
Let all know it! Poor Granada! In his Granada!

II

The Poet and Death

He was seen walking alone with her,
without fear of her scythe.
The sun was already on the towers; hammers
on the anvils, anvils and anvils of the forges.
Federico spoke,
flirting with death. She listened.
"Because the clapping of your dry palms
sounded yesterday in my verse, companion,
and you gave ice to my song and the edge
of your silver sickle to my tragedy,
I will sing you the flesh you do not have,
the eyes you lack,
the hair the wind was ruffling,
the red lips where they kissed you.
Today as before, gypsy, my death,
how good it is alone with you
in these winds of Granada, my Granada!"

III

He was seen walking . . .
        My friends, build
of stone and dream in the Alhambra,
a tomb for the poet,
over a fountain where water weeps
and says eternally:
The crime was in Granada, in his Granada!

SONG

The moon already rises
over the orange grove.
Venus shines
like a crystal bird.

Behind the distant range
the sky is amber and beryl,
and purple porcelain
on the quiet sea.

Night is in the garden,
water in the gargoyles!
Only the jasmine smells,
nightingale of perfumes.

How the war seems
to sleep from sea to sea,
while flowering Valencia
drinks the Guadalaviar!

Valencia of slender towers
and gentle nights, Valencia,
will I be with you
when I cannot see you,
where sand grows in the fields
and the violet sea fades away?

JUAN RAMÓN JIMÉNEZ (1881–) Like so many modern Spanish poets—Machado, Aleixandre, Lorca, Alberti—Juan Ramón Jiménez is an Andalusian by birth. Born in Moguer in 1881, he went to Madrid at eighteen, called there by Rubén Darío, who was his first master. Always sickly as a young man, he returned for his health to Moguer, where he wrote his famous book of poetic prose, *Platero y yo,* which holds in Spanish literature somewhat the same place as St. Exupéry's *Le Petit Prince.*

In 1916 Jiménez went to New York, where he married Zenobia Camprubí Aymar. With his wife he collaborated in the translation of works by Rabindranath Tagore, an important influence on his own prose and poetry. He traveled extensively in Europe and America. When civil war ravished Spain, though never a political writer, he accepted voluntary exile and was never to return to Spain. In 1956, while living and teaching in Puerto Rico, Juan Ramón Jiménez was awarded the Nobel Prize for literature.

Jiménez is the "pure" lyric poet of Spain. His early work, which made him by far the best-known poet of Spain between world wars, is delicate, luminous, sentimental, hypersensitive. Although such books as *Arias tristes* (1903), *Melancolía* (1912), and *Sonetos espirituales* (1917), won him his early reputation and eventually the Nobel Prize, it is precisely these works which, among contemporary writers, have put him under a literary cloud. But Jiménez developed beyond his early reputation to an extraordinary degree. His second period of *Piedra y cielo* (1919), *Eternidades* (1918), *Poesía* (1923), reveal a poet who has discarded conventional form to set down ideas and perceptions in bare, imaginative free forms. He is still the pure poet, but his punch is direct; sentimentality is gone. In the last works, *Animal de fondo* (1949) and later poems, the poet broods about death and his animal nature. The metaphysic is tortured and intimate; the lines flash with color, as in all his poems, but now they are crossed with savage pessimism and tense belief.

EDITOR'S NOTE. The poems by Jiménez were all translated by Willis Barnstone.

BIBLIOGRAPHY

Almas de violeta. Madrid, 1900.
Ninfeas. Madrid, 1900.
Rimas. Madrid, 1902.
Arias tristes. Madrid, 1903.
Jardines lejanos. Madrid, 1904.
Elegías puras. Madrid, 1908.
Elegías intermedias. Madrid, 1909.
Olvidanzas. Madrid, 1909.
Elegías lamentables. Madrid, 1910.
Baladas de primavera. Madrid, 1910.
La soledad sonora. Madrid, 1911.
Pastorales. Madrid, 1911.
Poemas mágicos y dolientes. Madrid, 1911.
Melancolía. Madrid, 1912.
Laberinto. Madrid, 1913.
Estío. Madrid, 1916.
Sonetos espirituales. Madrid, 1917.
Diario de un poeta recién casado. Madrid, 1917.
Eternidades. Madrid, 1918.
Piedra y cielo. Madrid, 1918.
Poesía. Madrid, 1923.
Belleza. Madrid, 1923.
La estación total con las canciones de la nueva luz. Buenos Aires, 1946.
Animal de fondo. Buenos Aires, 1949.
Tercera antología poética. Madrid, 1957.

❊ ❊ ❊

IDEAL EPITAPH FOR A SAILOR

To find your tomb one must
search the firmament.
Your death rains down from a star.
A gravestone does not oppress you, it is a universe
of dream.
In your ignorance, you are
in everything—sky, sea, and earth—dead.

FIRST DAWN

(*Dozing*)

We are arriving by train.
Shadowy cold, quiet.

And it is as if—
in a constant upheaval—
we arrive in life,
from death; we arrive
in death, from life.

Cocks crow; one doesn't know
whether in life, whether in death—
in a constant upheaval.
Shadowy cold, quiet.

DAWNING

The sun gilds honey
on mauve and green fields—
rock and vineyard, hill and plain.
Breezes make the blue flower
fresh and soft on livid stone walls.
There is no one now, or not yet,
in the enormous readied fields
which the lark decorates
with crystal wings.

   Here, there, open and deserted,
the red dazzling towns.

LIGHT

Outside, dark and ultimate wind wandered
toying with cold leaves.

Inside, an ecstasy of sunlight,
isolated, like an eternal
driven feeling in my soul,
within the turmoils of my flesh.

And the sun never departed, pure and pink.

DAWN

The sky in the oblivion
of my sleep, had
forgotten to be what it is.

Quickly, I opened
and raised my eyes, and a glory
also opened, a garland of green,
pure, blue secrets
touched my wakened forehead.

The sky was not a name,
but the sky.

YOU SEEMED

You seemed
passionate and still enraged,
a sunset behind the storm.

The red glow of your streaming eyes
illumined here and there your tragic shadow
in final coronation.
O vast nostalgia of a twilight
      (it!)
which was to come!

Where did I see such a city landscape—
quarters open to the western
sun at sea, with crystal portals streaked
with bleeding light—
horribly and gloriously unique
that seemed a woman?

That seemed an unknown woman.
O vast nostalgia of a woman
      (you!)
who were to come!

VIGIL

Night departs, a black bull—
full flesh of mourning, terror, mystery—
roaring with vast horror
at the sweating dread of all the slain;
and day comes in, a young child
begging trust, love, laughter,
a child in the remote
arcana
where ends and beginnings meet,

playing a moment
on some kind of field
of light and shadow
with the fleeing bull.

IT WAS THE SAME

It was the same
as an immense dusk of happy gold,
suddenly extinguished
in ashen clouds.

It left me with that gloom
of great anxieties
when they are shut up in the cage
of daily truth; with that burden
of ideally colored gardens
which an oil-filthy fire rubs out.

I did not give in,
I wept for it. I forced it. I saw ridiculous
unreason in the candid brotherhood
of man and life,
of death and man.

And here I am, ridiculously alive, waiting,
ridiculously dead, for death.

PRECISE WORD, ALIVE

Precise word, alive,
which the inner world exhales, the same
as a rose molded in a morning star:
cumulus—a serene mountain peak
in the heart—against the exact zenith;
final star in the upright jet
from the most profound fountain
of the soul!

HOW THE BIRD SINGING

How the bird singing
in the green poplar's peak of light
up to the gay sun of bright afternoon

splits my soul pleasantly in two—
and what musical blood pours out!
from the unturning zenith
down to the unchanging earth!

MOGUER DAWNINGS *

Silver poplar groves
breaking from the mist!
The solitary wind
moving through the marsh—
unreal earthquake—
widespread Huelva
remote and pink!
Above the sea, near la Rábida,
in the gray moist pearl
of the end-of-night sky
cold behind the raw dawn
(a horizon of pines!),
cold behind the white dawn,
the blazing moon.

SOUNDING BEHIND THE WALL

Sounding behind the wall
only your voice.

           Only a wall
cuts the sky from the world
yet what terror!

Everyone is on the other side
and neither you nor I can see.

* Moguer and Huelva are small cities in southern Andalusia, Spain.

PEDRO SALINAS (1892–1951) Pedro Salinas, like his lifelong friend Jorge Guillén, was a poet, professor, and excellent critic. Born in Madrid in 1892, he taught in Spanish and European universities before coming to teach at Wellesley College. Guillén succeeded him at Wellesley, and Salinas went to Johns Hopkins where he remained until his death in 1951.

Salinas is the poet of love. His poems, at once metaphysical and erotic, have the intimate colloquial tone of a telephone call; but the speech is exact, though easy, and meaningful on several levels. He is a poet of the modern world, which he mocks and loves—the Underwood girls and the Mabels of the Far West. The things of the world fascinate him. But no land or seascape wins his heart or imagination until the poet discovers the sea of Puerto Rico, which he celebrates in *El contemplado* (1947).

Salinas has been considered a disciple of Juan Ramón Jiménez and an exponent of *poésie pure*. The Jiménez accent is there, as well as the precise diction; more important, however, is the passionate, metaphysical "adventure toward the absolute," to use his definition of poetry.

EDITOR'S NOTE. The poems by Salinas were all translated by Willis Barnstone.

BIBLIOGRAPHY

Presagios. Madrid, 1923.
Seguro azar. Madrid, 1929.
Fábula yssigno. Madrid, 1931.
La voz a ti debida. Madrid, 1934.
Razón de amor. Madrid, 1936.
El contemplado. Mexico, 1946.
Todo más claro y otros poemas. Buenos Aires, 1949.
Poesías completas. Madrid, 1955.

❈   ❈   ❈

DISTANT SEA

It is not the sea but its image,
its imprint, wrongside, in the sky.

It is not the sea but its fragile
voice,
across the wide world,
broadcast through the winds.

It is not the sea but its name
in a lipless language,
townless,
with no other word than this:
sea.

It is not the sea but its idea
in fire, unfathomable, clean;
and I,
flaming, drowning inside it.

THE SHORE

If it were not for the weak
rose of white white foam
which it remotely invents,
who would tell me
that it moved its chest while
breathing, that it's
alive with an impulse inside,
that it craves the entire earth
and the blue quiet July sea?

VALLEY

In the tender landscape
—here, remaining—
the iron bridge.

Blue sky, green earth,
the bridge, O black!

On luxuriant hills
a will collapsing,
love on vacation,
life all in curves.

But walking, on, on, he
alone, bridge, straight.

EARTH. NOTHING MORE

Earth. Nothing more.
Earth. Nothing less.
And let that be enough for you.
For on the earth our feet are planted,
on our feet the torso straight,
on our torso the head firm,
and there, in our forehead's refuge
the pure idea, and in the pure idea
tomorrow, the key
—tomorrow—of eternity.
Earth. No more nor less.
And let that be enough for you.

ALMOST AVILA

The lofty walls,
intact, squander
vigils of stone
in front of deserted fields.
(And the enemies?)
From the watchtowers
the roads are seen
that carry slow
and humble herds.
(And the enemies?)
A great impregnable gate
is a passageway
for boring droves of beasts
—wine, oil, wheat.
(And the enemies?)
Perched on stones
of warring destinies,
some loving storks
made their peace
in the bed of winds.
(And the enemies?)
Fortified city,
faithful watchman
of centuries and lands;
and your enemies?

WATER IN THE NIGHT, IRRESOLUTE SNAKE

Water in the night, irresolute snake,
faint hissing and unknown path;
what day snow, what day ocean? Tell me.
What day cloud, echo
of you and a dry river bed?
Tell me.

I won't tell: you hold me between your lips,
I kiss you but no lucidity.
Let compassion in the night content you,
and leave the rest
in darkness, for I was made
for the thirst of lips that never question.

THE MISSING TREE

On the blade of an axe
they brought me
a piece of the world.
Cypress:
I see
long blue shadows
on a whitewashed wall.
I hear
the apical nightingale,
the frivolous songs.
I know by its secret mass
a vertical finger
of the constant landscape.
On the blade of an axe
they brought me everything.
I close my eyes
before whitewashed walls;
am buried in silence
of the flown nightingale.
I shudder, unmoving,
in the keyless landscape.

WAKE UP. DAY CALLS YOU

Wake up. Day calls you
to your life: your duty.

And to live, nothing more.
Root it out of the glum
night and the darkness
that covered your body
for which light waited
on tiptoe in the dawn.
Stand up, affirm the straight
simple will to be
a pure slender virgin.
Test your body's metal.
Cold, heat? Your blood
will tell against the snow,
or behind the window.
The color
in your cheeks will tell.
And look at people. Rest
doing no more than adding
your perfection to another
day. Your task
is to carry your life high,
and play with it, hurl it
like a voice to the clouds
so it may retrieve the light
already gone from us.
That is your fate: to live.
Do nothing.
Your work is you, nothing more.

I DON'T SEE YOU

I don't see you. But know
you are here behind
a skimpy wall made of
bricks and mortar, well within sound
of my voice, if I called you.
But I will not call.
I'll call you tomorrow
when, not seeing you,
I suppose you'll stay
close by my side;
and your voice today
is enough (which I
would not hear yesterday).

Tomorrow—when you are
there behind a skimpy
wall of winds,
of skies and years.

UNDERWOOD GIRLS

They are peacefully asleep,
those thirty round white keys.
Between them all
they uphold the world.
Watch them here in dream:
clouds,
round white; and inside:
destinies of thunder and fireflash,
of slow rain,
of snow, wind, signs.
Wake them
with springing contacts
of swift fingers
like ancient music.
They play another music:
metal phantasies,
stiff waltzes to dictation
Let them rise up from centuries
of sameness, be distinct
like seawaves
and a great secret soul
Let them think it is the letter,
the formula, as always.
So place
your fingers firmly
and seize and hurl
the thirty eternal nymphs
against the great vacuous world,
white on white.
At last they move to the pure deed,
wordless, senseless,
s, z, j, i . . .

DAILY SPRING

So many are spreading open: sky-
  gardens across the water!

Through the blueness, foam, tiny white clouds,
  so many white corollas!

Before full day comes, the meticulous
  twilight rises and goes

about its business: contriving futures.
  It gathers in and seeds

a few left-over stars, some bits of light
  through the sky, on the sea.

Waves and clouds are born with dawning.
  And spring, how swiftly!

That barely a bud—cloud—now a rose,
  in gold, in glory, explodes.

White dazzlings, fugacious flowers
  blossom in the earth-fields

of another blue. If foam is unleafed—
  petals along the beach—

a thousand open; they rise from a rosebush
  that is an endless plant.

The noon lays a crown of radiance
  on the work of the dawn.

Now the select harvest is a brilliance,
  a wave, a pageant, a cloud.

A season is abridged: it is an hour.
  What the earth takes so long

in turning into impatient stems
  the morning brings with it.

Dawn? It is the frequent and heavenly
  everyday spring;

without hope for Aprils, in the blue
  it releases Aprils.

Where is its power from, its precipitous
   driving force in the sap?

Obedience. To the light. Pure obedience;
   she in her zenith commands.

Spaces turn into night at her sign,
   at her sign grow bright.

The sea does not **breed** anything of shadow;
   it saves itself for light.

And she spreads on it her mythical truth:
   eternal magic, the light.

WHAT BIRDS?

Birds? Birds?
Is there only one bird in the world
flying with a thousand wings, singing
in innumerable trillings, always alone?
Are land and sky mirrors? Is air
a mirror of air, and does the great unique
bird multiply
its solitude in myriad appearances?
(Is that why
we call it birds?)

Or maybe there isn't one bird?
And are they
fatal plural immense, like the sea,
a numberless band, a surge of wings,
where one seeks a vision and the soul wants
to separate the truth of one lone bird
from its unending essence, from the one
   handsome bird?

ON THE DRY LAND

On the dry land
the soul of the wind
gave me sea news
with the shivering lips
of summer poplars.
Breaths of ocean

and longing for voyage,
keel, prow, wake,
Circe and gold fleece,
the wise poplars
all gave the lie
to the dry land.
And a white cloud
(a white sail)
on the horizon
with canvas gestures,
boasted of hurried flights
on choice routes
on the windless sea
of that dry sky
of the dry land
by summer poplars.

CÉSAR VALLEJO (1892–1938) Recently the place, and for the first time the date of birth of Vallejo were officially established: Santiago de Chuco, Departamento de La Libertad, Peru, March 19, 1892. His was a bitter life, warped by dire poverty, and full of persecutions and personal attacks. He studied first at the Colegio San Nicolás, Humachuco, and after 1912 at the University of San Marcos, Lima, but on discovering that he was not meant to be a scientist, he dropped out and took up literature at the University in Trujillo, from which he graduated in 1915. For a while he taught at the Colegio Nacional, in San Juan, but his only joy was in writing poems (somewhat imitative of Darío, Whitman, Lugones and Baudelaire) which he contributed to the various literary journals in Lima and the provinces. He also fell in love, twice, and even attempted to commit suicide. His return to Lima washed away some of his romanticism; he joined the vanguard Colonida group and sent to press his first collection of verse, *Heraldos negros* (1918). While paying a visit to his mother in his native Santiago de Chuco, he got in trouble with the local authorities and went into hiding for two months but was captured, and imprisoned for six months. While in jail he wrote constantly, and one of his odes, now included in his second book, *Trilce* (1922), was awarded a prize. *Trilce* is a strange book, the outpourings of a rebellious soul; he disregards grammar and syntax and often even logic and describes his poverty, his anguish, his anger at social inequities, and his sympathy for the underdogs. Soon thereafter he left Peru never to return.

From 1923 to 1930 he led a painful existence in Paris, trying to earn a living from his writings. When expelled from France, again for political reasons, he found a haven in Madrid. But life was not easier there: he contributed articles and stories for periodicals, wrote a novel, *Tungsteno;* a play, *Lockout;* and a book about his travel experiences in the Soviet Union in 1928 and 1929, *Rusia* (1931). Back in Paris in 1932 he struggled to keep alive, just when the Spanish civil war rushed him to join the Loyalists. The great upheaval inspired him with some of his most memorable verse: *España aparta de mi este cáliz* and *Poemas humanos,* published posthumously. He was rushed to Paris suffering from some strange disease and died at the Arago Clinic in Paris on Holy Friday, April 15, 1938.

BIBLIOGRAPHY

Works by Vallejo:
    Heraldos negros. 1918.
    Trilce. 1922 (2nd. ed., 1930).
    Poemas humanos. 1939.
    España aparta de mi este cáliz. 1940.
About Vallejo:
    Monguió, L. *César Vallejo, vida y obra.* New York, 1952.
    Nieto, L. C. *Poetas y escritores peruanos.* Cuzco, 1957.
    Zilio, G. M. *Stilo e poesia en César Vallejo.* Padua, 1961.

❈ ❈ ❈

THE SPIDER

There's a huge spider that crawls no more;
a colorless spider whose body,
a head and an abdomen, bleeds.

Today I saw it close up. And how vigorously
toward all sides
it stretched its countless feet.
And I thought of its invisible eyes,
the spider's fatal pilots.

It's a spider that trembled, stuck
on the edge of a stone,
the abdomen on one side
and the head on the other.

The poor creature has so many feet, yet it can't
make up its mind. And, seeing it
astonished in such a crisis,
I've been so anxious today about that traveler.

There's a huge spider whose abdomen
prevents it from following its head.
And I thought of its eyes
and its numerous feet.
And how anxious I am about that traveler!

TRANSLATED BY *Charles Guenther*

BLACK MESSENGERS

Life has blows, and such harsh ones . . . I cannot tell!
Blows like the hatred of God; as if before them,
The tidal surge of all suffering
Were to well up in the soul . . . I cannot tell!

They are few, yet they are there . . . They cleave dark furrows
In the proudest of faces and the strongest of backs.
Perhaps they will be the colts of barbarous Attilas,
Or the black messengers sent to us by Death.

They are the profound lapses of our soul's Christs,
From some adoring faith that Destiny blasphemes.
These sanguinary blows are the cracklings
Of some bread we are burning at the furnace door.

And man . . . Poor wretch . . . poor wretch! He turns his eyes, as
When we are summoned by a tap on the shoulder;
He turns mad eyes, and all experience
Wells up like a pool of guilt in his gaze.

Life has blows, and such harsh ones . . . I cannot tell!

TRANSLATED BY *Muriel Kittel*

OUR DAILY BREAD

I drink my breakfast . . . Damp earth
of the cemetery freezes the precious blood.
City of winter . . . the biting crusade
of a wheelbarrow appears, hauling
a feeling of starvation in chains.

I wish I could beat on all the doors,
and ask for somebody; and then
look at the poor, and, while they wept softly,
give bits of fresh bread to them.
And plunder the rich of their vineyards
with my two blessed hands
which, with one blow of light,
could blast nails from the Cross!

Eyelash of morning, Thou wilt not rise!
Give us our daily bread,
Lord . . . !

Every bone in me belongs to others;
and maybe I robbed them.

I came to take something for myself that maybe
was meant for some other man;
and so I start thinking that, if I had not been born,
another poor man could have drunk this coffee.
I feel like a dirty sneak-thief . . . Wherever I go!

And in this frigid hour, when the earth
transcends human dust and is so sorrowful,
I wish I could beat on all the doors
and beg pardon from someone,
and make bits of fresh bread with it
here, in the oven of my heart . . . !

TRANSLATED BY *James Wright*

AH THE FOUR WALLS OF THE CELL . . .

Ah the four white walls,
they can't help it, they always come out four.

Greenhouse of nerves, painful opening:
in the four corners they are always uprooted,
the arms and legs that are chained every day.

Loving woman, keeper of numberless keys,
if you were here, if you could just see
how the hours are these four walls.
We should lean on them together, the two of us,
we two more than ever. And you would not weep,
I swear, my saviour!

Ah the four walls of the cell.
Yet I pity the walls, and mostly, tonight,
those two long ones that hold
some shape of mothers who carry
the dead down slopes of bromide,
each one holding a little boy by the hand.

And I alone draw to one side, left back
holding up my right hand, that serves for both hands,
in search of a third arm
that will have to house, between my where and my when,
this sickly majority of man.

TRANSLATED BY *James Wright*

THE ETERNAL DICE

My God, I am weeping for the life that I live;
I am sorry to clutch at your bread;
but this wretched, thinking piece of clay
is not a crust leavened in your side:
you have no Mary-candles to darken.

My God, had you been man,
you, today, would know how to be God;
but you always lived so well,
that now you feel nothing of your own creation.
The man who suffers you—is God!

Today, when there are candles in my dazed eyes,
as in the eyes of a condemned man,
my God, you will light all your lamps,
and we will play with the old dice . . .

My God! when the whole universe is thrown,
maybe the circled eyes
of death will turn up,
like two final aces of clay.

My God, in this muffled, dark night,
you can't play any more, because the earth
is already a die nicked and rounded,
worn from rolling by chance,
and it can stop only in a hollow place,
in the hollow the enormous grave.

TRANSLATED BY *James Wright*

TO MY BROTHER MIGUEL IN MEMORIAM

Brother, today I sit on the brick bench of the house,
where you make a bottomless emptiness.
I remember we used to play at this hour, and mama
caressed us: "But, sons . . ."

Now I go hide
as before, from all evening
lectures, and I trust you not to give me away.
Through the parlor, the vestibule, the corridors.
Later, you hide, and I do not give you away.
I remember we made ourselves cry,
brother, from so much laughing.

Miguel, you went into hiding
one night in August, toward dawn,
but, instead of chuckling, you were sad.
And the twin heart of those dead evenings
grew annoyed at not finding you. And now
a shadow falls on my soul.

Listen, brother, don't be late
coming out. All right? Mama might worry.

TRANSLATED BY *James Wright*

IN THIS CORNER WHERE WE SLEPT
TOGETHER . . .

In this corner where we slept together
so many nights, it pleases me now to
wander about. The bed of the dead lovers
has been pushed aside or perhaps carried away.

You were always on time for other things,
yet you have not arrived. It was in this corner
where, one night by your side,
I read between your tender breasts
a tale by Daudet. This is the corner
we loved. Please don't deny it.

I have set myself to recording the summer days
now past, your coming and going,
small and brave and pale, through these rooms.

On this rainy night,
so far removed from both of us, I suddenly leap up,
there are two doors opening and closing,
two doors that come and go in the wind
shadow   to   shadow.

TRANSLATED BY *Lillian Lowenfels and Nan Braymer*

TRILCES XVI

I have faith in the strong
leave me crippled, wind, let me go.
I wear my zeros, my mouth a zero.
O dream give me your hardest diamond
your sense of unreality.

I have faith in the strong.
The colorless quantity
of a concave woman going by,
whose survival ends where mine begins.

I smack the bottom of a dusty Jesuit,
I pull down the green presidential banners,
All Death's crabs, the last flags,
turn the putrid posters face down.

I have faith in that I am,
and that I was useless.

O first of all.

TRANSLATED BY *Stanley Moss*

TRILCES XIV

What is my explanation? How did it happen?
That I am blistered and lacerated,
this way of walking on the edge,
those faces of brutes from temple dolls.
The blood cemented on my forehead, the quicksilver.
Those landladies pillowed on their buttocks.
What cannot be, was all along.
It was absurd.
Madness.
To walk all the way from Trujillo to Lima
to earn a wage less than money.

TRANSLATED BY *Stanley Moss*

THE LAST STEPS

My father's sleeping. His countenance
disfigures nothing;
he is gentle now . . .
if there is anything angry in him, it is I.

Today there is loneliness in the house and prayer.
There is no word from the children as usual.
My father wakes up, an innocent listening
for a flight to Egypt, a bloodless farewell.
He is closer now;
if anything is distant in him, it is I.

My mother walks near the cypresses,
tasting something already without taste.
She is so calm now,
light as a feather, so much farewell, so much love.

By the old stove loneliness, no sound,
or gossip, or green, or childhood.
Something's broken in the air this afternoon,
something lowers, something is crossed over,
somewhere two old roads curved and white.
Toward them my heart walks on foot.

TRANSLATED BY *Stanley Moss*

IF IT SHOULD RAIN TONIGHT . . .

If it should rain tonight, I would withdraw
A thousand years from here,
Better, a hundred, no more.
As if nothing had happened, I would
Imagine that I am yet to come.

Or with no mother, no lover, no obstinate desire
To squat waiting on the ground, with one
Intent,
Like this tonight, I would be combing
The Vedaic fiber,
The Vedaic yarn of my final finish, thread
Of the devil, an attempt to have held
By the nose
Two of Time's discordant clappers in one bell.

Whether I imagine my life
Or imagine that I am not yet born,
I shall not succeed in freeing myself.

It will not be what has not yet come, but
What has arrived and already gone,
But what has arrived and already gone.

TRANSLATED BY *Muriel Kittel*

THIS PIANO TRAVELS INSIDE . . .

This piano travels inside,
travels in glad leaps.
Then it meditates in ironclad repose,
fitted with ten horizons.

It goes on. It crawls under tunnels,
there under tunnels of pain,
under vertebrae that naturally fly off.

At other times its trumpets go,
slow yellow Asias of life,
go into eclipse,
and clean themselves of insectile nightmares,
now killed by thunder, herald of genesis.

Dark piano, whom are you watching
with your deafness that hears me,
with your dumbness that deafens me?
O mysterious pulse.

TRANSLATED BY *Charles Guenther*

I AM FREED FROM THE BURDENS
OF THE SEA . . .

I am freed from the burdens of the sea
when the waters come towards me.

We are always scattering salt. We season
the marvelous song, the good-luck song
on the lower lips of desire.
Oh beautiful virginity.
The saltless breeze passes.

From the distance, I breathe marrows,
hearing the profound score, as the surf
hunts for the keys.

And if we spoke this way of the nostrils
in the absurd,
we should cover our poverty with gold,
and hatch the still unborn wing
of the night, sister
of the orphaned wing of the day,
that is not really a wing, being alone.

TRANSLATED BY *James Wright*

TORMENTED FUGITIVE, COME IN, GO OUT . . .

Tormented fugitive, come in, go out
on the same quadrangular forge.
Doubt. The balance pierces and pierces
up to the hilt.

Sometimes I give in to all enemies,
and for a while I am the blackest of high peaks
in the accidental death of harmony.
Then my dark eyes are divinely irritated,

and the mountain range of my soul begins sobbing,
oxygen forces itself, delighted,
flaming, up and down, until
grief doubles up its peak with laughter.

But one day you will not be able to come
nor to leave, when I fling a handful of earth
into your eyes, fugitive!

TRANSLATED BY *James Wright*

A WOODEN THING MY PATIENCE . . .

A wooden thing my patience,
deaf and plant-like.

Day that has once been pure, a useless child,
that was born naked, now the miles of your march
are racing over your twelve extremities,
this frowning, grim deception
one day to be unravelled
into I know not what last winding-sheets.

Your mighty plumage, constellation formed
of curdled hemispheres beneath eternal
americas unpublished—you depart
and leave me reft of your ambiguous feelings
reft too, on Sunday, of your knot of dreams.

And moths consume my patience.
Again I cry: When will it come, that loud-mouthed
Sunday, silent as the tomb, to charge
this ragged Saturday, this horrible suture
which knits the pleasure that begets us by chance
and the pleasure that exiles us!

TRANSLATED BY *J. M. Cohen*

YOU PEOPLE ARE DEAD . . .

You people are dead.
What a strange manner of being dead. Anyone might say that
    you were not.
But, in truth, you are dead.

You float like nothing behind that membrane which, suspended from zenith to nadir,

comes and goes from dusk to dusk, trembling in front of the
sonorous box of a

wound which to you is painless. Well, I assure you that life is
in the mirror and

that you are the original: death.

While the wave goes and while the wave comes, with what
impunity one can be dead!

Only when the waters swell and break on the shores in front
of them, and when the

waves pile one on top of the other, then you transfigure yourselves and,

imagining you are about to die, you discover the sixth string
which does not belong

to you.

You are dead, never having at any time before this been alive.
Anyone might think

that since you do not exist now, you might have existed at
some other time.

But in truth you are the cadavers of a life that never was.
Pathetic fate, never to

have been anything at any time, but only dead! To be a dry
leaf without ever

at any time having been a green one. Orphaned beyond all
other orphans!

Yet for all that the dead are not, and cannot be, cadavers of
a life they have not

lived. They have forever died of life.

You are dead.

TRANSLATED BY *Thomas Merton*

BLACK STONE ON TOP OF A WHITE STONE

I shall die in Paris, in a rainstorm,
On a day I already remember.
I shall die in Paris—it does not bother me—
Doubtless on a Thursday, like today, in autumn.

It shall be a Thursday, because today, Thursday
As I put down these lines, I have set my shoulders
To the evil. Never like today have I turned,
And headed my whole journey to the ways where I am alone.

Cesar Vallejo is dead. They struck him,
All of them, though he did nothing to them.
They hit him hard with a stick and hard also
With the end of a rope. Witnesses are: the Thursdays,
The shoulder bones, the loneliness, the rain and the roads. . . .

TRANSLATED BY *Thomas Merton*

A MAN PASSES WITH A LOAF OF BREAD ON HIS SHOULDER . . .

A man passes with a loaf of bread on his shoulder.
Am I going thereafter to write about him, my double?

Another sits down, scratches himself, removes a louse from his
    armpit, kills it.
What good would it do to talk about psychoanalysis?

Another has attacked my chest with a club in his hand.
Shall I then discuss Socrates with the doctor?

A lame man gives his arm to a little boy.
After that, am I going to read André Breton?

A man shivers with cold, coughs, spits up blood.
Will it ever be fitting to allude to my inner soul?

Another scratches in the mud for husks and bones.
How then can I write about infinity?

A mason falls from the roof, dies before breakfast.
How then can I launch a new metaphor or rhythm?

A storekeeper cheats a customer of one gram.
How then can I talk about the Fourth Dimension?

A banker falsifies his accounts.
What tears are then left for the theater?

A cripple sleeps with one foot on his shoulder.
Shall I later on talk about Picasso, of all people?

Someone sobs at the side of a grave.
How can I consider my admission to the academy?

A man cleans his rifle in the kitchen.
What good would it do to talk more about it?

Someone walks by counting his fingers.
How can I think of the *not-me* without crying aloud?

TRANSLATED BY *Lillian Lowenfels and Nan Braymer*

PEACE, THE WASP, THE BUNG,
THE HILL SIDES . . .

Peace, the wasp, the bung, the hill sides,
The dead man, the ten litre bottles, the owl,
Places, the spider, the tombs, the tumbler, the dark women,
Unknowing, the kettle, the acolyte,
Drops, forgetfulness,
Power, the cousins, the archangel, the needle,
The Parish Priests, ebony, lack of skill
The part, the type, the stupor, the soul. . . .

Easy to handle, covered with saffron, everlasting, spotless,
Easy to carry, old, thirteen, covered with blood,
They have been photographed, made ready, they have swollen
    up,
Joined together, broad, they have put on ribbons, they are
    perfidious. . . .

Burning, comparing,
Living, flying in a rage,
Striking, analyzing, listening, meddling,
Dying, bearing up, getting themselves a place, weeping. . . .

After, these here,
After, up above,
Perhaps, while, behind, so much, so never,
Below, maybe, far,
Always, that one, tomorrow, how much,
How much. . . !

The horrible, the sumptuary, the very slow,
The portly, the fruitless,
The ill-fated, causing us to twitch, the wet, the fatal,
The all, the most-pure, the gloomy,
The bitter, the satanic, the tactile, the profound. . . .

TRANSLATED BY *Thomas Merton*

MASS

When the battle was over
and the fighter was dead, a man approached him
and said, "Don't die, I love you so!"
But the corpse, alas, kept dying.

Two came up to him and repeated,
"Don't leave us! Take heart, come back to life!"
But the corpse, alas, kept dying.

Twenty ran up to him, a hundred, a thousand, five hundred
    thousand,
crying out, "So much love and to be powerless against death!"
But the corpse, alas, kept dying.

Millions of individuals surrounded him
with a common petition, "Hold on, brother!"
But the corpse, alas, kept dying.

Then all men on earth
surrounded him; the sad corpse saw them and was moved;
he sat up slowly,
embraced the first man and started to walk . . .

TRANSLATED BY Charles Guenther

ANGER WHICH BREAKS A MAN
INTO CHILDREN . . .

Anger which breaks a man into children,
Which breaks the child into two equal birds,
And after that the bird into a pair of little eggs:
The poor man's anger
Has one oil against two vinegars.

Anger which breaks a tree into leaves
And the leaf into unequal buds
And the bud into telescopic grooves;
The poor man's anger
Has two rivers against many seas.

Anger which breaks good into doubts
And doubt into three similar arcs
And then the arc into unexpected tombs;
The poor man's anger
Has one steel against two daggers.

Anger which breaks the soul into bodies
And the body into dissimilar organs
And the organ into octave thoughts;
The poor man's anger
Has one central fire against two craters.

TRANSLATED BY Thomas Merton

WITH HIS INDEX FINGER HE USED TO WRITE ON THE AIR . . .

With his index finger he used to write on the air:
"Long live the comrades! Pedro Rojas."
Of Miranda del Ebro, father and man,
husband and man, railworker and man,
father—but even more man—Pedro and his two deaths.

A wind-borne scrap of paper, they killed him (this really
    happened)
A feather of flesh and blood, they killed him!
Go tell all the comrades at once!

A pole on which they hung their beam,
they killed him;
they killed him to the base of his forefinger!
At one and the same time they killed both Pedro and Rojas!

Long live the comrades
on the honor roll of the air!
May they live long with the *V* of the vulture in the guts
of Pedro
and of Rojas, hero and martyr!

Searching him after death, they surprised
within his body a body big enough to hold
the soul of the world,
and in his pocket an empty spoon.

Pedro also had the habit of eating
with the members of his family, of embellishing
his table and living pleasantly
like anyone else,
and that spoon stayed always in his jacket,
awake or asleep, always
that dead-alive spoon, with its symbolic meaning.
Inform all the comrades at once!
Let them bow before this spoon forever.

They killed him, forced death on him,
on Pedro, on Rojas, on the worker, the man, the one
who was once such a little baby, who looked at the sky,
and later grew up and became a Red,
struggling with every cell of his body, with his yeas and nays,
    his doubts, his hungers and the pieces of himself.

They killed him with finesse
amid the tresses of his wife, Juana Vasquez,
in the hour of fire, the year of the bullet,
and just when he was getting at the meaning of things.

Pedro Rojas, after his death,
raised himself up, kissed his bloody catafalque,
wept for Spain,
and once again wrote with his finger on the air:
"Long live the comrades! Pedro Rojas."

His dead body contains all of the world.

TRANSLATED BY *Lillian Lowenfels and Nan Braymer*

VICENTE HUIDOBRO (1893–1948) Born on January 10, 1893, of a well-to-do Chilean-French family, Huidobro was educated by the Jesuits in his native Santiago de Chile and, after nineteen, in Paris at the Lycée Berthelot. He graduated from the Law School but never practiced. Attracted by literature from the earliest, he began writing verse in Spanish or French in his teens. *Canciones de la noche* was privately printed in 1912 and in 1916 he became co-founder, with the literary rebels Guillaume Apollinaire and Pierre Reverdy, of the vanguard magazine *Nord-Sud*. Throughout World War I he resided in Paris, moving to Madrid in July, 1918, and causing there a literary revolt in the 1920's with his *"creacionismo,"* a trend not unlike the American imagism, only much wilder. This is the period when he signed manifestos and fought the "ultraists" (Gerardo Diego, Guillermo de Torre, Jorge Luis Borges), claiming priority over their movement. Later on he turned to prose and wrote extravagant biographies of Spain's national hero, the Cid, and of Cagliostro, both translated into English in the early 1930's: *Portrait of a Paladin* and *Mirror of a Magi*. During the civil war he helped the loyalists, returning to Chile at the war's termination. He died in Santiago on January 2, 1948, at the age of 54.

BIBLIOGRAPHY

Works by Huidobro:
  Canciones de la noche. 1912.
  La gruta del silencio. 1913.
  Las pagodas ocultas. 1914.
  Adán. 1916.
  Horizon carré. 1917.
  Tour Eiffel. 1918.
  El espejo de agua. 1918.
  Poemas árticos. 1918.
  Automne régulier. 1925.
  Tout à coup. 1925.
  Altazor. 1931.
  Temblor del cielo. 1931.
  Ver y palpar. 1941.
  El ciudadano del olvido. 1941.
About Huidobro:
  Holmes, H. A. *Vicente Huidobro and Creationism.* New York.
  del Valle, J. *Vicente Huidobro.* Santiago de Chile.

ARS POETICA

May verse be like a key
That opens a thousand doors.
A leaf falls; something goes by on the wing;
May all that eye can see be created,
And the hearer's soul stand trembling.

Invent new worlds and watch your word;
The adjective that bestows no life, destroys.

We are in the cycle of nerves.
Muscle hangs
Like a memento in museums;
But not for that have we less power:
True strength
Dwells in the head.

Why do you sing of the rose, oh poets?
Make it flower in the poem!

For us alone
Do all things live beneath the sun.

The poet is a little God.

TRANSLATED BY *Muriel Kittel*

SHE

She took two steps forward
Took two steps back
The first step said good morning sir
The second step said good morning madam
And the others asked how is your family
Today is as beautiful as a dove in the sky

She wore a burning chemise
She had eyes bringing sleep like the seas
She had hidden a dream in a dark cabinet
She had met a dead man in the middle of her head
When she came she left a lovelier part behind
When she left something formed on the horizon to wait for her
Her glances were wounded and bled on the hill
Her breasts were full and she sang the darknesses of her age
She was lovely as a sky under a dove

She had a mouth of steel
And a fatal flag outlined between her lips
She laughed like the sea that feels coals in its belly
Like the sea when the moon sees itself drowning
Like the sea that has nibbled all shores
The sea overflowing and falling in the void in times of
    abundance
When the stars murmur over our heads
Before the north wind opens its eyes
She was lovely in her horizons of bones
With her burning chemise and her glances like a tired tree
Like the sky riding on the doves

TRANSLATED BY *Charles Guenther*

GLANCES AND SOUVENIRS

    The sea
raising the sighs of travellers
runs in behind its waves swept by the wind
Infinity looks for a gull to hold aloft
one point of support, smooth and logical.

As we shall do
The sky clacks full of the wings it loves
        while I
look for my poem on foot
A star crunches like the wheel of
a car carrying away
the last souvenirs.

      Nothing will be encountered
The well of things lost will never be filled, never
with the glances and the echoes
      which move away
        above the fog
          and its great beasts.

TRANSLATED BY *Paul Blackburn*

IN

Heart of the bird
Heart shining in the bird
Heart of the night
Night of the bird
Bird of the heart of night

If night sings in the bird
In the bird forgotten in the sky
Sky lost in the night
I would tell you that what is in the heart shines in the bird

Night lost in the sky
Sky lost in the bird
Bird lost in the oblivion of the bird
Night lost in the night
Sky lost in the sky

But heart is the heart of the heart
And speaks through the mouth of the heart

TRANSLATED BY *Muriel Kittel*

From THE RONDO OF THE LAUGHING LIFE

Three hundred and sixty-five trees go into one forest
Three hundred and sixty-five forests go into one year
How many forests would make up a century?
A child could stay lost there for nearly a century
And could learn the songs of all of the birds
The trees bow their heads when the children throw stones
The stones greet the birds in mid-air and ask for a song
A song with blue eyes
A song with long hair
A song in parts like an orange
With a story full of smiles on the one hand and a story full of
    tears on the other
The tears wring their hands before drowning
And the smiles wave at people from far off like stones
Good morning and See you again are the offspring of mouths
    that are ready for falling in love
The sun says Good morning when the trees spread their wings
And it says See you again when the mountain is closing its eyes
See you again in the oil-covered waves of the sea
And I would say it myself because somewhere the sky holds a
    flag full of flowers
So that life is sweet a glass of orange juice with the stories of
    little boys between the teeth of little girls
So that it is joyful and can run between uncurbed colors like
    dogs
Or like rivers that flow towards my grandfather

The flowers give thanks at the side of the road

The trees murmur so clearly in front of our eyes that it would
be impossible not to understand them

The trees are fifteen years old and the flowers are learning to
walk

The trees say Good morning and beg the sun to take off its
necktie and put on its hat

So life is joyful

Life with its terrible speed

Life with three hundred and sixty-five trees to scamper up
happily

Life with its flowers like neckties

Life with its bellowing mounting the evening

Slow as the eyes of the evening

The sun says Good night and turns away until the trees resume
their places religiously

So life should be joyful

But men stare too hard with their bonfire eyes

They probe in corners with fingers like knives

They track down the sleeping trees to enslave them

Then we curse life and tighten our fists

Then we scream every night at the mountain

Long live death with its terrible speed

With its speed its terrible speed that will never run down

TRANSLATED BY *Jerome Rothenberg*

JORGE GUILLÉN (1893–) Born in Valladolid on January 18, 1893, Guillén developed quietly and studiously, first in Spain, studying in Valladolid and Madrid, and later abroad, as reader at the Sorbonne and Oxford, and since 1938 as professor in the United States, mainly at Wellesley College. An authority in the field of Spanish literature, he is thoroughly conversant with world literature and has to his credit splendid translations of Jules Supervielle and Paul Valéry, who has exerted a profound influence on him. All of Guillén's work is contained in one book, *Cántico*, originally published in 1928 after ten years of concentration and painful toil. The seventy-five original poems of this volume kept increasing with each new edition: to 125 in 1936, to 270 in 1945, to 332 in 1950—a situation quite exceptional for Spain where poets generally extemporize or, like uncontrollable geysers, spout forth their lyricism. Guillén has been accused of being cold, academic, intellectual by accusers who have been unable to discern the restrained emotion, the controlled passion which flow deep in the very substance of his verse.

BIBLIOGRAPHY

Works by Guillén:
   Cántico, 1928, 1936, 1945, 1950, 1956.
About Guillén:
   Alonso, A. *"Jorge Guillén, poeta esencial."* La Nación (Buenos Aires), April 21, 1929.
   Alonso, D. *Poetas españoles contemporáneos.* Madrid, 1952.
   Bergamín, J. *"La poética de Jorge Guillén."* La Gaceta Literaria (Madrid), January 1, 1929.
   Cano, J. L. *De Machado a Bousoño.* Madrid, 1955.
   Casalduero, J. *Jorge Guillén, Cántico.* Buenos Aires, 1946.
   Gullón, R., and Blecua, J. M. *La poesía de Jorge Guillén.* Zaragoza, 1949.
   Pleak, F. A. *The Poetry of Jorge Guillén.* Princeton University Press, 1942.

❊   ❊   ❊

OMEN

You are now all your destiny's fragrance.
Your life unlived and pure pulses
Within me, the tic-toc of no time.

What if the alien sun will never brighten
These figures, not of dream but, yes
Created by the two of us in pride!
   It does not matter. They are
   Truer than verisimilitudes of light
   Foreshortened here by chance and compromise.

Transformed into the omens of yourself,
You are sustained—oh, but without arcana!
By the invading total unity.

What of that immense and formless
Pullulation in the black of depths
Under the solitudes enhanced by stars?
   The celebrated stars, the stars
   Do not watch the candor of our night.
   Tranquilly exists so great a darkness.

Dark of eternity. Oh, not a celestial
Monster! For our souls, invisibly,
Conquest: their presence here among the things.

TRANSLATED BY *Patricia Terry*

ADVENT

Oh moon, how much April,
How vast and gentle the air!
All that I lost, when the birds
Return, will be mine again.

Yes, when the little birds
Choiring their aubade
Sweetly, sweetly persist
In grace released from art.

The moon is not far away,
Calm within our sky.
He who I was awaits me,
Buried in my mind.

The nightingale will sing
From the zenith of desire.
Dawn, the dawn light cleaving
Breezes and the sky.

And has that time been lost,
Though lost to me? Into
The hand, deft god,
Of the timeless moon.

TRANSLATED BY Patricia Terry

THIS MOON

The moon!
          When you unveil
The contours of the dark,
Even nameless shadow
Is friendly close to the course
Of your familiar radiance.
And always you refuse
To be that heaven-born refuge
Claimed by deluded lament.
Tranquilly you continue
Illuminating your round.
Who more nakedly displays
His truth than you, rotund
Countenance? And with a firm
Smile, contemplating face
To face so many, presiding,
You make the rounds of your nocturnal
Realm. For us all
You are the absolute omen
Graced by your so gentle
Apparition.
          Full moon!

TRANSLATED BY Patricia Terry

BEYOND

I

(Now to the body the soul
Returns, moving toward the eyes,
Makes contact.) Light! I by my whole
Being invaded. Wonder!

Intact it is, enormous,
Prowling time . . . Abruptly,
Noises. How they leap
Over the not yet

Sharp-bladed yellows
Of a sun now gentle
With its dawning rays
Through the room diffused,

While the substantial
Begins to appear
Which, disposed in things,
Will limit, center me!

And the chaos? Far away
From its source, I receive
Out of the turbulence of light
These chips of coolness. Day!

A certainty
Extending, grows, commands.
Magnificence confirms
The innuendo: morning.

And the weight of morning falls,
Vibrates on my eyes
Which once again will see
The extraordinary: all.

By centuries distilled, all
Rises totally
Here within this moment
Eternal and for me.

And I from the ceaseless
Flow of moments save
The present, eternity
Suspended in the air.

The blood hastens, hastens
With doomed avidity.
Blindly I accumulate
Destiny, willing to be.

To be; nothing more. Enough,
The absolute of joy.
With the essential in silence
So much is identified!

From rapids by caprice
Of unique destinies
Break loose, and with the force
Of being cast off time,

Irrevocably to fuse
With the last unyielding
Sonority: yes, yes, yes,
The syllable of the sea!

All communicates to me,
In conquest, made a world,
Valor, the will to be
In truth, in triumph, real.

I am; here and now. I breathe.
The profound is the air.
Reality invents me.
I am its legend. Hail!

II

No, not a dream. Creation's
Vigor consummates
Here its paradise:
Accustomed penumbra.

And this implacable being
To which I am once more
Surrendered—the obscure
Resolving into form

In surfaces of pillow,
The whiteness of a sheet,
A hand touching linen
And the extended body

Which remembering
The star asserts its weight—
This being, universal
Conqueror, maintains

Also in the concealed
Its plenitude: it is
Beyond always in truth
Mysterious, very real.

III

Beyond! Close at times
Very close, familiar,
Alluding to certain courteous
Enigmas: here they are.

Irreducible, and yet
Lengthy, broad, deep
Enigmas—in their masses.
I touch them, use them.

Toward my society
The room inclines.
So many objects! Named,
They submit to the mind.

Enigmas they are and here
Live to meet my need,
Amiable tranpierce
Whatever my surroundings

Constant with the mobile
Alliances of bonds
Affirming in the flux
Their equilibrium.

IV

The balcony, panes of glass,
Books, and a table.
That is all they are?
Yes, palpable wonders.

Jubilance of matter
Transforms into discrete
Planes the atoms, sad
Never to be seen.

And through a simple blade
Or for love of a curved
Handle, all the force
Of plenitude awakes.

Energy or its glory!
Shining in my domain
Peacefully within
The real, now, Monday.

And matter, with humility
Agile to define
The Grace of Apparition:
This is wicker, this is lime.

V

Along that wall,
Under a sun which flows,
Gilds and shadows warm
Clarities, the slow

Sunlit calm in flux.
Smiling goes the sun
Along the wall. Matter
Joyful in conjunction!

And, meanwhile, the summit
Of a tree—leaf by leaf
Sunning itself, surrendered,
All here and now—enchants me.

Soon I know a presence
Wandering through green
Will offer me its own
Being: the remote.

So remote it is
In itself beyond. The gift
Of a unique world: I follow
This passage to my soul!

VI

Oh perfection: I depend
On all that is beyond,
I depend on the things!
Without me they exist, and now

Propound themselves in volumes
Undreamed of by a hand
Rejoicing to appraise
The gesture of surprise!

I, in joy, require
The glass-paned balcony,
That luster promises
The longed-for to desire,

And is truly the diaphanous
Atmosphere of morning,
Eaves, and tile roofs,
Distances, there, clouds!

Touching the shore of April
That warbling trill dispersed
Through a fragility
Of foliage. (There is dew.)

But the day at last renews
Rotundity of human
Edifice, refers
Its forces to my view.

And so it reconciles,
Fuses distances;
Landscapes in their transit
Along the balcony glide.

Never does the sky
Obstruct, the sky that now
—Air that I breathe—
With planet overwhelms me.

Where lost, to wander, where?
My center is this point
At random. So entire
Always the world awaits.

A tranquility
Constant to affirm
Is beacon-guide to all
Who in the universe

Of web, in the eternal
Journey captives, under
The sun will to be
And to their love surrender

Condemned, but to soar
In joy with the earth and sea,
Take wing toward the infinite:
One ray of sunlight more.

It is the very light
Of Eden, still resplendent
Here before my face, upon this
Flower, in this garden.

And with a thrust empowered
By confluence of love
Hastens to the hallowed
Never ending now

All of creation
Which, when a man awakens,
Projects solitude toward
Tumults of accord.

TRANSLATED BY *Patricia Terry*

BONFIRES

Love contentedly turns
To fire. The wind burns.

And, so lightly, the flame
Rustles, perseveres along
Its branches to remain
   Itself, now a song.

   That wind
Painter of its flight!
In shadows flames deny
The stars alight.

          Stars in decay?
          Soirée!

Love contentedly on fire.
I, drawn by undulating flames.
Love embraced by the wind's desire.

     Stars.
     Ladies are
     So lovely
     As flames!

For, mute and suave, the yellows
   All grow dull.
To red the glowing coals
   Their luster lull.

Lovely are
Ladies in
Flames.
And the stars!

Love contentedly aflame
Always toward a dawning
Blush the winds embrace.

       Aurora with hints
        Of star-prints.

  That wind
Painter of its flight!
   That burning
Of dawn against the night!

For the eyes, a deity,
Dawn in potency,
The flames I contemplate
  Illuminate me.

Love contentedly turns
To fire. The wind burns.

TRANSLATED BY *Patricia Terry*

THE HORSES

Shaggy and heavily natural, they stand
Immobile under their thick and cumbrous manes,
Pent in a barbed enclosure which contains,
By way of compensation, grazing land.

Nothing disturbs them now. In slow increase
They fatten like the grass. Doomed to be idle,
To haul no cart or wagon, wear no bridle,
They grow into a vegetable peace.

Soul is the issue of so strict a fate.
They harbor visions in their waking eyes,
And with their quiet ears participate
In heaven's pure serenity, which lies
So near all things—yet from the beasts concealed.
Serene now, superhuman, they crop their field.

TRANSLATED BY *Richard Wilbur*

GERARDO DIEGO (1896–) Born on October 1, 1896, in Santander, Gerardo Diego was educated in Deusto by the Jesuits. From the earliest his interests were divided between music and literature, but he followed them both successfully, becoming an accomplished pianist and obtaining degrees from Spain's leading universities: the master's from Salamanca and the doctorate from Madrid. He began writing verse from his early twenties, and after printing privately three plaquettes, he won a wider audience with *Manual de espumas* (1924), which was awarded the National Prize. This collection of thirty poems may be considered the most brilliant and original contribution of "ultraísmo," the vanguard movement in the Spain of the 1920's, primarily an adaptation of Pierre Reverdy's experiments which, in turn, echoed the "new spirit" of Guillaume Apollinaire and the cubist painters. Since 1920 Diego has taught in several secondary schools (in Soria, Gijón, Santander, Madrid). In Soria he met the great poet Antonio Machado, who influenced him deeply and since then, although he was also temperamentally inclined, he has cultivated a classical type of poetry, except for *Fábula de Equis y Zeda* (1932), which has an unmistakable surrealist essence. In 1947 Diego became a member of the Spanish Academy.

BIBLIOGRAPHY

Works by Gerardo Diego:
   El romancero de la novia. 1920.
   Imagen. 1922.
   Soria. 1923.
   Manual de espumas. 1924.
   Versos humanos. 1925.
   Viacrucis. 1931.
   Fábula de Equis y Zeda and *Poemas adrede.* 1932.
   Angeles de Compostela. 1940.
   Alondra de verdad. 1941.
   Romances and *Primera Antología.* 1941.
   La sorpresa. 1944.
   La suerte de la muerte. 1948.
About Gerardo Diego:
   Alonso, D. *Ensayos sobre la poesía española.* Madrid, 1946.
   Gómez de Baquero, E. *Pen Club: los poetas.* Madrid, 1929.
   de la Peña, M. *El ultraísmo en España.* Madrid, 1925.
   de la Torre, G. *Literaturas europeas de vanguardia.* Madrid, 1925.

SPRING

Yesterday   Tomorrow
The infant days sing at my window

The houses are all made of paper
and the swallows come and go
folding and unfolding corners

Profaners of roses
Incessant enjoyers of the ivory of things
Behold the nest
built for you on the loveliest derrick

And from it you will all sing
in the hands of the wind

>   My life is a lemon
>   but my song is not yellow
>   Lemons and planets
>   on the branches of the sun
>   How often you sheltered
>   the green shade of my love
>   the green shade of my love

Spring is born
and on its body of light the rain grazes

The rainbow bursts forth from prison

And over the rooftops
my white hand is a hotel
for the doves of my faithless sky

TRANSLATED BY *Angel Flores*

TABLE

I traversed the seas
embarked in your hand
leaving on the tablecloths an ocean-taste

The fish turn around my lighthouse
But ships foundered on the map
and a murmur of waves unfurled my cloak

The sea no longer cares to be round

Think not of death

It's not easy to reach the bottom
nor to make a wheel of fortune from our carpet

The sun rises from the table
and the sunset-tree loses its withered leaves

   This is the cross of the sea
     Nor does it wax nor wane

Wait until the lamp finds its bearings

And then our plates
will revolve beautifully
to the precise music of the stars

TRANSLATED BY Angel Flores

PARADISE

Dance
      Captives of the bar-room

Life is a tower
and the sun but a dove-cot
Fling the hanging shirts to flight

Up the piano
let us climb daily with fresh feet

And leave behind
rusty wakes
and budding smoke

We must arrive noiselessly

Full well the insect-winged rowers know
they cannot sing
nor dares their prow to fly

They are the patient spinners of bays
hardy smokers of foam and days

Dance
      Captives of the bar-room

For the clouds sing
though be ever abated the wings of the sea

From one side of the world to the other
rainbows come and go
for all of you
who missed your trains

And for you also
my flute makes the trees dance
and dusk raises
breasts and marble

The clouds are birds
and the sun a dove-cot

Hurrah
                    Captives of the bar-room

Life is a tower
growing each day over the sea-level

TRANSLATED BY *Angel Flores*

RHYME

Your eyes peroxide the curls of the rain
and when the sun sets on your cheeks
your hair is not damp nor the afternoon yet blonde

    Love   Put out the moon

Do not drink your words
nor pour in my cup your eyes' bitter hollows
The morning with seeing you is turned brunette

Light up the sun   Love
and kill the dance

TRANSLATED BY *Angel Flores*

AUTUMN

Woman thick with hours
and ripe with fruits
like yesterday's sun

The clock of winds saw you blossom
when in its ancient cage
the stubborn twilight plucked its feathers

Awakener of paschal birds
this clock of winds
has encircled the world
and makes water-games in the advents

From your eyes sand flows in a sterile stream
And in your gaze have expired
so many heedless butterflies
that stars no longer shine

Woman sower
of seeds and dawns

Woman engendering the bees
that build the hours

Woman punctual as the full moon

Open your hair   source of winds
for my bee-hive awaits you
empty and untenanted

TRANSLATED BY *Angel Flores*

CHRISTMAS EVE

The child and the mill
have forgotten their only refrain

The wheel in c flat is silent
in the well
whence the water rises and the sun sinks

Hand on cheek
the chimneys think of flying some day

Today the moon will not come
nor will the drunkard pass
between the open gate and the cradle-song

Tired from the trip
the wind sat down
by the foot of the wall

Full of faith the watchman
jots down the names of new stars

And failing to cross the neighborhood
the fluvial carts
pitch in vain

Only the weather-vanes sing happily

The melancholy houses
comb their roofs

And one of them dies
unnoticed

Tonight the moon will not appear
nor will the street-lamp cradle the drunkard

TRANSLATED BY *Angel Flores*

CLOUDS

I   shepherd of boulevards
was setting loose the benches
and seated by the running shore of the walk
was allowing my scholar lambs to wander

All had come to an end
My notebook
                sole winterfrond
and the news-stand well anchored amid the foam

I was thinking of drifting beds forever fresh
in which to smoke my verses and count the stars

I was thinking of my clouds
                                tepid waves of the sky
that seek shelter without ceasing to fly

I was thinking of the folds of the beautiful mornings
ironed unlike my handkerchief

But in order to fly
the sun must swing
and our armillary sphere revolve in our hand

Already everything is different

My heart dancing confuses the star
and such is the fever and electricity
that the bottle glows incandescent

Neither the woodland tower
turning slowly distributes the winds
nor do my hands milk the recipient hours

We must await the parade
of blasts and prophecies
We must await the moonbirth
of the messiah bird

All things must come to pass

The cinema surge resembles the sea's
Faraway days cross the screen
Unseen banners perfume the air
and the telephone brings echoes of battle

The waves make the tour of the world
There are no longer explorers of strait and pole
and with guidebooks on their breast
the tourists perished
of an unknown disease

The waves make the tour of the world

I would like to go with them

They have seen everything
They never come back nor turn their head
dispossessed pillows and sandals of Christ

Leave me eternally reclining

I will smoke my verses and lead my clouds
through all the pathways of heaven and earth

And when the sun returns upon its white horse
my well-balanced bed will take off for flight

TRANSLATED BY *Angel Flores*

NOCTURNE

The stars are all here

Even those reserved for formal nights

So much smoke born from the sky
has oxidized my eyes

The stars are sensitive to touch
I can't type without them

They know everything
How to regulate the feverish sea
and how to cool my blood with their young snow

Night has opened the piano
and I bid them goodbye with my hand

TRANSLATED BY *Angel Flores*

FEDERICO GARCÍA LORCA (1898–1936) Born on January 5, 1898, in Fuentevaqueros (Granada), of a well-to-do family of the rural gentry, García Lorca found from the earliest a stimulating environment: his mother was an accomplished pianist and relatives and friends comprised personages of distinction in the arts and in philosophy: Fernando de los Ríos and Manuel de Falla, among others. From the time he was attending elementary school Federico performed his own plays at family reunions and parties. During his secondary-school days when the student body toured Spain, studying her architecture and arts, he drank in the very essence of folkloric Spain, most especially of gypsy Spain, collecting by ear the folk music of the various areas. Gifted in drawing, music (he sang, played the piano, composed), poetry, and the theater, he was extremely happy in the Residencia (the students' quarters) when he arrived in Madrid. His verse began to appear in magazines and later in book form: *Libro de poemas* (1921), *Canciones* (1927), and, most important, *Romancero gitano* (1928) and *Poemas del cante jondo* (1931), which won prizes and established him among Spain's loftiest poets. A brief sojourn in the United States (1929–1930) provided him with material for his surrealistic *Poeta en Nueva York* (1940). In 1931 the republican government sponsored his experimental theater group "La Barraca" and after that his genius and energy were devoted to the adaptation of Spanish classic plays and to his own playwriting: *Bodas de sangre, Yerma, La casa de Bernarda Alba,* and a dozen other plays. García Lorca was viciously executed in somewhat mysterious circumstances in August, 1936, during the chaotic civil war.

BIBLIOGRAPHY

Works by García Lorca:
  Libro de poemas. 1921.
  Canciones. 1927.
  Romancero gitano. 1928.
  Poema del cante jondo. 1931.
  Llanto para Ignacio Sánchez Mejías. 1935.
  Seis poemas galegos. 1935.
  Diván del Tamarit. 1936.
  Poeta en Nueva York. 1940.

Obras completas. 8 Volumes. 1942.
About García Lorca:

Barea, A. *Lorca, the Poet and his People.* London, 1944.
Bowra, C. M. *The Creative Experiment.* London and New York, 1929, pp. 189–219.
Campbell, R. *F. García Lorca.* Yale University Press, 1952.
Correa, G. *La poesía mítica de F. García Lorca.* Oregon University Monograph, 1957.
Crow, J. A. *F. García Lorca.* University of California Press, 1945.
Díaz-Plaja, G. *F. García Lorca, su vida e influencia en la poesía española.* Buenos Aires, 1954.
Flicniakoska, J. C. *L'Univers poétique de F. García Lorca.* Bordeaux, 1952.
Flys, J. M. *El lenguaje poético de F. García Lorca.* Madrid, 1955.
de la Guardia, A. *García Lorca.* Buenos Aires, 1941.
Honig, E. *Lorca.* New York, 1939.
Parrot, L. *F. García Lorca.* Paris, 1947.
Schonberg, J. *F. García Lorca.* Paris, 1956.

❊   ❊   ❊

SOMNAMBULE BALLAD

Green, how much I want you green.
Green wind. Green branches.
The ship upon the sea
and the horse in the mountain.
With the shadow on her waist
she dreams on her balcony,
green flesh, hair of green,
and eyes of cold silver.
Green, how much I want you green.
Beneath the gypsy moon,
all things look at her
but she cannot see them.

Green, how much I want you green.
Great stars of white frost
come with the fish of darkness
that opens the road of dawn.
The fig tree rubs the wind
with the sandpaper of its branches,
and the mountain, a filching cat,
bristles its bitter aloes.

But who will come? And from where?
She lingers on her balcony,
green flesh, hair of green,
dreaming of the bitter sea.

—Friend, I want to change
my horse for your house,
my saddle for your mirror,
my knife for your blanket.

Friend, I come bleeding,
from the passes of Cabra.
—If I could, young man,
this pact would be sealed.
But I am no more I,
nor is my house now my house.
—Friend, I want to die
decently in my bed.
Of iron, if it be possible,
with sheets of fine holland.
Do you not see the wound I have
from my breast to my throat?
—Your white shirt bears
three hundred dark roses.
Your pungent blood oozes
around your sash.
But I am no more I,
nor is my house now my house.
—Let me climb at least
up to the high balustrades:
let me come! Let me come!
up to the green balustrades.
Balustrades of the moon
where the water resounds.

Now the two friends go up
towards the high balustrades.
Leaving a trail of blood,
leaving a trail of tears.
Small lanterns of tin
were trembling on the roofs.
A thousand crystal tambourines
were piercing the dawn.

Green, how much I want you green,
green wind, green branches.
The two friends went up.
The long wind was leaving
in the mouth a strange taste
of gall, mint and sweet-basil.
Friend! Where is she, tell me,
where is your bitter girl?
How often she waited for you!
How often did she wait for you,
cool face, black hair,
on this green balcony!

Over the face of the cistern
the gypsy girl swayed.
Green flesh, hair of green,
with eyes of cold silver.
An icicle of the moon
suspends her above the water.
The night became as intimate
as a little square.
Drunken civil guards
were knocking at the door.
Green, how much I want you green.
Green wind. Green branches.
The ship upon the sea.
And the horse on the mountain.

TRANSLATED BY *Stephen Spender and J. L. Gili*

THE DEATH OF ANTOÑITO EL CAMBORIO

Voices of death resounded
near the Guadalquivir.
Ancient voices which surround
voice of manly carnation.
He nailed through their boots
bites of wild boar.
In the fight he leapt
like the slippery dolphin.
He bathed in enemy blood
his crimson tie,
but there were four daggers
and he could only succumb.

When the stars nail
spears on the grey water,
when the yearlings dream
verónicas of gilliflowers,
voices of death resounded
near the Guadalquivir.

—Antonio Torres Heredia,
an authentic Camborio,
dark of green moon,
voice of manly carnation:
Who took your life away
near the Guadalquivir?
—My four cousins the Heredias,
sons of Benamejí.
They did not envy in others
what they envied in me.
Raisin-coloured shoes,
ivory medallions
and this skin kneaded
of olive and jasmine.
—Ah, Antoñito of the Camborios
worthy of an Empress!
Remember the Virgin
because you are to die.
—Ah, Federico García,
call the Guardia Civil!
Already my waist has snapped
like a stalk of maize.

Three gushes of blood,
and he died in profile.
Living coin which never
will be repeated.
A swaggering angel places
his head on a cushion.
Others with a wearied blush
lighted an oil lamp.
And when the four cousins
arrive at Benamejí,
voices of death ceased
near the Guadalquivir.

TRANSLATED BY *Stephen Spender and J. L. Gili*

LAMENT FOR IGNACIO SANCHEZ MEJIAS

1. Cogida and Death

At five in the afternoon.
It was exactly five in the afternoon.
A boy brought the white sheet
at five in the afternoon.
A frail of lime ready prepared
at five in the afternoon.
The rest was death, and death alone
at five in the afternoon.

The wind carried away the cottonwool
at five in the afternoon.
And the oxide scattered crystal and nickel
at five in the afternoon.
Now the dove and the leopard wrestle
at five in the afternoon.
And a thigh with a desolate horn
at five in the afternoon.
The bass-string struck up
at five in the afternoon.
Arsenic bells and smoke
at five in the afternoon.
Groups of silence in the corners
at five in the afternoon.
And the bull alone with a high heart!
At five in the afternoon.
When the sweat of snow was coming
at five in the afternoon,
when the bull ring was covered in iodine
at five in the afternoon.
death laid eggs in the wound
at five in the afternoon.
At five in the afternoon.
Exactly at five o'clock in the afternoon.

A coffin on wheels is his bed
at five in the afternoon.
Bones and flutes resound in his ears
at five in the afternoon.
Now the bull was bellowing through his forehead
at five in the afternoon.
The room was iridescent with agony

at five in the afternoon.
In the distance the gangrene now comes
at five in the afternoon.
Horn of the lily through green groins
at five in the afternoon.
The wounds were burning like suns
at five in the afternoon,
and the crowd was breaking the windows
at five in the afternoon.
At five in the afternoon.
Ah, that fatal five in the afternoon!
It was five by all the clocks!
It was five in the shade of the afternoon!

2. The Spilled Blood

I will not see it!

Tell the moon to come
for I do not want to see the blood
of Ignacio on the sand.

I will not see it!

The moon wide open.
Horse of still clouds,
and the grey bull ring of dreams
with willows in the barreras.

I will not see it!

Let my memory kindle!
Warn the jasmines
of such minute whiteness!

I will not see it!

The cow of the ancient world
passed her sad tongue
over a snout of blood
spilled on the sand,
and the bulls of Guisando,
partly death and partly stone,
bellowed like two centuries
sated with treading the earth.
No.
I do not want to see it!
I will not see it!

Ignacio goes up the tiers
with all his death on his shoulders.
He sought for the dawn
but the dawn was no more.
He seeks for his confident profile
and the dream bewilders him.
He sought for his beautiful body
and encountered his opened blood.
I will not see it!
I do not want to hear it spurt
each time with less strength:
that spurt that illuminates
the tiers of seats, and spills
over the corduroy and the leather
of a thirsty multitude.
Who shouts that I should come near!
Do not ask me to see it!

His eyes did not close
when he saw the horns near,
but the terrible mothers
lifted their heads.
And across the ranches,
an air of secret voices rose,
shouting to celestial bulls,
herdsmen of pale mist.
There was no prince in Seville
who could compare with him,
nor sword like his sword
nor heart so true.
Like a river of lions
was his marvellous strength,
and like a marble torso
his firm drawn moderation.
The air of Andalusian Rome
gilded his head
where his smile was a spikenard
of wit and intelligence.
What a great torero in the ring!
What a good peasant in the sierra!
How gentle with the sheaves!
How hard with the spurs!
How tender with the dew!

How dazzling in the fiesta!
How tremendous with the final
banderillas of darkness!

But now he sleeps without end.
Now the moss and the grass
open with sure fingers
the flower of his skull.
And now his blood comes out singing;
singing along marshes and meadows,
sliding on frozen horns,
faltering soulless in the mist,
stumbling over a thousand hoofs
like a long, dark, sad tongue,
to form a pool of agony
close to the starry Guadalquivir.
Oh, white wall of Spain!
Oh, black bull of sorrow!
Oh, hard blood of Ignacio!
Oh, nightingale of his veins!
No.
I will not see it!
No chalice can contain it,
no swallows can drink it,
no frost of light can cool it,
nor song nor deluge of white lilies,
no glass can cover it with silver.
No.
I will not see it!

3. The Laid Out Body

Stone is a forehead where dreams grieve
without curving waters and frozen cypresses.
Stone is a shoulder on which to bear Time
with trees formed of tears and ribbons and planets.

I have seen grey showers move towards the waves
raising their tender riddled arms,
to avoid being caught by the lying stone
which loosens their limbs without soaking the blood.

For stone gathers seed and clouds,
skeleton larks and wolves of penumbra:
but yields not sounds nor crystals nor fire,
only bull rings and bull rings and more bull rings without
    walls.

Now, Ignacio the well born lies on the stone.
All is finished. What is happening? Contemplate his face:
death has covered him with pale sulphur
and has placed on him the head of a dark minotaur.

All is finished. The rain penetrates his mouth.
The air, as if mad, leaves his sunken chest,
and Love, soaked through with tears of snow,
warms itself on the peak of the herd.

What are they saying? A stenching silence settles down.
We are here with a body laid out which fades away,
Go, Ignacio; feel not the hot bellowing.
Sleep, fly, rest: even the sea dies!

4. Absent Soul

The bull does not know you, nor the fig tree,
nor the horses, nor the ants in your own house.
The child and the afternoon do not know you
because you have died for ever.

The back of the stone does not know you,
nor the black satin in which you crumble.
Your silent memory does not know you
because you have died for ever.

The autumn will come with small white snails,
misty grapes and with clustered hills,
but no one will look into your eyes
because you have died for ever.

Because you have died for ever,
like all the dead of the Earth,
like all the dead who are forgotten
in a heap of lifeless dogs.

Nobody knows you. No. But I sing of you.
For posterity I sing of your profile and grace.
Of the signal maturity of your understanding.
Of your appetite for death and the taste of its mouth.
Of the sadness of your once valiant gaiety.

It will be a long time, if ever, before there is born
an Andalusian so true, so rich in adventure.
I sing of his elegance with words that groan,
and I remember a sad breeze through the olive trees.

TRANSLATED BY *Stephen Spender and J. L. Gili*

VICENTE ALEIXANDRE (1900–) Born in Seville on April 26, 1900, Aleixandre completed his secondary studies in Málaga, and by the time he finished his law studies in Madrid, his poems, which he had begun writing in his teens, appeared in Spain's leading literary review, *Revista de Occidente*. Ill health forced him to give up his position with the railroad company and live in the country for several years. His first book, *Ámbito*, containing poems written in 1924–1927, appeared in 1928, but it was not until 1934 that his reading public widened: *La destrucción o el amor* was awarded the National Prize. A difficult poet, deeply influenced by Pablo Neruda, he endeavored to revive romanticism, a new brand of romanticism veering toward surrealism in a volcanic glow of mystic pantheism. Notwithstanding his novelty, his esotericism, and the dream quality of his world, Aleixandre was admitted to the Spanish Academy in 1949 and is today considered Spain's most remarkable poet.

BIBLIOGRAPHY

Works by Aleixandre:
   Ámbito. 1928.
   Espadas como labios. 1932.
   La destrucción o el amor. 1934.
   Pasión de la tierra. 1935 and 1946.
   Sombra del paraíso. 1944.
   Mundo a solas. 1950.
   Nacimiento último. 1953.
   Historia del corazón. 1954.
   Mis poemas mejores. 1956.
   Obras completas. 1961.
About Aleixandre:
   Alonso, D. *Poetas españoles contemporáneos.* Madrid, 1952.
   Alonso, D. *Ensayos sobre poesía española.* Madrid, 1944.
   Bousoño, C. *La poesía de Vicente Aleixandre.* Madrid, 1950.
   Cano, J. L. *De Machado a Bousoño.* Madrid, 1955.
   Corcel, the Valencian literary journal, devotes an entire issue to Aleixandre, 1944, 5–6.
   Díaz-Plaja, G. *Poesía lírica castellana.* 2nd Ed. Barcelona, 1948.
   Salinas, P. *Literatura española en el siglo XX.* Mexico, 1941.

❋ ❋ ❋

LIFE

A paper bird in my breast
says that the time for kisses hasn't come;
life, life, the sun crackles invisibly,
kisses or birds, early or late or never.
A little noise is enough to die,
that of another heart to be silent,
or this strange lap which on earth
is a ship gilded with red hair.
Sad head, gold temples, sun that's going to set;
here in the shade I dream with a river,
reeds of green blood that now rises,
I dream resting on your warmth or life.

TRANSLATED BY *Charles Guenther*

THE JUNGLE AND THE SEA

Out there among the remote
lights or steels not yet in use
tigers big as hate,
lions shaggy as a heart,
blood like an appeased sadness,
fight off the yellow hyena that puts on the form of the gluttonous sunset.

Oh the sudden whiteness,
the violet hollows under faded eyes,
when savage beasts bare their knives or teeth
like the poundings of a heart that ignores everything
except love
exposed on those necks, there where the artery pumps,
where you can't be sure if it's love or hate
flashing on the white fangs.

To stroke the scowling mane
while the powerful claw makes itself felt in the earth,
while the roots of the trees, quivering,
feel the deep nails
like a love making its invasion so.

To look into those eyes that only burn at night,
in which the small deer, long since devoured,
still exhibits its miniature image like gold in the night,
a departure flickering with posthumous tenderness.

The tiger, the hunter lion, the elephant wearing a soft necklace around its tusks,
the cobra that is like the warmest kind of love,
the eagle that caresses the hard brains of the rock,
the tiny scorpion that simply hopes to hold life tight, for one
instant, in its pliers,
the cowardly presence of a man's body that can never possibly
be taken for a jungle,
that lucky ground where the clear-sighted little vipers set up
their nests in an armpit of moss,
while the neat cochineal bug
steals down from a silky magnolia leaf . . .
Everything vibrates when the sound of the forest forever virgin
rises like two wings of gold,
wingsheaths, bronze or clear-toned conch,
before a sea that will never confuse its foams with the tender
little shoots.

The quiet waiting,
that hope forever green,
bird, paradise, luster of feathers never touched,
invents the tallest branch clusters,
where fangs of music,
where the powerful claws, love driven in,
the burning blood that spurts out of the wound,
will not reach, no matter how far up the jet stretches,
or those breasts half-open on the ground
extend their pain or greed towards the blue skies.

Bird of happiness,
blue bird or feather,
over a deafening hum of lonely beasts,
of love or punishment against the sterile trunks,
in front of the sea, a long way off, retreating like the light.

TRANSLATED BY *Hardie St. Martin*

BLACK HAIR

Why do I gaze at you, with your dark eyes,
living velvet in which I hurt my life?
Black hair, sorrow where I bury my mouth,
sad surge of waves where my kisses founder,
final shore where my voice at last is spent and
drenches your royal essence, O pillowed hair, O coils of power!

My restless desires
break on your border, as on some dark strand.
O, flooded as you are, you exist, you survive, you rule!
A triumph is wholly yours, like a rock towering in the seas.

TRANSLATED BY *Edwin Morgan*

TRUTH

Not walls, but shadows, stifle my heart; what is it
that smiles in these shadows? What loneliness lifts up
its moonless agony of arms and its loud cries
into the night? Who is it sings secretly in the leaves?
Birds? Hardly; but a memory of birds. What are you but
an echo, only an echo, unkempt feather, sorry dross, dull
dead matter here in my hands? Kissing ashes
is not kissing love. Gnawing a dry branch
is far from placing these lustrous lips above a breast
whose languid swell may add a sparkle to these
flashing ivories. The sun, the dazzling sun!

The dress is laid aside—a rustling, useless
relic of the city. The body lies shining,
naked, fluid as a spring where
ardent life is felt in the midst of branches
burning in the tropics, thrust from an equator.

Drink; drink up the heady passion of a midday
that shoots its lights into the zenith and inflames you
to an utter dizziness and dissolves you. Beautiful, vital death,
embers of day! Virgin forest, ending your life in flames!

TRANSLATED BY *Edwin Morgan*

TO A NAKED GIRL

How tenderly she looks
at me—you, girl with the dark eyes!
From the bank of that river, with waves mid-stream,
I can see your outline sharp above a harmony of green.
It is no nakedness come to sear the grass like a flame,
or like the startling falling ember, foreteller of ashes,
but rather you are set there in stillness, freshest
of morning primroses, come to perfection in a breath.

Fresh image of the softly blowing primrose.
Your body has a bed of secluded virgin turf
whose verges lie like a river flowing at peace.
Stretched out you lie, and your dear nakedness sings,
sweetly composed by the breezes of a valley.
Ah, girl of music, so graciously offered, and
the gift denied, there on that far-off shore!
Wild waves intervene, dividing me from you,
my sweet everlasting desire, body, bond of happiness,
resting like a heavenly star upon that grass.

TRANSLATED BY *Edwin Morgan*

DESTINY OF THE FLESH

No, it isn't that. I am not looking at
a heaven on the other side of the horizon.
My eyes are not fixed on quiet powerful eyes
that calm the savage waters bellowing here.
I am not looking at the waterfall of lights going
from a mouth to a breast down to soft, finite hands
that cup this world and weigh it like gold.

I see bodies everywhere, naked, faithful
to the world's weariness. Flesh passing, born
to be a spark of light perhaps, to burn
with love and be space, that has no memory,
beautiful rondure of light.
And which is here, right here, decayingly eternal,
continuing, constant, always, always exhausted.

It's useless for a distant wind, with vegetable shape, or a
    tongue
to lap its volume slowly and long, to give it an edge,
burnish, stroke it and make much of it.
Human bodies, tired rocks, grey bulks
aware always, at the sea's edge,
that life does not end, no, by inheriting itself.
Bodies that, repeated tomorrow, infinite bodies, always push on
like a slow foam that knows everything now.
Man's flesh always, without light. Always pushed
from out there, from an ocean without origin that sends
waves, waves, foams, tired bodies, walls
of a sea that never ends and gasps on its beaches, without rest.

Multiplied, repeated, continuing, you pile up your flesh,
your life, without hope, monotonously the same under dull
    skies that succeed each other with indifference.
On that sea of bodies that spill, without interruption, here,
    break
roundly here and are left, subject to death once more, on the
    beaches,
one never sees, no, the slippery skiff, light sailer,
slit, rip, and open the light's blood
with a keel of steel and escape in a flash
towards the deep horizon, towards the last
beginning of life, the eternal ocean's limit
that scatters their human grey
bodies. Towards the light, towards the ladder of climbing
    lights
that lifts from a kind of breast towards a mouth,
towards immense eyes, whole eyes that are fixed on something,
towards silent hands, finite hands that trap,
there where, forever tired but filled with life, we are still
    being born.

               TRANSLATED BY *Hardie St. Martin*

SING, BIRDS

Birds, the caresses of your free wings
can't take away my sad
memory. What bright lip-passion
the chirping speaks from your pure breast!
Sing for me, flashing birds
who summon joy in the burning woods
and, drunk with light, rise like clappers of a bell
in the blue that adopts you spiritedly.
Sing for me, birds who are born every day
and declare the world's innocence
in your cry. Sing, sing and be glad in your heart
that you uproot me, and don't return to earth.

               TRANSLATED BY *Charles Guenther*

TO DON LUIS DE GONGORA

What firm architecture rises
from the landscape, breaks the air's hard
reality, without haste, and takes its place?

The lines move solemnly. But from its site
the curve sprouts, rounds out its contour
at the top and leaves the rind intact,
prison for all that ceremony.

The tall sky spreads its plan of lights
in rhythm with sunsets that are in good taste
and reach their right peak high up.

The houses of the air, vibrating
unseen, give off their irisless shades of color
and the total perfect chord cries out.

TRANSLATED BY Hardie St. Martin

ETERNALLY

I gaze out mildly from this quiet farm
over this heavy landscape with its lingering clouds.
This blue was the earthly dominance and colour
of some eyes. This perennial green
was youth, was spring. Tranquilly here, tranquilly
I look at the soft outlines of the high mountains.
A natural roundness, carelessly laid bare? . . .
This smooth prairie, devoid of poplars, breathes.
My hand, familiar with the suave crust of the earth,
today holds up my head as I lean on my elbow.
Imperishable, a river gently shows the teeth
of love, singing and laughing towards another burst of foam.
Voices, far-off voices are the sweet reminder
of how the far-off girls are for ever in the eyes
of their rough heroes, who wait for them in the grove
and passionately take them in their boats
and sail them off. O river of the young—dawns
that never fade—how gladly they abound,
and never end, and never end!

. . . With my eyes opened.
TRANSLATED BY Edwin Morgan

EPITAPH

To cross out your name,
burning body who wait on earth
as a god awaits oblivion, I name you here,
boundary of a life; here, necessary
body that blazed. No tomb: free earth.

Leave at once the lingering gaze
which a hard stone will demand of you,
or a tree without birds requires,
pure in the night, in its naked vigilance.

The sound of a river is never heard here.
Death lives in the deep earth
like absolute earth.

Men, pass by:
your steps won't sound on a breast.

TRANSLATED BY *Charles Guenther*

RAFAEL ALBERTI (1902–) Born on December 16, 1902, in Puerto de Santa María (Cádiz), where he studied in a Jesuit school, bitterly evoked in his political poems of the 1930's, Alberti arrived in Madrid in 1917 in the hope of attaining fame as a painter. It was not until six years later that he fully realized his poetic gifts. This revelation dawned on him while taking a cure in the Guadarrama mountains for what the doctors feared to be consumption. At that time he wrote many of these lovely lyrics which form part of his first book, *Marinero en tierra,* winner of the National Prize in 1925. This is another way of saying that at the age of twenty-three Alberti had attained a wide reputation. Not unlike the poetry of García Lorca, that of Alberti echoed the folkloric then in vogue and found also in the old masters (Gil Vicente, Lope de Vega, Góngora), as in his great contemporary, Juan Ramón Jiménez. But in him this vein was less abiding than in García Lorca; Alberti was more chameleonlike, each book was entirely different from the previous one: from popularism he moved on into Gongorism, ultraism, socialism, surrealism, and so on. Bowra claimed the "brilliantly introspective" *Sobre los ángeles* (1929) to be Alberti's masterpiece, and he says further: "Alberti was from the start more intellectual than Lorca. . . . He lacked Lorca's instinctive joy and instinctive melancholy: his gifts were more varied and more conflicting." During the civil war Alberti was a militant Republican, and at the hour of defeat he fled to Buenos Aires, where he has been living since then.

BIBLIOGRAPHY

Works by Alberti:
   Marinero en tierra. 1925.
   La amante. 1926.
   El alba del alhelí. 1927.
   Cal y canto. 1929.
   Sobre los ángeles. 1929.
   Consignas. 1934.
   Poesías. 1934.
   Trece bandas y 48 estrellas. 1934.
   Verte y no verte. 1936.
   Entre el clavel y la espada. 1940.
   Pleamar. 1944.
   A la pintura. 1946.

Retornos. 1946.
Ora marítima. 1954.
About Alberti:

Bowra, C. M. *The Creative Experiment.* London and New York, 1949, pp. 220–253.

Díaz-Plaja, G. *Poesía lírica castellana.* Barcelona, 1938.

Larralde, P. *"El mar, el toro y la muerte," Sustancia* (Tucumán, Argentina), Año IV (1943), pp. 337–353.

Proff, E. *"Popularismo"* and *"Barroquismo"* in the Poetry of R. Alberti. 1942.

Sabella, A. *"La poesía de Rafael Alberti," Atenea,* August 1940, pp. 273–285.

❊   ❊   ❊

THE COLLEGIATE ANGELS

None of us understood the secret dark of the blackboards
nor why the armillary sphere seemed so remote when we
  looked at it.
We only knew that a circumference does not have to be round
and that an eclipse of the moon confuses the flowers
and speeds up the timing of birds.

None of ús understood anything:
nor why our fingers were made of India ink
and the afternoon closed compasses only to have the dawn
  open books.
We only knew that a straight line, if it likes, can be curved
  or broken
and that the wandering stars are children who don't know
  arithmetic.

TRANSLATED BY *Mark Strand*

THE BULL OF DEATH

Black bull, longing for wounds,
charging the water's landscapes,
examining papers and baggage
on trains that go to the bull rings.

What do you dream in your horns,
what hidden desires redden the journey,
what maritime system of ditches
and drains do your charges practice?

Longing for a man with a sword,
for femoral blood and gangrene,
not even the *mayoral* can stop you now.

Run, bull, to the sea, charge. Nothing.
But since you intend to wound,
here is a bullfighter of spume, salt and sand.
Kill him.

TRANSLATED BY *Mark Strand*

IF MY VOICE SHOULD DIE ON LAND

If my voice should die on land,
take it to sea-level
and leave it on the shore.

Take it to sea-level
and make it captain
of a white ship of war.

Oh my voice adorned
with naval insignia:
on the heart an anchor,
and on the anchor a star,
and on the star the wind,
and on the wind the sail!

TRANSLATED BY *Mark Strand*

TO MISS X, BURIED IN THE WEST WIND

Ah, Miss X, Miss X: 20 years old!

Blouses in the windows,
the hairdressers
are crying without your hair
—blond fire cut short—.

Ah, Miss X, hatless Miss X,
rougeless dawn,
alone,
so free,
you,
in the wind!

You never wore earrings.

The dressmakers, in white, on their balconies,
forgotten by heaven.
                    —Let's see!
                        At last!
                          What?
                            No!
                                It was only a bird,
                                not you,
                                little Miss X.

The barman, oh, how sad!
   (Beer.
   Lemonade.
   Whiskey.
   Gin Fizz.)
He has painted the bottles black.
And the flags,
prides of the bar,
black, at half-mast.

And the sky won't carry your radiogram!

Thirty ships,
forty seaplanes
and a sailboat loaded with oranges,
shouting all over the sea and the clouds.

                                    Nothing.

Ah, Miss X! Where have you gone?

His Majesty, the King of your country, isn't eating.
The King doesn't sleep.
He smokes.
He dies along the seacoast in a car.

Ministries,
Gold Exchanges,
Consulates,
Casinos,
Shops,
Parks,
closed.

And meanwhile, you, in the wind,
"Do your shoes pinch?"
Miss X, of the seas,
"Say, does the air hurt you?"

Ah, Miss X, Miss X, how dull!
I am yawning.

        Adios. . . .

                Goodbye. . . .

*(No one thinks of you anymore. The steel
butterflies
with broken wings
burning the air
settled on the wind's
swaying dahlias.
Electrocuted sun.
Carbonized moon.
Fear of winter's white bear.*

*Forbidden.
By Government declaration,
hunting by sea
or sky is prohibited.*

No one thinks of you anymore, little Miss X.)

                TRANSLATED BY *Mark Strand*

THE ANGEL OF NUMBERS

Virgins with rulers
and compasses watching
the heavenly blackboards.

And the angel of numbers,
thoughtful, flying
from 1 to 2, from 2
to 3, from 3 to 4.

Cold chalk and sponges
streaked and erased
the light of outerspace.

Not sun, not moon, not stars,
not the sudden green
of lightning,
not the air. Only mist.

Virgins without rulers,
without compasses, crying.

And on the dead blackboards,
the angel of numbers,
lifeless, shrouded
on the 1 and the 2,
on the 3, on the 4 . . .

TRANSLATED BY *Mark Strand*

BLUE

1
Blue arrived. And its time was painted.

2
How many blues did the Mediterranean give?

3
Venus, mother of the sea of the blues.

4
The blue of the Greeks
rests, like a god, on columns.

5
The delicate, medieval blue.

6
The Virgin brought her virginal blue:
blue Mary, blue Our Lady.

7
It fell to his palette. And brought
the most secret blue from the sky.
Kneeling, he painted his blues.
Angels christened him with blue.
They appointed him: Beato Blue Angelico.

8
There are celestial palettes like wings
descended from the white of clouds.

9
The blues of Italy,
the blues of Spain,
the blues of France . . .

10
Raphael had wings.
Perugino also had wings
in order to spread his blues around.

11

When they get color from you,
indigo blue, brushes are feathers.

12

Venice of golden Titian blue.

13

Rome of Poussin blues between the pines.

14

Tintoretto blues embitter me.

15

Sulphur alcohol phosphorous Greco blue.
Toxic verdigris blue Greco.

16

On the palette of Velasquez I have
another name: I am called Guadarrama.

17

When I wander through nacreous flesh,
I am called the merry blue vein of Rubens.

18

And in the dawn of the lakes,
with a blue awakening, the echoes
of darkness repeat: Patinir.

19

There is a virginal Murillo blue,
forerunner of the brilliance of the chromes

20

Tiepolo also gave blues to his century.

21

Thinned, delicate, I am a sash—
Goya's light blue ribbon.

22

I would say to you:
   —You are beautiful,
beautiful as the glorious blue of ceilings.

23

Explosions of blue in the allegories.

24

In Manet blue echoes sing
of a far off Spanish blue.

25

I am also called Renoir. They yell for me,
but I respond at times in lilac
with my blue voice made transparent.

26

I am the blue shadow,
the clear silhouette of your body.
For old eyes, the scandal.

27

The Balearics gave their blues to Painting.

28

Sometimes the sea invades the palette
of the painter and assigns him
a blue sky given only in secret.

29

The shadow is bluest when the body
that casts it has vanished.

30

Ecstatic blue, having been
pure blue in motion, is nostalgic.

31

Even if the blue is not in the picture,
it covers it like a screen of light.

32

One day blue said:
—Today I have a new name. They call me:
Blue Pablo Ruiz Blue Picasso.

TRANSLATED BY *Mark Strand*

BALLAD OF WHAT THE WIND SAID

Eternity could very well
be only a river,
be a horse forgotten
and the cooing
of a lost dove.

As for the man who leaves
his fellow men, the wind comes
telling him other things,
opening his ears
and eyes to other things.

Today I left my fellow men,
and alone, in this ravine,
began to look at the river
and saw a horse alone
and listened lonely

to the cooing
of a lost dove.

And then the wind came close
and, like someone in passing,
told me:
Eternity could very well
be only a river,
be a horse forgotten
and the cooing
of a lost dove.

TRANSLATED BY Mark Strand

JESUIT SCHOOL

We were the day pupils,
students from bourgeois families already in decline.
Christian charity gave us our culture free of charge,
piety opened to us the books and the classroom doors.
We were already of those who would one day be buried gratis.

We did not quite know why no gold-braid wound about our
    caps,
nor how it happened that none ran down the seams of our
    trousers.
We never saw our names printed,
only typewritten,
blue,
blurred.

We were the day pupils.

2

So much anger,
so much hate,
futilely spent biting our nails
while the blackboard whitened with numbers
and the margins of the books wearied of inkstains,
so much anger contained without weeping
brought us always to the sea, which cares nothing for square
    roots,
to the sky, liberated from theorems,
free from professors,
to the warm dunes
where in line we used to urinate, looking toward the school.

We were the day pupils.

3

Some of us had talent,
a good voice for singing,
a firm pulse,
steady,
able to draw a circle in one stroke,
also good at guarding goals,
receiving the sacrament each day at early mass
or stealing from the orchards at certain hours some oranges or
    plums.
Some of us had this much good or that much hypocrisy.
But Claudio,
Juan or Francisco Ponce de León,
Antonio,
Luis or Pedro Gómez,
all of them
were heirs, with land and cattle
far away
in the provinces.
So neither did you have a good voice for singing,
nor I some bit of talent
nor was the other fellow able to draw a circle in one stroke.

We were the day pupils.

4

Oh sea,
you could have surged up
burst into class some morning,
some evening,
at an hour when equations were forgotten,
when the atlases thought of themselves merely as colored card-
    board,
immovable illustrations that never would travel.
Now,
when there is no longer any remedy—
unless it be that of the bullet conspiring in the fist—
it occurs to me to invite you,
to propose to you this ingenious conquest of the blackboards,
of the dignified desks where suddenly there used to appear,
darkened,
angry,
the bespectacled eyes that always hated us.
I tell you this,

Oh sea,
sea that used to come to the gates of the school,
without ever thinking,
I suppose,
of coming into the classroom.

5

I see the years,
the same as those I now hear returning to me this afternoon,
  bedecked with cassocks,
dark scarecrows,
like pigs that had stuffed themselves with floating dead fish,
leaving behind them an inky trail spattered with semen and
  vomit.
I hear how crucifixes invade me,
pitiless penumbras of coughs mingled with prayers and via
  crucis,
and an odor of coffee,
a dry breakfast,
rotting in the tepid mouths of the confessors.
It is impossible that this scene could ever return,
reconquer for even one moment, its flyblown dream,
formaldehyde and smoke.
This is not possible again, this sordid latrine with belchings and
  tapioca soup.

It is impossible.
I do not want it.
It is impossible to wish for you such a childhood and death.

TRANSLATED BY *Ira S. Wallach*

METAMORPHOSIS OF THE CARNATION

I

By the side of the sea and a river in my early days,
I wanted to be a horse.
  The reed shores were made of wind and mares.
I wanted to be a horse.
  The towering tails swept the stars.
I wanted to be a horse.
  Listen, mother, to my long-paced trot.
I wanted to be a horse.
  Beginning tomorrow, mother, I'll live by the water.

I wanted to be a horse.
A whitefoot girl slept on the bottom.
I wanted to be a horse.

2

I left.
The shells are closed.
That blind odor of spume
always recalled me.
It always sought me out.
I left.
I'm squeezing lemons
into a dish of salt water.
I always remembered you.
I was always running into you.
I left.
The shells are still closed.

3

The horse asked for sheets,
crinkled as rivers.
White sheets.
I want to be a man for one night.
Call me at dawn.
The woman never called him.
(And he never returned to his stable.)

4

The dove misunderstood,
misunderstanding.
For north, it flew south
and took the wheat for water,
misunderstanding.
It believed the sea was the sky,
that night was morning,
misunderstanding.
That the stars were dew,
the drought a snowfall,
misunderstanding.
It thought your skirt was its blouse;
your heart its house.
It misunderstood.
(It fell asleep on the riverbank,
and you, at the top of a branch.)

5

At dawn, the cock was stunned.
His voice echoed back
the voice of a boy.

The cock, at dawn, detected
signs of manhood.

At dawn, the cock was stunned.

With eyes of love and warfare
he leapt to an orange tree.

From the orange to a lemon tree,
from the lemons to a patio,
from the patio to a bedroom
the cock flew.

The woman sleeping there
embraced him.

The cock was stunned.

6

The bull suckled, suckled
the milk of the highland woman.

The bull's eyes went mild
as those of a girl.

Now that you are a bull, my son,
thrust me with your horn.

You'll see I have another bull
inside me.

(The mother turned to grass,
and the bull to a water bull.)

TRANSLATED BY *Anthony Kerrigan*

JORGE CARRERA ANDRADE (1902–)   Born in Quito in 1902 and educated in a provincial town, Carrera Andrade started outgrowing his earliest influences, especially Hugo, Baudelaire, and Francis Jammes, when still in his teens. In his first volume, *Estanque inefable,* published by the Universidad Central of Quito in 1922, his voice sounds very much his own. From his twenties on, Carrera Andrade has lived away from his native country—in Europe, Asia, and several countries of the Western Hemisphere—in the diplomatic service of Ecuador. While in Japan in the 1940's, he was deeply impressed by the Japanese haiku, but this was a passing phase of *"microgramas,"* as he called his haikus, in the work of a poet of tremendous resources and the widest diapason, the author of some twenty volumes, all different and all exciting.

BIBLIOGRAPHY

Works by Carrera Andrade:
  Estanque inefable. 1922.
  La guirnalda del silencio. 1926.
  Boletines de mar y tierra. 1930.
  Rol de la manzana. 1935.
  El tiempo manual. 1935.
  Biografía para uso de los pájaros. 1937.
  La hora de las ventanas iluminadas. 1937.
  Microgramas. 1940.
  País secreto. 1940.
  Registro del mundo. 1940.
  Canto al puente de Oakland. 1941.
  Canto a las fortalezas volantes. 1944.
  Lugar de origen. 1945.
  Poesías escogidas. 1945.
  El visitante de niebla y otros poemas. 1947.
  Aquí yace la espuma. 1950.
  Familia de la noche. 1954.
  Moneda del forastero. 1958.
  Edades poéticas. 1958.
About Carrera Andrade:
  Carrera Andrade, J. *Edades poéticas.* Quito, 1958.
  Harth, D. E. *The Poetic World of Jorge Carrera Andrade.* Doctoral thesis, University of Syracuse, 1958.
  Pane, R. V. "Jorge Carrera Andrade, a bibliography." *Bulletin of Bibliography,* Vol. XVIII (1945), pp. 147–148.
  Salinas, P. Introduction to Carrera Andrade's *Poesías escogidas.* Caracas, 1945.

de Undurraga, A. *"La órbita poética de J. Carrera Andrade."*
Atenea, July 1942, pp. 31–47.

❊　❊　❊

THE WEATHERCOCK OF THE
CATHEDRAL OF QUITO

The cock on the weathervane
Cannot flap his wings
Even though today is a feast.

The sun spreads his great yellow
Carpet in the courtyard
As Anna del Campo passes by.

Gold quilts on the balconies,
Diamonds on the roofs
Domes and towers.

Anna del Campo has come
With her nose in the air
A dew damsel.

The cock would like to crow
Poor tin Don Juan
Stuck on his belfry.

Clouds wheel round him
In his blue hen-yard,
The burning bird flashes.

Silver cock in the wind,
Sun-cock, paralyzed
In a desert of roofs.

Cathedral ascetic
He knows no other corn
Than the sky's kind: hail.

Anna del Campo goes by:
He flashes sun-signals
To his friend, the lightning rod.

Anna: take me to the door
Of your house of flowers
Where bliss never ends.

Give me your cool dew
For my throat of sand:
Give me your lily-field!

TRANSLATED BY *Thomas Merton*

COCOA TREE

Cocoa tree
Archangel tutor of the green parrot,
Cool doctrine in a tropic land,
Adding colors, subtracting sounds
In a total of shade,
With a heavenly vocation you dictate
Fragrant lessons.

On your knees, hands joined,
Hearing the hum of secret hives of bees
You let your happiness grow.

Rich in almond-shaped thoughts
You write, upon the pages of the air,
The virgin jungle's novel
Even to the sweet smell of grandmothers' cups
In dining rooms, with silent doors,
Where the wall-clock drips
Like a half-orange.

TRANSLATED BY *Thomas Merton*

A MAN FROM ECUADOR BENEATH
THE EIFFEL TOWER

You turn into a plant on the coasts of time
With your goblet of round sky
Your opening for the tunnels of traffic
You are the biggest ceiba tree on earth.

Up go the painter's eyes
By your scissor-stair, into the blue.

Over a flock of roofs
You stretch your neck, a llama of Peru.

Robed in folds of winds,
A comb of constellations in your hair
You show yourself
To the circus of horizons.

Mast of an adventure above time!

Pride of five hundred and thirty cubits.

Pole of the tent set up by men
In a corner of history
Your gaslit drawing in the night
Copies the milky way.

First letter of a cosmic alphabet
Pointing in the direction of heaven;
Hope standing on stilts;
Glorification of the skeleton.

Iron to brand the flock of clouds
Or dumb sentinel of the industrial age.
The tides of heaven
Silently undermine your pillar.

TRANSLATED BY *Thomas Merton*

RETURN VOYAGE

My life was a geography
I studied now and again,
a book of maps or of dreams.
I woke up in America.

Did I dream those towns and rivers?
Were those countries not true?
Are there three ports in my life:
to dream, to wake up and to die?

I fell asleep among statues
and I woke up alone.
Where are those amiable shadows?
Is it true I was loved and in love?

It was a geography of dreams,
a history of magic.
I know by memory the islands and faces
that I saw or perhaps dreamed.

My senses sprawled out
on the loot of the universe—
fruit, women, immensity—
like drunken pirates.

I found you at last in a port,
my naked girl with your perfect form:
I slaked my human thirst
in your great, trembling waters.

Then she was a child of wheat,
a maiden of abundance,
but the eternal Other always
called to me from every doorway.

I saw the land of cities
from the snows to the palmtrees.
God cleaned the windows there
and no one wanted to die.

I saw the dry land of the bull—
last refuge of blueness—
and the land where the pinetree lifts
its green obelisk to the light.

Did I dream that face beyond the wall,
that hand against my flesh?
And that roadway of apples
and doves, did I dream that too?

The bays (that were) like slices
of a crystal watermelon,
and their islands like seeds,
were they nothing but dreams?

This dust still clinging to my feet,
is it mortal ashes?
Were the places where I anchored
not ports but years?

I studied nothing but solitude
in the most varied languages,
and graduated Doctor of Dreams.
I came to America to wake up.

But the thirst for life and for death
still burns in my throat,
and I humbly bend my knee
in this land of maize.

O land of fruit and of tombs,
sole property of the sun:
I come from the world—what a long dream!—
and a map unrolls in my voice.

TRANSLATED BY Lysander Kemp

JOHN WITHOUT HEAVEN

John is my name, John Everyman; not just
    A dweller on earth—its prisoner too I am
A shadow hung with clothes; a walking dust;
    One of the crowd; John Meek, John Mild, John Lamb.

Only my hand for every task: it knows
    How to move wheels, to mine deep-hidden ore;
It is my servant: it can pluck the rose
    And turn the key that opens the earth's door.

I tilled the firmament for my increase;
    Great wealth in clouds I owned; my fortune grew
With soaring flight, with blueness & with peace,
    And with that splintered sky, the morning dew.

Space was my farm, space without bounds or bars
    —O wide blue fields, perpetually sown
With corn that bore a crop of shining stars—
    And clouds my cattle were, my herds, my own.

Birds were my laborers; my granary
    Was Day, wide open, crammed from wall to wall
With fruit and grain of joy; the western sky
    Ripened and glowed like orchards in the Fall.

Then came the mirror-merchants, came the strange
    Hunters of angels, armed and merciless;
They seized my flowery farm, and in exchange
    They gave me tinsel, vapor, nothingness . . .

Word-coiners, executioners of the swan,
    Hooded and masked, they sacked my garnered gold;
My barns are empty; all my stars are gone;
    Scraps of the moon remain, stiffened and cold.

I lost my azure farm, I lost the height.
    The cattle-clouds, the brilliance freshly sown;
A whole celestial husbandry of light
    In empty space engulfed and overthrown.

I lost my claim-stake in the golden West;
   I lost the dew, and found the worm instead.
(John is my name, John, John the Dispossessed.)
   The treasure of long centuries is fled.

Only upon my back lies a blue weight,
   A dome of ice. Nothing but John am I—
The universal prey, disconsolate,
   John without heaven, John without the sky.

TRANSLATED BY Jan Struther

TRANSFORMATIONS

My work is done among two windows
on the street, ten yards of land,
a plate of moonlight each night
and the yawn of empty pitchers.

For me, each day is Monday:
always to begin over, steps in a circle
around myself in the ten yards
of my rented tomb with windows.

I abandoned the world for an eternal
chair in which I carry on
my work of bee and phantasm,
changing sighs into money

to buy the sun each Sunday
and to keep my country in a closet,
to meet love on the stairs,
to fend off lightning with an umbrella.

My work is done in a street
where rows of faces are sold
among houses that know by memory
the color of clothing and of clouds.

I am Inspector of Windows,
lost in the street of the street-signs:
each day is a round trip
toward nowhere, toward the night.

TRANSLATED BY Lysander Kemp

PABLO NERUDA (1904–)   Pablo Neruda—his real name
is Neftalí Reyes—was born in Parral, Chile, on July 12, 1904,
and attended the local schools and the Liceo of nearby Te-
muco. At the age of fifteen, and under the pseudonym "Pablo
Neruda," he sent his first batch of poems to the magazine
Selva Austral. In 1921, while attending the Instituto Pedagó-
gico of Santiago, he won a first prize for *"La canción de la
fiesta."* However, it was not until 1924, with his *Veinte poemas
de amor y una canción desesperada,* that his reputation became established. Soon thereafter he entered the diplomatic
corps, serving as consul in Burma, Siam, Cambodia, Anam,
Japan, China, and India. While serving as consul in Buenos
Aires, the Editorial Ercilla of Santiago brought out the first
volume of *Residencia en la tierra,* which contains the best of
his poems written between 1925 and 1931—a milestone in the
history of Spanish poetry. The second volume of *Residencia*
was completed in Madrid, where Neruda was then cultural
attaché—and where the poet saw the outbreak and also the
horrors of the Spanish civil war, which inspired his *España en
el corazón* (1937). After a few years in Mexico, Neruda
finally returned to Chile, where he has served as a senator. His
outstanding achievements of the last decade or so have been
his *Canto general* (1950), *Alturas de Macchu Picchu,* included here, and his four volumes of "elemental" Odes.

BIBLIOGRAPHY

Works by Neruda:
   La canción de la fiesta. 1921.
   Crepusculario [1919]. 1923.
   Veinte poemas de amor y una canción desesperada. 1924.
   Tentativa del hombre infinito. 1926.
   El hondero entusiasta [1923–24]. 1933.
   Residencia en la tierra (Vol. I, 1925–31). 1933.
   Residencia en la tierra (Vol. II, 1931–35). 1935.
   España en el corazón. 1937.
   Las furias y las penas. 1939.
   Tercera residencia [1935–45]. 1947.
   Alturas de Macchu Picchu. 1948.
   Canto general. 1950.
   Las uvas y el viento. 1954.
   Odas elementales. 1954.
   Nuevas odas elementales. 1955.

Libro tercero de las odas. 1957.
Estravagario. 1958.
Navegaciones y regresos. 1959.
About Neruda:

Alonso, A. *Poesía y estilo de Pablo Neruda.* Buenos Aires, 1940 (2nd ed., 1951).

Cardona Peña, A. "Pablo Neruda." *Cuadernos Americanos,* November–December 1950, pp. 257–289.

De Lellis, M. J. *Pablo Neruda.* Buenos Aires, 1957.

Ehrenburg, I. *Poesía política de Pablo Neruda.* Santiago de Chile, 1953.

Marcenac, J. *Pablo Neruda.* Paris, 1954.

Meléndez, C. "Pablo Neruda." *Revista Hispánica Moderna,* October 1936, pp. 1–34.

❊ ❊ ❊

SUMMITS OF MACCHU PICCHU *

I

From air to air, like an empty net,
between the streets and the atmosphere I went, reaching and
    departing
with the advent of autumn the farflung specie
of the leaves, and, between the springtime and the tassels of
    wheat,
that which the greatest love, as withiñ a falling
glove, brings to us like a long moon.

(In the distempered bodies
days of living splendor: their steel reduced
to the silence of acid:
nights ravelled to the ultimate flour:
injured stamens of the nuptial fatherland.)

Someone who awaited me amid the violins
uncovered a world like a buried tower
sinking its spiral deeper than all

* The ancient fortress of Macchu Pichu, cradle of the Inca Empire, is located more than 12,000 feet above sea-level in the most inaccessible corner of the Peruvian Andes. Built some 3,000 years B.C., this oldest American city was lost for many centuries before it was uncovered and excavated by Hiram Bingham in 1912. Although the roofs, which were thatched, are almost gone, the city is still virtually intact.

the leaves the color of raucous sulphur:
deeper still, into the gold of geology,
like a sword wrapt in meteors
I plunged my hand sweet and turbulent
into the inmost genital of the earth.
Into the deep waves I pressed my forehead,
falling like a drop down to the sulphuric peace,
and like a blindman I returned to the jasmine
of the spent springtime of man.

II

If flower to flower conveys its lofty germ
and the rock nurtures the disseminated flower
in its beaten cloak of diamond and sand,
man crumples the petal of light which he gathers
in the unceasing nautical springs
and grinds the throbbing metal into his hands.
And then, amid the garments and the smoke, upon the sunken
    table,
like a shuffled quantity, there remains the soul:
quartz and wakefulness, tears in the ocean
like pools of cold: nevertheless
he slays it and torments it with paper and with hate,
submerges it in the quotidian carpet, shreds it
on the hostile barbed wire of his clothes.

No: in corridors, air, sea, or roads,
who guards without a dagger (like the incarnadine
poppies) his blood? Fury attenuated
the sad trading of the seller of souls,
and from the height of the plumtree the dew
for a thousand years has been leaving its transparent message
upon the same branch that waits, O heart, O forehead crushed
between the cavities of autumn!

How many times in the streets of winter, or on
an omnibus or a boat at twilight, or in the thickest of
solitudes, that of a night of festivity, under the sound
of shadows and bells, in the very grotto of human pleasure,
have I longed to stop and seek the fathomless eternal vein
that once I touched in stone or in the lightning loosed by a kiss.
(That which in grain like a yellow tale
of small pregnant breasts reiterates a number
that endlessly is tenderness in germinal layers
and which, forever the same, is threshed in marble,

and that which in water is transparent fatherland—a bell
from the isolated snow to the bloody waves.)

I could snatch but a cluster of faces or masks
in flight, like rings of empty gold,
like wraps strewn by the daughters of a wild autumn
making the wretched tree of fearful races tremble.

I had no place to rest a hand,
a place which, gushing like the water of a dammed-up spring,
or hard as a grume of coal or crystal,
would have returned the warmth or cold of my outstretched
hand.
What was man? In what part of his conversation held
amid shops and whistles, in which of his metallic movements
dwelt the indestructible, the imperishable, life?

III

Man like an ear of corn was threshed in the endless
granary of lost deeds, of squalid
events, from one to seven, to eight,
and not one death but many deaths came to each one:
each day a little death, dust, worm, lamp
extinguished in the mud of the slums, a little death with fat
wings
entered each man like a short lance
and hounded by bread or by knife man was
the winner: son of the ports, obscure captain of the plough
or gnawer of thick streets,
each one fainted awaiting his death, his short daily death:
and their dreadful day-by-day ordeal
was like a black cup from which they drank trembling.

IV

Powerful death beckoned me many times:
it was like the unseen salt of the waves,
and the effusion of its unseen savor
was like halves of sinkings and of height
or vast constructions of wind and snowdrift.

I came to the ferrous edge, to the narrows
of the air, to the windingsheet of stone and agriculture,
to the astral emptiness of the last steps
and to the vertiginous spiral road:
but broad sea, O death! you come not wave on wave,
but like a burst of nocturnal clearness

or like the total numbers of the night.
You never came to rummage in the pocket,
your visit was not possible without raiment of red:
without auroral carpet of encompassing silence:
without high or buried legacies of tears.

I could not love in every being a tree
bearing its little autumn upon its back (the death of a
    thousand leaves),
all the false deaths and resurrections
without earth, without abyss:
I wanted to swim in the broadest lives,
in the widest river-mouths,
and when little by little man was denied me
and step and door barred lest my gushing hands
touch his wounded non-existence,
then through street and street and river and river
and city and city and bed and bed I went,
and my saline mask traversed the wilderness,
and in the last humiliated houses, without lamp, without fire,
without bread, without stone, without silence, alone,
I rolled over dying of my own death.

V

It was not you, sombre death, bird of iron plumage,
not you that the poor heir of the chambers
carried, between quick feedings, under his empty skin:
it was something, a poor petal of exterminated rope:
an atom of his breast which did not join the struggle
or crude dew that did not fall upon his brow.
It was that which could not be reborn, a particle
of little death with neither peace nor territory:
a bone, a bell that died within him.
I lifted the iodine bandages, immersed my hands
in the poor sufferings that murdered death,
and I found in the wound merely a cold gust
that entered by the vague interstices of his soul.

VI

Then up the ladder of the earth I climbed,
through the atrocious tangle of lost forests,
up to you, Macchu Picchu.
Lofty city of laddered stones,
ultimate abode of those not hidden
by earth in robes of sleep.

In you as in two parallel lines
the cradle of the lightning and of man
rocked in a wind of thorns.

Mother of stone, foam of the condors.

Lofty reef of the human dawn.

Shovel lost in the primal sand.

This was the home, this is the site:
here the broad kernels of corn arose
and fell again as red hail.

Here the gold thread came from the vicuña
to dress the loves, the tombs, the mothers,
the king, the prayers, the warriors.

Here man rested his feet at night
beside the feet of the eagle, in lofty carnivorous
lairs, and in the dawn
trod with feet of thunder the rarefied mist,
and touched the earth and the stones
unto recognition in the night or in death.

I see the garments and the hands,
the vestige of water in the thundering gorge,
the wall smoothed by the touch of a face
that watched with my eyes the terrestrial lamps,
that oiled with my hands the vanished
timbers: for everything, clothes, furs, pots,
words, wine, bread,
is gone, fallen to the ground!

And the air came in with orange-blossom
fingers over all the sleeping ones:
a thousand years of air, months, weeks of air,
of blue wind, of ferrous mountain range,
like gentle hurricanes of steps
polishing the lonely realm of stone.

VII

All you dead of one abyss, shades of a single chasm,
the deep one, as if to contain
your true dimension
the veritable, the all-encompassing
death came, and from the graven rocks,
from the scarlet capitals,

from the laddered aqueducts
you plummeted like an autumn
in a single death.
Today the empty air no longer weeps,
it knows no more your feet of clay,
forgotten now your jugs that drained the sky
when spilled by the lightning's knives,
and your mighty tree was consumed
by the mist, and cut down by the gale.

It lifted a hand which fell abruptly
from the summit to the end of time.
Now you are no more, spidery hands, gossamer
threads, tangled web:
all that you were has collapsed: customs, well worn
syllables, masks of dazzling light.

But a permanence of stone and of word:
raised like a glass by the hands
of all, the living, the dead, the silenced—sustained
by so much death: the city—a wall, by so much life wrought
of petals of stone: the permanent rose, the home:
this Andean reef of glacial settlements.

When the clay-colored hand
turned to clay, and the little eyelids closed
full of crude walls alive with castles,
and everything human lay jumbled in its hole,
exactitude remained on high:
the lofty site of the human dawn:
the loftiest cask containing silence:
a life of stone after so many lives.

VIII

Climb up with me, American love.
Kiss with me the secret stones.
The torrential silver of the Urubamba
strews pollen to the yellow cup.
Strewn the emptiness of the clinging vine,
the petrified plant, the hard wreath
over the silence of the mountain coffin.
Come, tiny life, between the wings
of earth, while crystal and cold—whipped air
cleaving adamant emeralds—
O wild water, you descend from the snow.

Love, love, unto the sudden night,
from the roaring Andean flint
to the rosy-kneed dawn,
you watch the blind son of the snow.

O Wilkamayu river of roaring strings,
when you shatter your lineal thunders
in white foam, like wounded snow,
when your steep blast
singing and lashing awakens the sky,
what tale do you bring to the ear scarcely
loosed from your Andean foam?

Who captured the lightning of the cold
and left it enchained on the summit,
doled out in glacial tears,
dashed its rapid swords,
stricken its martial stamens,
carried on its warrior's bed
overpowered to its end of rock?

What do your rippling flashings tell?
Did once your secret rebel lightning
travel vibrant with words?
Who is shattering the frozen syllables,
dark languages, golden banners,
fathomless mouths, muffled shouts
of your dainty arterial waters?
Who clips the floral eyelids
that come to watch from the earth?
Who is hurling the dead branches
that come cascading down in your hands
to thresh their night threshed
in the geological carbon?
Who is casting down the cluster of linkages?
Who is burying the farewells anew?

Love, love, do not touch the brink,
nor adore the sunken head:
let time fulfill its stature
in its parlor of broken brooks,
and, between the walls and the rushing torrents,
gather the air of the ravine,
the parallel sheets of the wind,
the blind canal of the mountain ranges,

the crude salute of the dew,
and climb, flower by flower, through the thicket,
trodding the cliff-fallen snake.

In the zone of cliffs, stone and forest,
dust of green stars, bright woods,
the Mantur bursts like a living lake
or a new floor of silence.

Come to my own being, to my very self,
to the crowning solitude.
The dead kingdom still lives.

And the sanguinary shadow of the condor
crosses the clock like a black ship.

IX

Sidereal eagle, vine of mist.
Lost bastion, blind scimitar.
Starry belt, solemn bread.
Torrential ladder, vast eyelid.
Triangular tunic, pollen of stone.
Lamp of granite, bread of stone.
Mineral serpent, rose of stone.
Buried ship, spring of stone.
Horse of the moon, light of stone.
Equinoctial T-square, vapor of stone.
Final geometry, book of stone.
Iceberg wrought by the gales.
Madrepore of submerged time.
Wall by fingers softened.
Roof by feathers assailed.
Clusters of mirrors, foundations of tempest.
Thrones overturned by the clinging vine.
Reign of the pitiless claw.
Whirlwind suspended on the slope.
Motionless cataract of turquoise.
Patriarchal bell of the sleepers.
Shackle of subjugated snows.
Iron lying upon its statues.
Inaccessible barred tempest.
Hands of puma, sanguinary rock.
Shade-giving tower, discussion of snow.
Night upraised in fingers and roots.
Window of the mists, hardened dove.

Nocturnal plant, statue of thunders.
Essential mountain-range, marine roof.
Architecture of lost eagles.
Twine of the sky, bee of the heights.
Bloody level, constructed star.
Mineral bubble, moon of quartz.
Andean serpent, forehead of amaranth.
Dome of silence, pure fatherland.
Beloved of the sea, tree of cathedrals.
Cluster of salt, cherry tree of black wings.
Snowy teeth, cold thunder.
Scratched moon, threatening stone.
Mane of the cold, stirring of the air.
Volcano of hands, dark cataract.
Wave of silver, direction of time.

X

Stone within the stone, man, where was he?
Air within the air, man, where was he?
Time within time, man, where was he?
Were you too the little piece
of unfinished man, of empty eagle
who through today's streets, through the footprints,
through the leaves of dead autumn
is crushing the soul to the grave?
Poor hand, foot, poor life . . .
Days of light wasted
upon you, like rain
on the flags of the carnival,
did they give petal by petal of their dim nourishment
to your empty mouth?
                    Hunger, man's shoal,
hunger, secret plant, woodcutters' root,
hunger, did the borders of your reef
climb these lofty landslid towers?

I ask you, salt of the roadways,
show me the spoon; allow me, architecture,
to gnaw with a stick the stamens of stone,
to mount all the rungs of the air to the void,
to probe the entrail till I touch the man.

Macchu Picchu, did you put
stone upon stone, and at the base, a rag?
Coal upon coal and in the foundation tears?

Fire in the gold and, within it trembling, the great
red splash of blood?

Relinquish to me the slave you buried!
Erupt from your soul the hard bread
of the wretched, show me the garb
of the serf, and his window.
Tell me how he slept when he was alive.
Tell me if his sleep was raucous, half-open, like a black hole
worn in the wall by weariness.
The wall, the wall! If upon his sleep
there weighed every layer of stone, and if he fell beneath it
as beneath a moon, with sleep!

Ancient America, buried bride,
did your fingers too,
on reaching from the forest toward the lofty void of the gods,
under the nuptial banners of light and decorum
mingled with the thunder of drums and lances,
did your fingers too, yours too—
those which the abstract rose and the line of cold
and the bleeding breast of the new grain carried
to the web of radiant weave, to the hard cavities—
did you too, buried America, you too, harbor in the humblest,
in the bitter intestine, like an eagle, hunger?

XI

Across the confused splendor,
into the stony night, let me plunge my hand
and let throb within me, like a bird imprisoned for a thousand
    years,
the ancient heart of the forgotten!
Let me now forget this joy, which is broader than the sea,
for man is broader than the sea and its islands,
and one must fall into him as into a well to emerge from the
    depths
with a spray of secret water and sunken truths.
Let me forget, broad stone, the mighty proportions,
the transcendental measure, the honeycombed stones,
and from the T-square let now my hand
slide down upon the hypotenuse of harsh blood and hairshirt.
When, like a horseshoe of red elytra, the frantic condor
strikes my temples in its flight
and its hurricane of bloodthirsty feathers sweeps the dark dust
from the sloping perron, I see not the swift beast,

I see not the blind cycle of its claws,
I see the ancient human being, the serf, the sleeper
in the fields, I see a body, a thousand bodies, a man, a thousand women,
under the black blast, black with rain and the night,
with the heavy stone of the statue:
John Stonecutter, son of Wiracocha,
John Coldeater, son of the green star,
John Barefoot, grandson of the turquoise,
rise with me, brother, to be born.

XII

Rise with me, brother, to be born.
Extend me your hand from the deep
realm of your widespread anguish.
You will not return from the rocky depths.
You will not return from subterranean time.
Your hardened voice will not return.
Your perforated eyes will not return.
Behold me from the depths of the earth,
ploughman, weaver, silent shepherd:
tamer of the tutelary llamas:
mason of the defiant scaffolding:
watercarrier of the Andean tears:
jeweler of the carven fingers:
sower quivering in the seed:
potter spilt into your clay:
bring your ancient buried cares
to the cup of this new life.
Show me your blood and your wrinkles,
tell me: here I suffered
because the jewel did not shine or the earth
yield the stone or the grain in time:
show me the stone on which you fell,
the wood upon which you were crucified,
kindle for me the ancient flints,
the ancient lamps, the whips embedded
in your wounds through the centuries
and the axes gleaming with blood.
I come to speak through your dead mouth.
From across the world gather all
the silent spilt lips
and from the depths talk to me all through this long night
as if I were there with you anchored,

tell me all, chain by chain,
link by link, and step by step,
sharpen the knives you used to keep,
place them on my breast and my hand,
like a river of yellow lightning bolts,
like a river of buried tigers,
and let me weep, hours, days, years,
blind ages, stellar centuries.

Give me your silence, your water, your hope.

Give me your struggle, your iron, your volcanoes.

Affix your bodies to mine like magnets.

Partake of my veins and my mouth.

Speak with my words and my blood.

TRANSLATED BY *Kate Flores*

MIGUEL HERNÁNDEZ (1910–1942) Born on October 30, 1910, in Orihuela, a village in Alicante, the son of a goatherd, Miguel Hernández saw little of school, yet enough to learn how to read and write. His activities followed his father's: tilling the soil, tending the goats, selling the milk from house to house. Of the books that went through his hands those of the Golden Age attracted him most, and soon he wanted to write his own and in 1932 he saw his name in print in the local newspaper. Encouraged by his first publication, he went on writing, and his collected verse, *Perito en lunas,* appeared in Murcia the following year. It attracted some attention and he moved to Madrid, where he was welcomed by Neruda, Aleixandre, and Bergamín and became secretary to the art critic José María de Cossío. Bergamín, the editor of the important journal *Cruz y Raya,* then published *"Quien te ha visto y quien te ve, o sombra de lo que eras"* (1934), an *"auto sacramental"* in the style of the religious plays of the Golden Age. However, it was not until *El rayo que no cesa* (1936) that his reputation was well established; but by then he was sucked into the maelstrom of the civil war. Ferociously militant, he wrote some of the most forceful verse favoring the Loyalist cause. But he was captured after the war and for years remained in prison, so poorly fed and lodged that his weak, tubercular organism was not able to withstand the punishment; he died in his cell on March 28, 1942, not quite thirty-two years old.

BIBLIOGRAPHY

Works by Hernández:
　Perito en lunas. 1933.
　El rayo que no cesa. 1936.
　Viento del pueblo. 1937.
　Obras escogidas. 1952.
　Obras completas. 1960.
About Hernández:
　Díaz-Plaja, G. *Poesía lírica española.* Barcelona, 1948.
　Buxó, José P. *"La poesía de Miguel Hernández." Ideas de México,* January–April 1955, pp. 60–71.

❊　❊　❊

From THE UNENDING LIGHTNING

I

Some flesh-eating knife
on tender killing wing
hovers steady, flashing
down upon my life.

This bolt of metal twitching,
swooping brilliantly,
picks and pecks at me,
like a sorrow nesting.

The bushy balcony
above my ears is dark
and thick, and yet my heart,
my heart is hoary gray.

In cruel kindness driven
by the lightning bolt,
I scramble back to childhood
like the moon to town.

My every eyelash gleans
the salt of souls and tears.
From cobwebs I cull flowers.
So I use my griefs.

Where can I go and not be
hounded by my doom?
As you sweep your room
I grapple with the sea.

No longer to resist
this raging love or hell
is inconceivable.
Pain keeps my grief ageless.

Yet in the end I'll drown
you, heart-swell, birdwing lightning.
For this I know: in dying
my last breath's my own.

Go on, then, winged knife,
swoop down, wound me; some day
yellow time will fade
against my photograph,

IV

You tossed me a bitter lemon
with a hand so warm and pure
I didn't dare disturb the sphere.
Yet I thought I'd try the rind.

One yellow nip and my blood switched
from sweet and slow to racing hot
and writhing. That big pointed teat
had bitten me at once, right back!

When glancing up I caught your smile,
unconscious of my greed and guile,
at all my lemonry-in-vain,

I felt my blood slump in my vest;
straight through the pores of that gold breast
shot one annihilating pain.

V

Your heart's a frozen orange—no light
or any sweetness fleshed within,
yet with its stippled rind so golden
how winsomely it charms the sight!

My heart's a feverish pomegranate,
open, waxy, pink and clustered,
offering each tender bead
so lovingly, so obstinate.

Then when I come to touch your heart,
how shattering to find it locked
in terrifying snow and frost!

On the fringes of my grief
waves this parched-dry handkerchief,
hoping my tears will drown its thirst.

XI

You kill me, you're so pure and chaste!
Though I confess, my love, I'm guilty.
I snatched that kiss; yes, it was I
who sipped the flower of your face.

I sipped the flower of your face,
and ever since that wondrous day
your face looks pale and squinched, grown heavy,
scruple yellow, with distress.

The ghost of that delinquent kiss
now haunts your cheekbone, growing ever
darker, deeper, obvious.

How zealously you stay awake!
How stubbornly you watch my lips
against the least indulgent break!

XXIII

Like the bull I was born to sorrow
and pain; like the bull I am marked
by a hellish brand in the ribs
and a masculine fruit in the groin.

Like the bull my immeasurable heart
finds the world too small, and in love
with a face I would kiss, like the bull
I must wrangle with you for your love.

Like the bull I have thrived on punishment,
my tongue has been bathed in the blood of my heart,
and I rush down the wind with my neck full of barbs.

Like the bull I have charged you, pursued you, while you
have left my desire for you on the sword,
and so, like the bull I am tricked, I am scorned.

XXVI

Gardeners go down the path.
Homeward. The sacred hour.
Blood sodden by the weight
of winter, summer, spring.

Gigantic labors piled behind them.
Homeward. To a song, a kiss.
Graven on the air behind them
the smell of tools and hands.

I go down another path.
Not homeward to a song, a kiss.
Marauder, destinationless.

A bull stands by the stream, apart.
Its huge face, tragic, wet,
forgets it is a bull, and virile.

XXVIII

This death, under a bull's hide
full of holes and the horns of his own
undoing, tramples and feeds
on a luminous bullfighters' field.

His roars are volcanic and steam
with the furious love he spreads
in a flame over everything living,
killing the gentlest ranchers.

Come, beast, with your ravenous love,
come feed on my heart's gnarled grass.
You may like its bitterness.

Like you, I am nagged by a love
for all, and my heart spreads out
over all its winding sheet.

TRANSLATED BY *Edwin Honig*

ELEGY FOR RAMÓN SIJÉ

(In Orihuela, where he and I were born, death like a
lightning flash deprived me of Ramón Sijé, so dear to me.)

I want to be the grieving gardener
of the earth you fill and fertilize,
    my dearest friend, so soon.

Mingling my helpless sorrow with the rain,
the snails, and all the organs of your body,
    I shall feed your heart

to the drooping poppies. Pain bunches up
between my ribs till every breath I draw
    becomes an aching stitch.

A brutal slam, a heavy frozen fist,
a sudden silent killing axe-blow sent
    you toppling to the ground.

Nothing gapes wider than my wounded cry,
this grief that plummets down to roots of death
    sunk deeper than my life.

Across the stubble of the dead I walk
uncomforted, leaving my heart behind,
    and go about my business.

Death touched you as it fled, so soon—oh, dawn
shot up so soon, so soon, and you were hurtled
   in this pit of earth.

I shan't forgive death's last caress; I shan't
forgive life's heedlessness—no, not the earth
   nor nothingness itself.

My hands scoop up a storm of lightning, boulders,
strident axes thirsting, hungering
   for catastrophes.

I want to dig the earth up with my teeth.
I want to scrape the dirt off bit by bit
   with sharp and burning teeth.

I'll hollow out this pit until I find you,
kiss your noble head, ungag your mouth,
   and bring you back to life.

Back to my orchard and the fig tree where
your soul will brush its wings high up among
   the blossoms, gathering

the wax and honey of angelic hives;
back to the murmuring at windows where
   the country lovers meet.

You'll bask beneath my sheltered glance and hear
your sweetheart and the bees exhaust the theme
   of your nobility.

Greedily my love cries out to you.
It calls your crumpled velvet heart: come to
   these drifting almond sprays;

come to the rosy petaled souls among
these curdling almond trees. I need you here.
We've still so many things to talk about,
   my friend, my dearest friend.

TRANSLATED BY *Edwin Honig*

LAST SONG

Painted, but not empty;
this house of mine is painted,
colored by great passions
and calamities.

It will be retrieved
from grief where it was borne
with one deserted table
and a shattered bed.

Kisses on the pillows
will plump them up again.
The sheet that wraps our bodies
will put forth a vine,
dense and fragrant, nightly.

Hatred will be scotched
behind the window pane.

Our wrangling will be gentle.

Let this be my hope.

TRANSLATED BY *Edwin Honig*

WAR

The aged in the villages.
The heart, ownerless.
Love has no object.
Grass, dust, crow.
And youth?

In the coffin.

A tree, withered and alone.
A woman like a log
Widowed in her bed.
Hatred has no end.
And youth?

In the coffin.

TRANSLATED BY *Edwin Honig*

THE TRAIN OF THE WOUNDED

Silence that is wrecked on the silence
of those mouths closed by the night.
It remains silent, even when crossed.
It speaks the drowned speech of the dead.

Silence.

Open the highways of deep cotton,
gag the wheels, the clocks,
hold back the sea's voice, the dove's:
touch the feelings of the night of dreams.

Silence.

The train, rainy with flying blood,
the fragile train of those who are bleeding,
the silent, painful, pale,
gagged train of sufferings.

Silence.

Train of the mortal paleness that grows:
paleness covers heads,
the *Ay!* covers the voice, the heart, the earth,
the heart of those who were badly hurt.

Silence.

They are dumping legs, arms, eyes,
dumping out parts all through the train.
They pass, leaving a trail of bitterness,
another milky way of limbs like stars.

Silence.

Hoarse train, passed out, stained red:
the coal is dying fast, smoke sighs,
and the engine sighs like a mother,
advances like a long discouragement.

Silence.

The long mother is dying to stop
under a tunnel and stretch out and sob.
There are no stops for it except
the hospital, except the breast.

Silence.

In order to live, one portion is enough:
a man can fit in a corner of the flesh.
A single finger, a single piece of wing
can start the body on its total flight.

Silence.

Stop that dying train whose long road
across the night never comes to an end.
Even the horse has been left without shoes,
sand gets into its hooves, into its breath.

TRANSLATED BY *Hardie St. Martin*

THE CEMETERY

The cemetery is close
to where you and I sleep,

among the prickly pears,
blue agaves and children
who shout uproariously
if a corpse clouds the road.

From here the cemetery
is all blue, golden, clean.
Four steps—and the dead.
Four steps—and the living.

Clean, blue and golden, there
my son becomes remote.

TRANSLATED BY *Willis Barnstone*

LULLABY OF THE ONION
(Dedicated to his son, after receiving a letter from his wife,
in which she wrote she had only bread and onion to eat.)

An onion is hoarfrost
constricted and poor.
Hoarfrost of your days
and my nights.
Hunger and onion,
black ice and hoarfrost
enormous and round.

My child was lying
in the cradle of hunger.
Nursing
on the blood of an onion.
But your blood
was a frosting of sugar,
onion and hunger.

A swarthy woman
dissolved in the moon
undoes herself thread by thread
over the crib.
Laugh, child,
you can swallow the moon
whenever you want.

Lark of my house,
laugh hard.
The laughter in your eyes
is the light of the world.
Laugh so that when
my soul hears,
it will thrash in space.

Your laughter frees me
and lends me wings.
It lessens my solitude
and crumbles my prison.
Mouth that flies,
heart that flashes lightning
on your lips.

Your laughter is the most
victorious sword,
vanquisher of flowers
and larks.
Rival of the sun.
The future of my bones
and my love.

The winged flesh,
the sudden eyelid,
live as never
in high color.
How many linnet birds
are flushed and flutter
from your body!

I awoke from being a child:
Don't you awake!
My mouth is sad:
Laugh forever!
In your cradle

defend laughter
feather by feather.

Soar so high,
so far,
let your flesh be the sky
just born.
If only I might
return to the beginning
of your flight!

In this eighth month you laugh
with five lemon blooms,
with five diminutive
ferocities.
With five teeth
like five adolescent
jasmine.

Tomorrow they will be
the frontier of kisses,
when your teeth
feel a weapon upon them.
When a fire
runs down from your teeth
searching the center.

Fly, child, on the double
moon of the breast;
it, sad with onion
you, satisfied and content.
Don't tumble down.
Don't even know what happens
or what goes on.

TRANSLATED BY *Anthony Kerrigan*

OCTAVIO PAZ (1914–) Born in Mexico City in 1914 and educated at the National University, Paz published his first verse collection, *Luna silvestre,* in 1933. After a year (1937) in Spain during the civil war, he returned to Mexico City and founded *Taller,* a magazine devoted to poetry and literary criticism. His *Raiz del hombre* (1937) and *Bajo tu clara sombra* (1938) established him as one of the most promising writers of his generation. With some of his friends (Xavier Villaurrutia, Octavio G. Barreda), he launched in 1940 the vanguard review *El Hijo Pródigo.* In 1942 he collected all his verse, with but a few exceptions, in *A la orilla del mundo.* Two years later he was awarded a Guggenheim Fellowship which permitted him to travel in the United States. Since 1946, when Paz entered the diplomatic service, he has lived in France and in India, where he lives now. With a one-act play based on Hawthorne's story, "Rappacini's Daughter," Paz tried his hand at playwriting. The same year (1957) also marked the publication of *Piedra de sol,* a mythical poem which has fascinated American poets, as can be seen from three different versions into English: by Peter Miller, Muriel Rukeyser, and Stephen Berg. In 1960 all of Paz' verse (*Luna silvestre* excepted) was collected in *Libertad bajo palabra.* Since then he has published *Salamandra* (1962).

BIBLIOGRAPHY

Works in Verse by Paz:
  Luna silvestre. 1933.
  Raiz del hombre. 1937.
  Bajo tu clara sombra. 1938.
  Entre la piedra y la flor. 1941.
  A la orilla del mundo. 1942.
  Libertad bajo palabra. 1949.
  Aguila o sol? 1951.
  Semillas para un himno. 1954.
  Piedra de sol. 1957.
  La estación violenta. 1958.
  Salamandra. 1962.

❀ ❀ ❀

THE STREET

Here is a long and silent street.
I walk in blackness and I stumble and fall

and rise, and I walk blind, my feet
trampling the silent stones and the dry leaves.
Someone behind me also tramples, stones, leaves:
if I slow down, he slows;
if I run, he runs. I turn: nobody.
Everything dark and doorless,
only my steps aware of me,
I turning and turning among these corners
which lead forever to the street
where nobody waits for, nobody follows me,
where I pursue a man who stumbles
and rises and says when he sees me: nobody.

TRANSLATED BY *Muriel Rukeyser*

From SUN STONE

. . . names, places,
street and streets; faces; streets; circles;
railway stations, a park, the single rooms,
stains on the wall, somebody combing her hair,
someone singing beside me, watching herself,
rooms, places, streets, names, rooms,

The scene: Madrid, in 1937,
on the Plaza del Angel seeing the women
doing their sewing and singing with their sons,
and then the shriek of the siren and their shriek,
houses brought down and kneeling in the dust,
the towers cloven, the faces running spittle
and the hurricane of engines, I hold forever;
you and I, we took our clothes off and made love
to defend with our lives our eternal portion,
our rationing of time and of paradise,
to touch our root, to reach ourselves in touching,
to recover our inheritance pirated
by robbers of life in a thousand centuries,
you and I, we took our clothes off and we kissed
because these nakednesses, woven together,
can overleap time and are invulnerable,
nothing can touch them, they go to the origins,
there is no You nor I, tomorrow, yesterday, names,
there truly two become only one body and soul,
O to be whole . . .

there are rooms that are adrift
among the great cities that go foundering,
furnished rooms, city streets, names striking like wounds,
the room whose windows look out on other rooms
all papered in the same discolored paper
where a man in shirtsleeves reads his newspaper
while a woman irons; the room lit bright in spring
and, entering, the branches of the peachtree;
the other rooms; outside it is always raining,
with rusted statues of three boys in the courtyard;
rooms that are ships, and that are rocking and singing
in a gulf of brilliance; o the submarines:
silence dispersed upon the greenness of waves
and everything that we touch phosphoresces;
memorials to a luxury whose pictures
are eaten away over the threadbare carpets;
trapdoors, cells, oubliettes, enchanted caverns,
cages of birds, and rooms with numbers on them,
everything is transfigured, everything is in flight,
all these moldings are clouds, and every door
opens on the sea, the field, the air; each meal
is now a celebration; sealed tight as shells,
time cannot hope, besieging them, to conquer,
there is no time here, no wall: space, space is here,
open your hand and gather these riches in,
cut all the fruits, this life is here to eat,
lie at the foot of this tree, and drink the water!

TRANSLATED BY *Muriel Rukeyser*

THE DAY IN UDAIPUR

White palace.
White on the black lake.
Lingam and yoni.

You surround me, night,
As the god the goddess.
The cool terrace.
You are immense immense
When measured.

Inhuman stars.
But the hours are ours.

I fall and get up,
I burn and drown. Have you
Only a body?

    Birds on the water,
    Dawn on the eyelids.

The marbles push forward,
Absorbed in themselves,
As tall as death.

    Are the palaces stranded?
    Whiteness drifting.

Women, children
On the roadways.
Scattered fruit.

    Rags or lightning-bolts?
    A parade on the black plain.

Silver bracelets,
Cool and tinkling,
On arms and ankles.

    A small boy arrives at his wedding
    In a rented suit.

Clean clothes
Spread out among the stones.
Look at them and shut up.

    Monkeys with red buttocks.
    Howling on the islet.

Flies. Blood.
A kid cavorts
In Kali's courtyard.

    Gods, men and beasts
    Eat from the same plate.

The headless black
Goddess dances
On the pallid god.

    Heat. An enormous humming.
    And those rotted mangoes . . .

A wasp-nest hangs
From the wall, a dark
And ardent sun.

My brow is also a sun
With black thoughts inside.

The marbles glow.
Palaces of death.
Hallucinations.

Hundreds of parrots:
Green, black, then green again.

Your brow. The lake.
Smooth, without thoughts.
A fish leaps.

Twilight. Lights
On the water.

Ripples. The plain
Is ochre. So is the crevice . . .
Your clothes nearby.

I am like a lamp
On your shadowed body.

Living scales:
Two bodies united
Over the emptiness.

The sky crushes us.
The water sustains us.

Open your eyes.
A forest of trees
Was born tonight.

Whiteness, you hide
What I see and say.

TRANSLATED BY *Lysander Kemp*

THE ENDLESS INSTANT

Between sleeping and waking, I hear an incessant river running between dimly discerned, looming forms, drowsy and
frowning.

It is the black and white cataract, the voices, the laughter,
the groans, of a confused world hurling itself from a height.

And my thoughts that gallop and gallop and get no further
also fall and rise, and turn back and plunge into the stagnant waters of language.

Words!—to stamp the world with an indelible seal or to fling
it wide open, syllables wrested from the tree of idiom, axes
against death, prows where the great wave of emptiness
breaks, wounds, water shoots, svelte comes that insomnia
raises!

A second ago it would have been easy to grasp a word and
repeat it once and then again,

any one of those phrases one utters alone in a room without
mirrors

to prove to oneself that it's not certain,
               that we are still alive after all,

but now with weightless hands night is lulling the furious tide,
and one by one images recede, one by one words cover their
faces.

The time is past already for hoping for time's arrival, the
time of yesterday, today and tomorrow,

yesterday is today, tomorrow is today, today all is today,
suddenly it came forth from itself and is watching me,

it doesn't come from the past, it is not going anywhere, today is here, it is not death

no one dies of death, everyone dies of life—it is not life—
instantaneous fruit, vertiginous and lucid rapture, the empty
taste of death gives more life to life—

today is not death nor life,

has no body, nor name, nor face, today is here, cast at my
feet, looking at me.

I am standing, quiet at the center of the circle I made in falling away from my thoughts,

I am standing and I have nowhere to turn my eyes to, not one
splintered fragment of the past is left,

all childhood has brought itself to this instant and the whole
future is these pieces of furniture nailed to their places,

the wardrobe with its wooden face, the chairs lined up waiting
for nobody,

the chubby armchair with its arms spread, obscene as if dead
in its bed,

the electric fan—conceited insect—the lying window, the
actual without chinks or cracks,

all has shut itself up in itself, I have come back to where I
began, everything is today and forever.

Way off there, on the other side, shores extend, immense as a
look of love,

there the night clothed in water displays its hieroglyphics a
hand's breadth away,

the river enters singing along the sleeping plain and moistens
the roots of the word freedom,

there enlaced bodies lose themselves in a forest of transparent
trees,

under the leaves of the sun we walk, my love, we are two reflections that cross swords with each other,

silver stretches bridges for us to cross the night, stones make
way for us,

there you are the tattooing on the jade breast fallen from the
moon, there the insomniac diamond yields

and in its empty center we are the eye that never blinks and
the transfixion of the instant held within itself in its
splendor.

All is far off, there is no way back, the dead are not dead, the
living are not alive,

there is a wall, an eye that is a well, all that is pulls downward, the body is heavy,

thoughts are heavy, all the years are this minute that is
dropping interminably down,

from that hotel room in San Francisco I stepped right into
Bangkok, today is yesterday,

reality is a staircase going neither up nor down, we don't
move, today is today, always is today,

always the sound of trains that depart each night towards
night,

the resort to toothless words,

the boring through of the wall, the comings and goings,
reality shutting doors,

putting in commas, the punctuation of time, all is far off, the
walls are enormous,

the glass of water is thousands of miles away, it will take me
 a thousand years to cross my room again,

what a remote sound the word life has, I am not here, there
 is no here, this room is somewhere else, here is nowhere,
 little by little I have been shutting myself and find no exit
 that doesn't give onto this instant,

this instant is I, I went out of myself all at once, I have no
 name and no face,

I am here, cast at my feet, looking at myself looking to see
 myself seen.

Outside, in the gardens that summer has ravaged, a cicada
 rages against the night.

Am I or was I here?

TRANSLATED BY Denise Levertov

JORGE LUIS BORGES (1899–   ) Born in Buenos Aires, Borges was educated in Argentina and later in Switzerland and France. A major writer of our century, he has published many collections of short stories, essays, and poems, which have, in turn, been translated into the world's main languages. Often his stories read like erudite essays, his essays like poems, and his poems like brief narrations. Contending that the distinction between poetry and prose is largely typographical, in recent volumes of poetry he has included sections in prose. Throughout his work, Borges explores real, mythical and metaphysical worlds, seeking absolute truths, key words, escape from the labyrinth of solitude. At the same time he knows his search, which justifies the "algebra of his being," will fail, for in our condition of Heraclitian flux, there is no single truth, word or escape from self. Borges began to lose his sight in 1955, the year he began to study Anglo-Saxon and Old Norse, whose themes have profoundly influenced his own work, especially his poetry. The poems reveal the metaphysical exploration, enormous erudition, and spoofing humor of his best *ficciones*, yet they also contain a personal pathos and self-delineation absent from other writing. Borges has received many international honors, including the International Publishers Prize in 1961, which he shared with Samuel Beckett. He was Charles Eliot Norton Professor of Poetry at Harvard in 1967–68 and has lectured widely at American universities. He has received many honorory degrees, including the degree of Doctor of Letters, *honoris causa*, from Columbia, Oxford and the University of Paris.

BIBLIOGRAPHY

Works by Borges:
  Fervor de Buenos Aires, 1923
  Luna de Enfrente, 1925
  Cuadernos San Martín, 1929
  Evaristo Carriego, 1930
  Discusión, 1932
  Historia Universal de la infamia, 1935
  Historia de la Eternidad, 1936
  Ficciones 1944
  El aleph, 1949
  Otras inquisiciones, 1952
  El hacedor, 1960

About Borges:
  Alazraki, Jaime. *La prosa narrativa de Jorge Luis Borges,*
    Madrid, 1968.
  Barrenechea, Ana María. *La expresión de la irrealidad en la
    obra de Jorge Luis Borges, Mexico,* 1957.
  Gertel, Zunilda. *Borges, y su retorno a la poesía,* New York,
    1967.

❊   ❊   ❊

REMORSE

I have committed the worst sin of all
That a man can commit. I have not been
Happy. Let the glaciers of oblivion
Drag me and mercilessly let me fall.
My parents bred and bore me for a higher
Faith in the human game of nights and days;
For earth, for air, for water, and for fire.
I let them down. I wasn't happy. My ways
Have not fulfilled their youthful hope. I gave
My mind to the symmetric stubbornness
Of art, and all its webs of pettiness.
They willed me bravery. I wasn't brave.
It never leaves my side, since I began:
This shadow of having been a brooding man.

                    TRANSLATED BY *Willis Barnstone*

A BLIND MAN

I do not know what face looks back at me
When I look at the mirrored face, nor know
What aged man conspires in the glow
Of the glass, with tired silent fury.
Slow in shadow, with my hand I explore

My invisible features. A sparkling ray
Reaches me. A glimmer of your hair is gray
And some is even gold. I've lost no more
Than just the useless surfaces of things.
This consolation is of great import:
It is the comfort Milton had. I resort
To letters and to roses—my wonderings.
I think . . . if I could see my face I soon
Would know who I am on this rare afternoon.

TRANSLATED BY *Willis Barnstone*

NIGHTMARE

I am dreaming of an ancient king. His crown
Is iron and his gaze is dead. There are
No faces like that now. His rigid sword
Will watch over him, loyal like his hound.
I do not know if he is from Norway
Or Northumberland. But from the north, I know.
His thick red beard capes his chest. He doesn't throw
A glance at me, not a blind glance my way.
From what blackened mirror or from what ship
On seas that were his gambling wilderness
Could this gray and grave man venture a trip
Toward me, imposing his past and bitterness?
I know he dreams and judges me, is drawn
Erect. Day breaks up night. He has not gone.

TRANSLATED BY *Willis Barnstone*

POEM WRITTEN IN A COPY OF BEOWULF

At times I ask myself what are the reasons,
During my wandering night, that now impel
Me to begin (expecting no miracle
Of perfection) to study the tongue of the harsh Saxons.
Exhausted by the years my memory
Allows the futilely repeated words
To slip away, the way my life first girds
And then ungirds its tired history.
I tell myself it must be that the soul,
In a sufficient and a secret way,
Knows it is immortal, that its vast, grave
Circle takes in and can accomplish all.
Beyond this longing and beyond this verse,
Waiting for me, inexhaustible: the universe.

TRANSLATED BY *Willis Barnstone*

A KEY IN EAST LANSING

I am a key whose steel has been filed out.
My uneven edge was not cut aimlessly.
I sleep my vague sleep in a closet I don't see
In which I am a captive held throughout
By my keychain. A lock waits for me within,
Only one. The door is made of forged steel
And tight glass. Inside, ready to reveal
Itself, is the hidden true house. Deep in
The scanty twilight, the uninhabited
Mirrors glare into the nights and days
And glare upon the photographs of the dead
And the tenuous past of photographs. In this maze,
One day I will push up against the rock—
Hard door, and slip inside to turn the lock.

East Lansing, Michigan
1976
TRANSLATED BY *Willis Barnstone*

EMANUEL SWEDENBORG

He was taller than the others were. When that
Unusual man walked among men he was remote
And now and then called angels by invok-
ing secret names. And he was looking at
What earthly eyes cannot see: feverishly bright
Geometry, the crystal labyrinth
Of God, and the disgusting vortex in
The whirlpool of a man's hellish delights.
He knew that Glory and Avernus must be
Inside the soul, with all their myths and blaze,
And like the Greek he also knew that days
Of time are mirrors of eternity.
In dry Latin he was examining
Beyond all why or when: the ultimate things.

TRANSLATED BY *Willis Barnstone*

CAMDEN, 1892

The smell of coffee and of newspapers.
Sunday and its boredom. It is morning.
Some allegorical verses are adorning
The skimmed over page: the vain pentameters
Of a happy colleague. The old man lies
Stretched out and white in his respectable

Poor man's room. Lazily he fills
The weary mirror with his gaze. His eyes
See a face. He thinks, now unsurprised: that face
Is me. With fumbling hand he reaches out
To touch the tangled beard and ravaged mouth.
The end is not far off. His voice declares:
I am almost gone, and yet my verses scan
Life and its splendor. I was Walt Whitman.

TRANSLATED BY *Willis Barnstone*

SPINOZA

Here in the twilight the translucent hands
Of the Jew polishing the crystal glass.
The dying afternoon is cold with bands
Of fear. Each day the afternoons all pass
The same. The hands and space of hyacinth
Paling in the confines of the Ghetto walls
Barely exist for the quiet man who stalls
There, dreaming up a brilliant labyrinth.
Fame does not disturb him (that reflection of
Dreams in the dream of another mirror), nor love,
The timid love of women. Gone the bars,
He's free, from metaphor and myth, to sit
Polishing a stubborn lens: the infinite
Map of the One who now is all His stars.

TRANSLATED BY *Willis Barnstone*

JOHANNES BRAHMS

I know I am an intruder in your gardens
Which redeem a young paradise that was vast,
Humble, low, in a primordial past,
And now is raised again by your violins.
My fate is silence. And it won't do,
That misery (which people like to save
By shrilly invoking art) to honor you.
To honor you one must be sound and brave.
I am a man, a coward. And I know
That nothing will excuse my resolution
To sing of the magnificent elation—
Fire and crystal—of your loving soul.
My servitude is the word, is the impure

Conjunction of a meaning and a sound.
Yours is the river that flows and will endure,
Not a symbol, not a mirror, not a moan.

TRANSLATED BY *Willis Barnstone*

HERACLITUS

Heraclitus is walking through the afternoon
Of Ephesos. With no intervention
Of his will the afternoon has left him
On the border of a soundless river
Whose destiny and name he does not know.
There is a stone Janus and some poplars.
He sees himself in the shifting mirror
And discovers and polishes the sentence
Which generations of mankind
Will not let slip away. His voice declares:
No one steps two times in the waters
Of the same river. He stops. He feels,
With the astonishment of a sacred horror,
That he too is a river and a flight.
He wants to recapture that morning
And its night and the night before. He cannot.
He repeats the sentence. He sees it printed
In future bright characters
On one of Burnet's pages.
Now Heraclitus does not know Greek. Janus,
God of the Gates, is a Latin god.
Heraclitus has no yesterday or now.
He is a mere artifice that a gray man
Dreamed on the shores of the Red Cedar River,
A man who is weaving pentameters
So as not to brood so much on Buenos Aires
And on the loved faces. One face is gone.

TRANSLATED BY *Willis Barnstone*

POEM OF THE GIFTS
To Maria Esther Vanquez

Let no one with tears or disapproval slight
This declaration of the majesty
Of God, who with magnificent irony
Granted me books and, at the same time, night.

He made this set of lightless eyes the lord
In this city of books, and they can only read
In the library of dreams where the dawns cede
These senseless paragraphs to unexplored

Wishful longings. Futilely the day
Squanders its infinite books on them in scripts
Elusive like the elusive manuscripts
Of Alexandria, which burned away.

A king among his fountains and greenery
Is dying of hunger and thirst (the Greek relates).
I lurch from side to side, lost in the straits
Of this towering, profound, blind library.

The encyclopedia, atlas, the Orient
And the West, centuries, the dynasties,
Symbols, cosmos, the cosmogonies
Salute the walls, yet all is impotent.

Slow in my darkness, I am exploring the
Thread of twilight with my faltering cane,
I who imagined Paradise was the domain
Under the heading of a library.

Something, which surely cannot be defined
By the word *chance,* presides over these things;
Some other man controlled, in shadowy evenings,
The multitude of books. He too was blind.

Straying through the slowness of these galleries
I often feel with unclear, holy dread
That I am the other, the dead man who tread
The same steps on the same days. Which of these

Two beings, which of us is writing this poem
Of a plural I and one lone shadow? I came
To ask: what difference if one name is my name
When our curse is indivisible, a single gloom?

Groussac or Borges, now I look upon
A dear world coming apart like smoldering trash,
Formless, burning to a vague, pale ash
That looks like sleep and like oblivion.

TRANSLATED BY *Willis Barnstone*

THE WATCHER

The light enters and I remember who I am; he is there.

He begins by telling me his name which (it should now be clear) is mine.

I revert to the servitude which has lasted more than seven times ten years.

He saddles me with his rememberings.

He saddles me with the miseries of every day, the human condition.

I am his old nurse; he requires me to wash his feet.

He spies on me in mirrors, in mahogany, in shop windows.

One or another woman has rejected him, and I must share his anguish.

He dictates to me now this poem, which I do not like.

He insists I apprentice myself tentatively to the stubborn Anglo-Saxon.

He has won me over to the hero worship of dead soldiers, people with whom I could scarcely exchange a single word.

On the last flight of stairs, I feel him at my side.

He is in my footsteps, in my voice.

Down to the last detail, I abhor him.

I am gratified to remark that he can hardly see.

I am in a circular cell and the infinite wall is closing in.

Neither of the two deceives the other, but we both lie.

We know each other too well, inseparable brother.

You drink the water from my cup and you wolf down my bread.

The door to suicide is open, but theologians assert that, in the subsequent shadows of the other kingdom, there will I be, waiting for myself.

TRANSLATED BY *Alastair Reid*

YOU

In all the world, one man has been born, one man has died.

To insist otherwise is nothing more than statistics, an impossible extension.

No less impossible than bracketing the smell of rain with your dream of two nights ago.

That man is Ulysses, Abel, Cain, the first to make constellations of the stars, to build the first pyramid, the man who contrived the hexagrams of the Book of Changes, the smith who engraved runes on the sword of Hengist, Einar Tamberskelver the archer, Luis de León, the bookseller who fathered Samuel Johnson, Voltaire's gardener, Darwin aboard the *Beagle*, a Jew in the death chamber, and, in time, you and I.

One man alone has died at Troy, at Metaurus, at Hastings, at Austerlitz, at Trafalgar, at Gettysburg.

One man alone has died in hospitals, in boats, in painful solitude, in the rooms of habit and of love.

One man alone has looked on the enormity of dawn.

One man alone has felt on his tongue the fresh quenching of water, the flavor of fruit and of flesh.

I speak of the unique, the single man, he who is always alone.

TRANSLATED BY *Alastair Reid*

1891

I catch a glimpse of him and then I lose him—
best black suit well-brushed and narrow-fitting,
nondescript neckerchief around the throat,
narrow forehead, straggling moustache,
he walks among the people of the evening,
lost in himself, not seeing anyone.
At a corner counter on the Calle Piedras
he takes a shot of spirits, out of habit.
Someone calls out to him. He doesn't answer.
Behind his eyes, an old resentment smolders.
Another block. A fragment of milonga
falls from a patio. Those cheap guitars
keep gnawing at the edges of his temper,
but still, his walk keeps time, unconsciously.
He lifts his hand and pats the solid handle
of the dagger in the collar of his waistcoat.
He goes to reclaim a debt. It is not far.
A few steps, and the man stops in his walking.
In the passageway, there is a flowering thistle.
He hears the clunk of a bucket in the cistern
and a voice already too well-known to him.
He pushes the far door, which is already open
as though he were expected. This very evening
perhaps they will have shown him his own death.

TRANSLATED BY *Alastair Reid*

they treat us as if we were offspring. They're spoiled and we're spoiled."

"They've been acting funny ever since you forbade them to take the rocket to New York a few months ago."

"They're not old enough to do that alone, I explained."

"Nevertheless, I've noticed they've been decidedly cool toward us since."

"I think I'll have David McClean come tomorrow morning to have a look at Africa."

"But it's not Africa now, it's Green Mansions country and Rima."

"I have a feeling it'll be Africa again before then."

A moment later they heard the screams.

Two screams. Two people screaming from downstairs. And then a roar of lions.

"Wendy and Peter aren't in their rooms," said his wife.

He lay in his bed with his beating heart. "No," he said. "They've broken into the nursery."

"Those screams—they sound familiar."

"Do they?"

"Yes, awfully."

And although their beds tried very hard, the two adults couldn't be rocked to sleep for another hour. A smell of cats was in the night air.

"Father?" said Peter.

"Yes."

Peter looked at his shoes. He never looked at his father any more, nor at his mother. "You aren't going to lock up the nursery for good, are you?"

"That all depends."

"On what?" snapped Peter.

"On you and your sister. If you intersperse this Africa with a little variety—oh, Sweden perhaps, or Denmark or China—"

"I thought we were free to play as we wished."

"You are, within reasonable bounds."

"What's wrong with Africa, Father?"

"Oh, so now you admit you have been conjuring up Africa, do you?"

"I wouldn't want the nursery locked up," said Peter coldly. "Ever."

"Matter of fact, we're thinking of turning the whole house off for about a month. Live sort of a carefree one-for-all existence."

"That sounds dreadful! Would I have to tie my own shoes instead of letting the shoe tier do it? And brush my own teeth and comb my hair and give myself a bath?"

"It would be fun for a change, don't you think?"

"No, it would be horrid. I didn't like it when you took out the picture painter last month."

"That's because I wanted you to learn to paint all by yourself, son."

"I don't want to do anything but look and listen and smell; what else is there to do?"

"All right, go play in Africa."

"Will you shut off the house sometime soon?"

"We're considering it."

"I don't think you'd better consider it any more, Father."

"I won't have any threats from my son!"

"Very well." And Peter strolled off to the nursery.

"Am I on time?" said David McClean.

"Breakfast?" asked George Hadley.

"Thanks, had some. What's the trouble?"

"David, you're a psychologist."

"I should hope so."

"Well, then, have a look at our nursery. You saw it a year ago when you dropped by; did you notice anything peculiar about it then?"

"Can't say I did; the usual violences, a tendency toward a slight paranoia here or there, usual in children because they feel persecuted by parents constantly, but, oh, really nothing."

They walked down the hall. "I locked the nursery up," explained the father, "and the children broke back into it during the night. I let them stay so they could form the patterns for you to see."

There was a terrible screaming from the nursery.

"There it is," said George Hadley. "See what you make of it."

They walked in on the children without rapping.

The screams had faded. The lions were feeding.

"Run outside a moment, children," said George Hadley. "No, don't change the mental combination. Leave the walls as they are. Get!"

With the children gone, the two men stood studying the lions clustered at a distance, eating with great relish whatever it was they had caught.

"I wish I knew what it was," said George Hadley. "Sometimes I can almost see. Do you think if I brought high-powered binoculars here and—"

David McClean laughed dryly. "Hardly." He turned to study all four walls. "How long has this been going on?"

"A little over a month."

"It certainly doesn't *feel* good."

"I want facts, not feelings."

"My dear George, a psychologist never saw a fact in his life. He only hears about feelings; vague things. This doesn't feel good, I tell you. Trust my hunches and my instincts. I have a nose for something bad. This is very bad. My advice to you is to have the whole damn room torn down and your children brought to me every day during the next year for treatment."

"Is it that bad?"

"I'm afraid so. One of the original uses of these nurseries was so that we could study the patterns left on the walls by the child's mind, study at our leisure, and help the child. In this case, however, the room has become a channel toward—destructive thoughts, instead of a release away from them."

"Didn't you sense this before?"

"I sensed only that you had spoiled your children more than most. And now you're letting them down in some way. What way?"

"I wouldn't let them go to New York."

"What else?"

"I've taken a few machines from the house and threatened them, a month ago, with closing up the nursery unless they did their homework. I did close it for a few days to show I meant business."

"Ah, ha!"

"Does that mean anything?"

"Everything. Where before they had a Santa Claus now they have a Scrooge. Children prefer Santas. You've let this room and this house replace you and your wife in your children's affections. This room is their mother and father, far more important in their lives than their real parents. And now you come along and want to shut it off. No wonder there's hatred here. You can feel it coming out of the sky. Feel that sun. George, you'll have to change your life. Like too many others, you've built it around creature comforts. Why, you'd starve tomorrow if something went wrong in your kitchen. You wouldn't know how to tap an egg. Nevertheless, turn everything off. Start new. It'll take time. But we'll make good children out of bad in a year, wait and see."

"But won't the shock be too much for the children, shutting the room up abruptly, for good?"

"I don't want them going any deeper into this, that's all."

The lions were finished with their red feast.

The lions were standing on the edge of the clearing watching the two men.

"Now *I'm* feeling persecuted," said McClean. "Let's get out of here. I never have cared for these damned rooms. Make me nervous."

"The lions look real, don't they?" said George Hadley. "I don't suppose there's any way . . ."

"What?"

". . . that they could *become* real?"

"Not that I know."

"Some flaw in the machinery, a tampering or something?"

"No."

They went to the door.

"I don't imagine the room will like being turned off," said the father.

"Nothing ever likes to die—even a room."

"I wonder if it hates me for wanting to switch it off?"

"Paranoia is thick around here today," said David McClean. "You can follow it like a spoor. Hello." He bent and picked up a bloody scarf. "This yours?"

"No." George Hadley's face was rigid. "It belongs to Lydia."

They went to the fuse box together and threw the switch that killed the nursery.

The two children were in hysterics. They screamed and pranced and threw things. They yelled and sobbed and swore and jumped at the furniture.

"You can't do that to the nursery, you can't!"

"Now, children."

The children flung themselves onto a couch, weeping.

"George," said Lydia Hadley, "turn on the nursery, just for a few moments. You can't be so abrupt."

"No."

"You can't be so cruel."

"Lydia, it's off, and it stays off. And the whole damn house dies as of here and now. The more I see of the mess we've put ourselves in, the more it sickens me. We've been contemplating our mechanical, electronic navels for too long. My God, how we need a breath of honest air!"

And he marched about the house turning off the voice clocks, the stoves, the heaters, the shoe shiners, the shoe lacers, the body scrubbers and swabbers and massagers, and every other machine he could put his hand to.

The house was full of dead bodies, it seemed. It felt like a mechanical cemetery. So silent. None of the humming hidden energy of machines waiting to function at the tap of a button.

"Don't let them do it!" wailed Peter at the ceiling, as if he was talking to the house, the nursery. "Don't let Father kill everything." He turned to his father. "Oh, I hate you!"

"Insults won't get you anywhere."

"I wish you were dead!"

"We were, for a long while. Now we're going to really start living. Instead of being handled and massaged, we're going to *live*."

Wendy was still crying, and Peter joined her again. "Just a moment, just one moment, just another moment of nursery," they wailed.

"Oh, George," said the wife, "it can't hurt."

"All right—all right, if they'll only just shut up. One minute, mind you, and then off forever."

"Daddy, Daddy, Daddy!" sang the children, smiling with wet faces.

"And then we're going on a vacation. David McClean is coming back in half an hour to help us move out and get to the airport. I'm going to dress. You turn the nursery on for a minute, Lydia, just a minute, mind you."

And the three of them went babbling off while he let himself be vacuumed upstairs through the air flue and set about dressing himself. A minute later Lydia appeared.

"I'll be glad when we get away," she sighed.

"Did you leave them in the nursery?"

"I wanted to dress, too. Oh, that horrid Africa. What can they see in it?"

"Well, in five minutes we'll be on our way to Iowa. Lord, how did we ever get in this house? What prompted us to buy a nightmare?"

"Pride, money, foolishness."

"I think we'd better get downstairs before those kids get engrossed with those damned beasts again."

Just then they heard the children calling, "Daddy, Mommy, come quick—quick!"

They went downstairs in the air flue and ran down the hall. The children were nowhere in sight. "Wendy? Peter!"

They ran into the nursery. The veldtland was empty save for the lions waiting, looking at them. "Peter, Wendy?"

The door slammed.

"Wendy, Peter!"

George Hadley and his wife whirled and ran back to the door.

"Open the door!" cried George Hadley, trying the knob. "Why, they've locked it from the outside! Peter!" He beat at the door. "Open up!"

He heard Peter's voice outside, against the door.

"Don't let them switch off the nursery and the house," he was saying.

Mr. and Mrs. George Hadley beat at the door. "Now, don't be ridiculous, children. It's time to go. Mr. McClean'll be here in a minute and . . ."

And then they heard the sounds.

The lions on three sides of them, in the yellow veldt grass, padding through the dry straw, rumbling and roaring in their throats.

The lions.

Mr. Hadley looked at his wife and they turned and looked back at the beasts edging slowly forward, crouching, tails stiff.

Mr. and Mrs. Hadley screamed.

And suddenly they realized why those other screams had sounded familiar.

"Well, here I am," said David McClean in the nursery doorway. "Oh, hello." He stared at the two children seated in the center of the open glade eating a little picnic lunch. Beyond them was the water hole and the yellow veldtland; above was the hot sun. He began to perspire. "Where are your father and mother?"

The children looked up and smiled. "Oh, they'll be here directly."

"Good, we must get going." At a distance Mr. McClean saw the lions fighting and clawing and then quieting down to feed in silence under the shady trees.

He squinted at the lions with his hand up to his eyes.

Now the lions were done feeding. They moved to the water hole to drink.

A shadow flickered over Mr. McClean's hot face. Many shadows flickered. The vultures were dropping down the blazing sky.

"A cup of tea?" asked Wendy in the silence.

The Golem

AVRAM DAVIDSON

*Eventually, every Jewish writer takes a crack at telling
his own version of this Yiddish myth. Mr. Davidson, I
think, is the first to transport it to Southern California.
   He also appears to be the first to realize that the
golem is not only horrible but funny too.*

The gray-faced person came along the street where old Mr.
and Mrs. Gumbeiner lived. It was afternoon, it was autumn,
the sun was warm and soothing to their ancient bones. Anyone
who attended the movies in the twenties or the early thirties
has seen that street a thousand times. Past these bungalows
with their half-double roofs Edmund Lowe walked arm in arm
with Leatrice Joy, and Harold Lloyd was chased by Chinamen
waving hatchets. Under these squamous palm trees Laurel
kicked Hardy and Woolsey beat Wheeler upon the head with
codfish. Across these pocket-handkerchief-sized lawns the ju-
veniles of the Our Gang Comedies pursued one another and
were pursued by angry fat men in golf knickers. On this same
street—or perhaps on some other one of five hundred streets
exactly like it.

Mrs. Gumbeiner indicated the gray-faced person to her
husband.

"You think maybe he's got something the matter?" she
asked. "He walks kind of funny, to me."

"Walks like a golem," Mr. Gumbeiner said indifferently.

The old woman was nettled.

"Oh, I don't know," she said. "*I* think he walks like your
cousin Mendel."

The old man pursed his mouth angrily and chewed on his
pipestem. The gray-faced person turned up the concrete path,
walked up the steps to the porch, sat down in a chair. Old Mr.
Gumbeiner ignored him. His wife stared at the stranger.

52

"Man comes in without a hello, goodbye or howareyou, sits himself down and right away he's at home. The chair is comfortable?" she asked. "Would you like maybe a glass tea?" She turned to her husband. "Say something, Gumbeiner!" she demanded. "What are you, made of wood?"

The old man smiled a slow, wicked, triumphant smile. "Why should *I* say anything?" he asked the air. "Who am I? Nothing, that's who."

The stranger spoke. His voice was harsh and monotonous. "When you learn who—or, rather, what—I am, the flesh will melt from your bones in terror." He bared porcelain teeth.

"Never mind about my bones!" the old woman cried. "You've got a lot of nerve talking about my bones!"

"You will quake with fear," said the stranger.

Old Mrs. Gumbeiner said that she hoped he would live so long. She turned to her husband once again. "Gumbeiner, when are you going to mow the lawn?"

"All mankind—" the stranger began.

"*Shah!* I'm talking to my husband. He talks *eppis* kind of funny, Gumbeiner, no?"

"Probably a foreigner," Mr. Gumbeiner said complacently.

"You think so?" Mrs. Gumbeiner glanced fleetingly at the stranger. "He's got a very bad color in his face, *nebbich*. I suppose he came to California for his health."

"Disease, pain, sorrow, love, grief—all are nought to—"

Mr. Gumbeiner cut in on the stranger's statement. "Gall bladder," the old man said. "Guinzburg down at the shul looked exactly the same before his operation. Two professors they had in for him, and a private nurse day and night."

"I am not a human being!" the stranger said loudly.

"Three thousand seven hundred fifty dollars it cost his son, Guinzburg told me. 'For you, Poppa, nothing is too expensive —only get well,' the son told him."

"*I am not a human being!*"

"Ai, is that a son for you!" the old woman said, rocking her head. "A heart of gold, pure gold." She looked at the stranger. "All right, all right, I heard you the first time. Gumbeiner! I asked you a question. When are you going to cut the lawn?"

"On Wednesday, *odder* maybe Thursday, comes the Japaneser to the neighborhood. To cut lawns is *his* profession. *My* profession is to be a glazier—retired."

"Between me and all mankind is an inevitable hatred," the stranger said. "When I tell you what I am, the flesh will melt —"

"You said, you said already," Mr. Gumbeiner interrupted.

"In Chicago where the winters were as cold and bitter as the Czar of Russia's heart," the old woman intoned, "you had strength to carry the frames with the glass together day in and day out. But in California with the golden sun, to mow the lawn when your wife asks, for this you have no strength. Do I call in the Japaneser to cook for you supper?"

"Thirty years Professor Allardyce spent perfecting his theories. Electronics, neuronics—"

"Listen how educated he talks," Mr. Gumbeiner said admiringly. "Maybe he goes to the university here?"

"If he goes to the university, maybe he knows Bud?" his wife suggested.

"Probably they're in the same class and he came to see him about the homework, no?"

"Certainly he must be in the same class. How many classes are there? Five *in ganzen:* Bud showed me on his program card." She counted off on her fingers. "Television Appreciation and Criticism, Small-Boat Building, Social Adjustment, The American Dance . . . The American Dance—*nu,* Gumbeiner —"

"Contemporary Ceramics," her husband said, relishing the syllables. "A fine boy, Bud. A pleasure to have him for a boardner."

"After thirty years spent in these studies," the stranger, who had continued to speak unnoticed, went on, "he turned from the theoretical to the pragmatic. In ten years' time he had made the most titanic discovery in history: he made mankind, *all* mankind, superfluous: he made *me.*"

"What did Tillie write in her last letter?" asked the old man.

The old woman shrugged. "What should she write? The same thing. Sidney was home from the Army, Naomi has a new boy friend—"

"He made ME!"

"Listen, Mr. Whatever-your-name-is," the old woman said, "maybe where you came from is different, but in *this* country you don't interrupt people the while they're talking—Hey. Listen, what do you mean, he *made* you? What kind of talk is that?"

The stranger bared all his teeth again, exposing the too-pink gums.

"In his library, to which I had a more complete access after his sudden and as yet undiscovered death from entirely natural causes, I found a complete collection of stories about androids, from Shelley's *Frankenstein* through Capek's *R.U.R.* to Asimov's—"

"Frankenstein?" said the old man, with interest. "There used to be Frankenstein who had the soda-*wasser* place on Halstead Street: a Litvack, *nebbich*."

"What are you talking?" Mrs. Gumbeiner demanded. "His name was Franken*thal*, and it wasn't on Halstead, it was on Roosevelt."

"—clearly shown that all mankind has an instinctive antipathy toward androids and there will be an inevitable struggle between them—"

"Of course, of course!" Old Mr. Gumbeiner clicked his teeth against his pipe. "I am always wrong, you are always right. How could you stand to be married to such a stupid person all this time?"

"I don't know," the old woman said. "Sometimes I wonder myself. I think it must be his good looks." She began to laugh. Old Mr. Gumbeiner blinked, then began to smile, then took his wife's hand.

"Foolish old woman," the stranger said, "why do you laugh? Do you not know I have come to destroy you?"

"What!" old Mr. Gumbeiner shouted. "Close your mouth, you!" He darted from his chair and struck the stranger with the flat of his hand. The stranger's head struck against the porch pillar and bounced back.

"When you talk to my wife, talk respectable, you hear?"

Old Mrs. Gumbeiner, cheeks very pink, pushed her husband back in his chair. Then she leaned forward and examined the stranger's head. She clicked her tongue as she pulled aside the flap of gray skinlike material.

"Gumbeiner, look! He's all springs and wires inside!"

"I *told* you he was a golem, but no, you wouldn't listen," the old man said.

"You said he *walked* like a golem."

"How could he walk like a golem unless he *was* one?"

"All right, all right. You broke him, so now fix him."

"My grandfather, his light shines from Paradise, told me

55

that when MoHaRaL—Moreynu Ha-Rav Löw—his memory for a blessing, made the golem in Prague, three hundred? four hundred years ago? he wrote on his forehead the Holy Name."

Smiling reminiscently, the old woman continued, "And the golem cut the rabbi's wood and brought his water and guarded the ghetto."

"And one time only he disobeyed the Rabbi Löw, and Rabbi Löw erased the *Shem Ha-Mephorash* from the golem's forehead and the golem fell down like a dead one. And they put him up in the attic of the shul and he's still there today if the Communisten haven't sent him to Moscow. This is not just a story," he said.

"*Avadda* not!" said the old woman.

"I myself have seen both the shul *and* the rabbi's grave," her husband said conclusively.

"But I think this must be a different kind golem, Gumbeiner. See, on his forehead: nothing written."

"What's the matter, there's a law I can't write something there? Where is that lump clay Bud brought us from his class?"

The old man washed his hands, adjusted his little black skull-cap, and slowly and carefully wrote four Hebrew letters on the gray forehead.

"Ezra the Scribe himself couldn't do better," the old woman said admiringly. "Nothing happens," she observed, looking at the lifeless figure sprawled in the chair.

"Well, after all, am I Rabbi Löw?" her husband asked deprecatingly. "No," he answered. He leaned over and examined the exposed mechanism. "This spring goes here . . . this wire comes with this one . . ." The figure moved. "But this one goes where? And this one?"

"Let be," said his wife. The figure sat up slowly and rolled its eyes loosely.

"Listen, Reb Golem," the old man said, wagging his finger. "Pay attention to what I say—you understand?"

"Understand . . ."

"If you want to stay here, you got to do like Mr. Gumbeiner says."

"Do-like-Mr.-Gumbeiner-says . . ."

"*That's* the way I like to hear a golem talk. Malka, give here the mirror from the pocketbook. Look, you see your face? You see on the forehead, what's written? If you don't do like Mr.

Gumbeiner says, he'll wipe out what's written and you'll be no more alive."

"No-more-alive . . ."

"*That's* right. Now, listen. Under the porch you'll find a lawnmower. Take it. And cut the lawn. Then come back. Go."

"Go . . ." The figure shambled down the steps. Presently the sound of the lawnmower whirred through the quiet air in the street just like the street where Jackie Cooper shed huge tears on Wallace Beery's shirt and Chester Conklin rolled his eyes at Marie Dressler.

"So what will you write to Tillie?" old Mr. Gumbeiner asked.

"What should I write?" Old Mrs. Gumbeiner shrugged. "I'll write that the weather is lovely out here and that we are both, blessed be the Name, in good health."

The old man nodded his head slowly, and they sat together on the front porch in the warm afternoon sun.

Helen O'Loy

LESTER DEL REY

There are a few stories which come up regularly in misty-eyed discussions of the real classics of sf. Lester del Rey has written two: Nerves (too long for inclusion here in its magazine version, and much more satisfactory as a novel anyhow), and this one.

I am an old man now, but I can still see Helen as Dave unpacked her, and still hear him gasp as he looked her over.

"Man, isn't she a beauty?"

She was beautiful, a dream in spun plastics and metals, something Keats might have seen dimly when he wrote his sonnet. If Helen of Troy had looked like that the Greeks must have been pikers when they launched only a thousand ships; at least, that's what I told Dave.

"Helen of Troy, eh?" He looked at her tag. "At least it beats this thing—K2W88. Helen . . . Mmmm . . . Helen of Alloy."

"Not much swing to that, Dave. Too many unstressed syllables in the middle. How about Helen O'Loy?"

"Helen O'Loy she is, Phil." And that's how it began—one part beauty, one part dream, one part science; add a stereo broadcast, stir mechanically, and the result is chaos.

Dave and I hadn't gone to college together, but when I came to Messina to practice medicine I found him downstairs in a little robot repair shop. After that we began to pal around, and when I started going with one twin he found the other equally attractive, so we made it a foursome.

When our business grew better, we rented a house near the rocket field—noisy but cheap, and the rockets discouraged apartment building. We liked room enough to stretch ourselves. I suppose if we hadn't quarreled with them we'd have married the twins in time. But Dave wanted to look over the

58

latest Venus-rocket attempt when his twin wanted to see a display stereo starring Larry Ainslee, and they were both stubborn. From then on we forgot the girls and spent our evenings at home.

But it wasn't until "Lena" put vanilla on our steak instead of salt that we got off on the subject of emotions and robots. While Dave was dissecting Lena to find the trouble, we naturally mulled over the future of the mechs. He was sure that the robots would beat men someday, and I couldn't see it.

"Look here, Dave," I argued. "You know Lena doesn't think—not really. When those wires crossed, she could have corrected herself. But she didn't bother; she followed the mechanical impulse. A man might have reached for the vanilla, but when he saw it in his hand, he'd have stopped. Lena has sense enough, but she has no emotions, no consciousness of self."

"All right, that's the big trouble with the mechs now. But we'll get around it, put in some mechanical emotions or something." He screwed Lena's head back on, turned on her juice. "Go back to work, Lena, it's nineteen o'clock."

Now, I specialized in endocrinology and related subjects. I wasn't exactly a psychologist, but I did understand the glands, secretions, hormones, and miscellanies that are the physical causes of emotions. It took medical science three hundred years to find out how and why they worked, and I couldn't see men duplicating them mechanically in much less time.

I brought home books and papers to prove it, and Dave quoted the invention of memory coils and veritoid eyes. During that year we swapped knowledge until Dave knew the whole theory of endocrinology and I could have made Lena from memory. The more we talked, the less sure I grew about the impossibility of *homo mechanensis* as the perfect type.

Poor Lena. Her cuproberyl body spent half its time in scattered pieces. Our first attempts were successful only in getting her to serve fried brushes for breakfast and wash the dishes in oleo oil. Then one day she cooked a perfect dinner with six wires crossed, and Dave was in ecstasy.

He worked all night on her wiring, put in a new coil, and taught her a fresh set of words. And the next day she flew into a tantrum and swore vigorously at us when we told her she wasn't doing her work right.

"It's a lie," she yelled, shaking a suction brush. "You're all liars. If you so-and-so's would leave me whole long enough, I might get something done around the place."

When we had calmed her temper and got her back to work, Dave ushered me into the study. "Not taking any chances with Lena," he explained. "We'll have to cut out that adrenal pack and restore her to normalcy. But we've got to get a better robot. A housemaid mech isn't complex enough."

"How about Dillard's new utility models? They seem to combine everything in one."

"Exactly. Even so, we'll need a special one built to order, with a full range of memory coils. And out of respect to old Lena, let's get a female case for its works."

The result, of course, was Helen. The Dillard people had performed a miracle and put all the works in a girl-modeled case. Even the plastic-and-rubberite face was designed for flexibility to express emotions, and she was complete with tear glands and taste buds, ready to simulate every human action, from breathing to pulling hair. The bill they sent with her was another miracle, but Dave and I scraped it together; we had to turn Lena over to an exchange to complete it, though, and thereafter we ate out.

I'd performed plenty of delicate operations on living tissues, and some of them had been tricky, but I still felt like a pre-med student as we opened the front plate of her torso and began to sever the leads of her "nerves." Dave's mechanical glands were all prepared, complex little bundles of radio tubes and wires that heterodyned on the electrical thought impulses and distorted them as adrenalin distorts the reaction of human minds.

Instead of sleeping that night, we pored over the schematic diagrams of her structures, tracing the thought mazes of her wiring, severing the leaders, implanting the heterones, as Dave called them. And while we worked, a mechanical tape fed carefully prepared thoughts of consciousness and awareness of life and feeling into an auxiliary memory coil. Dave believed in leaving nothing to chance.

It was growing light as we finished, exhausted and exultant. All that remained was the starting of her electrical power; like all the Dillard mechs, she was equipped with a tiny atomotor instead of batteries, and once started she would need no further attention.

Dave refused to turn her on. "Wait until we've slept and rested," he advised. "I'm as eager to try her as you are, but we can't do much studying with our minds half dead. Turn in, and we'll leave Helen until later."

Even though we were both reluctant to follow it, we knew the idea was sound. We turned in, and sleep hit us before the air conditioner could cut down to sleeping temperature. And then Dave was pounding on my shoulder.

"Phil! Hey, snap out of it!"

I groaned, turned over, and faced him. "Well? . . . Uh! What is it? Did Helen—"

"No, it's old Mrs. Van Styler. She 'visored to say her son has an infatuation for a servant girl, and she wants you to come out and give counterhormones. They're at the summer camp in Maine."

Rich Mrs. Van Styler! I couldn't afford to let that account down, now that Helen had used up the last of my funds. But it wasn't a job I cared for.

"Counterhormones! That'll take two weeks' full time. Anyway, I'm no society doctor, messing with glands to keep fools happy. My job's taking care of serious trouble."

"And you want to watch Helen." Dave was grinning, but he was serious too. "I told her it'd cost her fifty thousand!"

"*Huh?*"

"And she said okay, if you hurried."

Of course, there was only one thing to do, though I could have wrung fat Mrs. Van Styler's neck cheerfully. It wouldn't have happened if she'd used robots like everyone else—but she had to be different.

Consequently, while Dave was back home puttering with Helen, I was racking my brain to trick Archy Van Styler into getting the counterhormones, and giving the servant girl the same. Oh, I wasn't supposed to, but the poor kid was crazy about Archy. Dave might have written, I thought, but never a word did I get.

It was three weeks later instead of two when I reported that Archy was "cured," and collected on the line. With that money in my pocket, I hired a personal rocket and was back in Messina in half an hour. I didn't waste time in reaching the house.

As I stepped into the alcove, I heard a light patter of feet, and an eager voice called out, "Dave, dear?" For a minute I couldn't answer, and the voice came again, pleading, "Dave?"

I don't know what I expected, but I didn't expect Helen to meet me that way, stopping and staring at me, obvious disappointment on her face, little hands fluttering up against her breast.

"Oh," she cried. "I thought it was Dave. He hardly comes home to eat now, but I've had supper waiting hours." She dropped her hands and managed a smile. "You're Phil, aren't you? Dave told me about you when . . . at first. I'm so glad to see you home, Phil."

"Glad to see you doing so well, Helen." Now, what does one say for light conversation with a robot? "You said something about supper?"

"Oh, yes. I guess Dave ate downtown again, so we might as well go in. It'll be nice having someone to talk to around the house, Phil. You don't mind if I call you Phil, do you? You know, you're sort of a godfather to me."

We ate. I hadn't counted on such behavior, but apparently she considered eating as normal as walking. She didn't do much eating, at that; most of the time she spent staring at the front door.

Dave came in as we were finishing, a frown a yard wide on his face. Helen started to rise, but he ducked toward the stairs, throwing words over his shoulder.

"Hi, Phil. See you up here later."

There was something radically wrong with him. For a moment I'd thought his eyes were haunted, and as I turned to Helen hers were filling with tears. She gulped, choked them back, and fell to viciously on her food.

"What's the matter with him . . . and you?" I asked.

"He's sick of me." She pushed her plate away and got up hastily. "You'd better see him while I clean up. And there's nothing wrong with me. And it's not my fault, anyway." She grabbed the dishes and ducked into the kitchen; I could have sworn she was crying.

Maybe all thought is a series of conditioned reflexes—but she certainly had picked up a lot of conditioning while I was gone. Lena in her heyday had been nothing like this. I went up to see if Dave could make any sense out of the hodgepodge.

He was squirting soda into a large glass of apple brandy, and I saw that the bottle was nearly empty. "Join me?" he asked.

It seemed like a good idea. The roaring blast of an ion rocket overhead was the only familiar thing left in the house. From the look around Dave's eyes, it wasn't the first bottle he'd emptied while I was gone, and there were more left. He dug out a new bottle for his own drink.

"Of course, it's none of my business, Dave, but that stuff won't steady your nerves any. What's gotten into you and Helen? Been seeing ghosts?"

Helen was wrong; he hadn't been eating downtown—nor anywhere else. His muscles collapsed into a chain in a way that spoke of fatigue and nerves, but mostly of hunger. "You noticed it, eh?"

"Noticed it? The two of you jammed it down my throat."

"Uhmmm." He swatted at a nonexistent fly and slumped farther down in the pneumatic. "Guess maybe I should have waited with Helen until you got back. But if that stereo cast hadn't changed . . . Anyway, it did. And those mushy books of yours finished the job."

"Thanks. That makes it all clear."

"You know, Phil, I've got a place up in the country—fruit ranch. My dad left it to me. Think I'll look it over."

And that's the way it went. But finally, by much liquor and more perspiration, I got some of the story out of him before I gave him an amytal and put him to bed. Then I hunted up Helen and dug the rest of the story from her, until it made sense.

Apparently as soon as I was gone Dave had turned her on and made preliminary tests, which were entirely satisfactory. She had reacted beautifully—so well that he decided to leave her and go down to work as usual.

Naturally, with all her untried emotions, she was filled with with curiosity and wanted him to stay. Then he had an inspiration. After showing her what her duties about the house would be, he set her down in front of the stereovisor, tuned in a travelogue, and left her to occupy her time with that.

The travelogue held her attention until it was finished, and the station switched over to a current serial with Larry Ainslee, the same cute emoter who'd given us all the trouble with the twins. Incidentally, he looked something like Dave.

Helen took to the serial like a seal to water. This play-acting was a perfect outlet for her newly excited emotions. When that particular episode finished, she found a love story on another station and added still more to her education. The afternoon programs were mostly news and music, but by then she'd found my books; and I do have rather adolescent taste in literature.

Dave came home in the best of spirits. The front alcove was neatly swept, and there was the odor of food in the air that he'd missed around the house for weeks. He had visions of Helen as the superefficient housekeeper.

So it was a shock to him to feel two strong arms around his neck from behind and hear a voice all aquiver coo into his ears, "Oh, Dave, darling, I've missed you so, and I'm so *thrilled* that you're back." Helen's technique may have lacked polish, but it had enthusiasm, as he found when he tried to stop her from kissing him. She had learned fast and furiously— also, Helen was powered by an atomotor.

Dave wasn't a prude, but he remembered that she was only a robot, after all. The fact that she felt, acted, and looked like a young goddess in his arms didn't mean much. With some effort, he untangled her and dragged her off to supper, where he made her eat with him to divert her attention.

After her evening work, he called her into the study and gave her a thorough lecture on the folly of her ways. It must have been good, for it lasted three solid hours and covered her station in life, the idiocy of stereos, and various other miscellanies. When he had finished, Helen looked up with dewy eyes and said wistfully, "I know, Dave, but I still love you."

That's when Dave started drinking.

It grew worse each day. If he stayed downtown, she was crying when he came home. If he returned on time, she fussed over him and threw herself at him. In his room, with door locked, he could hear her downstairs pacing up and down and muttering; and when he went down, she stared at him reproachfully until he had to go back up.

I sent Helen out on a fake errand in the morning and got Dave up. With her gone, I made him eat a decent breakfast and gave him a tonic for his nerves. He was still listless and moody.

"Look here, Dave," I broke in on his brooding. "Helen isn't human, after all. Why not cut off her power and change a few memory coils? Then we can convince her that she never was in love and couldn't get that way."

"You try it. I had that idea, but she put up a wail that would wake Homer. She says it would be murder—and the hell of it is that I can't help feeling the same about it. Maybe she isn't human, but you wouldn't guess it when she puts on that martyred look and tells you to go ahead and kill her."

"We never put in substitutes for some of the secretions present in man during the love period."

"I don't know what we put in. Maybe the heterones backfired or something. Anyway, she's made this idea so much a part of her thoughts that we'd have to put in a whole new set of coils."

"Well, why not?"

"Go ahead. You're the surgeon of this family. I'm not used to fussing with emotions. Matter of fact, since she's been acting this way I'm beginning to hate work on any robot. My business is going to blazes."

He saw Helen coming up the walk and ducked out the back door for the monorail express. I'd intended to put him back in bed, but let him go. Maybe he'd be better off at his shop than at home.

"Dave's gone?" Helen did have that martyred look now.

"Yeah. I got him to eat, and he's gone to work."

"I'm glad he ate." She slumped down in a chair as if she were worn out, though how a mech could be tired beat me. "Phil?"

"Well, what is it?"

"Do you think I'm bad for him? I mean, do you think he'd be happier if I weren't here?"

"He'll go crazy if you keep acting this way around him."

She winced. Those little hands were twisting about pleadingly, and I felt like an inhuman brute. But I'd started, and I went ahead. "Even if I cut out your power and changed your coils, he'd probably still be haunted by you."

"I know. But I can't help it. And I'd make him a good wife, really I would, Phil."

I gulped; this was going a little too far. "And give him strapping sons to boot, I suppose. A man wants flesh and blood, not rubber and metal."

"Don't, please! I can't think of myself that way; to me, I'm a woman. And you know how perfectly I'm made to imitate a real woman—in all ways. I couldn't give him sons, but in every other way I'd try so hard, I know I'd make him a good wife."

I gave up.

Dave didn't come home that night, nor the next day. Helen was fussing and fuming, wanting me to call the hospitals and the police, but I knew nothing had happened to him. He always carried identification. Still, when he didn't come on the third day, I began to worry. And when Helen started out for his shop, I agreed to go with her.

Dave was there, with another man I didn't know. I parked Helen where he couldn't see her, but where she could hear, and went in as soon as the other fellow left.

Dave looked a little better and seemed glad to see me. "Hi, Phil—just closing up. Let's go eat."

Helen couldn't hold back any longer, but came trooping in. "Come on home, Dave. I've got roast duck with spice stuffing, and you know you love that."

"Scat!" and Dave. She shrank back, turned to go. "Oh, all right, stay. You might as well hear it, too. I've sold the shop. The fellow you saw just bought it, and I'm going up to the old fruit ranch I told you about, Phil. I can't stand the mechs any more."

"You'll starve to death at that," I told him.

"No, there's a growing demand for old-fashioned fruit, raised out of doors. People are tired of this water-culture stuff. Dad always made a living out of it. I'm leaving as soon as I can get home and pack."

Helen clung to her idea. "I'll pack, Dave, while you eat. I've got apple cobbler for dessert." The world was toppling under her feet, but she still remembered how crazy he was for apple cobbler.

Helen was a good cook; in fact she was a genius, with all the good points of a woman and a mech combined. Dave ate well enough, after he got started. By the time supper was over, he'd thawed out enough to admit he liked the duck and the cobbler, and to thank her for packing. In fact, he even let her kiss him goodbye, though he firmly refused to let her go to the rocket field with him.

Helen was trying to be brave when I got back, and we carried on a stumbling conversation about Mrs. Van Styler's servants for a while. But the talk began to lull, and she sat staring out of the window at nothing most of the time. Even the stereo comedy lacked interest for her, and I was glad enough to have her go off to her room. She could cut her power down to simulate sleep when she chose.

As the days slipped by, I began to realize why she couldn't believe herself a robot. I got to thinking of her as a girl and companion myself. Except for odd intervals when she went off by herself to brood, or when she kept going to the telescript for a letter that never came, she was as good a companion as a man could ask. There was something homey about the place that Lena had never put there.

I took Helen on a shopping trip to Hudson, and she giggled and purred over the wisps of silk and glassheen that were the fashion, tried on endless hats, and conducted herself as any normal girl might. We went trout fishing for a day, where she proved to be as good a sport and as sensibly silent as a man. I thoroughly enjoyed myself and thought she was forgetting Dave. That was before I came home unexpectedly and found her doubled up on the couch, threshing her legs up and down and crying to the high heavens.

It was then I called Dave. They seemed to have trouble in reaching him, and Helen came over beside me while I waited. She was tense and fidgety as an old maid trying to propose. But finally they located Dave.

"What's up, Phil?" he asked as his face came on the viewplate. "I was just getting my things together to—"

I broke him off. "Things can't go on the way they are, Dave. I've made up my mind. I'm yanking Helen's coils tonight. It won't be worse than what she's going through now."

Helen reached up and touched my shoulder. "Maybe that's best, Phil. I don't blame you."

Dave's voice cut in. "Phil, you don't know what you're doing!"

"Of course I do. It'll all be over by the time you can get here. As you heard, she's agreeing."

There was a black cloud sweeping over Dave's face. "I won't have it, Phil. She's half mine and I forbid it!"

"Of all the—"

"Go ahead, call me anything you want. I've changed my mind. I was packing to come home when you called."

Helen jerked around me, her eyes glued to the panel. "Dave, do you . . . are you . . ."

"I'm just waking up to what a fool I've been, Helen. Phil, I'll be home in a couple of hours, so if there's anything . . ."

He didn't have to chase me out. But I heard Helen cooing something about loving to be a rancher's wife before I could shut the door.

Well, I wasn't as surprised as they thought. I think I knew when I called Dave what would happen. No man acts the way

Dave had been acting because he hates a girl; only because he thinks he does—and thinks wrong.

No woman ever made a lovelier bride or a sweeter wife. Helen never lost her flare for cooking and making a home. With her gone, the old house seemed empty, and I began to drop out to the ranch once or twice a week. I suppose they had trouble at times, but I never saw it, and I know the neighbors never suspected they were anything but normal man and wife.

Dave grew older, and Helen didn't, of course. But between us we put lines in her face and grayed her hair without letting Dave know that she wasn't growing old with him; he'd forgotten that she wasn't human, I guess.

I practically forgot, myself. It wasn't until a letter came from Helen this morning that I woke up to reality. There, in her beautiful script, just a trifle shaky in places, was the inevitable that neither Dave nor I had seen.

Dear Phil,

As you know, Dave has had heart trouble for several years now. We expected him to live on just the same, but it seems that wasn't to be. He died in my arms just before sunrise. He sent you his greetings and farewell.

I've one last favor to ask of you, Phil. There is only one thing for me to do when this is finished. Acid will burn out metal as well as flesh, and I'll be dead with Dave. Please see that we are buried together, and that the morticians do not find my secret. Dave wanted it that way, too.

Poor, dear Phil, I know you loved Dave as a brother, and how you felt about me. Please don't grieve too much for us, for we have had a happy life together, and both feel that we should cross this last bridge side by side.

With love and thanks from

Helen

It had to come sooner or later, I suppose, and the first shock has worn off now. I'll be leaving in a few minutes to carry out Helen's last instructions.

Dave was a lucky man, and the best friend I ever had. And Helen—well, as I said, I'm an old man now and can view things more sanely; I should have married and raised a family, I suppose. But . . . there was only one Helen O'Loy.

The Cold Equations

TOM GODWIN

*I am reliably informed that this story, by a comparative
unknown, drew more reader mail than any other story
in the history of* Astounding Science Fiction. *I am also
reliably informed that it is possible to find a way out of
the dilemma the story poses. Unfortunately, the first
two methods proposed by my informant (who is not a
science-fiction writer, but a working physicist) do not
work.*

*This is not Mr. Godwin's only story; it is, however,
his best—and, as the nominations show, one of the best
of all time. It requires an unusual writer and an unusual
human being to look at the result which a situation demands rather than at one's own hopes (or, for that
matter, the downbeat trend being what it is in sf., one's
own fears). Mr. Godwin's gaze is steady, his understanding exact. When he or anybody else is going to
turn out another story this final and this complete I
have no idea. But I buy a good many science-fiction
magazines and books each month hoping to find out.*

He was not alone.

There was nothing to indicate the fact but the white hand
of the tiny gauge on the board before him. The control room
was empty but for himself; there was no sound other than
the murmur of the drives—but the white hand had moved. It
had been on zero when the little ship was launched from the
Stardust; now, an hour later, it had crept up. There was something in the supplies closet across the room, it was saying, some
kind of a body that radiated heat.

It could be but one kind of a body—a living, human body.

He leaned back in the pilot's chair and drew a deep, slow
breath, considering what he would have to do. He was an EDS
pilot, inured to the sight of death, long since accustomed to it

and to viewing the dying of another man with an objective lack of emotion, and he had no choice in what he must do. There could be no alternative—but it required a few moments of conditioning for even an EDS pilot to prepare himself to walk across the room and coldly, deliberately, take the life of a man he had yet to meet.

He would, of course, do it. It was the law, stated very bluntly and definitely in grim Paragraph L, Section 8, of Interstellar Regulations: *"Any stowaway discovered in an EDS shall be jettisoned immediately following discovery."*

It was the law, and there could be no appeal.

It was a law not of men's choosing but made imperative by the circumstances of the space frontier. Galactic expansion had followed the development of the hyperspace drive, and as men scattered wide across the frontier there had come the problem of contact with the isolated first colonies and exploration parties. The huge hyperspace cruisers were the product of the combined genius and effort of Earth and were long and expensive in the building. They were not available in such numbers that small colonies could possess them. The cruisers carried the colonists to their new worlds and made periodic visits, running on tight schedules, but they could not stop and turn aside to visit colonies scheduled to be visited at another time; such a delay would destroy their schedule and produce a confusion and uncertainty that would wreck the complex interdependence between old Earth and the new worlds of the frontier.

Some method of delivering supplies or assistance when an emergency occurred on a world not scheduled for a visit had been needed, and the Emergency Dispatch Ships had been the answer. Small and collapsible, they occupied little room in the hold of the cruiser; made of light metal and plastics, they were driven by a small rocket drive that consumed relatively little fuel. Each cruiser carried four EDS's, and when a call for aid was received the nearest cruiser would drop into normal space long enough to launch an EDS with the needed supplies or personnel, then vanish again as it continued on its course.

The cruisers, powered by nuclear converters, did not use the liquid rocket fuel, but nuclear converters were far too large and complex to permit their installation in the EDS's. The cruisers were forced by necessity to carry a limited amount of bulky rocket fuel, and the fuel was rationed with care, the cruiser's computers determining the exact amount of fuel each EDS would require for its mission. The computers considered the course coordinates, the mass of the EDS, the mass of pilot and cargo; they were very precise and accurate and omitted nothing from their calculations. They could not, however, forsee and allow for the added mass of a stowaway.

The *Stardust* had received the request from one of the exploration parties stationed on Woden, the six men of the party already being stricken with the fever carried by the green kala midges and their own supply of serum destroyed by the tornado that had torn through their camp. The *Stardust* had gone through the usual procedure, dropping into normal space to launch the EDS with the fever serum, then vanishing again in hyperspace. Now, an hour later, the gauge was saying there was something more than the small carton of serum in the supplies closet.

He let his eyes rest on the narrow white door of the closet. There, just inside, another man lived and breathed and was beginning to feel assured that discovery of his presence would now be too late for the pilot to alter the situation. It *was* too late; for the man behind the door it was far later than he thought and in a way he would find it terrible to believe.

There could be no alternative. Additional fuel would be used during the hours of deceleration to compensate for the added mass of the stowaway; infinitesimal increments of fuel that would not be missed until the ship had almost reached its destination. Then, at some distance about the ground that might be as near as a thousand feet or as far as tens of thousands feet, depending upon the mass of ship and cargo and the preceding period of deceleration, the unmissed increments of fuel would make their absence known; the EDS would expend its last drops of fuel with a sputter and go into whistling free fall. Ship and pilot and stowaway would merge together upon impact as a wreckage of metal and plastic, flesh and blood, driven deep into the soil. The stowaway had signed his own death warrant when he concealed himself on the ship; he could not be permitted to take seven others with him.

He looked again at the telltale white hand, then rose to his feet. What he must do would be unpleasant for both of them; the sooner it was over, the better. He stepped across the control room to stand by the white door.

"Come out!" His command was harsh and abrupt above the murmur of the drive.

It seemed he could hear the whisper of a furtive movement inside the closet, then nothing. He visualized the stowaway cowering closer into one corner, suddenly worried by the possible consequences of his act, his self-assurance evaporating.

"I said *out!*"

He heard the stowaway move to obey, and he waited with his eyes alert on the door and his hand near the blaster at his side.

The door opened and the stowaway stepped through it, smiling. "All right—I give up. Now what?"

It was a girl.

He stared without speaking, his hand dropping away from the blaster and acceptance of what he saw coming like a heavy and unexpected physical blow. The stowaway was not a man—she was a girl in her teens, standing before him in little white gypsy sandals, with the top of her brown, curly head hardly higher than his shoulder, with a faint, sweet scent of perfume coming from her, and her smiling face tilted up so her eyes could look unknowing and unafraid into his as she waited for his answer.

Now what? Had it been asked in the deep, defiant voice of a man he would have answered it with action, quick and efficient. He would have taken the stowaway's identification disk and ordered him into the air lock. Had the stowaway refused to obey, he would have used the blaster. It would not have taken long; within a minute the body would have been ejected into space—had the stowaway been a man.

He returned to the pilot's chair and motioned her to seat herself on the boxlike bulk of the drive-control units that were set against the wall beside him. She obeyed, his silence making the smile fade into the meek and guilty expression of a pup that has been caught in mischief and knows it must be punished.

"You still haven't told me," she said. "I'm guilty, so what happens to me now? Do I pay a fine, or what?"

"What are you doing here?" he asked. "Why did you stow away on this EDS?"

"I wanted to see my brother. He's with the government survey crew on Woden and I haven't seen him for ten years, not since he left Earth to go into government survey work."

"What was your destination on the *Stardust?*"

"Mimir. I have a position waiting for me there. My brother has been sending money home all the time to us—my father and mother and I—and he paid for a special course in linguistics I was taking. I graduated sooner than expected and I was offered this job on Mimir. I knew it would be almost a year before Gerry's job was done on Woden so he could come on to Mimir, and that's why I hid in the closet there. There was plenty of room for me and I was willing to pay the fine. There were only the two of us kids—Gerry and I— and I haven't seen him for so long, and I didn't want to wait another year when I could see him now, even though I knew I would be breaking some kind of a regulation when I did it."

I knew I would be breaking some kind of a regulation. In a way, she could not be blamed for her ignorance of the law; she was of Earth and had not realized that the laws of the space frontier must, of necessity, be as hard and relentless as the environment that gave them birth. Yet, to protect such as her from the results of their own ignorance of the frontier, there had been a sign over the door that led to the section of the *Stardust* that housed the EDS's; a sign that was plain for all to see and heed: UNAUTHORIZED PERSONNEL KEEP OUT!

"Does your brother know that you took passage on the *Stardust* for Mimir?"

"Oh, yes. I sent him a spacegram telling him about my graduation and about going to Mimir on the *Stardust* a month before I left Earth. I already knew Mimir was where he would be stationed in a little over a year. He gets a promotion then, and he'll be based on Mimir and not have to stay out a year at a time on field trips, like he does now."

There were two different survey groups on Woden, and he asked, "What is his name?"

"Cross—Gerry Cross. He's in Group Two—that was the way his address read. Do you know him?"

Group One had requested the serum; Group Two was eight thousand miles away, across the Western Sea.

"No, I've never met him," he said, then turned to the control board and cut the deceleration to a fraction of a gravity, knowing as he did so that it could not avert the ultimate end, yet doing the only thing he could do to prolong

73

that ultimate end. The sensation was like that of the ship suddenly dropping, and the girl's involuntary movement of surprise half lifted her from the seat.

"We're going faster now, aren't we?" she asked. "Why are we doing that?"

He told her the truth. "To save fuel for a little while."

"You mean we don't have very much?"

He delayed the answer he must give her so soon to ask, "How did you manage to stow away?"

"I just sort of walked in when no one was looking my way," she said. "I was practicing my Gelanese on the native girl who does the cleaning in the Ship's Supply office when someone came in with an order for supplies for the survey crew on Woden. I slipped into the closet there after the ship was ready to go and just before you came in. It was an impulse of the moment to stow away, so I could get to see Gerry—and from the way you keep looking at me so grim, I'm not sure it was a very wise impulse. But I'll be a model criminal—or do I mean prisoner?" She smiled at him again. "I intended to pay for my keep on top of paying the fine. I can cook and I can patch clothes for everyone and I know how to do all kinds of useful things, even a little bit about nursing."

There was one more question to ask:

"Did you know what the supplies were that the survey crew ordered?"

"Why, no. Equipment they needed in their work, I supposed."

Why couldn't she have been a man with some ulterior motive? A fugitive from justice, hoping to lose himself on a raw new world; an opportunist, seeking transportation to the new colonies where he might find golden fleece for the taking; a crackpot with a mission. Perhaps once in his lifetime an EDS pilot would find such a stowaway on his ship—warped men, mean and selfish men, brutal and dangerous men—but never before a smiling blue-eyed girl who was willing to pay her fine and work for her keep that she might see her brother.

He turned to the board and turned the switch that would signal the *Stardust*. The call would be futile, but he could not, until he had exhausted that one vain hope, seize her and thrust her into the air lock as he would an animal—or a man. The delay, in the meantime, would not be dangerous with the EDS decelerating at fractional gravity.

A voice spoke from the communicator. *"Stardust.* Identify yourself and proceed."

"Barton, EDS 34Gn. Emergency. Give me Commander Delhart."

There was a faint confusion of noises as the request went through the proper channels. The girl was watching him, no longer smiling.

"Are you going to order them to come back after me?" she asked.

The communicator clicked and there was the sound of a distant voice saying, "Commander, the EDS requests . . ."

"Are they coming back after me?" she asked again. "Won't I get to see my brother after all?"

"Barton?" The blunt, gruff voice of Commander Delhart came from the communicator. "What's this about an emergency?"

"A stowaway," he answered.

"A stowaway?" There was a slight surprise to the question. "That's rather unusual—but why the 'emergency' call? You discovered him in time, so there should be no appreciable danger, and I presume you've informed Ship's Records so his nearest relatives can be notified."

"That's why I had to call you, first. The stowaway is still aboard and the circumstances are so different—"

"Different?" the commander interrupted, impatience in his voice. "How can they be different? You know you have a limited supply of fuel; you also know the law as well as I do: 'Any stowaway discovered in an EDS shall be jettisoned immediately following discovery.' "

There was the sound of a sharply indrawn breath from the girl. *"What does he mean?"*

"The stowaway is a girl."

"What?"

"She wanted to see her brother. She's only a kid and she didn't know what she was really doing."

"I see." All the curtness was gone from the commander's voice. "So you called me in the hope I could do something?" Without waiting for an answer he went on, "I'm sorry—I can do nothing. This cruiser must maintain its schedule; the life of not one person but the lives of many depend on it. I know how you feel but I'm powerless to help you. You'll have to go through with it. I'll have you connected with Ship's Records."

The communicator faded to a faint rustle of sound, and he turned back to the girl. She was leaning forward on the bench, almost rigid, her eyes fixed wide and frightened.

"What did he mean, to go through with it? To jettison me . . . to go through with it—what did he mean? Not the way it sounded . . . he couldn't have. What did he mean—what did he really mean?"

Her time was too short for the comfort of a lie to be more than a cruelly fleeting delusion.

"He meant it the way it sounded."

"No!" She recoiled from him as though he had struck her, one hand half upraised as though to fend him off and stark unwillingness to believe in her eyes.

"It will have to be."

"No! You're joking—you're insane! You can't mean it!"

"I'm sorry." He spoke slowly to her, gently. "I should have told you before—I should have, but I had to do what I could first; I had to call the *Stardust*. You heard what the commander said."

"But you can't—if you make me leave the ship, I'll *die*."

"I know."

She searched his face, and the unwillingness to believe left her eyes, giving way slowly to a look of dazed horror.

"You know?" She spoke the words far apart, numb and wonderingly.

"I know. It has to be like that."

"You mean it—you really mean it." She sagged back against the wall, small and limp like a little rag doll, and all the protesting and disbelief gone. "You're going to do it—you're going to make me die?"

"I'm sorry," he said again. "You'll never know how sorry I am. It has to be that way and no human in the universe can change it."

"You're going to make me die and I didn't do anything to die for—I didn't *do* anything—"

He sighed, deep and weary. "I know you didn't, child. I know you didn't."

"EDS." The communicator rapped brisk and metallic. "This

is Ship's Records. Give us all information on subject's identification disk."

He got out of his chair to stand over her. She clutched the edge of the seat, her upturned face white under the brown hair and the lipstick standing out like a blood-red cupid's bow.

"Now?"

"I want your identification disk," he said.

She released the edge of the seat and fumbled at the chain that suspended the plastic disk from her neck with fingers that were trembling and awkward. He reached down and unfastened the clasp for her, then returned with the disk to his chair.

"Here's your data, Records: Identification Number T837—"

"One moment," Records interrupted. "This is to be filed on the gray card, of course?"

"Yes."

"And the time of the execution?"

"I'll tell you later."

"Later? This is highly irregular; the time of the subject's death is required before—"

He kept the thickness out of his voice with an effort. "Then we'll do it in a highly irregular manner—you'll hear the disk read first. The subject is a girl and she's listening to everything that's said. Are you capable of understanding that?"

There was a brief, almost shocked silence, then Records said meekly, "Sorry. Go ahead."

He began to read the disk, reading it slowly to delay the inevitable for as long as possible, trying to help her by giving her what little time he could to recover from her first horror and let it resolve into the calm of acceptance and resignation.

"Number T8374 dash Y54. Name, Marilyn Lee Cross. Sex, female. Born July 7, 2160." *She was only eighteen.* "Height, five-three. Weight, a hundred and ten." *Such a slight weight, yet enough to add fatally to the mass of the shell-thin bubble that was an EDS.* "Hair, brown. Eyes, blue. Complexion, light. Blood type, O." *Irrelevant data.* "Destination, Port City, Mimir." *Invalid data.*

He finished and said, "I'll call you later," then turned once again to the girl. She was huddled back against the wall, watching him with a look of numb and wondering fascination.

"They're waiting for you to kill me, aren't they? They want me dead, don't they? You and everybody on the cruiser want me dead, don't you?" Then the numbness broke and her voice was that of a frightened and bewildered child. "Everybody wants me dead and I didn't *do* anything. I didn't hurt anyone—I only wanted to see my brother."

"It's not the way you think—it isn't that way at all," he said. "Nobody wants it this way; nobody would ever let it be this way if it was humanly possible to change it."

"Then why is it? I don't understand. Why is it?"

"This ship is carrying kala fever serum to Group One on Woden. Their own supply was destroyed by a tornado. Group Two—the crew your brother is in—is eight thousand miles away across the Western Sea, and their helicopters can't cross it to help Group One. The fever is invariably fatal unless the serum can be had in time, and the six men in Group One will die unless this ship reaches them on schedule. These little ships are always given barely enough fuel to reach their destination, and if you stay aboard your added weight will cause it to use up all its fuel before it reaches the ground. It will crash then, and you and I will die and so will the six men waiting for the fever serum."

It was a full minute before she spoke, and as she considered his words the expression of numbness left her eyes.

"Is that it?" she asked at last. "Just that the ship doesn't have enough fuel?"

"Yes."

"I can go alone or I can take seven others with me—is that the way it is?"

"That's the way it is."

"And nobody wants me to have to die?"

"Nobody."

"Then maybe— Are you sure nothing can be done about it? Wouldn't people help me if they could?"

"Everyone would like to help you, but there is nothing anyone can do. I did the only thing I could do when I called the *Stardust*."

"And it won't come back—but there might be other cruisers, mightn't there? Isn't there any hope at all that there might be someone, somewhere, who could do something to help me?"

She was leaning forward a little in her eagerness as she waited for his answer.

"No."

The word was like the drop of a cold stone and she again leaned back against the wall, the hope and eagerness leaving her face. "You're sure—you *know* you're sure?"

"I'm sure. There are no other cruisers within forty light-years; there is nothing and no one to change things."

She dropped her gaze to her lap and began twisting a pleat of her skirt between her fingers, saying no more as her mind began to adapt itself to the grim knowledge.

It was better so; with the going of all hope would go the fear; with the going of all hope would come resignation. She needed time and she could have so little of it. How much?

The EDS's were not equipped with hull-cooling units; their speed had to be reduced to a moderate level before entering the atmosphere. They were decelerating at .10 gravity, approaching their destination at a far higher speed than the computers had calculated on. The *Stardust* had been quite near Woden when she launched the EDS; their present velocity was putting them nearer by the second. There would be a critical point, soon to be reached, when he would have to resume deceleration. When he did so the girl's weight would be multiplied by the gravities of deceleration, would become, suddenly, a factor if paramount importance, the factor the computers had been ignorant of when they determined the amount of fuel the EDS should have. She would have to go when deceleration began; it could be no other way. When would that be—how long could he let her stay?

"How long can I stay?"

He winced involuntarily from the words that were so like an echo of his own thoughts. How long? He didn't know; he would have to ask the ship's computers. Each EDS was given a meager surplus of fuel to compensate for unfavorable conditions within the atmosphere, and relatively little fuel was being consumed for the time being. The memory banks of the computers would still contain all data pertaining to the course set for the EDS; such data would not be erased until the EDS reached its destination. He had only to give the computers the new data—the girl's weight and the exact time at which he had reduced the deceleration to .10.

"Barton." Commander Delhart's voice came abruptly from the communicator as he opened his mouth to call the *Star*-

dust. "A check with Records shows me you haven't completed your report. Did you reduce the deceleration?"

So the commander knew what he was trying to do.

"I'm decelerating at point ten," he answered. "I cut the deceleration at seventeen fifty and the weight is a hundred and ten. I would like to stay at point ten as long as the computers say I can. Will you give them the question?"

It was contrary to regulations for an EDS pilot to make any changes in the course or degree of deceleration the computers had set for him, but the commander made no mention of the violation. Neither did he ask the reason for it. It was not necessary for him to ask; he had not become commander of an interstellar cruiser without both intelligence and an understanding of human nature. He said only, "I'll have that given the computers."

The communicator fell silent and he and the girl waited, neither of them speaking. They would not have to wait long; the computers would give the answer within moments of the asking. The new factors would be fed into the steel maw of the first bank and the electrical impulses would go through the complex circuits. Here and there a relay might click, a tiny cog turn over, but it would be essentially the electrical impulses that found the answer; formless, mindless, invisible, determining with utter precision how long the pale girl beside him might live. Then five little segments of metal in the second bank would trip in rapid succession against an inked ribbon and a second steel maw would spit out the slip of paper that bore the answer.

The chronometer on the instrument board read 18:10 when the commander spoke again.

"You will resume deceleration at nineteen ten."

She looked toward the chronometer, then quickly away from it. "Is that when . . . when I go?" she asked. He nodded and she dropped her eyes to her lap again.

"I'll have the course correction given you," the commander said. "Ordinarily I would never permit anything like this, but I understand your position. There is nothing I can do, other than what I've just done, and you will not deviate from these new instructions. You will complete your report at nineteen ten. Now—here are the course corrections."

The voice of some unknown technician read them to him, and he wrote them down on the pad clipped to the edge of the control board. There would, he saw, be periods of deceleration when he neared the atmosphere when the deceleration would be five gravities—and at five gravities one hundred ten pounds would become five hundred fifty pounds.

The technician finished and he terminated the contact with a brief acknowledgment. Then, hesitating a moment, he reached out and shut off the communicator. It was 18:13 and he would have nothing to report until 19:10. In the meantime, it somehow seemed indecent to permit others to hear what she might say in her last hour.

He began to check the instrument readings, going over them with unnecessary slowness. She would have to accept the circumstances, and there was nothing he could do to help her into acceptance; words of sympathy would only delay it.

It was 18:20 when she stirred from her motionlessness and spoke.

"So that's the way it has to be with me?"

He swung around to face her. "You understand now, don't you? No one would ever let it be like this if it could be changed."

"I understand," she said. Some of the color had returned to her face and the lipstick no longer stood out so vividly red. "There isn't enough fuel for me to stay. When I hid on this ship I got into some thing I didn't know anything about and now I have to pay for it."

She had violated a man-made law that said KEEP OUT, but the penalty was not for men's making or desire and it was a penalty men could not revoke. A physical law had decreed: *h amount of fuel will power an EDS with a mass of m safely to its destination;* and a second physical law had decreed: *h amount of fuel will not power an EDS with a mass of m plus x safely to its destination.*

EDS's obeyed only physical laws, and no amount of human sympathy for her could alter the second law.

"But I'm afraid. I don't want to die—not now. I want to live, and nobody is doing anything to help me; everybody is letting me go ahead and acting just like nothing was going to happen to me. I'm going to die and nobody *cares.*"

"We all do," he said. "I do and the commander does and the clerk in Ship's Records; we all care and each of us did what little he could to help you. It wasn't enough—it was almost nothing—but it was all we could do."

"Not enough fuel—I can understand that," she said, as though she had not heard his own words. "But to have to die for it. *Me* alone . . ."

How hard it must be for her to accept the fact. She had never known danger of death; had never known the environments where the lives of men could be as fragile and fleeting as sea foam tossed against a rocky shore. She belonged on gentle Earth, in that secure and peaceful society where she could be young and gay and laughing with the others of her kind; where life was precious and well guarded and there was always the assurance that tomorrow would come. She belonged in that world of soft winds and a warm sun, music and moonlight and gracious manners, and not on the hard, bleak frontier.

"How did it happen to me so terribly quickly? An hour ago I was on the *Stardust,* going to Mimir. Now the *Stardust* is going on without me and I'm going to die and I'll never see Gerry and Mama and Daddy again—I'll never see anything again."

He hesitated, wondering how he could explain it to her so she would really understand and not feel she had somehow been the victim of a reasonlessly cruel injustice. She did not know what the frontier was like; she thought in terms of safe-secure Earth. Pretty girls were not jettisoned on Earth; there was a law against it. On Earth her plight would have filled the newscasts and a fast black patrol ship would have been racing to her rescue. Everyone, everywhere, would have known of Marilyn Lee Cross, and no effort would have been spared to save her life. But this was not Earth and there were no patrol ships; only the *Stardust,* leaving them behind at many times the speed of light. There was no one to help her, there would be no Marilyn Lee Cross smiling from the newscasts tomorrow. Marilyn Lee Cross would be but a poignant memory for an EDS pilot and a name on a gray card in Ship's Records.

"It's different here; it's not like back on Earth," he said. "It isn't that no one cares; it's that no one can do anything to help. The frontier is big, and here along its rim the colonies and exploration parties are scattered so thin and far between. On Woden, for example, there are only sixteen men—sixteen men on an entire world. The exploration parties, the survey crews, the little first colonies—they're all fighting alien environments, trying to make a way for those who will follow after. The environments fight back, and those who go first usually make mistakes only once. There is no margin of safety along the rim of the frontier; there can't be until the way is made for the others who will come later, until the new worlds are tamed and settled. Until then men will have to pay the penalty for making mistakes, with no one to help them, because there is no one *to* help them."

"I was going to Mimir," she said. "I didn't know about the frontier; I was only going to Mimir and *it's* safe."

"Mimir is safe, but you left the cruiser that was taking you there."

She was silent for a little while. "It was all so wonderful at first; there was plenty of room for me on this ship and I would be seeing Gerry so soon. I didn't know about the fuel, didn't know what would happen to me . . ."

Her words trailed away, and he turned his attention to the viewscreen, not wanting to stare at her as she fought her way through the black horror of fear toward the calm gray of acceptance.

Woden was a ball, enshrouded in the blue haze of its atmosphere, swimming in space against the background of star-sprinkled dead blackness. The great mass of Manning's Continent sprawled like a gigantic hourglass in the Eastern Sea, with the western half of the Eastern Continent still visible. There was a thin line of shadow along the right-hand edge of the globe, and the Eastern Continent was disappearing into it as the planet turned on its axis. An hour before, the entire continent had been in view; now a thousand miles of it had gone into the thin edge of shadow and around to the night that lay on the other side of the world. The dark-blue spot that was Lotus Lake was approaching the shadow. It was somewhere near the southern edge of the lake that Group Two had their camp. It would be night there soon, and quick behind the coming of night the rotation of Woden on its axis would put Group Two beyond the reach of the ship's radio.

He would have to tell her before it was too late for her to talk to her brother. In a way, it would be better for both of them should they not do so, but it was not for him to decide. To each of them the last words would be something to hold and cherish, something that would cut like the blade of a knife yet would be infinitely precious to remember, she for her own brief moments to live and he for the rest of his life.

He held down the button that would flash the grid lines on the viewscreen and used the known diameter of the planet to estimate the distance the southern tip of Lotus Lake had yet to go until it passed beyond radio range. It was approximately five hundred miles. Five hundred miles; thirty minutes—and the chronometer read 18:30. Allowing for error in estimating, it would not be later than 19:05 that the turning of Woden would cut off her brother's voice.

The first border of the Western Continent was already in sight along the left side of the world. Four thousand miles across it lay the shore of the Western Sea and the camp of Group One. It had been in the Western Sea that the tornado had originated, to strike with such fury at the camp and destroy half their prefabricated buildings, including the one that housed the medical supplies. Two days before, the tornado had not existed; it had been no more than great gentle masses of air out over the calm Western Sea. Group One had gone about their routine survey work, unaware of the meeting of air masses out at sea, unaware of the force the union was spawning. It had struck their camp without warning—a thundering, roaring destruction that sought to annihilate all that lay before it. It had passed on, leaving the wreckage in its wake. It had destroyed the labor of months and had doomed six men to die and then, as though its task was accomplished, it once more began to resolve into gentle masses of air. But, for all its deadliness, it had destroyed with neither malice nor intent. It had been a blind and mindless force, obeying the laws of nature, and it would have followed the same course with the same fury had men never existed.

Existence required order, and there was order; the laws of nature, irrevocable and immutable. Men could learn to use them, but men could not change them. The circumference of a circle was always pi times the diameter, and no science of man would ever make it otherwise. The combination of chemical A with chemical B under condition C invariably produced reaction D. The law of gravitation was a rigid equation, and it made no distinction between the fall of a leaf and the ponderous circling of a binary star system. The nuclear conversion process powered the cruisers that carried men to the stars; the same process in the form of a nova would destroy a world with equal efficiency. The laws *were*, and the universe moved in obedience to them. Along the frontier were arrayed all the forces of nature, and sometimes they destroyed those who were fighting their way outward from Earth. The men of the frontier had long ago learned the bitter futility of cursing the forces that would destroy them, for the forces were blind and deaf; the futility of looking to the heavens for mercy, for the stars of the galaxy swung in their long, long sweep of two hundred million years, as inexorably controlled as they by the laws that knew neither hatred nor compassion. The men of the frontier knew—but how was a girl from Earth to fully understand? *H amount of fuel will not power an EDS with a mass of m plus x safely to its destination*. To himself and her brother and parents she was a sweet-faced girl in her teens; to the laws of nature she was *x*, the unwanted factor in a cold equation.

She stirred again on the seat. "Could I write a letter? I want to write to Mama and Daddy. And I'd like to talk to Gerry. Could you let me talk to him over your radio there?"

"I'll try to get him," he said.

He switched on the normal-space transmitter and pressed the signal button. Someone answered the buzzer almost immediately.

"Hello. How's it going with you fellows now—is the EDS on its way?"

"This isn't Group One; this is the EDS," he said. "Is Gerry Cross there?"

"Gerry? He and two others went out in the helicopter this morning and aren't back yet. It's almost sundown, though, and he ought to be back right away—in less than an hour at the most."

"Can you connect me through to the radio in his 'copter?"

"Huh-uh. It's been out of commission for two months— some printed circuits went haywire and we can't get any more until the next cruiser stops by. Is it something important—bad news for him, or something?"

"Yes—it's very important. When he comes in get him to the transmitter as soon as you possibly can."

"I'll do that; I'll have one of the boys waiting at the field with a truck. Is there anything else I can do?"

"No, I guess that's all. Get him there as soon as you can and signal me."

He turned the volume to an inaudible minimum, an act that would not affect the functioning of the signal buzzer, and unclipped the pad of paper from the control board. He tore off the sheet containing his flight instructions and handed the pad to her, together with pencil.

"I'd better write to Gerry too," she said as she took them. "He might not get back to camp in time."

She began to write, her fingers still clumsy and uncertain in the way they handled the pencil, and the top of it trembling a little as she poised it between words. He turned back to the viewscreen, to stare at it without seeing it.

She was a lonely little child trying to say her last goodbye, and she would lay out her heart to them. She would tell them how much she loved them and she would tell them to not feel badly about it, that it was only something that must happen eventually to everyone and she was not afraid. The last would be a lie and it would be there to read between the sprawling uneven lines: a valiant little lie that would make the hurt all the greater for them.

Her brother was of the frontier and he would understand. He would not hate the EDS pilot for doing nothing to prevent her going; he would know there had been nothing the pilot could do. He would understand, though the understanding would not soften the shock and pain when he learned his sister was gone. But the others, her father and mother—they would not understand. They were of Earth and they would think in the manner of those who had never lived where the safety margin of life was a thin, thin line—and sometimes not at all. What would they think of the faceless, unknown pilot who had sent her to her death?

They would hate him with cold and terrible intensity, but it really didn't matter. He would never see them, never know them. He would have only the memories to remind him; only the nights of fear, when a blue-eyed girl in gypsy sandals would come in his dreams to die again. . . .

He scowled at the viewscreen and tried to force his thoughts into less emotional channels. There was nothing he could do to help her. She had unknowingly subjected herself to the penalty of a law that recognized neither innocence nor youth nor beauty, that was incapable of sympathy or leniency. Regret was illogical—and yet, could knowing it to be illogical ever keep it away?

She stopped occasionally, as though trying to find the right words to tell them what she wanted them to know, then the pencil would resume its whispering to the paper. It was 18:37 when she folded the letter in a square and wrote a name on it. She began writing another, twice looking up at the chronometer as though she feared the black hand might reach its rendezvous before she had finished. It was 18:45 when she folded it as she had done the first letter and wrote a name and address on it.

She held the letters out to him. "Will you take care of these and see that they're enveloped and mailed?"

"Of course." He took them from her hand and placed them in a pocket of his gray uniform shirt.

"These can't be sent off until the next cruiser stops by, and the *Stardust* will have long since told them about me, won't it?" she asked. He nodded and she went on: "That makes the letters not important in one way, but in another way they're very important—to me, and to them."

"I know. I understand, and I'll take care of them."

She glanced at the chronometer, then back to him. "It seems to move faster all the time, doesn't it?"

He said nothing, unable to think of anything to say, and she asked, "Do you think Gerry will come back to camp in time?"

"I think so. They said he should be in right away."

She began to roll the pencil back and forth between her palms. "I hope he does. I feel sick and scared and I want to hear his voice again and maybe I won't feel so alone. I'm a coward and I can't help it."

"No," he said, "you're not a coward. You're afraid, but you're not a coward."

"Is there a difference?"

He nodded. "A lot of difference."

"I feel so alone. I never did feel like this before; like I was all by myself and there was nobody to care what happened to me. Always, before, there was Mama and Daddy there and my friends around me. I had lots of friends, and they had a going-away party for me the night before I left."

Friends and music and laughter for her to remember—and on the viewscreen Lotus Lake was going into the shadow.

"Is it the same with Gerry?" she asked. "I mean, if he should make a mistake, would he have to die for it, all alone and with no one to help him?"

"It's the same with all, along the frontier; it will always be like that so long as there is a frontier."

"Gerry didn't tell us. He said the pay was good, and he sent money home all the time because Daddy's little shop just brought in a bare living, but he didn't tell us it was like this."

"He didn't tell you his work was dangerous?"

"Well—yes. He mentioned that, but we didn't understand. I always thought danger along the frontier was something that was a lot of fun; an exciting adventure, like in the three-D shows." A wan smile touched her face for a moment. "Only it's not, is it? It's not the same at all, because when it's real you can't go home after the show is over."

"No," he said. "No, you can't."

Her glance flicked from the chronometer to the door of the air lock, then down to the pad and pencil she still held. She shifted her position slightly to lay them on the bench beside her, moving one foot out a little. For the first time he saw that she was not wearing Vegan gypsy sandals, but only cheap imitations; the expensive Vegan leather was some kind of grained plastic, the silver buckle was gilded iron, the jewels were colored glass. *Daddy's little shop just brought in a bare living . . .* She must have left college in her second year, to take the course in linguistics that would enable her to make her own way and help her brother provide for her parents, earning what she could by part-time work after classes were over. Her personal possessions on the *Stardust* would be taken back to her parents—they would neither be of much value nor occupy much storage space on the return voyage.

"Isn't it—" She stopped, and he looked at her questioningly. "Isn't it cold in here?" she asked, almost apologetically. "Doesn't it seem cold to you?"

"Why, yes," he said. He saw by the main temperature gauge that the room was at precisely normal temperature. "Yes, it's colder than it should be."

"I wish Gerry would get back before it's too late. Do you

really think he will, and you didn't just say so to make me feel better?"

"I think he will—they said he would be in pretty soon." On the viewscreen Lotus Lake had gone into the shadow but for the thin blue line of its western edge, and it was apparent he had overestimated the time she would have in which to talk to her brother. Reluctantly, he said to her, "His camp will be out of radio range in a few minutes; he's on that part of Woden that's in the shadow"—he indicated the viewscreen—"and the turning of Woden will put him beyond contact. There may not be much time left when he comes in—not much time to talk to him before he fades out. I wish I could do something about it—I would call him right now if I could."

"Not even as much time as I will have to stay?"

"I'm afraid not."

"Then—" She straightened and looked toward the air lock with pale resolution. "Then I'll go when Gerry passes beyond range. I won't wait any longer after that—I won't have anything to wait for."

Again there was nothing he could say.

"Maybe I shouldn't wait at all. Maybe I'm selfish—maybe it would be better for Gerry if you just hold him about it afterward."

There was an unconscious pleading for denial in the way she spoke and he said, "He wouldn't want you to do that, to not wait for him."

"It's already coming dark where he is, isn't it? There will be all the long night before him, and Mama and Daddy don't know yet that I won't ever be coming back like I promised them I would. I've caused everyone I love to be hurt, haven't I? I didn't want to—I didn't intend to."

"It wasn't your fault," he said. "It wasn't your fault at all. They'll know that. They'll understand."

"At first I was so afraid to die that I was a coward and thought only of myself. Now I see how selfish I was. The terrible thing about dying like this is not that I'll be gone but that I'll never see them again; never be able to tell them that I didn't take them for granted; never be able to tell them I knew of the sacrifices they made to make my life happier, that I knew all the things they did for me and that I loved them so much more than I ever told them. I've never told them any of those things. You don't tell them such things when you're young and your life is all before you—you're so very afraid of sounding sentimental and silly. But it's so different when you have to die—you wish you had told them while you could and you wish you could tell them you're sorry for all the little mean things you ever did or said to them. You wish you could tell them that you didn't really mean to ever hurt their feelings and for them to only remember that you always loved them far more than you ever let them know."

"You don't have to tell them that," he said. "They will know—they've always known it."

"Are you sure?" she asked. "How can you be sure? My people are strangers to you."

"Wherever you go, human nature and human hearts are the same."

"And they will know what I want them to know—that I love them?"

"They've always known it, in a way far better than you could ever put in words for them."

"I keep remembering the things they did for me, and it's the little things they did that seem to be the most important to me, now. Like Gerry—he sent me a bracelet of fire-rubies on my sixteenth birthday. It was beautiful—it must have cost him a month's pay. Yet I remember him more for what he did the night my kitten got run over in the street. I was only six years old and he held me in his arms and wiped away my tears and told me not to cry, that Flossy was gone for just a little while, for just long enough to get herself a new fur coat, and she would be on the foot of my bed the very next morning. I believed him and quit crying and went to sleep dreaming about my kitten coming back. When I woke up the next morning, there was Flossy on the foot of my bed in a brand-new white fur coat, just like he had said she would be. It wasn't until a long time later that Mama told me Gerry had got the pet-shop owner out of bed at four in the morning and, when the man got mad about it, Gerry told him he was either going to go down and sell him the white kitten right then or he'd break his neck."

"It's always the little things you remember people by; all the little things they did because they wanted to do them for you. You've done the same for Gerry and your father and mother; all kinds of things that you've forgotten about but that they will never forget."

"I hope I have. I would like for them to remember me like that."

"They will."

"I wish—" She swallowed. "The way I'll die—I wish they wouldn't ever think of that. I've read how people look who die in space—their insides all ruptured and exploded and their lungs out between their teeth and then, a few seconds later, they're all dry and shapeless and horribly ugly. I don't want them to ever think of me as something dead and horrible like that."

"You're their own, their child and their sister. They could never think of you other than the way you would want them to, the way you looked the last time they saw you."

"I'm still afraid," she said. "I can't help it, but I don't want Gerry to know it. If he gets back in time, I'm going to act like I'm not afraid at all and—"

The signal buzzer interrupted her, quick and imperative.

"Gerry!" She came to her feet. "It's Gerry now!"

He spun the volume control knob and asked, "Gerry Cross?"

"Yes," her brother answered, an undertone of tenseness to his reply. "The bad news—what is it?"

She answered for him, standing close behind him and leaning down a little toward the communicator, her hand resting small and cold on his shoulder.

"Hello, Gerry." There was only a faint quaver to betray the careful casualness of her voice. "I wanted to see you—"

"Marilyn!" There was sudden and terrible apprehension in the way he spoke her name. "What are you doing on that EDS?"

"I wanted to see you," she said again. "I wanted to see you, so I hid on this ship—"

"You *hid* on it?"

"I'm a stowaway . . . I didn't know what it would mean—"

"Marilyn!" It was the cry of a man who calls, hopeless and desperate, to someone already and forever gone from him. "What have you done?"

"I . . . it's not—" Then her own composure broke and the cold little hand gripped his shoulder convulsively. "Don't,

Gerry—I only wanted to see you; I didn't intend to hurt you. Please, Gerry, don't feel like that—"

Something warm and wet splashed on his wrist and he slid out of the chair, to help her into it and swing the microphone down to her level.

"Don't feel like that. Don't let me go knowing you feel like that—"

The sob she had tried to hold back choked in her throat, and her brother spoke to her. "Don't cry, Marilyn." His voice was suddenly deep and infinitely gentle, with all the pain held out of it. "Don't cry, Sis—you mustn't do that. It's all right, honey—everything is all right."

"I—" Her lower lip quivered and she bit into it. "I didn't want you to feel that way—I just wanted us to say goodbye, because I have to go in a minute."

"Sure—sure. That's the way it'll be, Sis. I didn't mean to sound the way I did." Then his voice changed to a tone of quick and urgent demand. "EDS—have you called the *Stardust*? Did you check with the computers?"

"I called the *Stardust* almost an hour ago. It can't turn back, there are no other cruisers within forty light-years, and there isn't enough fuel."

"Are you sure that the computers had the correct data—sure of everything?"

"Yes—do you think I could ever let it happen if I wasn't sure? I did everything I could do. If there was anything at all I could do now, I would do it."

"He tried to help me, Gerry." Her lower lip was no longer trembling and the short sleeves of her blouse were wet where she had dried her tears. "No one can help me and I'm not going to cry any more and everything will be all right with you and Daddy and Mama, won't it?"

"Sure—sure it will. We'll make out fine."

Her brother's words were beginning to come in more faintly, and he turned the volume control to maximum. "He's going out of range," he said to her. "He'll be gone within another minute."

"You're fading out, Gerry," she said. "You're going out of range. I wanted to tell you—but I can't now. We must say goodbye so soon—but maybe I'll see you again. Maybe I'll come to you in your dreams with my hair in braids and crying because the kitten in my arms is dead; maybe I'll be the touch of a breeze that whispers to you as it goes by; maybe I'll be one of those gold-winged larks you told me about, singing my silly head off to you; maybe, at times, I'll be nothing you can see, but you will know I'm there beside you. Think of me like that, Gerry; always like that and not— the other way."

Dimmed to a whisper by the turning of Woden, the answer came back:

"Always like that, Marilyn—always like that and never any other way."

"Our time is up, Gerry—I have to go now. Good—" Her voice broke in mid-word and her mouth tried to twist into crying. She pressed her hand hard against it and when she spoke again the words came clear and true:

"Goodbye, Gerry."

Faint and ineffably poignant and tender, the last words came from the cold metal of the communicator:

"Goodbye, little sister . . ."

She sat motionless in the hush that followed, as though listening to the shadow-echoes of the words as they died away, then she turned away from the communicator, toward the air lock, and he pulled down the black lever beside him. The inner door of the air lock slid swiftly open, to reveal the bare little cell that was waiting for her, and she walked to it.

She walked with her head up and the brown curls brushing her shoulders, with the white sandals stepping as sure and steady as the fractional gravity would permit and the gilded buckles twinkling with little lights of blue and red and crystal. He let her walk alone and made no move to help her, knowing she would not want it that way. She stepped into the air lock and turned to face him, only the pulse in her throat to betray the wild beating of her heart.

"I'm ready," she said.

He pushed the lever up and the door slid its quick barrier between them, enclosing her in black and utter darkness for her last moments of life. It clicked as it locked in place and he jerked down the red lever. There was a slight waver to the ship as the air gushed from the lock, a vibration to the wall as though something had bumped the outer door in passing, then there was nothing and the ship was dropping true and steady again. He shoved the red lever back to close the door on the empty air lock and turned away, to walk to the pilot's chair with the slow steps of a man old and weary.

Back in the pilot's chair he pressed the signal button of the normal-space transmitter. There was no response; he had expected none. Her brother would have to wait through the night until the turning of Woden permitted contact through Group One.

It was not yet time to resume deceleration, and he waited while the ship dropped endlessly downward with him and the drives purred softly. He saw that the white hand of the supplies-closet temperature gauge was on zero. A cold equation had been balanced and he was alone on the ship. Something shapeless and ugly was hurrying ahead of him, going to Woden where its brother was waiting through the night, but the empty ship still lived for a little while with the presence of the girl who had not known about the forces that killed with neither hatred nor malice. It seemed, almost, that she still sat, small and bewildered and frightened, on the metal box beside him, her words echoing hauntingly clear in the void she had left behind her:

I didn't do anything to die for . . . I didn't do anything . . .

The Dwindling Sphere

WILLARD HAWKINS

This, fellow readers, is what the Golden Age was like. The great flowering of Astounding Science Fiction *in the 1940s began with stories like Mr. Hawkins' fascinating speculation—which, by the way, has never been previously reprinted.*

EXTRACTS FROM THE DIARY OF
FRANK BAXTER, B.S., M.Sc.

June 23, 1945. I thought today I was on the track of something, but the results, while remarkable in their way, were disappointing. The only thing of importance I can be said to have demonstrated is that, with my new technique of neutron bombardment, it is unnecessary to confine experiments to the heavier elements. This broadens the field of investigation enormously. Substituted a lump of common coal for uranium in today's experiment, and it was reduced to a small cinder. Probably oxidized, owing to a defect in the apparatus or in my procedure.

However, it seems remarkable that, despite the almost instantaneous nature of the combustion, there was no explosion. Nor, as far as I could detect, was any heat generated. In fact, I unthinkingly picked up the cinder—a small, smooth buttonlike object—and it was scarcely warm.

June 24, 1945. Repeated yesterday's experiment, carefully checking each step, with results practically identical to yesterday's. Can it be that I am on the verge of success? But that is absurd. If—as might be assumed from the evidence—my neutron bombardment started a self-perpetuating reaction which continued until every atom in the mass had been subjected to fission, enormous energy would have been generated. In fact, I would no longer be here, all in one piece, to tell about it. Even the combustion of my lump of coal at such a practically instantaneous rate would be equivalent to exploding so much dynamite.

It is very puzzling, for the fact remains that the lump has been reduced to a fraction of its original weight and size. There is, after all, only one possible answer: the greater part of its mass must have been converted into energy. The question, then, is what became of the energy?

June 28, 1945. Have been continuing my experiments, checking and rechecking. I have evidently hit upon some new principle in the conversion of matter into energy. Here are some of the results thus far:

Tried the same experiment with a chunk of rock—identical result. Tried it with a lump of earth, a piece of wood, a brass doorknob. Only difference in results was the size and consistency of the resulting cinder. Have weighed the substance each time, then the residue after neutron bombardment. The original substance seems to be reduced to approximately one twentieth of its original mass, although this varies somewhat according to the strength of the magnetic field and various adjustments in the apparatus. These factors also seem to affect the composition of the cinder.

The essence of the problem, however, has thus far baffled me. Why is it that I cannot detect the force generated? What is its nature? Unless I can solve this problem, the whole discovery is pointless.

I have written to my old college roommate, Bernard Ogilvie, asking him to come and check my results. He is a capable engineer and I have faith in his honesty and common sense—even though he appears to have been lured away from scientific pursuits by commercialism.

July 15, 1945. Ogilvie has been here now for three days. He is greatly excited, but I am sorry that I sent for him. He has given me no help at all on my real problem—in fact, he seems more interested in the by-products than in the experiment itself. I had hoped he would help me to solve the mystery of what becomes of the energy generated by my process. Instead, he appears to be fascinated by those little chunks of residue—the cinders.

When I showed that it was possible, by certain adjustments in the apparatus, to control their texture and substance, he was beside himself with excitement. The result is that I have spent all my time since his arrival in making these cinders. We have produced them in consistency ranging all the way from hard little buttons to a mushy substance resembling cheese.

Analysis shows them to be composed of various elements, chiefly carbon and silica. Ogilvie appears to think there has been an actual transmutation of elements into this final result. I question it. The material is simply a form of ash—a residue.

We have enlarged the apparatus and installed a hopper, into which we shovel rock, debris—in fact, anything that comes handy, including garbage and other waste. If my experiment after all proves a failure, I shall at least have the ironic satisfaction of having produced an ideal incinerator. Ogilvie declares there is a fortune in that alone.

July 20, 1945. Bernard Ogilvie has gone. Now I can get down to actual work again. He took with him a quantity of samples and plans for the equipment. Before he left, he revealed what is on his mind. He thinks my process may revolutionize the plastics industry. What a waste of time to have called him in! A fine mind spoiled by commercialism. With an epochal discovery in sight, all he can think of is that here is an opportunity to convert raw material which costs practically nothing into commercial gadgets. He thinks the stuff can be molded and shaped—perhaps through a matrix principle incorporated right in the apparatus.

Partly, I must confess, to get rid of him, I signed the agreement he drew up. It authorizes him to patent the process in my name, and gives me a major interest in all subsidiary devices and patents that may be developed by his engineers. He himself is to have what he calls the promotion rights, but there is some sort of a clause whereby the control reverts wholly to me or to my heirs at his death. Ogilvie says it will mean millions to both of us.

He undoubtedly is carried away by his imagination. What could I do with such an absurd sum of money? However, a few thousand dollars might come in handy for improved equipment. I must find a means of capturing and controlling that energy.

EXTRACTS FROM THE DIARY OF QUENTIN BAXTER, PRESIDENT OF PLASTOSCENE PRODUCTS, INC.

August 3, 2065. I have made a discovery today which moved me profoundly—so profoundly that I have opened this journal so that my own thoughts and reactions may be likewise recorded for posterity. Diary-keeping has heretofore appeared to me as a rather foolish vanity—it now appears in an altogether different light.

The discovery which so altered my viewpoint was of a diary kept by my great-grandfather, Frank Baxter, the actual inventor of plastoscene.

I have often wondered what sort of a man this ancestor of mine could have been. History tells us almost nothing about him. I feel now that I know him as intimately as I know my closest associates. And what a different picture this diary gives from the prevailing concept!

Most of us have no doubt thought of the discoverer of the plastoscene principle as a man who saw the need for a simple method of catering to humanity's needs—one which would supplant the many laborious makeshifts of his day—and painstakingly set out to evolve it.

Actually, the discovery appears to have been an accident. Frank Baxter took no interest in its development—regarded it as of little account. Think of it! An invention more revolutionary than the discovery to fire, yet its inventor failed entirely to grasp its importance! To the end of his days it was to him merely a by-product. He died considering himself a failure, because he was unable to attain the goal he sought—the creation of atomic power.

In a sense, much of the credit apparently belongs to his friend Bernard Ogilvie, who grasped the possibilities inherent in the new principle. Here again, what a different picture the diary gives from that found in our schoolbooks! The historians would have us regard Frank Baxter as a sort of master mind, Bernard Ogilvie as his humble disciple and man Friday.

Actually, Ogilvie was a shrewd promoter who saw the possibilities of the discovery and exploited them—not especially to benefit humanity, but for personal gain. We must give him credit, however, for a scrupulous honesty which was amazing for his time. It would have been easy for him to take advantage of the impractical, dreamy scientist. Instead, he arranged that the inventor of the process should reap its rewards, and it is wholly owing to his insistence that control reverted to our family, where it has remained for more than a century.

All honor to these two exceptional men!

Neither, it is true, probably envisioned the great changes that would be wrought by the discovery. My ancestor remained to the end of his days dreamy and aloof, concerned solely with his futile efforts to trap the energy which he was sure he had released. The wealth which rolled up for him through Plastoscene Products, Inc.—apparently the largest individual fortune of his time—was to him a vague abstraction. I find a few references to it in his diary, but they are written in a spirit of annoyance. He goes so far as to mention once—apparently exasperated because the responsibilities of his position called him away from his experiments for a few hours—that he would like to convert the millions into hard currency and pour them into a conversion hopper, where at least they might be turned into something useful.

It is strange, by the way, that the problem he posed has never been demonstrably solved. Scientists still are divided in their allegiance to two major theories—one, that the force generated by this conversion of elements escapes into the fourth dimension; the other that it is generated in the form of radiations akin to cosmic rays, which are dissipated with a velocity approaching the infinite. These rays do not affect ordinary matter, according to the theory, because they do not impinge upon it, but instead pass through it, as light passes through a transparent substance.

August 5, 2065. I have read and reread my grandfather's diary, and confess that I more and more find in him a kindred spirit. His way of life seems to me infinitely more appealing than that which inheritance has imposed upon me. The responsibilities resting on my shoulders, as reigning head of the Baxter dynasty, become exceedingly onerous at times. I even find myself wondering whether plastoscene has, after all, proved such an unmixed blessing for mankind.

Perhaps the greatest benefits may lie in the future. Certainly each stage in its development has been marked by economic readjustments—some of them well-nigh world-shattering. I have often been glad that I did not live through those earlier days of stress, when industry after industry was wiped out by the remorseless juggernaut of technological progress. When, for example, hundreds of thousands were thrown out of employment in the metal-mining and -refining and allied industries. It was inevitable that plastoscene substitutes, produced at a fraction of the cost from common dirt of the fields, should wipe out this industry—but the step could have been taken, it seems to me, without subjecting the dispossessed workers and employers to such hardship, thereby precipitating what amounted to a civil war. When we pause to think of it, almost every article in common use today represents one or more of those industries which was similarly wiped out, and on which vast numbers of people depended for their livelihood.

We have, at length, achieved a form of stable society—but I, for one, am not wholly satisfied with it. What do we have? A small owning class—a cluster of corporations grouped around the supercorporation, Plastoscene Products, Inc., of which I am—heaven help me!—the hereditary ruler. Next, a situation-holding class, ranging from scientists, executives and technicians down to the mechanical workers. Here again—because there are so few situations open, compared with the vast reservoir of potential producers—the situation holders have developed what amounts to a system of hereditary succession. I am told that it is almost impossible for one whose father was not a situation holder even to obtain the training necessary to qualify him for any of the jealously guarded positions.

Outside of this group is that great, surging mass, the major part of human society. These millions, I grant, are fed and clothed and housed and provided with a standard of living which their ancestors would have regarded as luxurious. Nevertheless, their lot is pitiful. They have no incentives; their status is that of a subject class. Particularly do I find distasteful the law which makes it a crime for any member of this enforced leisure group to be caught engaging in useful labor. The appalling number of convictions in our courts for this crime shows that there is in mankind an instinct to perform useful service, which cannot be eradicated merely by passing laws.

The situation is unhealthy as well from another standpoint. To me it seems a normal thing that society should progress. Yet we cannot close our eyes to the fact that the most highly skilled scientific minds the world has ever known have failed to produce a worth-while advance in technology for over a quarter of a century. Has science become sterile? No. In fact, every schoolboy knows the answer.

Our scientists do not dare to announce their discoveries. I am supposed to shut my eyes to what I know—that every vital discovery along the lines of technology has been suppressed. The plain, blunt truth is that we dare not introduce any technical advance which would eliminate more situation holders. A major discovery—one that reduced an entire class of situation holders to enforced leisure—would precipitate another revolution.

Is human society, as a result of its greatest discovery, doomed to sterility?

October 17, 2089. It has been nearly a quarter of a century since I first read the diary of my great-grandfather, Frank Baxter. I felt an impulse to get it out to show to my son, and before I realized it I had reread the volume in its entirety. It stirred me even more than it did back in my younger days. I must preserve its crumbling pages in facsimile, on permanent plastoscene parchment, so that later descendants—finding our two journals wrapped together—will thrill as I have thrilled to that early record of achievement.

The reading has crystallized thoughts long dormant in my mind. I am nearing the end of the trail. Soon I will turn over the presidency of Plastoscene Products, Inc., to my son— if he desires it. Perhaps he will have other ideas. He is now a full-fledged Pl. T.D. Doctor of Plastoscene Technology. It may be that power and position will mean as little to him as they have come to mean to me. I shall send for him tomorrow.

October 18, 2089. I have had my discussion with Philip, but I fear I bungled matters. He talked quite freely of his experiments. It seems that he has been working along the line of approach started by Levinson some years ago. As we know, the plastoscene principle in use involves the making of very complex adjustments. That is to say, if we wish to manufacture some new type of object—say a special gyroscope bearing—the engineer in charge first sets the machine to produce material of a certain specific hardness and temper, then he adjusts the controls which govern size and shape, and finally, having roughly achieved the desired result, he refines the product with micrometer adjustments—but largely through the trial-and-error method—until the quality, dimensions and so on meet the tests of his precision instruments. If the object involved is complex—involving two or more compounds, for example—the adjustments are correspondingly more difficult. We have not succeeded in producing palatable foodstuffs, though our engineers have turned out some messes which are claimed to have nourishing qualities. I suspect that the engineers have purposely made them nauseous to the taste.

True, once the necessary adjustments have been made, they are recorded on microfilm. Thereafter, it is only necessary to feed this film into the control box, where the electric eye automatically makes all the adjustments for which the skill of the technician was initially required. Levinson, however, proposed to reproduce natural objects in plastoscene by photographic means.

It is this process which Philip apparently has perfected. His method involves a three-dimensional "scanning" device which records the texture, shape and the exact molecular structure of the object to be reproduced. The record is made on microfilm, which then needs only to be passed through the control box to re-create the object as many times as may be required.

"Think of the saving of effort!" Philip remarked enthusiastically. "Not only can objects of the greatest intricacy be reproduced without necessity of assembling, but even natural foods can be created in all their flavor and nourishing quality. I have eaten synthetic radishes—I have even tasted synthetic chicken—that could not be told from the original which formed its matrix."

"You mean," I demanded in some alarm, "that you can reproduce life?"

His face clouded. "No. That is a quality that seems to elude the scanner. But I can reproduce the animal, identical with its live prototype down to the last nerve tip and hair, except that it is inert—lifeless. The radishes I spoke of will not grow in soil—they cannot reproduce themselves—but chemically and in cell structure they image the originals."

"Philip," I declared, "this is an amazing achievement! It removes the last limitation upon the adaptability of plastoscene. It means that we can produce not merely machine parts but completely assembled machines. It means that foodstuffs can be—"

I stopped, brought to myself by his sudden change in expression.

"True, Father," he observed coldly, "except that it happens to be a pipe dream. I did not expect that you would be taken in by my fairy tale. I have an engagement and must go."

He hurried from the room before I could get my wits about me.

October 23, 2089. Philip has been avoiding me, but I managed at last to corner him.

I began this time by mentioning that it would soon be necessary for me to turn over the burden of Plastoscene Products, Inc., to him as my logical successor.

He hesitated, then blurted, "Father, I know this is going to hurt you, but I don't want to carry on the succession. I prefer to remain just a cog in the engineering department."

"Responsibility," I reminded him, "is something that cannot be honorably evaded."

"Why should it be my responsibility?" he demanded vehemently. "I didn't ask to be your son."

"Nor," I countered, "did I ask to be my father's son, nor the great-grandson of a certain inventor who died in the twentieth century. Philip, I want you to do one thing for me. Take this little book, read it, then bring it back and tell me what you think of it." I handed him Frank Baxter's diary.

October 24, 2089. Philip brought back the diary today. He admitted that he had sat up all night reading it.

"But I'm afraid the effect isn't what you expected," he told me frankly. "Instead of instilling the idea that we Baxters have a divine mission to carry on the dynasty, it makes me feel that our responsibility is rather to undo the damage already caused by our meddling. That old fellow back there—

Frank Baxter—didn't intend to produce this hideous stuff."

"Hideous stuff?" I demanded.

"Don't be shocked, Father," he said, a trifle apologetically. "I can't help feeling rather deeply about this. Perhaps you think we're better off than people in your great-grandfather's time. I doubt it. They had work to do. There may have been employment problems, but it wasn't the enforced idleness of our day. Look at Frank Baxter—he could work and invent things with the assurance that he was doing something to advance mankind. He wasn't compelled to cover up his discoveries for fear they'd cause further—"

He stopped suddenly, as if realizing that he had said more than he intended.

"My boy," I told him, speaking slowly, "I know just how you feel—and knowing it gives me more satisfaction than you can realize."

He stared at me, bewildered. "You mean—you don't want me to take on the succession?"

I unfolded my plan.

FROM THE DIARY OF RAN RAXLER, TENTH-RANKING HONOR STUDENT, NORTH-CENTRAL FINALS, CLASS OF 2653

December 28, 2653. I have had two thrills today—an exciting discovery right on the heels of winning my diploma in the finals. Being one of the high twenty practically assures me of a chance to serve in the production pits this year.

But the discovery—I must record that first of all. It consists of a couple of old diaries. I found them in a chestful of family heirlooms which I rescued as they were about to be tossed into the waste tube. In another minute, they would have been on their way to the community plastoscene converter.

There has been a legend in our family that we are descended from the original discoverer of plastoscene, and this find surely tends to prove it. Even the name is significant. Frank Baxter. Given names as well as surnames are passed down through the generations. My grandfather before me was Ran Raxler. The dropping of a letter here, the corruption of another there, could easily have resulted in the modification of Frank Baxter to Ran Raxler.

What a thrill it will be to present to the world the authentic diary of the man who discovered the plastoscene principle! Not the impossible legendary figure, but the actual, flesh-and-blood man. And what a shock it will be to many! For it appears that Frank Baxter stumbled upon this discovery quite by accident, and regarded it to the end of his days as an unimportant by-product of his experiments.

And this later Baxter—Quentin—who wrote the companion diary and sealed the two together. What a martyr to progress he proved himself—he and his son, Philip. The diary throws an altogether different light on their motives than has been recorded in history. Instead of being selfish oligarchs who were overthrown by a mass uprising, this diary reveals that they themselves engineered the revolution.

The final entry in Quentin Baxter's diary consists of these words: "I unfolded my plan." The context—when taken with the undisputed facts of history—makes it clear what the plan must have been. As I reconstruct it, the Baxters, father and son, determined to abolish the control of plastoscene by a closed corporation of hereditary owners, and to make it the property of the whole people.

The son had perfected the scanning principle which gives plastoscene its present unlimited range. His impulse was to withhold it—in fact, it had become a point of honor among technicians to bury such discoveries, after showing them to a few trusted associates. Incomprehensible? Perhaps so at first, but not when we understand the upheavals such discoveries might cause in the form of society then existing. To make this clear, I should, perhaps, point to the record of history, which proves that up to the time of plastoscene, foodstuffs had been largely produced by growing them in the soil. This was accomplished through a highly technical process, which I cannot explain, but I am told that the University of Antarctica maintains an experimental laboratory in which the method is actually demonstrated to advanced classes. Moreover, we know what these foods were like through the microfilm matrices which still reproduce some of them for us.

The right to produce such foods for humanity's needs was jealously guarded by the great agricultural aristocracy. And, of course, this entire situation-holding class, together with many others, would be abolished by Philip's invention.

We know what happened. Despite the laws prohibiting the operation of plastoscene converters except by licensed technicians and situation holders, contraband machines suddenly began to appear everywhere among the people. Since these machines were equipped with the new scanning principle, it is obvious, in view of the diary, that they must have been deliberately distributed at strategic points by the Baxters.

At first, the contraband machines were confiscated and destroyed—but since they were, of course, capable of reproducing themselves through the matrix library of microfilm which was standard equipment, the effort to keep pace with their spread through the masses was hopeless. The ruling hierarchies appealed to the law, and to the Baxters, whose hereditary control of the plastoscene monopoly had been supposedly a safeguard against its falling into the hands of the people as a whole. The Baxters, father and son, then played their trump card. They issued a proclamation deeding the plastoscene principle in perpetuity to all the people. History implies that they were forced to do this—but fails to explain how or why. There was a great deal of confusion and bloodshed during this period; no wonder that historians jumped at conclusions—even assuming that the Baxters were assassinated by revolutionists, along with others of the small owning group who made a last stand, trying to preserve their monopolies. In light of Quentin Baxter's diary, there is far better ground for believing that they were executed by members of their own class, who regarded them as traitors.

We should be thankful indeed that those ancient days of war and bloodshed are over. Surely such conditions can never reappear on Earth. What possible reason can there be for people to rise up against each other? Just as we can supply all our needs with plastoscene, so can our neighbors on every continent supply theirs.

March 30, 2654. I have completed my service in the production pits, and thrilling weeks they have been. To have a part in the great process which keeps millions of people alive, even for a brief four weeks' period, makes one feel that life has not been lived in vain.

One could hardly realize, without such experience, what

enormous quantities of raw material are required for the sustenance and needs of the human race. How fortunate I am to have been one of the few to earn this privilege of what the ancients called "work."

The problem must have been more difficult in the early days. Where we now distribute raw-material concentrates in the form of plastoscene-B, our forefathers had to transport the actual rock as dredged from the gravel pits. Even though the process of distribution was mechanical and largely automatic, still it was cumbersome, since material for conversion is required in a ratio of about twenty to one as compared with the finished product.

Today, of course, we have the intermediate process, by which soil and rock are converted at the pits into blocks of plastoscene-B. This represents, in a sense, the conversion process in an arrested stage. The raw material emerges in these blocks reduced to a tenth of its original weight and an even smaller volume than it will occupy in the finished product—since the mass has been increased by close packing of molecules.

A supply of concentrate sufficient to last the ordinary family for a year can now easily be stored in the standard-sized converter, and even the huge community converters have a capacity sufficient to provide for all the building, paving of roadways, recarpeting of recreation grounds, and like purposes, that are likely to be required in three months' time. I understand that experimental stations in South America are successfully introducing liquid concentrate, which can be piped directly to the consumers from the vast production pits.

I was amused on my last day by a question asked by a ten-year-old boy, the son of one of the supervisors. We stood on a rampart overlooking one of the vast production pits, several hundred feet deep and miles across—the whole space filled with a bewildering network of towers, girders, cranes, spires and cables, across and through which flashed transports of every variety. Far below us, the center of all this activity, could be discerned the huge conversion plant, in which the rock is reduced to plastoscene-B.

The little boy looked with awe at the scene, then turned his face upward, demanding, "What are we going to do when this hole gets so big that it takes up the whole world?"

We laughed, but I could sympathize with the question.

Man is such a puny creature that it is difficult for him to realize what an infinitesimal thing on the Earth's surface is a cavity which to him appears enormous. The relationship, I should say, is about the same as a pinprick to a ball which a child can toss in the air.

FROM THE INTRODUCTION TO OUR EIGHTY YEARS' WAR, *SIGNED BY GLUX GLUXTON, CHIEF HISTORIAN, THE NAPHALI INSTITUTE OF SCIENCE (DATED AS OF THE SIXTH DAY, SIXTH LUNAR MONTH, YEAR 10,487)*

The Eighty Years' War is over. It has been concluded by a treaty of eternal amity signed at Latex on the morning of the twenty-ninth day of the fifth month.

By the terms of the treaty, all peoples of the world agree to subject themselves to the control by the World Court. The Court, advised through surveys continuously conducted by the International Institute of Science, will have absolute authority over the conversion of basic substance into plastoscene, to the end that further disputes between regions and continents shall be impossible.

To my distinguished associates and to myself was allotted the task of compiling a history of the causes behind this prolonged upheaval and of its course. How well we have succeeded posterity must judge. In a situation so complex, how, indeed, may one declare with assurance which were the essential causes? Though known as *the* Eighty Years' War, a more accurate expression would be "the Eighty Years *of* War," for the period has been one marked by a constant succession of wars—of outbreaks originating spontaneously and from divers causes in various parts of the world.

Chief among the basic causes, of course, were the disputes between adjoining districts over the right to extend their conversion pits beyond certain boundaries. Nor can we overlook the serious situation precipitated when it was realized that the Antarctican sea-water conversion plants were sucking up such great quantities that the level of the oceans was actually being lowered—much as the Great Lakes once found on the North American continent were drained of their water centuries ago. Disputes, alliances and counteralliances, regions arrayed against each other, and finally engines of war raining fearful destruction. What an unprecedented bath of blood the world has endured!

The whole, aim, from this time forth, will be to strip off the earth's surface evenly, so that it shall become smooth and even, not rough and unsightly and covered with abandoned pits as now viewed from above. To prevent a too rapid lowering of sea level, it is provided that Antarctica and some other sections which have but a limited amount of land surface shall be supplied with concentrate from the more favored regions.

Under such a treaty, signed with fervent good will by the representatives of a war-weary world population, is it far-fetched to assert that permanent peace has been assured? Your historian holds that it is not.

FROM THE REPORT OF RAGNAR DUGH, DELEGATE TO THE WORLD PEACE CONFERENCE, TO THE 117th DISTRICT (CIRCUIT 1092, REV. 148)

Honored confrères: It gives me pleasure to present, on behalf of the district which has honored me as its representative, concurrence in the conditions for peace as proposed in the majority report.

As I view your faces in the televisor, I see in them the same sense of deep elation that I feel in the thought that this exhausting era of bloodshed and carnage has run its course, and that war is to be rendered impossible from this time forth. Is this too strong a statement? I read in your eyes that it is not, for we are at last abolishing the cause of war—namely, the overcrowding of the earth's surface.

The proposed restrictions may seem drastic, but the human race will accustom itself to them. And let us remember that they would be even more drastic if the wars themselves had not resulted in depopulating the world to a great extent. I am glad that it has not been found necessary to impose a ten-year moratorium on all childbearing. As matters stand, by limiting childbirth to a proportion of one child per circuit of the sun for each three deaths within any given district, scientists agree that the population of the earth will be reduced at a sufficient rate to relieve the tension.

The minority report, which favors providing more room for

the population by constructing various levels or concentric shells, which would gird the world's surface and to which additional levels would be added as needed, I utterly condemn. It is impractical chiefly for the reason that the conversion of so much material into these various dwelling surfaces would cause a serious shrinkage in the earth's mass.

Let us cast our votes in favor of the majority proposition, thus insuring a long life for the human race and for the sphere on which we dwell, and removing the last cause of war between peoples of the earth.

FROM THE MEMOIRS OF XLAR XVII, PRINCEP OF PLES

Cycle 188, 400-43. What an abomination is this younger generation! I am glad the new rules limit offspring to not more than one in a district per cycle. My nephew, Ryk LVX, has been saturating himself with folklore at the Museum of Antiquity, and had the audacity to assure me that there are records which suggest the existence of mankind before plastoscope. Why will people befog their minds with the supernatural?

"There is a theory," he brazenly declared, "that at one time the world was partly composed of food, which burst up through its crust ready for the eating. It is claimed that even the carpet we now spread over the earth's surface had its correspondence in a substance which appeared there spontaneously."

"In that case," I retorted sarcastically, "what became of this—this exudation of the rocks?"

Of course, he had an answer ready: "Plastoscene was discovered and offered mankind an easier method of supplying its needs, with the result that the surface of the earth, containing the growth principle, was stripped away. I do not say that this is a fact," he hastened to add, "but merely that it may have some basis."

Here is what I told my nephew. I sincerely tried to be patient and to appeal to his common sense. "The basis in fact is this: It is true that the earth's surface has been many times stripped during the long existence of the human race. There is only one reasonably theory of life on this planet. Originally man—or rather his evolutionary predecessor—possessed within himself a digestive apparatus much wider in scope than at present. He consumed the rock, converted it into food, and thence into the elements necessary to feed his tissues, all within his own body. Eventually, as he developed intelligence, man learned how to produce plastoscene by mechanical means. He consumed this product as food, as well as using it for the myriad other purposes of his daily life. As a result, the organs within his own body no longer were needed to produce plastoscene directly from the rock. They gradually atrophied and disappeared, leaving only their vestiges in the present digestive tract."

This silenced the young man for a time, but I have no doubt he will return later with some other fantastic delusion. On one occasion it was the legend that, instead of being twin planets, our earth and Luna were at one time of differing sizes, and that Luna revolved around the earth as some of the distant moons revolve around their primaries. This theory has been thoroughly discredited. It is true that there is a reduction of the earth's mass every time we scrape its surface to produce according to our needs; but it is incredible that the earth could ever have been several times the size of its companion planet, as these imaginative theorists would have us believe. They forget, no doubt, that the volume and mass of a large sphere is greater, in proportion to its area and consequent human population, than that of a smaller sphere. Our planet even now would supply man for an incomprehensible time, yet it represents but a tiny fraction of such a mass as these theorists would have us believe in. They forget that diminution would proceed at an ever-mounting rate as the size decreased; that such a huge sphere as they proposed would have lasted forever.

It is impossible. As impossible as to imagine that a time will come when there will be no more Earth for man's conversion—

Requiem

ROBERT A. HEINLEIN

Robert A. Heinlein received more nominations for this anthology than any other author, a fact that does not surprise anybody. So many Heinlein stories were listed that picking one becomes a very individual business. My own favorite Heinlein short story is "They," but "They," like most of Mr. Heinlein's work, is readily available elsewhere, as the Honor Roll will tell you. I finally picked, in order to duck out of as many fights as possible, the single Heinlein story which received the most votes. This is it.

Mr. Heinlein was once called by Alfred Bester "the Kipling of science fiction." This seems to me one of the most accurate statements made recently about any writer in or out of sf. I cannot think of anything to add to it, except my own admiration for the man who has, in great part, spent the last twenty-seven years in showing the rest of us what science fiction can be.

On a high hill in Samoa there is a grave. Inscribed on the marker are these words:

> Under the wide and starry sky
> Dig my grave and let me lie.
> Glad did I live and gladly die
> And I lay me down with a will!
>
> This be the verse which you grave for me:
> Here he lies where he longed to be,
> Home is the sailor, home from the sea,
> And the hunter home from the hill.

These lines appear another place—scrawled on a shipping tag

torn from a compressed-air container and pinned to the ground with a knife.

It wasn't much of a fair, as fairs go. The trottin' races didn't promise much excitement, even though several entries claimed the blood of the immortal Dan Patch. The tents and concession booths barely covered the circus grounds, and the pitchmen seemed discouraged.

D. D. Harriman's chauffeur could not see any reason for stopping. They were due in Kansas City for a directors' meeting. That is to say, Harriman was. The chauffeur had private reasons for promptness, reasons involving darktown society on Eighteenth Street. But the Boss not only stopped but hung around.

Bunting and a canvas arch made the entrance to a large enclosure beyond the race track. Red and gold letters announced:

This way to the
MOON ROCKET!!!!
See it in actual flight!
Public Demonstration Flights
Twice Daily
This is the ACTUAL TYPE used by the
First Man to Reach the MOON!!!
YOU can ride it!!—$50.00

A boy nine or ten years old hung around the entrance and stared at the posters.

"Want to see the ship, son?"

The kid's eyes shone. "Gee, mister, I sure would."

"So would I. Come on." Harriman paid out fifty dollars for two pink tickets which entitled them to enter the enclosure and examine the rocket ship. The kid took his and ran on ahead with the single-mindedness of youth. Harriman looked over the stubby curved lines of the ovoid body. He noted with a professional eye that she was a single-jet type with fractional controls around her midriff. He squinted through his glasses at the name painted in gold on the carnival red of the body. *Carefree*. He paid another quarter to enter the control cabin. When his eyes had adjusted to the gloom caused by the strong ray filters of the ports, he let them rest lovingly on the keys of the console and the semicircle of dials above. Each beloved gadget was in its proper place. He knew them—graven in his heart.

While he mused over the instrument board, with the warm liquid of content soaking through his body, the pilot entered and touched his arm.

"Sorry, sir. We've got to cast loose for the flight."

"Eh?" Harriman started, then looked at the speaker. Handsome devil, with a good skull and strong shoulders—reckless eyes and a self-indulgent mouth, but a firm chin. "Oh, excuse me, Captain."

"Quite all right."

"Oh, I say, Captain, er uh—"

"McIntyre."

"Captain McIntyre, could you take a passenger this trip?" The old man leaned eagerly toward him.

"Why, yes, if you wish. Come along with me." He ushered Harriman into a shed marked "Office" which stood near the gate. "Passenger for a checkover, Doc."

Harriman looked startled, but permitted the medico to run a stethoscope over his thin chest and strap a rubber bandage around his arm. Presently he unstrapped it, glanced at McIntyre, and shook his head.

"No go, Doc?"

"That's right, Captain."

Harriman looked from face to face. "My heart's all right—that's just a flutter."

The physician's brows shot up. "It is? But it's not just your heart; at your age your bones are brittle, too brittle to risk a take-off."

"Sorry, sir," added the pilot "but the Bates County Fair Association pays the doctor here to see to it that I don't take anyone up who might be hurt by the acceleration."

The old man's shoulders drooped miserably. "I rather expected it."

"Sorry, sir." McIntyre turned to go, but Harriman followed him out.

"Excuse me, Captain—"

"Yes?"

"Could you and your, uh, engineer have dinner with me after your flight?"

The pilot looked at him quizzically. "I don't see why not. Thanks."

"Captain McIntyre, it is difficult for me to see why anyone would quit the earth-moon run." Fried chicken and hot biscuits in a private dining room of the best hotel the little town of Butler afforded, three-star Hennessey and Corona-Coronas had produced a friendly atmosphere in which three men could talk freely.

"Well, I didn't like it."

"Aw, don't give him that, Mac—you know it was Rule G that got you." McIntyre's mechanic poured himself another brandy as he spoke.

McIntyre looked sullen. "Well, what if I did take a couple o' drinks? Anyhow, I could have squared that—it was the dern persnickety regulations that got me fed up. Who are you to talk? Smuggler!"

"Sure I smuggled! Who wouldn't with all those beautiful rocks just aching to be taken back to Earth? I had a diamond once as big as— But if I hadn't been caught I'd be in Luna City tonight. And so would you, you drunken blaster—with the boys buying us drinks, and the girls smiling . . ." He put his face down and began to weep quietly.

McIntyre shook him. "He's drunk."

"Never mind." Harriman interposed a hand. "Tell me, are you really satisfied not to be on the run any more?"

McIntyre chewed his lip. "No—he's right, of course. This barn-storming isn't what it's all cracked up to be. We've been hopping junk at every pumpkin doin's up and down the Mississippi Valley—sleeping in tourist camps and eating at greaseburners. Half the time the sheriff has an attachment on the ship, the other half the Society for the Prevention of Something or Other gets an injunction to keep us on the ground. It's no sort of a life for a rocket man."

"Would it help any for you to get to the moon?"

"Well . . . yes. I couldn't get back on the earth-moon run, but if I was in Luna City I could get a job hopping ore for the company—they're always short of rocket pilots for that, and they wouldn't mind my record. If I kept my nose clean, they might even put me back on the run, in time."

Harriman fiddled with a spoon, then looked up. "Would you young gentlemen be open to a business proposition?"

"Perhaps. What is it?"

"You own the *Carefree?*"

"Yeah. That is, Charlie and I do—barring a couple of liens against her. What about it?"

"I want to charter her . . . for you and Charlie to take me to the moon!"

Charlie sat up with a jerk. "D'joo hear what he said, Mac? He wants us to fly that old heap to the Moon!"

McIntyre shook his head. "Can't do it, Mr. Harriman. The old boat's worn out. You couldn't convert to escape fuel. We don't even use standard juice in her—just gasoline and liquid air. Charlie spends all of his time tinkering with her at that. She's going to blow up someday."

"Say, Mr. Harriman," put in Charlie, "what's the matter with getting an excursion permit and going in a company ship?"

"No, son," the old man replied, "I can't do that. You know the conditions under which the U.N. granted the company a monopoly on lunar exploitation—no one to enter space who was not physically qualified to stand up under it. Company to take full responsibility for the safety and health of all citizens beyond the stratosphere. The official reason for granting the franchise was to avoid unnecessary loss of life during the first few years of space travel."

"And you can't pass the physical exam?"

Harriman shook his head.

"Well—if you can afford to hire us, why don't you just bribe yourself a brace of company docs? It's been done before."

Harriman smiled ruefully. "I know it has, Charlie, but it won't work for me. You see, I'm a little too prominent. My full name is Delos D. Harriman."

"What? *You* are old D. D.? But you own a big slice of the company yourself—you practically *are* the company; you ought to be able to do anything you like, rules or no rules."

"That is a not unusual opinion, son, but it is incorrect. Rich men aren't more free than other men; they are less free, a good deal less free. I tried to do what you suggest, but the other directors would not permit me. They are afraid of losing their franchise. It costs them a good deal in—uh—political-contact expenses to retain it, as it is."

"Well, I'll be a— Can you tie that, Mac? A guy with lots of dough, and he can't spend it the way he wants to."

McIntyre did not answer, but waited for Harriman to continue.

"Captain McIntyre, if you had a ship, would you take me?"

McIntyre rubbed his chin. "It's against the law."

"I'd make it worth your while."

"Sure he would, Mr. Harriman. Of course you would, Mac. Luna City! Oh, baby!"

"Why do you want to go to the moon so badly, Mr. Harriman?"

"Captain, it's the one thing I've really wanted to do all my life—ever since I was a young boy. I don't know whether I can explain it to you or not. You young fellows have grown up to rocket travel the way I grew up to aviation. I'm a great deal older than you are, at least fifty years older. When I was a kid practically nobody believed that men would ever reach the moon. You've seen rockets all your lives, and the first to reach the moon got there before you were a young boy. When I was a boy they laughed at the idea. But I believed—I believed. I read Verne, and Wells, and Smith, and I believed that we could do it—that we *would* do it. I set my heart on being one of the men to walk on the surface of the moon, to see her other side, and to look back on the face of the earth hanging in the sky. I used to go without my lunches to pay my dues in the American Rocket Society, because I wanted to believe that I was helping to bring the day nearer when we would reach the moon. I was already an old man when that day arrived. I've lived longer than I should, but I would not let myself die . . . I will not!—until I have set foot on the moon."

McIntyre stood up and put out his hand. "You find a ship, Mr. Harriman. I'll drive 'er."

"Atta' boy, Mac! I told you he would, Mr. Harriman."

Harriman mused and dozed during the half-hour run to the north into Kansas City, dozed in the light troubled sleep of old age. Incidents out of a long life ran through his mind in vagrant dreams. There was that time . . . oh, yes, 1910 . . . A little boy on a warm spring night: "What's that, Daddy?" "That's Halley's comet, Sonny." "Where did it come from?" "I don't know, son. From way out in the sky somewhere." "It's *beyooootiful,* Daddy. I want to touch it." " 'Fraid not, Son."

"Delos, do you mean to stand there and tell me you put the money we have saved for the house into that crazy rocket company?" "Now, Charlotte, please! It's not crazy; it's a sound business investment. Someday soon rockets will find the sky. Ships and trains will be obsolete. Look what happened to the men that had the foresight to invest in Henry Ford." "We've been all over this before." "Charlotte, the day will come when men will rise up off the earth and visit the moon, even the planets. This is the beginning." "Must you shout?" "I'm sorry, but—" "I feel a headache coming on. Please try to be a little quiet when you come to bed."

He hadn't gone to bed. He had sat out on the veranda all night long, watching the full moon move across the sky. There would be the devil to pay in the morning, the devil and a thin-lipped silence. But he'd stick by his guns. He'd given in on most things, but not on this. But the night was his. Tonight he'd be alone with his old friend. He searched her face. Where was Mare Crisium? Funny, he couldn't make it out. He used to be able to see it plainly when he was a boy. Probably needed new glasses—this constant office work wasn't good for his eyes.

But he didn't need to see, he knew where they all were: Crisium, Mare Fecunditatis, Mare Tranquilitatis—that one had a satisfying roll!—the Apennines, the Carpathians, old Tycho with its mysterious rays. Two hundred and forty thousand miles—ten times around the earth. Surely men could bridge a little gap like that. Why, he could almost reach out and touch it, nodding there behind the elm trees.

Not that he could help. He hadn't the education.

"Son, I want to have a little serious talk with you." "Yes, Mother." "I know you had hoped to go to college next year" (Hoped! He had lived for it. The University of Chicago to study under Moulton, then on to the Yerkes Observatory to work under the eye of Dr. Frost himself), "and I had hoped so, too. But with your father gone and the girls growing up, it's harder to make ends meet. You've been a good boy, and worked hard to help out. I know you'll understand." "Yes, Mother."

"Extra! Extra! Stratosphere Rocket Reaches Paris! Read aaaaa-lllll about 't." The thin little man in the bifocals snatched at the paper and hurried back to the office. "Look at

this, George." "Huh? Hmm, interesting, but what of it?"
"Can't you see? The next stage is to the moon!" "God, but
you're a sucker, Delos. The trouble with you is you read too
many of those trashy magazines. Now, I caught my boy reading one of 'em just last week, *Stunning Stories* or some such
title, and dressed him down proper. Your folks should have
done you the same favor."—Harriman squared his narrow
middle-aged shoulders. "They will so reach the moon!"—His
partner laughed. "Have it your own way. If baby wants the
moon, Papa bring it for him. But you stick to your discounts
and commissions; that's where the money is."

The big car droned down the Paseo and turned off on
Armour Boulevard. Old Harriman stirred uneasily in his sleep
and muttered to himself.

"But, Mr. Harriman—" The young man with the notebook
was plainly perturbed.

The old man grunted. "You heard me. Sell 'em. I want
every share I own realized in cash as rapidly as possible.
Spaceways, Spaceways Provisioning Company, Artemis Mines,
Luna City Recreations—the whole lot of them."

"It will depress the market. You won't realize the full value
of your holdings."

"Don't you think I know that? I can afford it."

"What about the shares you had earmarked for Richardson
Observatory and for the Harriman Scholarships?"

"Oh, yes. Don't sell those. Set up a trust. Should have done
it long ago. Tell young Kamens to draw up the papers. He
knows what I want."

The interoffice visor flashed into life. "The gentlemen are
here, Mr. Harriman."

"Send 'em in. That's all Ashley. Get busy."

Ashley went out as McIntyre and Charlie entered. Harriman got up and trotted forward to greet them.

"Come in, boys, come in. I'm so glad to see you. Sit down.
Sit down. Have a cigar."

"Mighty pleased to see you, Mr. Harriman," acknowledged
Charlie. "In fact, you might say we need to see you."

"Some trouble, gentlemen?" Harriman glanced from face to
face.

McIntyre answered him. "You still mean that about a job
for us, Mr. Harriman?"

"Mean it? Certainly I do. You're not backing out on me?"

"Not at all. We need that job now. You see, the *Carefree* is lying in the middle of the Osage River with her jet split clear back to the injector."

"Dear me! You weren't hurt?"

"No, aside from sprains and bruises. We jumped."

Charlie chortled. "I caught a catfish with my bare teeth."

In short order they got down to business. "You two will have to buy a ship for me. I can't do it openly; my colleagues would figure out what I mean to do and stop me. I'll supply you with all the cash you need. You go out and locate some sort of a ship that can be refitted for the trip. Work up some good story about how you are buying it for some playboy as a stratosphere yacht, or that you plan to establish an Arctic-Antarctic tourist route. Anything as long as no one suspects that she is being outfitted for space flight. Then, after the Department of Transport licenses her for strato flight, you move out to a piece of desert out West—I'll find a likely parcel of land and buy it—and then I'll join you. Then we'll install the escape-fuel tanks, change the injectors and timers and so forth, to fit her for the hop. How about it?"

McIntyre looked dubious. "It'll take a lot of doing, Charlie. Do you think you can accomplish that change-over without a dockyard and shops?"

"Me? Sure I can—with your thick-fingered help. Just give me the tools and materials I want, and don't hurry me too much. Of course, it won't be fancy—"

"Nobody wants it to be fancy. I just want a ship that won't blow when I start slapping the keys. Isotope fuel is no joke."

'It won't blow, Mac."

"That's what you thought about the *Carefree*."

"That ain't fair, Mac. I ask you, Mr. Harriman—that heap was junk, and we knew it. This'll be different. We're going to spend some dough and do it right. Ain't we, Mr. Harriman?"

Harriman patted him on the shoulder. "Certainly we are, Charlie. You can have all the money you want. That's the least of our worries. Now, do the salaries and bonuses I mentioned suit you? I don't want you to be short."

". . . As you know, my clients are his nearest relatives and have his interests at heart. We contend that Mr. Harriman's conduct for the past several weeks, as shown by the evidence here adduced, gives clear indication that a mind once brilliant in the world of finance has become senile. It is therefore with the deepest regret that we pray this honorable court, if it pleases, to declare Mr. Harriman incompetent and to assign a conservator to protect his financial interests and those of his future heirs and assigns." The attorney sat down, pleased with himself.

Mr. Kamens took the floor. "May it please the court, if my esteemed friend is *quite* through, may I suggest that in his last few words he gave away his entire thesis: 'financial interests of future heirs and assigns.' It is evident that the petitioners believe that my client should conduct his affairs in such a fashion as to insure that his nieces and nephews, and their issue, will be supported in unearned luxury for the rest of their lives. My client's wife has passed on, he has no children. It is admitted that he has provided generously for his sisters and their children in times past, and that he has established annuities for such near kin as are without means of support. But now, like vultures—worse than vultures, for they are not content to let him die in peace—they would prevent my client from enjoying his wealth in whatever manner best suits him for the few remaining years of his life. It is true that he has sold his holdings; is it strange that an elderly man should wish to retire? It is true that he suffered some paper losses in liquidation. 'The value of a thing is what that thing will bring.' He was retiring and demanded cash. Is there anything strange about that? It is admitted that he refused to discuss his actions with his so-loving kinfolk. What law or principle requires a man to consult with his nephews on anything? Therefore we pray that this court will confirm my client in his right to do what he likes with his own, deny this petition, and send these meddlers about their business."

The judge took off his spectacles and polished them thoughtfully. "Mr. Kamens, this court has as high a regard for individual liberty as you have, and you may rest assured that any action taken will be solely in the interests of your client. Nevertheless, men do grow old, men do become senile, and in such cases must be protected. I shall take this matter under advisement until tomorrow. Court it adjourned."

From the *Kansas City Star:*

ECCENTRIC MILLIONAIRE DISAPPEARS

. . . failed to appear for the adjourned hearing. The bailiffs returned from a search of places usually frequented by Harriman with the report that he had not been seen since the previous day. A bench warrant under contempt proceedings has been issued and . . .

A desert sunset is a better stimulant for the appetite than a hot dance orchestra. Charlie testified to this by polishing the last of the ham gravy with a piece of bread. Harriman handed each of the younger men cigars and took one himself.

"My doctor claims that these weeds are bad for my heart condition," he remarked as he lighted it, "but I've felt so much better since I joined you boys here on the ranch that I am inclined to doubt him." He exhaled a cloud of blue-gray smoke and resumed. "I don't think a man's health depends so much on what he does as on whether he wants to do it. I'm doing what I want to do."

"That's all a man can ask of life," agreed McIntyre.

"How does the work look now, boys?"

"My end's in pretty good shape," Charlie answered. "We finished the second pressure tests on the new tanks and the fuel lines today. The ground tests are all done, except the calibration runs. Those won't take long—just the four hours to make the runs if I don't run into some bugs. How about you, Mac?"

McIntyre ticked them off on his fingers. "Food supplies and water on board. Three vacuum suits, a spare, and service kits. Medical supplies. The buggy already had all the standard equipment for strato flight. The late lunar ephemerides haven't arrived yet."

"When do you expect them?"

"Any time—they should be here now. Not that it matters. This guff about how hard it is to navigate from here to the moon is hokum to impress the public. After all, you can *see* your destination—it's not like ocean navigation. Gimme a sextant and a good radar and I'll set you down anyplace on the moon you like, without cracking an almanac or a star table, just from a general knowledge of the relative speeds involved."

"Never mind the personal buildup, Columbus," Charlie told him. "We'll admit you can hit the floor with your hat. The general idea is, you're ready to go now. Is that right?"

"That's it."

"That being the case, I *could* run those tests tonight. I'm getting jumpy—things have been going too smoothly. If you'll give me a hand, we ought to be in bed by midnight."

"O.K., when I finish this cigar."

They smoked in silence for a while, each thinking about the coming trip and what it meant to him. Old Harriman tried to repress the excitement that possessed him at the prospect of immediate realization of his lifelong dream.

"Mr. Harriman—"

"Eh? What is it, Charlie?"

"How does a guy go about getting rich, like you did?"

"Getting rich? I can't say; I never tried to get rich. I never wanted to be rich, or well known, or anything like that."

"Huh?"

"No, I just wanted to live a long time and see it all happen. I wasn't unusual; there were lots of boys like me—radio hams, they were, and telescope builders, and airplane amateurs. We had science clubs, and basement laboratories, and science-fiction leagues—the kind of boys who thought there was more romance in one issue of the *Electrical Experimenter* than in all the books Dumas ever wrote. We didn't want to be one of Horatio Alger's get-rich heroes either, we wanted to build spaceships. Well, some of us did."

"Jeez, Pop, you make it sound exciting."

"It was exciting, Charlie. This has been a wonderful, romantic century, for all of its bad points. And it's grown more wonderful and more exciting every year. No, I didn't want to be rich; I just wanted to live long enough to see men rise up to the stars, and, if God was good to me, to go as far as the moon myself." He carefully deposited an inch of white ash in a saucer. "It has been a good life. I haven't any complaints."

McIntyre pushed back his chair. "Come on, Charlie, if you're ready."

"O.K."

They all got up. Harriman started to speak, then grabbed at his chest, his face a dead gray-white.

"Catch him, Mac!"

"Where's his medicine?"

"In his vest pocket."

They eased him over to a couch, broke a small glass capsule into a handkerchief, and held it under his nose. The volatile released by the capsule seemed to bring a little color into his face. They did what little they could for him, then waited for him to regain consciousness.

Charlie broke the uneasy silence. "Mac, we ain't going through with this."

"Why not?"

"It's murder. He'll never stand up under the initial acceleration."

"Maybe not, but it's what he wants to do. You heard him."

"But we oughtn't to let him."

"Why not? It's neither your business nor the business of this blasted paternalistic government to tell a man not to risk his life doing what he really wants to do."

"All the same, I don't feel right about it. He's such a swell old duck."

"Then what d'yuh want to do with him—send him back to Kansas City so those old harpies can shut him up in a laughing academy till he dies of a broken heart?"

"N-no-o-o—not that."

"Get out there and make your setup for those test runs. I'll be along."

A wide-tired desert runabout rolled in the ranch-yard gate the next morning and stopped in front of the house. A heavy-set man with a firm but kindly face climbed out and spoke to McIntyre, who approached to meet him.

"You James McIntyre?"

"What about it?"

"I'm the deputy federal marshal hereabouts. I got a warrant for your arrest."

"What's the charge?"

"Conspiracy to violate the Space Precautionary Act."

Charlie joined the pair. "What's up, Mac?"

The deputy answered. "You'd be Charles Cummings, I guess. Warrant here for you. Got one for a man named Harriman, too, and a court order to put seals on your spaceship."

"We've no spaceship."

"What d'yuh keep in that shed?"

"Strato yacht."

"So? Well, I'll put seals on her until a spaceship comes along. Where's Harriman?"

"Right in there." Charlie obliged by pointing, ignoring McIntyre's scowl.

The deputy turned his head. Charlie couldn't have missed the button by a fraction of an inch, for the deputy collapsed quietly to the ground.

Charlie stood over him, rubbing his knuckles and mourning. "That's the finger I broke playing shortstop. I'm always hurting that finger."

"Get Pop into the cabin," Mac cut him short, "and strap him into his hammock."

"Aye aye, Skipper."

They dragged the ship by tractor out of the hanger, turned, and went out on the desert plain to find elbow room for the take-off. They climbed in. McIntyre saw the deputy from his starboard conning port. He was staring disconsolately after them.

McIntyre fastened his safety belt, settled his corset, and spoke into the engine-room speaking tube. "All set, Charlie?"

"All set, Skipper. But you can't raise ship yet, Mac—*she ain't named!*"

"No time for your superstitions!"

Harriman's thin voice reached them. "Call her the *Lunatic*. It's the only appropriate name!"

McIntyre settled his head into the pads, punched two keys, then three more in rapid succession, and the *Lunatic* raised ground.

"How are you, Pop?" Charlie searched the old man's face anxiously.

Harriman licked his lips and managed to speak. "Doing fine, son. Couldn't be better."

"The acceleration is over; it won't be so bad from here on. I'll unstrap you so you can wiggle around a little. But I think you'd better stay in the hammock." He tugged at buckles.

Harriman partially repressed a groan.

"What is it, Pop?"

"Nothing. Nothing at all. Just go easy on that side."

Charlie ran his fingers over the old man's side with the

125

sure, delicate touch of a mechanic. "You ain't foolin' me none, Pop. But there isn't much I can do until we ground."

"Charlie—"

"Yes, Pop?"

"Can't I move to a port? I want to watch the earth."

"Ain't nothin' to see yet; the ship hides it. As soon as we turn ship, I'll move you. Tell you what: I'll give you a sleepy pill, and then wake you when we do."

"No!"

"Huh?"

"I'll stay awake."

"Just as you say, Pop."

Charlie clambered monkey fashion to the nose of the ship and anchored to the gimbals of the pilot's chair.

McIntyre questioned him with his eyes.

"Yeah, he's alive all right," Charlie told him, "but he's in bad shape."

"How bad?"

"Couple of cracked ribs, anyhow. I don't know what else. I don't know whether he'll last out the trip, Mac. His heart was pounding something awful."

"He'll last, Charlie. He's tough."

"Tough? He's delicate as a canary."

"I don't mean that. He's tough way down inside—where it counts."

"Just the same, you'd better set her down awful easy if you want to ground with a full complement aboard."

"I will. I'll make one full swing around the moon and ease her in on an involute approach curve. We've got enough fuel, I think."

They were now in a free orbit; after McIntyre turned ship, Charlie went back, unslung the hammock, and moved Harriman, hammock and all, to a side port. McIntyre steadied the ship about a transverse axis so that the tail pointed toward the sun, then gave a short blast on two tangential jets opposed in couple to cause the ship to spin slowly about her longitudinal axis, and thereby create a slight artificial gravity. The initial weightlessness when coasting commenced had knotted the old man with the characteristic nausea of free flight, and the pilot wished to save his passenger as much discomfort as possible.

But Harriman was not concerned with the condition of his stomach.

There it was, all as he had imagined it so many times. The moon swung majestically past the view port, wider than he had ever seen it before, all of her familiar features cameo clear. She gave way to the earth as the ship continued its slow swing, the earth itself as he had envisioned her, appearing like a noble moon, many times as wide as the moon appears to the earthbound, and more luscious, more sensuously beautiful than the silver moon could be. It was sunset near the Atlantic seaboard—the line of shadow cut down the coast line of North America, clashed through Cuba, and obscured all but the west coast of South America. He savored the mellow blue of the Pacific Ocean, felt the texture of the soft green and brown of the continents, admired the blue-white cold of the polar caps. Canada and the northern states were obscured by cloud, a vast low-pressure area that spread across the continent. It shone with an even more satisfactory dazzling white than the polar caps.

As the ship swung slowly around, Earth would pass from view, and the stars would march across the port—the same stars he had always known, but steady, brighter, and unwinking against a screen of perfect, live black. Then the moon would swim into view again to claim his thoughts.

He was serenely happy in a fashion not given to most men, even in a long life time. He felt as if he were every man who has ever lived, looked up at the stars, and longed.

As the long hours came and went he watched and dozed and dreamed. At least once he must have fallen into deep sleep, or possibly delirium, for he came to with a start, thinking that his wife, Charlotte, was calling to him. "Delos!" the voice had said "Delos! Come in from there! You'll catch your death of cold in that night air."

Poor Charlotte! She had been a good wife to him, a good wife. He was quite sure that her only regret in dying had been her fear that he could not take proper care of himself. It had not been her fault that she had not shared his dream and his need.

Charlie rigged the hammock in such a fashion that Harriman could watch from the starboard port when they swung around the far face of the moon. He picked out the landmarks made familiar to him by a thousand phtographs with nostalgic pleasure, as if he were returning to his own country. McIntyre brought her slowly down as they came back around to the earthward face, and prepared to land east of Mare Fecunditatis, about ten miles from Luna City.

It was not a bad landing, all things considered. He had to land without coaching from the grounds, and he had no second pilot to watch the radar for him. In his anxiety to make it gentle he missed his destination by some thirty miles, but he did his cold-sober best. But at that it was bumpy.

As they grounded and the pumice dust settle around them, Charlie came up to the control station.

"How's our passenger?" Mac demanded.

"I'll see, but I wouldn't make any bets. That landing stunk, Mac."

"Damn it, I did my best."

"I know you did, Skipper. Forget it."

But the passenger was alive and conscious, although bleeding from the nose and with a pink foam on his lips. He was feebly trying to get himself out of his cocoon. They helped him, working together.

"Where are the vacuum suits?" was his first remark.

"Steady, Mr. Harriman. You can't go out there yet. We've got to give you some first aid."

"Get me that suit! First aid can wait."

Silently they did as he ordered. His left leg was practically useless, and they had to help him through the lock, one on each side. But, with his inconsiderable mass having a lunar weight of only twenty pounds, he was no burden. They found a place some fifty yards from the ship where they could prop him up and let him look, a chunk of scoria supporting his head.

McIntyre put his helmet against the old man's and spoke. "We'll leave you here to enjoy the view while we get ready for the trek into town. It's a forty-miler, pretty near, and we'll have to break out spare air bottles and rations and stuff. We'll be back soon."

Harriman nodded without answering and squeezed their gauntlets with a grip that was surprisingly strong.

He sat very quietly, rubbing his hands against the soil of the moon and sensing the curiously light pressure of his body against the ground. At long last there was peace in his heart. His hurts had ceased to pain him. He *was* where he had longed to be—he had followed his need. Over the western horizon hung the earth at last quarter, a green-blue giant moon. Overhead the sun shone down from a black and starry sky. And underneath the moon the soil of the moon itself. He was on the moon!

He lay back, still, while a bath of content flowed over him like a tide at flood and soaked to his very marrow.

His attention strayed momentarily, and he thought once again that his name was called. Silly, he thought, I'm getting old—my mind wanders.

Back in the cabin Charlie and Mac were rigging shoulder yokes on a stretcher. "There. That will do," Mac commented. "We'd better stir Pop out; we ought to be going."

"I'll get him," Charlie replied. "I'll just pick him up and carry him. He don't weigh nothing."

Charlie was gone longer than McIntyre had expected him to be. He returned alone. Mac waited for him to close the lock and swing back his helmet. "Trouble?"

"Never mind the stretcher, Skipper. We won't be needin' it."

"Yeah, I mean it," he continued. "Pop's done for. I did what was necessary."

McIntyre bent down without a word and picked up the wide skis necessary to negotiate the powdery ash. Charlie followed his example. Then they swung the spare air bottles over their shoulders and passed out through the lock.

They didn't bother to close the outer door of the lock behind them.

Theory of Rocketry

C. M. KORNBLUTH

The peculiar reality of Cyril Kornbluth's sf led one editor to comment that Mr. Kornbluth was writing stories aimed at The Saturday Evening Post *of the year 2100. I don't think he has ever done better than in this bitter, precise and perfectly real picture of a future very near and quite entirely possible.*

Mr. Edel taught six English classes that year at Richard M. Nixon High School, and the classes averaged seventy-five pupils each. That was four hundred and fifty boys and girls, but Mr. Edel still tried to have the names down cold by at least the third week of the semester. As English 308 stormed into his room he was aware that he was not succeeding, and that next year he would even stop trying, for in 1978 the classes would average eighty-two pupils instead of seventy-five.

One seat was empty when the chime sounded; Mr. Edel was pleased to notice that he remembered whose it was. The absent pupil was a Miss Kahn, keyed into his memory by "Kahnstipated," which perhaps she was, with her small pinched features centered in a tallow acre of face. Miss Kahn slipped in some three seconds late; Edel nodded at his intern, Mrs. Giovino, and Mrs. Giovino coursed down the aisle to question, berate and possibly demerit Miss Kahn. Edel stood up, the Modern Revised Old Testament already open before him.

"You're blessed," he read, "*if you're excused for your wrong-doing and your sin is forgiven. You're blessed if God knows that you're not evil and sly any more. I, King David, used to hide my sins from God while I grew old and blustered proudly all day. But all day and all night too your hand was heavy on me, God . . .*"

It would be the flat, crystal-clear, crystal-blank M.R.O.T. all this week; next week he'd read (with more pleasure) from the Roman Catholic Knox translation; the week after that, from the American Rabbinical Council's crabbed version heavy with footnotes; and the week after that, back to M.R.O.T. Thrice blessed was he this semester that there were no Moslems, Buddhists, militant atheists or miscellaneous cultists to sit and glower through the reading or exercise their legal right to wait it out in the corridor. This semester the classes were All-American: Protestant, Catholic, Jewish—choice of one.

"Amen," chorused the class, and they sat down; two minutes of his fifty-minute hour were gone forever.

Soft spring was outside the windows, and they were restless. Mr. Edel "projected" a little as he told them, "This is the dreaded three-minute impromptu speech for which English Three Oh Eight is notorious, young ladies and gentlemen. The importance of being able to speak clearly on short notice should be obvious to everybody. You'll get nowhere in your military service if you can't give instructions and verbal orders. You'll get less than nowhere in business if you can't convey your ideas crisply and accurately." A happy thought struck him: great chance to implement the Spiritual-Values Directive. He added, "You may be asked to lead in prayer or say grace on short notice." (He's add *that* one to his permanent repertoire; it was a natural.) "We are not asking the impossible. Anybody can talk interestingly, easily and naturally for three minutes if they try. Miss Gerber, will you begin with a little talk on your career plans?"

Miss Gerber ("Grapefruit" was the mnemonic) rose coolly and driveled about the joys of motherhood until Mrs. Giovino passed her card to Edel and called time.

"You spoke freely, Miss Gerber, but perhaps not enough to the point," said Edel. "I'm pleased, though, that you weren't bothered by any foolish shyness. I'm sure everybody I call on will be able to talk right up like you did." (He liked that *"like"* the way you like biting on a tooth that aches; *he'd* give them Artificial-Grammar De-emphasis . . .) "Foster, may we hear from you on the subject of your coming summer vacation?" He jotted down a C for the Grapefruit.

Foster ("Fireball") rose and paused an expert moment. Then in a firm and manly voice he started with a little joke

("If I survive English Three Oh Eight . . ."), stated his theme ("A vacation is not a time for idling and wasted opportunity"), developed it ("harvest crew during the day for *physical*—my Science Search Project during the evenings for *mental*"), elevated it ("no excuse for neglecting one's regular attendance at one's place of worship") and concluded with a little joke ("should be darned glad to get back to school!").

The speech clocked 2:59. It was masterly; none of the other impromptus heard that morning came close to it.

"And," said Mr. Edel at lunch to his semi-crony Dr. Fuqua, biology, "between classes I riffled through the grade cards again and found I'd marked him F. Of course I changed it to A. The question is, *why?*"

"Because you'd made a mistake," said Fuqua absently. Something was on his mind, thought Edel.

"No, no. Why did I make the mistake?"

"Well, Fured, in *The Psychology of Everyday*—"

"Roland, please, I know all that. Assume I do. Why do I unconsciously dislike Foster? I should get down on my knees and thank God for Foster."

Fugua shook his head and began to pay attention. "Foster?" he said. "You don't know the half of it. I'm his faculty adviser. Quite a boy, Foster."

"To me just a name, a face, a good recitation every time. You know: seventy-five to a class. What's he up to here at dear old Tricky Dicky?"

"Watch the funny jokes, Edel," said Fuqua, alarmed.

"Sorry. It slipped out. But Foster?"

"Well, he's taking an inhuman pre-engineering schedule. Carrying it with ease. Going out for all the extracurricular stuff the law allows. R.O.T.C. Drill Team, Boxing Squad, Math Club, and there I had to draw the line. He wanted on the Debating Team too. I've seen him upset just once. He came to me last year when the school dentist wanted to pull a bad wisdom tooth he had. He made me make the dentist wait until he had a chance to check the dental requirements of the Air Force Academy. They allow four extractions, so he let the dentist yank it. Fly boy. Off we go into the whatsit. He wants it bad."

"I see. Just a boy with motivation. How long since you've seen one, Roland?"

Dr. Fuqua leaned forward, his voice low and urgent. "To

hell with Foster, Dave. I'm in trouble. Will you help me?"

"Why, of course, Roland. How much do you need?" Mr. Edel was a bachelor and had found one of the minor joys of that state to be "tiding over" his familied friends.

"Not that kind of trouble, Dave. Not yet. They're sharpening the ax for me. I get a hearing this afternoon."

"Good God! What are you supposed to have done?"

"Everything. Nothing. It's one of those 'best interests' things. Am I taking the Spiritual-Values Directive *seriously* enough? Am I *thinking* about patting any adolescent fannies? Exactly *why* am I in the lowest quarter for my seniority group with respect to voluntary hours of refresher summer courses? Am I *happy* here?"

Edel said, "These things always start somewhere. Who's out to get you?"

Fuqua took a deep breath and said in a surprisingly small voice, "Me, I suppose."

"Oh?"

Then it came out with a rush. "It was the semester psychometrics. I'd been up all night almost, fighting with Beth. She does *not* understand how to handle a fifteen-year-old boy— never mind. I felt sardonic, so I did something sardonic. And stupid. Don't ever get to feeling sardonic, Dave. I took the psychometric and I checked their little boxes and I told the goddamned truth right down the line. I checked them where I felt like checking them and not where a prudent biology teacher *ought* to check them."

"You're dead," Mr. Edel said after a pause.

"I thought I could get a bunch of the teachers to say they lie their way through the psychometrics. Start a real stink."

"I'd make a poor ditch digger, Roland, but—if you can get nine others, I'll speak up. No, make that six others. I don't think they could ignore eight of us."

"You're a good man," Dr. Fuqua said. "I'll let you know. There's old McGivern—near retirement. I want to try him." He gulped his coffee and headed across the cafeteria.

Edel sat there, mildly thunderstruck at Fuqua's folly and his own daring. Fuqua had told them the kind of bird he was by checking "Yes" or "No" on the silly-clever statements. He had told them that he liked a drink, that he thought most people were stupider than he, that he talked without thinking first, that he ate too much, that he was lazy, that he had an eye for a pretty ankle—that he was a human being not much better or worse than any other human being. But that wasn't the way to do it, and damned well Fuqua had known it. You simply told yourself firmly, for the duration of the test, "*I am a yuk. I have never had an independent thought in my life; independent thinking scares me. I am utterly monogamous and heterosexual. I go bowling with the boys. Television is the greatest of the art forms. I believe in installment purchasing. I am a yuk.*"

That these parlor games were taken seriously by some people was an inexplicable but inexorable fact of life in the twentieth century. Edel had yukked his way through scholarships, college admissions, faculty appointment and promotions and had never thought the examination worse than a bad cold. Before maturity set in, in the frat house, they had eased his qualms about psychometric testing with the ancient gag "You ain't a man until you've had it three times."

Brave of him, pretty brave at that, to back up Fuqua—if Roland could find six others.

Roland came to him at four o'clock to say he had not even found one other. "I don't suppose— No. I'm not asking you to, Dave. Two—it wouldn't be any good."

He went into the principal's office.

The next day a bright young substitute was teaching biology in his place and his student advisees had been parceled out among other teachers. Mr. Edel found that young Foster had now become his charge.

The seventy-two pupils in his English 114 class sat fascinated and watched the television screen. Dr. Henley Ragen was teaching them *Macbeth,* was teaching about nine hundred English 114 classes throughout the state *Macbeth,* and making them like it. The classroom rapport was thick enough to cut and spread with a shingle. The man's good, Edel thought, but *that* good? How much is feedback from their knowing he's famous for his rapport, how much is awe of his stupendous salary, still nowhere equal to nine hundred teachers' salaries?

Dr. Henley Ragen, *el magnifico,* portentously turned a page; there was grim poetry in the gesture. He transfixed the classroom (nine hundred classrooms) with Those Eyes.

Abruptly he became Macbeth at the Banquet prepar'd. With nervous hilarity he shouted at his guests, *"You know your own degrees; sit down! At first and last, the hearty welcome!"* Stockstill at a lectern he darted around the table, bluffly rallying the company, slipped off to chat, grimly merry, with the First Murtherer at the door, returned to the banquet, stood in chilled horror at the Ghost in the chair, croaked, *"The table's full."*

Mr. Edel studied the faces of his seventy-two English 114ers. They were in hypnotic states of varying depths, except Foster. The Fireball was listening and learning, his good mind giving as well as taking. The intelligent face was alive, the jaw firm, and around him eyes were dull and jaws went slack. Foster could speak and write an English sentence, which perhaps was the great distinguishing mark between him and the rest of English 114. Blurted fragments of thought came from them, and the thoughts were clichés a hundred times out of a hundred.

Dr. Henley Ragen growled at them, *"We are yet but young in deed . . ."* and his eyes said the rest, promising horrors to come. He snapped the book shut like a pistol's bang; the 114ers popped out of their trances into dazed attentiveness. "Notebooks!" said Ragen (*qua* Ragen) and, seventy-two gunfighters quick on the draw, they snapped out books and poised their pens. Ragen spoke for ten minutes about the scene; every so often Those Eyes and an intensification of That Voice cued them to write a word or a phrase, almost without glancing at the paper. (Later each would look at his notes and not be surprised to find them lucid, orderly, even masterful summations of the brief lecture.)

As Dr. Henley Ragen bluffly delivered a sort of benediction from the altar of leaning, Mr. Edel thought, Well, they've got the Banquet Scene now; they'll own it forever. The way they own the Prologue to *The Canterbury Tales,* the "Ode to the West Wind," *Arrowsmith.* A good deal better than nothing; *pauca sed matura.* Or so he supposed.

That afternoon from three to five Mr. Edel was available to his advisees. It was a period usually devoted to catching up on his paperwork; beyond making out the students' assignment schedule, a task traditionally considered beyond the capacity of the young, he had done no advising in years. And Foster appeared.

His handshake was manly, his grin was modest but com-

135

pelling. He got to the point. "Mr. Edell, do you think I could swing an Enrichment Project in English?"

The teacher hardly knew what he meant. "Enrichment? Well, we haven't been doing that lately, Foster. I suppose it's still in the optional curriculum—"

"Yes, sir, Form Sixty-eight, English, Paragraph Forty-five, Section Seven. *'Opportunities shall be afforded to students believed qualified by advisers to undertake projects equivalent to College Freshman English term papers, and the grades therefor shall be entered on the students' records and weighed as evidence in assigning students' positions in the graduating class.'*"

Mr. Edel had found Foster's card by then and was studying it. The boy's schedule was brutal, but his grade average was somewhere between B-plus and A. "Foster," he told him, "there's such a thing as a breaking point. I—I understand you want very much to go to Colorado Springs." (Poor Fuqua! What had become of . . . ?)

"Very much, sir. They expect the best—they have a right to expect the best. I'm not complaining, Mr. Edel, but there are girls with straight-A averages who aren't working as hard as I am. Well, I've just got to beat them at their own game."

Mr. Edel understood. It wasn't just girls, though mostly it was. There was a type of student who was no trouble, who did the work, every smidgen of it, who read every word of every assigned page, who turned in accurate, curiously dead, echoless, unresonant papers which you could not in decency fault though you wanted to tear them up and throw them in their authors' bland faces. You had a curious certainty that the adeptly memorized data they reeled back on demand vanished forever once the need for a grade was gone, that it never by any chance became bone of their bone to strengthen them against future trials. Often enough when you asked them what they hoped to be they similingly said, "I am going to teach."

Foster, now. A boy who *fought* with the material and whipped it. He said, "Why so strong, Foster? What's it about?"

The boy said, "Space, partly. And my father. Two big challenges, Mr. Edel. I think I'm a very lucky fellow. Here I am with a new frontier opening up, but there are lot's of fellows my age who don't see it. I see it because of my father. It's wonderful to have a challenge like that: Can I be the man he is? Can I learn even more, be a better leader, a better engineer?"

Mr. Edel was moved deeply. "Your father just missed space flight, is that it?"

"By a whisker," Foster said regretfully. "Nothing can be done about it except what I'm doing."

"He's an aeroengineer?"

"He can do *anything*," Foster said positively. "And he has!"

A picture of the elder Foster was forming in Mr. Edel's mind—young Fireball grown taller, solider and grizzled, the jaw firmed and controlled, the voice more powerful and sure. And, unquestionably, leather puttees.

Foster's card said he had no mother, which made it more understandable. This fine boy was hard material honed to an edge, single-purposed. Did he have a young Hap Arnold here in his office? A Curtis LeMay? They had to come from somewhere, those driving, wide-ranging leaders and directors of millions. The slow-rolling conquest of space needed such men, first to navigate and pilot so no navigator or pilot would ever be able to snow them, then to move up step by step through research to command, then to great command.

"I'll bet on you, Foster," he said abruptly. "We can't let the—the future *English* teachers outpoint you with their snap courses. You'll do me a term paper on . . . on *Henry V*. First, read it. Read *hell* out of it and take notes. Get in touch with me when you think you're ready to talk it over. I happen to be a bachelor; I have time in the evenings. And talk it over with your father, if you can persuade him to read along with you."

Foster laughed. "I'm afraid Dad's much too busy for Shakespeare, but I'll try. Thanks, Mr. Edel." He left.

Mr. Edel, with considerable trouble, found a pad of forms in his desk which covered Enrichment Projects, English, Adviser's Permission for. He filled one out for Foster, looked it over and said, surprised, "Again, damn it!" He had checked the box for "Permission denied." He tore up the form—it was discolored anyway from being so long on the top of the pad—and meticulously made out another, checking the various boxes with exquisite care.

That night after dinner he tried to telephone Roland Fuqua, but service to his number had been discontinued.

Alarmed, he buzzed over on his scooter to Fuqua's apartment, one of a quarter million in the Dearborn Village Development of Metropolitan Life and Medical. Roland's hulking, spoiled and sullen boy Edward (who had unilaterally changed his name last year to Rocky) was the only person there, and he was on his way out—"to an orgy with some pigs," if you believed him. He said "Little Rollo" was now a night-shift lab assistant in a pet-food company's quality-control department and this was his mother's Bingo night. "You want I should give a message?" he asked satirically, overplaying the role of intolerable burdened youth.

"If it won't break your back," Mr. Edel said, "please ask your father to give me a ring sometime."

Again in his own small apartment, Mr. Edel thought of many things. Of the ancient papyrus which, when decoded, moaned: *"Children are not now as respectful and diligent as they were in the old days."* Of *Henry V*. Of Dr. Fuqua drudging away on pet-food protein determinations and lucky to be doing that. Of his own selfish, miserable, lonely comfort in his castle. Of Foster, the hero-king to be, and of himself, Aristotle to the young Alexander. Had there been a dozen such in his twenty years? There had not. Marie Perrone still sent him her novels, and they were almost popular and very bad. Jim Folwell had gone to Princeton and into the foreign service and that was that. Janice Reeves and Ward Dreiman were married and both teaching at Cornell. What had happened to the hundred thousand others he had taught only God and themselves knew. If they all dropped dead at this instant, tomorrow morning some trucks would not roll for an hour or two, some advertising agencies would come near to missing a few deadlines, some milk would sour and some housewives would bang, perplexed, on the doors of shops that should be open, a few sales would languish unclosed, a few machines would growl for lack of oil. But Foster might land on the moons of Jupiter.

Therefore let him learn, make him learn, how to be great. He would meet his Pistols, Bardolphs, Fluellens, a few Exeters, and without doubt his Cambridges and Scroops: clowns, fussbudgets, friends and traitors. It could matter to nobody except herself if her agent ripped poor arty Marie Perrone up her back; it might matter a great deal to—he shied at the alternatives—to, let us say, man, if Foster trusted a Pistol to do his work, or passed over a Fluellen for his mannerisms, or failed to know a Scroop when he saw one.

We will arm the young hero-king, he thought comfortably just before sleep claimed him.

Rolan Fuqua had been transferred to Toledo by the pet-food company. He wrote to Edel:

Instinct tells me not to queer my luck by talking about it, but anyway—I really believe I'm moving up in the organization. The other day a party from Sales came through the QC labs and one of them, just an ordinary-looking Joe, stopped to talk to me about the test I was running—asked very intelligent questions. You could have knocked me over with a Folin-Wu pipette when they told me who he was afterward: just John McVey himself, Assistant Vice-President in Charge of Sales! Unaccustomed as I am to pipe dreams, it can't be a coincidence that it was me he talked to instead of half a dozen other lab men with seniority; I don't know what he has in mind exactly, maybe some kind of liaison job between QC and Sales, which would put me on Staff level instead of Hourly-Rated. . . .

Mr. Edel felt sick for him. He would have to answer the letter at once; if he put it off he would put it off again and their correspondence would peter out and Fuqua would be betrayed. But what could he tell him—that he *was* pipe-dreaming, that "coincidences" like that happen to everybody a hundred times a day, that Rolan Fuqua, Ph.D., would never, at forty-five, move from the quality-control lab to the glittering world of sales?

He stalled for time by stamping and addressing the envelope first, then hung over the typewriter for five minutes of misery. It was Wednesday night; Foster was due for the twelfth and last of his Enrichment sessions. Mr. Edel tried not to cause Fuqua pain by dwelling on the world of teaching he had lost—but *what* else was there to write about?

I'm sure you remember Foster—the fly boy? I've been taking him, on one of those Enrichment things, through Henry

V. This is supposed to win him .001 of a place higher on the graduating-class list and get him into the Academy, and I suppose it will. Things are very simple for Foster, enviably so. He has a titan of engineering for a father who appears to commute between the Minas Gerais power station in Brazil, his consulting service in the city and trouble spots in the I. T. and T. network—maybe I should say commutate. I honestly do not believe that Foster has to lie his way through the personality profiles like the rest of us mortals—

Now, there was a hell of a thing to put down. He was going to rip the page out and start again, then angrily changed his mind. Fuqua wasn't a cripple; it wasn't Bad Form to mention his folly; it would be merely stupid to pretend that nothing had happened. He finished out the page with a gush of trivia. Sexy little Mrs. Dickman who taught Spanish was very visibly expecting. New dietician in the cafeteria, food cheaper but worse than ever. Rumored retirement of Old Man Thelusson again and one step up for history teachers if true. Best wishes good luck regards to Beth and the youngster, Dave. He whipped the page into folds, slipped it into the envelope and sealed the flap fast, before he could change his mind again. It was time to stop treating Fuqua like a basket case; if convalescence had not begun by now it never would.

His bell rang: Foster was on time, to the minute.

They shook hands rather formally. "Like a cup of coffee, Foster?" Mr. Edel asked.

"No thank you, sir."

"I'll make one for myself, then. Brought your paper? Good. Read it to me."

While he compounded coffee Foster began to read. After much discussion they had settled on "Propaganda and Reality in *Henry V*" as his topic. The boy had read Holinshed where relevant, articles in *The Dictionary of National Biography* and appropriate history texts. Beyond suggesting these, Mr. Edel had left him alone in the actual treatment of his paper. He did not quite know what to expect from Foster beyond careful organization and an absence of gross blunders; he waited with interest.

The paper was a short one—fifteen hundred words, by request. Nevertheless it gave Mr. Edel a few painful shocks.

There were two sneers at "deluded groundlings," much reveling in the irony of the fictional Henry's affection for his Welsh captain as against the real Henry who had helped to crush Glendower and extinguish the Welsh as a nation, and fun with the Irishman Macmorris who came loyally from Shakespeare's pen in 1599 while "the general of our gracious empress" was doing his best to extinguish the Irish as a nation. Henry's *we have now no thoughts in us but France (save those to God)* was evaluated as "the poet's afterthought." The massacre of the French prisoners at Agincourt, Henry's brutal practical joke with the pretended glove of a French nobleman, his impossibly compressed and eloquent courtship of Katharine, were all somehow made to testify to a cynical Shakespeare manipulating his audience's passions.

The great shock was that Foster approved of all this. *"It was a time of troubles and England was besieged from without and threatened from within. The need of the time was a call to unity, and this Shakespeare provided in good measure. The London mob and the brotherhood of apprentices, always a potential danger to the Peace, no doubt were inspired and pacified for a time by the Shakespearean version of a successful aggressor's early career."*

Modestly Foster folded his typescript.

It was ground into Mr. Edel that you start by saying whatever words of praise are possible and then go on to criticize. Mechanically he said warm things about the paper's organization, its style, its scholarly apparatus. "But—aren't you taking a rather too utilitarian view of the play? It is propaganda to some extent, but should you stop short with the propaganda function of the play? I'm aware that you're limited by your topic and length, but I wish there had been some recognition of the play's existence as a work of art."

Foster said, smiling, "Well, I'm new at this, Mr. Edel. I didn't know I was supposed to stray. Should I revise it?"

"Oh, no," Mr. Edel said quickly. "I didn't mean to imply that you're unarguably mistaken in anything you said. I don't know why I'm fussing at you about it at all. I suppose you've taken a sort of engineering approach to literature, which is natural enough. Did you ever succeed in engaging your father in the project?"

"I'm afraid not, Mr. Edel. You can imagine."

"He's been away?"

"Why, no." Foster was surprised. But *didn't* his father go away now and then? He thought Foster had said—or *almost* said—

He took the paper from him and leafed through it. "This is quite good enough for a pass, Foster. It'll be read by somebody in the English chairman's office, but that's a formality. Let's say you've completed your Enrichment Option." He stuck out his hand and Foster took it warmly. "That, then, is that. Do you have to run now?"

"With all rods out," Foster said. "I've got to prepare for the Math Team meet, a hundred things. Can I mail that for you?"

It was the letter to Fuqua on his desk. "Why, thanks."

"Thank *you,* Mr. Edel, for the time you've taken with me."

Well worth it, son, Mr. Edel thought after the door closed. There aren't many like you. The paper was a little cold and cynical, but you'll learn. Criticism's heady stuff. Speaking quite objectively, you've done a piece thoroughly consistent with College Freshman English work, and that's what you were supposed to do. If it helps get you into Colorado Springs, I've done my job.

He turned in the paper the next day to the English chairman's office and the assistant chairman read it while he waited, mumbled "Seems quite competent" and entered a "Completed" on Foster's grade card. He let his eyes run over the other grades and whistled. "A beaver," he said.

"All rods out," Mr. Edel smugly corrected him, and went to the door. A freshman girl who knew him, on messenger duty with the principal's office, intercepted him in the corridor. The message: he would please report at once to the principal; Mrs. Giovino would be advised to take such classes as he might be obliged to miss.

"*Classes?*" he asked the girl, unbelievingly.

She knew nothing.

The assistant principal for teaching personnel received him at once, alone in his two-window office. He was a gray man named Sturgis whose pride was getting to the point. "Edel," he asked, "are you sure you're *happy* here?"

Mr. Edel said, recognizing a sheet of typing on Sturgis' desk, "May I ask how you got that letter of mine?"

"Surely. Your young friend Foster turned it in."

"But why? Why?"

"I shall quote: *'I honestly do not believe that Foster has to lie his way through the personality profiles like the rest of us mortals.'* If you believed this, Edel, why did you counsel him to lie? Why did you show him this letter as proof that you lied yourself?"

"Counsel him to lie? I never. I never."

His stammering was guilt; his sweating was guilt. Sturgis pitied him and shook his head. "He kept a little record," Sturgis said. "Ha, a 'log' he called it—he's quite space-minded; did you know?"

"I know. I demand a hearing, goddammit!"

Sturgis was surprised. "Oh, you'll get a hearing, Edel. We always give hearings; you know that."

"I know that. Can I get back to my classes now?"

"Better not. If you're not *happy* here . . ."

Mr. Edel and Foster met that afternoon in the soda shop two blocks from the school. Mr. Edel had been waiting for him, and Foster saw the teacher staring at him from a booth. He excused himself politely from the Math Team crowd around him and joined Mr. Edel.

"I feel I owe you an explanation, sir," Foster said.

"I agree. How could you—why—?"

Foster said apologetically, "They like you to be a little ruthless at the Academy. This will stand out on my record as a sign of moral fiber. No, Mr. Edel, don't try to hit me. I'll make things look that much worse at the hearing. Goodbye, sir."

He rejoined his handsome, quiet crowd at the counter; in a moment they were talking busily about elliptic functions and Fourier series. Mr. Edel slunk from the place knowing that there was only one court of appeal.

3379 Seneca Avenue turned out to be a shocking slum tenement back of a municipal bus garage. The apartment, Mr. Edel thought, after his initial surprise, would be one of those "hideaways"—probably a whole floor run together, equipped with its own heating and air-conditioning, plumbing replaced . . . after all, would Foster Senior give a damn about a fancy address? Not that engineer.

But the Foster apartment, or so said a card tacked to a rust-stiffened bed-pull, was only one of a dozen like it on the cabbage-reeking fifth floor. And the paunchy, unshaven, undershirted man who came to the door and stood reeling in the doorway said: "Yah, I'm Ole Foster. Yah, I got a boy in Nixon High. What the crazy kid do now? He's crazy, that kid. Maybe I get a little drunk sometime, I got a little pension from I hurt my back driving the buses, people don't appreciate, don't realize. You wanna drink? What you say you come for?"

"About your son . . ."

"So I beat him up!" the man yelled, suddenly belligerent. "Ain't I his father? He talks smart to me, I got a right to beat him some, ain't I? People don't appreciate . . ."

Old Foster lost interest and, mumbling, closed the door.

Mr. Edel walked slowly down the stairs, not able to forgive, but feeling at least the beginnings of eventual ease from the knowledge of why he was being destroyed.

Don't Look Now

HENRY KUTTNER

Henry Kuttner could do anything. Anyhow, he could write any sort of story, from sober and thoughtful examinations like "Private Eye" to wildly funny stories like "Mimsy Were the Borogoves," to mention only two of the yarns nominated for this anthology. "Don't Look Now" stands somewhere in the middle—a fine, horrifying notion carried off with great good humor. This, a difficult trick for anybody, was a specialty of Mr. Kuttner's, and it results in a tone he made peculiarly his own.

The man in the brown suit was looking at himself in the mirror behind the bar. The reflection seemed to interest him even more deeply than the drink between his hands. He was paying only perfunctory attention to Lyman's attempts at conversation. This had been going on for perhaps fifteen minutes before he finally lifted his glass and took a deep swallow.

"Don't look now," Lyman said.

The brown man slid his eyes sidewise toward Lyman, tilted his glass higher, and took another swig. Ice cubes slipped down toward his mouth. He put the glass back on the red-brown wood and signaled for a refill. Finally he took a deep breath and looked at Lyman.

"Don't look at what?" he asked.

"There was one sitting right beside you," Lyman said, blinking rather glazed eyes. "He just went out. You mean you couldn't see him?"

The brown man finished paying for his fresh drink before he answered. "See who?" he asked, with a fine mixture of boredom, distaste and reluctant interest. "Who went out?"

"What have I been telling you for the last ten minutes? Weren't you listening?"

145

"Certainly I was listening. That is—certainly. You were talking about—bathtubs. Radios. Orson—"

"Not Orson. H. G. Herbert George. With Orson it was just a gag. H. G. *knew*—or suspected. I wonder if it was simply intuition with him? He couldn't have had any proof—but he did stop writing science fiction rather suddenly, didn't he? I'll bet he knew once, though."

"Knew what?"

"About the Martians. All this won't do us a bit of good if you don't listen. It may not anyway. The trick is to jump the gun—with proof. Convincing evidence. Nobody's ever been allowed to produce the evidence before. You *are* a reporter, aren't you?"

Holding his glass, the man in the brown suit nodded reluctantly.

"Then you ought to be taking it all down on a piece of folded paper. I want everybody to know. The whole world. It's important. Terribly important. It explains everything. My life won't be safe unless I can pass along the information and make people believe it."

"Why won't your life be safe?"

"Because of the Martians, you fool. They own the world."

The brown man sighed. "Then they own my newspaper too," he objected, "so I can't print anything they don't like."

"I never thought of that," Lyman said, considering the bottom of his glass, where two ice cubes had fused into a cold, immutable union. "They're not omnipotent, though. I'm sure they're vulnerable, or why have they always kept under cover? They're afraid of being found out. If the world had convincing evidence—Look, people always believe what they read in the newspapers. Couldn't you—"

"Ha," said the brown man with deep significance.

Lyman drummed sadly on the bar and murmured, "There must be some way. Perhaps it I had another drink . . ."

The brown-suited man tasted his Collins, which seemed to stimulate him. "Just what is all this about Martians?" he asked Lyman. "Suppose you start at the beginning and tell me again. Or can't you remember?"

"Of course I can remember. I've got practically total recall. It's something new. Very new. I never could do it before. I can even remember my last conversation with the Martians." Lyman favored the brown man with a glance of triumph.

"When was that?"

"This morning."

"I can even remember conversations I had last week," the brown man said mildly. "So what?"

"You don't understand. They make us forget, you see. They tell us what to do and we forget about the conversation—it's post-hypnotic suggestion, I expect—but we follow their orders just the same. There's the compulsion, though we think we're making our own decisions. Oh, they own the world, all right, but nobody knows it except me."

"And how did you find out?"

"Well, I got my brain scrambled, in a way. I've been fooling around with supersonic detergents, trying to work out something marketable, you know. The gadget went wrong—from some standpoints. High-frequency waves, it was. They went through and through me. Should have been inaudible, but I could hear them, or rather—well, actually I could *see* them. That's what I mean about my brain being scrambled. And after that, I could see and hear the Martians. They've geared themselves so they work efficiently on ordinary brains, and mine isn't ordinary any more. They can't hypnotize me, either. They can command me, but I needn't obey—now. I hope they don't suspect. Maybe they do. Yes, I guess they do."

"How can you tell?"

"The way they look at me."

"How do they look at you?" asked the brown man, as he began to reach for a pencil and then changed his mind. He took a drink instead. "Well? What are they like?"

"I'm not sure. I can see them, all right, but only when they're dressed up."

"Okay, okay," the brown man said patiently. "How do they look, dressed up?"

"Just like anybody, almost. They dress up in—in human skins. Oh, not real ones—imitations. Like the Katzenjammer Kids zipped into crocodile suits. Undressed, I don't know. I've never seen one. Maybe they're invisible even to me then, or maybe they're just camouflaged. Ants or owls or rats or bats or—"

"Or anything," the brown man said hastily.

"Thanks. Or anything, of course. But when they're dressed

147

up like humans—like that one who was sitting next to you a while ago, when I told you not to look—"

"That one was invisible, I gather?"

"Most of the time they are, to everybody. But once in a while, for some reason, they—"

"Wait," the brown man objected. "Make sense, will you? They dress up in human skins and then sit around invisible?"

"Only now and then. The human skins are perfectly good imitations. Nobody can tell the difference. It's that third eye that gives them away. When they keep it closed, you'd never guess it was there. When they want to open it, they go invisible—like *that*. Fast. When I see somebody with a third eye, right in the middle of his forehead, I know he's a Martian and invisible, and I pretend not to notice him."

"Uh-huh," the brown man said. "Then for all you know I'm one of your visible Martians."

"Oh, I hope not!" Lyman regarded him anxiously. "Drunk as I am, I don't think so, I've been trailing you all day, making sure. It's a risk I have to take, of course. They'll go to any length—any length at all—to make a man give himself away. I realize that. I can't really trust anybody. But I had to find *someone* to talk to, and I—" He paused. There was a brief silence. "I could be wrong," Lyman said presently. "When the third eye's closed, I can't tell if it's there. Would you mind opening your third eye for me?" He fixed a dim gaze on the brown man's forehead.

"Sorry," the reporter said. "Some other time. Besides, I don't know you. So you want me to splash this across the front page, I gather? Why don't you go to see the managing editor? My stories have to get past the desk and rewrite."

"I want to give my secret to the world," Lyman said stubbornly. "The question is, how far will I get? You'd expect they'd have killed me the minute I opened my mouth to you—except that I didn't say anything while they were here. I don't believe they take us very seriously, you know. This must have been going on since the dawn of history, and by now they've had time to get careless. They let Fort go pretty far before they cracked down on him. But you noticed they were careful never to let Fort get hold of genuine proof that would convince people."

The brown man said something under his breath about a

human-interest story in a box. He asked, "What do the Martians do besides hang around bars all dressed up?"

"I'm still working on that," Lyman said. "It isn't easy to understand. They run the world, of course, but why?" He wrinkled his brow and stared appealingly at the brown man. "Why?"

"If they do run it, they've got a lot to explain."

"That's what I mean. From our viewpoint, there's no sense to it. We do things illogically, but only because they tell us to. Everything we do, almost, is pure illogic. Poe's "Imp of the Perverse"—you could give it another name beginning with M. Martian, I mean. It's all very well for psychologists to explain why a murderer wants to confess, but it's still an illogical reaction. Unless a Martian commands him to."

"You can't be hypnotized into doing anything that violates your moral sense," the brown man said triumphantly.

Lyman frowned. "Not by another human, but you can by a Martian. I expect they got the upper hand when we didn't have more than ape-brains, and they've kept it ever since. They evolved as we did, and kept a step ahead. Like the sparrow on the eagle's back who hitchhiked till the eagle reached his ceiling, and then took off and broke the altitude record. They conquered the world, but nobody ever knew it. And they've been ruling ever since."

"But—"

"Take houses, for example. Uncomfortable things. Ugly, inconvenient, dirty, everything wrong with them. But when men like Frank Lloyd Wright slip out from under the Martians' thumb long enough to suggest something better, look how the people react. They hate the thought. That's their Martians, giving them orders."

"Look. Why should the Martians care what kind of houses we live in? Tell me that."

Lyman frowned. "I don't like the note of skepticism I detect creeping into this conversation," he announced. "They care, all right. No doubt about it. They *live* in our houses. We don't build for our convenience, we build, under order, for the Martians, the way they want it. They're very much concerned with everything we do. And the more senseless, the more concern. Take wars. Wars don't make sense from any human viewpoint. Nobody really wants wars. But we go right on having them. From the Martian viewpoint, they're useful.

149

They give us a spurt in technology, and they reduce the excess population. And there are lots of other results, too. Colonization, for one thing. But mainly technology. In peacetime, if a guy invents jet propulsion it's too expensive to develop commercially. In wartime, though, it's *got* to be developed. Then the Martians can use it whenever they want. They use us the way they'd use tools or—or limbs. And nobody ever really wins a war—except the Martians."

The man in the brown suit chuckled. "That makes sense," he said. "It must be nice to be a Martian."

"Why not? Up till now, no race ever successfully conquered and ruled another. The underdog could revolt or absorb. If you know you're being ruled, then the ruler's vulnerable. But if the world doesn't know—and it doesn't . . ."

"Take radios," Lyman continued, going off at a tangent. "There's no earthly reason why a sane human should listen to a radio. But the Martians make us do it. They like it. Take bathtubs. Nobody contends bathtubs are comfortable—for us. But they're fine for Martians. All the impractical things we keep on using, even though we know they're impractical—"

"Typewriter ribbons," the brown man said, struck by the thought. "But not even a Martian could enjoy changing a typewriter ribbon."

Lyman seemed to find that flippant. He said that he knew all about the Martians except for one thing—their psychology.

"I don't know *why* they act as they do. It looks illogical sometimes, but I feel perfectly sure they've got sound motives for every move they make. Until I get that worked out I'm pretty much at a standstill. Until I get evidence—proof—and help. I've got to stay under cover till then. And I've been doing that. I do what they tell me, so they won't suspect, and I pretend to forget what they tell me to forget."

"Then you've got nothing much to worry about."

Lyman paid no attention. He was off again on a list of his grievances.

"When I hear the water running in the tub and a Martian splashing around, I pretend I don't hear a thing. My bed's too short and I tried last week to order a special length, but the Martian that sleeps there told me not to. He's a runt, like most of them. That is, I think they're runts. I have to deduce, because you never see them undressed. But it goes on like that constantly. By the way, how's your Martian?"

The man in the brown suit set down his glass rather suddenly.

"My Martian?"

"Now, listen. I may be just a little bit drunk, but my logic remains unimpaired. I can still put two and two together. Either you know about the Martians or you don't. If you do, there's no point in giving me that 'What, *my* Martian?' routine. I know you have a Martian. Your Martian knows you have a Martian. My Martian knows. The point is, do *you* know? Think hard," Lyman urged solicitously.

"No, I haven't got a Martian," the reporter said, taking a quick drink. The edge of the glass clicked against his teeth.

"Nervous, I see," Lyman remarked. "Of course you *have* got a Martian. I suspect you know it."

"What would I be doing with a Martian?" the brown man asked with dogged dogmatism.

"What would you be doing without one? I imagine it's illegal. If they caught you running around without one they'd probably put you in a pound or something until claimed. Oh, you've got one, all right. So have I. So has he, and he, and he—and the bartender." Lyman enumerated the other barflies with a wavering forefinger.

"Of course they have," the brown man said. "But they'll all go back to Mars tomorrow and then you can see a good doctor. You'd better have another dri—"

He was turning toward the bartender when Lyman, apparently by accident, leaned close to him and whispered urgently, *"Don't look now!"*

The brown man glanced at Lyman's white face reflected in the mirror before them.

"It's all right," he said. "There aren't any Mar—"

Lyman gave him a fierce, quick kick under the edge of the bar. "Shut up! One just came in!"

And then he caught the brown man's gaze and with elaborate unconcern said, "—so naturally, there was nothing for me to do but climb out on the roof after it. Took me ten minutes to get it down the ladder, and just as we reached the bottom it gave one bound, climbed up my face, sprang from the top of my head, and there it was again on the roof, screaming for me to get it down."

"What?" the brown man demanded with pardonable curiosity.

"My cat, of course. What did you think? No, never mind, don't answer that." Lyman's face was turned to the brown man's, but from the corners of his eyes he was watching an invisible progress down the length of the bar toward a booth at the very back.

"Now, why did he come in?" he murmured. "I don't like this. Is he anyone you know?"

"Is who—?"

"That Martian. Yours, by any chance? No, I suppose not. Yours was probably the one who went out a while ago. I wonder if he went to make a report and sent this one in? It's possible. It could be. You can talk now, but keep your voice low, and stop squirming. Want him to notice we can see him?"

"I can't see him. Don't drag me into this. You and your Martians can fight it out together. You're making me nervous. I've got to go, anyway." But he didn't move to get off the stool. Across Lyman's shoulder he was stealing glances toward the back of the bar, and now and then he looked at Lyman's face.

"Stop watching me," Lyman said. "Stop watching him. Anybody'd think you were a cat."

"Why a cat? Why should anybody—Do I look like a cat?"

"We were talking about cats, weren't we? Cats can see them, quite clearly. Even undressed, I believe. They don't like them."

"Who doesn't like who?"

"Whom. Neither likes the other. Cats can see Martians—sh-h!—but they pretend not to, and that makes the Martians mad. I have a theory that cats ruled the world before Martians came. Never mind. Forget about cats. This may be more serious than you think. I happen to know my Martian's taking tonight off, and I'm pretty sure that was your Martian who went out some time ago. And have you noticed that nobody else in here has his Martian with him? Do you suppose—" His voice sank. "Do you suppose they could be *waiting for us outside?*"

"Oh, Lord," the brown man said. "In the alley with the cats, I suppose."

"Why don't you stop this yammer about cats and be serious

for a moment?" Lyman demanded, and then paused, paled, and reeled slightly on his stool. He hastily took a drink to cover his confusion.

"What's the matter now?" the brown man asked.

"Nothing." Gulp. "Nothing. It was just that—he *looked* at me. With—you know."

"Let me get this straight. I take it the Martian is dressed in—is dressed like a human?"

"Naturally."

"But he's invisible to all eyes but yours?"

"Yes. He doesn't want to be visible just now. Besides—" Lyman paused cunningly. He gave the brown man a furtive glance and then looked quickly down at his drink. "Besides, you know, I rather think you *can* see him—a little, anyway."

The brown man was perfectly silent for about thirty seconds. He sat quite motionless, not even the ice in the drink he held clinking. One might have thought he did not even breathe. Certainly he did not blink.

"What makes you think that?" he asked in a normal voice, after the thirty seconds had run out.

"I—did I say anything? I wasn't listening." Lyman put down his drink abruptly. "I think I'll go now."

"No you won't," the brown man said, closing his fingers around Lyman's wrist. "Not yet you won't. Come back here. Sit down. Now. What was the idea? Where were you going?"

Lyman nodded dumbly toward the back of the bar, indicating either a jukebox or a door marked "Men."

"I don't feel so good. Maybe I've had too much to drink. I guess I'll—"

"You're all right. I don't trust you back there with that— that invisible man of yours. You'll stay right here until he leaves."

"He's going now," Lyman said brightly. His eyes moved with great briskness along the line of an invisible but rapid progress toward the front door. "See, he's gone. Now let me loose, will you?"

The brown man glanced toward the back booth.

"No," he said, "he isn't gone. Sit right where you are."

It was Lyman's turn to remain quite still, in a stricken sort of way, for a perceptible while. The ice in *his* drink, however, clinked audibly. Presently he spoke. His voice was soft, and rather soberer than before.

153

"You're right. He's still there. You can see him, can't you?"

The brown man said, "Has he got his back to us?"

"You *can* see him, then. Better than I can, maybe. Maybe there are more of them here than I thought. They could be anywhere. They could be sitting beside you anywhere you go, and you wouldn't even guess, until—" He shook his head a little. "They'd want to be *sure*," he said, mostly to himself. "They can give you orders and make you forget, but there must be limits to what they can force you to do. They can't make a man betray himself. They'd have to lead him on— until they were sure."

He lifted his drink and tipped it steeply above his face. The ice ran down the slope and bumped coldly against his lip, but he held it until the last of the pale, bubbling amber had drained into his mouth. He set the glass on the bar and faced the brown man.

"Well?" he said.

The brown man looked up and down the bar.

"It's getting late," he said. "Not many people left. We'll wait."

"Wait for what?"

The brown man looked toward the back booth and looked away again quickly.

"I have something to show you. I don't want anyone else to see."

Lyman surveyed the narrow, smoky room. As he looked the last customer besides themselves at the bar began groping in his pocket, tossed some change on the mahogany and went out slowly.

They sat in silence. The bartender eyed them with stolid disinterest. Presently a couple in the front booth got up and departed, quarreling in undertones.

"Is there anyone left?" the brown man asked in a voice that did not carry down the bar to the man in the apron.

"Only—" Lyman did not finish, but he nodded gently toward the back of the room. "He isn't looking. Let's get this over with. What do you want to show me?"

The brown man took off his wrist watch and pried up the metal case. Two small glossy photograph prints slid out. The brown man separated them with a finger.

"I just want to make sure of something," he said. "First—

why did you pick me out? Quite a while ago, you said you'd been trailing me all day, making sure. I haven't forgotten that. And you knew I was a reporter. Suppose you tell me the truth now."

Squirming on his stool, Lyman scowled. "It was the way you looked at things," he murmured. "On the subway this morning—I'd never seen you before in my life, but I kept noticing the way you looked at things, the wrong things, things that weren't there, the way a cat does, and then you'd always look away—I got the idea you could see the Martians, too.

"Go on," the brown man said quietly.

"I followed you. All day. I kept hoping you'd turn out to be—somebody I could talk to. Because if I could *know* that I wasn't the only one who could see them, then I'd know there was still some hope left. It's been worse than solitary confinement. I've been able to see them for three years now. Three years. And I've managed to keep my power a secret even from them. And, somehow, I've managed to keep from killing myself, too."

"Three years?" the brown man said. He shivered.

"There was always a little hope. I knew nobody would believe—not without proof. And how can you get proof? It was only that I—I kept telling myself that maybe you could see them, too, and if you could, maybe there were others—lots of others, enough so we might get together and work out some way of proving to the world . . ."

The brown man's fingers were moving. In silence he pushed a photograph across the mahogany. Lyman picked it up unsteadily.

"Moonlight?" he asked after a moment. It was a landscape under a deep, dark sky with white clouds in it. Trees stood white and lacy against the darkness. The grass was white as if with moonlight, and the shadows blurry.

"No, not moonlight," the brown man said. "Infrared. I'm strictly an amateur, but lately I've been experimenting with infrared film. And I got some very odd results."

Lyman stared at the film.

"You see, I live near—" The brown man's finger tapped a certain quite common object that appeared in the photograph. "And something funny keeps showing up now and then against it. But only with infrared film. Now, I know chlorophyll reflects so much infrared light that grass and leaves

155

photograph white. The sky comes out black, like this. There are tricks to using this kind of film. Photograph a tree against a cloud, and you can't tell them apart in the print. But you can photograph through a haze and pick out distant objects the ordinary film wouldn't catch. And sometimes, when you focus on something like this"—he tapped the image of the very common object again—"you get a very odd image on the film. Like that. A man with three eyes."

Lyman held the print up to the light. In silence he took the other one from the bar and studied it. When he laid them down he was smiling.

"You know," Lyman said in a conversational whisper, "a professor of astrophysics at one of the more important universities had a very interesting little item in the *Times* the other Sunday. Name of Spitzer, I think. He said that if there were life on Mars, and if Martians had ever visited earth, there'd be no way to prove it. Nobody would believe the few men who saw them. Not, he said, unless the Martians happened to be photographed." Lyman looked at the brown man thoughtfully. "Well," he said, "it's happened. You've photographed them."

The brown man nodded. He took up the prints and returned them to his watch case. "I thought so, too. Only, until tonight I couldn't be sure. I'd never seen one—fully—as you have. It isn't so much a matter of what you call getting your brain scrambled with supersonics as it is of just knowing where to look. But I've been seeing *part* of them all my life, and so has everybody. It's that little suggestion of movement you never catch except just at the edge of your vision, just out of the corner of your eye. Something that's *almost* there —and when you look fully at it, there's nothing. These photographs showed me the way. It's not easy to learn, but it can be done. We're conditioned to look directly at a thing—the particular thing we want to see clearly, whatever it is. Perhaps the Martians gave us that conditioning. When we see a movement at the edge of our range of vision, it's almost irresistible not to look directly at it. So it vanishes."

"Then they can be seen—by anybody?"

"I've learned a lot in a few days," the brown man said. "Since I took those photographs. You have to train yourself. It's like seeing a trick picture—one that's really a composite, after you study it. Camouflage. You just have to learn how.

Otherwise we can look at them all our lives and never see them."

"The camera does, though."

"Yes, the camera does. I've wondered why nobody ever caught them this way before. Once you see them on film, they're unmistakable—that third eye."

"Infrared film's comparatively new, isn't it? And then I'll bet you have to catch them against that one particular background—you know—or they won't show on the film. Like trees against clouds. It's tricky. You must have had just the right lighting that day, and exactly the right focus, and the lens stopped down just right. A kind of minor miracle. It might never happen again exactly that way. But— Don't look now."

They were silent. Furtively, they watched the mirror. Their eyes slid along toward the open door of the tavern.

And then there was a long, breathless silence.

"He looked back at us," Lyman said very quietly. "He looked at us . . . that third eye!"

The brown man was motionless again. When he moved, it was to swallow the rest of his drink.

"I don't think that they're suspicious yet," he said. "The trick will be to keep under cover until we can blow this thing wide open. There's got to be some way to do it—some way that will convince people."

"There's proof. The photographs. A competent cameraman ought to be able to figure out just how you caught that Martian on film and duplicate the conditions. It's evidence."

"Evidence can cut both ways," the brown man said. "What I'm hoping is that the Martians don't really like to kill—unless they have to. I'm hoping they won't kill without proof. But—" He tapped his wrist watch.

"There's two of us now, though," Lyman said. "We've got to stick together. Both of us have broken the big rule, *Don't look now*."

The bartender was at the back, disconnecting the jukebox. The brown man said, "We'd better not be seen together unnecessarily. But if we both come to this bar tomorrow night at nine for a drink—that wouldn't look suspicious, even to them."

"Suppose—" Lyman hesitated. "May I have one of those photographs?"

"Why?"

"If one of us had—an accident, the other one would still have the proof. Enough, maybe, to convince the right people."

The brown man hesitated, nodded shortly, and opened his watch case again. He gave Lyman one of the pictures.

"Hide it," he said. "It's—evidence. I'll see you here tomorrow. Meanwhile, be careful. Remember to play safe."

They shook hands firmly, facing each other in an endless second of final, decisive silence. Then the brown man turned abruptly and walked out of the bar.

Lyman sat there. Between two wrinkles in his forehead there was a stir and a flicker of lashes unfurling. The third eye opened slowly and looked after the brown man.

Seven-Day Terror

R. A. LAFFERTY

R. A. Lafferty is, comparatively, a new writer. Like most recent arrivals, he spends a good deal of his time in taking new, and very fresh, looks at the sort of thing everybody else has been looking at for years. Some of our most cherished traditions have been reduced to a kind of meaningless and farcical Brownian movement under the hands of this peculiar gentleman.

Judy Merril reprinted this one before I could get to it. I salute, as I am sometimes found doing, her taste, and I admire her speed.

"Is there anything you want to make disappear?" Clarence Willoughby asked his mother.

"A sinkful of dishes is all I can think of. How will you do it?"

"I just built a disappearer. All you do is cut the other end out of a beer can. Then you take two pieces of red cardboard with peepholes in the middle and fit them in the ends. You look through the peepholes and blink. Whatever you look at will disappear."

"Oh."

"But I don't know if I can make them come back. We'd better try it on something else. Dishes cost money."

As always, Myra Willoughby had to admire the wisdom of her nine-year-old son. She would not have had such foresight herself. He always did.

"You can try it on Blanche Manners' cat outside there. Nobody will care if it disappears except Blanche Manners."

"All right."

He put the disappearer to his eye and blinked. The cat disappeared from the sidewalk outside.

His mother was interested. "I wonder how it works. Do you know how it works?"

"Yes. You take a beer can with both ends cut out and put in two pieces of cardboard. Then you blink."

"Never mind. Take it outside and play with it. You hadn't better make anything disappear in here till I think about this."

But when he had gone his mother was oddly disturbed.

"I wonder if I have a precocious child. Why, there's lots of grown people who wouldn't know how to make a disappearer that would work. I wonder if Blanche Manners will miss her cat very much?"

Clarence went down to the Plugged Nickel, a pothouse on the corner.

"Do you have anything you want to make disappear, Nokomis?"

"Only my paunch."

"If I make it disappear it'll leave a hole in you and you'll bleed to death."

"That's right, I would. Why don't you try it on the fireplug outside?"

This in a way was one of the happiest afternoons ever in the neighborhood. The children came from blocks around to play in the flooded streets and gutters, and if some of them drowned (and we don't say that they *did* drown) in the flood (and brother! it was a flood), why, you have to expect things like that. The fire engines (who ever heard of calling fire engines to put out a flood?) were apparatus-deep in the water. The policemen and the ambulance men wandered around wet and bewildered.

"Resuscitator, resuscitator, anybody wanna resuscitator?" chanted Clarissa Willoughby.

"Oh, shut up," said the ambulance attendants.

Nokomis, the barman in the Plugged Nickel, called Clarence aside.

"I don't believe, just for the moment, I'd tell anyone what happened to the fireplug," he said.

"I won't tell if you won't tell," said Clarence.

Officer Comstock was suspicious. "There's only seven possible explanations. One of the seven Willoughby kids did it. I dunno how. It'd take a bulldozer to do it, and then there'd be something left of the plug. But however they did it, one of them did it."

Officer Comstock had a talent for getting near the truth of dark matters. This is why he was walking a beat out here in the boondocks instead of sitting in a chair downtown.

"Clarissa!" said Officer Comstock in a voice like thunder.

"Resuscitator, resuscitator, anybody wanna resuscitator?" chanted Clarissa.

"Do you know what happened to that fireplug?" asked Officer C.

"I have an uncanny suspicion. As yet it is no more than that. When I am better informed I will advise you."

Clarissa was eight years old and much given to uncanny suspicions.

"Clementine, Harold, Corinne, Jimmy, Cyril," he asked the five younger Willoughby children, "do you know what happened to that fireplug?"

"There was a man around yesterday. I bet he took it," said Clementine.

"I don't even remember a fireplug there. I think you're making a lot of fuss about nothing," said Harold.

"City Hall's going to hear about this," said Corinne.

"Pretty dommed sure," said Jimmy, "but I won't tell."

"Cyril!" cried Officer Comstock in a terrible voice. Not a terrifying voice, a terrible voice. He felt terrible now.

"Great green bananas," said Cyril, "I'm only three years old. I don't see how it's even my responsibility."

"Clarence," said Officer Comstock.

Clarence gulped.

"Do you know where that fireplug went?"

Clarence brightened. "No, sir. I don't know where it went."

A bunch of smart alecks from the Water Department came out and shut off the water for a few blocks around and put some kind of cap on in place of the fireplug. "This sure is going to be a funny-sounding report," said one of them.

Officer Comstock walked away discouraged. "Don't bother me, Miss Manners," he said. "I don't know where to look for your cat. I don't even know where to look for a fireplug."

"I have an idea," said Clarissa, "that when you find the cat you will find the fireplug the same place. As yet it is only an idea."

Ozzie Murphy wore a little hat on top of his head. Clarence pointed his weapon and winked. The hat was no longed there, but a little trickle of blood was running down the pate.

"I don't believe I'd play with that any more," said Nokomis.

"Who's playing?" said Clarence. "This is for real."

This was the beginning of the seven-day terror in the heretofore obscure neighborhood. Trees disappeared from the parkings; lampposts were as though they had never been; Wally Waldorf drove home, got out, slammed the door of his car, and there was no car. As George Mullendorf came up the walk to his house his dog, Pete, ran to meet him and took a flying leap to his arms. The dog left the sidewalk, but something happened; the dog was gone and only a bark lingered for a moment in the puzzled air.

But the worst were the fireplugs. The second plug was installed the morning after the disappearance of the first. In eight minutes it was gone and the flood waters returned. Another one was in by twelve o'clock. Within three minutes it had vanished. The next morning fireplug number four was installed.

The water commissioner was there, the city engineer was there, the chief of police was there with a riot squad, the president of the Parent-Teachers Association was there, the president of the university was there, the mayor was there, three gentlemen of the F.B.I., a newsreel photographer, eminent scientists and a crowd of honest citizens.

"Let's see it disappear now," said the city engineer.

"Let's see it disappear now," said the police chief.

"Let's see it disa— It did, didn't it?" said one of the eminent scientists.

And it was gone and everybody was very wet.

"At least I have the picture sequence of the year," said the photographer. But his camera and apparatus disappeared from the midst of them.

"Shut off the water and cap it," said the commissioner. "And don't put in another plug yet. That was the last plug in the warehouse."

"This is too big for me," said the mayor. "I wonder that Tass doesn't have it yet."

"Tass has it," said a little round man. "I am Tass."

"If all of you gentlemen will come into the Plugged Nickel," said Nokomis, "and try one of our new Fire Hydrant Highballs you will all be happier. These are made of good corn whiskey, brown sugar and hydrant water from this very gutter. You can be the first to drink them."

Business was phenomenal at the Plugged Nickel, for it was in front of its very doors that the fireplugs disappeared in floods of gushing water.

"I know a way we can get rich," said Clarissa several days later to her father, Tom Willoughby. "Everybody says they're going to sell their houses for nothing and move out of the neighborhood. Go get a lot of money and buy them all. Then you can sell them again and get rich."

"I wouldn't buy them for a dollar each. Three of them have disappeared already, and all the families but us have their furniture moved out in their front yards. There might be nothing but vacant lots in the morning."

"Good, then buy the vacant lots. And you can be ready when the houses come back."

"Come back? Are the houses going to come back? Do you know anything about this, young lady?"

"I have a suspicion verging on a certainty. As of now I can say no more."

Three eminent scientists were gathered in an untidy suite that looked as though it belonged to a drunken sultan.

"This transcends the metaphysical. It impinges on the quantum continuum. In some ways it obsoletes Boff," said Dr. Velikof Vonk.

"The contingence on the intransigence is the most mystifying aspect," said Arpad Arkabaranan.

"Yes," said Willy McGilly. "Who would have thought that you could do it with a beer can and two pieces of cardboard? When I was a boy I used an oatmeal box and red Crayola."

"I do not always follow you," said Dr. Vonk. "I wish you would speak plainer."

So far no human had been injured or disappeared—except for a little blood on the pate of Ozzie Murphy, on the lobes of Conchita when her gaudy earrings disappeared from her very ears, a clipped finger or so when a house vanished as the front doorknob was touched, a lost toe when a neighborhood boy kicked at a can and the can was not; probably not more than a pint of blood and three or four ounces of flesh all together.

Now, however, Mr. Buckle the grocery man disappeared before witnesses. This was serious.

Some mean-looking investigators from downtown came out to the Willoughbys'. The meanest-looking one was the mayor. In happier days he had not been a mean man, but the terror had now reigned for seven days.

"There have been ugly rumors," said one of the mean investigators, "that link certain events to this household. Do any of you know anything about them?"

"I started most of them," said Clarissa. "But I didn't consider them ugly. Cryptic, rather. But if you want to get to the bottom of this just ask me a question."

"Did you make those things disappear?" asked the investigator.

"That isn't the question," said Clarissa.

"Do you know where they have gone?" asked the investigator.

"That isn't the question, either," said Clarissa.

"Can you make them come back?"

"Why, of course I can. Anybody can. Can't you?"

"I cannot. If you can, please do so at once."

"I need some stuff. Get me a gold watch and a hammer. Then go down to the drugstore and get me this list of chemicals. And I need a yard of black velvet and a pound of rock candy."

"Shall we?" asked one of the investigators.

"Yes," said the mayor. "It's our only hope. Get her anything she wants."

And it was all assembled.

"Why does she get all the attention?" asked Clarence. "I was the one that made all the things disappear. How does she know how to get them back?"

"I knew it!" cried Clarissa with hate. "I knew he was the one that did it. He read in my diary how to make a disappearer. If I was his mother, I'd whip him for reading his little sister's diary. That's what happens when things like that fall into irresponsible hands."

She poised the hammer over the gold watch of the mayor on the floor.

"I have to wait a few seconds. This can't be hurried. It'll be only a little while."

The second hand swept around to the point that was preordained for it before the world began. Clarissa suddenly brought down the hammer with all her force on the beautiful gold watch.

"That's all," she said. "Your troubles are over. See, there is Blanche Manners' cat on the sidewalk just where she was seven days ago."

And the cat was back.

"Now let's go down to the Plugged Nickel and watch the fireplug come back."

They had only a few minutes to wait. It came from nowhere and clanged into the street like a sign and a witness.

"Now I predict," said Clarissa, "that every single object will return exactly seven days from the time of its disappearance."

The seven-day terror had ended. The objects began to reappear.

"How," asked the mayor, "did you know they would come back in seven days?"

"Because it was a seven-day disappearer that Clarence made. I also know how to make a nine-day, a thirteen-day, a twenty-seven-day, and an eleven-year disappearer. I was going to make a thirteen-day one, but for that you have to color the ends with the blood from a little boy's heart, and Cyril cried every time I tried to make a good cut."

"You really know how to make all of these?"

"Yes. But I shudder if the knowledge should ever come into unauthorized hands."

"I shudder too, Clarissa. But tell me, why did you want the chemicals?"

"For my chemistry set."

"And the black velvet?"

"For doll dresses."

"And the pound of rock candy?"

"How did you ever get to be mayor of this town if you have to ask questions like that? What do you think I wanted the rock candy for?"

"One last question," said the mayor. "Why did you smash my gold watch with the hammer?"

"Oh," said Clarissa, "that was for dramatic effect."

Coming Attraction

FRITZ LEIBER

This story, which was one of the five stories most often nominated, does not strike me as a warning, but as a prophecy.

The coupe with the fishhooks welded to the fender shouldered up over the curb like the nose of a nightmare. The girl in its path stood frozen, her face probably stiff with fright under her mask. For once my reflexes weren't shy. I took a fast step toward her, grabbed her elbow, yanked her back. Her black skirt swirled out.

The big coupe shot by, its turbine humming. I glimpsed three faces. Something ripped. I felt the hot exhaust on my ankles as the big coupe swerved back into the street. A thick cloud like a black flower blossomed from its jouncing rear end, while from the fishhooks flew a black shimmering rag.

"Did they get you?" I asked the girl.

She had twisted around to look where the side of her skirt was torn away. She was wearing nylon tights.

"The hooks didn't touch me," she said shakily. "I guess I'm lucky."

I heard voices around us:

"Those kids! What'll they think up next?"

"They're a menace. They ought to be arrested."

Sirens screamed at a rising pitch as two motor police, their rocket-assist jets full on, came whizzing toward us after the coupe. But the black flower had become an inky fog obscuring the whole street. The motor police switched from rocket assists to rocket brakes and swerved to a stop near the smoke cloud.

"Are you English?" the girl asked me. "You have an English accent." Her voice came shudderingly from behind the sleek black satin mask. I fancied her teeth must be chattering. Eyes that were perhaps blue searched my face from behind the black gauze covering the eyeholes of the mask.

I told her she'd guessed right.

She stood close to me. "Will you come to my place tonight?" she asked rapidly. "I can't thank you now. And there's something else you can help me about."

My arm, still lightly circling her waist, felt her body trembling. I was answering the plea in that as much as in her voice when I said, "Certainly."

She gave me an address south of Inferno, an apartment number and a time. She asked me my name and I told her.

"Hey, you!"

I turned obediently to the policeman's shout. He shooed away the small clucking crowd of masked women and barefaced men. Coughing from the smoke that the black coupe had thrown out, he asked for my papers. I handed him the essential ones.

He looked at them and then at me. "British Barter? How long will you be in New York?"

Suppressing the urge to say, "For as short a time as possible." I told him I'd be here for a week or so.

"May need you as a witness," he explained. "Those kids can't use smoke on us. When they do that, we pull them in."

He seemed to think the smoke was the bad thing. "They tried to kill the lady," I pointed out.

He shook his head wisely. "They always pretend they're going to, but actually they just want to snag skirts. I've picked up rippers with as many as fifty skirt snags tacked up in their rooms. Of course, sometimes they come a little too close.

I explained that if I hadn't yanked her out of the way she'd have been hit by more than hooks. But he interrupted. "If she'd thought it was a real murder attempt, she'd have stayed here."

I looked around. It was true. She was gone.

"She was fearfully frightened," I told him.

"Who wouldn't be? Those kids would have scared old Stalin himself."

"I mean frightened of more than 'kids.' They didn't look like kids."

167

"What did they look like?"

I tried without much success to describe the three faces. A vague impression of viciousness and effeminacy doesn't mean much.

"Well, I could be wrong," he said finally. "Do you know the girl? Where she lives?"

"No," I half lied.

The other policeman hung up his radiophone and ambled toward us, kicking at the tendrils of dissipating smoke. The black cloud no longer hid the dingy façades with their five-year-old radiation flash burns, and I could begin to make out the distant stump of the Empire State Building, thrusting up out of Inferno like a mangled finger.

"They haven't been picked up so far," the approaching policeman grumbled. "Left smoke for five blocks, from what Ryan says."

The first policeman shook his head. "That's bad," he observed solemnly.

I was feeling a bit uneasy and ashamed. An Englishman shouldn't lie, at least not on impulse.

"They sound like nasty customers," the first policeman continued in the same grim tone. "We'll need witnesses. Looks as if you may have to stay in New York longer than you expect."

I got the point. I said, "I forgot to show you all my papers," and handed him a few others, making sure there was a five-dollar bill in among them.

When he handed them back a bit later, his voice was no longer ominous. My feelings of guilt vanished. To cement our relationship, I chatted with the two of them about their job.

"I suppose the masks give you some trouble," I observed. "Over in England we've been reading about your new crop of masked female bandits."

"Those things get exaggerated," the first policeman assured me. "It's the men masking as women that really mix us up. But, brother, when we nab them, we jump on them with both feet."

"And you get so you can spot women almost as well as if they had naked faces," the second policeman volunteered. "You know, hands and all that."

"Especially all that," the first agreed with a chuckle. "Say, is it true that some girls don't mask over in England?"

"A number of them have picked up the fashion," I told him. "Only a few, though—the ones who always adopt the latest style, however extreme."

"They're usually masked in the British newscasts."

"I imagine it's arranged that way out of deference to American taste," I confessed. "Actually, not very many do mask."

The second policeman considered that. "Girls going down the street bare from the neck up." It was not clear whether he viewed the prospect with relish or moral distaste. Likely both.

"A few members keep trying to persuade Parliament to enact a law forbidding all masking," I continued, talking perhaps a bit too much.

The second policeman shook his head. "What an idea. You know, masks are a pretty good thing, brother. Couple of years more and I'm going to make my wife wear hers around the house."

The first policeman shrugged. "If women were to stop wearing masks, in six weeks you wouldn't know the difference. You get used to anything, if enough people do or don't do it."

I agreed, rather regretfully, and left them. I turned north on Broadway (old Tenth Avenue, I believe) and walked rapidly until I was beyond Inferno. Passing such an area of undecontaminated radioactivity always makes a person queasy. I thanked God there weren't any such in England, as yet.

The street was almost empty, though I was accosted by a couple of beggars with faces tunneled by H-bomb scars, whether real or of make-up putty I couldn't tell. A fat woman held out a baby with webbed fingers and toes. I told myself it would have been deformed anyway and that she was only capitalizing on our fear of bomb-induced mutations. Still, I gave her a seven-and-a-half-cent piece. Her mask made me feel I was paying tribute to an African fetish.

"May all your children be blessed with one head and two eyes, sir."

"Thanks," I said, shuddering, and hurried past her.

". . . There's only trash behind the mask, so turn your head, stick to your task: Stay away, stay away—from—the—girls!"

This last was the end of an anti-sex song being sung by

some religionists half a block from the circle-and-cross insignia of a femalist temple. They reminded me only faintly of our small tribe of British monastics. Above their heads was a jumble of billboards advertising predigested foods, wrestling instruction, radio handies and the like.

I stared at the hysterical slogans with disagreeable fascination. Since the female face and form have been banned on American signs, the very letters of the advertiser's alphabet have begun to crawl with sex—the fat-bellied, big-breasted capital *B*, the lascivious double *O*. However, I reminded myself, it is chiefly the mask that so strangely accents sex in America.

A British anthropologist has pointed out that, while it took more than five thousand years to shift the chief point of sexual interest from the hips to the breasts, the next transition, to the face, has taken less than fifty years. Comparing the American style with Moslem tradition is not valid; Moslem women are compelled to wear veils, the purpose of which is to make a husband's property private, while American women have only the compulsion of fashion and use masks to create mystery.

Theory aside, the actual origins of the trend are to be found in the antiradiation clothing of World War III, which led to masked wrestling, now a fantastically popular sport, and that in turn led to the current female fashion. Only a wild style at first, masks quickly became as necessary as brassieres and lipsticks had been earlier in the century.

I finally realized that I was not speculating about masks in general, but about what lay behind one in particular. That's the devil of the things; you're never sure whether a girl is heightening loveliness or hiding ugliness. I pictured a cool, pretty face in which fear showed only in widened eyes. Then I remembered her blond hair, rich against the blackness of the satin mask. She'd told me to come at the twenty-second hour—10 P.M.

I climbed to my apartment near the British Consulate; the elevator shaft had been shoved out of plumb by an old blast, a nuisance in these tall New York buildings. Before it occurred to me that I would be going out again, I automatically tore a tab from the film strip under my shirt. I developed it just to be sure. It showed that the total radiation I'd taken that day was still within the safety limit. I'm no phobic about it, as so many people are these days, but there's no point in taking chances.

I flopped down on the daybed and stared at the silent speaker and the dark screen of the video set. As always, they made me think, somewhat bitterly, of the two great nations of the world. Mutilated by each other, yet still strong, they were crippled giants poisoning the planet with their respective dreams of an impossible equality and an impossible success.

I fretfully switched on the speaker. By luck, the news-caster was talking excitedly of the prospects of a bumper wheat crop, sown by planes across a dust bowl moistened by seeded rains. I listened carefully to the rest of the program (it was remarkably clear of Russian telejamming), but there was no further news of interest to me. And, of course, no mention of the moon, though everyone knows that America and Russia are racing to develop their primary bases into fortresses capable of mutual assault and the launching of alphabet bombs toward Earth. I myself knew perfectly well that the British electronic equipment I was helping trade for American wheat was destined for use in spaceships.

I switched off the newscast. It was growing dark, and once again I pictured a tender, frightened face behind a mask. I hadn't had a date since England. It's exceedingly difficult to become acquainted with a girl in America, where as little as a smile often can set one of them yelping for the police—to say nothing of the increasingly puritanical morality and the roving gangs that keep most women indoors after dark. And, naturally, the masks, which are definitely not, as the Soviets claim, a last invention of capitalist degeneracy, but a sign of great psychological insecurity. The Russians have no masks, but they have their own signs of stress.

I went to the window and impatiently watched the darkness gather. I was getting very restless. After a while a ghostly violent cloud appeared to the south. My hair rose. Then I laughed. I had momentarily fancied it a radiation from the crater of the Hell-bomb, though I should instantly have known it was only the radio-induced glow in the sky over the amusement and residential area south of Inferno.

Promptly at twenty-two hours I stood before the door of my unknown girl friend's apartment. The electronic say-who-please said just that. I answered clearly, "Wysten Turner," wondering if she'd given my name to the mechanism. She evidently had, for the door opened. I walked into a small empty living room, my heart pounding a bit.

The room was expensively furnished with the latest pneumatic hassocks and sprawlers. There were some midgie books on the table. The one I picked up was the standard hard-boiled detective story in which two female murderers go gunning for each other.

The television was on. A masked girl in green was crooning a love song. Her right hand held something that blurred off into the foreground. I saw the set had a handie, which we haven't in England as yet, and curiously thrust my hand into the handie orifice beside the screen. Contrary to my expectations, it was not like slipping into a pulsing rubber glove, but rather as if the girl on the screen actually held my hand.

A door opened behind me. I jerked out my hand with as guilty a reaction as if I'd been caught peering through a keyhole.

She stood in the bedroom doorway. I think she was trembling. She was wearing a gray fur coat, white-speckled, and a gray velvet evening mask with shirred gray lace around the eyes and mouth. Her fingernails twinkled like silver.

It hadn't occurred to me that she'd expect us to go out.

"I should have told you," she said softly. Her mask veered nervously toward the books and the screen and the room's dark corners. "But I can't possibly talk to you here."

I said doubtfully, "There's a place near the Consulate. . . ."

"I know where we can be together and talk," she said rapidly. "If you don't mind."

As we entered the elevator I said, "I'm afraid I dismissed the cab."

But the cab driver hadn't gone, for some reason of his own. He jumped out and smirkingly held the front door open for us. I told him we preferred to sit in back. He sulkily opened the rear door, slammed it after us, jumped in front and slammed the door behind him.

My companion leaned forward. "Heaven," she said.

The driver switched on the turbine and televisor.

"Why did you ask if I were a British subject?" I said, to start the conversation.

She leaned away from me, tilting her mask close to the window. "See the moon," she said in a quick, dreamy voice.

"But why, really?" I pressed, conscious of an irritation that had nothing to do with her.

"It's edging up into the purple of the sky."

"And what's your name?"

"The purple makes it look yellower."

Just then I became aware of the source of my irritation. It lay in the square of writhing light in the front of the cab beside the driver.

I don't object to ordinary wrestling matches, though they bore me, but I simply detest watching a man wrestle a woman. The fact that the bouts are generally "on the level," with the man greatly outclassed in weight and reach and the masked females young and personable, only makes them seem worse to me.

"Please turn off the screen," I requested the driver.

He shook his head without looking around. "Uh-uh, man," he said. "They've been grooming that babe for weeks for this bout with Little Zirk.

Infuriated, I reached forward, but my companion caught my arm. "Please," she whispered frightenedly, shaking her head.

I settled back, frustrated. She was closer to me now, but silent, and for a few moments I watched the heaves and contortions of the powerful masked girl and her wiry masked opponent on the screen. His frantic scrambling at her reminded me of a male spider.

I jerked around, facing my companion. "Why did those three men want to kill you?" I asked sharply.

The eyeholes of her mask faced the screen. "Because they're jealous of me," she whispered.

"Why are they jealous?"

She still didn't look at me. "Because of him."

"Who?"

She didn't answer.

I put my arm around her shoulders. "Are you afraid to tell me?" I asked. "What *is* the matter?"

She still didn't look my way. She smelled nice.

"See here," I said laughingly, changing my tactics, "you really should tell me something about yourself. I don't even know what you look like."

I half playfully lifted my hand to the band of her neck. She gave it an astonishingly swift slap. I pulled it away in sudden pain. There were four tiny indentations on the back. From one of them a tiny bead of blood welled out as I watched. I looked at her silver fingernails and saw they were actually delicate and pointed metal caps.

"I'm dreadfully sorry," I heard her say, "but you frightened me. I thought for a moment you were going to . . ."

At last she turned to me. Her coat had fallen open. Her evening dress was Cretan Revival, a bodice of lace beneath and supporting the breasts without covering them.

"Don't be angry," she said, putting her arms around my neck. "You were wonderful this afternoon."

The soft gray velvet of her mask, molding itself to her cheek, pressed mine. Through the mask's lace the wet warm tip of her tongue touched my chin.

"I'm not angry," I said. "Just puzzled and anxious to help."

The cab stopped. To either side were black windows bordered by spears of broken glass. The sickly purple light showed a few ragged figures slowly moving toward us.

The driver muttered, "It's the turbine, man. We're grounded." He sat there hunched and motionless. "Wish it had happened somewhere else."

My companion whispered, "Five dollars is the usual amount."

She looked out so shudderingly at the congregating figures that I suppressed my indignation and did as she suggested. The driver took the bill without a word. As he started up, he put his hand out the window and I heard a few coins clink on the pavement.

My companion came back into my arms, but her mask faced the television screen, where the tall girl had just pinned the convulsively kicking Little Zirk.

"I'm so frightened," she breathed.

Heaven turned out to be an equally ruinous neighborhood, but it had a club with an awning and a huge doorman uniformed like a spaceman, but in gaudy colors. In my sensuous daze I rather liked it all. We stepped out of the cab just as a drunken old woman came down the sidewalk, her mask awry. A couple ahead of us turned their heads from the half-revealed face as if from an ugly body at the beach. As we followed them in I heard the doorman say, "Get along, Grandma, and cover yourself."

Inside, everything was dimness and blue glows. She had said we could talk here, but I didn't see how. Besides the inevitable chorus of sneezes and coughs (they say America is fifty per cent allergic these days), there was a band going full blast in the latest robop style, in which an electronic composing machine selects an arbitrary sequence of tones into which the musicians weave their raucous little individualities.

Most of the people were in booths. The band was behind the bar. On a small platform beside them a girl was dancing, stripped to her mask. The little cluster of men at the shadowy far end of the bar weren't looking at her.

We inspected the menu in gold script on the wall and pushed the buttons for breast of chicken, fried shrimps and two Scotches. Moments later, the serving bell tinkled. I opened the gleaming panel and took out our drinks.

The cluster of men at the bar filed off toward the door, but first they stared around the room. My companion had just thrown back her coat. Their look lingered on our booth. I noticed that there were three of them.

The band chased off the dancing girls with growls. I handed my companion a straw and we sipped our drinks.

"You wanted me to help you about something," I said. "Incidentally, I think you're lovely."

She nodded quick thanks, looked around, leaned forward. "Would it be hard for me to get to England?"

"No," I replied, a bit taken aback. "Provided you have an American passport."

"Are they difficult to get?"

"Rather," I said, surprised at her lack of information. "Your country doesn't like its nationals to travel, though it isn't quite as stringent as Russia."

"Could the British Consulate help me get a passport?"

"It's hardly their—"

"Could you?"

I realized we were being inspected. A man and two girls had paused opposite our table. The girls were tall and wolfish-looking, with spangled masks. The man stood jauntily between them like a fox on its hind legs.

My companion didn't glance at them, but she sat back. I noticed that one of the girls had a big yellow bruise on her

175

forearm. After a moment they walked to a booth in the deep shadows.

"Know them?" Is asked. She didn't reply. I finished my drink. "I'm not sure you'd like England," I said. "The austerity's altogether different from your American brand of misery."

She leaned forward again. "But I must get away," she whispered.

"Why?" I was getting impatient.

"Because I'm so frightened."

There was chimes. I opened the panel and handed her the fried shrimps. The sauce on my breast of chicken was a delicious steaming compound of almonds, soy and ginger. But something must have been wrong with the radionic oven that had thawed and heated it, for at the first bite I crunched a kernel of ice in the meat. These delicate mechanisms need constant repair and their aren't enough mechanics.

I put down my fork. "What are you really scared of?" I asked her.

For once her mask didn't waver away from my face. As I waited I could feel the fears gathering without her naming them, tiny dark shapes swarming through the curved night outside, converging on the radioactive pest spot of New York, dipping into the margins of the purple. I felt a sudden rush of sympathy, a desire to protect the girl opposite me. The warm feeling added itself to the infatuation engendered in the cab.

"Everything," she said finally.

I noded and touched her hand.

"I'm afraid of the moon," she began, her voice going dreamy and brittle, as it had in the cab. "You can't look at it and not think of guided bombs."

"It's the same moon over England," I reminded her.

"But it's not England's moon any more. It's ours and Russia's. You're not responsible. Oh, and then," she said with a tilt of her mask, "I'm afraid of the cars and the gangs and the loneliness and Inferno. I'm afraid of the lust that undresses your face. And"—her voice hushed—"I'm afraid of the wrestlers."

"Yes?" I prompted softly after a moment.

Her mask came forward. "Do you know something about the wrestlers?" she asked rapidly. "The ones that wrestle women, I mean. They often lose, you know. And then they have to have a girl to take their frustration out on. A girl who's soft and weak and terribly frightened. They need that, to keep them men. Other men don't want them to have a girl. Other men want them just to fight women and be heroes. But they must have a girl. It's horrible for her."

I squeezed her fingers tighter, as if courage could be transmitted—granting I had any. "I think I can get you to England," I said.

Shadows crawled onto the table and stayed there. I looked up at the three men who had been at the end of the bar. They were the men I had seen in the big coupe. They wore black sweaters and close-fitting black trousers. Their faces were as expressionless as dopers. Two of them stood about me. The other loomed over the girl.

"Drift off, man," I was told. I heard the other inform the girl, "We'll wrestle a fall, sister. What shall it be? Judo, slapsie or kill-who-can?"

I stood up. There are times when an Englishman simply must be maltreated. But just then the foxlike man came gliding in like the star of a ballet. The reaction of the other three startled me. They were acutely embarrassed.

He smiled at them thinly. "You won't win my favor by tricks like this," he said.

"Don't get the wrong idea, Zirk," one of them pleaded.

"I will if it's right," he said. "She told me what you tried to do this afternoon. That won't endear you to me, either. Drift."

They backed off awkwardly. "Let's get out of here," one of the said loudly as they turned. "I know a place where they fight naked with knives."

Little Zirk laughed musically and slipped into the seat beside my companion. She shrank from him, just a little. I pushed my feet back, leaned forward.

"Who's your friend, baby?" he asked, not looking at her.

She passed the question to me with a little gesture. I told him.

"British," he observed. "She's been asking you about getting out of the country? About passports?" He smiled pleasantly. "She likes to start running away. Don't you, baby?" His small hand began to stroke her wrist, the fingers bent a little, the tendons ridged, as if he were about to grab and twist.

"Look here," I said sharply. "I have to be grateful to you for ordering off those bullies, but—"

"Think nothing of it," he told me. "They're no harm except when they're behind steering wheels. A well-trained fourteen-year-old girl could cripple any one of them. Why, even Theda here, if she went in for that sort of thing . . ." He turned to her, shifting his hand from her wrist to her hair. He stroked it, letting the strands slip slowly through his fingers. "You know I lost tonight, baby, don't you?" he said softly.

I stood up. "Come along," I said to her. "Let's leave."

She just sat there. I couldn't even tell if she was trembling. I tried to read a message in her eyes through the mask.

"I'll take you away," I said to her. "I can do it. I really will."

He smiled at me. "She'd like to go with you," he said. "Wouldn't you, baby?"

"Will you or won't you?" I said to her. She still just sat there.

He slowly knotted his fingers in her hair.

"Listen, you little vermin," I snapped at him. "Take your hands off her."

He came up from the seat like a snake. I'm no fighter. I just know that the more scared I am, the harder and straighter I hit. This time I was lucky. But as he crumped back I felt a slap and four stabs of pain in my cheek. I clapped my hand to it. I could feel the four gashes made by her dagger finger caps, and the warm blood oozing out from them.

She didn't look at me. She was bending over Little Zirk and cuddling her mask to his cheek and crooning, "There, there, don't feel bad, you'll be able to hurt me afterward."

There were sounds around us, but they didn't come close. I leaned forward and ripped the mask from her face.

I really don't know why I should have expected her face to be anything else. It was very pale, of course, and there weren't any cosmetics. I suppose there's no point in wearing any under a mask. The eyebrows were untidy and the lips chapped. But as for the general expression, as for the feelings crawling and wriggling across it . . .

Have you ever lifted a rock from damp soil? Have you ever watched the slimy white grubs?

I looked down at her, she up at me. "Yes, you're so

frightened, aren't you?" I said sarcastically. "You dread this little nightly drama, don't you? You're scared to death."

And I walked right out into the purple night, still holding my hand to my bleeding cheek. No one stopped me, not even the girl wrestlers. I wished I could tear a tab from under my shirt and test it then and there, and find I'd taken too much radiation, and so be able to ask to cross the Hudson and go down New Jersey, past the lingering radiance of the Narrows Bomb, and so on to Sandy Hook to wait for the rusty ship that would take me back over the seas to England.

Politics

MURRAY LEINSTER

This story was written in 1932. In it you'll discover something that works very much like radar, and you'll also note the computer-aimed guns. You will also be involved in a World War II which never happened.

Murray Leinster has been writing sf for quite a long time and has been noted for most of that time for the strong and delightful sense of adventure which his work carries. What has, comparatively, escaped notice is his concern with what man is doing to other men and what man is doing to himself—a concern displayed with enviable passion and control in this story, which has never been reprinted.

1

The War of the Pacific has at least taught one lesson on naval strategists. No naval force can ever be said to be inconsiderable, if officered and manned by a capable and determined personnel.—Grahame, Modern Sea Power (*New York, 1937.*)

Lieutenant MacReady saw the enemy from the *Minnesota's* fighting top and rejoiced with a bitter rejoicing at the sight. This was in August of 1934, you see, just four days after the Battle of Hungars' Bank, and the *Minnesota's* whole ship company thirsted for vengeance, both upon the enemy and upon the politicians who had sacrificed the rest of the fleet to win an election. The politicians were safe, but the enemy was here, and the *Minnesota* tore through the water toward them with the speed and fury of an avenging nemesis.

"Enemy in sight, sir," he said crisply into the transmitter strapped to his chest. "Bearing . . ."

"Reported and ranged," said a curt voice in the earphones.

MacReady looked down. The guns of the top forward turret were winding up to extreme range. The top turret was coming around. . . . He felt the shock of the discharge before the blast of sound from the explosion struck him. Three guns, fourteen-inchers, had sent out a ranging salvo. The shells were invisible screaming demons of steel and explosive, hurtling upward now, but they would descend nearly twenty miles away and it was Lieutenant MacReady's task to watch their fall. Or it had been his task before the new range finders were installed while the wreckage of that boiler explosion was being repaired. And it might at any instant be his task again.

He counted the seconds; refocused his glasses; wet his lips. Somehow he knew that the guns were swinging below him. Grim, gray-painted tubes were moving slowly to position. . . . He saw the enemy vessels vaguely. There was what looked like a melee of ships on the horizon's edge. Two huge bulks, one of them listing visibly even at this distance. That would be the *Langley*, an aircraft carrier. The other was the *Saratoga*, also a carrier. Over and about the distant ship tiny motes danced. Aircraft. Army planes from shore, carrying on dogfights in the place of the Navy planes that had shared in the disaster of Hungars' Bank. And there was the *Seattle*, on fire but fighting savagely. He saw the flashes of her guns. The *St. Louis* was with her. They were fighting a rear-guard action to enable the aircraft carriers to get away. Those tiny specks were the destroyers. American destroyers. Half-wrecked and battered but fighting gamely as they limped homeward. . . .

The ranging salvo splashed. Three tremendous waterspouts, rising simultaneously, high above the fighting tops of any ship afloat.

"Right six, up two—" snapped MacReady.

The *Minnesota* burst into flame beneath him. Lieutenant MacReady started at the blast of sound. He was dazed by the mere shock, but he knew that every gun that could be brought to bear ahead had fired in one colossal burst of flame. And before his range correction was completed!

His earphones barked, *"Range that salvo."*

"Y-yes, sir," said Lieutenant MacReady.

He began to count the seconds. The lower forward turret was shifting slightly. Twenty-two, twenty-three . . . The three guns spouted flame and dingy-brown smoke. This was the very latest constant-pressure powder, guaranteed by the ordnance department not to vary more than one thousand pounds to the square inch breech pressure even under service conditions. Fifty-eight, fifty-nine . . .

The *Minnesota* was making twenty-eight knots. Blue water flowed past her with a deceptive smoothness. One of the distant aircraft carriers began to spit tiny flames from its antitorpedo battery. There was a flurry of destroyers—American destroyers meeting an attack. Lieutenant MacReady could see the enemy ships clearly now. Four big ones besides the destroyers. Pocket battleships, ten thousand tons, with more speed, more armor, more hitting power than anything else twice their size afloat. But the *Minnesota* was a forty-thousand-ton ship, the biggest battleship in the world. She was, incidentally, the only first-line ship left to the American Navy after the Battle of Hungars' Bank.

The salvo struck. A monstrous mound of water rose to an incredible height. The stern of an enemy ship showed from behind it. The rest of the enemy vessel was hidden behind the broadside splash. It seemed one single, volcanic eruption of water.

"Right one half," said Lieutenant MacReady into the transmitter before him. "Up . . ."

The mound of water began to fall. The stern of the enemy ship tilted with its descent. It rose upward till the keel showed. It dived slowly . . .

"By God, sir!" said Lieutenant MacReady shrilly. "She's sunk!"

Sixteen-inch shells are good medicine for pocket battleships. MacReady swung his glasses swiftly. There was a ranging salvo of shells still aloft. It was his duty to spot their fall . . .

He saw the splashes. Two of them. One was short. One was an over. The third . . . The stern of the enemy ship grew suddenly hazy.

"Straddled!" barked Lieutenant MacReady.

But the terrific concussion of the ship's whole forward battery tore at his chest. He felt something warm trickling down his chin. His nose was bleeding. He counted seconds with a strained attention. Another ranging blast below. There was a sudden roaring overhead. Two enemy bombers with a six-fighting-planes escort were racing toward the ship. The Army planes from shore were diving for it. The whole antiaircraft battery of the *Minnesota* barked savagely twice. MacReady heard terrific concussions and the sound of a dogfight going on somewhere up aloft.

I'd be happy, thought MacReady in savage satisfaction, if only some of our politicians were on those ships out there. We're shooting like a streak. We couldn't miss if those damned pol—"

A monster mound of water rose up, obliterating one of the three remaining pocket battleships. MacReady's lips formed the word *"Straddled!,"* but there seemed hardly any need. The mound slowly flattened out, and the sea was clean where it had been. A pocket battleship can stand an amazing lot of pounding, but there simply isn't any armor that will keep out a sixteen-inch shell. And when several of them strike at once the result is deplorable. Seconds later the third pocket battleship was silhouetted by splashes. The whole fabric of the *Minnesota* shuddered beneath MacReady as for the third time every gun that could be brought to bear was fired in one world-filling blast of sound. And seconds later a fourth ranging salvo.

Splashes began to rise about the *Minnesota* herself. But a ten-thousand-ton ship is not a steady firing platform, and though it may carry armament far out of proportion to its size it is really designed for fleet work, with smoke screens, aircraft spotters and other aids to efficiency. The *Minnesota* was a self-contained fighting unit, capable of fighting like a whirlwind, and it was taking the offensive. Which was an advantage in itself. One shell fell fifty yards from the *Minnesota's* side. The next salvo from the ship that fired it should have done some damage. But then the third broadside struck, and when the sea subsided a pocket battleship was rolling over with a grave dignity, to turn turtle and sink. And seconds later the fourth ranging salvo struck, and as its splashes leaped upward the *Minnesota* roared for the fourth time.

Lieutenant MacReady was dazed and dizzy. He felt the ship changing course beneath him. Three broadsides had struck and three ships were sunk! Of course, the *Minnesota* carried the heaviest metal of any ship afloat, but it wasn't natural! There'd been no time for the spotting of shells and the correction of range. Just a ranging salvo, and as it sent splashes skyward the whole forward battery of the *Minnesota* flamed. No delay. No waiting. Above all, no error! The *Minnesota* fired every gun that could bear. Twenty miles away and a long time later four acres of sea arose mountainously, with scattering splashes outside, and anything afloat in that four acres of sea simply ceased to exist.

It happened again now. The fourth broadside struck, it seemed squarely. When the turmoil of its arrival ceased, the fourth enemy pocket ship was still afloat, but explosions were coming from it with lightninglike rapidity. And suddenly it vomited flame from somewhere amidships, broke jaggedly in half—and the sea was clean.

The *Minnesota* had already changed course. There were only enemy destroyers afloat now, after only four broadsides. The distant American ships drew to one side, fighting savagely as they moved. A torpedo struck home somewhere out there, and a thin sliver of metal which was an American destroyer upended and went down in a clean dive. And the air seemed suddenly full of buzzings as of a myriad mosquitos.

"*Lieutenant MacReady,*" said the curt voice in his headphones. "*You will not be required to spot ranges as long as the new range finders function. You will, however, search for possible subs, and especially for torpedo trails.*"

"Yes, sir," said Lieutenant MacReady exultantly.

He turned to grin at his fellow spotter in the forward fighting top. A ringside seat at the big show! Enemy aircraft were racing for the *Minnesota,* but the Army ships from shore were taking a deadly toll. MacReady glanced back at the distant thin line of the coast. Motes were visible in the sky. More Army planes, coming out from land. Fighting planes all, save one squadron of heavy bombers with a haze of tiny pursuit planes whirling before it for protection.

A pall of blackness arose far away upon the sea. The enemy destroyers were making a smoke screen. The *Seattle* and the *St. Louis* were the targets toward which the lengthening spearhead of blackness reached out. They had been under heavy fire from the pocket ships before the *Minnesota* came out. If the destroyers could sink them and the aircraft carriers, it would amount to victory. Destroyer attacks in daylight against ships like the *Minnesota* are unhealthy, but the lesser and already crippled American ships might be wiped out.

But the *Minnesota* spouted flame from fifty gun muzzles. The antiaircraft guns barked in one monstrous volley. They barked again. There were terrific concussions up aloft, and Lieutenant MacReady saw a huge ball of yellow smoke— T.N.T. smoke—spreading with an enormous velocity in mid-air.

"Got a bomber!" he whispered to himself. He wiped the blood off his face and grinned from ear to ear with sheer excitement.

The broadside landed, fifteen miles away. And it struck not as a concentrated blast of sheer destruction, but as a barrage. Separate splashes rose in glittering similitude of stalagmites on a limestone cavern floor. But each pinnacle, shining in the sun, represented the point of fall of a six-inch shell (they were small and few) or an eight-inch shell (there were more of them) or of mighty sixteen-inch shells themselves. The broadside of the *Minnesota* had deliberately been spread out to cover a huge area thinly. But a destroyer does not need much pounding to be put out of action. The tip of the spearhead of smoke heading for the American destroyers simply ceased to be. And the *Minnesota* flamed again, and again, and again. Six times, at fifteen-second intervals, she belched out coruscating waves of fire. A long time later the broadsides fell.

The antiaircraft batteries barked savagely. Firing like the heavy guns; simultaneous salvos at single targets at single instants. Picking out the enemy bombers and leaving the enemy single-seaters to the Army ships. Over and above the droning of many motors there was now the intermittent sound of colossal explosions. Enemy two-thousand-pound bombs were going off in mid-air as the bombers that carried them were wrecked by screaming hails of metal.

MacReady fixed his glasses upon the distant smoke screen. It was ragged and torn. A single enemy destroyer showed clearly for an instant. It was changing course and streaking for the far horizon. The rest were gone! The forward turret boomed a ranging salvo. MacReady watched feverishly. Army ships coming out from shore in a never-ending stream. Some-where far aloft— The ranging salvo struck! A quarter mile over! But the forward battery crashed forth for the tenth time in this action. Every gun bearing ahead crashed.

MacReady was bleeding at the nose and ears from the concussions that had battered at him. He was bruised all over. He was deafened and his bloodshot eyes streamed water, but he sat in a stilly glow of satisfaction, wishing only that certain politicians could be upon that panic-stricken destroyer that fled from a hail of death.

He saw the shells land. The fleeing destroyer was emitting a dense cloud of smoke to conceal its trail. But it was lifted a hundred and fifty feet clear as contact-fused shells went off in an inferno of destruction. It was flung above even its own smoke screen. MacReady saw it break in pieces and vanish again behind the smoke.

And then there was only the buzzing of a multitude of motors aloft and all around. The tearing, rasping chatter of machine guns became audible. MacReady gazed upward and saw the Army planes hunt down ruthlessly and relentlessly every enemy plane that was aloft. With bitter satisfaction he watched the flying things go fluttering helplessly downward, or dive as plummets of flame into the sea. His satisfaction was tempered with only a slight regret when the last enemy pilot fought a magnicent lone duel with an Army formation, and entangled two of them in his final, blazing fall.

The *Minnesota* shepherded the other American ships toward the Golden Gate, gleaming and unmarred and belligerent. There were two scout cruisers under her protection, the *Seattle* and the *St. Louis*. The *Seattle* was still on fire, but was getting it under some control. There were two aircraft carriers, one of them listing heavily. There were seven half-wrecked destroyers. That was all. They went limping slowly toward the shore, through waters littered for a space with wave-wetted wings.

They went ahead of the *Minnesota* and entered the harbor. They anchored, watched by silent, stunned, almost panic-stricken crowds which thronged the waterfront and did not cheer at all.

Because this was four days after the Battle of Hungars' Bank. The enemy fleet held the Pacific. The *Minnesota* alone excepted, the whole first line of the American battle fleet was at the bottom of the sea. Save for a few submarines and perhaps half a dozen still-fugitive destroyers—now being hunted down by the victorious enemy—these limping, shattered carcasses of ships constituted the Navy of the United States of America.

And, one day before, the enemy had scornfully broadcast the terms on which it would make peace. Hawaii, Guam, the

Philippines and the Panama Canal were the only territorial demands, but an indemnity was insisted on and the enemy also required the surrender of the *Minnesota* and a pledge that the United States would never build more than a minimum number of small, slow cruisers in the future.

Throughout a panic-stricken nation, strong pacifist political pressure was being brought to bear to force Congress to accept those terms.

2

There have been in the past, and there will be in the future, attempts by politicians to dictate naval and military policies for other than naval and military ends. But never again will a civilian official of the United States dare issue a direct order governing naval or military operations! He would be impeached at least. In the present temper of the populace, he would probably be lynched.
—*Address to graduating class, U.S. Naval Academy, by the Secretary of the Navy, 1938.*

Lieutenant MacReady had been at Annapolis with the commander of the torpedo-boat-destroyer *Wasp*. In those far-off days MacReady had been a lowly plebe, while the destroyer skipper was an upperclassman, but they forgathered on equal terms in MacReady's quarters on the *Minnesota*. MacReady offered libation, and the *Wasp*'s commander raised his arm.

"Here's hell to politicians," he said grimly. "They sank our fleet!"

MacReady made an appropriate gesture, accepting the toast.

"Now shoot it," he commanded. "What happened?"

"If you want to know," said the *Wasp*'s commander bitterly, "they sent the battle fleet out with orders to avoid an action. An election is coming on. Pacifists are strong politically. If we blew the enemy out of the water, they'd denounce us as murderers, vote against the Administration, and change the political complexion of Congress. Therefore the Admiral was told to avoid a fleet action until after elections if he could, and

187

if he couldn't to make sure it wasn't a decisive defeat for the enemy. Isn't that pretty?"

"Damn pretty," said MacReady ironically. "Oh, damn pretty!"

"The enemy fleet was spoiling for a scrap," went on the *Wasp*'s commander more bitterly still. "They've been building pocket battleships, playing with 'em like kids with a new toy. On paper they had more gun power than we did, in more but smaller ships. We had the weight and the punishing power. They thought they could lick us. They came over to force a fleet action. They ignored Hawaii and came on with a supply fleet ten miles long behind 'em. And you can't handle a modern fleet, with destroyer screens and the like, without using wireless! We were picking up their code stuff and trying to decode it. They were doing the same with ours. Both sides were using radio direction finders, of course. They knew where we were, and we knew where they were. But they wanted a fight, and we were ordered to avoid one. It couldn't be avoided!"

" 'Hit first, hit hard, hit often!' " quoted MacReady. "But tell me, old man, *why* did the Admiral split his fleet?"

"Direct, specific orders from Washington!" snapped the *Wasp*'s commander. "We knew the enemy was determined on a fleet action and headed straight for us. The Admiral reported to Washington that a general engagement was absolutely unavoidable and an attempt at anything but a decisive victory was stark madness. He got detailed orders—the plan that sank the fleet! Signed by the President as commander in chief. Politics! Armchair strategy that looked all right on paper, but—my God! The battle fleet was to proceed northwest, with its radio silent. The two aircraft carriers, with escorting destroyers, were to proceed southwest. The carriers were to keep planes aloft, with their wireless outfits going, simulating a battle fleet in movement. The enemy would head for them. At the logical instant they would cut off their wireless and run. And the battle fleet would make a demonstration proving its actual position to be a thousand miles or so from where the enemy thought it was. A trick to gain time. A trick to postpone a battle until after election. That's all! They say the Admiral cried when he read the order."

"Here's hell to politicians," said MacReady morosely. "Why didn't it work?"

"An air photo from forty thousand feet," said the *Wasp's* commander sardonically, "is of no ordinary use to anybody. It's taken through an infrared filter that fog or clouds can't bother, but the Army doesn't use 'em because they don't give enough detail. But they'll tell the difference between a battle fleet and a pair of aircraft carriers, all right!"

MacReady groaned. The *Wasp's* skipper went on grimly: "That must have been how they did it. Silenced high-altitude planes and photos taken through eight miles of haze. Anyhow, six hours after the battlefleet headed northwest, the enemy fleet split up, too. They duplicated our maneuver. They sent their supply fleet to meet us, with its wireless going full blast to simulate a battle fleet, and they sent their battle fleet to meet ours, full speed ahead and with its wireless shut off, too. But they didn't leave their carriers behind!"

MacReady groaned again.

"The dirigible *Akron* sighted them," said the destroyer skipper coldly. "They got her in twenty minutes, after she'd sent the alarm back and crashed twelve planes that attacked her. But that was too late. We were eight hundred miles away, with the whole air service! You should have seen those carriers shoot planes into the air! One-two-three they went up! Streaking for the fight! It'd be four hours before the fastest of them got there, but they went! And the damned thing was nearly over when they arrived. Our ships had gone into action with only the ship planes to spot and fight for them. The enemy had four carriers—little ones, but they carried a hell of a lot of planes. Twenty minutes after the opening gun, they'd wiped the skies clean above our fleet. There were only six planes spotting for our whole fleet during the second half hour of the action. With smoke screens in use, you know what that meant! There were only three during the last hour! The enemy laid down smoke screens and potted at our ships from behind 'em. Our destroyers went through the screens and tried to do the spotting the air service should have done. Suicide, but we got two of their pocket ships and one of their superdreadnaughts that way. Meanwhile our boats were going to hell and gone. When the air fleet arrived there was only the old *New York* and the *Michigan* above-water in the first line, and we'd lost two thirds of our destroyers. But they stayed afloat, those two old tubs, taking all the punishment the whole enemy fleet could give 'em, and passing out all they had. Until our planes ran out of gas! It was all over then. They'd flown eight hundred miles to get to the fight. They were nearly out of fuel when they got there. And the enemy expected to gather them in when they made forced landings. Pretty idea, wasn't it?"

Lieutenant MacReady said pungent words.

"They did get three," said the commander of the *Wasp* calmly. "But the rest somehow got blown up or crashed by their pilots before they jumped for the water. It annoyed the enemy. They left the pilots—in the water."

Lieutenant MacReady said more pungent words, much more pungent.

"Meanwhile we on the decoy fleet had been tipped off. Oh, a hell or a time we had! Orders first were to try to join the battle fleet. An hour later the old Admiral knew he couldn't hold out until the air fleet got there, and ordered us to streak for home. The planes couldn't be turned back. They were gone, anyway. He tried to save the carriers and ships with them. We turned and ran." The destroyer skipper gesticulated bitterly. "Then the destroyers from the supply fleet hit us. We'd sent every plane we had to the fleet action. They'd done nearly the same. So we fought 'em off. For four days we'd been running away from them, fighting night and day, when the *Minnesota* turned up. Those pocket ships only got here this morning. Four days and nights of fighting, Mac! We sank three of their destroyers for every two of us they got, but there were twenty-four of us when we started out, and there were seven of us who came in, and the pocket ships would have finished us if the *Minnesota* hadn't blown hell out of them!"

There was silence. There was no noise anywhere on the *Minnesota* except an unplaceable dim whine which was a dynamo running somewhere. Out the porthole of MacReady's cabin could be seen the dim bulks of the two aircraft carriers that had been brought into port that day. The *Langley* still listed heavily to port, but there were lighters clustered about her side and arc lamps burned brightly. At three separate points, clusters of arc lamps burned vividly on the harbor water.

There was a droning hum overhead. It passed on and out to sea.

"Army planes," the commander of the *Wasp* said heavily.

"Doing naval patrol. At least the Army can smother their air force if they try any bombing. But what good'll it do? I haven't got a ship any more. My engines were shot to hell. They're cutting off the bow of the *Wasp* with an underwater torch. They're going to weld it in place of the *Waddy*'s bow, which looks like a full-blown rose. And our stern goes to replace the *Stingray*'s tail. Out of three wrecks they'll make two ships that can steam. It'll take four days, with underwater welding. But what good will it do?"

"It depends," said MacReady without hope, "on our shooting. *And* on politics. You saw our shooting today?"

The *Wasp*'s commander nodded. "I thought of you up there in the fighting top, spotting shells. The air was clear and you could do it—"

"I didn't spot a damned shell," said MacReady. "The new range finders have taken my job away from me and do it ten times as well. We've got fire power now, old horse! And fire control! We've got the new range finders in. Those parallel-beam finders they've been working on for years."

His companion looked puzzled.

"All electrical," explained MacReady. "No observer at all. Two telescopes, one at each end of a baseline, and mounted exactly parallel. Fitted with photoelectric cells instead of eyepieces. You swing the baseline around and they sweep the horizon. And a ship on the horizon changes the amount of light that goes through a narrow slit to the photoelectric cell. It registers the instant the first telescope hits the stern of the ship. A fraction of a second later, because the telescopes are exactly parallel, the ship image registers on the other cell. Both cells register exactly the same changes in current output, but one is a fraction of a second behind the other. Knowing the rate of sweep in seconds or mils or arc, if one photoelectric cell lags behind the other one mil, and you know the baseline, you work out the distance in a hurry. See?"

"Complicated," commented the destroyer skipper distastefully.

"Complicated as hell," agreed MacReady readily. "But, man, does it work! Those range finders sweep their field ten times per second, ranging each way. We range the enemy ship twenty times per second and get electric impulses to read off. But, better than that, we range our own shell splashes and the target together, with the same instrument, at the same time! See the point?"

"M-m-m-m. That looks good!"

"It's even better!" insisted MacReady. "We get electric impulses, instantaneous, instead of observer's figures. The impulses go to an integrator that calculates the range and declination. That feeds into a computer that works up the firing data—barometer, wind, humidity, and so on—and that goes to a relay that lays the gun! All working at the same time! The gun's laid on the target from the first second or two. Constant ranging gives speed and course of the target. The computer dopes 'em out, shifts the gun to where the target will be when the shells land, and we fire a salvo. And then the splashes get ranged by the same outfit in relation to the target! Errors in the firing data and powder lot—even wear on the gun gears—are automatically corrected! Then we let go a broadside. It blows hell out of the target! Gun for gun and ship for ship, the *Minnesota*'s the top fighting machine in the world! And half our superiority comes from those finders. Why, man, our antiaircraft finders range a plane, compute its course and speed in three dimensions, lay twenty guns on its most probable position at the time of shell burst, and fire the guns, all in two fifths of a second! They can do everything but play 'Home Sweet Home' on a piccolo!"

"Then," said the commander of the *Wasp*, "Why in hell weren't the other ships fitted with them?"

"Dear heart," protested MacReady in fine irony, "haven't you ever heard of politics? We have a few men with guts in Washington. We have also a large number of elderly maiden ladies with pants on. The range finders were in production. They were shipped here to be fitted. War broke out. There was a wave of popular sentiment against the rude and brutal practice of defending one's country against anybody else. The fleet was ordered to sea at once, because if it didn't get to sea the pacifists might manage to forbid its sailing! With the old range finders and air spotting we were on equal terms with the enemy. We could fight, anyhow! But even after the fleet had sailed the political pacifists managed to get those orders issued that you wot of, which sank our fleet. Politics, you see! It's sweet and pretty! And the *Minnesota* has the range finders installed simply because one of our boilers blew up. It killed sixteen men. We had to be left in port, and while we were getting the mess cleaned up and repaired the skipper put in the new finders. That's why we're damned near a match for the whole enemy navy!"

"And what good does it do?" asked the commander of the *Wasp* bitterly. "You're making 'em a present. The peace terms call for the surrender of the *Minnesota,* and these damned politicians are going to accept 'em!"

Lieutenant MacReady leaned forward confidentially.

"Old boy," he said under his breath, "the Secretary of the Navy is *not* an elderly maiden lady with pants on. There has never yet been an American warship surrendered without a fight. Our skipper has told him we can have some destroyers ready to fight again in six days, and asked permission to commit suicide in his own ship. The Army's going to help, by fighting off enemy planes if an action takes place within a hundred miles of shore. So if the enemy wants the *Minnesota* he'll have to take her! The Secretary thinks he can hold off surrender, in Washington, for those six days. If he can't, we go out before, without the destroyers, and smash our wireless so we can't be ordered to come back. And it will be suicide, and highly immoral, to fight against a gallant enemy who has sunk our ships and left our plane pilots to drown because they blew up their ships rather than hand them over, but—well, it'll be better than the other thing, won't it?"

"You're damn right!" said the commander of the *Wasp* hungrily. "I can shovel coal, or wash mess dishes, or—or—"

"I think," said Lieutenant MacReady magnanimously, "that it can be arranged. The Secretary of the Navy will be fired. The pacifists will write in the school history books that we were murderers. But maybe, if we work it right, the politicians won't object. Because we'll be sunk. I know *I'd* hate to be a politician and have a Navy man look me in the eye!"

The commander of the *Wasp* stood up.

"I'm going back to slave-drive my men," he said feverishly. "We've got to get those destroyers ready. Only time for one more. Here's hell to politicians!"

3

A politician is a man who believes that the greatest catastrophe that can possibly befall his country is the election of somebody else to the office he wants.—Leinster, Politics *(New York, 1931).*

The *Minnesota* lay at anchor in San Francisco Harbor. The sun shone down placidly upon the scene. There were flags flying everywhere. Some of them were "peace flags" and they flew brightly. Some were American flags; they were at half-mast. The city was still and dead. Newspapers came out at frequent intervals with huge hundred-and-twenty-point head-lines and very nearly identical contents. Two destroyers had made port in Alaska. They had refueled and gone to sea again. One destroyer, battered and in a sinking condition, had made the port of Vancouver, B.C., and was unable to put out again. She was interned. It was rumored that American submarines had located the enemy fleet with radio direction finders and had submerged in its path. Motors silent and men still as death, they had allowed the screen of destroyers and light craft to pass overhead. They had risen among the capital ships of the enemy navy. They had sunk three ships before they were de-stroyed. Then enemy command denied the rumor. There was no other war news. Peace news was oratory in print, accounts of meetings and resolutions and other activities of the persons opposed to war even in self-defense.

In San Francisco the only signs of life or energy were displayed in two places only. One was the Navy Yard, where men worked frantically against time with electric-welding and oxyacetylene apparatus, doing work that required months of time and elaborate equipment in days instead and with make-shift materials. The *Langley* was having a patch made for the torpedo blast in her side. It was being welded in one piece on shore. It would be sunk alongside and welded in place by Ells-worth underwater torches in the hands of divers. The *Wasp* was a fragment of herself, her bow and stern cut away and only her shell-torn middle section beached in shallow water to rust away. Every one of the returned vessels was aswarm with men. Their own crews were laboring like madmen to get them in shape to steam. They did not hope to attain to real battle efficiency. They only hoped to patch them up so they could share in the last foray of the fighting forces of the United States Navy. If they could steam, and if they could fire a gun, the crews of these ships would mutiny if forbidden a place at the suicide of the fleet.

The other spot where activity was in order was the headquarters of those organizations which opposed the prosecution of war against even a declared enemy. Speakers bustled in and out. Banners flew and gaudy placards smote the eye. Orators moved to strategic points to explain to half-stunned crowds that war was evil in itself and that the disaster of Hungars' Bank was the direct act of Providence, disapproving of America. Suitably edited portions of Scripture were available for distribution. And constantly through that activity for the service of abstract good ran the threat of political action, and an insistence upon the power of little mean men at the polls to undo the actions of bigger men who were deaf to the clamor of fanatics.

The orators ranged everywhere. Marine sentries stopped them at the Navy Yard gates, firmly refusing entry even to deputations of sad-eyed, hysterically righteous women intent upon pleading with the sailors not to murder the sons of other women, regardless of the fact that those sons of other women had not hesitated to sink the American battle fleet. It was uncomfortable anywhere to be in a military or naval uniform, because of the reproaches of convinced opponents of war. Pacifism had become respectable within the past four years, and its proponents took full advantage of the immunity accorded to respectable men. An enthusiastic orator even had himself rowed alongside the *Minnesota* and began a moving speech addressed to the sailors, advocating mutiny and the consistent violation of all the articles of war, and was lured below the slop chute by a sergeant of marines. It was pure accident, of course, that the ship's garbage was discharged at just that time, but an indignant protest was immediately telegraphed to the Secretary of the Navy and all other Cabinet officers.

That was in San Francisco. In Washington there were

parades in favor of peace. The President, being by American custom not only a government executive but also the leader of a political party, was forced for the sake of his party's chances in the coming elections to devote four hours in one day to the hearing of spokesmen for different groups of antiwar delegates from antiwar societies throughout the nation. The War and Navy departments were picketed by determined, passionately sincere advocates of peace at any price. Senators and members of the House of Representatives were besieged by opponents of carnage.

In London, the American ambassador was dryly informed that the British Government, though in sympathy with the present embarrassments of the American Government, would delay for the present the taking up of the unquestionably just claims of British subjects against the states which while in the Confederacy had sold bonds in England and later repudiated them. The American ambassador took the hint and cabled desperately that if the United States announced its renunciation of self-defense its standing before the world would be forever gone. In Germany there was laughter and ironically bitter comments in the journals. In France there was alarm and indignation at the threatened disappearance of an ally through what its official press termed national suicide. In Central and South America there was pure panic. Republics which heretofore had maintained a chip-on-the-shoulder attitude toward the United States now made frantic representations that the Monroe Doctrine would be without force behind it. They begged, they implored, they pleaded with the United States not to adopt a course which would ultimately involve their ruin with its own.

But in the United States foreign opinion had no weight. Pacifism was an issue which would decide an election. It would determine whether Tweedledum should stay in office or be thrown out for Tweedledee. It was a matter of politics, and therefore much more important than national prestige or national security or the national honor itself to all the Tweedledums in office and all the Tweedledees without.

The Secretary of the Navy was fighting for time, with the Secretary for War ably seconding him. These two men, at least, would lose their political status with the triumph of a no-defense attitude in the coming elections. Their place was to be taken—so the righteous had it—by a Secretary for Peace. And they fought tooth and nail, by argument and persuasion and browbeating and cajoling, to stem the panic of Congressmen in terror of political oblivion. But on the fourth day the Secretary of the Navy wired to San Francisco in code: *"Peace proposals considered in Congress tomorrow. Will probably be accepted the day after. I take responsibility of ordering you to use your own judgment in operations against the enemy."*

The Secretary of the Navy would have committed political suicide when the order became known. But he would be able to look at himself in a mirror without shrinking. The captain of the *Minnesota* read the telegram with a grin and weary smile. He tossed it across his desk.

"We'll go out in the morning. The only question is, is that crazy MacReady right? And how many destroyers will we have?"

"Two, sir, plus the scout cruisers and the aircraft carriers. And the planes that went out to try MacReady's idea are due back at any moment, sir."

The message from the Secretary of the Navy neither interrupted nor intensified the feverish labor going on upon the battered ships that had limped into port four days before. An interruption would have slowed things up. An intensification would have been impossible. Repairs were being made with a reckless disregard for mere deficiencies in materials or means. One marvelous assemblage of plates and machinery had parts of six separate vessels in it. Another was repaired from four, one of them a troop transport stolen from the Army while somebody painstakingly looked the other way. Depth-bomb sowers were being equipped for a new purpose, and a strictly improvised munitions plant was unloading Army shells of one type and reloading their contents into naval shells of another sort entirely, which lacked full charges.

And Lieutenant MacReady was rapidly attaining to a state approaching heaven. A flight of Navy planes had gone out to sea, far beyond the view of pacifists and politicians. They had laid down a smoke screen of the thickest and heaviest sort, and made certain tests. Then they laid down a second and made other tests. And they went roaring back to shore with Lieutenant MacReady filled with a stilly rapture.

He found the commander of the *Wasp* in his quarters, picking threads out of one sleeve of his uniform coat.

"Pulling off some gold braid," he said ruefully to MacReady. "Mac, there's no room for me on this damned ship. So I'm pulling some gold braid off. I'll look like a petty officer without it, and I'm stowing away till the action begins."

"Hold on," said MacReady unsteadily. "I'm sort of dizzy with success. But you've a right to share in it. You gave me the idea first. I'll go to the skipper and ask."

"What idea? What in hell?"

"You talked about the enemy using an infrared filter to photograph the battle fleet through eight miles of haze. It made me think. Have you ever seen the sun through a smoke screen?"

"Of course! It's red."

"Quite true," said MacReady. "The blue rays are filtered out by a smoke screen or by dust. Only reds remain. The sun gets redder as the smoke screen gets thicker, because only the very longest of visible rays get through. The question came up, did infrared rays get stopped at all?"

"Mac!"

"The photoelectric cells in our range finders," said MacReady with a strange precision, "are sensitive to infrared. We went out to sea with a baby range finder. We put on camera filters that shut off everything but the infrared rays. The range finder worked perfectly well. Then we laid down a smoke screen. The finder still worked. Then we laid down another one, thick and wide and deep. And the finder still worked. We're going to fight the last fight of the *Minnesota* that way. We'll be independent of aircraft for spotting, even if we're deep in the middle of a smoke screen ourselves. And so I'll see if I've got a pull with the skipper."

A long time later he came back. His eyes were glowing.

"You'll sit up in the fighting top with me, old horse. We go into action at dawn."

The commander of the *Wasp* started up. "Praise God! You're sure?"

"At the present," said MacReady evenly, "the enemy fleet is bombarding Seattle. The word came through five minutes ago. It's steaming past on the way south. Every ship, as it passes, flings a few broadsides into the town. The present estimate is that half the civilian population is wiped out—

and the fleet is still passing. The enemy intention is evidently to hasten our acceptance of their peace terms."

The *Wasp's* commander clenched his fists and swore helplessly.

"We'll sail in time to meet them just after dawn," said MacReady calmly. "The *Minnesota* and what destroyers we've patched up, against the battle fleet that sank our own. Old horse, we ought to have a gaudy suicide. And so—" he poured libation—"here's hell to politicians!"

4

Strategy was defined by General Forrest, C.S.A., as "getting the mostest men there the firstest." Fire superiority may be similarly explained as getting the most shells to the target first. And fire superiority is the lesson to be learned from the Battle of the California Coast.—Grahame, Modern Sea Power.

The dawn came quietly over the hills to eastward. In a vast silence the darkness thinned and the stars paled, and little winking shore lights faded to obscurity as the sky turned gray, and nearly white, and then took on its normal blueness with only a small pinkish glow above the sun itself.

The *Minnesota* was headed north. Ahead of her there were five destroyers in line, with a scout cruiser at either end. The monster aircraft carriers trailed behind her, their decks white with land planes. More tiny destroyers darted here and there about them. In the rear, again, two fleet submaries plowed along at twenty knots. They had come into harbor with their crews bleary-eyed from exhaustion just three hours before the *Minnesota* sailed. And they were going out again, refueled and with their torpedo racks refilled, with half their crews sleeping the twitching slumber of exhaustion in their bunks. Fresh men would navigate them until the action began. Then the exhausted men would rise and share in it. It was their right, and they had demanded it.

The rim of the sun peered over the eastern horizon. Vividly scarlet, it was not the dull-red ball that presages a sultry morning. It came slowly and heavily up over the edge of the world and like some monstrous balloon broke awkwardly free and swam upward into the sky. The sea became abruptly a cerulean blue, and the waves glittered and flashed in the sunshine.

Lieutenant MacReady, up in the *Minnesota's* fighting top, turned to the former skipper of the *Wasp*. He pointed to a trailing wake of gulls, fluttering tirelessly after the ship.

"I've watched those things for hours, in my time," he observed. "They'll see something today. Thank God we've got clear weather! Old horse, we've got a fine day to die in!"

The skipper of the *Wasp* was searching the sky ahead through binoculars.

"The enemy," he said briefly. "See?"

He pointed. An infinitesimal speck against the pale-blue sky was hovering too steadily to be a gull. Lieutenant MacReady spoke crisply into the transmitter trapped to his chest. There was a sudden flurry over on one of the aircraft carriers. Half a dozen planes shot upward, climbing steeply. They passed nearly over the *Minnesota*. The two in the fighting top could see the helmeted, goggled head of the last pilot as he went streaking in the wake of the rest.

"Never had much use for the Army," said MacReady absently, with his eyes searching the skyline ahead, "but they're turning out pretty good eggs. They do like a scrap, anyhow."

The tiny fleet moved steadily onward. The sun shone upon the vessels, and they were gleaming and defiant in its early rays. But the *Minnesota* alone was unblemished. Patches showed clearly on the rest. A sailor was absorbedly engaged in painting something on the *Stingray*. He was trying to cover up a rust spot that had appeared almost overnight on an unpainted weld.

Silence and stillness. Far overhead, the fighting planes from the carrier were mere specks, as tiny as the ship they had gone up to destroy. That enemy observation-plane turned tail and fled. The American planes raced after it. They went beyond the horizon and disappeared.

The clamor of a gong sounded below. Lieutenant MacReady turned to his companion and grinned. "Mess! But they'll send something up for us."

The fleet went on. Fifteen minutes. Half an hour. An hour. The sea was clean before them. Then tiny pinpoints appeared on the horizon.

"Enemy destroyers," said MacReady. He spoke into his strapped-on transmitter and looked down at the guns. They remained motionless. The *Minnesota* went on steadily, ignoring the distant tiny ships, awaiting enemies worthy of her steel. Her destroyer escort kept formation. The attitude of the American fleet was that of scorn.

More pinpoints. More destroyers. They drew closer, but not too close. They spread about, keeping to a thirty-thousand-yard range. They hemmed in the horizon ahead and to westward. Heavier ships appeared—scout cruisers. The sea seemed speckled with enemy craft. Light ships closed in the horizon behind the *Minnesota*.

"That's so they can mop up if we try to run for it," said MacReady. "Read for torpedo attacks at the end of the action. Lord! There're a bunch of them!"

There were a bunch of them. Three fourths of the destroyer force that had come across the Pacific. As many as the American battle fleet had taken into the Battle of Hungars' Bank. They turned the horizon on three sides of the *Minnesota* into something fancifully resembling a picket fence.

Enemy pocket battleships came into view, steaming at full speed to be in at the death. They deployed in line ahead, cutting off the *Minnesota* from the open sea. But they did not fire a gun. Now little specks began to appear in the air above the enemy fleet, and still there was no offensive movement. Then the six full-sized battleships of the enemy came grandly over the edge of the world. They moved for an apparently predetermined position.

"This isn't to be a battle," said MacReady. "They're figuring it as an execution—a beautiful example of fire superiority and fire control. Considering the psychology of our gallant foes, I imagine they'll try to blow us out of the water with a simultaneous broadside from every ship in the fleet. It would be neat, and probably effective. Or do you suppose they think we came out to surrender?"

The ten destroyers with the *Minnesota* suddenly belched forth black smoke from their funnels and shot ahead. Weaving back and forth, darting here and there, they began to make an impenetrable smoke screen between the *Minnesota* and her enemies. MacReady flung back his head to look at the land. Yes! A long black thread-like line was lengthening from the shore. Army planes. Five miles from the *Minnesota* that line bifurcated—split in two.

"God bless 'em!" said MacReady comfortably." They're just on time! They'll give the destroyers a busy morning. Every bomber the Army owns is in that line! We've got air superiority in this action!"

The *Minnesota* was in the center of perhaps a square mile of open sea, with a growing wall of blackness about her. But from the fighting top MacReady could see over it.

He watched the enemy ships building up a precise, cere-monial formation for the destruction of the *Minnesota*. Mac-Ready's eyes gleamed suddenly. The top forward turret swung in place and its guns wound up to nearly maximum elevation.

"They do love ceremony, the enemy," he said gently. "They're arranging themselves for our destruction as if it were a review. If I were the Old Man, I'd not bother about ranging salvos after the first spotting. We've got them all ranged, anyhow, and with one salvo for wind and barometer and so on, I'd fire broadsides only."

The *Minnesota's* top turret guns flashed ear-splittingly—the first ranging salvo. The destroyers were weaving madly about, extending and thickening the smoke screen about her. It would have blinded any other ship in the world and made her utterly dependent upon aircraft observation. But spotting is exacting work, and the Army observers wouldn't be ef-ficient in spotting for the Navy anyhow. The enemy evidently counted upon it. The smoke screen was wide and thick. Here and there it billowed upward enough to obscure the horizon. But a long time later MacReady saw three splashes rising mountainously near one of the pocket battleships of the enemy. He opened his mouth automatically to telephone a correction, but before he could speak the *Minnesota* let loose. And this time she was broadside on to her target. Not only her forward battery, but fore and aft, with all her main and secondary battery, she flung a hurtling hell of steel and flame toward the enemy. The recoil made her whole vast fabric shudder. Fifteen seconds later she flamed again. Fifteen seconds; the air split asunder with the same concussion. Fifteen seconds . . . With unvarying, mathematical precision, she let go twelve broadsides in three minutes. It was impossible to discover that her gun muzzles shifted.

She came about in a long sweep. MacReady and the skipper

of the *Wasp* ignored their bleeding noses and the bruises of sheer concussion. They swept the horizon, quivering like hounds on the scent.

"One—two—three!" MacReady counted in an awed voice. "Three of them sunk, by God! Thank God for heavy metal! And another one's out of action, or I'm a Swede! *Ah-h-h-h!*"

An apparently uninjured speck, against the very edge of the world, tore itself apart with a sudden vehemence. There was a flash and a monstrous ball of dense black smoke. Then there was another gap in the ceremonial formation which was to execute the *Minnesota*. Either it had forgotten that the American ship was the most powerful war vessel in the world or it had counted upon no more than human accuracy in its shellfire. But there was no human factor-of-error in the gun-laying on the *Minnesota* now. She was a machine, and the most deadly fighting machine on earth.

Flashes appeared along that distant line of ships. The *Minnesota* dived into the smoke screen all about. A destroyer darted aside to give it room. The smoke screen had been laid in long spreading trails of blackness. From aloft it would look like a rather untidily executed maze. MacReady caught a glimpse of the foredeck of the *Langley*—its afterdeck was blotted out by a hill of densest black—and plane after plane after plane was taking off with the regularity and precision of bullets going out of a machine gun. He saw a spreading fan of planes rising from another spot—the other carrier. Then the *Minnesota* vanished from beneath him as it went swiftly into darkness. A long distance away he saw the other fighting top above a sea of black. Black billows rolled lazily about the horizon. He saw a ship on fire, in the enemy line. That was the work of one of the fleet subs. The enemy did not know of their existence or escape. They took a heavy toll between them, and one of them blew itself to atoms beneath the pocket battleship that rammed it. Which was not healthy for the pocket battleship.

MacReady heard his companion shouting. He was chattering excitedly into the telephone transmitter strapped to his chest. A concussion wave struck him. The ship was firing again. The gas blasts from the guns blew the smoke screen crazily about. One; fifteen seconds—two; fifteen seconds—three . . . Six broadsides the *Minnesota* fired from the thickest of its own smoke screen.

Hell broke loose a half mile astern. A six-inch shell screamed between the fighting tops of the *Minnesota*. That was a stray. The storm of fire from the capital ships of the enemy fleet was pouring into the ocean where the *Minnesota* might have been, but wasn't. They couldn't see her. Her smoke screen hid her before they had fired ranging salvos. And range readings by even trained observers are not much good without trial salvos and spottings. The *Minnesota* had started the action on her own terms, which, with air superiority on her side, were much better than the enemy had intended.

Two minutes of silence save for the screaming of enemy shells searching for the ship. The smoke screen was lengthening and spreading. The *Minnesota* had four square miles of blackness in which to hide, but it was blackness only to the enemy. MacReady caught a glimpse of a monstrous dogfight going on aloft. Enemy aircraft could not spot the *Minnesota* from above their own ships. So intricately woven was her protecting screen that a position nearly vertically above her was essential. The enemy aircraft were trying to get it. The Army ships were keeping them from it. The solitary American battleship was using tactics which not only were entirely new, they were tactics which were impossible to a ship without control of the air, without eyes to penetrate the screen and prevent collision with her tiny consorts, and without utterly perfect spotting for her shells.

Enemy shells shrieked all about. An eight-incher landed somewhere and burst with a sickening detonation. The whole sea seemed to be boiling. Shell splashes leaped upward above the smoke screen, glittering in the sunlight. They were visible to the enemy, but not especially helpful without a sight of their target. There was a flickering ball of madly fighting planes a mile and a half to the right. Something huge and winged burst out of it and raced toward the *Minnesota*'s fighting tops, with a dozen Army single-seaters pouring lead at it and two enemy combat planes dying magnificently in the attempt to protect it.

The big ship's antiaircraft battery crashed venomously. There was a colossal, an incredible explosion. The huge winged thing vanished in an expanding ball of flame. Two combat ships shriveled and fell with it. Another reeled and a wing came off, and it began to descend, whirling crazily like a maple leaf. The rest of them turned and went madly back toward the ball of roaring, crackling fighting things.

The *Minnesota* shuddered again. And again. And again. Broadsides of every gun that would bear fired from abysmal blackness into the bright sunshine. Storms of screaming metal, flying shieking through space, to fall twenty miles away. From the tail of his eye MacReady saw a magnificent duel of two fighting planes ended in the fraction of a second as the trajectory of some ship's broadside passed through the area of their combat. They were annihilated. But MacReady could not see it all. He was battered at and pounded by waves of sheer concussion. He heard a voice beside him, thinly, and it was the commander of the *Wasp*, but MacReady could not make out what he was saying and did not try. Then he caught a glimpse of the enemy fleet as the rolling billows of the smoke screen lowered for an instant.

The noise did not lessen for an instant, and it was like the din of all hell let loose. But MacReady did not hear it, because something huge over in the enemy lines was pointing its bow skyward and going down slowly by the stern. A monstrous mound of water rose above it as a broadside struck. The mound subsided, and that monstrous ship was only a third of a ship above-water. It was going down and down . . . A pocket battleship was on fire. A broadside struck one of the enemy's big ships. Fifteen seconds later, another. Fifteen seconds later still, a third. Fifteen seconds later still, a fourth. . . .

"Fire power!" cried MacReady exultantly amid the tumult of ten thousand explosions. "We've got it! The heaviest broadside in the world! Infrared screens. Beam range finders that spot our own shells with the targets they strike. Powder that varies less than a thousand pounds' pressure at the breech! Six ships we've sunk, old horse! Six ships! And we're barely scratched! Why doesn't the enemy use his destroyers? Their big ships are no good! If they want to finish us, why don't they bring on their destroyers?"

As if to answer him, he saw. The *Minnesota* ran into an area where its smoke screen had partly settled down and spread out. It was still not in view of the enemy capital ships. Only the fighting tops and a quarter of the masts were clear. But the smoke ended a half mile away and the line of enemy destroyers were in full charge. Full speed ahead, bones in their teeth, straining every nerve for the velocity needed to make a success of their suicidal dash for the *Minnesota*. Twenty of them in a magnificent squadron plunging for the target of their fleet.

One of them rose and buckled as a thousand-pound bomb exploded in the sea in contact with its hull. The Army bombers were at work. A second lost its tail and came to a halt, spitting smoke and stream and bitterly despairing streams of antiaircraft shells. A third ran into an aerial bomb and started a dive that ended on the bottom. The *Minnesota's* antitorpedo battery exploded thunderously. Again. Again. Again. . . . Six terrific volleys. Six destroyers died. The bombers got to work again on what were left. The smoke screen heaved slowly upward and blotted out the view.

There were twenty square miles of smoke screen for the *Minnesota* to play in now, and the Army held the air against the most desperate assaults of an enemy now in actually a desperate position. The American battleship was the most powerful battleship on earth—even on paper. She could range her shots and spot them through a smoke screen that made her invisible to the enemy. The Army had held the air above her from the first. Now it was fighting for the air above the enemy. American air bombs sank one enemy aircraft carrier. A pocket battleship's steering gear was wrecked by a bombing squadron who went on about their other business and left a flight of torpedo planes to finish her off. The enemy fleet was in exactly the position into which, with the assistance of American politicians, it had maneuvered the American battle fleet off Hungars' Bank. The *Minnesota* had control of the air and fought not only behind but in a smoke screen. The enemy ships were necessarily firing nearly at random, despite their enormous numerical superiority, while the *Minnesota* fired broadside after broadside with an uncanny accuracy. And its broadside was the heaviest afloat. In this action, because of the unhuman accuracy of its range-finder spotting, it secured a larger percentage of hits than any other vessel had ever made, in action or out of it.

"All they've got left," panted the commander of the *Wasp*, "is subs!" He was hoarse, though he could never remember speaking a word before, and much less shouting. "They've tried everything else. They'll try their subs now!"

MacReady's nose and ears were bleeding from concussion.

His eyes were bloodshot and watering from the same cause. He was gory and horrible to look at, but he grinned exultantly.

"The wind's blowing the smoke screen southward at fourteen knots. We're moving with it. There's no sub on earth can travel fourteen knots submerged, and you can bet your other collar, old horse, that no sub's going to get to us on the surface!"

A faint howl came up from below. It sounded even above the tumult of explosions all about and the uproar of aircraft aloft. There was no fighting above the *Minnesota* now. The fighting was taking place above the enemy fleet. The howl came up again, thin and reedy but triumphant. MacReady recognized it. It was a simultaneous roar of pure delight from the officers and men of the *Minnesota*. And MacReady's earphones gave him the cause of it an instant later:

"The enemy has formed a smoke screen for his own protection from our fire!"

And Lieutenant MacReady and the commander of the now trisected *Wasp* arose and danced clumsily about the fighting top of the *Minnesota* and shrieked themselves hoarse from pure joy.

Because, of course, if the *Minnesota*'s range finders could range and spot shells through a smoke screen to direct her fire out of it, they could also work through two to direct her fire into another. And the enemy's control of the air was gone forever, so his only possible hope would be to destroy the accuracy of the *Minnesota*'s fire. It was incredible. It was impossible. But it was true.

So the action of the ninth of August, 1934, more commonly known as the Battle of the California Coast, was completed with two blankets of blackness floating upon the sea. The *Minnesota* remained deep in one mass of impenetrable darkness, and her guns boomed and boomed and boomed, sending shells screaming to the targets futilely hiding in the heart of another darkness or with even greater futility trying to flee.

The action had started at half past six in the morning. At three in the afternoon—it was seven o'clock by Washington time—an official order reached the *Minnesota* by wireless and in the official naval code. There had been a stormy, a tumultuous session in Congress. The bombardment of Seattle had had the effect the enemy anticipated. Instead of two days of debate, a conclusion was reached in one. A resolution had been passed accepting the preliminary peace terms of the enemy. The President of the United States was commanded to issue the orders meeting the enemy's requirements for an armistice.

As commander in chief of the military and naval forces of the United States, he issued the historic order:

TO THE SENIOR OFFICER COMMANDING AMERICAN VESSELS OF WAR IN THE PACIFIC OCEAN.
Immediately on receipt of this order you will surrender all vessels under your command to the officer in command of the enemy battle fleets off our coasts.

And the captain of the *Minnesota* radioed his even more historic reply:

TO THE PRESIDENT OF THE UNITED STATES.
There is no longer an enemy battle fleet off our coasts. We have destroyed it.

As a matter of politics, the Battle of the California Coast had the extraordinary result of making pacifism no longer respectable. In any case it immediately ceased to be a political issue, because America instantly backslid into patriotism. Our politicians, in the remaining three days before election, vied with each other in patriotic fervor. Where before they had competed for the noblest expressions of resignation to the will of Providence, now they struggled to outdo each other in the ingenuity of the demands they proposed we should make upon the enemy as the price of peace. And they were voted for on that basis.

But at any rate, until America forgets, the Army and the Navy are not toys for politicians any longer.

Memento Homo

WALTER M. MILLER, JR.

The work of Walter M. Miller, Jr., is beginning to receive from fans the sort of respect which it has for some years received from authors and editors. His earnest poetry has made itself felt in one novel (the best-selling A Canticle for Leibowitz) *and two volumes of short stories. Here is a fine example of his shorter work, not included in either of his collections.*

. . . quia pulvis es et in pulverem reverteris.

Old Donegal was dying. They had all known it was coming, and they watched it come—his haggard wife, his daugher, and now his grandson, home on emergency leave from the pre-astronautics academy. Old Donegal knew it, too, and had known it from the beginning, when he had begun to lose control of his legs and was forced to walk with a cane. But most of the time he pretended to let them keep the secret they shared with the doctors—that the operations had all been failures, and that the cancer that fed at his spine would gnaw its way brainward until the paralysis engulfed vital organs, and then Old Donegal would cease to be. It would be cruel to let them know that he knew.

Once, weeks ago, he had joked about the approaching shadows. "Buy the plot back where people won't walk over it, Martha," he said. "Get it way back under the cedars—next to the fence. There aren't many graves back there yet. I want to be alone."

"Don't *talk* that way, Donny!" his wife had choked. "You're not dying."

His eyes twinkled maliciously. "Listen, Martha, I want to be buried face down. I want to be buried with my back to space, understand? Don't let them lay me out like a lily."

"Donny, *please!*"

"They oughta face a man the way he's headed," Donegal grunted. "I been up—*way* up. Now I'm going straight down."

Martha had fled from the room in tears. He had never done it again, except to the interns and nurses, who, while they insisted that he was going to get well, didn't mind joking with him about it.

Martha can bear my death, he thought, can bear preknowledge of it. But she couldn't bear thinking that he might take it calmly. If he accepted death gracefully, it would be like deliberately leaving her, and Old Donegal had decided to help her believe whatever would be comforting to her in such a troublesome moment.

"When'll they let me out of this bed again?" he complained.

"Be patient, Donny," she sighed. "It won't be long. You'll be up and around before you know it."

"Back on the moon run, maybe?" he offered. "Listen, Martha, I been planetbound too long. I'm not too old for the moon run, am I? Sixty-three's not so old."

That had been carrying things too far. She knew he was hoaxing, and dabbed at her eyes again. The dead must humor the mourners, he thought, and the sick must comfort the visitors. It was always so.

But it was harder, now that the end was near. His eyes were hazy, and his thoughts unclear. He could move his arms a little, clumsily, but feeling was gone from them. The rest of his body was lost to him. Sometimes he seemed to feel his stomach and his hips, but the sensation was mostly an illusion offered by higher nervous centers, like the "ghost arm" that an amputee continues to feel. The wires were down, and he was cut off from himself.

He lay wheezing on the hospital bed, in his own room, in his own rented flat. Gaunt and unshaven, gray as winter twilight, he lay staring at the white net curtains that billowed gently in the breeze from the open window. There was no sound in the room but the sound of breathing and the loud ticking of an alarm clock. Occasionally he heard a chair scraping on the stone terrace next door, and the low mutter of voices, sometimes laughter, as the servants of the Keith mansion arranged the terrace for late-afternoon guests.

With considerable effort he rolled his head toward Martha, who sat beside the bed, pinch-faced and weary.

"You ought to get some sleep," he said.

"I slept yesterday. Don't talk, Donny. It tires you."

"You ought to get more sleep. You never sleep enough. Are you afraid I'll get up and run away if you go to sleep for a while?"

She managed a brittle smile. "There'll be plenty of time for sleep when . . . when you're well again." The brittle smile fled and she swallowed hard, like swallowing a fishbone. He glanced down, and noticed that she was squeezing his hand spasmodically.

There wasn't much left of the hand, he thought. Bones and ugly tight-stretched hide spotted with brown. Bulging knuckles with yellow cigarette stains. My hand. He tried to tighten it, tried to squeeze Martha's thin one in return. He watched it open and contract a little, but it was like operating a remote-control mechanism. Goodbye, hand, you're leaving me the way my legs did, he told it. I'll see you again in hell. How hammy can you get, Old Donegal? You maudlin ass.

"Requiescat," he muttered over the hand, and let it lie in peace.

Perhaps she heard him. "Donny," she whispered, leaning closer, "won't you let me call the priest now? Please."

He rattled a sigh and rolled his head toward the window again. "Are the Keiths having a party today?" he asked. "Sounds like they're moving chairs out on the terrace."

"Please, Donny, the priest?"

He let his head roll aside and closed his eyes, as if asleep. The bed shook slightly as she quickly caught at his wrist to feel for a pulse.

"If I'm not dying, I don't need a priest," he said sleepily.

"That's not right," she scolded softly. "You know that's not right, Donny. You know better."

Maybe I'm being too rough on her? he wondered. He hadn't minded getting baptized her way, and married her way, and occasionally priest-handled the way she wanted him to when he was home from a space run; but when it came to dying, Old Donegal wanted to do it his own way.

He opened his eyes at the sound of a bench being dragged across the stone terrace. "Martha, what kind of a party are the Keiths having today?"

"I wouldn't know," she said stiffly. "You'd think they'd

have a little more respect. You'd think they'd put it off a few days."

"Until—?"

"Until you feel better."

"I feel fine, Martha. I like parties. I'm glad they're having one. Pour me a drink, will you? I can't reach the bottle any more."

"It's empty."

"No it isn't, Martha, it's still a quarter full. I know. I've been watching it."

"You shouldn't have it, Donny. Please don't."

"But this is a party, Martha. Besides, the doctor says I can have whatever I want. Whatever I want, you hear? That means I'm getting well, doesn't it?"

"Sure, Donny, sure. Getting well."

"The whiskey, Martha. Just a finger in a tumbler, no more. I want to feel like it's a party."

Her throat was rigid as she poured it. She helped him get the tumbler to his mouth. The liquor seared his throat, and he gagged a little as the fumes clogged his noise. Good whiskey, the best—but he couldn't take it any more. He eyed the green stamp on the neck of the bottle on the bed table and grinned. He hadn't had whiskey like that since his space days. Couldn't afford it now, not on a blastman's pension.

He remembered how he and Caid used to smuggle a couple of fifths aboard for the moon run. If they caught you it meant suspension, but there was no harm in it, not for the blast-room men who had nothing much to do from the time the ship acquired enough velocity for the long, long coaster ride until they started the rockets again for lunar landing. You could drink a fifth, jettison the bottle through the trash lock, and sober up before you were needed again. It was the only way to pass the time in the cramped cubicle, unless you ruined your eyes trying to read by the glow lamps. Old Donegal chuckled. If he and Caid had stayed on the run, Earth would have a ring by now, like Saturn—a ring of Old Granddad bottles.

"You said it, Donny-boy," said the misty man by the billowing curtains. "Who else knows the Gegenschein is broken glass?"

Donegal laughed. Then he wondered what the man was doing there. The man was lounging against the window, and his unzipped space rig draped about him in an old familiar way. Loose plug-in connections and hose ends dangled about his lean body. He was freckled and grinning.

"Caid," Old Donegal breathed softly.

"What did you say, Donny?" Martha answered.

Old Donegal blinked hard and shook his head. Something let go with a soggy snap, and the misty man was gone. I'd better take it easy on the whiskey, he thought. You got to wait, Donegal, old lush, until Nora and Ken get here. You can't get drunk until they're gone, or you might get them mixed up with memories like Caid's.

Car doors slammed in the street below. Martha glanced toward the window.

"Think it's them? I wish they'd get here. I wish they'd hurry."

Martha arose and tiptoed to the window. She peered down toward the sidewalk, put on a sharp frown. He heard a distant mutter of voices and occasional laughter, with group footsteps milling about on the sidewalk. Martha murmured her disapproval and closed the window.

"Leave it open," he said.

"But the Keiths' guests are starting to come. There'll be such a racket." Se looked at him hopefully, the way she did when she prompted his manners before company came.

Maybe it wasn't decent to listen in on a party when you were dying, he thought. But that wasn't the reason. Donegal, your chamber pressure's dropping off. Your brains are in your butt end, where a spacer's brains belong, but your butt end died last month. She wants the window closed for her own sake, not yours.

"Leave it closed," he grunted. "But open it again before the moon run blasts off. I want to listen."

She smiled and nodded, glancing at the clock. "It'll be an hour and a half yet. I'll watch the time."

"I hate that clock. I wish you'd throw it out. It's loud."

"It's your medicine clock, Donny." She came back to sit down at his bedside again. She sat in silence. The clock filled the room with its clicking pulse.

"What time are they coming?" he asked.

"Nora and Ken? They'll be here soon. Don't fret."

"Why should I fret?" He chuckled. "That boy—he'll be a good spacer, won't he, Martha?"

213

Martha said nothing, fanned at a fly that crawled across his pillow. The fly buzzed up in an angry spiral and alighted on the ceiling. Donegal watched it for a time. The fly had natural-born space legs. I know your tricks, he told it with a smile, and I learned to walk on the bottomside of things before you were a maggot. You stand there with your magnasoles hanging to the hull, and the rest of you's in free fall. You jerk a sole lose, and your knee flies up to your belly, and reaction spins you half around and near throws your other hip out of joint if you don't jam the foot down fast and jerk up the other. It's worse'n trying to run through knee-deep mud with snowshoes, and a man'll go nuts trying to keep his arms and legs from taking off in odd directions. I know your tricks, fly. But the fly was born with his magnasoles, and he trotted across the ceiling like Donegal never could.

"That boy Ken—he ought to make a damn good space engineer," wheezed the old man.

Her silence was long, and he rolled his head toward her again. Her lips tight, she stared down at the palm of his hand, unfolded his bony fingers, felt the cracked calluses that still welted the shrunken skin, calluses worn there by the linings of space gauntlets and the handles of fuel valves, and the rungs of get-about ladders during free fall.

"I don't know if I should tell you," she said.

"Tell me what, Martha?"

She looked up slowly, scrutinizing his face. "Ken's changed his mind, Nora says. Ken doesn't like the academy. She says he wants to go to medical school."

Old Donegal thought it over, nodded absently. "That's fine. Space medics get good pay." He watched her carefully.

She lowered her eyes, rubbed at his calluses again. She shook her head slowly. "He doesn't want to go to space."

The clock clicked loudly in the closed room.

"I thought I ought to tell you, so you won't say anything to him about it," she added.

Old Donegal looked grayer than before. After a long silence, he rolled his head away and looked toward the limp curtains.

"Open the window, Martha," he said.

Her tongue clucked faintly as she started to protest, but she said nothing. After frozen seconds, she sighed and went to open it. The curtains billowed, and a babble of conversation blew in from the terrace of the Keith mansion. With the sound came the occasional brassy discord of a musician tuning his instrument. She clutched the window sash as if she wished to slam it closed again.

"Well! Music!" grunted Old Donegal. "That's good. This is some shebang. Good whiskey and good music and you." He chuckled, but it choked off into a fit of coughing.

"Donny, about Ken—"

"No matter, Martha," he said hastily. "Space medic's pay is good."

"But, Donny—" She turned from the window, stared at him briefly, then said, "Sure, Donny, sure," and came back to sit down by his bed.

He smiled at her affectionately. She was a man's woman, was Martha—always had been, still was. He had married her the year he had gone to space—a lissome, wistful, old-fashioned lass, with big violet eyes and gentle hands and gentle thoughts—and she had never complained about the long and lonely weeks between blast-off and glide-down, when most spacers' wives listened to the psychiatrists and soap operas and soon developed the symptoms that were expected of them, either because the symptoms were chic or because they felt they should do something to earn the pity that was extended to them. "It's not so bad," Martha had assured him. "The house keeps me busy till Nora's home from school, and then there's a flock around till dinner. Nights are a little empty, but if there's a moon I can always go out on the porch and look at it and know where you are. And Nora gets out the telescope you built her, and we make a game of it. 'Seeing if Daddy's still at the office' she calls it."

"Those were the days," he muttered.

"What, Donny?"

"Do you remember that Steve Farran song?"

She paused, frowning thoughtfully. There were a lot of Steve Farran songs, but after a moment she picked the right one and sang it softly . . .

> "O moon whereo'er the clouds fly,
> Beyond the willow tree,
> There is a ramblin' space guy
> I wish you'd save for me.

Mare Tranquilitatis,
O dark and tranquil sea,
Until he drops from heaven,
Rest him there with thee . . ."

Her voice cracked, and she laughed. Old Donegal chuckled weakly.

"Fried mush," he said. "That one made the cats wilt their ears and wail at the moon. I feel real crazy," he added. "Hand me the king kong, fluffmuff."

"Keep cool, Daddy-O, you've had enough." Martha reddened and patted his arm, looking pleased. Neither of them had talked that way, even in the old days, but the outdated slang brought back memories—school parties, dances at the Rocketport Club, the early years of the war when Donegal had jockeyed an R-43 fighter in the close-space assaults against the Soviet satellite project. The memories were good.

A brassy blare of modern "slide" arose suddenly from the Keith terrace as the small orchestra launched into its first number. Martha caught an angry breath and started toward the window.

"Leave it," he said. "It's a party. Whiskey, Martha. Please —just a small one."

She gave him a hurtful glance.

"Whiskey. Then you can call the priest."

"Donny, it's not right. You know it's not right—to bargain for such as that."

"All right. Whiskey. Forget the priest."

She poured it for him, and helped him get it down, and then went out to make the phone call. Old Donegal lay shuddering over the whiskey taste and savoring the burn in his throat. Jesus, but it was good.

You old bastard, he thought, you got no right to enjoy life when nine tenths of you is dead already, and the rest is foggy as a thermal dust-rise on the lunar *mare* at hell-dawn. But it wasn't a bad way to die. It ate your consciousness away from the feet up; it gnawed away the present, but it let you keep the past, until everything faded and blended. Maybe that's what eternity is, he thought—one man's subjective past, all wrapped up and packaged for shipment, a single space-time entity, a one-man microcosm of memories, when nothing else remains.

"If I've got a soul, I made it myself," he told the gray nun at the foot of his bed.

The nun held out a pie pan, rattled a few coins in it. "Contribute to the Radiation Victims' Relief?" the nun purred softly.

"I know you," he said. "You're my conscience. You hang around the officers' mess, and when we get back from a sortie you make us pay for the damage we did. But that was forty years ago."

The nun smiled, and her luminous eyes were on him softly. "Mother of God!" he breathed, and reached for the whiskey. His arm obeyed. The last drink had done him good. He had to watch his hand to see where it was going, and squeezed the neck until his fingers whitened so that he knew that he had it, but he got it off the table and onto his chest, and he got the cork out with his teeth. He had a long pull at the bottle, and it made his eyes water and his hands grow weak. But he got it back to the table without spilling a bit, and he was proud of himself.

The room was spinning like the cabin of a gyro-gravved ship. By the time he wrestled it to a standstill, the nun was gone. The blare of music from the Keith terrace was louder, and laughing voices blended with it. Chairs scraping and glasses rattling. A fine party, Keith, I'm glad you picked today. This shebang would be the younger Keith's affair. Ronald Tonwyler Keith III, scion of Orbital Engineering and Construction Company—builders of the moonshuttle ships that made the run from the satellite station to Luna and back.

It's good to have such important neighbors, he thought. He wished he had been able to meet them while he was still up and about. But the Keiths' place was walled in, and when a Keith came out he charged out in a limousine with a chauffeur at the wheel, and the iron gate closed again. The Keiths built the wall when the surrounding neighborhood began to grow shabby with age. It had once been the best of neighborhoods, but that was before Old Donegal lived in it. Now it consisted of sooty old houses and rented flats, and the Keith place was really not a part of it any more. Nevertheless, it was really something when a pensioned blastman could say, "I live out close to the Keiths—you know, the *Ronald* Keiths." At least, that's what Martha always told him.

The music was so loud that he never heard the doorbell ring, but when a lull came he heard Nora's voice downstairs and listened hopefully for Ken's. But when they came up, the boy was not with them.

"Hello, skinny-britches," he greeted his daughter.

Nora grinned and came over to kiss him. Her hair dangled about his face, and he noticed that it was blacker than usual, with the gray streaks gone from it again.

"You smell good," he said.

"You don't, Pops. You smell like a sot. Naughty!"

"Where's Ken?"

She moistened her lips nervously and looked away. "He couldn't come. He had to take a driver's lesson. He really couldn't help it. If he didn't go, he'd lose his turn, and then he wouldn't finish before he goes back to the academy." She looked at him apologetically.

"It's all right, Nora."

"If he missed it, he wouldn't get his copter license until summer."

"It's okay. Copters! Hell, the boy should be in jets by now!"

Several breaths passed in silence. She gazed absently toward the window and shook her head. "No jets, Pop. Not for Ken."

He glowered at her. "Listen! How'll he get into space? He's got to get his jet licenses first. Can't get in rockets without 'em."

Nora shot a quick glance at her mother. Martha rolled her eyes as if sighing patiently. Nora went to the window to stare down toward the Keith terrace. She tucked a cigarette between scarlet lips, lit it, blew nervous smoke against the pane.

"Mom, can't you call them and have that racket stopped?"

"Donny says he likes it."

Nora's eyes flitted over the scene below. "Female butterflies and puppy-dogs in sport jackets. And the cadets." She snorted. "Cadets! Imagine Ron Keith the Third ever going to space. The old man buys his way into the academy, and they throw a brawl as if Ronny passed the Compets."

"Maybe he did," growled Old Donegal.

"Hah!"

"They live in a different world, I guess," Martha sighed.

"If it weren't for men like Pops, they'd never've made their fortune."

"I like the music, I tell you," grumbled the old man.

"I've half a mind to go over there and tell them off," Nora murmured.

"Let them alone. Just so they'll stop the racket for blast-away."

"Look at them! Polite little pattern-cuts, all alike. They take pre-space because it's the thing to do. Then they quit before the payoff comes."

"How do you know they'll quit?"

"That party—I bet it cost six months' pay, spacer's pay," she went on, ignoring him. "And what do real spacers get? Oley gets killed, and Pop's pension wouldn't feed the Keiths' cat."

"You don't understand, girl."

"I lost Oley. I understand enough."

He watched her silently for a moment, then closed his eyes. It was no good trying to explain, no good trying to tell her the dough didn't mean a damn thing. She'd been a spacer's wife, and that was bad enough, but now she was a spacer's widow. And Oley? Oley's tomb revolved around the sun in an eccentric orbit that spun in close to Mercury, then reached out into the asteroid belt, once every 725 days. When it came within rocket radius of Earth, it whizzed past at close to fifteen miles a second.

You don't rescue a ship like that, skinny-britches, my darling daughter. Nor do you salvage it after the crew stops screaming for help. If you use enough fuel to catch it, you won't get back. You just leave such a ship there forever, like an asteroid, and it's a damn shame about the men trapped aboard. Heroes all, no doubt—but the smallness of the widow's monthly check failed to confirm the heroism, and Nora was bitter about the price of Oley's memory, perhaps.

Ouch! Old Donegal, you know she's not like that. It's just that she can't understand about space. You ought to make her understand.

But did he really understand, himself? You ride hot in a roaring blast room, hands tense on the mixer controls and the pumps, eyes glued to instruments, body sucked down in a four-gravity thrust, and wait for the command to choke it off. Then you float free and weightless in a long nightmare as the beast coasts moonward, a flung javelin.

The "romance" of space—drivel written in the old days.

When you're not blasting, you float in a cramped hotbox, crawl through dirty mazes of greasy pipe and cable to tighten a lug, scratch your arms and bark your shins, get sick and choked up because no gravity helps your gullet get the food down. Liquid is worse, but you gag your whiskey down because you have to.

Stars? You see stars by squinting through a viewing lens, and it's like a photo transparency, and if you aren't careful you'll get an eyeful of Old Blinder and back off with a punch-drunk retina.

Adventure? Unless the skipper calls for course correction, you float around in the blast cubicle with damn little to do between blast-away and moon-down, except sweat out the omniscient accident statistics. If the beast blows up or gets gutted in space, a statistic had your name on it, that's all, and there's no fighting back. You stay outwardly sane because you're a hog for punishment; if you weren't, you'd never get past the psychologists.

"Did you like horror movies when you were a kid?" asked the psych. And you'd damn well better answer yes, if you want to go to space.

Tell her, old man, you're her pop. Tell her why it's worth it, if you know. You jail yourself in a coffin-size cubicle, and a crazy beast thunders berserk for uncontrollable seconds, and then you soar in ominous silence for the long long hours. Grow sweaty, filthy, sick, miserable, idle—somewhere out in Big Empty, where man's got no business except the trouble he always makes for himself wherever he goes. Tell her why it's worth it, for pay less than a good bricklayer's. Tell her why Oley would do it again.

"It's a sucker's run, Nora," he said. "You go looking for kicks, but the only kicks you get to keep is what Oley got. God knows why—but it's worth it."

Nora said nothing. He opened his eyes slowly. Nora was gone. Had she been there at all?

He blinked around at the fuzzy room and dissolved the shifting shadows that sometimes emerged as old friendly faces, grinning at him. He found Martha.

"You went to sleep," said Martha. "She had to go. Kennie called. He'll be over later, if you're not too tired."

"I'm not tired. I'm all head. There's nothing much to get tired."

"I love you, Old Donegal."

"Hold my hand again."

"I'm holding it, old man."

"Then hold me where I can feel it."

She slid a thin arm under his neck and bent over his face to kiss him. She was crying a little, and he was glad she could do it now without fleeing the room.

"Can I talk about dying now?" he wondered aloud.

She pinched her lips together and shook her head.

"I lie to myself, Martha. You know how much I lie to myself?"

She nodded slowly and stroked his gray temples.

"I lie to myself about Ken, and about dying. If Ken turned spacer, I wouldn't die—that's what I told myself. You know?"

She shook her head. "Don't talk, Donny, please."

"A man makes his own soul, Martha."

"That's not true. You shouldn't say things like that."

"A man makes his own soul, but it dies with him, unless he can pour it into his kids and his grandchildren before he goes. I lied to myself. Ken's a yellow-belly. Nora made him one, and the boots won't fit."

"Don't, Donny. You'll excite yourself again."

"I was going to give him the boots—the overboots with magnasoles. But they won't fit him. They won't ever fit him. He's a lily-livered lapdog, and he whines. Bring me my boots, woman."

"Donny!"

"The boots, they're in my locker in the attic. I want them."

"What on earth!"

"Bring me my goddam space boots and put them on my feet. I'm going to wear them."

"You can't; the priest's coming."

"Well, get them anyway. What time is it? You didn't let me sleep through the moon-run blast, did you?"

She shook her head. "It's half an hour yet. I'll get the boots if you promise not to make me put them on you."

"I want them on."

"You can't, until Father Paul's finished."

"Do I have to get my feet buttered?"

She sighed. "I wish you wouldn't say things like that. I wish you wouldn't, Donny. It's sacrilege, you know it is."

"All right—'anointed'," he corrected wearily.

"Yes, you do."

"The boots, woman, the boots."

She went to get them. While she was gone, the doorbell rang, and he heard her quick footsteps on the stairs, and then Father Paul's voice asking about the patient. Old Donegal groaned inwardly. After the priest, the doctor would come, at the usual time, to see if he were dead yet. The doctor had let him come home from the hospital to die, and the doctor was getting impatient. Why don't they let me alone? he growled. Why don't they let me handle it in my own way, and stop making a fuss over it? I can die and do a good job of it without a lot of outside interference, and I wish they'd quit picking at me with syringes and sacraments and enemas. All he wanted was a chance to listen to the orchestra on the Keith terrace, to drink the rest of his whiskey, and to hear the beast blast away for the satellite on the first lap of the run to Luna.

It's going to be my last day, he thought. My eyes are going fuzzy, and I can't breathe right, and the throbbing's hurting my head. Whether he lived through the night wouldn't matter, because delirium was coming over him, and then there would be the coma, and the symbolic fight to keep him pumping and panting. I'd rather die tonight and get it over with, he thought, but they probably won't let me go.

He heard their voices coming up the stairs:

"Nora tried to get them to stop it, Father, but she couldn't get in to see anybody but the butler. He told her he'd tell Mrs. Keith, but nothing happened. It's just as loud as before."

"Well, as long as Donny doesn't mind . . ."

"He just says that. You know how he is."

"What're they celebrating, Martha?"

"Young Ronald's leaving—for pre-space training. It's a going-away affair."

They paused in the doorway. The small priest smiled in at Donegal and nodded. He set his black bag on the floor inside, winked solemnly at the patient.

"I'll leave you two alone," said Martha. She closed the door, and her footsteps wandered off down the hall.

Donegal and the young priest eyed each other warily.

"You look like hell, Donegal," the padre offered jovially. "Feeling nasty?"

"Skip the small talk. Let's get this routine over with."

The priest humphed thoughtfully, sauntered across to the bed, gazed down at the old man disinterestedly. "What's the matter? Don't want the 'routine'? Rather play it tough?"

"What's the difference?" he growled. "Hurry up and get out. I want to hear the beast blast off."

"You won't be able to," said the priest, glancing at the window, now closed again. "That's quite a racket next door."

"They'd better stop for it. They'd better quiet down for it. They'll have to turn it off for five minutes or so."

"Maybe they won't."

It was a new idea, and it frightened him. He liked the music, and the party's gaiety, the nearness of youth and good times—but it hadn't occurred to him that it wouldn't stop so he could hear the beast.

"Don't get upset, Donegal. You know what a blast-off sounds like."

"But it's the last one. The last time. I want to hear."

"How do you know it's the last time?"

"Hell, don't I know when I'm kicking off?"

"Maybe, maybe not. It's hardly your decision."

"It's not, eh?" Old Donegal fumed. "Well, bigawd, you'd think it wasn't. You'd think it was Martha's and yours and that damfool medic's. You'd think I got no say-so. Who's doing it, anyway?"

"I would guess," Father Paul grunted sourly, "that Providence might appreciate His fair share of the credit."

Old Donegal made a surly noise and hunched his head back into the pillow to glower.

"You want me?" the priest asked. "Or is this just a case of wifely conscience?"

"What's the difference? Give me the business and scram."

"No soap. Do you want the sacrament, or are you just being kind to your wife? If it's for Martha, I'll go *now*."

Old Donegal glared at him for a time, then wilted. The priest brought his bag to the bedside.

"Bless me, Father, for I have sinned."

"Bless you, son."

"I accuse myself . . ."

Tension, anger, helplessness—they had piled up on him, and now he was feeling the aftereffects. Vertigo, nausea, and the black confetti—a bad spell. The whiskey—if he could only reach the whiskey. Then he remembered he was receiving a sacrament and struggled to get on with it. Tell him, old man, tell him of your various rottennesses and vile transgressions, if you can remember some. A sin is whatever you're sorry for, maybe. But, Old Donegal, you're sorry for the wrong things, and this young Jesuitical gadget wouldn't like listening to it. I'm sorry I didn't get it instead of Oley, and I'm sorry I fought in the war, and I'm sorry I can't get out of this bed and take a belt to my daughter's backside for making a puny whelp out of Ken, and I'm sorry I gave Martha such a rough time all these years—and wound up dying in a cheap flat, instead of giving her things like the Keiths had. I wish I had been a sharpster, contractor, or thief . . . instead of a common laboring spacer, whose species lost its glamor after the war.

Listen, old man, you made your soul yourself, and it's yours. This young dispensor of oils, Substances and mysteries wishes only to help you scrape off the rough edges and gouge out the bad spots. He will not steal it, nor distort it with his supernatural chisels, nor make fun of it. He can take nothing away, but only cauterize and neutralize, he says, so why not let him try? Tell him the rotten messes.

"Are you finished, my son?"

Old Donegal nodded wearily, and said what he was asked to say, and heard the soft mutter of Latin that washed him inside and behind his ghostly ears—". . . *ego te absolvo in Nomine Patris* . . ."—and he accepted the rest of it lying quietly in the candlelight and the red glow of the sunset through the window, while the priest anointed him and gave him Bread, and read the words of the soul in greeting its Spouse: "I was asleep, but my heart waked; it is the voice of my beloved calling: come to me, my love, my dove, my undefiled . . ." and from beyond the closed window came the sarcastic wail of a clarinet painting hot slides against a rhythmic background.

It wasn't so bad, Old Donegal thought when the priest was done. He felt like a schoolboy in a starched shirt on Sunday morning, and it wasn't a bad feeling, though it left him weak.

The priest opened the window for him again and repacked his bag. "Ten minutes till blast-off," he said. "I'll see what I can do about the racket next door."

When he was gone Martha came back in, and he looked at

her face and was glad. She was smiling when she kissed him, and she looked less tired.

"Is it all right for me to die now?" he grunted.

"Donny, don't start that again."

"Where's the boots? You promised to bring them."

"They're in the hall. Donny, you don't want them."

"I want them, and I want a drink of whiskey, and I want to hear them fire the beast." He said it slow and hard, and he left no room for argument.

When she had got the huge boots over his shrunken feet, the magnasoles clanged against the iron bedframe and clung there, and she rolled him up so that he could look at them, and Old Donegal chuckled inside. He felt warm and clean and pleasantly dizzy.

"The whiskey, Martha, and for God's sake make them stop the noise till after the firing. Please!"

She went to the window and looked out for a long time. Then she came back and poured him an insignificant drink.

"Well?"

"I don't know," she said. "I saw Father Paul on the terrace, talking to somebody."

"Is it time?"

She glanced at the clock, looked at him doubtfully and nodded. "Nearly time."

The orchestra finished a number, but the babble of laughing voices continued. Old Donegal sagged. "They won't do it. They're the Keiths, Martha. Why should I ruin their party?"

She turned to stare at him, slowly shook her head. He heard someone shouting, but then a trumpet started softly, introducing a new number. Martha sucked in a hurt breath, pressed her hands together and hurried from the room.

"It's too late," he said after her.

Her footsteps stopped on the stairs. The trumpet was alone. Donegal listened, and there was no babble of voices, and the rest of the orchestra was silent. Only the trumpet sang—and it puzzled him, hearing the same slow bugle notes of the call played at the lowering of the colors.

The trumpet stopped suddenly. Then he knew it had been for him.

A brief hush—then thunder came from the blast station two miles to the west. First the low reverberation, rattling the windows, then the rising growl as the sleek beast knifed skyward on a column of blue-white hell. It grew and grew until it drowned the distant traffic sounds and dominated the silence outside.

Quit crying, you old fool, you maudlin ass . . .

"My boots," he whispered, "my boots . . . please . . ."

"You've got them on, Donny."

He sank quietly then. He closed his eyes and let his heart go up with the beast, and he sank into the gravity padding of the blast room, and Caid was with him, and Oley. And when Ronald Keith III instructed the orchestra to play "Blast-Room Man," after the beast's rumble had waned, Old Donegal was on his last moon run, and he was grinning. He'd had a good day.

Martha went to the window to stare out at the thin black trail that curled starward above the blast station through the twilight sky. Guests on the terrace were watching it, too.

The doorbell rang. That would be Ken, too late. She closed the window against the chill breeze and went back to the bed. The boots, the heavy, clumsy boots—they clung to the bedframe, with his feet half out of them. She took them off gently and set them out of company's sight. Then she went to answer the door.

The Bright Illusion

C. L. MOORE

C. L. Moore (Mrs. Henry Kuttner) is the only author nominated each of whose stories was nominated more than once. Both "Vintage Season" and "No Woman Born" have been republished several times and are almost as available as they ought to be.

"The Bright Illusion," a rather earlier story, was published in 1934 and has never been reprinted. I can't undestand this state of affairs, but I am extremely happy to remedy it.

Through the blinding shimmer of sun upon sand, Dixon squinted painfully at the curious mirage ahead. He was reeling with thirst and heat and weariness, and about him the desert heaved in long, blurred waves, but through the haze of his own weakness, and through the sun haze upon the desert, he peered anxiously at the thing and could not make it out.

Nothing he had ever seen or heard of could cause such a mirage as this. It was a great oval of yellow light, bulging up convexly from the earth like some translucent golden egg half buried in the sand. And over its surface there seemed to be an immense busyness, as if it was covered with tiny, shimmering things that moved constantly. He had never seen anything remotely resembling it before.

As he toiled through the sand toward the bright illusion, he became aware of darker specks around it haphazardly, specks that as he approached took on the aspect of men grotesquely sprawled in attitudes of death. He could not make it out. Of course it was a mirage, yet it did not recede as he advanced, and the details of those sprawled bodies became clearer and clearer, and the great translucent oval loomed up against the sky mystifyingly.

He thought he must be dreaming, or perhaps a little unbalanced by the heat and thirst. He had been struggling through this burning sand under this burning sun for a long while now, and there were times when the rush of illusion swallowed him up, and he could hear water splashing and fountains tinkling in the empty desert about him. This must be a hallucination, then, for it could scarcely be a mirage. He was almost upon it, and it had so real a look—those bodies, sprawling—

He stumbled over the first, for somehow his muscles did not co-ordinate very well now. It was the sun-withered body of an old man in the Legion uniform, his kepi fallen forward over his face. The next was that of an Arab in a tangle of dirty white garments, and beyond him was the almost-fresh corpse of a boy in khaki shorts and sun helmet.

Dixon wondered duly what had happened to them and why the bodies were in such varying stages of decomposition. He lifted a dragging head and peered at the great egg-shape thing bulging up from the sand. It reminded him of a huge bubble of golden water, save that bubbles were round, and—

Belatedly, caution returned to him. These dead men must have met their deaths somehow through the presence of the great egg. He had better advance more cautiously or— And then the pull seized him. He had come too near. Something inexorable and slow was dragging him forward—or was it that the great bubble was advancing toward him?

Sky and sand reeled. And the distance between him and the great egg-shaped thing lessened and lessened and—and somehow he found himself flat against a great golden translucency that shivered against him with the strangest motion, as if it was alive and hungry for—

He felt that he should be afraid, yet somehow he was not aware of fear at all. The golden light was closing over him and around him with a queer, engulfing motion. He shut his eyes and relaxed utterly in the impassive grip of the thing.

Dixon was lying motionless in the midst of a golden radiance that seemed crystal clear, yet so obstructed his vision that he could see only a few yards away, and the desert landscape outside was as unreal as a dream. The most delicious sensation of rest and well-being was surging through him in slow waves that succeeded one another like ripples on a shore, each leaving an increasing residue of serenity and luxurious comfort. Thirst and hunger and weariness had vanished in a breath. He knew no fear or anxiety. In a trancelike calm he lay there, feeling the waves flow through him unbroken, staring up into the lucid golden light without wonder or surprise.

How long he lay there he never knew. In the perfect peace of the glow enfolding him, he was very dimly aware that the all-penetrating waves were washing through him in a way which queerly suggested searching. They permeated every atom of him, flooding his brain with light and calmness.

In his tranced quiet he knew, without actually realizing, that memory in lightning flashes was reeling through his mind. Abstract memories of things he had learned in college and in afterlife. Snatches of literature, fragments of sciences. Mathematical problems solved in breathtaking speed and supplanted by chemical formulas that melted into the bits of psychology remembered from schooldays. Impassively he lay there, scarcely realizing the flashing reviews that passed through his light-flooded brain.

And then the tempo of the ripples that went over him began to change. His mind awoke by degrees from its pleasant coma, though his body still lay relaxed. And now the wavelets in the queerest way were beating upon his brain tantalizingly. Little fragments of thoughts not his own blew through his mind and faded.

He struggled to grasp them. He clutched at the vanishing tags, striving to weld them together, feeling obscurely that if he could retain each small flutter as it wavered through his mind, if he could put them together and fuse them in a unit, he might understand.

Very slowly he succeeded. Very slowly the waves as they flowed through him began to surrender their meanings to his clutching mind: meanings that solidified and amplified with each succeeding wave, building themselves up slowly as ripple after ripple washed serenely through the straining brain that was learning so painfully to comprehend their significance.

By degrees Dixon realized that some intelligence was striving to communicate with him. The knowledge did not come in words or even word forms introduced into his brain. But it came, slowly and inexorably, building up and up as wave after measured wave flowed through him and vanished, leaving a residue of knowledge to be increased by the next.

And the vast, the almost divine, impersonality of it staggered him. This being—intelligence, presence—was so utterly abstract a thing that even in the knowledge it imparted to him there was no hint of personality or consciousness of individual being. There could have been no "I" in its supervocabulary of thought ripples. Divinely serene, divinely abstract, it allowed knowledge to flow through the brain of the man suspended in its heart. And by measured degrees that knowledge build itself up in his mind.

He had been chosen. For a long while this being had been waiting here, trapping the men who came near enough, sending its light waves in floods through their minds to illuminate their thoughts and their capacity for knowledge, probing their intelligences. All those others lying outside had been found wanting. The being had discarded them and waited, in its serene passivity, until the right man came by.

This much flowed through his brain. Then there was a hiatus, to permit him to absorb the knowledge, to understand. After a while the wavelets began to beat through him again in their measured slowness. He became aware of vast, dim voids, blank stretches empty of space or time or any of the myriad dimensions. He knew that through these, while long periods elapsed which yet had no relation to the time he understood, the great light-bubble had traveled from some origin unthinkably far away, on a quest. He realized that it had at last emerged from those gray, formless voids into the interstellar space of his own universe; that it had made its way here, driven by a vast purpose he could not grasp, and had come to rest upon the desert sands, to lie in wait.

Again there was a gap in the thought waves, and again Dixon lay still, assimilating that stunning knowledge. And yet, somehow, he was not greatly surprised or in the remotest way skeptical. He waited.

Presently the flow began again. There was, in another part of space, a world which this being desired—or no, not desired; there was nothing so human or personal a thing as desire about it. A world which it meant to have; a very alien world, he gathered, from the sort he knew. Peopled by alien creatures and built in other dimensions than those which formed his own universe.

These people worshiped a powerful god. And it was this worship—this godhood—which the being that enfolded him meant to possess. It tried to give him a glimpse of why, but the thought waves which flowed through his brain were incomprehensible and remote—not knowledge, but a jumble of unrelated impressions, without coherence. After a few vain attempts to instill the reason for its purpose into his mind, the being apparently dismissed the point as unnecessary and went on.

This god which it meant to dispossess was very powerful; so powerful that of itself the being could do nothing to overthrow it, could not even pass the barriers set up to guard the strange world. It had need of an intelligent, animate creature from a world different enough in structure so that the god's peculiar powers would have no effect upon him.

Gradually the measured beats made it clear to Dixon that he was the chosen envoy. He was to be transported there, armed in potent ways, sent out into the new world to overthrow the god's domain and make way for his sponsor to take possession.

There was a long hiatus after that. Dixon lay quiet, rather stunned by the magnitude of the thing. The being which engulfed him must have sensed the growing rebellion in his mind, for after a while the beats began again. And Dixon knew that the proposition was not a compulsory one. But—the knowledge flowed casually through him—though he was free to be released and set back upon his journey if he refused the plan, he would inevitably die soon, die very unpleasantly.

There was no water within any possible reach, and a band of veiled Tuaregs was scouring the desert nearby in search of that Arab who lay in a huddle of dirty white robes outside the egg-shaped bubble. If he did not die of thirst before they caught him, he would die in a manner infinitely more undesirable at their hands. But, of course, if he so desired, he was free to go.

Dixon digested this information thoughtfully, hesitatingly, through he knew he had no choice. His blind stumbling through the desert could have no other end than slow death, as he had been aware even before he came upon the great bubble. And if there were Tuaregs near— Even in the bodily trance that cradled him he shuddered. He had seen victims of

231

Tuareg tortures, miraculously alive after days and days of—
He turned his mind from that. No; he had no choice.

And gradually a little spark of excitement began to burn in
him. What an adventure! And though death might lie at the
end of it, there was at least a hope for life, and he knew he
had not even that if he refused. Consent was forming in his
mind, but, even before it crystallized, the being must have
known, for about him the lucid radiance suddenly began to
cloud and change. Milkiness flooded through it and through
his body and his brain. Oblivion swallowed him up.

When realization returned to Dixon it came slowly. Layer
by layer the oblivion melted from his mind. He had a vague
impression of vast spaces traversed and barriers surmounted,
and somehow he sensed an indefinable difference in the space
that surrounded the bubble, though it was indefinite how he
knew it. A little beat quivered through him, and another,
clearing away the fogs of his consciousness. Then knowledge
began to pulse again through him in measured flow.

They had crossed gulfs greater than he could comprehend.
They were suspended now above the world of their destination. He was to look briefly upon it, for even through the
protecting walls of the light-bubble the thing that he would
see was so alien to him that in his present form he could not
bear to gaze upon it long.

Then the light about Dixon cleared to translucence, and
somehow he was looking out and down upon a scene that
stunned his eyes with its violence. He had an instant's impression of a land that shrieked and raved with maniacal color
beyond any conception of color as he knew it. He turned his
eyes wincingly away and stared down at the scene immediately
below. And though in point of actual space it must have been
very far away, he could see everything quite clearly and with
a wider radius of vision than he was accustomed to. It was as
if in one glance he encompassed the whole circle of the horizon.

The world below was one vast city that reeled away in
terrace below crazy terrace out to a skyline that shimmered
with white dazzle. And the colors that blazed and howled and
agonized over the insane angles of the place turned him sick
and dizzy. They were incredible angles and impossible colors,

the tints and the tilts of madness—wild, staggering lines and arcs and jagged peaks, crazy inclines broken by ridges of eruptive color, zigzag bridges, buildings that leaned out in gravity-defying angles.

All these incredible terraces mounted up and up in diminishing arcs to the topmost tier of all. This was small and smooth, though over its pavement the insane colors sprawled blotchily. And in the very center a mighty column rose, blacker than any darkness he had ever seen before. On its height burned a pale flame.

But the inhabitants! Dixon could see them quite clearly despite the distance. They were sinuous and serpentine, and their motions were blurs of swiftness, poems of infinite grace. They were not men—they had never been men in any stage of their evolution. And if the colors of the buildings were agony to his eyes, the living, unstable hues that writhed and crawled over the beings below were so frightful that his gaze rebelled. For this reason he never knew just how they were shaped.

There was one standing just below the great black pillar whereon burned the flame, and of this he had the clearest view. It was boneless and writhing, livid with creeping color. Its single great eye, lucid and expressionless, stared from an unfeatured, mouthless face, half scarlet and half purple, between which two shades a wedge of nameless green broadened as he looked away.

He had seen this much before the pellucid crystal began to cloud about him once more and the slow knowledge began its beat through his brain. He must look no longer, or something disastrous might happen to his benumbed senses. He understood by now that it was not in his own form that he was to go out into the crazy land. He was sure, even without that seeping knowledge, that his own body could never endure the colors of the place, nor could his own material feet tread the dizzy angles. Many of the streets and bridges were too steep for human feet to walk.

And he was understanding, as the slow waves flowed on, how different these people were from his own kind. Not only in appearance; their very substance was different from flesh and blood, the atoms arranged in different patterns. They obtained nourishment in an incomprehensible way from some source he could not understand. Their emotions and habits and purposes were alien to all his experience, and among them even the sexes were not those he knew. They were more numerous than mankind's two, and their functions were entirely different. Reproduction here was based on an utterly alien principle.

When the pause came in the waves of knowledge. Dixon was a little dizzy with the complete strangeness of this place and with wonder how he would be enabled to enter it. He lay still, wondering, until the flow began again.

Then the knowledge of the way he was to be introduced into the strange god's domain began to surge in deliberate beats through his brain. It seemed simple, yet the magnitude of it was staggering. A sort of veil of illusion was to be dropped between him and these alien beings. To them, his form would seem one of their own. Through the veil his speech would be filtered and changed into their indescribable mode of communication. And to him they would have the appearance of humanity, their speech would be understandable, their curious emotions translated into familiarity.

Even their multiple sexes would be resolved arbitrarily into two. For though this being could not approach any nearer the strange god whose flame burned upon the pillar, it seemed to have immense power even from this distance in the crazy world below.

The slow-beating waves made him aware that during his sojourn in the strange place he would be guided and in a measure protected, and that this knowledge would still flow through his brain. All this was possible, he understood, because of his own complete difference from anything in this world—such a difference that he would not cause even a ripple upon the surface of the god's consciousness until the time came for his overthrow.

Then again the cloudiness began to clear, until Dixon was looking out through crystal walls upon that reeling city below. For an instant it shuddered with mad colors before his aching eyes. And then over the whole crazy panorama the queerest blurring came. He looked down upon a changing world wherein the wild colors faded and ran together and the staggering angles of that mighty vista below were obscured in structural changes whose purpose he began to understand.

Before his eyes a splendid and stately city was taking shape. Out of the ruin of eye-wrenching color rose tier beyond tier of white pillars and translucent domes. Roofs of alabaster formed themselves under a sky whose pallor was deepening into blue.

When he tore his eyes away from that magnificent vista, terrace dropping away below terrace, crowned with domes and spires and columns wreathed in green, far out to the distant horizon, he saw that over the crowded streets with their swarms of multicolored horrors a stranger change was falling. Out of the mingling indistinctnesses of those colors without name, the semblance of humanity grew. People of noble stature and stately bearing, robed in garments of shining steel, took form before his eyes.

In less time than it takes to tell, a metropolis of familiar aspect stretched invitingly under his gaze. That nightmare of colors was gone as a nightmare goes, leaving no faintest trace behind. Yet he knew as he looked down that in reality nothing was changed. The writhing people still flashed with infinite speed and grace through tiptilted streets of gravity-defying angles. He blinked and looked again, but the illusion held steady—a stupendous city, smiling under a blue, familiar sky.

Slowly through his consciousness beat the realization that, once down there in the metamorphosed world, he must search out the temple of the god, find its vulnerable spot, provide as it were a window, so that through his eyes the being which had brought him here could see its enemy's weakness and instruct Dixon further. And it was impressed upon him, too, that all possible speed must be made, for though there was little danger that the god would realize the inimical presence, yet his very safeguard was his greatest danger. Dixon was so alien to the ultimate particles of his being that, though this protected him from the god, it made his maintenance in the strange world very difficult. It was a strain even upon the vast powers of the light-bubble being to keep that veil of illusion stretched protectingly between him and this world, the very sight and touch of which would send him mad if he was exposed to it long unguarded.

There was a little pause after this, and Dixon lay still, awed by the unthinkable difference between his own structure of mind and body and that of the strange place and people below. Then with breathtaking abruptness, darkness dropped over him. One instant he lay serenely cradled in golden radiance, the next he was dropping through blackness with a queer, high scream in his ears as if he fell through some resisting atmosphere which was not air. Physically he was protected, but he could hear the thin sound of it in varying intensities.

And then without warning the darkness broke, and he found his feet upon solid ground without any hint of jar. He was simply standing upon a marble pavement under a clear blue sky and looking out over a breath-stopping vista of world-city, dropping away in terrace below shining terrace to a distant skyline, out and away in broadening tiers. Light shimmered dazzlingly upon faraway steel figures moving through the streets below, away and away until they were no more than tiny pinpricks of shimmer on the horizon's edge. From each broad circular terrace a marble ramp led down to the next beneath, and over these the steel-bright people were swarming in busy hordes.

And Dixon knew, even as he stared with caught breath at the magnificence of it, that in reality he stood at the apex of a city of madness that reeled away below him in tier after crazy tier, a nightmare of meaningless angles and raving color, through whose streets things writhing and dreadful and acrawl with living hues were flashing with movements of blurring speed. All this splendor was a veil across his eyes. What unknowable activities were really taking place below? On what nameless errands were these busy crowds bound? Then a little sound at his side turned him from the dizzy thoughts tormenting his brain, and he flashed an abrupt glance sidewise, alert for danger. Then he caught his breath and stared.

She was slim as a sword blade in her steel robe, standing under the mighty tower of the black pillar, and she was lovelier than a dream. Her hair swung in black page-boy curls to her shoulders, and from under the darkness of it eyes as blue as steel met his unwaveringly. She was all bright metal to his first glance, steel-molded curves of her under the armored robe, steel lights upon her burnished hair, steel-bright eyes shining. All steel and brightness—but Dixon saw that her mouth was soft and colored like hot embers. And for an instant he wanted to burst into crazy song. It was an inexplicable feeling that he had never known before, a heady delight in being alive. But even through the exultation, he knew that he looked upon an illusion. He knew that she was a faceless, crawling thing, without sex, without any remotest kinship to anything he knew. And yet this illusion was very lovely and—

She was looking up at him with startled eyes, and now she spoke, a little breathlessly, in a sweet, tinkling voice. "You— you have come? Oh, whence have you come?" And he thought that she was striving hard not to believe something which she wanted with all her soul to think true.

There was no answer he could give. He glanced around helplessly at the blue, empty sky, at the great pillar rising behind her, at the pale flame burning so steadily upon its summit. The blaze held him for an instant, and in the instant he stood with eyes uplifted the girl must have thought she had her answer, for she caught her breath in a gasp that was half a sob, and in one swift motion she fell to her knees before him, a miracle of sliding grace in that close gown of steel, so that the light rippled all down her sweet, slim body and lay bluely on the wings of her hair that swung forward as she bent her head.

"I knew it! I knew!" she breathed. "I knew my god would send you! Oh, praise great IL, who has sent me such an envoy!"

Dixon looked down upon the bent black head, his eyes troubled. If she believed him a messenger from the god, it would simplify his task enormously. And yet . . . He had entertained no scruples about displacing the god of a maniacal world peopled with writhing monstrosities, but this was different, somehow. This girl . . .

"I am the high priestess of our god," she murmured, as if in answer to his half-formed query. "I have served IL with all my heart for many cycles now, but only he knows how I have prayed for the coming of an envoy among us. Such honor is enough to—to—" The sweet voice choked suddenly on a sob, as if the answer to her prayer was too much for her to endure unmoved.

Dixon bent and took her chin in his hand, lifting her face to his. The steel-bright eyes were dazzling with diffused tears. The red mouth trembled. She was looking up at him with awe and worship upon her face, and suddenly he knew that he wanted no worship from her. He resented that look of respect and awe. He wanted—well, he wanted her to see a man, not a divine messenger. He wanted to—

Then the queerest madness came over him, deliciously—

and he acted. He stooped swiftly and set his lips over the trembling red lips of the girl, and for an instant the whole strange world reeled and swam in a heady pleasure like nothing he had ever known before.

When he straightened and stood looking down upon her, she met his eyes with purest bewilderment in hers, one hand hovering at her lips and incomprehension radiant in every line of her. Her blue gaze was traveling over him from head to foot in swift, puzzled glances.

And then realization swept back upon him tremendously. To her he wore the writhing shape that was hers in reality. That troubled blue gaze was the gaze of a single pale eye which traveled over the crawling limbs of a monster. He was not even sure that, to her, kneeling denoted homage and wondered in what alien way she was actually expressing her awe.

It was an uncanny feeling which was to haunt him through all his hours here—the knowledge that what he looked upon was unreal, the wonder as to what was actually taking place behind the mask of humanity which only he could see. That kiss—how had it seemed to her? What nameless gesture had he seemed to perform before her eyes—her eye? For he had kissed a monstrosity that had no mouth. Remembering the glimpse he had caught of a one-eyed, featureless face crawling with alive colors, he shuddered and turned back to the kneeling girl as if for reassurance.

Dixon was aware of a curious emptiness within him because of this beauty which was only an illusion—had never been, would never be. He was looking straight into her steel-blue eyes now, and she was smiling very tremulously and with that puzzled look still upon her face. He could see the little shimmering tumult her heart made under the dazzle of her robe. And she was not even female! He narrowed his eyes and strove to pierce the mirage for a moment; to convince himself that here knelt a colored horror of sinuosity and sexlessness. And everything within him cried out protestingly. She was human—she was lovely—she was everything desirable and sweet. And she did not even exist save as a crawling horror upon whom in her normal guise he could never dare to look.

Then, as if to refute that, she flashed up at him a small, uncertain smile which made her so unmistakably human and sweet that he disbelieved everything but her own reality, and she said, "What—what was the meaning of that, O divine envoy?"

He frowned. "You are to call me Dixon," he said. "And that was—well, just a form of greeting."

"The way they greet one another in great IL's domain—in Paradise? Then . . ." She rose in one swift motion. Before he realized what was happening she had risen upon her sandaled toes and her warm mouth was brushing his. "Then I return your greeting, O Dixon."

Involuntarily his arms closed around her. Her body was firm and soft and warm in his clasp—the body of a living human girl, a mirage more real than reality. And again he wondered what nameless rites she was actually performing behind the illusory veil which masked her real, writhing self. And because she felt so pleasant in his arms he released her abruptly and stepped back, knowing the first quickening of uneasiness. Good heaven, could it be possible for a man to fall in love with a hallucination?

She looked up at him serenely, evidntly feeling that she had mastered a difficult point of divine etiquette.

"How pleasant a thing is this new way of greeting!" she murmured, half to herself. "And now, O Dixon, you have but to command me in all things. What would you in IL's world-city?"

Dixon debated swiftly with himself. After all, lovely though she seemed, she was—and he must bear this in mind constantly, lest something dangerous befall—she was a sinuous, faceless thing, a creeping horror with the tints of an incredible spectrum. She was no more than this, and he must find his way, by her help, into the god IL's temple and let the light-being look through his eyes so that he might find IL's vulnerable spot. After that—well, he must do as he was commanded. IL would be overthrown, his own sponsor would usurp the godship, and that would be all. As for these beings which peopled the world, no doubt the change of gods would be a startling thing, but there was no help for it. He had but to perform his own part and then go.

"O Dixon!" the sweet, light voice of the girl broke in upon his thoughts. "O Dixon, would you see how IL's temple is kept by his worshipers? Would you see how devoutly his world adores him?"

"Yes," said Dixon thankfully. "You may lead me to IL's temple."

She genuflected again, a poem of grace in that steel gown along which the light slid in long lines as she moved, and the dark hair swung forward about her face. Then she turned and crossed the terrace toward a ramp which led down into the city. They went down the slope of it—what eye-tormenting angles of spanning actually led downward he could not even guess—and emerged upon a broad street lined with pillared buildings. There were throngs of steel-robed people here who parted in devout rows as the priestess came down the ramp.

She paused at the head of the street and lifted her arms, and Dixon heard her voice ringing clearly over the crowd. "Great IL has answered our prayers at last," she cried. "He has sent us an envoy from his own divinity. Here is the messenger from our god!"

A murmur went over the crowd—a murmur of awe and rejoicing. And then they knelt in long, sinuous rows as if a wind had blown across a field of sword blades. And with incredible swiftness the whisper ran back along the street, from mouth to mouth. He imagined it rippling out and out, down and down, from terrace to terrace, until it reached the ultimate limits of the whole tiered world.

They stepped down among the kneeling throngs, walking a lane of steel worshipers, and by the time they had reached the end of the street Dixon could see flecks of light far away below hurrying upward as the news spread. Up through the pillared streets and the green terraces they came swarming, men and women in robes of linked metal, with intent, awe-struck faces upturned. Dixon moved on with a long stride, a divine messenger from a god marching in triumph through a city without ends or boundaries, for as far as he could see the steel flecks that were people flashed up through the buildings below. And their multitudes were breathtaking. The whole vast city swarmed with living steel as wave after wave of armored people rolled upward toward the heights. His brain reeled with the numbers of them.

Over the bowed heads of the throngs as they advanced, Dixon glanced curiously at the buildings which lined the streets, casting about for some clue to the sort of life those people led. He found nothing. The marble pillars and walls rose as blankly as stage sets along the streets. A mask had been set for him over the realities of the place, but it was not a living mask. There were no shops, no markets, no residences. Rows of noncommittal pillars faced him blankly, betraying no secrets. Apparently the light-being had been unable to do more than mask the strangeness of this world. It could not infuse into it the spirit of a daily life so utterly alien as man's.

They went on through the dead-faced streets, down another ramp, and always the people dropped to their knees, perfectly the illusion of humanity. What, he wondered, were they actually doing? In what weird, incredible way were they really expressing their devotion? It was, of course, better not to know.

Dixon watched the girl before him walking proudly and lightly through the homage-stricken throngs, her dark head high, the steel robe rippling over the loveliness of her body as she moved. Presently she paused for him, smiling over her shoulder in a way that made his heart quicken, and turned in under the great arch of a doorway.

It was not a particularly imposing structure; no more than a marble-columned building with a huge dark portal. But, once inside, Dixon stopped in stunned astonishment at the vastness spread out before him.

It must have occupied the whole interior of all the terraces above—a mighty dome about which the buildings and streets overhead were the merest shell. In the dimness he could not descry the limits of it, but he saw that the whole vast temple was built in the shape of a great dome. For temple it must be. He knew that instinctively. There was the shadow of divinity in it, somehow—a vast calm. And for an instant, as he stared about the great place, he forgot even the presence of the girl at his side.

In the very center of the wide, dark floor lay a pool of pale radiance which somehow gave the impression that it seethed and boiled, though its surface lay untroubled under the lofty dome of the roof. And above the pool the ceiling was shaped like a burning lens to gather and concentrate the radiance arising from it. This centered at the apex of the roof in a dazzle of light at which he could not look directly. He realized that the center of this burning brilliance must be just under the pillar which crowned the topmost terrace—the pillar upon which burned the flame of IL.

Beyond the column of light rising from the pool, Dixon saw

dimly in the gloom of the great temple the glimmer of steel robes. There was an arch in the far wall, so distant he could scarcely make it out, and in this doorway a small steel figure stood. As he watched, the sonorous boom of a gong rang through the dimness. The air trembled with sound, and through the shaking twilight the figure stepped out resolutely, crossing the floor with even, unhurried strides. He could not tell at the distance if it was man or woman, but it approached the radiant pool with, somehow, a sort of restrained eagerness that he was at a loss to understand. It reached the brink and did not pause. The haze of light rising from the pool swallowed it without a flicker. And the great dome was empty again save for themselves.

Dixon turned, awe-struck, to the girl, questions hovering on his mouth. Just in time he remembered his role and rephrased the query: "And how do you interpret this, priestess?"

She smiled up at him bewilderingly. It irritated him that his heart made that odd little leap whenever she smiled so, and he missed the first of her answer in watching the way her lips moved to frame the words she spoke.

". . . continually, at every beat of the signal," she was saying, "so that there is never an interval through all time when one of us has not completed his cycles and is ready to return into the flame." The gong sounded above her light voice. "See? Here comes another. And for countless ages it has been so, for our numbers are great enough so that the stream of voluntary sacrifices need never falter. So we nourish IL's flame and keep it burning."

Dixon said nothing. His eyes were upon her, but the bright illusion was swimming curiously in a mist that was closing down over him, and he was becoming aware of a strange pulsing of his own blood, as if—yes, as if familiar waves of knowledge were beginning their beat through his receptive brain. For a timeless interval he stood rigid, receiving that intelligence, feeling all he had seen and heard draining out of him into the vast reservoir of knowledge which was the light-being, feeling the voiceless commands of it flowing in. Ripple after ripple of the incoming tide rose in his brain. And gradually, in measured beats, he learned that this pool was the source of the pale flame burning upon the pillar, but that it was not essentially a part of it. The god IL drew his power from the dissolving lives of those people who sacrificed themselves—and this was the only way to destroy them, for they could not die otherwise—but IL was not present in the pool. IL was the flame on the column, no more, feeding upon the reflection from below. And if the rising light could be cut off temporarily IL's power would fail at its source. The invader could make an entrance and fight it out with him.

And now for an instant all the thought flow ceased; then in sharply clear ripples of intense emphasis came the syllables of a word. It was a word without meaning to Dixon, a word whose very sounds were unlike those of any language that man speaks. But he knew that he must speak it, and that the cadences of the sound would somehow open the way for the light-being to enter. With the impression of that word upon him the ripples ceased. A profound quiet reigned in his mind.

Out of that quiet the great domed temple slowly took form about him again. He heard the gong notes trembling through the air and saw another steel-robed figure pacing toward the pool. He turned his head and looked down into the high priestess' face at his shoulder. He had only to speak the word now and accomplish IL's overthrow—and then leave. Leave her—never see her again, except perhaps in dreams.

Her eyes met his with a little kindling under the blueness of them, and her mouth trembled into a smile as she met his gaze. She had the look of one eager and taut and waiting, and there was perfect faith in her eyes. And in that instant he knew he could not betray it.

"No," he murmured aloud. "No, my dear; I can't—I simply can't do it!"

Her brows drew together in exquisite bewilderment. "Do what?" she asked in a light whisper, to match his own lowered tone. "Do what?" But somehow the answer seemed not to interest her, for she did not pause for a reply. She had met his eyes and was staring up in a sort of dazed surprise, her blue gaze plunging into his with rigid intensity. And slowly she began to speak, in a tiny, breathless murmur. "I think . . . I think I see, O Dixon, the strangest things . . . in your eyes. Dreadful things and shapes without meaning . . . and something like a veil between us. . . . Dixon . . . nothing is clear . . . and yet—and yet, Dixon, my own face is looking back at me out of your eyes."

He caught his breath suddenly in a painful gasp, and in one involuntary motion he had her in his arms. She clung to him blindly. He could feel the trembling that shivered through her steel-sheathed body, and her heart's pounding shook them both.

"I am afraid, Dixon—I am afraid!" she wailed softly. "What is it that frightens me so, Dixon?"

He did not answer. There was no answer. But he hugged her close and felt the sweet firmness of her body against his and knew helplessly that he loved the illusion that was herself and would always love it.

Dixon was frightened, too; frightened at the depth of the emotion that shook him, for he was remembering the clinging of her soft mouth to his, and how beautifully her body curved under the embrace of her metal robe, and that the loveliness which filled his arms and his heart was no more than an illusion to mask something so grotesque that he could never bear to look upon it unmasked. Lovely body, lovely face, sweet, warm mouth upon his—was this all? Could love rise from no more than a scrap of beautifully shaped flesh? Could any man love more than that with such intensity as shook him now?

He loosed her from one arm and set his finger under her chin, lifting her face to his. Her eyes met his own, blue and puzzled and afraid, and shining with something very splendid which all but blotted out her bewilderment and her terror.

"I love you," he murmured. "I don't care—I love you."

"Love?" she echoed in her light whisper. "Love?" And he saw in her eyes that the word had no meaning for her.

The room reeled about him for an instant. Somehow he had never thought of that. Knowing as he did of the immense gulf between them and the strangeness of the emotions which swayed these creatures of such alien race, yet it had not occurred to him that anywhere throughout the cosmos where living beings dwelt there could be a species to which love had no meaning. Was she, then, incapable of feeling it? Good heaven, was he doomed to love an empty body, soulless, the mirage masking a sexless being who could not return any emotion he knew?

He looked down and saw the diffused radiance behind her eyes, shining and very tender, and the bewilderment upon her face, and he thought, somehow, that he was hovering on the very brink of something vaster than anything he had ever known before—an idea too splendid to be grasped. Yet when he looked down into her eyes he thought he understood—almost—

Suddenly all about him the world trembled. It was as if the whole vast place were the reflection in a pool, and a ripple had passed blurringly over the surface. Then everything righted itself. But he understood. He had been here too long. The veil between him and this alien world was wearing thin.

"No—I *can't* go!" he groaned and gripped the girl closer in his arms.

He must have spoken aloud, for he felt her stir against him and heard her anxious voice. "Go? O Dixon, Dixon—take me with you! Don't leave me, Dixon!"

Some fantastic hope flowered suddenly within him. "Why not?" he demanded. "Why not? Tell me!" And he shook her a little in his urgency.

"I don't know," she faltered. "I only know that—that—O Dixon, that I shall be so lonely when you have gone. Take me—please take me!"

"Why?" he demanded inexorably. For he thought now that he was hovering very near the understanding of the vast and splendid thing which had almost dawned upon him before the world shook.

"Because I . . . because . . . I don't understand it, Dixon, I can't tell you why—I haven't the words. But since you came I—is it that I have been waiting for you always? For I never knew until you came how lonely I had been. And I cannot let you go without me. O Dixon, is this what you call love?"

There was pain in her voice and in her veiled eyes. And the thought came to him that love was like an infectious germ, spreading pain wherever it rooted itself. Had he brought it to her—infected her too with the hopeless passion he knew? For it was wildly hopeless. In a moment or so he must leave this alien place forever, and no power existent could maintain very long the illusory veil through which they knew love.

Could his own new love for her endure the sight of her real self? And what would happen to this strange flowering of an emotion nameless and unknown to her—her love for him? Could it bear the look of his human shape, unmasked? And yet, he asked himself desperately, could a love as deep and sincere as the love he bore her be so transient a thing that he could not endure the sight of her in another guise? Could—

245

Again that queer flickering flashed over the world. Dixon felt the ground underfoot tilt dangerously, and for a moment insane colors stabbed at his eyes and the whole room reeled and staggered. Then it was still again. He had scarcely noticed. He swung her around to face him, gripping her shoulders and staring down compellingly into her eyes.

"Listen!" he said rapidly, for he knew his time was limited now, perhaps to seconds. "Listen! Have you any idea what you are asking?"

"Only to go with you," she said. "To be with you, wherever you are. And if you are indeed IL's messenger—perhaps a part of his godhead—then shall I enter the flame and give myself to IL? In that way can I join you and be one with you?"

He shook his head. "I am not from IL. I have been sent to destroy him. I'm a man from a world so different from yours that you could never bear to look upon me in my real form. You see me as an illusion, just as I see you. And I must go back to my own world now—alone."

Her eyes were dizzy with trying to understand.

"You are—not from IL? Not as you seem? Another world? Oh, but take me with you! I must go—I must!"

"But, my dearest, I can't. Don't you understand? You couldn't live an instant in my world—nor I much longer in yours."

"Then I will die," she said calmly. "I will enter the flame and wait for you in death. I will wait forever."

"My darling, not even that." He said it gently. "Not even in death can we be together. For when you die you go back to IL, and I go—I go—back to another god, perhaps. I don't know. But not to IL."

She stood, blank-eyed, in his grasp, trying to force her mind into the incredible belief. When she spoke, the words came slowly, as if her thoughts were speaking aloud.

"I don't understand," she said. "But I know . . . you speak the truth. If I die by the flame—in the only way there is for me to die—we are parted forever. I can't! I won't! I will not let you go! Listen to me—" and her voice dropped to a soft whisper—"you say you came to destroy IL? Why?"

"As the envoy of another god, who would take his place."

"I have given my whole life to the worship of IL," she murmured to herself, very gently. And then, in a stronger voice: "But destroy him, Dixon! There may be a chance that way—there is none now. Oh, I may be a traitor—worse than a traitor. There is no word to describe one who betrays his god into destruction, no word terrible enough. But I would do it—yes, gladly, now. Destroy him, and let me seek another death somewhere, somehow—let me die as you die. Perhaps your god can release me into your sort of death, and I can wait for you there until you come. Oh, Dixon, please!"

The idea was a staggering one, but for a wild moment Dixon knew hope again. Might it not be that—that—

Quite suddenly he understood. He looked down on the loveliness of her with unseeing eyes. In these past few moments of insanity, learning that she loved him, too, enough that she begged death of him if in that way they might be united, in these few moments he came to realize that the flesh meant nothing. It was not her body he loved. And a great relief flooded him, to be sure that—sure that it was not merely infatuation, or desire for the loveliness which did not exist save as a mirage before his eyes. No, it was love, truly and completely, despite the shape she wore, despite the nameless sex that was hers. Love for herself—the essential self, however deeply buried beneath whatever terrible guise. And though her very substance was alien to him, and though no creature in all her ancestry had ever known love before, she loved him. Nothing else mattered.

And then without warning the great dome before him wavered and contorted into impossible angles, like the reflections in a flawed mirror. And Dixon felt the firm curved body in his arms melting fluidly into a different form and texture. It squirmed . . .

He stood at the entrance to a mighty room that staggered with frantic color, reeling with eye-stunning angles and incredible planes. And in his arms— He looked down. He clasped a creature at which he could not bear to look directly, a thing whose wild-looped limbs and sinuous body rippled and crawled with the moving tints of madness. It was slippery and horrible to the touch, and from the midst of a shifting, featureless face a great lucid eye stared up at him with desperate horror, as if it was looking upon something so frightful that the very sight was enough to unseat its reason.

Dixon closed his eyes after that one revolting glimpse, but he had seen in the eye upturned to him enough of dawning comprehension to be sure that it was she whom he held. And he thought that despite the utter strangeness of that one staring eye there was somewhere in the clarity of it, and the steadfastness, a glimmer of the innermost spark which was the being he loved—that spark which had looked from the blue gaze he had seen in its human shape. With that inner spark of life she was the same.

He tightened his grip upon her—or it—though his flesh crept at the contact and he knew that the feel was as revolting to it as to himself, and looked out over that shallow, color-stained head upon the vast room before him. His eyes throbbed savagely from those fierce colors never meant for human eyes to see. And though the creature in his arms hung acquiescent, he knew the effort it must cost to preserve that calm.

A lump rose in his throat as he realized the significance of that—such utter faith in him, though he wore a shape terrible enough to bring the fear of madness into that great lucid eye when it rested upon him. But he knew he could not stand there long and retain his own sanity. Already the colors were raving almost audibly through his brain, and the ground heaved underfoot, and he was sure that neither of them could endure much more of this. So he gripped the dreadful thing which housed the being he loved, and almost of itself he felt that incredibly alien word rip itself from his lips.

It was not a word to be set down in any written characters. Its sound to his ears was vague and indeterminate, like a whisper heard over too great distances to have any form. But the moment it left his lips he felt a vast, imponderable shifting in the substance of the temple. And, like a shutter's closing, the room went black. Dixon gave one involuntary sob of relief as the maniacal colors ceased their assault upon his brain, and he felt the dreadful thing in his arms go rigid in the utter blackness. For a moment everything was still as death.

And then through the dark around them a tiny shiver ran, the least little stir of motion, the thinnest thread of sound. It pierced Dixon's very eardrums and shuddered thrillingly along his nerves. And with incredible swiftness that tiny stirring and that infinitesimal sound grew and swelled and ballooned into a maelstrom of rushing tumult, louder and louder, shriller and shriller. Around them in the blackness swooped and stormed the sounds of a mightier conflict than any living man could ever have heard before—a battle of gods, invisible in the blackness of utter void.

That stunning uproar mounted and intensified until he thought his head would burst with the infinite sound of it, and forces beyond comprehension stormed through the air. The floor seemed to dissolve under him, and space whirled in the dark so that he was conscious of neither up nor down. The air raved and shrieked. Blind and deafened and stunned by the magnitude of the conflict, Dixon hugged his dreadful burden and waited.

How long it went on he never knew. He was trying to think as the turmoil raged around his head, trying to guess what would come next; if the light-being in its victory could unite them in any way, in life or in death. He could think of that quite calmly now, death and union. For life without her, he knew unquestioningly, would be a sort of living death, alone and waiting. Living was where she was, and if she were dead, then life lay only in death for him. His head reeled with the wild wonderings and with the noise of battle raving about them both. For eternities, it seemed to him, the whole universe was a maelstrom, insanity shrieked in his ears, and all the powers of darkness swooped and screamed through the void about him. But, after an endless while, very gradually he began to realize that the tumult was abating. The roaring in his ears faded slowly; the wild forces storming through the dark diminished. By infinite degree the uproar died away. Presently again the stillness of death descended through the blackness upon the two who waited.

There was a long interval of silence, nerve-racking, ear-tormenting. And then, at long last, out of that darkness and silence spoke a voice, vast and bodiless and serene. And it was not the voice of the light-being. It spoke audibly in Dixon's brain, not in words, but in some nameless speech which used instead of syllables some series of thought forms that were intelligible to him.

"My chosen priestess," said the voice passionlessly, "so you would have had me destroyed?"

Dixon felt the convulsive start of the creature in his arms and realized dimly that the same wordless speech, then, was intelligible to them both. He realized that only vaguely, with one corner of his mind, for he was stunned and overwhelmed with the realization that it must be the god IL speaking—that his own sponsor had been overcome.

"And you, Dixon," the voice went on evenly, "sent by my enemy to open the way. You are a very alien creature, Dixon. Only by the power I wrested from that being which assaulted me can I perceive you at all, and your mind is a chaos to me. What spell have you cast over my chosen priestess, so that she no longer obeys me?"

"Have you never heard of love?" demanded Dixon aloud.

The query faded into the thick darkness without an echo, and a profound stillness followed in its wake. He stood in the blind dark and utter silence, clutching his love, waiting. Out of that quiet the god-voice came at last:

"Love"—in a musing murmur. "Love—no! there is no such thing in all my universe. What is it?"

Dixon stood helpless, mutely trying to frame an answer. For who can define love? He groped for the thought forms, and very stumblingly he tried to explain, knowing as he did so that it was as much for the benefit of her he held in his arms as for the god, because, although she loved, she could not know the meaning of love, or what it meant to him. When he had ceased, the silence fell again heavily.

At last IL said, "So—the reigning principle of your own system and dimension. I understand that much. But there is no such thing here. Why should it concern you? Love is a thing between the two sexes of your own race. This priestess of mine is of another sex than those you understand. There can be no such thing as this love between you."

"Yet I saw her first in the form of a woman," said Dixon. "And I love her."

"You love the image."

"At first it may be that I did. But now—no; there's much more of it than that. We may be alien to the very atoms. Our minds may be alien, and all our thoughts, and even our souls. But, after all, alien though we are, that alienage is of superficial things. Stripped down to the barest elemental beginning, we have one kinship—we share life. We are individually alive, animate, free-willed. Somewhere at the very core of our beings is the one vital spark of life, which in the last analysis is *self*, and with that one spark we love each other."

The deepest silence fell again when he had ended—a silence of the innermost brain.

Out of it at last IL said, "And you, my priestess? What do you say? Do you love him?"

Dixon felt the shape in his arms shudder uncontrollably. She—he could not think of her as "it"—stood in the very presence of her god, heard him address her in the black blindness of his presence, and the awe and terror of it was almost enough to shake her brain. But after a moment she answered in a small, faltering murmur, the very ghost of a reply, and in some curious mode of speech which was neither vocal nor entirely thought transfer. "I—I do not know that word, O mightly IL. I know only that there is no living for me outside his presence. I would have betrayed your godhead to free me, so that I might die in his way of death, and meet him again beyond—if there can be any beyond for us. I would do all this again without any hesitation if the choice was given me. If this is what you call love—yes; I love him."

"He is," said IL, "a creature of another race and world and dimension. You have seen his real form, and you know."

"I do not understand that," said the priestess in a surer voice. "I know nothing except that I cannot—will not live with him. It is not his body I . . . love, nor do I know what it is which commands me so. I know only that I do love him."

"And I you," said Dixon. It was a very strange sensation to be addressing her thus, from brain to brain. "The sight of you was dreadful to me, and I know how I must have looked to you. But the shock of that sight has taught me something. I know now. The shape you wear and the shape you seemed to wear before I saw you in reality are both illusions, both no more than garments which clothe that . . . that living, vital entity which is yourself—the real you. And your body does not matter to me now, for I know that it is no more than a mirage."

"Yes," she murmured. "Yes, I understand. You are right. The bodies do not matter now. It goes so much deeper than that."

"And what," broke in the voice of IL, "is your solution of this problem?"

It was Dixon who broke the silence that fell in mute answer to the query. "There can be no such thing as union for us anywhere in life. In death, perhaps—but I do not know. Do you?"

"No," said IL surprisingly.

"You—you do not? You—a god?"

"No. I have taken these beings who worship me back into the flame. The energy which was theirs in life supports me—but something escapes. I do not know what. Something too intangible even for me to guess at. No—I am a god, and I do not know what comes after death."

Dixon pondered that for a long while. There was an implication in it somewhere which gave him hope, but his brain was so dazed he could not grasp it. At last the light broke, and he said joyfully, "Then—why, then you cannot keep us apart! We can die and be free."

"Yes. I have no hold over you. Even if I would wreak vengence upon you for your part in my betrayal, I could not. For death will release you into—I do not know what. But it will be release."

Dixon swallowed hard. Half-doubts and hesitations crowded his mind, but he heard his own voice saying steadily, "Will you do that for us—release us?"

In the silence as he waited for an answer he was trying to realize that he stood on the threshold of death; trying to understand, his mind probing ahead eagerly for the answer which might lie beyond. And in the timeless moment he waited he was very sure, for whatever lay ahead could not be extinction and surely not separation. This was the beginning; surely it could not end so soon, unfulfilled, all the questions unanswered.

No; this love which linked them, two beings so alien, could not flicker out with their lives. It was too great—too splendid, far too strong. He was no longer uncertain, no longer afraid, and hope began to torment him exquisitely. What lay beyond? What vast existences? What starry adventures, together? Almost impatiently he poised on the brink of death.

Through this IL's voice spoke with a vast, passionless calm. "Die, then," said IL.

For an instant the darkness lay unbroken about them. Then a little flicker ran indescribably through it. The air shook for a breathless moment.

And IL was alone.

And Now The News

THEODORE STURGEON

I suppose "And Now the News" is the oddest story in this collection. This is perfectly natural: its author has apparently made a specialty of arriving from new directions with peculiar, even unique, treasures. I am not at all sure, as a matter of fact, that this story is sf at all. I would like to hope it is, but it seems uncomfortably plausible.

A great many of Mr. Sturgeon's stories were nominated for inclusion here. Check the Honor Roll for availability and hunt them up. They're worth the search.

The man's name was MacLyle, which by looking at you can tell wasn't his real name, but let's say this is fiction, shall we? MacLyle had a good job in, well, a soap concern. He worked hard and made good money and got married to a girl called Esther. He bought a house in the suburbs, and after it was paid for he rented it to some people and bought a home a little farther out and a second car and a freezer and a power mower and a book on landscaping and settled down to the worthy task of giving his kids all the things he never had.

He had habits and he had hobbies, like everybody else and (like everybody else) his were a little different from anybody's. The one that annoyed his wife the most, until she got used to it, was the news habit, or maybe hobby. MacLyle read a morning paper on the eight-fourteen and an evening paper on the six-ten, and the local paper his suburb used for its lost dogs and auction sales took up forty after-dinner minutes. And when he read a paper he read it, he didn't mess with it. He read page one first and page two next, and so on all the way through. He didn't care too much for books, but he respected them in a mystical sort of way, and he used to say a newspaper was a kind of book, and so would raise particular hell if a section was missing or in upside down, or if the pages were out of line. He also heard the news on the radio. There were three stations in town with hourly broadcasts, one on the hour, and he was usually able to catch them all. During these five-minute periods he would look you right in the eye while you talked to him and you'd swear he was listening to you, but he wasn't. This was a particular trial to his wife, but only for five years or so. Then she stopped trying to be heard while the radio talked about floods and murders and scandal and suicide. Five more years and she went back to talking right through the broadcasts, but by the time people are married ten years things like that don't matter; they talk in code anyway, and nine tenths of their speech can be picked up anytime like ticker tape. He also caught the seven-thirty news on Channel 2 and the seven-forty-five news on Channel 4 on television.

Now, it might be imagined from all this that MacLyle was a crotchety character with fixed habits and a neurotic neatness, but this was far from the case. MacLyle was basically a reasonable guy who loved his wife and children and liked his work and pretty much enjoyed being alive. He laughed easily and talked well and paid his bills. He justified his preoccupation with the news in a number of ways. He would quote Donne: ". . . *any man's death diminishes me, because I am involved in mankind* . . . ," which is pretty solid stuff and hard to argue down. He would point out that he made his trains and his trains made him punctual, but that because of them he saw the same faces at the same time day after endless day, before, during, and after he rode those trains, so that his immediate world was pretty circumscribed, and only a constant awareness of what was happening all over the earth kept him conscious of the fact that he lived in a bigger place than a thin straight universe with his house at one end, his office at the other, and a railway track in between.

It's hard to say just when MacLyle started to go to pieces, or even why, though it obviously had something to do with all that news he exposed himself to. He began to react, very slightly at first; that is, you could tell he was listening. He'd *shh!* you, and if you tried to finish what you were saying he'd run and stick his head in the speaker grille. His wife and kids learned to shut up when the news came on, five minutes before the hour until five after (with MacLyle switching stations) and every hour on the half hour, and from seven-thirty to eight for the TV, and during the forty minutes it took him to read the local paper. He was not so obvious about it when he read his paper, because all he did was freeze over the pages like a catatonic, gripping the top corners until the sheets shivered, knotting his jaw and breathing from his nostrils with a strangled whistle.

Naturally all this was a weight on his wife Esther, who tried her best to reason with him. At first he answered her, saying mildly that a man has to keep in touch, you know; but very quickly he stopped responding altogether, giving her the treatment a practiced suburbanite gets so expert in, as when someone mentions a lawn mower just too damn early on Sunday morning. You don't say yes and you don't say no, you don't even grunt, and you don't move your head or even your eyebrows. After a while your interlocutor goes away. Pretty soon you don't hear these ill-timed annoyances any more than you appear to.

It needs to be said again here that MacLyle was, outside of his pecularity, a friendly and easy going character. He liked people and invited them and visited them, and he was one of those adults who can really listen to a first-grade child's interminable adventures and really care. He never forgot things like the slow leak in the spare tire or antifreeze or anniversaries, and he always got the storm windows up in time, but he didn't rub anyone's nose in his reliability. The first thing in his whole life he didn't take as a matter of course was this news thing that started so small and grew so quickly.

So after a few weeks of it his wife took the bull by the horns and spent the afternoon hamstringing every receiver in the house. There were three radios and two TV sets, and she didn't understand the first thing about them, but she had a good head and she went to work with a will and the can-opening limb of a pocket-knife. From each receiver she removed one tube, and, one at a time, so as not to get them mixed up, she carried them into the kitchen and meticulously banged their bases against the edge of the sink, being careful to crack no glass and bend no pins, until she could see the guts of the tube rolling around loose inside. Then she replaced them and got the back panels on the sets again.

MacLyle came home and put the car away and kissed her and turned on the living-room radio and then went to hang up his hat. When he returned the radio should have been warmed up, but it wasn't. He twisted the knobs a while and bumped it and rocked it back and forth a little, grunting, and then noticed the time. He began to feel a little frantic and raced back to the kitchen and turned on the little ivory radio on the shelf. It warmed up quickly and cheerfully and gave him a clear sixty-cycle hum, but that was all. He behaved badly from then on, roaring out the information that the sets didn't work, either of them, as if that wasn't pretty evident by that time, and flew upstairs to the boys' room, waking them explosively. He turned on their radio and got another sixty-cycle note, this time with a shattering microphonic when he rapped the case, which he did four times, whereupon the set went dead altogether.

Esther had planned the thing up to this point, but no further, which was the way her mind worked. She figured she could handle it, but she figured wrong. MacLyle came downstairs like a pallbearer, and he was silent and shaken until seven-thirty, time for the news on TV. The living-room set wouldn't peep, so up he went to the boys' room again, waking them just as they were nodding off again, and this time the little guy started to cry. MacLyle didn't care. When he found out there was no picture on the set, he almost started to cry, too, but then he heard the sound come in. A TV set has an awful lot of tubes in it and Esther didn't know audio from video. MacLyle sat down in front of the dark screen and listened to the news. *"Everything seemed to be under control in the riot-ridden border country in India,"* said the TV set. Crowd noises and a background of Beethoven's "Turkish March." *"And then . . ."* Cut music. Crowd noise up: *gabble-wurra* and a scream. Announcer over: *"Six hours later, this was the scene."* Dead silence, going on so long that MacLyle reached out and thumped the TV set with the heel of his hand. Then, slow swell, Ketelby's "In a Monastery Garden." *"On a more cheerful note, here are the six finalists in the Miss Continuum contest."* Background music, "Blue Room," interminably, interrupted only once, when the announcer said through a childish chuckle, *"And she meant it!"* MacLyle pounded himself on the temples. The little guy continued to sob. Esther stood at the foot of the stairs wringing her hands. It went on for thirty minutes like this. All MacLyle said when he came downstairs was that he wanted the paper—that would be the local one. So Esther faced the great unknown and told him frankly she hadn't ordered it and wouldn't again, which of course led to full and righteous confession of her activities of the afternoon.

Only a woman married better than fourteen years can know a man well enough to handle him so badly. She was aware that she was wrong, but that was quite overridden by the fact that she was logical. It would not be logical to continue her patience, so patience was at an end. That which offendeth thee, cast it out, yea, even thine eye and thy right hand. She realized too late that the news was so inextricably part of her husband that in casting it out she cast him out, too. And out he went, while whitely she listened to the rumble of the garage door, the car door speaking its sharp syllables, clear as *"Exit"* in a playscript; the keen of a starter, the mourn of a motor. She said she was glad and went into the kitchen and tipped the useless ivory radio off the shelf and retired, weeping.

And yet, because true life offers few clean cuts, she saw him once more. At seven minutes to three in the morning she became aware of faint music from somewhere; unaccountably it frightened her, and she tiptoed about the house looking for it. It wasn't in the house, so she pulled on MacLyle's trench coat and crept down the steps into the garage. And there, just outside in the driveway, where steel beams couldn't interfere with radio reception, the car stood where it had been all along, and MacLyle was in the driver's seat dozing over the wheel. The music came from the car radio. She drew the coat tighter around her and went to the car and opened the door and spoke his name. At just that moment the radio said *"And now the news . . . ,"* and MacLyle sat bolt upright and shh'd furiously. She fell back and stood a moment in a strange transition from unconditional surrender to total defeat. Then he shut the car door and bent forward, his hand on the volume control, and she went back into the house.

After the news report was over and he had recovered himself from the stab wounds of a juvenile delinquent, the grinding agonies of a derailed train, the terrors of the near-crash of a C-119, and the fascination of a Cabinet officer, charter member of the We Don't Trust Nobody Club, saying in exactly these words that there's a little bit of good in the worst of us and a little bit of bad in the best of us, all of which he felt keenly, he started the car (by rolling it down the drive, because the battery was almost dead) and drove as slowly as possible into town.

At an all-night garage he had the car washed and greased while he waited, after which the Automat was open and he sat in it for three hours drinking coffee, holding his jaw set until his back teeth ached, and making occasional, almost inaudible noises in the back of his throat. At nine he pulled himself together. He spent the entire day with his astonished attorney, going through all his assets, selling, converting, establishing, until when he was finished he had a modest packet of cash and his wife would have an adequate income until the children went to college, at which time the house would be sold, the tenants in the older house evicted, and Esther would be free to move to the smaller home with the price of the larger one added to the basic capital. The lawyer might have entertained fears for MacLyle except for the fact that he was jovial and loquacious throughout, behaving like a happy man—a rare form of insanity, but acceptable. It was hard work, but they did it in a day, after which MacLyle wrung the lawyer's hand and thanked him profusely and checked into a hotel.

When he awoke the following morning he sprang out of bed, feeling years younger, opened the door, scooped up the morning paper and glanced at the headlines.

He couldn't read them.

He grunted in surprise, closed the door gently, and sat on the bed with the paper in his lap. His hands moved restlessly on it, smoothing and smoothing until the palms were shadowed and the type hazed. The shouting symbols marched across the page like a parade of strangers in some unrecognized lodge uniform, origins unknown, destination unknown, and the occasion for marching only to be guessed at. He traced the letters with his little finger, he measured the length of a word between his index finger and thumb and lifted them up to hold them before his wondering eyes. Suddenly he got up and crossed to the desk, where signs and placards and printed notes were trapped like a butterfly collection under glass— the breakfast menu, something about valet service, something about checking out. He remembered them all and had an idea of their significance—but he couldn't read them. In the drawer was stationery, with a picture of the building and no other buildings around it, which just wasn't so, and an inscription which might have been in Cyrillic for all he knew. Telegram blanks, a bus schedule, a blotter, all bearing hieroglyphs and runes as far as he was concerned. A phone book full of strangers' names in strange symbols.

He requested of himself that he recite the alphabet. "A," he said clearly, and "Eh?" because it didn't sound right and he couldn't imagine what would. He made a small foolish grin and shook his head slightly and rapidly, but grin or no, he felt frightened. He felt glad, or relieved—most happy, anyway, but still a little frightened.

He called the desk and told them to get his bill ready, and dressed and went downstairs. He gave the doorman his parking check and waited while they brought the car round. He got in and turned the radio on and started to drive west.

He drove for some days, in a state of perpetual, cold, and (for all that) happy fright—roller-coaster fright, horror-movie fright—remembering the significance of a stop sign without being able to read the word STOP across it, taking caution from the shape of a railroad-crossing notice. Restaurants look like restaurants, gas stations like gas stations; if Washington's picture denotes a dollar and Lincoln's five, one doesn't need to read them. MacLyle made out just fine. He drove until he was well into one of those square states with all the mountains and cruised until he recognized the section where, years before he was married, he had spent a hunting vacation. Avoiding the lodge he had used, he took back roads until, sure enough, he came to that deserted cabin in which he had sheltered one night, standing yet, rotting a bit but only around the edges. He wandered in and out of it for a long time, memorizing details because he could not make a list, and then got back into his car and drove to the nearest town, not very near and not very much of a town. At the general store he bought shingles and flour and nails and paint—all sorts of paint, in little cans, as well as big containers of house paint—and canned goods and tools. He ordered a knock-down windmill and a generator, eighty pounds of modeling clay, two loaf pans and a mixing bowl, and a war-surplus jungle hammock. He paid cash and promised to be back in two weeks for the things the store didn't stock, and wired (because it could be done over the phone) his lawyer to arrange for the predetermined eighty dollars a month which was all he cared to take for himself from his assets. Before he left he stood in wonder before a monstrous piece of musical plumbing called an ophicleide which stood, dusty and majestic, in a corner. (While it might be easier on the reader to make this a French horn or a sousaphone—which would answer narrative purposes quite as well—we're done telling lies here. MacLyle's real name is concealed, his home town cloaked, and his occupation disguised, and dammit, it really was a twelve-keyed, 1824, fifty-inch, obsolete brass ophicleide.) The storekeeper explained how his great-grandfather had brought it over from the old country and nobody had played it for two generations except an itinerant tuba player who had turned pale green on the first three notes and put it down as if it was full of percussion caps. MacLyle asked how it sounded and the man told him terrible. Two weeks later MacLyle was back to pick up the rest of his stuff, nodding and smiling and saying not a word. He still couldn't read, and now he couldn't speak. Even more, he had lost the power to understand speech. He had paid for the purchases with a hundred-dollar bill and a wistful expression, and then another hundred-dollar bill, and the storekeeper, thinking he had turned deaf and dumb, cheated him roundly but at the same time felt so sorry for him that he gave him the ophicleide. MacLyle loaded up his car happily and left. And that's the first part of the story about MacLyle's being in a bad way.

MacLyle's wife Esther found herself in a peculiar position. Friends and neighbors offhandedly asked her questions to which she did not know the answers, and the only person who had any information at all, MacLyle's attorney, was under bond not to tell her anything. She had not, in the full and legal sense, been deserted, since she and the children were provided for. She missed MacLyle, but in a specialized way; she missed the old reliable MacLyle, and he had, in effect, left her long before that perplexing night when he had driven away. She wanted the old MacLyle back again, not this untrolleyed stranger with the grim and spastic pre-occupation with the news. Of the many unpleasant facets of this stranger's personality, one glowed brightest, and that was that he was the sort of man who would walk out the way he did and stay away as long as he had. Ergo, he was that undesirable person just as long as he stayed away, and tracking him down would, if it returned him against his will, return to her only a person who was not the person she missed.

Yet she was dissatisfied with herself, for all that she was the injured party and had wounds less painful than the pangs of conscience. She had always prided herself on being a good wife and had done many things in the past which were counter to her reason and her desires, purely because they were consistent with being a good wife. So as time went on she gravitated away from the "What shall I do?" area into the "What ought a good wife to do?" spectrum and, after a great deal of careful thought, went to see a psychiatrist.

He was a fairly intelligent psychiatrist, which is to say he caught on to the obvious a little faster than most people. For example, he became aware in only four minutes of conversation that MacLyle's wife Esther had not come to him on her own behalf, and, further, decided to hear her out completely before resolving to treat her. When she had quite finished and he had dug out enough corroborative detail to get the picture, he went into a long silence and cogitated. He matched the broad pattern of MacLyle's case with his reading and his experience, recognized the challenge, the clinical worth of the case, the probable value of the heirloom-diamond pendant worn by his visitor. He placed his finger tips together, lowered his fine young head, gazed through his eyebrows at MacLyle's wife Esther, and took up the gauntlet. At the prospects of getting her husband back safe and sane, she thanked him quietly and left the office with mixed emotions. The fairly intelligent psychiatrist drew a deep breath and began making arrangements with another head-shrinker to take over his other patients, both of them, while he was away, because he figured to be away quite a while.

It was appallingly easy for him to trace MacLyle. He did not go near the lawyer. The solid foundation of all skip tracers and bureaus of missing persons, in their *modus operandi*, is the piece of applied psychology which dictates that a man might change his name and his address, but he will seldom—can seldom—change the things he does, particularly the things he does to amuse himself. The ski addict doesn't skip to Florida, though he might make Banff instead of a habitual Mont Tremblant. A philatelist is not likely to mount butterflies. Hence when the psychiatrist found among MacLyle's papers some snapshots and brochures, dating from college days, of the towering Rockies, of bears feeding by the roadside, and especially of season after season's souvenirs of a particular resort to which he had never brought his wife and which he had not visited since he married her, it was worth a feeler, which went out in the form of a request to that state's police for information on a man of such-and-such a description driving so-and-so with out-of-state plates, plus a request that the man not be detained or warned, but only that he, the fairly intelligent psychiatrist, be notified. He He threw out other lines, too, but this is the one that hooked the fish. It was a matter of weeks before a state patrol car happened by MacLyle's favorite general store; after that it was a matter of minutes before the information was in the hands of the psychiatrist. He said nothing to MacLyle's wife Esther except goodbye for a while, and this bill is payable now, and then took off, bearing with him a bag of tricks.

He rented a car at the airport nearest MacLyle's hideout and drove a long, thirsty, climbing way until he came to the general store. There he interviewed the proprietor, learning some eighteen hundred items about how bad business could get, how hot it was, how much rain hadn't fallen and how much was needed, the tragedy of being blamed for high markups when anyone with the brains God gave a goose ought to know it cost plenty to ship things out here, especially in the small quantities necessitated by business being so bad and all; and betwixt and between he learned eight or ten items about MacLyle—the exact location of his cabin, the fact that he seemed to have turned into a deaf-mute who was also unable to read, and that he must be crazy because who but a crazy man would want eighty-four different half-pint cans of house paint or, for that matter, live out here when he didn't have to?

The psychiatrist got loose after a while and drove off, and the country got higher and dustier and more lost every mile, until he began to pray that nothing would go wrong with the car, and, sure enough, ten minutes later something did. Any car that made a noise like the one he began to hear was strictly a shot-rod, and he pulled over to the side to worry about it. He turned off the motor and the noise went right on, and he began to realize that the sound was not in the car or even near it, but came from somewhere uphill. There was a mile and a half more of the hill to go, and he drove it in increasing amazement, because that sound got louder and more impossible all the time. It was sort of like music, but like no music currently heard on this or any other planet. It was a solo voice, brass, with muscles. The upper notes, of which there seemed to be about two octaves, were wild and unmusical, the middle was rough, but the lowtones were like the speech of these mountains themselves, big up to the sky, hot, and more natural than anything ought to be, basic as a bear's fang. Yet all the notes were perfect, their intervals were perfect—this awful noise was tuned like an electronic organ. The psychiatrist had a good ear, though for a while he wondered how long he'd have any ears at all, and he realized all these things about the sound, as well as the fact that it was rendering one of the more primitive fingering studies from Czerny, Book One, the droning little horror that goes: *do mi fa sol la sol fa mi, re fa sol la ti la sol fa, mi sol la* . . . , inchworming up the scale and then descending hand over hand.

He saw blue sky almost under his front tires and wrenched the wheel hard over, and found himself in the grassy yard of a made-over prospector's cabin; but that he didn't notice right away, because sitting in front of it was what he described to himself, startled as he was out of his professional detachment, as the craziest-looking man he had ever seen.

He was sitting under a parched, wind-warped Engelmann spruce. He was barefoot up to the armpits. He wore the top half of a skivvy shirt and a hat the shape of one of those conical Boy Scout tents when one of the Boy Scouts had left the pole home. And he was playing, or anyway practicing, the ophicleide, and on his shoulders was a little moss of spruce needles, a small shower of which descended from the tree every time he hit on or under the low B flat. Only a mouse trapped inside a tuba during band practice can know precisely what's it's like to stand that close to an operating ophicleide.

It was MacLyle, all right, looming well fed and filled out. When he saw the psychiatrist's car he went right on playing, but, catching the psychiatrist's eye, he winked, smiled with the small corner of lip which showed from behind the large cup of the mouthpiece, and twiddled three fingers of his right hand, all he could manage of a wave without stopping. And he didn't stop, either, until he had scaled the particular octave he was working on and let himself down the other side. Then he put the ophicleide down carefully and let it lean against the spruce tree, and got up. The psychiatrist had become aware, as the last stupendous notes rolled away down the mountain, of his extreme isolation with this offbeat patient, of the unconcealed health and vigor of the man, and of the presence of the precipice over which he had almost driven his car a moment before, and had rolled up his window and buttoned the door lock and was feeling grateful for them. But the warm good humor and genuine welcome on MacLyle's sunburned face drove away fright and even caution, and almost before he knew what he was doing the psychiatrist had the door open and was stooping up out of the car, thinking, *Merry* is a disused word, but that's what he is, by God, a merry man. He called him by name, but MacLyle either didn't hear him or didn't care; he just put out a big warm hand and the psychiatrist took it. He could feel hard flat calluses in MacLyle's hand, and the controlled strength an elephant uses to lift a bespangled child in its trunk; he smiled at the image, because after all MacLyle was not a particularly large man, there was just that feeling about him. And once the smile found itself there it wouldn't go away.

He told MacLyle that he was a writer trying to soak up some of the magnificent country and had just been driving wherever the turn of the road led him, and here he was; but before he was half through he became conscious of MacLyle's eyes, which were in some indescribable way very much on him but not at all on anything he said; it was precisely as if he had stood there and hummed a tune. MacLyle seemed to be willing to listen to the sound until it was finished, and even to enjoy it, but that enjoyment was going to be all he got out of it. The psychiatrist finished anyway, and MacLyle waited a moment as if to see if there would be any more, and when there wasn't he gave out more of that luminous smile and cocked his head toward the cabin. MacLyle led the way, with his visitor bringing up the rear with some platitudes about nice place you got here. As they entered, he suddenly barked at that unresponsive back, "Can't you hear me?" and MacLyle, without turning, only waved him on.

They walked into such a clutter and clabber of colors that

the psychiatrist stopped dead, blinking. One wall had been removed and replaced with glass panes; it overlooked the precipice and put the little building afloat on haze. All the walls were hung with plain white chenille bedspreads, and the floor was white, and there seemed to be much more light indoors here than outside. Opposite the large window was an oversized easel made of peeled poles, notched and lashed together with baling wire, and on it was a huge canvas, most nonobjective, in the purest and most uncompromising colors. Part of it was unquestionably this room, or at least its air of colored confusion here and all infinity yonder. The ophicleide was in the picture, painstakingly reproduced, looking like the hopper of some giant infernal machine, and in the foreground some flowers; but the central figure repulsed him—more, it repulsed everything which surrounded it. It did not look exactly like anything familiar and, in a disturbed way, he was happy about that.

Stacked on the floor on each side of the easel were other paintings, some daubs, some full of ruled lines and overlapping planes, but all in this achingly pure color. He realized what was being done with the dozens of colors of house paint in little cans which had so intrigued the storekeeper.

In odd places around the room were clay sculptures, most mounted on pedestals made of sections of tree trunks large enough to stand firmly on their sawed ends. Some of the pedestals were peeled, some painted, and in some the bark texture or the bulges or clefts in the wood had been carried right up into the model, and in others clay had been knived or pressed into the bark all the way down to the floor. Some of the clay was painted, some not, some ought to have been. There were free forms and gollywogs, a marsupial woman and a guitar with legs, and some, but not an overweening number, of the symbolisms which preoccupy even fairly intelligent psychiatrists. Nowhere was there any furniture per se. There were shelves at all levels and of varying lengths, bearing nail kegs, bolts of cloth, canned goods, tools and cooking utensils. There was a sort of table, but it was mostly a workbench, with a vise at one end and, at the other, half finished, a crude but exceedingly ingenious foot-powered potter's wheel.

He wondered where MacLyle slept, so he asked him, and again MacLyle reacted as if the words were not words but a series of pleasant sounds, cocking his head and waiting to see if there would be any more. So the psychiatrist resorted to sign language, making a pillow of his two hands, laying his head on it, closing his eyes. He opened them to see Mac-Lyle nodding eagerly, then going to the white-draped wall. From behind the chenille he brought a hammock, one end of which was fastened to the wall. The other end he carried to the big window and hung on a hook screwed to a heavy stud between the panes. To lie in that hammock would be to swing between heaven and earth like Mahomet's tomb, with all that sky and scenery virtually surrounding the sleeper. His admiration for this idea ceased as MacLyle began making urgent indications for him to get into the hammock. He backed off warily, expostulating, trying to convey to MacLyle that he only wondered, he just wanted to know—no, *no*, he wasn't tired, dammit; but MacLyle became so insistent that he picked the psychiatrist up like a child sulking at bedtime and carried him to the hammock. Any impulse to kick or quarrel was quenched by the nature of this and all other hammocks to be intolerant of shifting burdens, and by the proximity of the large window, which he now saw was built leaning outward, enabling one to look out of the hammock straight down a minimum of four hundred and eighty feet. So all right, he concluded, if you say so. I'm sleepy.

So for the next two hours he lay in the hammock watching MacLyle putter about the place, thinking more or less professional thoughts.

He doesn't or can't speak (he diagnosed): aphasia, motor. He doesn't or can't understand speech: aphasia, sensory. He won't or can't read and write: alexia. And what else?

He looked at all that art—if it *was* art, and any that was, was art by accident—and the gadgetry: the chuntering windmill outside, the sashweight door closer. He let his eyes follow a length of clothesline dangling unobtrusively down the leaning center post to which his hammock was fastened, and the pulley and fittings from which it hung, and its extension clear across the ceiling to the back wall, and understood finally that it would, when pulled, open two long, narrow horizontal hatches for through ventilation. A small door behind the chenille led to what he correctly surmised was a primitive powder room, built to overhang the precipice, the most perfect no-plumbing solution for that convenience he had ever seen.

He watched MacLyle putter. That was the only word for it, and his actions were the best example of puttering he had ever seen. MacLyle lifted, shifted, and put things down, backed off to judge, returned to lay an approving hand on the thing he had moved. Net effect, nothing tangible—yet one could not say there was no effect, because of the intense satisfaction the man radiated. For minutes he would stand, head cocked, smiling slightly, regarding the half-finished potter's wheel, then explode into activity, sawing, planing, drilling. He would add the finished piece to the cranks and connecting rods already completed, pat it as if it were an obedient child, and walk away, leaving the rest of the job for some other time. With a wood rasp he carefully removed the nose from one of his dried clay figures and meticulously put on a new one. Always there was this absorption in his own products and processes, and the air of total reward in everything. And there was time, there seemed to be time enough for everything, and always would be.

Here is a man, thought the fairly intelligent psychiatrist, in retreat, but in a retreat the like of which my science has not yet described. For observe: he has reacted toward the primitive in terms of supplying himself with his needs with his own hands and by his own ingenuity, and yet there is nothing primitive in those needs themselves. He works constantly to achieve the comforts which his history has conditioned him to in the past—electric lights, cross-ventilation, trouble-free waste disposal. He exhibits a profound humility in the low rates he pays himself for his labor: he is building a potter's wheel apparently in order to make his own cooking vessels, and, since wood is cheap and clay free, his vessel can cost him less than engine-turned aluminum only by a very low evaluation of his own efforts.

His skills are less than his energy (mused the psychiatrist). His carpentry, like his painting and sculpture, shows considerable intelligence, but only moderate training; he can construct but not beautify, draw but not draft, and reach the artistically pleasing only by not erasing the random shake, the accidental cut; so that real creation in his work is, like any random effect, rare and unpredictable. Therefore his reward is in the area of satisfaction—about as wide a generalization as one can make.

What satisfaction? Not in possessions themselves, for this

man could have bought better for less. Not in excellence in itself, for he obviously could be satisfied with less than perfection. Freedom, perhaps, from routine, from dominations of work? Hardly, because for all that complexity of this cluttered cottage, it had its order and its system; the presence of an alarm clock conveyed a good deal in this area. He wasn't dominated by regularity—he used it. And his satisfaction? Why, it must lie in this closed circle, himself to himself, and in the very fact of noncommunication!

Retreat . . . retreat. Retreat to savagery and you don't engineer your cross-ventilation or adjust a five-hundred-foot gravity flush for your john. Retreat into infancy and you don't design and build a potter's wheel. Retreat from people and you don't greet a stranger like—

Wait.

Maybe a stranger who had something to communicate, or some way of communication, wouldn't be so welcome. An unsettling thought, that. Running the risk of doing something MacLyle didn't like would be, possibly, a little more unselfish than the challenge warranted.

MacLyle began to cook.

Watching him, the psychiatrist reflected suddenly that this withdrawn and wordless individual was a happy one, in his own matrix; further, he had fulfilled all his obligations and responsibilities and was bothering no one.

It was intolerable.

It was intolerable because it was a violation of the prime directive of psychiatry—at least, of that school of psychiatry which he professed, and he was not going to confuse himself by considerations of other, less-tried theories—*It is the function of psychiatry to adjust the aberrate to society, and to restore or increase his usefulness to it.* To yield, to rationalize this man's behavior as balance, would be to fly in the face of science itself; for this particular psychiatry finds its most successful approaches in the scientific method, and it is unprofitable to debate whether or not it is or is not a science. To its practitioner it is, and that's that; it has to be. Operationally speaking, what has been found true, even statistically, must be Truth, and all other things, even Possible, kept the hell out of the toolbox. No known Truth allowed a social entity to secede this way, and, for one, this fairly intelligent psychiatrist was not going to give this—this *suicide* his blessing.

He must, then, find a way to communicate with MacLyle, and when he had found it he must communicate to him the error of his ways. Without getting thrown over the cliff.

He became aware that MacLyle was looking at him, twinkling. He smiled back before he knew what he was doing, and obeyed MacLyle's beckoning gesture. He eased himself out of the hammock and went to the workbench, where a steaming stew was set out in earthenware bowls. The bowls stood on large plates and were surrounded by a band of carefully sliced tomatoes. He tasted them. They were obviously vine-ripened and had been speckled with a dark-green paste which, after studious attention to its aftertaste, he identified as fresh basil mashed with fresh garlic and salt. The effect was symphonic.

He followed suit when MacLyle picked up his own bowl, and they went outside and squatted under the old Engelmann spruce to eat. It was a quiet and pleasant occasion, and during it the psychiatrist had plenty of opportunity to size up his man and plan his campaign. He was quite sure now how to proceed, and all he needed was opportunity, which presented itself when MacLyle rose, stretched, smiled, and went indoors. The psychiatrist followed him to the door and saw him crawl into the hammock and fall almost instantly sleep.

The psychiatrist went to his car and got out his bag of tricks. And so it was that late in the afternoon, when MacLyle emerged stretching and yawning from his nap, he found his visitor under the spruce tree, hefting the ophicleide and twiddling its keys in a perplexed and investigatory fashion. MacLyle strode over to him and lifted the ophicleide away with a pleasant I'll-show-you smile, got the monstrous contraption into position, and ran his tongue around the inside of the mouthpiece, large as a demitasse. He had barely time to pucked up his lips at the strange taste there before his irises rolled up completely out of sight and he collapsed like a grounded parachute. The psychiatrist was able only to snatch away the ophicleide in time to keep the mouthpiece from knocking out MacLyle's front teeth.

He set the ophicleide carefully against the tree and straightened MacLyle's limbs. He concentrated for a moment on the pulse, and turned the head to one side so saliva would not drain down the flaccid throat, and then went back to his bag of tricks. He came back and knelt, and MacLyle did not even twitch at the bite of the hypodermics: a careful blend of the nonsoporific tranquilizers Frenquel, chlorpromazine and Reserpine, and a judicious dose of scopolamine, a hypnotic.

The psychiatrist got water and carefully sponged out the man's mouth, not caring to wait out another collapse the next time he swallowed. Then there was nothing to do but wait, and plan.

Exactly on schedule, according to the psychiatrist's wrist watch, MacLyle groaned and coughed weakly. The psychiatrist immediately and in a firm quiet voice told him not to move. Also not to think. He stayed out of the immediate range of MacLyle's unfocused eyes and explained that MacLyle must trust him, because he was there to help, and not to worry about feeling mixed-up or disoriented. "You don't know where you are or how you got here," he informed MacLyle. He also told MacLyle, who was past forty, that he was thirty-seven years old, but he knew what he was doing.

MacLyle just lay there obediently and thought these things over and waited for more information. He didn't know where he was or how he had got here. He did know that he must trust this voice, the owner of which was here to help him; that he was thirty-seven years old; and his name. In these things he lay and marinated. The drugs kept him conscious, docile, submissive and without guile. The psychiatrist observed and exulted: oh you azacyclonol, he chanted silently to himself, you pretty piperidyl, handsome hydrochloride, subtle Serpasil . . . Confidently he left MacLyle and went into the cabin, where, after due search, he found some decent clothes and some socks and shoes, and brought them out and wrapped the supine patient in them. He helped MacLyle across the clearing and into his car, humming as he did so, for there is none so happy as an expert faced with excellence in his specialty. MacLyle sank back into the cushions and gave one wondering glance at the cabin and at the blare of late light from the bell of the ophicleide; but the psychiatrist told him firmly that these things had nothing to do with him, nothing at all, and MacLyle smiled relievedly and fell to watching the scenery go by, passive as a Pekingese. As they passed the general store MacLyle stirred, but said nothing about it. Instead he asked the psychiatrist if the Ardsmere station was open yet, whereupon the psychiatrist could barely answer him for the impulse to purr like a cat: the Ardsmere station, two stops before MacLyle's suburban town, had burned down and been rebuilt almost six years ago; so now he knew for sure that MacLyle was living in a time preceding his difficulties—a time during which, of course, MacLyle had been able to talk. He crooned his appreciation for chlorpromazine (which had helped MacLyle be tranquil) and he made up a silent song, "O Doll o' Mine, Scopolamine"—which had made him so very suggestible. But all of this the psychiatrist kept to himself, and he answered gravely that yes, they had the Ardsmere station operating again. And did he have anything else on his mind?

MacLyle considered this carefully, but since all the immediate questions were answered—unswervingly he *knew* he was safe in the hands of this man, whoever he was, he knew (he thought) his correct age and that he was expected to feel disoriented, and he was also under a command not to think—he placidly shook his head and went back to watching the road unroll under their wheels. "Fallen Rock Zone," he murmured as they passed a sign. The psychiatrist drove happily down the mountain and across the flats, back to the city where he had hired the car. He left it at the railroad station ("Rail Crossing Road," murmured MacLyle) and made reservations for a compartment on the train, aircraft being too open and public for his purposes and far too fast for the hourly rate he suddenly decided to apply.

They had time for a silent and companionable dinner before train time, and then at last they were aboard, solid ground beneath, a destination ahead, and the track joints applauding.

The psychiatrist turned off all but one reading lamp and leaned forward. MacLyle's eyes dilated readily to the dimmer light, and the psychiatrist leaned back comfortably and asked him how he felt. He felt fine and said so. The psychiatrist asked him how old he was and MacLyle told him thirty-seven, but he sounded doubtful.

Knowing that the scopolamine was wearing off but the other drugs, the tranquilizers, would hang on for a bit, the psychiatrist drew a deep breath and removed the suggestion;

271

he told MacLyle the truth about his age and brought him up to the here and now. MacLyle just looked puzzled for a few minutes and then his features settled into an expression that can only be described as not unhappy. "Porter," was all he said, gazing at the push button on the partition with its little metal sign, and he announced that he could read now.

The psychiatrist nodded sagely and offered no comment, being quite willing to let a patient stew in his own juice as long as he produced essence.

MacLyle abruptly demanded to know why he had lost the powers of speech and reading. The psychiatrist raised his eyebrows a little and his shoulders a good deal and smiled one of those you-tell-me smiles, and then got up and suggested they sleep on it. He got the porter in to fix the beds and as an afterthought told the man to come back with the evening papers. Nothing can orient a cultural expatriate better than the evening papers. The man did. MacLyle paid no attention to this, one way or the other. He just climbed into the psychiatrist's spare pajamas thoughtfully and they went to bed.

The psychiatrist didn't know if MacLyle had awakened him on purpose or whether the train's slowing down for a watering stop had done it, or both; anyway, he awoke about three in the morning to find MacLyle standing beside his bunk looking at him fixedly. He closed his eyes and screwed them tight and opened them again, and MacLyle was still there, and now he noticed that MacLyle's reading lamp was lit and the papers were scattered all over the floor.

MacLyle said, "You're some kind of a doctor," in a flat voice.

The psychiatrist admitted it.

MacLyle said, "Well, this ought to make some sense to you. I was skiing out here years ago when I was a college kid. Accident, fellow I was with broke his leg. Compound. Made him comfortable as I could and went for help. Came back, he'd slid down the mountain, thrashing around, I guess. Crevasse, down in the bottom; took two days to find him, three days to get him out. Frostbite. Gangrene."

The psychiatrist tried to look as if he were following this.

MacLyle said, "The one thing I always remember, him pulling back the bandages all the time to look at his leg. Knew it was gone, couldn't keep himself from watching the stuff spread around and upward. Didn't like to; *had* to. Tried to stop him, finally had to help him or he'd hurt himself. Every ten, fifteen minutes all the way down to the lodge, fifteen hours, looking under the bandages."

The psychiatrist tried to think of something to say and couldn't, so he looked wise and waited.

MacLyle said, "That Donne, that John Donne I used to spout, I always believed that."

The psychiatrist began to misquote the thing about send not to ask for whom the bell . . .

"Yeah, that, but especially *'any man's death diminishes me, because I am involved in mankind.'* I believed that," MacLyle repeated. "I believed more than that. Not only death. Damn foolishness diminishes me because I am involved. People all the time pushing people around diminishes me. Everybody hungry for a fast buck diminishes me." He picked up a sheet of newspaper and let it slip away; it flapped off to the corner of the compartment like a huge grave-moth. "I was getting diminished to death and I had to watch it happening to me like that kid with the gangrene, so that's why." The train, crawling now, lurched suddenly and yielded. MacLyle's eyes flicked to the window, where neon beer signs and a traffic light were reluctantly being framed. MacLyle leaned close to the psychiatrist. "I just had to get uninvolved with mankind before I got diminished altogether, everything mankind did was my fault. So I did and now here I am involved again." MacLyle abruptly went to the door. "And for that, thanks."

From a dusty throat the psychiatrist asked him what he was going to do.

"Do?" asked MacLyle cheerfully. "Why, I'm going out there and diminish mankind right back." He was out in the corridor with the door closed before the psychiatrist so much as sat up. He banged it open again and leaned in. He said in the sanest of all possible voices, "Now, mind you, doctor, this is only one man's opinion," and was gone. He killed four people before they got him.

The Custodian

WILLIAM TENN

William Tenn has written, as far as I know, stories of three kinds. Many of them are funny, even farcical (and good farce is a very rare thing in sf, or, indeed, anywhere else). Some of them are thoughtful, quiet, intense explorations of an idea, a tendency, or a human being. A few of them, unfortunately, are standard reworkings of standard sf themes. These last received no nominations in this poll. A great many of Mr. Tenn's fine stories also received no nominations. Among the nominated stories, though, "The Custodian" stands out.

For one thing, it has never been reprinted in an anthology. For another, it is a blend of the first and second types mentioned. It is, regardless of what you may believe after the first reading, a serious and even, possibly, important exploration. It is also, in its own way, an extremely funny story. I don't know why it's funny, or even how the humor is managed. I wish I did know.

If you haven't read this one before, and possibly you haven't, you can find it again in Mr. Tenn's collection Of All Possible Worlds. *You can also find a great many other good stories there and in other collections by this many-sided and astonishingly bearded gnome.*

May 9, 2190—Well, I did it! It was close, but fortunately I have a very suspicious nature. My triumph, my fulfillment, was almost stolen from me, but I was too clever for them. As a result, I am happy to note in this, my will and testament, I now begin my last year of life.

No, let me be accurate. This last year of my life, the year that I will spend in an open tomb, really began at noon today. Then, in the second sub-basement of the Museum of Modern Astronautics, I charged a dial for the third successive time and got a completely negative response. That meant that I,

Fiyatil, was the only human being alive on Earth. What a struggle I have had to achieve that distinction!

Well, it's all over now, I'm fairly certain. Just to be on the safe side, I'll come down and check the anthropometer every day or so for the next week, but I don't think there's a chance in the universe that I'll get a positive reading. I've had my last, absolutely my final and ultimate battle with the forces of righteousness—and I've won. Left in secure, undisputed possession of my coffin, there's nothing for me to do now but enjoy myself. And that shouldn't be too hard. After all, I've been planning the pleasures for years!

Still, as I tugged off my suit of berrillit blue and climbed upstairs into the sunlight, I couldn't help thinking of the others. Gruzeman, Prejaut, and possibly even Mo-Diki— they'd have been here with me now if only they'd had a shade less academic fervor, a touch more of intelligent realism.

Too bad, in a way. And yet it makes my vigil more solemn, more glorious. As I sat down on the marble bench between Rozinski's heroic statues of the Spaceman and Spacewoman, I shrugged and dismissed the memories of Gruzeman, Prejaut, and Mo-Diki.

They had failed. I hadn't.

I leaned back, relaxing for the first time in more than a month. My eyes swept over the immense bronze figures towering above me, two pieces of sculpture yearning agonizingly for the stars, and I burst into a chuckle. The absolute incongruity of my hiding place hit me for the first time— imagine, the Museum of Modern Astronautics! Multiplied by the incredible nervous tension, the knuckle-biting fear of the past five days, the chuckle bounced up and down in my throat and became a giggle, then a splutter, and finally a reverberating, chest-heaving laugh that I couldn't stop. It brought all the deer out of the museum park to stand in front of the marble bench where Fiyatil, the last man on Earth, choked and coughed and wheezed and cackled at his senile accomplishment.

I don't know how long the fit might have held me, but a cloud, merely in the course of its regular duties as a summer cloud, happened to slide in front of the sun. That did it. I stopped laughing, as if a connection had been cut, and glanced upward.

The cloud went on, and the sunlight poured down as warmly as ever, but I shivered a bit.

Two pregnant young does came a little closer and stood watching as I massaged my neck. Laughter had given it a crick.

"Well, my dears," I said, tossing them a quotation from one of my favorite religions, "it would seem that in the midst of life we are at last truly in death."

They munched at me impassively.

May 11, 2190—I have spent the last two days putting myself and my supplies in order and making plans for the immediate future. Spending a lifetime in sober preparation for the duties of custodianship is one thing. Finding suddenly that you have become *the* custodian, the last of your sect as well as your race, and yet, peculiarly, the fulfillment of them both—that is quite another thing. I find myself burning with an insane pride. And a moment later I turn cold with the incredible, the majestic responsibility that I face.

Food will be no problem. In the commissary of this one institution there are enough packaged meals to keep a man like myself well fed for ten years, let alone twelve months. And wherever I go on the planet, from the Museum of Buddhist Antiquities in Tibet to the Panorama of Political History in Sebastopol, I will find a similar plenty.

Of course, packaged meals are packaged meals: somebody else's idea of what my menu should be. Now that the last Affirmer has gone, taking with him his confounded austerity, there is no longer any need for me to be a hypocrite. I can at last indulge my taste for luxury and bathe my tongue in gustatory baubles. Unfortunately I grew to manhood under Affirmer domination, and the hypocrisies I learned to practice in sixty cringing years have merged with the essential substance of my character. I doubt, therefore, that I will be preparing any meals of fresh food from the ancient recipes.

And then, too, meals of fresh food would involve the death of creatures that are currently alive and enjoying themselves. This seems a bit silly under the circumstances. . . .

Nor did I need to put any of the automatic laundries into operation. Yet I have. Why clean my clothes, I asked myself, when I can discard a tunic the moment it becomes slightly soiled and step into a newly manufactured garment, still stiff in memory of the machine matrix whence it came? Habit told me why I couldn't. Custodian concepts make it impossible for me to do what an Affirmer in my position would find easiest: shrug out of the tunic on a clear patch of ground and leave it lying behind me like a huge, brightly colored dropping. On the other hand, much Affirmer teaching that my conscious mind has been steadfastly rejecting for decades, I find to my great annoyance, has seeped into the unconscious osmotically. The idea of deliberately destroying anything as functional, if relatively unaesthetic, as a dirty Tunic, Male, Warm-Season, Affirmer Ship-Classification Number 2352558.3, appalls me—even against my will.

Over and over again I tell myself that Affirmer Ship-Classification Numbers now mean nothing to me. Less than nothing. They are as meaningless as cargo symbols on the Ark to the stevedores who loaded it, the day after Noah sailed.

Yet I step into a one-seater flyball for a relaxing tour of the museum grounds, and something in my mind says, Number 58184.72. I close my teeth upon a forkful of well-seasoned Luncheon Protein Component and note that I am chewing Ship-Classification Numbers 15762.94 through 15763.01. I even remind myself that it is a category to be brought aboard among the last, and only when the shipboard representative of the Ministry of Survival and Preservation has surrendered his command to the shipboard representative of the Ministry of the Journey.

Not a single Affirmer walks the earth at the moment. Together with their confounded multiplicity of government bureaus—including the one in which all people professing Custodianism had to be registered, the Ministry of Antiquities and Useless Relics—they are now scattered among a hundred or so planetary systems in the galaxy. But all this seems to matter not a bit to my idiotically retentive mind, which goes on quoting texts memorized decades ago for Survival Placement Examinations long since superseded and forgotten by those in authority.

They are so efficient, the Affirmers, so horribly, successfully efficient. As a youngster, I confided to my unfortunately loquacious comrade, Ru-Sat, that I had begun creative painting on canvas in my leisure hours. Immediately my parents, in collaboration with my recreational adviser, had me volunteered into the local Children's Extra Work for Extra Survival Group, where I was assigned to painting numbers and symbols on packing cases. "Not pleasure but persistence, persistence, persistence will preserve the race of man," I had to repeat from the Affirmer catechism before I was allowed to sit down to any meal from that time on.

Later, of course, I was old enough to register as a conscientious Custodian. "Please," my father choked at me when I told him, "don't come around any more. Don't bother us. I'm speaking for the entire family, Fiyatil, including your uncles on your mother's side. You've decided to become a dead man: that's your business now. Just forget you ever had parents and relatives—and let us forget we had a son."

This meant I could free myself from Survival chores by undertaking twice as much work with the microfilm teams that traveled from museum to museum and archaeological site to skyscraper city. But still there were the periodic Survival Placement Exams, which everyone agreed didn't apply to Custodians but insisted we take as a gesture of good will to the society which was allowing us to follow our consciences. Exams which necessitated putting aside a volume entitled *Religious Design and Decoration in Temples of the Upper Nile* for the dreary, dingy, well-thumbed *Ship-Classification Manual and Uniform-Cargo-Stowage Guide*. I had given up the hope of being an artist myself, but those ugly little decimals took up time that I wished to spend contemplating the work of men who had lived in less fanatic and less frenzied centuries.

They still do! So powerful is habit that, now that I have no questions on dehydration to answer ever again, I still find myself doing the logarithmic work necessary to find out where a substance is packed once its water is removed. It is horribly frustrating to be mired after all in an educational system from which I turned completely away!

Of course, the studies I am involved in at the moment probably don't help very much. Yet it is very important for me to pick up enough information from the elementary educatories in this museum, for example, to insure my not having to worry about the possibility of a flyball breakdown over a jungle area. I'm no technician, no trouble shooter. I have to learn instead how to choose equipment in good working order and how to start operating it without doing any damage to delicate components.

This technological involvement irritates me. Outside, the abandoned art of seventy thousand years beckons—and here I sit, memorizing dull facts about the power plants of worker robots, scrutinizing blueprints of the flyballs' antigrav screws, and acting for all the world like an Affirmer captain trying to win a commendation from the Ministry of the Journey before he blasts off.

Yet it is precisely this attitude that is responsible for my being here now, instead of sitting disconsolately aboard the Affirmer scout ship with Mo-Diki, Gruzeman and Prejaut. While they exulted in their freedom and charged about the planet like creaky old colts, I made for the Museum of Modern Astronautics and learned how to operate and read an anthropometer and how to activate the berrillit blue. I hated to waste the time, but I couldn't forget how significant to an Affirmer, especially a modern one, is the concept of the sacredness of human life. They had betrayed us once; they were bound to come back to make certain that the betrayal left no loose ends in the form of Custodians enjoying fulfillment. I was right then, and I know I am right now—but I get so bored with the merely useful.

Speaking of the anthropometer, I had a nasty shock two hours ago. The alarm went off—and stopped. I scurried downstairs to it, shaking out the berrillit-blue suit as I ran and hoping desperately that I wouldn't blow myself up in the course of using it a second time. By the time I got to the machine, it had stopped caterwauling. I charged the all-directional dial over ten times and got no response. Therefore, according to the anthropometer manual, nothing human was moving about anywhere in the entire solar system. I had keyed the machine to myself electroencephalographically so that I wouldn't set off the alarm. Yet the alarm *had* gone off, indisputably recording the presence of humanity other than myself, however temporary its existence had been. It was very puzzling.

My conclusion is that some atmospheric disturbance or faulty connection inside the anthropometer set the machine off. Or possibly, in my great joy over being left behind a few days ago, I carelessly damaged the apparatus. I heard the Affirmer scout ship radio the news of the capture of my

279

colleagues to a mother vessel waiting beyond Pluto; I *know* I'm the sole survivor on Earth. Besides, if it had been skulking Affirmers who set the alarm off, their own anthropometer would have detected me at the same time, since I had been walking about unprotected by the insulating effect of berrillit blue. The museum would have been surrounded by flyball crews and I'd have been caught almost immediately.

No, I cannot believe I have anything more to fear from Affirmers. They have satisfied themselves with their last-moment return of two days ago, I am positive. Their doctrine would forbid any further returns, since they would be risking their own lives. After all, there are only 363 days left—at most—before the sun goes nova.

May 15, 2190—I am deeply disturbed. In fact, I am frightened. And worst of it is, I do not know of what. All I can do now is wait.

Yesterday I left the Museum of Modern Astronautics for a preliminary tour of the world. I planned to spend two or three weeks hopping about in my flyball before I made any decision about where I would stay for the bulk of my year.

My first error was the choice of a first destination. Italy. It is very possible that if my little problem had not come up I would have spent eleven months there before going on with my preliminary survey. The Mediterranean is a dangerous and sticky body of water to anyone who had decided that, his own talents being inadequate or aborted, he may most fittingly spend his life cherishing the masterpieces presented to humanity by other, much more fortunate individuals.

I went to Ferrara first, since the marshy, reclaimed plain outside the city was a major Affirmer launching site. I lingered a little while at one of my favorite buildings, the Palazzo dei Diamanti, shaking my head as helplessly as ever at the heavy building stones of which it is constructed and which are cut and faceted like so many enormous jewels. To my mind, the city itself is a jewel, now somewhat dulled, that sparkled madly in the days of the Este court. One little city, one tiny, arrogant court—I would so happily have traded them for the two billion steadfastly boorish Affirmers. Over sixty years of almost unchallenged political control, and did an entire planetful of them produce a single competitor for a Tasso or an Ariosto? And then I realized that at least one native Ferraran would have felt at ease in the world that has just departed from me, its last romantic. I remembered that Savonarola had been born in Ferrara. . . .

The plain outside Ferrara also reminded me of the dour Dominican. The launching field, stretching away for quite a few flat miles, was strewn with enough possessions discarded at the last moment to make a truly towering Bonfire of Vanities.

But what pathetic vanities! Here, a slide rule that some ship's commander had ordered thrown out before take-off because the last inspection had revealed it to be in excess of what the *Ship-Classification Manual* listed as the maximum number of slide rules necessary for a vessel of that size. There, a mimeographed collection of tally sheets that had been dropped out of the closing air lock after every last item had been checked off as per regulations—one check *before* the item by the Ministry of Survival and Preservation, and one check *after* the item by the Ministry of the Journey. Soiled clothing, somewhat worn implements, empty fuel and food drums lay about on the moist ground. Highly functional articles all, that had somehow come in the course of time to sin against function—and had fallen swiftly from use. And, surprisingly, an occasional doll, not looking very much like a doll, to be sure, but not looking like anything that had an objective purpose either. Staring about me at the squalid debris dotted so rarely with sentiment, I wondered how many parents had writhed with shame when, despite their carefully repeated admonitions and advance warnings, the last search had discovered something in the recesses of a juvenile tunic that could only be called an old toy—or, worse yet, a keepsake.

I remembered what my recreational adviser had said on that subject, long years ago: "It's not that we believe that children shouldn't have toys, Fiyatil; we just don't want them to become attached to any particular toy. Our race is going to leave this planet that's been its home from the beginning. We'll be able to take with us only such creatures and objects as are usable to make other creatures and objects which we'll need for sustenance wherever we come down. And because we can't carry more than so much weight in each ship, we'll have to select from among the usable objects those which are essential.

"We won't take anything along because it's pretty, or because a lot of people swear by it, or because a lot of people *think* they need it. We'll take it along only because nothing else will do an important job so well. That's why I come to your home every month or so to inspect your room, to make certain that your bureau drawers contain only new things, that you're not falling into dangerous habits of sentimentality that can lead only to Custodianism. You've got far too nice a set of folks to turn into *that* kind of person."

Nonetheless, I chuckled to myself, I had turned into that kind of person. Old Tobletej had been right: the first step on the road to ruin had been bureau drawers crammed with odds and ends of memory. The twig on which had sat the first butterfly I'd ever caught, the net with which I'd caught him, and the first butterfly himself. The wad of paper that a certain twelve-year-old lady had thrown at me. A tattered copy of a real printed book—no facsimile broadcast, this, but something that had once known the kiss of type instead of the hot breath of electrons. The small wooden model of Captain Karma's starship, *Man's Hope*, which an old space hand at Lunar Line launching field had given me along with much misinformation. . . .

Those paunchy bureau drawers! How my parents and teachers had tried to teach me neatness and a hatred of possessions! And here was I, now grown into man's estate, smug over my possession of a quantity of artistic masterpieces the like of which no Holy Roman Emperor, no Grand Khan, would have dared to dream about.

I chuckled once more and started looking for the launching-site robots. They were scattered about, almost invisible in the unimportant garbage of the spaceship field. After loading the ship, they had simply wandered about until they had run down. I activated them once more and set them to cleaning the field. This is something I will do in every one of the two hundred or so launching sites on Earth, and this is the chief reason I have been studying robotics. I want Earth to look as pretty as possible when she dies. I never could be an Affirmer, I am afraid; I form strong attachments.

Feeling as I did, I just couldn't continue on my trip without taking the quickest, the most cursory glance at Florence.

Naturally. But, as I should have expected, I got drunk on oils and marbles and metalwork. Florence was empty of Florentines, but the glorious galleries were still there. I walked across the fine Ponte Vecchio, the only one of the famous Arno bridges to have escaped destruction in the Second World War. I came to Giotto's campanile and the baptistery doors by Ghiberti and I began to feel despair, desperation. I ran to the Church of Santa Croce to see Giotto's frescoes and the Convent of St. Mark's for Fra Angelico. What good was one year, what could I see of even a single city like this in a bare twelve months? I could view, I could gallop by, but what would I have time to *see?* I was in the Boboli gardens trying frantically to decide whether to look up Michelangelo's "David," which I'd seen once before, or some Donatello which I hadn't, when the alarms went off.

Both of them.

The day before I'd left, I'd put together a small anthropometer that had originally been developed for locating lost colonists in the Venusian swamps. It was based on an entirely different design than the big machine that I'd found in the Hall of Gadgets. Since the circuits were unlike, and they had been planned for use in entirely different atmospheres, I believed they would serve as excellent checks on each other. I'd set the alarms to the frequency of my flyball communicator and had left the museum fairly confident that the only thing that could make both anthropometers go off would be the presence of a man other than myself.

I flew back to the museum, feeling very confused. Both pieces of equipment had responded the same way. The alarm had gone off, indicating the sudden materialization of man on the planet. Then, when the stimulus had disappeared, both alarms had stopped. No matter how many times I charged the directional dials on each anthropometer, there was not the faintest suspicion of mankind within their extreme range, which is a little under one half of a light-year.

The initial confusion had given way to a strong feeling of discomfort. Something is very wrong here on Earth, something other than the sun's getting ready to explode in a year. Possibly I have the nontechnician's blind faith in a piece of apparatus which I don't fully understand, but I don't believe that the anthropometers should be acting this way unless something really abnormal is occurring.

It has pleased me to look upon this planet as an oceangoing ship about to sink, and myself as the gallant captain determined to go down with her. Abruptly, I feel as if the ship were beginning to act like a whale.

I know what I must do. I'll move a supply of food down to the Hall of Gadgets and sleep right under the anthropometers. The alarm usually lasts for a minute or two. I can leap to my feet, charge the all-direction dials and get enough of a reading right then to know exactly where the stimulus is coming from. Then I will pop into my flyball and investigate. It's really very simple.

Only, I don't *like* it.

May 17, 2190—I feel thoroughly ashamed of myself, as only an old man who has been seeing ghosts in the graveyard should be ashamed. That, in fact, is the only excuse I can make of myself. I have, I suppose, been thinking too much about death recently. The coming extinction of Earth and the solar system; my death, which is inevitably involved with it; the death by the million of creatures of uncounted species, the death of proud old cities that man has reared and occupied for centuries . . . Well, perhaps the association with ghosties and beasties and other strange phenomena is understandable. But I *was* getting frightened.

When the alarms went off again this morning, I got a directional reading. My destination was the Appalachian Mountain region in eastern North America.

The moment I got out of the flyball and took in the pale-azure fog covering the cave mouth in front of me, I began to understand—and feel ashamed. Through the fog, which thinned in one place and thickened in others as I watched, I could see several bodies lying on the floor of the cave. Obviously, one of them had to be alive for the anthropometer to have reacted as soon as a patch of berrillit blue got meager enough to make the presence of a human mind detectable. I walked round to the back of the cave and found no exit.

I went back to the museum in the flyball and returned with the necessary equipment. I deactivated the berrillit blue fog at the entrance and walked inside cautiously.

The interior of the cave, which had evidently been furnished as a domestic and comfortable hideout, was completely wrecked. Somebody had managed to get an activator as well as a quantity of berrillit blue which had not been given any particular shape and which, therefore, was about as stable as hydrogen and oxygen—if it is permissible to use a metaphor from chemistry to illustrate negative-force-field concepts. The berrillit blue had been activated as a sort of curtain across the mouth of the cave and had blown up immediately. But, since the activator was still operating and the entrance was fairly narrow, it continued to function as a curtain of insulating negative force, a curtain which had holes in it through which one could occasionally "peek" by means of the anthropometer at the people imprisoned inside.

There were three bodies near the entrance, two male and one female, rather youthful-looking. From the quantity and type of statuary on the walls of the cave, it was easy to deduce that these people had belonged to one of the numerous religious Custodian groups, probably the Fire in the Heavens cult. When, in the last week of the exodus, the Affirmers had denounced the Crohiik Agreement and stated that the Affirmation of Life required that even those who didn't Affirm had to be protected against themselves, these people had evidently taken to the mountains. Evading the subsequent highly effective search, they had managed to stay hidden until the last great vessel left. Then, suspecting as I had that at least one scout ship would return for a final roundup, they had investigated the properties of the anthropometer and found out about the only insulator, berrillit blue. Unfortunately, they had not found out enough.

Deep in the rear of the cave, a body twisted brokenly to meet me. It was a young woman. My first reaction was absolute astonishment at the fact that she was still alive. The explosion seemed to have smashed her thoroughly below the waist. She had crawled from the cave mouth to the interior, where the group had stored most of their food and water. As I teetered, momentarily undecided whether to leave her and get medication and blood plasma from a hospital in the region or to risk moving her immediately, she rolled over on her back.

She had been covering a year-old infant with her body, evidently uncertain when the berrillit might blow again. And somehow, in spite of what must have been tremendous agony, she had been feeding the child.

I bent down and examined the baby. He was quite dirty and covered with his mother's blood, but otherwise unharmed. I picked him up and, in answer to the question in the woman's eyes, I nodded.

"He'll be all right," I said.

She started what may have been a nod in reply and stopped halfway through to die. I examined her carefully and, I will admit, a shade frantically. There was no pulse—no heartbeat.

I took the child back to the museum and constructed a sort of playpen for him out of empty telescope sections. Then I went back to the cave with three robots and had the people buried. I admit the gesture was superfluous, but it wasn't only a matter of neatness. However fundamental our differences, we were all of Custodian persuasion, generally speaking. It somehow made me feel as if I were snapping my fingers in the face of the entire smug Affirmation to respect Fire in Heavens eccentricities in this fashion.

After the robots had completed their work, I placed a piece of the religious statuary (it was remarkably badly done, by the way) at the head of each grave and even said a short prayer, or rather a sermon. I developed the thought that I had suggested approximately a week earlier to some deer—to wit, that in the midst of life we are in death. I did not joke about it, however, but spoke seriously on the subject for several minutes. The robots who were my audience seemed even less excited by the intelligence than the deer had been.

May 21, 2190—I am annoyed. I am very, very annoyed, and my great problem at the moment is that I lack an object on which to expend my annoyance.

The child has been an incredible amount of trouble.

I took him to the largest medical museum in the Northern Hemisphere and had him thoroughly examined by the best pediatric diagnostic machinery. He seems to be in excellent health, which is fortunate for both of us. And his dietary requirements, while not the same as mine, are fairly simple. I got a full tape on the kind of food he needs and, after a few readjustments in the commissary of the Museum of Modern Astronautics, I have arranged for this food to be prepared and delivered to him daily. Unfortunately, he does not seem to regard this arrangement, which took up an inordinate amount of my time, as wholly satisfactory.

For one thing, he will not accept food from the regulation robot nursemaid which I have activated for him. This, I suspect, is because of his parents' odd beliefs: he probably has never encountered mechanical affection before. He will eat only when I feed him.

That situation alone is intolerable, but I have found it almost impossible to leave him guarded by the robot nursemaid. Though he does little more than crawl, he manages to do this at a surprisingly fast pace and is always disappearing into dark corridors of the museum. Then an alarm is flashed to me and I have to break off my examination of the gigantic palace of the Dalai Lama, the Potala, and come scudding back from Lhasa halfway across the world to the museum. Even then it would take us hours to find him—and by "us" I mean every robot at my disposal—if I were not able to resort to the anthropometer. This admirable gadget points out his hiding place very swiftly; and so, pulling him out of the firing chamber of the Space Howitzer in the Hall of Weapons, I return him to his playpen. Then, if I dare, and if it is not time for him to be fed, I may return—briefly—to the Tibetan plateau.

I am at present engaged in constructing a sort of enormous cage for him, with automatic heating and toilet facilities and devices that will screen out undesirable animals, insects, and reptiles. Though this is taking far too much of my time, it will be an excellent investment, I believe.

I don't know quite what to do about the feeding problem. The only solution I can find in any of the literature on the subject that offers promise is the one about letting him go hungry if he refuses food from normal sources. After a brief experiment, however, in which he seemed cheerfully resigned to starvation, I was forced to give in. I now handle every one of his meals.

The trouble is that I don't know whom to blame. Since I have been a Custodian from early manhood, I failed to see the need to reproduce. I have never been interested even slightly in children. I know very little about them and care less.

I have always felt that my attitude was admirably summed up by Socrates' comments in the *Symposium:*

Who, upon reflecting on Homer and Hesiod and other such great poets, would not rather have their children than ordinary human ones? Who would not like to emulate them in the creation of children such as theirs, which have preserved their memory and given them everlasting glory? . . . Many are the temples which have been raised in their honor for the sake of such children as they have had, which were never raised in honor of anyone for the sake of his mortal children.

Unfortunately, we are the only two humans alive on Earth, this child and I. We are going to our doom together; we ride the same round tumbril. And the treasures of the world, which were wholly mine less than a week ago, now belong at least partially to him. I wish we could discuss the matters at issue, not only to arrive at more equitable arrangements, but also for the sheer pleasure of the discussion. I have come to the conclusion that I began this journal out of unconscious terror when I discovered, after the Affirmers left, that I was completely alone.

I find myself getting very wistful for conversation, for ideas other than my own, for opinions against which mine might be measured. Yet according to the literature on the subject, while this child may begin talking on any day now, we will be immersed in catastrophe long before he learns to argue with me. I find that sad, however inevitable.

How I wander! The fact is that once again I am being prevented from studying art as I would like. I am an old man and should have no responsibilities; I have all but laid down my life for the privilege of this study. It is extremely vexing.

And conversation. I can just imagine the kind of conversation I might be having with an Affirmer at the moment, were one to have been stranded here with me. What dullness, what singleminded biological idiocy! What crass refusal to look at, let alone admit, the beauty his species has been seventy millennia in the making! The most he might have learned if he is European, say, is a bit about the accepted artists of his culture. What would he know of Chinese paintings, for example, or cave art? Would he be able to understand that in each there were primitive periods followed by eras of lusty development, followed in turn by a consolidation of artistic gains and an increase in formalization, the whole to be rounded off by a decadent, inner-groping epoch which led almost invariably into another primitive and lusty period? That these have occurred again and again in the major cultures, so that even the towering genius of a Michelangelo, a Shakespeare, a Beethoven will likely be repeated—in somewhat different terms—in another complete cycle? That there was a Michelangelo, a Shakespeare, and a Beethoven in each of several different flower periods in ancient Egyptian art?

How could an Affirmer understand such concepts when he lacks the basic information necessary to understanding? When their ships departed from the moribund solar system laden only with artifacts immediately usable? When they refused to let their offspring keep childhood treasures for fear of developing sentimentality, so that when they came to colonize Procyon XII there would be no tears for either the world that had died or the puppy that had been left behind?

And yet history plays such incredible jokes on man. They who ran away from their museums, who kept nothing but a cold microfilm record of what lay in their investment houses of culture, will learn that man's sentimentality is not to be frustrated. The bleak, efficient ships that brought them to these alien worlds will become museums of the past as they oxydize out of existence on the strange sands. Their cruelly functional lines will become the inspiration for temples and the cause of alcoholic tears.

What in the world is happening to me? How I run on! After all, I merely wanted to explain why I was annoyed.

May 29, 2190—I have made several decisions. I don't know if I shall be able to implement the most important of them, but I will try. In order, however, to give myself what I most need at the moment, time, I shall write much less in this journal, if I write any more at all. I will try very hard to be brief.

To begin with the least important decision: I have named the child Leonardo. Why I chose to name him after a man who, for all his talents—in fact, *because* of his talents—I regard as the most spectacular failure in the history of art, I do not know. But Leonardo was a well-rounded man, something which the Affirmers are not—and something which I am beginning to admit I am not.

By the way, the child recognizes his name. He is not yet able to pronounce it, but it is positively miraculous the way he recognizes it. And he makes a sound which is very like mine. In fact, I might say——

Let me go on.

I have decided to attempt an escape from Earth—with Leonardo. My reasons are many and complex, and I'm not certain that I understand them all, but one thing I do know: I have felt responsibility for a life other than my own and can no longer evade it. This is not a tardy emergence into Affirmer doctrine, but in a very real sense my own ideas come to judgment. Since I believe in the reality of beauty, especially beauty made with the mind and hands of man, I can follow no other course.

I am an old man and shall achieve little with the rest of my life. Leonardo is an infant: he represents raw potential; he might become anything—a song beyond Shakespeare's, a thought above Newton, above Einstein, or an evil beyond Gilles de Retz, a horror past Hitler. But the potential should be realized. I think that under my tutelage it is less likely to be evil, and that there *I* have a potential to be realized. In any case, even if Leonardo represents a zero personally, he may *carry* the germ plasm of a Buddha, of a Euripides, of a Freud. And *that* potential must be realized. . . .

There is a ship. Its name is *Man's Hope* and it was the first ship to reach the stars, almost a century ago when it had just been discovered that our sun would explode and become a nova in a little less than a hundred years. It was the ship that discovered for man the heart-quickening fact that other stars have planets and that many of those planets are habitable to him.

It was a long time ago that Captain Karma brought his starship back down on the soil of Earth with the news that escape was possible. That was long before I was born, long before humanity divided unequally into Custodian and Affirmer and long, long before either group were the unwinking fanatics they had become five years ago.

The ship is in the Museum of Modern Astronautics. I know it has been kept in good condition. I also know that twenty years ago, before the Affirmers had developed the position that absolutely nothing might be taken physically from a museum, the ship was equipped with the latest Léugio Drive. The motive was that, if it were needed on Exodus Day, it might make the trip to a star in months instead of the years it had required originally.

The only thing that I do not know is whether I, Fiyatil, the Custodian of Custodians and art critic extraordinary, can learn to run it in the time that Leonardo and I have left. But as one of my favorite comic characters remarked about the possibility of a man chopping his own head off: a man can *try*. . . .

There is something else on my mind, even more exciting in a way, but this comes first. I find myself looking at the sun a good deal these days, and very searching, too! Very!

November 11, 2190—I can do it. With the help of two robots which I will modify for the purpose, I can do it. Leonardo and I could leave immediately. But I have my other project to complete.

And this is my other project: I am going to use all the empty space in the ship. It was built originally for different motors and a very large crew, and I am going to use that space as a bureau drawer. Into that bureau drawer I will stuff the keepsakes of humanity, the treasures of its childhood and adolescence—at least, as many as I can get in.

For weeks I have been collecting treasures from all over the world. Incredible pottery, breathtaking friezes, glorious statuary, and oil paintings almost beyond counting litter the corridors of the museum. Brueghel is piled on Bosch, Bosch on Dürer. I am going to bring a little of everything to that star toward which I point my ship, a little to show what the real things were like. I am including things like the holograph manuscripts of Jane Austen's *Pride and Prejudice*, Beethoven's Ninth Symphony, Gogol's *Dead Souls*, Mark Twain's *Huckleberry Finn*, and holographs of Dickens' letters and Lincoln's speeches. There are many others, but I cannot take everything. Within responsible limits, I must please myself.

Therefore, I am not taking anything from the Sistine Chapel ceiling. I have carved out two bits of the "Last Judgment" instead. They are my favorites: the soul that suddenly realizes that it is condemned, and the flayed skin on which Michelangelo painted his own portrait. The only trouble is that fresco weighs so much! Weight, weight, weight—it is almost all I think about now. Even Leonardo follows me about and says, "Weight, weight, weight!" He pronounces nothing else so well.

Still, what should I take of Picasso? A handful of oils, yes, but I must take the "Guernica." And there is more weight.

I have some wonderful Russian copper utensils and some Ming bronze bowls. I have a lime spatula from eastern New Guinea made of oiled wood that has a delightfully carved handle (it was used in chewing betel nut and lime). I have a wonderful alabaster figure of a cow from ancient Sumer. I have an incredible silver Buddha from northern India. I have some Dahoman brass figures of a grace to shame Egypt and Greece. I have a carved-ivory container from Benin, West Africa, showing a thoroughly fifteenth-century-European Christ on the Cross. I have the Venus of Willendorf, Austria, the figure that was carved in the Aurignacian epoch of the Paleolithic and which is part of the artistic tradition of the Venus art of prehistoric mankind.

I have miniatures by Hilliard and Holbein, satiric prints by Hogarth, a beautiful Kangra painting of the eighteenth century on paper that shows astonishingly little Mughal influence, Japanese prints by Takamaru and Hiroshige—and where may I stop? How may I choose?

I have pages from the Book of Kells, which is an illuminated hand-executed manuscript of almost unmatched beauty; and I have pages from the Gutenberg Bible, put together in the infancy of printing, which has illuminated pages to give the *effect* of a hand-copied manuscript, because the printers didn't want their invention discovered. I have a tughra of Suleiman the Magnificent, a calligraphic emblem that formed headings for his imperial edicts; and I have a Hebrew Scroll of the Law whose calligraphy outshines the jewels which encrust the poles on which it is wound.

I have Coptic textiles of the sixth century and Alençon lace of the sixteenth. I have a magnificent red krater vase from one of Athens' maritime colonies and a wooded figurehead of a minister from a New England frigate. I have a Rubens nude and "Odalisque" by Matisse.

In architecture I am taking the Chinese *Compendium of Architecture,* which I think has never been equaled as a text, and a model of a Le Corbusier house built by him. I would love to take one building, the Taj Mahal, but I *am* taking the pearl that the Mogul gave to her for whom he built the ineffable tomb. It is a reddish pearl, shaped like a pear and about three and a half inches long; shortly after it was buried with her, it turned up in the possession of an emperor of China who set it on gold leaves and surrounded it with jade and emeralds. At the turn of the nineteenth century it was sold somewhere in the Near East for a tiny, ridiculous sum and ended in the Louvre.

And a tool: a small stone fish ax, the first thing known to have been made by human creatures.

All this I have collected near the ship. But I've stored none of it. And, I suddenly remember, I have collected as yet no furniture, no decorated weapons, no etched glass . . .

I must hurry, hurry!

November 2190—Shortly after I finished the last enry, I glanced upward. There were green specks on the sun, and strange orange streamers seemed to plume out to all points of the compass. Evidently there was not to be a year. These were the symptoms of death that the astronomers had predicted.

So there was an end to my collecting—and my sorting was done in less than a day. The one thing I suddenly found I had to do, when it became obvious that my sections of Michelangelo would be too heavy, was to go to the Sistine Chapel ceiling after all. This time I cut out a relatively tiny thing— the finger of the Creation as it stabs life into Adam. And I decided to take da Vinci's "La Gioconda," even though his "Beatrice d'Este" is more to my taste: the Mona Lisa's smile belongs to the world.

All posters are represented by one Toulouse-Lautrec. I dropped the "Guernica"; Picasso is represented instead by an oil from his blue period and a single striking ceramic plate. I dropped Harold Paris' "The Eternal Judgment" because of its bulk; all I have of his now is the print *Buchenwald No. 2, "Where Are We Going?"* And somehow or other, in my last-minute haste, I seemed to have selected a large number of Safavid bottles from Iran of the sixteenth and seventeenth centuries. Let future historians and psychologists puzzle out the reason for my choices; they are now irrevocable.

We are proceeding toward Alpha Centauri and should arrive in five months. How will we and all our treasures be received, I wonder? I suddenly feel insanely cheerful. I don't think it has anything to do with my rather belated realization that I, who have so little talent and have failed so miserably in the arts, will achieve a place in the history of art like no other man—a kind of aesthetic Noah. No, it is the fact that I am carrying both the future and the past to a rendezvous where they still have a chance to come to terms.

A moment ago Leonard bounced a ball against the visiplate and, looking at it, I observed that old Sol was expanding apoplectically. As I remarked to him then, "I find, to my astonishment, that in the midst of death I am—at last, at last!—truly in life."

The New Accelerator

H. G. WELLS

*The notion behind "The New Accelerator" is no longer
novel. The breezy reality given to it, however, is an
original patent of the author.*

*As always, Mr. Wells seems to be prophesying in a
number of directions at once; the final lines of the story
bring to memory instantly all of the discussions regarding scientific irresponsibility to which we have all grown
so used these last twenty years.*

*Mr. Wells, of course, needs no introduction. If not
the founder, he remains the first great popularizer of
modern sf, and an author, by the way, whose mass of
work outside this field deserves and will almost certainly
get revival.*

Certainly, if ever a man found a guinea when he was looking
for a pin it is my good friend Professor Gibberne. I have
heard before of investigators over-shooting the mark, but
never quite to the extent that he has done. He has really, this
time at any rate, without any touch of exaggeration in the
phrase, found something to revolutionise human life. And
that when he was simply seeking an all-round nervous stimulant to bring languid people up to the stresses of these pushful
days. I have tasted the stuff now several times, and I cannot
do better than describe the effect the thing had on me. That
there are astonishing experiences in store for all in search of
new sensations will become apparent enough.

Professor Gibberne, as many people know, is my neighbour
in Folkestone. Unless my memory plays me a trick, his portrait at various ages has already appeared in *The Strand Magazine*—I think late in 1899; but I am unable to look it up
because I have lent that volume to some one who has never

sent it back. The reader may, perhaps, recall the high forehead and the singularly long black eyebrows that give such a Mephistophelian touch to his face. He occupies one of those pleasant detached houses in the mixed style that makes the western end of the Upper Sandgate Road so interesting. His is the one with the Flemish gables and the Moorish portico, and it is in the room with the mullioned bay window that he works when he is down here, and in which of an evening we have so often smoked and talked together. He is a mighty jester, but, besides, he likes to talk to me about his work; he is one of those men who find a help and stimulus in talking, and so I have been able to follow the conception of the New Accelerator right up from a very early stage. Of course, the greater portion of his experimental work is not done in Folkestone, but in Gower Street, in the fine new laboratory next to the hospital that he has been the first to use.

As everyone knows, or at least as all intelligent people know, the special department in which Gibberne has gained so great and deserved a reputation among physiologists is the action of drugs upon the nervous system. Upon soporifics, sedatives, and anæsthetics he is, I am told, unequalled. He is also a chemist of considerable eminence, and I suppose in the subtle and complex jungle of riddles that centres about the ganglion cell and the axis fibre there are little cleared places of his making, glades of illumination, that, until he sees fit to publish his results, are inaccessible to every other living man. And in the last few years he has been particularly assiduous upon this question of nervous stimulants, and already, before the discovery of the New Accelerator, very successful with them. Medical science has to thank him for at least three distinct and absolutely safe invigorators of unrivalled value to practising men. In cases of exhaustion the preparation known as Gibberne's B Syrup has, I suppose, saved more lives already than any lifeboat round the coast.

"But none of these things begin to satisfy me yet," he told me nearly a year ago. "Either they increase the central energy without affecting the nerves or they simply increase the available energy by lowering the nervous conductivity; and all of them are unequal and local in their operation. One wakes up the heart and viscera and leaves the brain stupefied, one gets at the brain champagne fashion and does nothing good for the solar plexus, and what I want—and what, if it's an earthly possibility, I mean to have—is a stimulant that stimulates all round, that wakes you up for a time from the crown of your head to the tip of your great toe, and makes you go two—or even three to everybody else's one. Eh? That's the thing I'm after."

"It would tire a man," I said.

"Not a doubt of it. And you'd eat double or treble—and all that. But just think what the thing would mean. Imagine yourself with a little phial like this"—he held up a bottle of green glass and marked his points with it—"and in this precious phial is the power to think twice as fast, move twice as quickly, do twice as much work in a given time as you could otherwise do."

"But is such a thing possible?"

"I believe so. If it isn't, I've wasted my time for a year. These various preparations of the hypophosphites, for example, seem to show that something of the sort . . . Even if it was only one and a half times as fast it would do."

"It *would* do," I said.

"If you were a statesman in a corner, for example, time rushing up against you, something urgent to be done, eh?"

"He could dose his private secretary," I said.

"And gain—double time. And think if *you*, for example, wanted to finish a book."

"Usually," I said, "I wish I'd never begun 'em."

"Or a doctor, driven to death, wants to sit down and think out a case. Or a barrister—or a man cramming for an examination."

"Worth a guinea a drop," said I, "and more—to men like that."

"And in a duel again," said Gibberne, "where it all depends on your quickness in pulling the trigger."

"Or in fencing," I echoed.

"You see," said Gibberne, "if I get it as an all-round thing it will really do you no harm at all—except perhaps to an infinitesimal degree it brings you nearer old age. You will just have lived twice to other people's once."

"I suppose," I meditated, "in a duel—it would be fair?"

"That's a question for the seconds," said Gibberne.

I harked back further. "And you really think such a thing *is* possible?" I said.

"As possible," said Gibberne, and glanced at something that

297

went throbbing by the window, "as a motor-bus. As a matter of fact—"

He paused and smiled at me deeply, and tapped slowly on the edge of his desk with the green phial. "I think I know the stuff. . . . Already I've got something coming." The nervous smile upon his face betrayed the gravity of his revelation. He rarely talked of his actual experimental work unless things were very near the end. "And it may be, it may be—I shouldn't be surprised—it may even do the thing at a greater rate than twice."

"It will be rather a big thing," I hazarded.

"It will be, I think, rather a big thing."

But I don't think he quite knew what a big thing it was to be, for all that.

I remember we had several subsequent talks about the stuff. "The New Accelerator" he called it, and his tone about it grow more confident on each occasion. Sometimes he talked nervously of unexpected physiological results its use might have, and then he would get a bit unhappy; at others he was frankly mercenary, and we debated long and anxiously how the preparation might be turned to commercial account. "It's a good thing," said Gibberne, "a tremendous thing. I know I'm giving the world something, and I think it only reasonable we should expect the world to pay. The dignity of science is all very well, but I think somehow I must have the monopoly of the stuff for, say, ten years. I don't see why *all* the fun in life should go to the dealers in ham."

My own interest in the coming drug certainly did not wane in the time. I have always had a queer twist towards metaphysics in my mind. I have always been given to paradoxes about space and time, and it seemed to me that Gibberne was really preparing no less than the absolute acceleration of life. Suppose a man repeatedly dosed with such a preparation: he would live an active and record life indeed, but he would be an adult at eleven, middle-aged at twenty-five, and by thirty well on the road to senile decay. It seemed to me that so far Gibberne was only going to do for anyone who took his drug exactly what Nature has done for the Jews and Orientals, who are men in their teens and aged by fifty, and quicker in thought and act than we are all the time. The marvel of drugs has always been great to my mind; you can madden a man, calm a man, make him incredibly strong and alert or a helpless log, quicken this passion and allay that, all by means of drugs, and here was a new miracle to be added to this strange armoury of phials the doctors use! But Gibberne was far too eager upon his technical points to enter very keenly into my aspect of the question.

It was the seventh or eighth of August when he told me the distillation that would decide his failure or success for a time was going forward as we talked, and it was on the tenth that he told me the thing was done and the New Accelerator a tangible reality in the world. I met him as I was going up the Sandgate Hill towards Folkestone—I think I was going to get my hair cut; and he came hurrying down to meet me—I suppose he was coming to my house to tell me at once of his success. I remember that his eyes were unusually bright and his face flushed, and I noted even then the swift alacrity of his step.

"It's done," he cried, and gripped my hand, speaking very fast; "it's more than done. Come up to my house and see."

"Really?"

"Really!" he shouted. "Incredibly! Come up and see."

"And it does—twice?"

"It does more, much more. It scares me. Come up and see the stuff. Taste it! Try it! It's the most amazing stuff on earth." He gripped my arm and, walking at such a pace that he forced me into a trot, went shouting with me up the hill. A whole charabancful of people turned and stared at us in unison after the manner of people in charabancs. It was one of those hot, clear days that Folkestone sees so much of, every colour incredibly bright and every outline hard. There was a breeze, of course, but not so much breeze as sufficed under these conditions to keep me cool and dry. I panted for mercy.

"I'm not walking fast, am I?" cried Gibberne, and slackened his pace to a quick march.

"You've been taking some of this stuff," I puffed.

"No," he said. "At the utmost a drop of water that stood in a beaker from which I had washed out the last traces of the stuff. I took some last night, you know. But that is ancient history now."

"And it goes twice?" I said, nearing his doorway in a grateful perspiration.

"It goes a thousand times, many thousand times!" cried

Gibberne, with a dramatic gesture, flinging open his Early English carved-oak gate.

"Phew!" said I, and followed him to the door.

"I don't know how many times it goes," he said, with his latch-key in his hand.

"And you—"

"It throws all sorts of light on nervous physiology, it kicks the theory of vision in a perfectly new shape! . . . Heaven knows how many thousand times. We'll try all that after— The thing is to try the stuff now."

"Try the stuff?" I said, as we went along the passage.

"Rather," said Gibberne, turning on me in his study. "There it is in that little green phial there! Unless you happen to be afraid?"

I am a careful man by nature, and only theoretically adventurous. I *was* afraid. But on the other hand there is pride.

"Well," I haggled. "You say you've tried it?"

"I've tried it," he said, "and I don't look hurt by it, do I? I don't even look livery and I *feel*—"

I sat down. "Give me the potion," I said. "If the worst comes to the worst it will save having my hair cut, and that I think is one of the most hateful duties of a civilised man. How do you take the mixture?"

"With water," said Gibberne, whacking down a carafe.

He stood up in front of his desk and regarded me in his easy chair; his manner was suddenly affected by a touch of the Harley Street specialist. "It's rum stuff, you know," he said.

I made a gesture with my hand.

"I must warn you in the first place as soon as you've got it down to shut your eyes, and open them very cautiously in a minute or so's time. One still sees. The sense of vision is a question of length of vibration, and not of multitude of impacts; but there's a kind of shock to the retina, a nasty giddy confusion just at the time if the eyes are open. Keep 'em shut."

"Shut," I said. "Good!"

"And the next thing is, keep still. Don't begin to whack about. You may fetch something a nasty rap if you do. Remember you will be going several thousand times faster than you ever did before, heart, lungs, muscles, brain—everything —and you will hit hard without knowing it. You won't know it, you know. You'll feel just as you do now. Only everything in the world will seem to be going ever so many thousand times slower than it ever went before. That's what makes it so deuced queer."

"Lor'," I said. "And you mean——"

"You'll see," said he, and took up a measure. He glanced at the material on his desk. "Glasses," he said, "water. All here. Mustn't take too much for the first attempt."

The little phial glucked out its precious contents. "Don't forget what I told you," he said, turning the contents of the measure into a glass in the manner of an Italian waiter measuring whiskey. "Sit with the eyes tightly shut and in absolute stillness for two minutes," he said. "Then you will hear me speak."

He added an inch or so of water to the dose in each glass.

"By-the-bye," he said, "don't put your glass down. Keep it in your hand and rest your hand on your knee. Yes—so. And now——"

He raised his glass.

"The New Accelerator," I said.

"The New Accelerator," he answered, and we touched glasses and drank, and instantly I closed my eyes.

You know that blank non-existence into which one drops when one has taken "gas." For an indefinite interval it was like that. Then I heard Gibberne telling me to wake up, and I stirred and opened my eyes. There he stood as he had been standing, glass still in hand. It was empty, that was all the difference.

"Well?" said I.

"Nothing out of the way?"

"Nothing. A slight feeling of exhilaration, perhaps. Nothing more."

"Sounds?"

"Things are still," I said. "By Jove! yes! They *are* still. Except the sort of faint *pat, patter*, like rain falling on different things. What is it?"

"Analysed sounds," I think he said, but I am not sure. He glanced at the window. "Have you ever seen a curtain before a window fixed in that way before?"

I followed his eyes, and there was the end of the curtain, frozen, as it were, corner high, in the act of flapping briskly in the breeze.

"No," said I; "that's odd."

"And here," he said, and opened the hand that held the glass. Naturally I winced, expecting the glass to smash. But, so far from smashing, it did not even seem to stir; it hung in mid-air—motionless. "Roughly speaking," said Gibberne, "an object in these latitudes falls sixteen feet in the first second. This glass is falling sixteen feet in a second now. Only, you see, it hasn't been falling yet for the hundredth part of a second. That gives you some idea of the pace of my Accelerator." And he waved his hand round and round, over and under the slowly sinking glass. Finally he took it by the bottom, pulled it down and placed it very carefully on the table. "Eh?" he said to me, and laughed.

"That seems all right," I said, and began very gingerly to raise myself from my chair. I felt perfectly well, very light and comfortable, and quite confident in my mind. I was going fast all over. My heart, for example, was beating a thousand times a second, but that caused me no discomfort at all. I looked out of the window. An immovable cyclist, head down and with a frozen puff of dust behind his driving-wheel, scorched to overtake a galloping charabanc that did not stir. I gaped in amazement at this incredible spectacle. "Gibberne," I cried, "how long will this confounded stuff last?"

"Heaven knows!" he answered. "Last time I took it I went to bed and slept it off. I tell you, I was frightened. It must have lasted some minutes, I think—it seemed like hours. But after a bit it slows down rather suddenly, I believe."

I was proud to observe that I did not feel frightened—I suppose because there were two of us. "Why shouldn't we go out?" I asked.

"Why not?"

"They'll see us."

"Not they. Goodness, no! Why, we shall be going a thousand times faster than the quickest conjuring trick that was ever done. Come along! Which way shall we go? Window, or door?"

And out by the window we went.

Assuredly of all the strange experiences that I have ever had, or imagined, or read of other people having or imagining, that little raid I made with Bibberne on the Folkestone Leas, under the influence of the New Accelerator, was the strangest and maddest of all. We went out by his gate into the road, and there we made a minute examination of the statuesque passing traffic. The tops of the wheels and some of the legs of the horses of this charabanc, the end of the whip-lash and the lower jaw of the conductor—who was just beginning to yawn—were perceptibly in motion, but all the rest of the lumbering conveyance seemed still. And quite noiseless except for a faint rattling that came from one man's throat! And as parts of this frozen edifice there were a driver, you know, and a conductor, and eleven people! The effect as we walked about the thing began by being madly queer and ended by being—disagreeable. There they were, people like ourselves and yet not like ourselves, frozen in careless attitudes, caught in mid-gesture. A girl and a man smiled at one another, a leering smile that threatened to last for evermore; a woman in a floppy capeline rested her arm on the rail and stared at Gibberne's house with the unwinking stare of eternity; a man stroked his moustache like a figure of wax, and another stretched a tiresome stiff hand with extended fingers towards his loosened hat. We stared at them, we laughed at them, we made faces at them, and then a sort of disgust of them came upon us, and we turned away and walked round in front of the cyclist towards the Leas.

"Goodness!" cried Gibberne, suddenly; "look there!"

He pointed, and there at the tip of his fingers and sliding down the air with wings flapping slowly and at the speed of an exceptionally languid snail—was a bee.

And so we came out upon the Leas. There the thing seemed madder than ever. The band was playing in the upper stand, though all the sound it made for us was a low-pitched, wheezy rattle, a sort of prolonged last sigh that passed at times into a sound like the slow, muffled ticking of some monstrous clock. Frozen people stood erect; strange, silent, self-conscious-looking dummies hung unstably in mid-stride, promenading upon the grass. I passed close to a poodle dog suspended in the act of leaping, and watched the slow movement of his legs as he sank to earth.

"Lord, look *here!*" cried Gibberne, and we halted for a moment before a magnificent person in white faint-striped flannels, white shoes, and a Panama hat, who turned back to wink at two gaily dressed ladies he had passed. A wink, studied with such leisurely deliberation as we could afford, is an unattractive thing. It loses any quality of alert gaiety, and one remarks that the winking eye does not completely close, that under its drooping lid appears the lower edge of an eyeball and a line of white.

"Heaven give me memory," said I. "and I will never wink again."

"Or smile," said Gibberne, with his eye on the lady's answering teeth.

"It's infernally hot, somehow," said I. "Let's go slower."

"Oh, come along!' said Gibberne.

We picked our way among the bath-chairs in the path. Many of the people sitting in the chairs seemed almost natural in their passive poses, but the contorted scarlet of the bandsmen was not a restful thing to see. A purple-faced gentleman was frozen in the midst of a violent struggle to refold his newspaper against the wind; there were many evidences that all these people in their sluggish way were exposed to a considerable breeze, a breeze that had no existence so far as our sensations went. We came out and walked a little way from the crowd, and turned and regarded it. To see all that multitude changed to a picture, smitten rigid, as it were, into the semblance of realistic wax, was impossibly wonderful. It was absurd, of course; but it filled me with an irrational, an exultant sense of superior advantage. Consider the wonder of it! All that I had said and thought and done since the stuff begun to work in my veins had happened, so far as those people, so far as the world in general went, in the twinkling of an eye.

"The New Accelerator—" I began, but Gibberne interrupted me.

"There's that infernal old woman!" he said.

"What old woman?"

"Lives next door to me," said Gibberne. "Has a lapdog that yaps. Gods! The temptation is strong!"

There is something very boyish and impulsive about Gibberne at times. Before I could expostulate with him he had dashed forward, snatched the unfortunate animal out of visible existence, and was running violently with it towards the cliff of the Leas. It was most extraordinary. The little brute, you know, didn't bark or wriggle or make the slightest sign of vitality. It kept quite stiffly in the attitude of somnolent repose, and Gibberne held it by the neck. It was like running about with a dog of wood.

"Gibberne," I cried, "put it down!" Then I said something

else. "If you run like that, Gibberne," I cried, "you'll set your clothes on fire. Your linen trousers are going brown as it is!"

He clapped his hand on his thigh and stood hesitating on the verge.

"Gibberne," I cried, coming up, "put it down. This heat is too much! It's our running so! Two or three miles a second! Friction of the air!"

"What?" he said, glancing at the dog.

"Friction of the air," I shouted. "Friction of the air. Going too fast. Like meteorites and things. Too hot. And, Gibberne! Gibberne! I'm all over pricking and a sort of perspiration. You can see people stirring slightly. I believe the stuff's working off! Put that dog down."

"Eh?" he said.

"It's working off," I repeated. "We're too hot and the stuff's working off! I'm wet through."

He stared at me. Then at the band, the wheezy rattle of whose performance was certainly going faster. Then with a tremendous sweep of the arm he hurled the dog away from him and it went spinning upward, still inanimate, and hung at last over the grouped parasols of a knot of chattering people. Gibberne was gripping my elbow. "By Jove!" he cried. "I believe it is! A sort of hot pricking and—yes. That man's moving his pocket-handkerchief! Perceptibly. We must get out of this sharp."

But we could not get out of it sharply enough. Luckily perhaps! For we might have run, and if we had run we should, I believe, have burst into flames. Almost certainly we should have burst into flames! You know, we had neither of us thought of that. . . . But before we could even begin to run the action of the drug had ceased. It was the business of a minute fraction of a second. The effect of the New Accelerator passed like the drawing of a curtain, vanished in the movement of a hand. I heard Gibberne's voice in infinite alarm. "Sit down," he said, and flop, down upon the turf at the edge of the Leas I sat—scorching as I sat. There is a patch of burnt grass there still where I sat down. The whole stagnation seemed to wake up as I did so, the disarticulated vibration of the band rushed together into a blast of music, the promenaders put their feet down and walked their ways, the papers and flags began flapping, smiles passed into words, the winker finished his wink and went on his way complacently, and all the seated people moved and spoke.

The whole world had come alive again, was going as fast as we were, or rather we were going no faster than the rest of the world. It was like slowing down as one comes into a railway station. Everything seemed to spin round for a second or two, I had the most transient feeling of nausea, and that was all. And the little dog which had seemed to hang for a moment when the force of Gibberne's arm was expended fell with a swift acceleration clean through a lady's parasol!

That was the saving of us. Unless it was for one corpulent old gentleman in a bath-chair, who certainly did start at the sight of us and afterwards regarded us at intervals with a darkly suspicious eye, and finally, I believe, said something to his nurse about us, I doubt if a solitary person remarked our sudden appearance among them. Plop! We must have appeared abruptly. We ceased to smoulder almost at once, though the turf beneath me was uncomfortably hot. The attention of everyone—including even the Amusements Association band, which on this occasion, for the only time in its history, got out of tune—was arrested by the amazing fact, and the still more amazing yapping and uproar caused by the fact, that a respectable, over-fed lapdog sleeping quietly to the east of the bandstand should suddenly fall through the parasol of a lady on the west—in a slightly singed condition due to the extreme velocity of its movements through the air. In these absurd days, too, when we are all trying to be as psychic and silly and supersitious as possible! People got up and trod on other people, chairs were overturned, the Leas policeman ran. How the matter settled itself I do not know—we were much too anxious to disentangle ourselves from the affair and get out of range of the eye of the old gentleman in the bath-chair to make minute inquiries. As soon as we were sufficiently cool and sufficiently recovered from our giddiness and nausea and confusion of mind to do so we stood up and, skirting the crowd, directed our steps back along the road below the Metropole towards Gibberne's house. But amidst the din I heard very distinctly the gentleman who had been sitting beside the lady of the ruptured sunshade using quite unjustifiable threats and language to one of those chair-attendants who have "Inspector" written on their caps. "If you didn't throw the dog," he said, "who *did?*"

The sudden return of movement and familiar noises, and our natural anxiety about ourselves (our clothes were still dreadfully hot, and the fronts of the thighs of Gibberne's white trousers were scorched a drabbish brown), prevented the minute observations I should have liked to make on all these things. Indeed, I really made no observations of any scientific value on that return. The bee, of course, had gone. I looked for that cyclist, but he was already out of sight as we came into the Upper Sandgate Road, or hidden from us by traffic; the charabanc, however, with its people now all alive and stirring, was clattering along at a spanking pace almost abreast of the nearer church.

We noted, however, that the window-sill on which we had stepped in getting out of the house was slightly singed, and that the impressions of our feet on the gravel of the path were unusually deep.

So it was I had my first experience of the New Accelerator. Practically we had been running about and saying and doing all sorts of things in the space of a second or so of time. We had lived half an hour while the band played, perhaps, two bars. But the effect it had upon us was that the whole world had stopped for our convenient inspection. Considering all things, and particularly considering our rashness in venturing out of the house, the experience might certainly have been much more disagreeable than it was. It showed, no doubt, that Gibberne has still much to learn before his preparation is a manageable convenience, but its practicability it certainly demonstrated beyond all cavil.

Since that adventure he has been steadily bringing its use under control, and I have several times, and without the slightest bad result, taken measured doses under his direction; though I must confess I have not yet ventured abroad again under its influence. I may mention, for example, that this story has been written at one sitting and without interruption, except for the nibbling of some chocolate, by its means. I began at six-twenty-five, and my watch is now very nearly at the minute past the half-hour. The convenience of securing a long, uninterrupted spell of work in the midst of a day full of engagements cannot be exaggerated. Gibberne is now working at the quantitative handling of his preparation, with especial reference to its distinctive effects upon different types of constitution. He then hopes to find a Retarder with which to dilute its present rather excessive potency. The Retarder will, of course, have the reverse effect to the Accelerator; used alone it should enable the patient to spread a few seconds over many hours of ordinary time, and so to maintain an apathetic inaction, a glacierlike absence of alacrity, amidst the most animated or irritating surroundings. The two things together must necessarily work an entire revolution in civilised existence. It is the beginning of our escape from that Time Garment of which Carlyle speaks. While this Accelerator will enable us to concentrate ourselves with tremendous impact upon any moment or occasion that demands our utmost sense of vigour, the Retarder will enable us to pass in passive tranquillity through infinite hardship and tedium. Perhaps I am a little optimistic about the Retarder, which has indeed still to be discovered, but about the Accelerator there is no possible sort of doubt whatever. Its appearance upon the market in a convenient, controllable, and assimilable form is a matter of the next few months. It will be obtainable of all chemists and druggists, in small green bottles, at a high but, considering its extraordinary qualities, by no means excessive price. Gibberne's Nervous Accelerator it will be called, and he hopes to be able to supply it in three strengths: one in two hundred, one in nine hundred, and one in two thousand, distinguished by yellow, pink, and white labels respectively.

No doubt its use renders a great number of very extraordinary things possible; for, of course, the most remarkable and, possibly, even criminal proceedings may be effected with impunity by thus dodging, as it were, into the interstices of time. Like all potent preparations it will be liable to abuse. We have, however, discussed this aspect of the question very thoroughly, and we have decided that this is purely a matter of medical jurisprudence and altogether outside our province. We shall manufacture and sell the Accelerator, and, as for the consequences—we shall see.

THE HONOR ROLL

I know perfectly well that the listings which follow are not complete. I've made them as complete as possible, and I hope they'll enable you to know something about the history of the stories in the Honor Roll, and to hunt up and find the ones which I've not been able to include and which you haven't already read.

The Honor Roll comes in three sections. First is a listing of those stories which received the most nominations, as well as a separate listing for nominations of a given author. (This proved necessary to give anything like a true picture of the choices; as you'll note—to provide one example—eleven people agreed that Theodore Sturgeon should be in this list, but only two of those eleven agreed on the same story.) Second is the full Honor Roll, containing such information about original publication, anthology and collection reprints, etc., as I've been able to unearth. (Any additions will be gratefully received.) And third is a bibliography of all anthologies and authors' collections mentioned.

Once again: my regret at being unable to include more than one volume's worth of stories is greater than I can say. I can give you no better advice than—having read this selection—to go out and hunt up all the others. I did, and I'm grateful to have had the chance.

L.M.J.

TOP-VOTED STORIES

4 VOTES EACH
Nightfall, by Isaac Asimov
The Cold Equations, by Tom Godwin
Coming Attraction, by Fritz Leiber
Vintage Season, by C. L. Moore
A Martian Odyssey, by Stanley G. Weinbaum

3 VOTES EACH
The Enormous Radio, by John Cheever
Helen O'Loy, by Lester del Rey
Requiem, by Robert A. Heinlein

The Mindworm, by C. M. Kornbluth
The Twonky, by Henry Kuttner
Vengeance for Nikolai, by Walter M. Miller, Jr.
No Woman Born, by C. L. Moore

2 VOTES EACH

Poor Little Warrior, by Brian Aldiss
The Quest for St. Aquin, by Anthony Boucher
The Veldt, by Ray Bradbury
Who Goes There?, by John W. Campbell, Jr.
The Nine Billion Names of God, by Arthur C. Clarke
By His Bootstraps, by Robert A. Heinlein
Lifeline, by Robert A. Heinlein
They, by Robert A. Heinlein
As Easy as ABC, by Rudyard Kipling
The Country of the Kind, by Damon Knight
The Marching Morons, by C. M. Kornbluth
Don't Look Now, by Henry Kuttner
Mimsy Were the Borogoves, by Henry Kuttner
The Night He Cried, by Fritz Leiber
The Colour out of Space, by H. P. Lovecraft
Casey Agonistes, by Richard McKenna
A Canticle for Leibowitz, by Walter M. Miller, Jr.
The Bright Illusion, by C. L. Moore
He Walked Around the Horses, by H. Beam Piper
E for Effort, by T. L. Sherred
A Saucer of Loneliness, by Theodore Sturgeon
Generation of Noah, by William Tenn

TOP-VOTED AUTHORS

Votes
Received

14 Robert A. Heinlein
11 Fritz Leiber, Theodore Sturgeon
9   Henry Kuttner, C. L. Moore
8   C. M. Kornbluth
7   Walter M. Miller, Jr.
6   Isaac Asimov, William Tenn
4   Brian Aldiss, Ray Bradbury, Avram Davidson, Lester del Rey, Tom Godwin, Damon Knight, Stanley G. Weinbaum
3   John Cheever, George P. Elliott, Judith Merril, H. G. Wells
2   Poul Anderson, Alfred Bester, James Blish, Anthony Boucher, Arthur C. Clarke, Rudyard Kipling, Katherine Maclean, Richard Matheson, Richard McKenna, Robert Sheckley, Clifford B. Simak, A. E. Van Vogt, Jack Williamson